COMPETITION POLICY IN THE GLOBAL ECONOMY

International agreements on competition law and policy are notoriously difficult to implement. This collection examines the complexities involved when international coordination and harmonization of competition law and policy are considered.

Presenting an analysis of the issues surrounding cooperation and convergence, a number of key factors are examined. They include the impact of differing antitrust laws across borders on trade and investment, the effects on competition policy of international strategic alliances, mergers and acquisitions, the trade-off between firm privacy and antitrust needs in coordinating information flow across borders. The final section addresses major policy themes in the context of how to proceed in the future.

Drawing on the work of leading economists and lawyers, the research presented here is supported by the Japan Foundation International Bar Association and the World Bank.

Leonard Waverman is Professor of Economics and Director, Centre for International Studies, University of Toronto. **William S. Comanor** is Professor of Economics, University of California, Santa Barbara, and Professor of Health Services, School of Public Health, UCLA. **Akira Goto** is Professor of Economics at Hitotsubashi University and Director of Research, National Institute of Science and Technology Policy, Japan.

ROUTLEDGE STUDIES IN THE MODERN WORLD ECONOMY

INTEREST RATES AND BUDGET DEFICITS
A study of the advanced economies
Kanhaya L. Gupta and Bakhtiar Moazzami

WORLD TRADE AFTER THE URUGUAY ROUND
Prospects and policy options for the twenty-first century
Edited by Harald Sander and András Inotai

THE FLOW ANALYSIS OF LABOUR MARKETS
Edited by Ronald Schettkat

INFLATION AND UNEMPLOYMENT
Contributions to a new macroeconomic approach
Edited by Alvaro Cencini and Mauro Baranzini

MACROECONOMIC DIMENSIONS OF PUBLIC FINANCE
Essays in honour of Vito Tanzi
Edited by Mario I. Blejer and Teresa M. Ter-Minassian

FISCAL POLICY AND ECONOMIC REFORMS
Essays in honour of Vito Tanzi
Edited by Mario I. Blejer and Teresa M. Ter-Minassian

COMPETITION POLICY IN THE GLOBAL ECONOMY
Modalities for cooperation
Edited by Leonard Waverman, William S. Comanor and Akira Goto

COMPETITION POLICY IN THE GLOBAL ECONOMY

Modalities for cooperation

Edited by Leonard Waverman,
William S. Comanor and Akira Goto

London and New York

First published 1997
by Routledge
11 New Fetter Lane, London EC4P 4EE

Simultaneously published in the United States and Canada
by Routledge
29 West 35th Street, New York, NY 10001

Typeset in Times by
Mathematical Composition Setters Ltd, Salisbury, Wiltshire, UK

Printed and bound in Great Britain by
Redwood Books, Trowbridge, Wiltshire, UK

British Library Cataloguing in Publication Data
A catalogue record for this book is available from the British Library

Library of Congress Cataloging in Publication Data
Competition policy in the global economy : modalities for cooperation
/ edited by Leonard Waverman, William S. Comanor, and Akira Goto.
    p.   cm. — (Routledge studies in the modern world economy,
ISSN 1359-7965 ; 7)
Includes bibliographical references and index.
    1. Competition, International.
    2. Foreign trade regulation.
    3. International cooperation.
    4. Consolidation and merger of
corporations. I. Waverman, Leonard. II. Comanor, William S.
    III. Goto, Akira, 1945–   . IV. Series.
HF1414.C6623   1996
338.8′8—dc20
                                                          95-26831
                                                              CIP

ISBN 0-415-14226-1

CONTENTS

Part III R&D consortia

Part IV Vertical arrangements

Part V Cooperation, harmonization, convergence?

CONTENTS

LIST OF FIGURES

LIST OF TABLES

LIST OF TABLES

CONTRIBUTORS

Donald I. Baker Baker & Miller, Washington, DC

Annette Bongardt Centro de Estudos Europens, Universidade Católica Portuguesa, Lisbon

A. Neil Campbell McMillan Bull Casgrain, Toronto

William S. Comanor Department of Economics, University of California, Santa Barbara and School of Public Health, UCLA, Los Angeles

Eleanor M. Fox School of Law, New York University

Calvin S. Goldman Davies Ward & Beck, Toronto

Akira Goto Department of Economics, Hitotsubashi University, Tokyo and National Institute of Science and Technology Policy, Tokyo

Thomas M. Jorde Law & Economics Consulting Group Inc., Emeryville, CA

Shyam Khemani Private Sector Development, World Bank

Rainer Markl University of Frankfurt am Main

Stephen Martin Centre for Industrial Economics, Institute of Economics, University of Copenhagen

Werner Meißner University of Frankfurt am Main

Damien Neven Département d'économétrie et d'économie politique (DEEP), Université de Lausanne and CEPR, London

Hiroyuki Odagiri Institute of Socio-Economic Planning, University of Tsukuba, Ibaraki

Janusz A. Ordover Department of Economics, New York University

Sylvia Ostry Centre for International Studies, University of Toronto and Canadian Institute for Advanced Research

Patrick Rey CREST, CNRSEP40, Paris and CEPR, London

Michael J. Reynolds Allen & Overy, Brussels

James F. Rill Collier Shannon Rill & Scott, Washington, DC

J. William Rowley McMillan Bull Casgrain, Toronto

A. Edward Safarian Centre for International Studies, University of Toronto and Canadian Institute for Advanced Research

Paul Seabright Faculty of Economics & Politics, Cambridge University and CEPR, London

Kotaro Suzumura Institute of Economic Research, Hitotsubashi University, Tokyo

David J. Teece Center for Research in Management, University of California, Berkeley

Michael J. Trebilcock Faculty of Law, University of Toronto

Leonard Waverman Centre for International Studies, University of Toronto

1

INTRODUCTION

Leonard Waverman, William S. Comanor and Akira Goto

Globalization – the increasing integration of national markets – has undergone various phases, until recently largely fuelled by the explosion of world trade following the implementation of GATT and successive tariff-reducing rounds of multilateral negotiations. As Ostry (1989, 1990) points out, we are now in a phase of globalization dominated not by trade, but by foreign direct investment (FDI) under the aegis of multinational enterprises (MNEs). The multinationals of today are not searching for resource inputs as in the earlier portion of the twentieth century (see Krugman 1990) but are spreading the economies of scale and scope of increasingly technology-driven production across borders and among firms. This increasing globalization of product and capital markets, combined with the accelerating rhythm of technological innovation, has significantly altered the competitive environment of the large corporate enterprise.

This spread of technology-driven FDI is manifesting itself in a wide array of horizontal global organizational forms, including mergers, joint ventures, strategic alliances, research consortia and production consortia. Besides these horizontal manifestations of FDI, differing vertical arrangements (producer–supplier relationships) are also being put in place. Together, new 'networks' of corporate affiliations are proliferating, with the traditional structure of the firm becoming blurred.

Important conflicts exist between these new intrafirm and interfirm relationships, driven by global forces and existing national competition policies, primarily between Japan and the United States but also involving the European Union and other OECD nations.[1] These conflicts intermingle trade policy and competition policy and may interfere with the free flow of FDI and technology. Conflict between national competition policies is a crucial issue of global concern, especially critical to Japan–US relations. The purpose of this book is to investigate how domestic competition policies mesh in a world of increasingly international domestic markets. Do domestic competition policies interfere with FDI and trade, can they represent advantages to domestic firms, and if there is a case for coordination or harmonization of these domestic laws, how do we go about doing that?

1

In 1990 the US Federal Trade Commission launched an investigation of Japanese *keiretsu*, arguing that these long-term alliances may be exclusionary and employ discriminatory vertical (buyer–seller) practices. Also in 1990, the US FTC specifically began to investigate the purchasing practices of Japanese auto transplants in the United States to determine whether the 'exclusive' relationships they established with component manufacturers were consistent with US antitrust law. The United States has shown that competition policy and trade policy are inexorably linked. In the trade talks on Japanese structural impediments to US exports to Japan (SII) the United States has demanded and has received a commitment from Japan to enforce its competition policy more aggressively and to amend the law to increase penalties. In the 1990 SII talks Japan agreed 'to specify and make clear the practices that are unlawful in the distribution system in Japan and within the system of *keiretsu* ...'[2]

An example of the potential for uncoordinated domestic competition laws to interfere with investment lies in merger policy, which differs so markedly in its interpretation across countries (and across jurisdictions within a country such as the United States) that multinational mergers require multiple applications to competition authorities, taking time and adding uncertainty. Some form of harmonization among jurisdictions may be required.[3] In addition, new forms of corporate affiliation such as strategic alliances where firms enter into longer-term cooperation to share or develop technological developments are not well captured in traditional antitrust nets. Thus the issues of cooperation and competition, in particular with respect to interfirm arrangements and innovation, are as yet little researched. As a result, traditional competition policy may prove unable to deal adequately with innovation-driven mergers, strategic alliances and vertical integration. As there is no multinational competition authority, cross-border ventures (such as strategic alliances) may cause international competition problems (such as a dominant position) which require examination and solution.

Today, as Sylvia Ostry has stated, we are on a path to moving 'Beyond the Border'[4] or more appropriately 'Inside the Border'. Increasingly, what were once considered as purely domestic policies – policies such as patent laws, the setting of standards for high-tech products, government procurement, trade-related investment measures (TRIMS), subsidies and competition policy – are all on the international negotiations agenda. Competition law and policy may be at the top of the agenda because market access has become such a crucial subject and because domestic competition laws are seen as important in setting the terms of market access.[5] Yet there is little agreement on the appropriate arena for discussion of these issues or what aspects of domestic competition policy should be on the negotiating table. In this book we examine both of these issues, primarily the latter, concentrating on the analytic questions of whether various forms of interfirm relationships (mergers, joint ventures and strategic alliances, vertical arrangements) can raise cross-border issues amenable to bilateral or multilateral disposition.

The arena for discussions is a crucial subject (see Chapter 15). The recently signed GATT/WTO undertakings do not address competition policy explicitly although several sections are clearly related. Villambrosa (1994) sees the Agreement on Trade Related Investment Measures (TRIMS) as having clear competition policy consequences, since these measures were introduced to affect the business practices of MNEs. Villambrosa suggests that domestic competition law will be necessary in the aftermath of the disappearance of TRIMS. The Trade Related Intellectual Property Measures (TRIPS) section of the GATT/WTO agreements provides for consultations between governments where there is reason to believe that licensing practices or conditions pertaining to intellectual property rights constitute an abuse of these rights and have an adverse effect on competition (Villambrosa 1994: 3).

Other sections of the agreements – on the new subsidies codes (the traffic lights), the revised anti-dumping agreement (which some see as a backward step) – are all consistent with reducing trade and investment barriers to foreign firms.

Still there is no coherent understanding of the role of competition law and policy in the GATT/WTO agreement. Ostry (1994) suggests, after Hoekman and Mavroidis (1994), that GATT Article XXIII:1(b) on 'nullification and impairment' of benefits could be used to bring a complaint to the GATT dispute resolution process about some anti-competitive practice. In addition, the dispute resolution process in the WTO is likely to be open to a complaint brought forward on some aspect of another country's domestic anti-competitive behaviour. However, rather than being dragged, without analysis and without discussion, into some form of 'top-down' finding on the merits or demerits of a particular business practice, it is wise to begin analysing the international aspects of domestic competition policy. The recent trade dispute on market access to the domestic Japanese auto parts sector mixed market access and competition policy issues and would have been a difficult test case for the new WTO.

Bilateral and trilateral cooperation on competition policy has already started among countries and regimes. Among Asia–Pacific countries, Australia and New Zealand have harmonized their competition laws and policies as part of the ANZCERTA agreement. The NAFTA also has provisions regarding cooperation on competition policy. Broader multilateral cooperation has yet to begin but initiatives are being proposed. In the report of the Eminent Persons Group (EPG) of APEC, it was recommended that APEC 'consider adopting a policy based on the existing models of international cooperation on competition policy' (1993: 43, Recommendation 6). Bilateral codes exist between the United States and Canada, the European Union and the United States and are near finalization between the

EU and Canada.[6] The OECD has played an important role in developing dialogue and informal cooperation among competition policy authorities and sponsoring research and analysis. The OECD is likely to play an increasingly crucial role in the next stage – formal multilateral cooperation.

PRESSURES FOR AN INTERNATIONAL COMPETITION POLICY AGENDA

Besides globalization, other pressures exist which increase the desire to place competition law and policy on the international bargaining agenda:

1 *Policy awareness* – economies, such as the US, which were once less involved in world trade are now deep in trade. One may argue that the US views of the origins of its trade deficit are misplaced (see Krugman 1992) but now other countries' trade, investment, and domestic policies are breakfast table discussion in policy corridors.
2 *Policy fairness* – the concept of what is 'reciprocal is fair' and what is 'level [as in a playing field] is fair' has now arisen and will not be done away with. Therefore countries can no longer claim 'sovereignty' or 'that it is purely domestic' as the excuse for not discussing the impact of regulatory, purchasing, or competition policy regimes.
3 *Effective access*[7] – along with globalization, awareness and fairness has come the recognition that the end of the process must be *effective access*, that true national treatment requires the opening of markets. The speed of opening and the impediments to the large MNEs while domestic economies prepare for competition is open for discussion.
4 *Spillovers* – as the activities of MNEs become more important and cross over many borders, the spillovers from domestic policies such as competition policy become greater. Examples will be given below, but a simple case is a proposed merger where the multilateral nature of the corporations involved requires the approval and consent of many antitrust authorities. Thus any antitrust authority acting alone can end the merger even if it has benefits in the other jurisdictions. In addition, a fear exists that others will compete towards the lowest common regime in order to acquire footloose investment (see Trachtman 1994).
5 *New forms of interfirm arrangements* – new and evolving patterns of interfirm behaviour, collaboration and alliances are emerging (see Chapter 3 below), making effective analysis of interfirm behaviour difficult (see Bureau of Competition Policy, Canada, *Draft Guidelines on Strategic Alliances* 1995). Thus enforcement by a single national antitrust authority may be constrained as many of the new forms of behaviour cross borders.
6 *Dumping* – 95 per cent of observers would likely agree that anti-dumping practices as commonly employed are basically, although not exclusively, protectionist, raise domestic prices and lower welfare (see Council of

Economic Advisers, *Report to the President* 1994). In addition, anti-dumping is inconsistent with free trade and violates principles of national treatment (Waverman 1994). Ninety-five per cent of observers also agree that replacing anti-dump by competition policy procedures would be superior. To do this, however, requires some overall international competition policy agenda and a competition policy in each country which addresses predatory practices.

7 *Strategic dumping* – 'strategic dumping essentially involves subsidizing exports through higher home prices sustained by collusive price behaviour and a protected home market' (Ostry 1994: 15). The view that strategic dumping exists is growing and thus must be dealt with through rational analysis and discussion.

8 *Competitive exclusionary practices* – a danger exists that without competition policy convergence, nations will act unilaterally to defend what they consider to be their strategic interest. For example, the European Commission has complained that recent US competition law legislation (in this case the National Cooperative Production Act of 1994 extending permissive antitrust treatment to the production end of R&D collaborations) was conditioning the principle of national treatment so as to assist US firms (Services of the European Commission, *Report on US Barriers to Trade and Investment*, April 1994).

9 *Extraterritoriality* – as a function of all the points raised above, national governments are unilaterally extending the reach of their laws, including antitrust laws. In 1991 the US Federal Trade Commission concluded a consent decree with Institut Mérieux of France, which purchased Connaught Laboratories of Canada, neither having production facilities in the United States, and without informing the Canadian counterpart agency. In 1994 the US Department of Justice concluded a consent decree with Pilkington UK, a decree which stated that Pilkington's restrictive business practices affected the ability of US firms to export technology to build turnkey glass plants overseas. No impact on welfare in the United States was discussed.

THIS BOOK

The purposes of this book are threefold – first, to analyse the role of national competition policies in a world of increasingly interconnected markets; second, to produce a consistent framework to investigate the differences in domestic competition policies in the United States, Japan, the European Union and Canada, that impact competitiveness, international trade, investment and innovation; third, to propose alternative policies designed to reduce system friction.[8] This investigation of conflicts and frictions is based on the modern tools of industrial organization and strategic trade theory, focusing primarily on issues of dynamic efficiency.[9]

The chapters of this book are both an examination of legal differences in competition policies and an analysis of the impacts of globalization on domestic markets and competition. Researchers today do not analyse domestic macroeconomic policies without consideration of the global capital market. Similarly, one cannot discuss the impacts of domestic competition policies which affect real capital flows and innovation without an understanding of the constraints imposed by international markets and global competition. Moreover, unlike capital markets, goods markets can be impacted by market power. Thus we examine both the need for harmonization of domestic competition policies as well as the need (if any) for control of the degree of competition in multinational markets.

Below, we highlight the major issues which are examined under the headings of *the trends in the forms of international corporate organization* (how prevalent are cross-border intercorporate ties), *mergers* (ownership of horizontally connected means of production), *other horizontal arrangements* (joint ventures, consortia and alliances), *vertical arrangements* (ties between pieces of a vertically connected chain) and *policy* (the potential steps which are feasible in reducing undesirable barriers created by domestic antitrust policy). In each of these parts of the book the impact of competition policies on static and dynamic efficiency, innovation and technical advance is stressed. While each part has a different structure, several themes are maintained – what are the economic motivations for differences in observed structures; do domestic competition laws affect FDI, the uses of productive assets and the pace of innovation and, if so, what are the options to minimize conflict; are there international competition implications and if so, what can be done?

The chapters of the book are much more than a set of individual writings; they evolved over several years through a set of workshops and presentations. An Advisory Board was organized from key members of the legal and Competition Law Agency communities to provide comments on early drafts. The workshops (Santa Barbara, January 1993; Paris, May 1993; Tokyo, April 1994) proved so animated that a number of Advisory Board members decided to write papers for the volume (Goldman and Rill, Baker, Campbell, Reynolds and Rowley). We, the editors are indebted to the authors and Advisory Board members for the amount of time and energy that they put into the volume and the discussions. The majority of the funding was supplied by the Centre for Global Partnership of the Japan Foundation and we are extremely indebted to their generosity and their interest in the subject. We are also deeply grateful to the Bureau of Competition Policy in Canada, which provided the seed money for the project, and Howard Wetston, then its Director.

The workshops proved effective not just for the participants. The researchers and Advisory Board met with the Fair Trade Commission in Tokyo (May 1993), the International Trade Research Institute in Beijing

(April 1994), the World Bank (November 1994) and the Chinese Taipei Fair Trade Commission and the Pacific Economic Cooperation Council (Taipei, April 1995). As well several members of the group made presentations to the OECD committee on Competition Law and Policy in 1993.

Because there is a real need to maintain research, analysis and advice in the core area of the international aspects of domestic competition law, this group is now organized as the Global Forum on Trade and Competition Policy, with support from the International Bar Association and the World Bank. The Global Forum is designed as a non-governmental, non-partisan group of experts whose aims are to produce fundamental analyses of the interplay between trade and competition policy and to press for international policies which will maximize growth and efficiency.

Trends in the forms of international corporate organization

Two chapters form the first part of the book. In Chapter 2 *Sylvia Ostry* sets out the central case, the case that she was first in the world to raise, that the boundary between 'external' and 'domestic' policies is now irrelevant, that the rules of the game, including domestic R&D policy and competition policy, affect market access, trade and investment, the need to discuss how these 'domestic' issues affect access/trade/investment and why coordination/harmonization is on the agenda and is best dealt with openly. Dr Ostry considers that the substance of competition policy and its enforcement must both be dealt with but that the problems in harmonization are profound, since the overall objectives of competition policy vary not only in the efficiency principles utilized but also as to whether and which social policy goals are also part of competition policy objectives. Dr Ostry reminds us that 'the variation in enforcement in both the structural and behavioural instruments of competition policy is probably greater than that in objectives'. Dr Ostry discusses the issue of effective market access, *keiretsu* and argues that 'the crucial issue becomes a trade-off between efficiency and exclusion, or ... a conflict between the objectives of national policy and the important trade issue of effective market access'.

In Chapter 3 *A. Edward Safarian*, one of the leaders in the world studying MNEs and FDI, gathers and analyses new data examining the set of relationships used by MNEs in traditional FDI and in alliances. He finds that International Cooperation Agreements (ICAs) have grown, relative to FDI, over the 1982 to 1992 period. As we know FDI has grown far more than trade. ICAs have exploded albeit from a small base. Safarian analyses why ICAs are found for technology intensive products. He argues that the competition issues of ICAs are likely minor, as usually discussed by analysts, but suggests that, where such alliances are a part of state policy, strategic issues have to be carefully dealt with.

7

Broadly, firms can organize their international affiliations in arm's-length trade as well as in ownership and control-related affiliates (foreign direct investment), and various intermediate collaborative forms. In the past several decades the first has come to be significantly carried out through the second, while more recently the third appears to have gained relative to the second. Safarian summarizes the work which has been done to date on the reasons for the expansion of collaborative ventures, motives which range from reducing the costs of research and development (R&D) to enhancing market access. Here Safarian consolidates data on foreign direct investment and the most important component thereof, international mergers and acquisitions. There are large gaps and other defects in such data, but some clarification is possible by comparing IMF, OECD and other private and public studies.

Mergers

Merger policy has long differed across countries. However, a merger today can involve operations spanning a host of countries, thus involving applications to competition authorities in many jurisdictions at the regional, national and subnational level (for example, Siemens and GEC referred their bid for Plessey separately to the British, German, French and Italian governments, and in addition to the European Commission). Moreover, mergers and acquisitions are the main instrument of FDI today. Any authority acting in isolation can terminate the merger, including individual US states (in the United States private parties also have standing to challenge mergers).[10]

Two recent cases are illustrative of the issue. On August 31, 1990, the US FTC issued an order requiring a French firm with no production facilities in the United States, Institute Mérieux, which purchased a Canadian company – Connaught Laboratories (also with no production facilities in the United States), first, to lease a rabies vaccine business in Toronto to a third party and second, to give the FTC jurisdiction 'over any future acquisition Mérieux may make for 10 years' (Rosenthal 1990: 2). In 1989 a private antitrust case launched in New York state successfully prevented a merger not challenged by the US, British or EC competition authorities (Minorca, a hostile acquisition of Consolidated Gold Fields PLC).

In short, parties to an international merger face the possibility of multiple reviews and challenges to a proposed transaction under the domestic competition laws of various jurisdictions, with concomitant increases in uncertainty, cost and time delay.

'International merger' is, however, a somewhat imprecise term. The purchase of a local US business by a Japanese firm with no prior presence in the US market might be described as an international merger. At the other extreme, an international merger could involve two multinational enterprises which engage in production and sales activities in numerous common countries. Thus in Chapter 5 *Neil Campbell and Michael Trebilcock* develop a taxonomy of international merger transactions and identify the nature of the potential anti-competitive effects associated with each. These classifications provide a foundation for assessing which policy initiatives would be most appropriate for overcoming barriers to FDI and innovation.

The main body of this chapter consists of a comparative assessment of merger regulation in the United States, Japan, the European Union and Canada but with the focus on the international impact, spillovers across borders and problems of enforcement across borders. The purpose of this review is to identify major similarities and, more important, differences which impose constraints on FDI and innovation. This analysis is based primarily on the competition legislation in each jurisdiction as well as any delegated legislation or jurisprudence which is relevant. Enforcement guidelines and practices are examined, since they can have a substantial *de facto* impact on merger policy. For example, enforcement authorities in the United States adopted a substantially more lenient posture towards mergers in the 1980s without any prompting from legislative amendments or judicial decisions.

The comparative analysis is organized around a generic framework of the major substantive, procedural and remedial issues which arise in the review of anti-competitive mergers. In the substantive area, key issues include the definition of a merger, identification of relevant markets, the threshold used to identify anti-competitiveness, and the treatment of efficiency gains.[11]

Campbell and Trebilcock develop a series of coordination models or strategies for reducing the barriers to FDI and innovation resulting from differences in domestic merger policies.[12] Such strategies may range from informal cooperation between enforcement authorities at one extreme to a formal supranational merger review system at the other end of the spectrum. In between would be harmonization strategies of various types. For example, a weak form of harmonization might focus purely on procedural issues such as time limits and disclosure requirements. A strong form of harmonization, in contrast, might involve major substantive and/or remedial matters as well. Important issues consist of the ability to share information between jurisdictions, the standards to be applied and the criteria – national, regional or global competition and welfare (see OECD 1991: 4). The taxonomy of international mergers and the assessment of differences between domestic merger law regimes are a major contribution to the literature.

In Chapter 4 *Hiroyuki Odagiri* examines mergers and acquisitions in Japan. Odagiri begins, 'Mergers and acquisitions are by no means rare in Japan.' While hostile acquisitions are rare, the number of 'friendly' acquisitions is high (2,003 in 1992) although most are mergers of small firms. A survey of the motives for mergers emphasized 'sub-optimal scale, management difficulty, or simply bad management' (66 per cent) or 'growth constraints' (25 per cent). These main motives appear to explain purchases: diversification, marketing-orientated and technology-orientated. Odagiri argues that the three main features of the Japanese labour system – lifetime employment, seniority and enterprise unionism – make it difficult to merge unless a firm is experiencing severe problems.

Odagiri then turns to the anti-monopoly law in Japan and its enforcement. 'Has Japanese anti-monopoly regulation been effective in preventing anti-competitive mergers and acquisitions?' The answer is yes – through two channels: publication of the guidelines and informal consultation. 'In 1992 for example the JFTC brought one case (not an M&A) to court, issued thirty-seven recommendations, and warnings and admonitions in ninety-four cases.' Odagiri suggests that a more open process involving prior notification of large-scale acquisitions be implemented. Similarly, business alliances without share ownership, for which no notification is currently required, are not easy to detect by the FCC.

Joint ventures, strategic alliances and consortia

A merger is a share or asset sale which effectively eliminates a corporation. Other intercorporate forms of integration are increasing. Jorde and Teece (1990) discuss joint ventures, strategic alliances, research consortia and production consortia. These are all distinguishable from mergers in that they do not lead to the dissolution of a firm and can be temporary, 'assembled and disassembled as circumstances warrant' (Jorde and Teece 1990: 85). A recent phenomenon has been corporate capital linkages through minority share holdings – either cross-holdings of shares or a one-way minority participation. An example is the minority cross-holding negotiated between Renault and Volvo in 1991 as well as the Mitsubishi purchase of a significant minority ownership in Volvo.

There has not been a clear analysis of the differences between these various forms of organization and of what they mean for FDI. Joint ventures, research and production consortia and strategic alliances, as Safarian notes, seem to be becoming more prevalent, larger in size and possibly dominant in some high-tech industries. Experts differ in their views of the efficacy of current domestic competition policy in this area. Jorde and Teece (1990) saw antitrust laws in the United States as needlessly inhibiting 'interfirm agreements designed to develop and commercialize new technology' (p. 85) and suggested that the US National Cooperative Research Act of 1984 was only a minimal response to the problem. Broadly (1990) and Shapiro and Willig (1990) argue that one cannot ignore the 'cartel-like' impacts of consortia, especially those aimed at production, not research. Baumol (1990) examines 'technology cartels', i.e. 'consortia of firms willing to reveal their technological secrets to the other members, who may or may not be direct competitors, on the condition that the others reciprocate' (p. 2). Baumol finds that these technology cartels have advantages over single competitors, seem likely to contribute to economic efficiency and that 'this may be one way in which antitrust activity, as currently conducted (in the United States) does indeed inhibit innovation and productivity growth' (p. 35).

As a starting point two problems have to be carefully examined. The first concerns the motives that cause a firm to prefer a particular type of cooperation over another. A major determinant would appear to be the existence of transaction costs and firms' desire to restrict uncertainty and opportunistic behaviour. Government regulation and other strategic considerations may give important motives, as do the sharing of economies of scale, risk and technological knowledge.

The second problem is the impact that these various arrangements have on welfare. In order to identify the social benefits and costs, one has to distinguish sharply not only between the different forms of collaboration but also between the different goals that are aimed at. Let us take the example of *joint ventures*, one formed to promote R&D and the other to cooperate in production.

Intuitively, cooperative R&D arrangements have three beneficial effects. First, they allow firms to overcome the well known free rider problem associated with R&D when patent protection is imperfect. Spillovers of research results to rival competitors create an external effect that reduces the incentives to innovate. R&D cooperation may serve here as a means to solve this appropriability problem by committing firms to payment before the R&D is conducted, and hence before any spillovers can occur.

Second, cooperative research may allow the participants to enjoy substantial economies of joint action, especially when synergies or complementarities are present. By exploiting economies of scale and avoiding socially wasteful duplication of effort R&D cooperation can tend to improve the efficiency of the research process.

Third, research joint ventures guarantee diffusion and thus help to overcome the public good problem that arises after discovery. Because the use of information embodied in the results of a particular R&D process by one party does not exclude others from exploiting the same know-how, economic efficiency calls for widespread diffusion. The more firms that participate in the venture, the stronger is downstream competition via diffusion and the more will final consumers benefit from cooperative R&D arrangements.

Even though these effects are beneficial, research joint ventures raise some antitrust concerns. The first is that of dynamic inefficiency in the R&D market. Ventures in an already concentrated industry where the firms are aware of their interdependence may help rivals to avoid competing in the

R&D market. The result is a slowdown in the pace of technological innovation, which clearly has negative effects.

The second anti-competitive danger is that an R&D contract may facilitate horizontal collusion in the output market. This is especially true when the venture agreement incorporates ancillary restraints, which may be socially undesirable but nevertheless, under certain conditions, necessary to provide a proper incentive to undertake the research project at all.

In contrast to a cooperative arrangement that is formed to promote R&D, a conventional production joint venture seems to raise neither appropriability nor public good considerations and therefore the potential benefits of collaboration may be reduced. Moreover, the anti-competitive threat that a cooperative arrangement could pose is more apparent. Even if the parents of the joint venture avoid direct collusion there is still the danger that the venture could transfer its output to the parents at a sufficiently high price to cause them to charge higher prices to their customers. In the United States it took many attempts to bring joint production ventures under the National Cooperative Research Act to allow risk sharing, realization of economies of scale, economies of scope, and 'synergies arising from complementary skills or assets of the parties' (Rill 1990: 5). Academic economists are still clearly divided as to the social efficiency of production joint ventures.

International policy harmonization or guidelines are needed in this area. First, if competition policies on these horizontal, quasi-horizontal (or horizontal–vertical) arrangements differ across countries, friction will develop and technology development may be hampered. This is especially true when national joint ventures are formed in industries with large export shares. Foreign governments may then interpret a permissive attitude towards cooperative arrangements as a form of strategic trade policy intended to improve the relative position of domestic suppliers (their competitors). Another crucial competition issue exists, however. Where these ventures are cross-country or dominant in an industry, no national authority may be able to analyse or deal with the venture properly. One possible route for both these concerns is extraterritoriality: the attempted extension of one country's laws across its borders. Extraterritoriality is not an adequate answer but is possible today. An alternative is policy harmonization bolstered by global institutions that are able to promote this policy. The EU policy, through still unsatisfactory, may serve here as a useful example of intercountry coordination.

In Chapter 6 *Shyam Khemani and Leonard Waverman* study the competition policy issues surrounding the International Strategic Alliances (ISAs) which are found important in Chapter 3. They examine the motives for ISAs and whether competition policy concerns would require new forms of domestic competition law for these new forms of harmonization. They argue that any anti-competitive effects of ISAs (and few if any have been found) would be well covered by existing laws and processes. They consider notification rules but argue against these largely because of the difficulty of defining what an ISA is and the real potential for diminishing pro-competitive ISAs in such a process.

In Chapter 7 *James Rill and Calvin Goldman*, two ex-heads of the competition authorities in the United States and Canada, respectively, analyse deeply the confidentiality issues and the potential conflict between firm privacy and antitrust needs in coordinating an information request across one or several borders. They examine the operations of the Canadian–US Mutual Legal Assistance Treaty, the Canadian–US and the US–EU Antitrust Cooperation Agreements and the new US International Enforcement Assistance Act, which calls for increased information sharing among antitrust authorities. Rill and Goldman discuss the trade-offs between promoting competition though strong enforcement and perhaps limiting competition by making firms wary of undertaking certain activities. The authors also discuss the recent cooperation between Canada and the United States in joint investigation (fax paper), and coordinated raids (the plastic dinnerware case), both involving criminal charges.

In Chapter 8 *Kotaro Suzumura and Akira Goto* study a little known subject – the extent and nature of collaborative R&D consortia in Japan. Given Japanese success in 'high-tech' and the high visibility of cooperative R&D in Japan, many countries see Japanese policy as worthy of emulation. The authors begin by reminding us of basic economic principles: joint R&D can increase efficiency and be consistent with national welfare where collaboration aids diffusion and avoids wasteful duplication. However, joint decision-making could reduce innovation activity through spillovers into production decisions, thus raising prices and reducing well-being. Most R&D collaboration in Japan until recently did not involve joint research but coordinated in-house research. Of the 114 Joint Research Associations (JRAs) established before 1990, only twelve had joint R&D labs. The significance, size and extent of government subsidies to these JRAs have changed over the decades; in the 1980s the number, size and riskiness of research increased. The Japanese JRAs 'rarely realized' scale economies or brought together 'complementary assets'. The authors state that many of these JRAs are unlikely to have reduced wasteful duplication of effort. Why do JRAs exist in Japan? The authors conclude: 'The JRA scheme is an investment policy tool though which the government can promote some specific industrial policy goals'.

The authors turn to the potential anti-competitive effects of JRAs by examining the 1993 Japanese Fair Trade Commission (JFTC) Guidelines on joint R&D. The JFTC states that if the market share of competitors is below 20 per cent, cooperation problems are unlikely. In R&D collaborations where the participants have more than 20 per cent, the JFTC will look at restrictions on complementary activities or price and output restrictions. The authors approve of the new transparency in the guidelines but disagree with two thrusts – first, the emphasis on horizontal agreements rather than vertical R&D alliances which could prove anti-competitive, and, second, examining the pro-competitive nature of R&D alliances, not their effect on national welfare.

In Chapter 9 *Werner Meißner and Rainer Markl* examine the international trade and investment implications of R&D cooperation. They argue that national cooperation may well turn out to be a 'beggar thy neighbour' policy which increases the national well-being at the expense of foreigners. Thus a national R&D cooperation which excludes foreign companies is strategic trade policy and is at the expense of other nations. However, since MNEs are footloose and can expend their R&D resources anywhere (and R&D expenditures are becoming less concentrated in home countries), countries have an incentive to attract investment and R&D with a permissive antitrust policy. Thus the authors 'call for a quick and strong convergence of different national antitrust policies' in this area.

In Chapter 10 *Stephen Martin* continues the R&D theme. Martin provides a user-friendly guide to the recent theoretical economics literature on the potential efficiency-enhancing but competition-reducing effects of joint R&D&P (R&D and production). Martin extends this literature as well by showing in simple numerical simulation examples how both effects are possible. He feels that the literature shows 'that there is no compelling reason to think that joint R&D and production will in general improve static or dynamic market performance'. Joint R&D&P for very costly innovations could be socially desirable, but for other, less costly, projects, Martin argues, the potential anti-competitive efforts of joint R&D&P are large. Martin then analyses the antitrust policies towards joint R&D&P in the European Union, Japan and the United States. He contends that the institutional framework in Japan and the implicit antitrust limits on cooperation in the European Union are consistent with the pro-competitive effects of joint R&D&P. However, Martin suggests that US policy towards collaborative agreements 'lacks the central brake on anti-competitive agreements' of the EU and could threaten the rivalry which has been the source of US competitiveness.

In Chapter 11 *Thomas Jorde and David Teece* suggest that harmonization requires competition policy across national states to embed within it (1) common goals and (2) a shared vision of economic reality. Increasingly, economic welfare (rather than diffused political goals) has come to be accepted as the central goal of competition policy. However, a shared vision of economic reality has yet to emerge. Jorde and Teece express the hope that dynamic competition, i.e. competition fuelled by technological and organizational innovation, will be the vision of economic reality around which nations coalesce. Indeed, the authors express some confidence that industrial policy will be shelved and replaced by competition policy which embeds the historical goals of industrial policy within it.

Vertical interfirm arrangements and innovation

In the Triad one observes that the tightness of vertical control arrangements of customer–supplier relations varies (vertical integration, exclusive dealerships, resale price maintenance, refusal to supply, tying arrangements). Even at the expense of some oversimplification, one may distinguish the following categories on the continuum of control, namely a high degree of control in customer–supplier relations in Japan, a low one in the United States and United Kingdom and an intermediate degree in continental Europe. In addition, vertical arrangements range from fleeting to contractual, to ownership, to long-lasting Japanese informal consortia. These vertical arrangements are also handled very differently under antitrust law in the United States, in Japan, in the EU and in Canada. The differences appear particularly strong in the case of the Japanese form of ownership and production (the *keiretsu* corporate relationships). As noted, the US Federal Trade Commission investigated whether Japanese *keiretsu* relationships constitute anti-competitive behaviour, since *keiretsu* involve long-term exclusive supply arrangements and possibly different prices. The FTC was concerned that such practices may be exclusionary and discriminatory.

What explains these differences in vertical arrangements? Do the different relationships reflect cost minimization or increased market power? Do they affect trade? Are different forms of vertical arrangements (e.g. Anglo-Saxon contractual versus Japanese informal) necessarily inconsistent with each other (see Professor Kenichi Imai of Hitotsubashi University, 'An age of competition between variant systems of capitalism has begun', quoted in the *Globe and Mail*, Saturday, September 22, 1990, p. B-1).

The academic debate about the motivations for vertical restraints and their impact on economic welfare is quite passionate. Roughly speaking, on one side it is asserted that markets are necessarily competitive, so that new business practices can emerge only if they improve economic efficiency. Along this line of thinking, businessmen 'know their business' better than economists or regulators do, and the best possible regulatory policy is no regulation at all. On the other side, the advice is to rule out any kind of arrangement which may restrict one party's freedom of trade – which, for example, is the case with practically any provision in a franchise contract. The controversy reflects the opposition between different schools of economic thought, but it also hinges on divergences in the appreciation of the context of these relationships and of the nature of the underlying economic analysis.

The diversity of positions is mirrored in the diversity in the legal status of these vertical restraints in the various countries – and, also, in the change in attitudes over time, in a given country. In the United States, for instance, case law has developed separately for each type of restriction, and different case law for different types has evolved somewhat independently. (At least, the cases which serve as benchmarks are not necessarily the same for each type of restriction; moreover, the changes in attitude towards price and non-price restrictions have not always been coincidental.)

For many years, vertical restraints were treated in the United States in much the same manner as horizontal restraints. Just as the latter are considered to be *per se* violations of the Sherman Act, so vertical restraints received the same treatment. Indeed, vertical price restraints, including resale price maintenance, are still *per se* illegal in the United States. However, in the past fifteen years, vertical non-price restraints and other types of vertical restrictions have been adjudicated differently and are now evaluated under the rule of reason. Through this means, the anti-competitive effect of a specific restraint must be evaluated before it can be considered a violation of the antitrust laws.

While there is much to be said for this approach, since one can determine circumstances in which vertical restraints have both negative and positive consequences for consumer welfare, the question is more difficult than that. Cases adjudicated under the *per se* doctrine are generally won by plaintiffs, while those determined under the rule of reason tend to favour defendants. Therefore the specific rule employed has major implications for the final outcome. One's judgement as to the frequency and severity of the anti-competitive effects of such restraints has therefore an important bearing on the judicial rule employed, even despite the recognition that there are some circumstances where vertical restraints can be innocuous and others where they can have major anti-competitive results.

The approach of the European Union, on the other hand, is to treat vertical restraints according to the kind of relationship which is involved. Most vertical restraints are *a priori* illegal, according to the Treaty of Rome. However, various groups of vertical restrictions can be allowed when they are part of a selective distribution or franchising agreement. (There exist so-called 'block exemptions' for some categories of special types of producer–distributor relationship.)

To illustrate the diversity of legal attitudes, we review below the attitude of several countries or zones towards two particular types of restriction – exclusive territories (territorial restrictions) and exclusive dealing arrangements – for simplicity assuming that they are part of a franchise contract.

Territorial restrictions

Broadly speaking, territorial restrictions, which tend to reduce intrabrand competition, benefit from a *relatively permissive status* when part of a franchise agreement. Substantial differences can, however, be mentioned, in particular according to the kind of exclusive arrangements which are involved.

In the United States, *Continental Television* v. *GTE Sylvania* was the first case where the Supreme Court mentioned the possible pro-competitive effects of territorial restrictions on interbrand competition, and substituted the rule of reason for the *per se* illegality established in the *Schwinn* case. The Supreme Court also stressed the adverse effects that a *per se* rule may have on small and independent business.

The Australian Trade Practices Commission stressed that although Coca-Cola granted each franchisee a monopoly position in each territory, the franchise agreement had pro-competitive effects as well. It is interesting to note that the TPC insists that territorial exclusivity must be limited to a 'reasonable' period, generally not exceeding five years. The lack of complaints by competitors, cited by the Commission, should, however, be treated with caution, since these territorial restrictions may indeed serve to decrease interbrand competition as well as intrabrand competition.

The Canadian example provides sharp differences in approach. Although franchise agreements benefit from a favourable view in general, the antitrust authority will interfere when a substantial part of the franchiser's market is affected by the franchise arrangement. It will not interfere, however, when the agreement covers only a limited period of time, in order to facilitate the entry of new products or new firms. It may, however, be too early to assess the feasibility of implementing this contingent rule.

The European Commission and Court of Justice set a borderline between 'absolute' and 'limited' or 'passive' exclusive territory (a franchisee is allowed to sell 'passively' if he is allowed to accept orders from outside his territory – such a distinction was, however, suggested by Justice White in his concurring judgement in the Sylvania case). Therefore, although the commission recognizes that reducing intrabrand competition may in some contexts increase interbrand competition, it nevertheless insists on maintaining a substantial amount of intrabrand competition.[13]

Exclusive dealing arrangements

Exclusive dealing can be socially as well as privately beneficial when it serves to ensure a minimum level of distribution services or when it protects the producer's rights on a specific investment in a form of know-how. On the other hand it can have a negative impact on interbrand competition when a producer uses exclusive contracts to foreclose his market, by preempting outlet locations or prominent franchisees. This latter feature is likely to be the most harmful when used by well established producers, and when there is a shortage, even a transitory one, of possible distributors.

Several countries indeed aim at distinguishing between the situation of franchisers well established in their markets ('major suppliers') and the situation of new entrants, and are apparently succeeding in doing so. Article 49.4.a of the Canadian Competition Act allows the competition authorities to exempt exclusive dealing provisions, for a reasonable period, when the provisions mainly serve to facilitate the entry of a new firm or of a new product. This approach was successfully used to allow Bombardier to have exclusive dealers for its new Ski-doo product.

In the United States the decisions of the Supreme Court (*Tampa Electric v. Nashville Coal*) and FTC (Beltone Electronics) are generally in the same direction, although without providing substantial analytical tools.[14]

The European Union case is slightly more complex. There exclusive dealing agreements can be exempted as such by the exclusive dealing block exemption regulation, but they are not necessarily exempted when they are part of a larger franchising arrangement. In this latter case the Commission draws a distinction between those products which are at the core of the franchise agreement, on the one side, and secondary products such as accessories or spare parts, on the other side; exclusive agreements cannot be employed for the secondary products. The Commission also requires that a certain number of conditions must be satisfied; in particular, the exclusivity clause must be necessary for the protection of the franchiser's rights, and it must be impossible to achieve similar goals in different ways, such as for instance the specification of objective quality standards.

This quick survey shows substantive economic and legal differences between countries in their examination of vertical restraints. Thus an international examination of vertical arrangements takes on a new urgency today, since there appear to be growing differences in the treatment of vertical restraints across countries at the same time as global investment and other considerations are causing firms to produce in many markets. Since each of these markets is a unique arena for vertical distribution/supplier arrangements, multinational firms must adapt their vertical arrangements in different countries, likely at a loss of efficiency, or policy must converge.

The fact that different countries or zones have different policies towards vertical business practices creates several types of serious problems from the point of view of international trade, investment and innovation.

First, of course differences in competition law increase the costs associated with production across national borders. If a firm wants to expand in a new country, it has to learn the new acceptable behaviour and adapt. Adaptation may be costly. Second, a more favourable attitude towards vertical restraints in a given country can give a firm an artificial advantage over foreign competitors. This may enable a firm to compete in an unfair way in foreign countries. But, perhaps more important, it may favour incumbent firms at the expense of foreign firms and give rise to some form of hidden protectionism. The debate about the Japanese *keiretsu* and the SS1 negotiation is quite illustrative of this latter aspect. Policy convergence here may be a remedy. Policy convergence, however, depends on the definition and possible harmonization of laws relating to vertical practices, not an easy task.

There is also a growing and strong relationship between vertical arrangements and horizontal relationships. For example, the Mitsubishi *keiretsu* has been involved in numerous cooperative ventures, the most significant with Daimler-Benz in aerospace, automobiles and electronics. Various parts of these two huge vertically aligned firms were to cooperate with each other. This set of horizontal/vertical ties between large multinationals may raise complex competition concerns, at an international level beyond the jurisdiction of any single competition authority.

Three chapters in this volume examine the vertical arena. In Chapter 12 *Annette Bongardt* details a crucial arena – automobile production in Japan and Europe. The essential elements of the Japanese supply chain in auto production are well known – long-run relationships and bilateral price negotiations (among other crucial elements). The author provides new information and analysis of the changing supply relationship in the EU car supply chain. 'Supply structures in the EU car industry resemble overlapping and unstructured pyramids ... the EU components industry is presently undergoing a shake-out'. Real and potential competition from Japanese producers is causing deep shifts in existing methods of out-sourcing. While the technological capabilities of EU component producers are high, the sequential management of the R&D process is inefficient and final costs are high. The example of Mercedes-Benz demonstrates how new coordination of suppliers into 'learning networks' is proceeding in Europe. There is, however, far more sharing of suppliers across supply chains in Europe than in Japan, and this pattern is likely to remain. Hence any possibilities of 'exclusion' are lower in Europe. Moreover, actual networks, including those of Japanese producers in Europe, are via contracts rather than the 'vertical' *keiretsu* type. Bongardt analyses EU competition law on vertical restraints and finds that 'it is this gap in EU competition legislation to grant block exemptions for typified single-sourcing agreements in the vertical chain that implies that European networks are prejudicated in terms of transaction costs and time compared with networks based beyond the European Union that benefit from laxer legislation'.

In Chapter 13 *William Comanor and Patrick Rey* summarize the present state of economic theory on 'vertical restraints' (i.e. the differing contractual limitations placed on the activities of distributors and retailers by manufacturers, such as exclusive distribution, territorial restrictions, etc.; such contracts could also flow from dealers imposing contracts upstream). Economic theory suggests that, where interbrand competition is high, limits on interbrand competition are unlikely to be anti-competitive. That is, upstream firms can increase efficiency and the well-being of consumers by ensuring that distributors/retailers have sufficient margins to undertake demand-enhancing activities such as advertising, point-of-sale promotion and service, warranties, etc. However, in a number of cases, interbrand competition may not be sufficient or may be altered, the authors argue, by vertical restraints. In particular, the practice of exclusive distribution by groups of domestic firms may limit market access by foreigners. Comanor and Rey use the exclusive distribution arrangements that existed in the

1950s and 1960s among US car producers and their subsequent demise to argue that this reduced the costs of entry by foreign car producers into the US market. Hence they conclude that vertical restraints can act as implicit trade barriers.

In Chapter 14 *Akira Goto and Kotaro Suzumura* examine the operations of the *keiretsu* in Japan, a subject not well researched in the existing economics literature. They begin, 'Unfortunately the term *keiretsu* is more journalistic than academic and is not well defined.' They analyse the two types – horizontal (alliances of large firms belonging to different industries, the pre-World War II *zaibatsu*) and vertical (large manufacturing firms and their suppliers). The authors discuss the many characteristics of both types, concentrating on the issues of intragroup sales and purchases, 'a practice which is often the focus of trade talks'. Data on intragroup sales and purchases among horizontal *keiretsu* (11.1 per cent and 8.1 per cent respectively) suggest high trade with outsiders. However, these data do not shed light 'on whether member firms prefer to deal with other group members when alternatives exist'. A 1992 JFTC survey showed that among horizontal *keiretsu* which include computer manufacturers 'while group firms may prefer to deal with each other, in reality they buy from outside firms when they are not satisfied with the group firm's product'. Among vertical *keiretsu* long-run manufacturer–supplier relationships exist. However these are not exclusive and 'entry and exit are not uncommon'.

Goto and Suzumura explain horizontal *keiretsu* as a response to a different market for corporate control and a different legal and institutional framework than in the United States, for example, which gives Japanese firms few options to counter takeover and greenmail threats. The reasons for the vertical *keiretsu* are well known: cost reduction. The authors suggest several potential antitrust problems of *keiretsu*. First, vertical *keiretsu* may be a response of firms to the organizations of other competitors and while these vertical organizations are efficient their effects on prices to consumers (whether cost reductions are passed on in terms of lower final goods prices) are not known. Second, 'a certain degree of foreclosure is inevitable'. (However, 'foreclosure' is not bad if costs fall as a result and overall welfare increases.)

The authors end by arguing that the term *keiretsu* includes highly different organizational forms and diverse market effects. 'It is necessary to find the way to maintain their diversity and at the same time guarantee the compatibility of diverse market economics.'

Policy

The OECD has recently stated (March 1991) that 'International cooperation in competition policy is high on the agenda of the current debate on strengthening the rules of the game for economic relations' (p. 1). If, as the first three parts of this book suggest, the various horizontal and vertical relationships among multinationals affect domestic and international competition, what sets of policies could be put in place to minimize conflicts and maximize benefits – trade, investment, innovation and economic growth? One possible policy is harmonization. This does not necessarily mean that domestic policies should be identical. Conflicts and friction may be reduced by providing a consistent framework, a consistent reporting requirement, opening lines of communication between national competition authorities. More complete policy harmonization is another option to be examined. Campbell and Trebilcock in Chapter 5 provide an ordered topology of the various ways in which policy could be harmonized.

It is not necessary to have a set of completely harmonized competition policies across all countries. Such is not needed and likely counterproductive. The reason is simple. Economists in this volume and elsewhere disagree as to some of the essential fundamental principles of industrial organization – such as when vertical restraints are competitive or anti-competitive; whether R&D alliances are welfare-enhancing or welfare-reducing. The divergence in theory suggests that harmonizing competition policy to some tight standard is impossible and not beneficial – 'competition among competition policies' is still required. Also some elements of competition policy reflect essential domestic ways of operating an economy. The best example of this is merger law – the Anglo-Saxon model of corporate governance stresses the need for hostile takeovers to ensure managerial efficiency while the German/Japanese model stresses long-term alliances and frowns on hostile takeovers. Surely competition policy is going too far if the basic corporate governance of a nation has to be altered to some other model.

Yet, as we have stressed above, domestic anti-competitive abuses can have clear international ramifications – they can be barriers to trade and investment. Moreover, the spillovers also discussed above require some closer coordination.

Countries can no longer 'avoid' competition policies if firms domiciled there are free to contravene antitrust laws in other jurisdictions. The extension of domestic competition law through extraterritoriality is natural, since a country must be able to protect itself against companies' or other anti-competitive behaviour launched from outside the country. However, extraterritoriality can abuse another country's jurisdiction and laws. The principle of 'comity', taking another sovereign's interests into account, is difficult to make enforceable and concrete. The United States and the European Union have been particularly aggressive in extraterritorial applications of domestic competition law. The recently announced consent accord between Pilkington and the US Department of Justice signals a new extension of the extraterritorial application of antitrust law to the arena of patents and trade secrets. Several chapters in this volume address these policy concerns.

21

In Chapter 15 *Damien Neven and Paul Seabright* ask two crucial questions – first, whether trade policies and competition policies are complements or substitutes and, second, what organizational form (GATT, WTO, OECD, etc.) and institutional arrangement (formal, informal) best permit effective coordination. They show that 'in a number of instances the removal of trade barriers does indeed enhance the possibility that firms will indulge in predation and other forms of undesirable behaviour towards foreign competitors, so that trade and supranational competition policies may act as complements'. Hence opening borders (such as many LDCs or dynamic newly emerging economies are now doing) requires, in a number of theoretical instances, strong competition law.

The case for international cooperation or harmonization is that spillovers across national borders are high. The authors argue for the principle of subsidiarity – there are few reasons to centralize internationally those competition policy concerns which have only local effects. As spillovers do exist – and, indeed, as Ostry and others argue, are more prevalent than many consider – appropriate international mechanisms are necessary. Neven and Seabright argue that coordination problems among many players are high; 'this may be one reason why the European Union has felt the need to centralize its merger control procedures'. They argue that cooperative mechanisms will work only if a 'reasonable homogeneity of interests exists between the members of a few international groups'. Thus they are pessimistic that an organization such as the GATT can be effective in coordinating antitrust policy among countries.

In Chapter 16 *Janusz Ordover and Eleanor Fox* examine the wide variety of arguments, pro and con, for accommodation, coordination and harmonization of competition law among countries. They examine, in detail, the advantages and disadvantages of moving towards process harmonization, accommodating other countries' interests in domestic decision-making (positive and negative comity) and actual harmonization of domestic laws. They argue that the case is weak and the probability low for substantive harmonization but the authors offer sets of procedures and agreements, particularly on a process which could minimize conflicts.

In Chapter 17 Baker *et al.* set themselves a different agenda from Ordover and Fox: if one had agreed internationally to harmonize the enforcement of domestic competition law, how would one go about it? The chapter explores the many important procedural issues which arise when antitrust agencies seek to cooperate and coordinate enforcement efforts. The authors discuss the ways in which enforcement cooperation can contribute to the objective of maximizing global economic welfare, and suggest six fundamental principles which should guide enforcement cooperation initiatives. The chapter also examines methods of achieving greater cooperation, including bilateral and multilateral treaties and memoranda of understanding. A lengthy appendix applies these general concepts to the area of merger review. The authors present specific proposals for operationalizing an 'International Merger Review System' which would be based on the concept of mutual recognition (e.g. of common forms and time limits for reviewing international transactions) rather than complete harmonization.

NOTES

1 The OECD produced an initial report on the interaction of trade and competition policy in 1984.
2 D. Rosenthal and R. Lipstein, *M&A Today*, April 23, 1990.
3 Sir Leon Brittan, Commissioner of the European Union for competition policy recently proposed that the European Union and the United States examine means to resolve conflicts over merger laws (April 6, 1990). In late 1990 the American Bar Association launched a study examining the legal issues of the international coordination of competition policy.
4 Ostry, *Governments and Corporations in a Shrinking World: Trade and Innovation Policies in the United States, Europe and Japan* (1990).
5 The OECD has stated that 'International cooperation in competition policy is high on the agenda of the current debate on strengthening the rules of the game for economic relations' (March 1991). Peter Sutherland, the past Director General of GATT, has stated that competition policy should be on the next agenda for future multilateral discussions of harmonization.
6 Chapter 7 below analyses the difficult issues faced in establishing bilateral or multilateral agreements.
7 See Ostry (1994), pp. 8–17.
8 Sylvia Ostry coined the term 'system friction' (1990). An example of the frictions developing can be seen in the remarks of the EC Commissioner responsible for Competition Policy, who has stated that without 'truly equal or analogous rules of behaviour, it will be difficult to exempt EFTA countries from EC trade-policy action' (Sir Leon Brittan, January 29, 1990).
9 Teece (Jorde and Teece 1990) argues that existing US competition policy is aimed at price competition, not product competition or dynamic efficiency.
10 In April 1990 the US Supreme Court ruled that states as well as consumers or competitors had the right under US antitrust law to take civil action to undo a merger. Prior to this decision, states could only sue to prevent a merger from occurring.
11 The latter issue is particularly significant, since there is theoretical consensus that pro-competitive, efficiency-enhancing mergers ought to be encouraged, but distinguishing such transactions from those which are anti-competitive is an exercise which is difficult to operationalize in practice. (The efficiency gains defence in the Canadian legislation provides a unique and innovative model for comparisons in this area.)
12 Note that Article 24 of the EU merger regulation is designed to enhance harmonization of competition laws, since it allows the Commission to negotiate 'comparable treatment' (read competition policy treatment). The EU merger regulation places great weight on competition issues in assessing mergers. If a non-EU country used its authority to ban a takeover by an EU firm on general issues, not competition policy, the European Union could then 'negotiate

comparable treatment'. Also note that Wolfgang Kartte, president of Germany's cartel office, has proposed the creation of a multilateral competition agency (see Rosenthal 1990: 9).

13 European Economic Community Commission decision on *Pronuptia*, Official Journal No. L 13/39, at 37. Regulation No. 4087/98 on the application of Article 85(3) of the Treaty of Rome to categories of franchising agreements, November 30, 1988, published in Official Journal No. L 359/46, December 28, 1988, p. 282 (point 12). *Ibid.*, p. 285.

14 The exemption regulation therefore does not apply when the franchisee can buy from other suppliers items which conceivably meet reasonable and explicit quality requirements (except, of course, if the goal of the franchisee consists exactly in distributing the franchiser's products). In the same spirit, even if the aim of the franchisee is the distribution of the franchiser's products, the franchiser cannot prevent his franchisees from buying the franchiser's products from other franchisees or retail outlets.

REFERENCES

William J. Baumol (1990) 'Technology-sharing Cartels', paper presented at the European Association of Industrial Economics Conference, Lisbon, September 2.

Joseph F. Broadly (1990) 'Antitrust Law and Innovation Cooperation', *Journal of Economic Perspectives* 4 (3).

Bureau of Competition Policy, Canada (1995) *Guidelines on Strategic Alliances*, Ottawa.

Council of Economic Advisors (1994) *Report to the President*, Washington.

B. Hoekman and P.C. Mavroidis (1994) 'Competition, Competition Policy and the GATT', *World Economy* 17, 121–50.

Thomas M. Jorde and David J. Teece (1990) 'Innovation and Cooperation: Implications for Competition and Antitrust', *Journal of Economic Perspectives* 4 (3).

Paul Krugman (1990) 'Multinational Corporations – The Old and the New', *Journal of the North American Economics and Finance Association*, December.

Paul Krugman (1992) *Age of Diminished Expectations: US Economic Policy in the 1990s*. Cambridge, Mass.; London: MIT Press.

OECD (1991) 'Towards an International Framework for Competition Policy', Committee on Competition Law and Policy, March 15.

Sylvia Ostry (1989) *Governments and Corporations in a Shrinking World: Trade and Innovation Policies in the United States, Europe and Japan*. New York: Council on Foreign Relations Press.

Sylvia Ostry (1990) 'Beyond the Border: The New International Policy Arena', paper presented at OECD, Forum for the Future, Paris, October 30.

Sylvia Ostry (1994) 'New Dimensions of Market Access: Overview from a Trade Policy Perspective', OECD Roundtable on the New Dimensions of Market Access in a Globalizing World Economy. Paris, June 30–July 1.

Douglas E. Rosenthal (1990) 'The Potential for Jurisdictional Conflicts in Multistate International Merger Transactions', mimeo, Washington.

James F. Rill (1990) Statement Concerning Joint Production Ventures Before the Subcommittee on Antitrust, Monopolies and Business Rights, Committee on the Judiciary, United States Senate, July 17.

Carl Shapiro and Robert D. Willig (1990) 'On the Antitrust Treatment of Production Joint Ventures', *Journal of Economic Perspectives* 4 (3).

Joel Trachtman (1993) 'International Regulatory Competition, Externalization, and Jurisdiction', *Harvard International Law Journal* 34 (Winter), 47–104, Harvard International Law Journal 0017-8063.

Villambrosa, R. (1994) 'Interactions between Competition and other Economic Policies: Trade and Competition Policies', paper prepared for an Informal Workshop with Dynamic Non-member Economies, Competition Policy. OECD Paris, November 25.

Waverman, L. (1994) 'Post NAFTA: "Can the USA, Canada and Mexico Deepen their Economic Relationships?"', paper prepared for the Inter-American Dialogue. Washington, March 2.

Part I

THE ISSUES

2

GLOBALIZATION, DOMESTIC POLICIES AND THE NEED FOR HARMONIZATION

Sylvia Ostry

When I made my original proposal for domestic policy convergence some years ago, I did so in the context of the evolution of innovation policies in the Triad.[1] That rationale also emerged in the OECD project on Technology and the Economy, or TEP, which had focused on the pervasive implications of technological change, especially in information and communication technologies (ICT), on governments, the economy and society. As a consequence, at their 1991 meeting OECD Ministers recommended that one follow-up of the TEP exercise should be a determination of whether policy harmonization in selected areas, including most obviously competition policy, was desirable and feasible. The objective of such analysis would be to propose new international 'rules of the game'. These proposals were sent to Ministers for adoption at the 1994 annual meeting but thus far little has emerged.

This policy convergence idea stemmed from the 1980s debate over globalization, competitiveness and rivalry among multinational firms, mainly from the Triad, for market share in leading edge sectors. These developments had generated a new kind of international friction, much broader than trade protectionism, which I called 'system friction'.[2] The term 'system friction' underlined that there were several different market models, the differences stemming from both historical and cultural legacies as well as divergence in a range of domestic policies. System differences affected a firm's international competitiveness, which was derived from the interaction between the firm's own capabilities and the broad institutional context of its home country. Since it would be neither feasible nor desirable to seek convergence in the cultural and historical dimension of different systems, the best, though perhaps limited, avenue for reducing or ameliorating system friction would be through harmonization of the relevant government policies. Relevance was defined as those policies which significantly affected the firm's *innovative capability*, to be determined by analysis. A second, and logical, objective of such analysis would also be to answer the

29

question 'Convergence to what?', i.e. to produce a set of normative proposals aimed at achieving more innovation-orientated policies.

While I still would defend the proposal on convergence premised on enhancing innovation, I recognize that one should not ignore the noise from 'system friction' on the trade and investment front. And, of course, there is a blurring of boundaries among different policy domains such as trade, investment and high-tech industrial policy. So I'd like to focus on the intersect between trade, investment and competition policies and raise some questions about harmonization and new international rules of the game in that context rather than primarily in the innovation framework. In doing so I come to the conclusion that harmonization of domestic policies, in this case competition policy, is probably a necessary but not a sufficient condition to ameliorate system friction.

THE NEW TRADE AGENDA

The ongoing analysis of the globalization of the international economy in the 1980s, marked especially by a surge of foreign direct investment after 1983, is introducing some new concepts into trade policy discourse. These new concepts have also been influenced by the Uruguay Round negotiations which began in 1986 and by bilateral policy initiatives, especially the US–Japan Structural Impediments Initiative, or SII.

One of these concepts is *effective market access*, originating from the experience with the negotiations on trade in services, which emphasized that both domestic regulations and the option of establishment were legitimate areas for negotiating access for services, and also from the SII, which, for example, dealt with problems such as Japanese regulations concerning large retail stores as impediments to imports (the so-called store wars furore). Effective market access is a 'soft' concept – soft and even slippery – but none the less has become part of the trade policy lexicon and will, I believe, at some time become part of the negotiating agenda both multilaterally, after the Uruguay Round, and perhaps bilaterally and regionally.

Effective market access begins from the premise that barriers to the entry of imports are no longer confined to the border: effective market barriers can arise from both statutory and institutional impediments as well as impediments to foreign direct investment or market *presence*. Of course, it will be noted that barriers to entry are also a concept relevant to competition policy, where, however, it has a rather different meaning related to the theory of contestability and the entry (and exit) of firms.

Effective market access and/or presence, it is argued, is a more appropriate concept in a globalizing world characterized by accelerating technological change and increasingly fierce international competition. In such a world, multinational firms in leading edge sectors need access or presence at least in each of the three regions of the Triad in order to capture economies of scale and scope; to respond to changing consumer tastes for customized products and after-sales service; and to access technology from various sources, including government-funded research consortia. Barriers to exports or investment in one or more of these strategic markets, it is argued, may inflict a significant and perhaps irreversible blow to competitiveness. Thus behind this new concept of effective market access or presence is a rather complex – and quite new – view of reciprocity embracing both trade and investment.

The implications of this new concept are far-ranging. Thus, to secure effective market access via *exports*, a number of domestic impediments must be considered, including, for example, differences in distribution systems; the role of trading companies which impede close consumer contact necessary for customization and service; vertical arrangements between suppliers and producers or between producers and distributors, etc. Market *presence* by investment or other means, rather than access by exporting, is essential for knowledge and technology transfer, which travels many routes, including suppliers and customers, as well as the more traditional science and technology installations. So foreign direct investment is particularly important in sectors of continuous product and process innovation. Up for consideration and possible negotiation, then, would be impediments to investment including not only overt barriers, such as those precluding foreign ownership in particular sectors, but also more complex structural phenomena related to financial markets and markets for corporate control. The latter are important in determining ease of access via mergers and acquisitions.

In addition to the notion of effective market access and/or presence, another new item in trade policy discussions is the concept of *strategic dumping*. Strategic dumping, motivated by monopolizing intent, essentially involves subsidizing exports through higher home prices sustained by collusive price behaviour and a protected home market. To deter entry, high fixed costs – for example, by coordinated R&D expenditure – would also produce significant dynamic economies of scale. The closed home market, the large sunk costs, and the advantages derived from learning by doing could all serve to discourage investment in this sector in both the importing and third countries.

Thus an essential dimension of strategic dumping is the *exporting country policies*: trade policy and competition policy, both substance and enforcement. The injury to the *importing* country's firms involves both restriction of exports and diminished competitiveness because of inadequate investment in innovation. Moreover, the use of price as a monopolizing tool may not be necessary, so the conventional rationale for dumping in both price and injury terms would be inappropriate. Yet it is also clear how very complex and difficult it would be to spell out alternative clean, clear and balanced rules to tackle this complex scenario of strategic behaviour.

One option would be for the importing country to undertake a form of harassment as a policy of deterrent – strategic anti-dumping. It is not difficult – given the lack of precision in the current GATT code and the technical ingenuity of expert lawyers and bureaucrats – to 'prove' that dumping has taken place under virtually any pricing behaviour of exporters.[3] The manipulation of trade rules, however, is hardly an acceptable policy route. Moreover, strategic anti-dumping policy will likely induce investment by the exporting firms into the importing country to escape harassment. This seems to be what happened during the 1980s in Europe, especially in semiconductors.[4] Unfortunately this unintended investment policy may lead to other problems, especially overcapacity.

It should be noted that these three concepts – effective market access, effective market presence and strategic dumping – are all interrelated. For example, effective market access by exports used to be considered as an alternative to effective market presence by investment. During the 1980s wave of multinationalization it became apparent that in many sectors they were complements and not substitutes. Moreover, strategic dumping behaviour depends on impediments to either effective access through exports or impediments to effective presence through foreign direct investment. And all these trade concepts are related to firm competitiveness through their impact on economies of scale and scope; customization; technology transfer and innovation. Finally, a truly level playing field for multinational firms would require not only reasonable symmetry of access for trade and investment but also, as noted in the discussion of strategic dumping, prevention of collusive behaviour and other abuses of dominant market position, thereby necessitating harmonization of competition policies. So let me now turn to a discussion of some policy options.

SYSTEM FRICTION: SOME POLICY OPTIONS

Essentially, there are three policy instruments available for tackling the problems arising from asymmetry of access for trade and investment and from strategic dumping. These are trade policy, competition policy and investment policy. My purpose in this concluding section is not to present detailed proposals for policy initiatives but rather to highlight some of the changes which might be explored and, more significantly in the present context, to suggest why even these or other policy changes in these instruments will leave us with some basic dilemmas in coping with system friction through new international rules of the game.

Trade policy

During the early discussions in the Uruguay Round, the United States proposed that a separate negotiating agenda item should be high-technology goods. Because there was no clear rationale presented for this proposal it was opposed by a number of countries and eventually dropped. The reason for recalling this historical episode is that, whatever prompted the US proposal, one could argue today that it might be revived because a quite cogent rationale could be formulated through the concept of strategic dumping.

In order to remove the barriers to access into the exporter's market the first step would be to agree to a list of *industry* characteristics; for example, degree of concentration as measured by exporting firms' share of home market; exporting firms' share of world market (which would affect alternative third country producers); extent and nature of barriers to entry of new firms or expansion of existing firms; degree of import penetration; prices in the exporting country's home market relative to prices elsewhere, etc. The purpose of selecting specific industries would be to focus the negotiations on eliminating protection for sectors where strategic behaviour is feasible, i.e. sectors with oligopolistic structures, high entry barriers, significant static and dynamic efficiencies and dominance in global markets.

From this agreed industry list one could then assemble a group of products and for these compile a list of specific import barriers. This would then form the basis for a 'zero for zero' negotiation, i.e. the removal of all border restraints on a reciprocal basis. The negotiations could begin with a small group of countries, say the OECD, and then they could decide whether the agreement should be conditional or full MFN. If conditional, the agreement should be open to all countries willing to accede to the zero tariffs.

The removal of trade barriers will not, on its own, remove the threat of strategic dumping. As we have seen, this type of activity also requires action on competition policy in the exporting market which will be discussed below. It is of some interest to note, however, that there are two Bills now being considered in the US Senate which seem to be targeted at strategic dumping. One, sponsored by Senator Howard M. Metzenbaum, is the International Fair Competition Act, which would amend the Anti-dumping Act to allow for the collection of triple damages by US firms injured by below-cost pricing of foreign products. Companies suing under the Metzenbaum legislation would have to prove that foreign dumping results from 'extracting profits from a *closed home market*'.[5] The other Bill, sponsored by Senator Charles Grassley, would allow US firms to sue under the Sherman Antitrust Act those foreign companies whose actions violate their own government's competition law which has not been enforced and which 'inhibits competition by US firms in that jurisdiction'.[6] Both these approaches to dumping involve the extraterritorial reach of US competition policy rather than either trade policy *per se* or trade policy plus negotiated harmonization of competition policies. It would, *ceteris paribus*, seem more effective and less contentious to use trade policy for reducing border impediments and competition policy convergence for restraining collusive behaviour in all relevant markets.

Competition policy

The harmonization of competition policy, the objective of the ongoing OECD initiative launched in 1991 as a follow-up to TEP,[7] must deal with divergence in both substance and enforcement.

Substantive convergence must first confront the fact that the overall *objectives* of competition policy vary from country to country (and, indeed, have varied in the same country over time). For example, while most countries include efficiency as an objective, there is a distinction made between static and dynamic efficiency in only a few jurisdictions. Further, objectives other than efficiency are included in many countries but these social and political objectives vary across countries and may often conflict with the target of promoting efficiency. Again, while competition policy is focused on the private sector in most countries, the EU mandate includes government behaviour such as subsidization. It is of interest to note, moreover, that while there is virtually unanimous agreement on the objective of prohibition of price-fixing, there are such significant differences in the process of enforcement among the OECD countries that significant variation in actual firm behaviour is quite common.

Indeed, the variation in enforcement in both the structural and the behavioural instruments of competition policy is probably greater than that in objectives. And, as is usually the case, the devil is in the process detail! The differing legal traditions among countries are an important factor in this divergence, with the United States unique in its emphasis on private avenues of enforcement and triple damage suits. Here is an instance, perhaps, where the distinction between government policy and the cultural–institutional legacy is decidedly blurred. This important difference between the United States and most other countries is undoubtedly one reason for the greater American predisposition to extraterritoriality.

Assuming that the OECD convergence project achieved success by 1994 – a very heroic assumption, no doubt – a number of unsolved problems would remain in this policy domain. For example, is a supranational jurisdiction required to tackle the issue of global dominance in, say, the merger area? (The importance and difficulty of this issue are amplified by the trend to transnational mergers and strategic alliances which erode the notion of corporate citizenship and perhaps also the concern by national governments about potential abuse of a dominant position.) Is a supranational dispute settlement mechanism required because of conflict between competition policy objectives and effective market access or presence? Put another way, will the aggregation of domestic welfare equal a maximization of global welfare?

The current and ongoing debate about the Japanese *keiretsu* provides a useful example of the dilemma created by the pressure to adapt national policies to a global economy. So let me conclude with a brief description of the '*keiretsu* issue' and the implications for both trade and investment or effective market access and effective market presence.

Keiretsu and effective market access

There has been, in the past few years, a virtual flood of articles about the Japanese *keiretsu* and the implications of this form of industrial organization for world trade and investment. The views expressed by different authors range from dismissing their impact as virtually negligible – a non-issue, in effect – to the revisionist school, which represents the *keiretsu* as a near-impenetrable barrier to market access in Japan. It is clear that this debate will continue for some time and that it is well beyond the scope of this chapter to review and assess it. What I want to do, instead, is highlight the main characteristics of differing *keiretsu* forms which impact on effective access and presence, the new trade and investment policy agenda.[8]

While there are many different forms of *keiretsu*, or patterns of intercorporate relationships in Japan, the impact on market access via exports is best illustrated by the vertical *keiretsu* of two kinds: production *keiretsu*, or hierarchies of several tiers of subcontractors that supply parent firms with equipment or intermediate products, and the distribution *keiretsu* which link production firms and retail or wholesale distributors.

The production *keiretsu*, in the motor industry in particular, have been the subject of intensive US–Japanese negotiation. US officials have argued that they are exclusionary, i.e. prevent imports into Japan of US auto parts, and should be subject to more effective antitrust enforcement by Japanese authorities. A counter-argument is that they are simply a different form of industrial organization, an intermediate between the vertically integrated firm and fully decentralized markets and, indeed, other auto producers are adopting a form of the Japanese model as, for example, the recent GM restructuring illustrates.

This intermediate form of industrial organization is governed by long-term, reciprocal, contractual relations which, in some respects, may be more efficient (especially in a dynamic sense) than either vertical integration or price-focused market transactions. The issue of collusion should, therefore, be directed only at the final product market and essentially concerns *horizontal* behaviour. If competition in final products exists there is no role for competition policy in dealing with production *keiretsu*. Indeed, if the role of domestic competition policy is to enhance efficiency, the vertical *keiretsu* may be a desirable form of organization. Essentially the same case is made with respect to distribution *keiretsu*, where the information technology at the point of sale opens up major opportunities for enhancing product innovation through more rapid adaptation of production to changing consumer buying preferences. The fact remains, however, that the long-term contractual relations will impede market access, especially for intermediate products like auto parts and semiconductors and some consumer goods which cannot access distribution networks.

Paul Sheard distinguishes between the exclusionary effects of previous contracts, or 'second order exclusion' and exclusion from competition for contract renewal or 'first order exclusion' and argues that only the latter raises issues which may be relevant to competition authorities.[9] But 'first order exclusion' involves a significant loss of time when long-term contracts are involved and the element of time may be very important, imposing significant forgone costs of dynamic efficiencies in industries where continuing improvement in process and product is the essential characteristic of innovation. Competitiveness delayed may be competitiveness denied in some circumstances.

None the less if one accepts the argument that long-term contractual relations are simply a different and, in some respects, more efficient and effective form of organization, the crunch issue becomes a trade-off between efficiency and exclusion or, to get back to our unsolved dilemmas, a conflict between the objectives of national policy and the important international trade issue of effective market access. Thus convergence of competition policy alone will not reduce the system friction which stems from profound differences in institutional legacies.

This conclusion is strengthened as we turn from trade to investment issues.

Keiretsu and effective market presence

There is a marked disparity between the inward foreign investment stock of Japan as compared with that of Europe and the United States. In 1989 the Japanese stock was estimated at $28 billion as compared with $249 billion in the European Community and $347 billion in the United States.[10] This low level of foreign investment in Japan is in part a result of many decades of official restrictions, most of which were removed during the 1980s. Thus today investment policy in Japan has been largely liberalized. Yet there was still an enormous disparity between the inward flows of investment as between Japan and other OECD countries during the 1980s wave of transnationalization: the total inflow between 1986 and 1990 was $275 billion into the European Community; $259 billion into the United States and $1.6 billion into Japan![11] There are a number of reasons for this striking difference[12] but divergence in current official investment policy is not one of them.

The intermarket or horizontal *keiretsu*, which involves groupings of firms in diverse industries around a major bank, are a fundamental aspect of Japanese capitalism. The lead bank is not only an important source of capital but performs other functions with respect to the client firm's needs, such as facilitating access to other banks, assisting in restructuring if required, providing management assistance if necessary, etc. In addition to this long-term reciprocal relationship with the lead bank in the *keiretsu*, cross-shareholding among intermarket *keiretsu* members is very extensive, ranging from 30 per cent to 65 per cent in the six major horizontal *keiretsu*.[13] As a number of analysts have demonstrated, the combination of these two aspects of the Japanese form of industrial organization – the complex and extended role of the lead bank and the cross-shareholding among *keiretsu* members – results in a model of corporate governance strikingly different from the Anglo-Saxon model in which equity markets and other phenomena such as takeovers, shareholders' rights, extensive disclosure regulations, etc., create active markets for corporate control. The issue here is not whether the Japanese model is more or less efficient – although some would argue that it encourages a long view which facilitates innovation by providing 'patient' capital, while others would point out that it may be grossly inefficient and encourage excess investment and hence serious overcapacity. But, efficiency aside, the issue in the present context of asymmetry in effective market presence is that as a consequence of this difference in governance systems there are major barriers to foreign direct investment by its most common form of merger and acquisition.

It is thus difficult to see how reducing divergence in investment policies (an ongoing process in several multilateral fora, including the GATT and the OECD) or harmonization of competition policies, which have no mandate in the financial market arena, will significantly reduce the increasing system friction emanating from impediments to investment. It should be noted, by the way, that a similar asymmetry to investment access through the M&A route is a matter of concern in the European Union because of differences between the United Kingdom and many Continental models of corporate governance, but especially that of Germany.[14] As a result, a number of changes will be undertaken in an effort to achieve more convergence over the long-term to a 'European model' which will combine elements of different structural and regulatory arrangements.

Indeed, more generally, there is growing debate in both the United Kingdom and the United States about the need to reform the corporate governance model and, in Japan, changes are taking place largely as a consequence of the serious after-effects of the asset price inflation of the 1980s. The latter may well have the effect (perhaps unintended!) of facilitating access by merger and acquisition. In addition, the Japanese government has announced a number of measures to encourage greenfield investment by foreigners. It is, of course, too early to judge whether the final result of these separate national developments will significantly reduce the current striking asymmetry of effective market presence within the Triad. The timing is opportune for a multilateral effort of analysis and discussion of corporate governance within the OECD – perhaps using the European Union as a 'case study' in convergence efforts. My own view is that the problem of asymmetry of investment access will be far more difficult to solve than the trade issues, because corporate governance lies at the heart of the different capitalist models, with deep historical, cultural and behavioural roots highly resistant to change. Incremental regulatory measures and long-run market-led evolutionary change may be the wisest approach.

CONCLUSION

This survey of some of the issues which straddle the ever more complex nexus of trade, investment and innovation issues confirms the desirability of promoting convergence in competition policy. But I also want to stress the point that achieving this objective will still leave a number of unsolved problems. There is a big agenda of unfinished work to be tackled in order to avoid the potentially serious and destabilizing consequences of continuing system friction.

NOTES

1 Sylvia Ostry, *Government and Corporations in a Shrinking World: Trade and Innovation Policies in the United States, Europe and Japan*, Council on Foreign Relations, New York, 1990, pp. 79–99.
2 See Sylvia Ostry, 'Exploring the Policy Options for the 1990s', in OECD Forum for the Future, *Support Policies for Strategic Industries: Systemic Risks and Emerging Issues*, Paris, 1991. See also OECD TEP, *Technology in a Changing World*, Paris, 1991, pp. 13–35.
3 See John H. Jackson and Edwin A. Vermulst (eds), *Antidumping Law and Practice: A Comparative Approach*, Ann Arbor, Michigan, University of Michigan Press, 1989.
4 See Ostry, *Governments and Corporations*, pp. 46–52.
5 *Inside U.S. Trade*, Washington, May 8, 1992, p. 8, emphasis added.
6 *Ibid.*
7 See OECD Press Release, Ministerial *Communiqué*, Paris, June 5, 1991, 'Policy Statement on Technology and the Economy', pp. 19–20.
8 Most of my presentation comes from an excellent survey by Michael L. Gerlach, *The keiretsu: A Primer*, Japan Society, New York, 1992. See also Paul Sheard, '*Keiretsu* and Closedness of the Japanese Market: An Economic Appraisal', Institute of Social and Economic Research, Osaka University, Japan, Discussion Paper No. 273, June, 1992.
9 Sheard, *Keiretsu*, pp. 36–7.
10 United Nations, *World Investment Report, 1992, Transnational Corporations as Engines of Growth*, New York, 1992, p. 20.
11 *Ibid*, p. 311.

12 See, for example, Dennis J. Encarnation, *Rivals beyond Trade: America versus Japan in Global Competition*, Cornell University Press, New York, 1992, especially chapters one and two.
13 Gerlach, *The keiretsu*, p. 18.
14 See Commission of the European Communities, *Study on Obstacles to Takeover Bids in the European Community, Executive Summary*, December, 1989.

3

TRENDS IN THE FORMS OF INTERNATIONAL BUSINESS ORGANIZATION

A. Edward Safarian

The contrast between markets and hierarchies has long been noted in the literature on the forms of domestic and international business organization. That literature has always included various alliance forms of organization, such as licences and joint ventures. During the 1980s there was increasing emphasis on international corporate alliances between independent firms (henceforth ICAs).[1]

In this chapter the trends in these various forms of international business organization are considered. The main emphasis of the chapter is on providing data on relative rates of increase, sectoral concentrations, countries of origin and receipt, and other patterns of change. Some of the significant problems in the quality of data will be noted. In terms of issues, we note that growth in ICAs relative to foreign direct investment (FDI) poses some interesting questions for the most widely accepted view on why firms (hierarchies) are favoured for technology-intensive products in particular. We conclude by noting briefly one aspect of the competition implications of such expansion.

The data in this chapter are presented for individual countries in nominal currencies and have not been deflated to allow comparisons of real figures. Problems of inflation, exchange rate conversions, and different valuation methods beset many of the figures noted below. In some cases the lack of data prevents normalization: measures of the degree of multinationalization of an economy require comparisons of the stock of FDI with total corporate assets, for example, data which often are available on a partial basis at best. In other cases one is hard pressed to know how to deflate data such as the stock of FDI, since it is book value of investments made over time. We have not attempted such normalization. In terms of what is of primary interest here, the main problem is that value data do not exist at all for the ICAs, limiting the comparisons which are possible with other organizational forms.

One issue which will be examined below is the extent to which the MNE organizational form is losing out to the ICA organizational form, a point

40

some authors have emphasized. A second issue is that, despite the recognition of the role which such organizational forms can play in enhancing trade and investment, many national barriers exist limiting their spread. Some of these barriers reflect differences in national competition policies, differences which have been addressed more slowly than other matters affecting trade and investment.

TRENDS IN FDI, FOREIGN TRADE AND DOMESTIC PRODUCTION

Data on FDI, both stocks and flows, are the longest and broadest of any of the sets of data noted in this chapter.[2] Official data in some countries go back for three-quarters of a century and private estimates even further, and there is considerable detail by sectors and in other respects. Yet these data also leave much to be desired for analytical purposes. Some countries report reinvested earnings as part of their inward and outward FDI flows, others do not. Some countries use a figure of 10 per cent of equity held abroad to define effective voting control hence FDI, others use 25 or 50 per cent.[3] Sectoral coverage is uneven, especially in services. Data on stocks are available for fewer countries and create additional differences in what is reported by country, notably in definitions of book values and in sample survey methods. Comparative analyses are greatly affected by such problems. For example, FDI flows purporting to measure the same thing between pairs of countries (outward from X, inward to Y) often differ widely in reported amounts, in the changes from year to year, and even in sign. The first two points can also be made with regard to stocks, which are less volatile than flows.[4]

A variety of sources have suggested that FDI has been rising more rapidly than foreign trade and domestic production. Much depends, of course, on the beginning and end years chosen, and we know there is significant overlap between these magnitudes. One set of estimates is given in Table 3.1. It shows that FDI outflows and related technology payments rose more rapidly than world trade, world production and domestic investment during the late 1980s. FDI outflows declined in 1991–2 (a setback reversed in 1993, as noted in Table 3.2) but stocks continued to rise.

The developed countries dominate the outflows side. Between 95 and 98 per cent of global outflows were from such countries in the 1981–92 period. Of course, the set of developed countries changes over time. Japan was classified as a developing country in 1960 but in the 1986–90 period supplied 19 per cent of the world's outward FDI flows (see Table 3.4). Outflows from the developing countries have increased from 2 per cent to 5 per cent of the total. Some of the Asian newly industrialized countries, in particular, have become significant home countries for MNEs. On the inflow side, there has been a marked shift to the developing countries, from

Table 3.1 Worldwide foreign direct investment and selected economic indicators, 1992, and growth rates, 1981–92

Indicator	Value at current prices, 1992	Annual growth rate (%)			
		1981–5[a]	1986–90[a]	1990–1	1991–2
FDI outflows	171	3	24	−17	−11
FDI outward stock	2,125[b]	5	11	10	6
Sales of foreign affiliates of TNCs[c]	4,800[d]	2[e]	15	−13	−
Current gross domestic product at factor cost	23,300	2	9	4	5
Gross domestic investment	5,120	0.4	10	4	5
Exports of goods and non-factor services	4,500[d]	−0.2	13	3	−
Royalty and fee receipts	37	0.1	19	8	5

Source: UNCTAD, Division on Transnational Corporations and Investment (1994, p. 4).
Notes:
[a] Compound growth rate estimates, based on a semi-logarithmic regression equation.
[b] 1993.
[c] Estimated by extrapolating the worldwide sales of foreign affiliates of TNCs from Germany, Japan and the United States on the basis of the relative importance of these countries in worldwide outward FDI stock.
[d] 1991.
[e] 1982–5.

26 per cent of the global inflows in 1981–5 to 41 per cent in 1993, or 44 per cent if Central and Eastern Europe are included in this group (Table 3.2).[5]

In terms of country composition, there have been some very large changes over time. The home countries for FDI have diversified. In the 1960s the United States accounted for 66 per cent of OECD outward flows of FDI. That had fallen to only 16 per cent in 1981–90. Japan and the United Kingdom made up much of the difference, although several other OECD countries increased their shares of outward flows (Table 3.3). On the inward side, by contrast, host country recipients of FDI become more concentrated over these periods. In particular, the US share of OECD investments soared from 15 per cent in the 1960s to 45 per cent in the 1980s, with the declines in shares for Australia, Canada and Germany accounting for most of the difference.

These trends were beginning to change in the late 1980s and early 1990s, based on preliminary data. In 1991–3 the five major home countries continued to account for close to two-thirds of global outward flows.[6] However, the United States reasserted its position as the largest exporter of FDI, France continued its expansion as a major home country, while the UK and Japanese shares fell significantly (Table 3.4).

Table 3.2 Inflows and outflows of foreign direct investment, annual averages, 1981–93

Country	Value ($ billions)								Share in total (%)				
	1981–5	1986–90	1988	1989	1990	1991	1992	1993[a]	1981–5	1986–90	1991	1992	1993
Developed countries													
Inflows	37	130	131	168	176	121	102	109	74	84	74	65	56
Outflows	47	163	162	212	222	185	162	181	98	96	96	95	–
Developing countries													
Inflows	13	25	28	27	31	39	51	80	26	16	24	32	41
Outflows	1	6	6	10	10	7	9	14	2	4	4	5	–
Central and Eastern Europe[b]													
Inflows	0.02	0.1	0.015	0.3	0.3	2	4	5	0.04	0.1	1	3	3
Outflows	0.004	0.02	0.02	0.02	0.04	0.01	0.03	–	0.01	0.01	0.005	0.02	–
All countries													
Inflows	50	155	159	196	208	162	158	194	100	100	100	100	100
Outflows	48	168	168	222	232	192	171	195	100	100	100	100	–

Source: UNCTAD, Division on Transnational Corporations and Investment (1994, p. 12).
[a] Based on preliminary estimates.
[b] Former Yugoslavia is included in developing countries.
Note: The levels of worldwide inward and outward FDI flows and stocks should balance; however, in practice, they do not. The causes of the discrepancy include differences between countries in the definition and valuation of FDI; the treatment of unremitted branch profits in inward and outward direct investment; treatment of unrealized capital gains and losses; the recording of transactions of 'offshore' enterprises; the recording of reinvested earnings in inward and outward direct investment; the treatment of real estate and construction investment; and the share-in-equity threshold in inward and outward direct investment.

Table 3.3 Shares of selected countries in cumulative inward and outward flows of FDI for OECD countries, 1961–90 (%)

	Inward flows			Outward flows		
	1961–70	*1971–80*	*1981–90*	*1961–70*	*1971–80*	*1981–90*
Australia	12.8	6.0	4.8	0.7	0.8	2.2
Canada	13.1	2.9	1.8	2.1	3.7	4.5
France	6.7	9.0	6.2	3.7	4.6	9.0
Germany	15.0	7.4	3.6	5.8	7.7	9.7
Italy	8.6	3.0	2.9	2.4	1.2	2.8
Japan	1.5	0.8	0.4	2.0	6.0	17.3
Netherlands	5.5	5.8	4.7	3.8	9.2	6.6
UK	10.2	21.6	14.4	10.5	18.2	17.9
USA	14.9	30.0	44.5	66.3	44.4	16.0

Source: OECD (1987: 72), OECD (1990), UN (1992) *World Investment Directory* III. Included are all OECD countries which accounted for 5 per cent or more of the OECD total inward FDI in 1961–70 or of OECD outward FDI in 1981–8.

Table 3.4 Outflows of foreign direct investment from the five major home countries, 1981–93

	Share in world total (%)				
Country	*1981–5*[a]	*1986–90*[a]	*1991*	*1992*	*1993*[b]
France[c]	6	10	12	18	11
Germany	9	9	12	9	9
Japan[c]	11	19	16	10	6
UK	19	17	8	9	13
USA[d]	23	13	17	19	25
Total[e]	67	68	66	66	64

Source: UNCTAD, Division on Transnational Corporations and Investment (1994, p. 17).
Notes:
[a] Compounded growth rate estimates, based on a semi-logarithmic regression equation.
[b] Based on preliminary estimates.
[c] Not including reinvested earnings. In the case of France, reinvested earnings are not reported after 1982.
[d] Excluding outflows to the finance (except banking), insurance and real estate industries of the Netherlands Antilles. Also excludes currency translation adjustments.
[e] Totals may not add up, due to rounding.

More dramatic changes have been occurring on the inward side. The world's ten largest recipients of FDI in the early 1990s are shown in Figure 3.1. The most striking change has been in the position of China, which moved to the position of fourth largest recipient in 1992 and second largest in 1993. It is also of interest that two Latin American countries, Mexico and Argentina, are among the top ten, a situation which did not exist a few years earlier.[7]

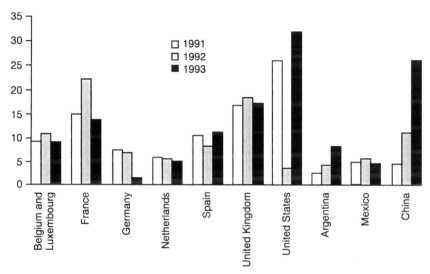

Figure 3.1 The world's ten largest recipients of foreign direct investment inflows in the 1990s ($ billion)
Source: UNCTAD, Division on Transnational Corporations and Investment 1994, p. 69

Table 3.5 Sectoral composition of outward foreign direct investment stock of the major home countries, various years (%)

Home country	Year	Primary sector	Secondary sector	Tertiary sector
France	1987	4	50	46
	1991	9	44	47
Germany	1985	4	43	53
	1992	2	39	59
Japan[a]	1985	17	29	52
	1993[b]	5	27	66
UK	1984	33	32	35
	1991	18	36	46
USA[c]	1985	15	44	41
	1992	7	42	51

Source: UNCTAD, Division on Transnational Corporations and Investment (1994, p. 18).
Notes:
[a] Based on notifications. Does not include branches and direct purchase of real estate. Therefore, total does not add up to 100 per cent.
[b] As of September.
[c] Excluding investment stock in the finance (except banking), insurance and real estate industries of the Netherlands Antilles.

In sectoral terms, there has been a marked shift in the composition of FDI from resources and manufacturing in the earlier decades to services in the 1980s. In the 1950s the stock of FDI was mainly in primary products and resource-based manufactures. The emphasis then shifted to secondary manufactures. In the 1980s the concentration has been in services, whose share of the world's stock of FDI rose from about a quarter to about 50 per cent from the early 1970s to the late 1980s. FDI in services accounted for 55–60 per cent of annual flows in the late 1980s (UN 1991: 15). Sectoral and country data on FDI in services are not as well developed as those for manufactures. We do know that by 1991 the share of the tertiary sector was between 46 and 66 per cent of the outward stock for the five major home countries (Table 3.5).

INTERNATIONAL MERGERS AND ACQUISITIONS

FDI entry by international mergers and acquisitions (IMAs) has become the dominant form of corporate entry to a country, exceeding greenfield entry by a wide margin in value terms. It was noted above that the US share of the value of OECD inward FDI had risen to 54 per cent in the 1980s. The acquisitions share of that total in value terms was about 85 per cent in the late 1980s (US *Survey of Current Business*, May 1990).[8] In Canada in the late 1980s acquisitions were about 80 per cent of the value of inward FDI. For the developed countries as a whole, IMAs rose to 86 per cent of the value of inward FDI in 1988 before falling sharply to only 41 per cent in 1991 (Table 3.6). If one considers the global data flows in previous tables, it is clear that the upswing of FDI in the late 1980s and the decline in the first few years of the 1990s were largely driven by IMAs.[9]

Comparing merger activity in different countries is difficult enough, given the varying definitions of such activities, differences in coverage and timing, and other problems (for example, OECD 1984; Cooke 1988). IMAs pose even larger statistical problems. Few official sources exist and these differ in the periods covered and methods used.[10] The private sources of data cover

Table 3.6 Value of worldwide cross-border acquisitions and foreign direct investment inflows to the developed countries, 1986–92

Item	1986	1987	1988	1989	1990	1991	1992
Worldwide cross-border acquisitions ($ billions)	39	71	113	122	113	50	75
FDI inflows to developed countries ($ billions)	67	109	131	168	176	121	102
Acquisitions as % FDI	58	65	86	73	64	41	74

Source: UNCTAD, Division on Transnational Corporations and Investment (1994, p.21).

relatively short periods and differ significantly in coverage and other ways as noted below. Nevertheless, the available sources point to some interesting, if necessarily qualified, conclusions for our purposes.

First, there was a clear increase in the number of mergers and acquisitions in the major industrial countries during the 1980s, including an increase in larger transactions. This trend has been examined in various studies (Khemani 1991; Cooke 1988). It is clearly related in part to the 'globalization' process described by many writers, in the sense that a significant portion of the mergers and acquisitions noted in such studies are IMAs.

More can be said about international mergers if we utilize private data sources also. Once again we must keep in mind several data problems. Different types of transactions are included in various series, coverage in the Triad is more complete than elsewhere, and (judging by revisions) coverage improves significantly with time. For these and other reasons it is difficult to reconcile various series, including those shown here. Turning to international mergers and acquisitions, some very marked differences appear for the United States, the European Union and Japan. The US series shown in Table 3.7 has a break in 1986, when the minimum size of transaction reported was raised. This break is noticeable in the domestic mergers and acquisitions. Domestic mergers rose by about 50 per cent in numbers and 150 per cent by value in the period 1982–5. These increases are well beyond what one sees on inward and outward IMAs, except for the value figure on the inward side. From 1986 to 1990, by contrast, inward and outward IMAs far outstripped domestic mergers and acquisitions, both in number and in value. This is consistent with the relatively rapid growth of FDI noted earlier. Both domestic and international mergers show declines in 1991 and 1992 and recovery in 1993.

Table 3.8 considers data gathered by the European Commission on mergers for the 1,000 largest industrial firms in the European Community, ranked by turnover, the 500 largest firms worldwide, and the largest firms in the service sector (represented by banking, distribution and insurance). The longest series is for the industrial sector. In this case the numbers of both intra-Community and international majority acquisitions (including mergers) are low in the early 1980s. For example, mergers in these two categories combined fell short of national mergers each year until 1988/9. For the next three years the intra-Community and international mergers far outstripped the national mergers. Particularly notable are the intra-Community mergers, whose value rose sixfold from 1982/3 to 1989/90. Even in the distribution, banking and insurance sectors, where state restrictions on majority acquisitions and mergers were more frequent than in most types of industry, the rate of increase in numbers of mergers was impressive, especially for intra-Community acquisitions. It is well known that some of the continental European capital markets are not very conducive to takeovers

Table 3.7 US merger and acquisition completions, 1982–93

Year	1982	1983	1984	1985	1986	1987	1988	1989	1990	1991	1992	1993
US acquires non-US												
Number	138	149	154	199	127	182	237	371	410	424	497	580
Value ($ billion)	1.0	1.4	2.2	1.2	3.6	6.9	11.9	27.3	20.3	14.7	14.2	18.4
Non-US acquires US												
Number	227	116	190	215	352	375	547	703	791	513	373	327
Value ($ billion)	5.4	2.2	8.4	19.4	31.3	53.7	66.2	69.6	56.4	28.9	15.6	21.6
US acquires US												
Number	1,934	2,130	2,832	3,076	2,046	1,956	2,224	2,724	3,086	2,576	2,808	3,023
Value ($ billion)	54.3	49.1	115.5	125.5	185.2	134.2	193.4	214.1	123.7	94.7	95.0	128.7
Total												
Number	2,299	2,395	3,176	3,490	2,521	2,513	3,008	3,798	4,287	3,513	3,678	3,930
Value ($ billion)	60.7	52.7	126.1	146.1	220.1	194.8	271.5	311.0	200.4	138.3	124.8	168.7

Source: Mergers and Acquisitions, *Journal of Corporate Venture*, Philadelphia: MLR Publishing Co., 1990–3.
Note: Up to 1985 all information is based on all completed mergers and acquisitions valued at $1 million or more. Partial acquisitions of 5 per cent or more of a company's capital stock are included if the payments are $1 million or more. From 1986 on only transactions valued at $5 million or more are reported, as well as purchases of partial interest that involve at least a 40 per cent stake in the target company or an investment of at least $100 million.

Table 3.8 Breakdown of national, Community and international majority mergers and acquisitions (combined turnover greater than ECU 1 billion, ECU 2 billion, ECU 5 billion and ECU 10 billion) (numbers)

Category	Year	National[b]					Community[c]					International[d]					Total[a]
		>1	>2	>5	>10	Total[a]	>1	>2	>5	>10	Total[a]	>1	>2	>5	>10	Total[a]	Total[a]
Industry	1982/1983					59					38					20	117
	1983/1984					101					29					25	155
	1984/1985					146					44					18	208
	1985/1986					145					52					30	227
	1986/1987	111	73	42	18	211	52	42	24	13	75	8	3	2	—	17	303
	1987/1988	135	84	48	24	214	86	61	34	22	111	47	40	28	15	58	383
	1988/1989	163	118	60	29	233	148	110	72	53	197	62	60	38	24	66	496
	1989/1990	183	117	66	44	241	212	158	102	70	257	118	109	56	26	124	622
	1990/1991	158	118	75	42	186	145	107	65	37	170	94	89	60	37	99	455
	1991/1992	155	114	72	36	175	102	86	57	37	119	48	45	30	16	49	343
Distribution banking and insurance	1984/1985					47					16					4	67
	1985/1986					44					13					13	70
	1986/1987	33	21	13	6	79	5	4	3	1	15	11	8	5	3	18	112
	1987/1988	35	26	13	6	107	22	19	10	4	34	17	10	7	2	34	175
	1988/1989	48	37	14	1	119	15	13	7	2	28	13	12	8	4	27	174
	1989/1990	36	30	17	12	112	25	18	13	4	58	9	7	3	1	41	211
	1990/1991	34	27	17	5	94	20	20	14	10	28	7	6	4	2	19	141
	1991/1992	33	28	21	10	113	20	17	13	6	40	1	1	1	1	11	164
Total	1984/1985					193					60					22	275
	1985/1986					189					65					43	297
	1986/1987	144	94	55	24	290	57	46	27	14	90	19	11	7	3	35	415
	1987/1988	170	110	61	30	321	108	80	44	26	145	64	50	35	17	92	558
	1988/1989	211	155	74	30	352	163	123	79	55	225	75	72	46	28	93	670
	1989/1990	219	147	83	56	353	237	176	115	74	315	127	116	59	27	165	833
	1990/1991	192	145	92	47	280	165	127	79	47	198	101	95	64	39	118	596
	1991/1992	188	142	93	46	288	122	103	70	43	159	49	46	31	17	60	507

Source: Report on Competition Policy, Commission of European Communities, Brussels (various issues).
Notes:
[a] Breakdown by size not available before 1986/7. Totals include acquisitions of more than ECU 1 billion and also those which are less. Data are for twelve months ending 1 June of each year.
[b] Operations of firms from the same member states.
[c] Operations of firms from different member states.
[d] Operations of firms from member states and third countries with effect on the Community market.

in general and hostile takeovers in particular, for reasons such as state policy and the existing high degree of concentration of share ownership (see Safarian 1993a, part II and chapter 11). The United States and United Kingdom, by contrast, have more active markets in the purchase and sale of larger firms, including cross-border activity. If one looked at data for the mid or early 1980s, for example, the United Kingdom would far exceed other EC countries in cross-border merger activity in particular. More recent data suggest that UK firms were still the most active in IMAs, but French firms in particular had become equally active in value terms on the outward side and firms in several other European countries were engaging in major cross-border mergers and acquisitions.[11]

Some useful work could be done in further integrating data and analysis of FDI with the domestic literature on mergers and acquisitions. Research on both the theory and the welfare effects of FDI would be enriched thereby, and there might well be equivalent benefits in the reverse direction. Recent efforts at such integration are evident in Waverman (1991).

Japan has had a lower rate of domestic merger activity, at least among larger firms, and a substantially lower rate of inward mergers and acquisitions. The data in Table 3.9 show that, while the number of mergers and acquisitions had become very similar to that of the United States by 1987, the value of acquisitions was far less in Japan, with the average value in that year at $10.4 million, compared with $80.6 million in the United States.[12] Table 3.10, using a different Japanese data base for larger firms, shows only about twenty

Table 3.9 US and Japanese merger and acquisition activity, 1981–8

Year	No.		Value ($ billions)		Average value ($ millions)		No. of large deals	
	US	Japan	US	Japan[a]	US	Japan[a]	US[b]	Japan[c]
1981	2,395	1,815	82.6	10.1	34.49	5.58	113	50
1982	2,346	919	53.8	13.3	22.93	14.50	116	47
1983	2,533	1,722	73.1	8.9	28.86	5.14	138	63
1984	2,543	1,886	122.2	10.4	48.05	5.52	200	81
1985	3,001	1,920	179.8	15.0	59.91	7.80	270	79
1986	3,336	2,083	173.1	27.2	51.89	13.06	346	112
1987	2,032	2,299	163.7	24.0	80.56	10.42	301	131
1988		2,364		27.2		11.49		

Source: Japan Economic Institute (1990) as cited in Lawrence (1993: 93).
Notes:
[a] The dollar values of Japanese deals were calculated using current exchange rates from the International Monetary Fund, *International Financial Statistics* (various issues); Japanese data are for fiscal years.
[b] Deal of $100 million-plus.
[c] Deal of ¥50 billion-plus; ¥50 billion = $220 million, $210 million, and $346 million in 1980, 1985 and 1987, respectively.

Table 3.10 Numbers of mergers and acquisitions involving Japanese firms, 1981, 1985–90

Year	Japanese firms acquire Japanese firms	Japanese firms acquire foreign firms	Foreign firms acquire Japanese firms	Total
1981	122	48	6	176
1985	163	100	26	289
1986	226	204	21	451
1987	219	228	22	469
1988	223	315	17	555
1989	240	405	15	660
1990	293	440	18	751

Source: Yamaichi Securities Co., cited in Japan Economic Institute (1991).

purchases of Japanese firms per year by foreigners in the last half of the 1980s, although Japanese purchases of both Japanese and foreign firms rose rapidly. A survey by MITI in 1991 of all businesses which had a foreign capital ratio of 50 per cent or more showed that only 7 per cent of the total number began through the acquisition of Japanese firms, while 44 per cent and 49 per cent respectively began as joint ventures and as greenfield investments (cited in Lawrence 1993: 99–100). Lawrence relates this particularly to stock cross-holdings among keiretsu members and other Japanese firms, with the consequence that hostile takeovers in particular are more difficult.

INTERNATIONAL CORPORATE ALLIANCES

Terminology and coverage have not yet been standardized for what we call ICAs. Mariti and Smiley (1983: 437) have defined them as 'any long-term, explicit agreement amongst two or more firms', excluding the parent–subsidiary relation. Mowery (1988: 2–3) also uses a broad definition for what he terms international collaborative ventures, namely 'interfirm collaboration in product development, manufacture, or marketing that spans national boundaries, is not based on arm's-length market transactions, and includes substantial contributions by partners of capital, technology, or other assets'. He goes on to note that this excludes exports, FDI (where one firm has control) and licensing. Somewhat narrower definitions are adopted by other writers. Hagedoorn and Schakenraad (1991: appendix I) define ICAs as common interests between independent (industrial) partners which are not connected through (majority) ownership. In addition, they include only arrangements involving technology transfer or joint research. They exclude production and marketing joint ventures, collusion to set prices or limit entry and other forms which, they note, may be side effects of ICAs. Mytelka (1991: 1) also uses a narrower definition; 'strategic partnerships' cover situations where sharing of knowledge is involved and the alliance is an attempt to improve the competitive position of the firm.

Keeping in mind such differences, we note in Table 3.11 some of the trends in ICAs. This table provides for various years from 1974 to 1992 the number of ICAs reported in a variety of sources. These sources cover not only different time periods but different types of agreements or sectors, and also use different methodologies. None of the sources is a worldwide survey in practice; many are limited to a particular sector or to a particular home country, and coverage may improve over time in some cases. Some of these differences are brought out in the notes to the table. Taken at face value, however, very high rates of increase in numbers of agreements are evident in all but one of the series.

Some of the more inclusive data bases can be used to show more detail on such ICAs. Data collected by the Maastricht Institute, shown in more detail in Table 3.12, cover interfirm agreements, including ICAs, with the emphasis on technological ties. This series indicates that joint R&D, along with technology arrangements, has grown relative to joint ventures and research corporations, minority ownerships and cross-holdings, and perhaps customer–supplier relationships. Note that almost half of the agreements were formed in 1985–8 alone. These agreements are heavily concentrated by sector, given the emphasis on technology transfer and joint research. For example, about 40 per cent of the interfirm agreements are in information technology industries, 20 per cent in biotechnology, 10 per cent each in new materials and chemicals, and the remaining 20 per cent in various manufacturing sectors. Studies which used a broader definition of agreements also show a concentration in research-intensive areas, while giving weight to the production and marketing agreements excluded in the Maastricht data base.[13]

Some further detail on organizational forms is brought out in Tables 3.13–14 for two sectors, biotechnology and semiconductors, where detailed data have been collected on ICAs. Marketing agreements are far more common for alliance start-ups in biotechnology than for such start-ups in semiconductors. In the former case the firms need the support of large pharmaceutical companies to secure regulatory approval as well as to market their products. A variety of licensing, research and development alliances are also common. In semiconductors, licensing, R&D agreements and technology exchange form about 60 per cent of the alliances. A major motive for cooperation is the need to establish a proprietary standard as a technology (Kogut et al. 1993: 72–3, 85). US firms dominate start-ups in both sectors. While alliances with European and Japanese firms are significant, the great majority of such alliances in the 1980s were with other US firms (Kogut et al. 1993: 85–9).

Freeman and Hagedoorn (1994) make a distinction between two largely different forms of technology cooperation. Strategic technology partnerships

Table 3.11 Evolution of cooperative agreements established annually

Year	(a)	(b)	(c)	(d)	(e)	(f)	(g)	(h)	(i)	(j)
1974			37				169[1]			
1975	3		14							
1976	7		16			31				
1977	7		15							
1978	7	2	14						30	
1979	13	1	27				317[2]		30	
1980	22	4	34	85		94		15	30	
1981	28	22	40	169				31	60	22
1982	23	19	35	197				58	100	58
1983	39	16		292	46			97	150	49
1984	66	42		346	69		1504[3]	131	195	69
1985				487	82			149	245	90
1986				438	81					
1987					90	180				
1988					111					
1989					129		2629[4]			
1990					156					
1991					145					
1992					103					

Sources: Gugler and Dunning (1993: 125) for columns (a) to (g) and Chesnais (1988: 63) for columns (h) to (j). More detail appears in these two sources, but the following may be noted here.

(a) Alexis Jacquemin, Marleen Lammerant and Bernard Spinoit, *Compétition européenne et coopération entre entreprises en matière de recherche-développement*, Commission des Communautés européennes, Document, Luxembourg, 1986: data on 212 cooperative agreements formed between 1978 and 1984 by at least one EC firm.

(b) C.S. Haklisch, *Technical Alliances in the Semiconductor Industry*, mimeo, New York University, 1986: Cooperative agreements formed by the forty-one major world semiconductor producers.

(c) Karen J. Hladik, *International Joint Ventures*, Lexington Books, Lexington Mass., 1985: US International Joint Ventures created in high income countries between 1974 and 1982.

(d) G.C. Cainarca, M.G. Colombo, S. Mariotti, C. Ciborra, G. De Michelis and M.G. Losano, *Technologie dell'Informazion e accordi tra imprese*, Fondazione Adriano Olivetti, Edizioni di Comunità, Milan, 1989: Arpa data base on 2,014 agreements formed between 1980 and 1986 in the information technologies sectors (semiconductors, computers and telecommunications).

(e) Commission's Reports on the EC's Competition Policy. See for example: Commission des Communautés européennes, *Dix-huitième Rapport sur la politique de concurrence*, Brussels and Luxembourg, 1989.

(f) Karen J. Hladik and Lawrence H. Linden, 'Is an international joint venture in R&D for you?', *Research Technology Management* 32, No. 4, July–August 1989, page 12: McKinsey Studies on US international joint ventures created in 1976, 1980 and 1987.

(g) John Hagedoorn and Jos Schakenraad, *Leading Companies and the Structure of Strategic Alliances in Core Technologies*, MERIT. University of Limburg, 1990: CATI database on 9,000 agreements formed up to July 1989.

(h) LAREA–CEREM (University of Paris, Nanterre) Agreements involving European firms in research-intensive industries.

(i) Venture Economics, corporate venture capital investment agreements.

(j) Schiller, international agreements with US small biotech firms.

Notes:
[1] Before 1974.
[2] 1975–9.
[3] 1980–1984.
[4] 1985–9.

Table 3.12 Increase in the number of interfirm agreements by form of cooperation (absolute numbers and percentages)

Modes of cooperation	Before 1972	1973–6	1977–80	1981–4	1985–8	Total
Joint ventures and research corporations	83 53.2%	64 41.8%	112 22.6%	254 20.8%	345 17.8%	858 21.6%
Joint R&D	14 9.0%	22 14.4%	65 13.1%	255 20.9%	653 33.7%	1,009 25.5%
Technology exchange arrangements	6 3.8%	4 2.6%	33 6.7%	152 12.4%	165 8.5%	360 9.1%
Direct investment (minority and cross holdings)	27 17.3%	29 19.0%	168 33.9%	170 13.9%	237 12.2%	631 15.9%
Customer–supplier relationship	5 3.2%	19 12.4%	47 9.5%	133 10.9%	265 13.7%	469 11.8%
One directional technology flows	21 13.5%	15 9.8%	71 14.3%	259 21.2%	271 14.0%	637 16.1%
Total	156 100%	153 100%	496 100%	1,223 100%	1,936 100%	3,964 100%
	3.9%	3.9%	12.5%	30.9%	48.8%	100%

Source: Hagedoorn (1990), p. 20. About half of these agreements are within Western Europe, the United States and Japan, rather than between these areas. See Hagedoorn and Schakenraad (1989), p. 8.

Table 3.13 Alliance type by semiconductor start-ups

Year	M&A	JV	EQT	MFG	MKT	LIC	R&D	TECHEX	SCND
1979	0	0	0	0	0	1	0	0	1
1980	0	0	0	1	0	1	0	0	0
1981	0	0	1	2	0	0	3	1	0
1982	1	0	0	0	0	3	0	2	3
1983	1	0	4	3	5	7	10	5	4
1984	1	0	2	3	1	2	7	5	7
1985	1	1	4	8	4	10	15	5	6
1986	5	3	5	3	1	5	34	15	7
1987	5	8	3	6	3	10	21	6	7
1988	1	0	1	1	1	0	5	1	1
1989	0	0	1	4	5	5	8	2	1
Total	15	12	21	31	20	44	103	42	37

Source: Dataquest, as reproduced in Kogut *et al.* (1993: 86).
Key: *M&A* = mergers and acquisitions; *JV* = joint venture; *EQT* = equity (minority) investment; *MFG* = manufacturing agreement; *MKT* = marketing agreement; *LIC* = licensing; *R&D* = R&D agreement; *TECHEX* = technology exchange; *SCND* = second-sourcing.

Table 3.14 Alliance type by biotechnology start-ups

Year	JV	MFG	MKT	LIC	RES	DEV
1981	3	1	0	0	1	1
1982	0	2	4	0	2	4
1983	3	1	4	13	8	9
1984	5	4	14	13	8	19
1985	4	5	21	24	13	18
1986	14	11	43	38	32	52
1987	5	8	28	19	27	40
1988	3	4	16	9	11	35
Total	37	36	130	116	102	178

Source: Bioscan, as reproduced in Kogut *et al.* (1993: 83).
Key: *JV* = joint venture; *MFG* = manufacturing agreement; *MKT* = marketing agreement; *LIC* = licensing; *RES* = research agreement; *DEV* = development agreement.

involve joint R&D agreements and other shared innovative activities which are likely to have a long-term effect on the market position of one or all parties. Other agreements, by contrast, allow one firm to access the technology of a second on agreed terms – licensing is a primary form. The Maastricht data base shows that the more R&D-intensive alliances were very largely concentrated in the developed countries in the 1980s (Table 3.15). This data base, as already noted, includes only arrangements involving technology transfer or joint research. Some of the joint ventures shown in

Table 3.15 Distribution of different modes of strategic technology alliances, international regions, 1980–9

Mode of cooperation	Number of alliances	Share for developed economies (%)	Share for Triad–NICs (%)	Share for Triad–LDC (%)
Joint ventures	1,224 (29.2%)	27.7	61.9	67.2
Joint R&D	1,752 (41.8%)	43.2	9.3	10.9
Minority investments	684 (16.3%)	16.3	14.4	20.3
Other	532 (12.7%)	12.8	14.4	1.6
Total	4,192 (100%)	100.0	100.0	100.0

Source: MERIT–CATI as shown in Freeman and Hagedoorn (1994: 775).

the table were formed solely to share R&D, but generally they have a number of corporate objectives. Joint R&D pacts are the most research-intensive forms, minority investments usually involve an interest by a large firm in a smaller firm's technology, and the 'other' category (namely R&D contracts and second-sourcing agreements) also involves technology sharing (Freeman and Hagedoorn 1994: 774). The main point is that the more research-intensive forms are concentrated in the developed countries. Other

Table 3.16 Patterns of interfirm agreements: geographical distribution

Geographical areas	High-tech industries		All industries	
	No.	%	No.	%
Intra-area				
US	254	23.9	352	18.7
EEC	150	14.1	282	15.0
Japan	18	1.7	59	3.1
Inter-area				
US–EEC	276	26.0	413	21.9
US–Japan	141	13.3	202	8.6
EEC–Japan	87	8.2	162	10.8
With other areas	135	12.8	413	21.9
Total	1,061	100.0	1,883	100.0

Source: Studies by E. Ricotta and colleagues noted in Chesnais (1988: 68), covering 1,883 agreements set up in 1982–5 between firms in the more industrialized countries.

studies, such as that noted in Table 3.16, arrive at similar conclusions. These and other sources may underestimate the number of ICAs from or in the developing countries, given the sources and definitions used; for example, agreements between firms in developing countries may not be fully reported, and the informal trust relations characteristic of some types of transactions in Asian countries are not easily identified. Nevertheless, based on present sources, a high degree of concentration in the developed countries, and especially in the Triad, seems likely for the research-intensive ICAs especially. If this is the case, it raises a question on just how helpful these newer forms of business organization will be for many less developed countries as they attempt to catch up with the developed economies.

IS THE MULTINATIONAL COMPANY LOSING GROUND?

Some writers have read a great deal into the rapid increase in ICAs in recent years. Both FDI and international mergers are seen as receding in importance while cooperative agreements in one form or another become more important. Moreover, ICAs are seen not as some intermediate form embodying elements of markets and hierarchies but as a new form where elements such as trust and various forms of non-rivalrous behaviour play important roles. If this is the case, something quite significant has happened to the preference of many MNEs for FDI over other forms of organization. The implications for the theory of FDI will be far-reaching.[14]

Briefly, the most commonly accepted theory of FDI is that the specific advantages possessed by oligopolistic firms, notably their investment in intangibles such as R&D and management skills, can often be exploited more profitably through subsidiaries than through markets or other organizational forms such as ICAs. One view is that markets for transferring such assets are imperfect, especially for newer or more complex technologies. In addition, firms may fear imitation and other opportunistic behaviour by others if markets or ICAs are used. Non-subsidiary forms also limit transfer pricing and other forms of opportunistic behaviour by the firm. One would expect parent–subsidiary relations to prevail where interdependence between the parties is large and where the costs of internalization are not excessive.[15]

This approach to international business organization has always allowed scope for other forms, such as joint ventures and one-directional licensing, but in limited contexts.[16] These older cooperative forms have been expanding across industrial sectors and sometimes in more flexible ways. There has also been a substantial growth in newer or more complex alliance forms, which often appear to involve technology sharing between firms as against a largely unilateral transfer. Whether one is prepared to accept all of this as diminishing the relative role of FDI depends in part on how one interprets the data presented above.

There are several reasons why one might question whether the relative role of FDI has decreased, or at least suspend judgement on the question.

1 It is apparent that FDI experienced a major recovery from the global problems of the early 1980s, and, in particular, branched out substantially into the services sector. The recovery appears to have resumed after an interruption in the first year or two of the 1990s.

2 The data presented above for the various organizational forms are not comparable. One result is that comparisons tend, perhaps erroneously, to favour growth in ICAs relative to FDI. Available ICA figures are very largely by number of agreements. It is difficult to know how one would put a value on them. The FDI figures are in value terms, as well as numbers; some specific cases of international mergers run into billions of dollars. Moreover, the ICA figures typically cover a limited number of sectors, usually goods-producing sectors undergoing rapid technological change, while FDI covers the entire range of production of goods and services. It is not difficult to find a set of newly liberalized service sectors, for example, where FDI growth has been phenomenal in the past decade or two.

3 As suggested in Table 3.16, a majority of the ICAs involve US firms – perhaps as much as 70 per cent in high-tech industries and 60 per cent in all industries, depending on how one allocates the residual for inter-area agreements in that table. Meanwhile, the US share of world outward FDI stock was falling towards 30 per cent during the 1980s. If ICAs are as widespread a phenomenon as is sometimes claimed, it is surprising to see them so highly concentrated on one country.[17]

4 Finally, the great majority of the ICAs reported above have been established in the 1980s, notably since 1985 (see, for example, Tables 3.11–12 above). Many are also apparently short-term in nature; that is, they dissolve once they have attained a specific short-term objective or objectives. It seems premature to judge their importance as a new organizational form.

It is suggested that the multinational enterprise should continue to be regarded as the central private institution in international economic activity. As such, it will utilize arm's-length dealings, subsidiary ties and interfirm agreements as a variety of political, economic and technological circumstances dictate. There is certainly scope for improvement in the theory of FDI: at a minimum, given the data above, it should be able to explain not only the circumstances in which firms prefer the subsidiary form of organization but also those in which they prefer ICAs. There is also enough evidence of major use of ICAs by larger firms, in a sufficiently wide range of activities, to warrant much further analysis.[18] The boundaries of the firm are clearly more flexible than was once thought. Such flexibility raises a number of conflicting issues for traditional antitrust policies, as the chapters of this volume indicate. The need for further study is complicated by the problems in data collection. Some of the private studies of ICAs noted above, such as those collected by the Maastricht Institute and at LAREA–CEREM in Nanterre, have not been updated because of the expense involved and the difficulties in improving the data. Competition authorities have collected such data only in a limited way as part of customary antitrust proceedings. Further analysis is likely to depend in good part on the willingness of such authorities and international organizations to collect such data in a systematic way.

BARRIERS TO INTERNATIONAL TRANSACTIONS

Many issues could be highlighted in relation to the data presented above. One which is central to the present volume is the continuance, despite apparent liberalization in recent years, of many barriers to FDI and ICAs.

It is true that, whatever barriers exist, they have clearly not prevented a major expansion of the international transactions noted above. That expansion has been driven by many forces. In policy terms, one can note that there was a marked shift in government attitudes to inward FDI in the late 1970s and throughout the 1980s. Most review agencies for such investment were ended or substantially liberalized. Indeed, incentives to investment, including those to FDI, have been increased and also been applied more selectively. Privatization, deregulation and modification of requirements regarding domestic ownership have opened a number of industries to at least partial foreign ownership. Even firms once considered strategic in terms of industrial policy are now able to negotiate closer ties with foreign firms.[19]

This apparent openness may be deceptive in some important respects. Cross-border mergers and acquisitions still face significant legal obstacles in a number of countries. Some of these obstacles are clearly directed at cross-border mergers as distinct from those within a country. The existence of foreign investment review on entry and subsequent merger in some countries is one example. Such review agencies are also typically more welcoming to greenfield investment than to IMAs. In addition, differences in competition and related policy areas (among others) often impose substantial uncertainty and other costs on international mergers. Such a merger may require multiple approvals in widely different national legal systems involving, at times, many jurisdictions in one or more federal states (see Chapters 5 and 7 in this volume).

In addition to all of this, however, one can also note that there are wide differences in state holdings of shares between countries, and also in the concentration of shareholdings in banks and other groups. Such close holdings appear to be more extensive in Japan, and also in Germany and some other European countries, than they are in either the United States or the United Kingdom, with Canada probably in an intermediate position. On a related point, it is also evident that there are wide differences between countries in the disclosure, voting and other rights of shareholders, often a critical issue in the effectiveness of takeovers in general and hostile takeovers in particular.[20]

Finally, we note that, while often reducing general review or sectoral restrictions on foreign firms, most countries are now targeting certain high-technology sectors with extensive subsidies, non-tariff barriers and other support. In many cases the sectoral consortia which are formed are designed to limit the participation of foreign-owned firms or those from outside the region involved.

This way of putting the issue begs some questions about the desirability of foreign ownership and international mergers, whether generally or in particular cases. It also leaves open the question whether there are potential economic advantages to close (national) holdings and particularly whether and how to reconcile differences in national systems in any harmonization of international merger review. In terms of the former, for example, Caves's (1982: chapter 4) analysis of the effects of multinationals on competition leads mainly to positive, or at least neutral, conclusions. Hughes *et al.* (1980: chapter 11), in analysing the effects of mergers across countries, conclude there is a case for common policies across countries but also for different national policies because of 'macrodynamic economic considerations' or political philosophy. Our point is simply that, given the broad acceptance of the role which the various organizational forms can play in expediting trade, investment and innovation, considerable work needs to be done on how far and how best to reduce existing obstacles to their spread. This volume is intended, in fact, as a contribution to such work.

Similar points can be made about ICAs. A central question on the competitive effects of ICAs is whether those which focus on technology agreements of various kinds help or hinder innovation. Many of the studies which focus on technological ICAs of various kinds appear to regard them favourably in welfare terms, at least so far as competitive effects are concerned. They may refer to possible anti-competitive effects, but their classification of the various motives for ICAs appears to downgrade such effects. For example, Ciborra (1991: 53, 59–61) recognizes that market power can be enhanced by ICAs but argues that emphasis on control of opportunistic behaviour in designing ICAs would block the learning, innovation and trust which are central to them. Where competition is limited it tends to be regarded as benevolent in the sense of spurring innovation. By contrast, Porter has argued that the mergers and alliances spurred by the prospect of a single European market are likely to restrict competition in knowledge-intensive industries, most notably the innovation needed to compete on a world scale.[21] Chapter 6 of this volume deals with these issues at length.

Any attempt to develop more competition policy on ICAs, or to harmonize national policies, is going to have to cope with one additional problem. Some of the ICAs are an integral part of most state policies to develop or maintain a presence in the high-technology areas. They are, in effect, aspects of industrial policy, along with the strategic aspects of trade and multinational investment policy. It is one thing to agree on how best to apply competition policy, including its international aspects, to private firms. It is quite another to decide how best to agree on international aspects of competition which involves government–firm collaboration, often in the context of competition among high-technology firms in the Triad. Yet these very issues of national and regional treatment of other countries' firms and production, whether in trade, investment or alliances, and the impact on competition and innovation, are what much of the debate in the EU, GATT and other organizations is all about. Competition policy, it is clear, is only part of a larger international agenda, and one which has been addressed more slowly than some other issues.

NOTES

1 See Williamson (1975) for a classic statement on the differences between markets and hierarchies, and Caves (1982) and various studies by Dunning (e.g. 1993) for applications to the theory and effects of multinational enterprises (MNEs). For early general statements on ICAs, see Oman (1984) and Mariti and Smiley (1983).

2 The IMF and OECD publish widely used sets of data. Dunning and Cantwell (1987) perform a major service by assembling and explaining the data in a systematic way. See also the extensive data sets in the successive surveys of *Transnational Corporations and World Development*, *World Investment Report*, and *World Investment Directory*, published by UNCTAD, Division on Transnational Corporations and Investment (formerly the UN Centre on Transnational Corporations).

3 Parent–subsidiary relationships are usually defined in terms of effective voting control of the subsidiary, hence of appointment of its board and chief executive. A long-term interest in the affiliate is usually involved. In practice, control can be exercised through a variety of other measures, and varies considerably among subsidiaries.

4 For examples of the problems see Kinniburgh and Ribeiro (1986).

5 This picture would be modified if the less volatile stock data were used. In 1960 the developed countries as a whole (including the United States) and the United States alone accounted for 99 per cent and 47 per cent of the outward world stock respectively, while in 1992 the figures were 97 per cent and 25 per cent. In 1975 the developed countries and the United States accounted for 75 per cent and 11 per cent of the inward world stock, while by 1992 the figures were 78 per cent and 22 per cent respectively.

6 Table 3.4 shows the share of global flows, Table 3.3 of OECD flows, which account for about 95 per cent of global outward flows.

7 The ranking appears to be based on the average for 1991–3, the third year of

which is preliminary and unpublished. If 1991–2 were used, for example, Canada would rank above three of the countries shown and Singapore beside Mexico.

8 A different picture is given if one considers numbers of IMAs and particularly if one also gives other categories than IMAs and new plants. See UN (1989), pp. 31–2, which gives US Department of Commerce data indicating foreign M&As in the United States, excluding real estate, were 45 per cent of the number of direct investments in 1985–7.

9 See UNCTAD, Division on Transnational Corporations and Investments (1994: 22–4), for an analysis of the role of IMAs in FDI.

10 A study based on data available in 1980 noted that only seven OECD countries were able to show the number of international mergers separately from those which were domestic (OECD 1984: 55). The situation had improved only moderately by 1989 (United Nations 1989: Part II).

11 This statement is based on data in KPMG *Dealwatch* (London), various issues for 1989 to 1993 inclusive. For other evidence on the pick-up in cross-border activity in the late 1980s see Smith and Walter (1990). In this connection, Geroski and Vlassopoulos (1993, first published in 1990) appear to understate the importance of cross-border mergers, especially in value terms, for both the United States and Europe, and also overstate the importance of UK acquisitions compared with those of other European countries.

12 Lawrence (1993: 92) adds that the difference could reflect a bias in the samples, since the Japanese data are comprehensive, while the US data may not be.

13 See Chesnais (1988: 62–8) for several such studies. However, the INSEAD Business School Study which apparently used a broad definition for 839 agreements in 1975–86 also found a high concentration in computers, motor vehicles, electrical, aerospace and telecommunications. (Hergert and Morris 1988: 105.)

14 See, for example, several studies in Mytelka (1991), notably those by Michalet and Ciborra. The implications for an internalization approach to FDI are examined in Delapierre and Michalet (1989).

15 See Safarian (1990) for a more extensive statement and evidence. Theories derived from industrial organization are not the only ones, but seem to be most widely accepted.

16 Kogut (1988) notes that over 45 per cent of a sample of 150 joint ventures did not continue beyond five years.

17 The argument can be turned around, of course, to suggest US multinationals are simply anticipating trends in ICAs.

18 That process has been under way for some time, as our sources suggest. One area where significant work has been done is the motives for cooperation between often competing firms. For a summary and extension, see Hagedoorn (1993). This work clearly ties in with extension of the traditional theory of FDI.

19 See Safarian (1991, 1993b) for the changed policy environment of the 1980s and some effects on policy.

20 See the data from Investor Responsibility Research Centre noted in the *Economist*, April 29, 1989, p. 76. The United States, United Kingdom and Canada rank well above most of Western Europe and Japan in this study in terms of shareholder rights. See also UK Department of Trade and Industry (1989).

21 Porter's doubts about European coalitions were already evident in Porter and Fuller (1986: 342) but are expressed most forcefully in the *Economist*, June 9, 1990, pp. 17–19. See also the critique in the same publication, June 30, 1990, p. 6.

REFERENCES

Caves, R.E. (1982) *Multinational Enterprise and Economic Analysis*. Cambridge University Press.

Chesnais, (1988) 'Technical Cooperation Agreements Between Firms', OECD, *STI Review* 4, 51–120.

Ciborra, C. (1991) 'Alliances as Learning Experiences: Cooperation, Competition and Change in Hightech Industries', in L. Mytelka (ed.) *Strategic Partnerships.*

Cooke, T.E. (1988) *International Mergers and Acquisitions*. Oxford, Basil Blackwell.

Delapierre, M. and C.-A. Michalet (1989) 'Vers un changement des structures des multinationales: le principe d'internalisation en question', *Revue d'Economie Industrielle* 47, 1, 27–43.

Dunning, J.H. (1993) *Multinational Enterprise and the Global Economy*. Reading, Mass., Addison-Wesley.

Dunning, J. and J. Cantwell (1987) *IRM Directory of Statistics of International Investment and Production*. London, Macmillan.

Freeman, C. and J. Hagedoorn (1994) 'Catching up or Falling Behind: Patterns in International Interfirm Technology Partnering', *World Development* 22, 5, 771–80.

Geroski, P. and A. Vlassopoulos (1993) 'Recent Patterns of European Merger Activity', in M. Bishop and J. Kay (eds) *European Mergers and Merger Policy*, Oxford University Press.

Gugler, P. and J.H. Dunning (1993) 'Technology-based Cross-border Alliances', in R. Culpan (ed.) *Multinational Strategic Alliances*. New York, International Business Press.

Hagedoorn, J. (1990) 'Organizational Modes of Interfirm Cooperation and Technology Transfer', *Technovation* 10, 1, 17–30.

Hagedoorn, J. (1993) 'Understanding the Rationale of Strategic Technology Partnering: Interorganizational Modes of Cooperation and Sectoral Differences', *Strategic Management Journal* 14, 371–85.

Hagedoorn, J. and J. Schakenraad (1989) 'Some Remarks on Co-operative Agreements and Technology Indicators (CATI) Information Systems' (mimeo). Maastricht, MERIT.

Hagedoorn, J. and J. Schakenraad (1990) 'Technology Cooperation, Strategic Alliances and their Motives: Brother, Can You Spare a Dime or Do You Have a Light?' Paper for SMS Conference, Stockholm, 24–7 September. Maastricht, MERIT.

Hagedoorn, J. and J. Schakenraad (1991) 'The Economic Effects of Strategic Partnerships and Technology Cooperation' (mimeo). Maastricht, MERIT.

Hergert, M. and D. Morris (1988) 'Trends in International Collaborative Agreements', in F.J. Contractor and P. Lorange (eds) *Cooperative Strategies in International Business*. Lexington Books.

Hughes, A., Dennis C. Mueller and A. Singh (1980), 'Competition Policy in the 1980s: the Implications of the International Merger Wave', in D.C. Mueller, *The Determinants and Effects of Mergers*. Cambridge, Oelgeschager Gunn & Hain.

Japan Economic Institute (1990) 'Japan and Mergers: Oil and Water?' *JEI Report*, April 6.

Japan Economic Institute (1991) 'Foreign Direct Investment in Japan', *JEI Report*, September 20.

Katzenbach, E., H.-E. Scharrer and L. Waverman (eds) (1993) *Competition Policy in an Interdependent World Economy*. Baden-Baden, Nomos Verlag.

Khemani, R.S. (1991) 'Recent Trends in Mergers and Acquisition Activity in

Canada and in Selected Countries', in L. Waverman (ed.) *Corporate Globalization Through Mergers and Acquisitions.*

Kinniburgh J. and V.B. Ribeiro (1986) 'Data on FDI', *UNCTC Reporter* (autumn, 16–19).

Kogut, B. (1988) 'A Study of the Life Cycle of Joint Ventures', in F.J. Contractor and P. Lorange (eds) *Cooperative Strategies in International Business.* Lexington Books.

Kogut, B., W. Shan and G. Walker (1993) 'Knowledge in the Network and the Network as Knowledge: the Structuring of New Industries', in G. Grabher (ed.) *The Embedded Firm: On the Socioeconomics of Industrial Networks.* London, Routledge.

Lawrence, R.Z. (1993) 'Japan's Low Levels of Inward Investment: The Role of Inhibitions on Acquisitions', in K.A. Froot (ed.) *Foreign Direct Investment,* University of Chicago Press.

Mariti P. and R.H. Smiley (1983) 'Co-operative Agreements and the Organization of Industry', *Journal of Industrial Economics* 31, 4, 437–51.

Michalet, C.-A. (1991) 'Strategic Partnerships and the Changing Internationalization Process', in L. Mytelka (ed.) *Strategic Partnerships.*

Mowery D.C. (1988) 'Collaborative Ventures Between U.S. and Foreign Manufacturing Firms: an Overview', in D.C. Mowery (ed.) *International Collaborative Ventures in U.S. Manufacturing.* Cambridge, Mass., Ballinger.

Mytelka, L., ed. (1991) *Strategic Partnerships: States, Firms and International Competition.* London, Pinter Publishers.

OECD (1984) *Merger Policies and Recent Trends in Mergers.* Paris, OECD.

OECD (1987) *International Investment and the Multinational Enterprises: Recent Trends in International Investment.* Paris, OECD.

OECD (1990) *The 1990 Review of The OECD 1976 Declaration and Decisions on International Investments and Multinational Enterprises.* Paris, OECD.

Oman (1984) *New Forms of International Investment in Developing Countries.* Paris, OECD.

Porter, M.E. and M.B. Fuller (1986) 'Coalitions and Global Strategy', in M.E. Porter (ed.) *Competition in Global Industries.* Cambridge, Mass., Harvard Business School Press.

Safarian, A.E. (1990) 'The Investment Decisions of Multinational Enterprises', *North American Review of Economics and Finance* 1, 2, 253–66.

Safarian, A.E. (1991) 'Firm and Government Strategies', in B. Bürgenmeier and J.L. Mucchielli (eds) *Multinationals and Europe 1992: Strategies for the Future.* London, Routledge.

Safarian, A.E. (1993a) *Multinational Enterprise and Public Policy.* Cheltenham, Edward Elgar.

Safarian, A.E. (1993b) 'Have Transnational Mergers or Joint Ventures Increased?' In E. Katzenbach *et al.* (eds) *Competition Policy in an Interdependent World Economy.*

Smith, C.S. and I. Walter (1990) 'Economic Restructuring in Europe and the Market for Corporate Control', *Journal of International Securities Markets,* winter, 291–313.

UK Department of Trade and Industry (1989) *Barriers to Takeovers in the European Community,* a study prepared by Coopers & Lybrand, London, HMSO.

United Nations (1988) *Transnational Corporations in World Development.* New York, UNCTC.

United Nations (1989) *The Process of Transnationalization and Transnational Mergers.* New York, UNCTC.

United Nations (1991) *World Investment Report: the Triad in Foreign Direct Investment*. New York, UNCTC.

United Nations (1992) *World Investment Report: Transnational Corporations as Engines of Growth*. New York, United Nations, Transnational Corporations and Management Division.

United Nations (1992) *World Investment Directory* III, *Developed Countries*. New York, UNCTC.

United Nations (1993) *World Investment Report: Transnational Corporations and Integrated International Production*. New York, United Nations, Programme on Transnational Corporations.

UNCTAD, Division on Transnational Corporations and Investment (1994) *World Investment Report: Transnational Corporations, Employment and the Workplace*. United Nations, New York and Geneva.

Waverman, L., ed. (1991) *Corporate Globalization Through Mergers and Acquisitions*. Calgary, University of Calgary Press, for Investment Canada.

Williamson, O.E. (1975) *Markets and Hierarchies: Analysis and Antitrust Implications*. New York, Free Press.

ACKNOWLEDGEMENTS

Research for this chapter was supported by a grant from the Bureau of Competition Policy, Ottawa. I am grateful also to Leonard Waverman for comments on earlier drafts, and to Walid Hejazi and Ata Mazaheri for research assistance.

Part II

MERGERS

4

MERGERS AND ACQUISITIONS IN JAPAN AND THE ANTI-MONOPOLY POLICY

Hiroyuki Odagiri

This chapter discusses some aspects of mergers and acquisitions (M&As) in Japan and public policy towards them, chiefly the anti-monopoly regulation. The first four sections discuss the numbers, sizes, types, objectives, and other characteristics of M&As in Japan and how they are related to the structure of Japanese firms, in particular their human resource structure. The regulations on M&As are discussed in the following two sections, with the fifth section describing the regulations in the Japanese Anti-monopoly Law concerning M&As, stockholdings, and interlocking directorates, and the sixth discussing the two major merger cases – the Nippon Steel case of 1970 and two more recent mergers in the paper industry. The chapter concludes with some assessment of the policies.

ARE MERGERS FEWER IN JAPAN?

Mergers and acquisitions are by no means rare in Japan. This is a fact not fully realized outside the country. It is true that *hostile* acquisitions are very rare in today's Japan. Still, hostile share acquisitions did take place in Japan, often for the purpose of greenmailing, which prompted corporate managers to increase the share of *stable* or friendly owners through mutual stock purchase.[1] Even in the United States and United Kingdom, friendly acquisitions have been far more common in recent years than hostile takeovers, despite much publicity associated with a number of hostile takeovers.

It is extremely difficult to compare the number of M&As across countries because official statistics are limited. Probably the only reliable data are the number of mergers in Japan. The Anti-monopoly Law in Japan stipulates in Section 15 that 'every company in Japan, which is desirous of becoming a party to a merger, shall, in accordance with the provisions of the Rules of the Fair Trade Commission, file a notification with the Commission' and this requirement is considered to be well observed; therefore, the number of

69

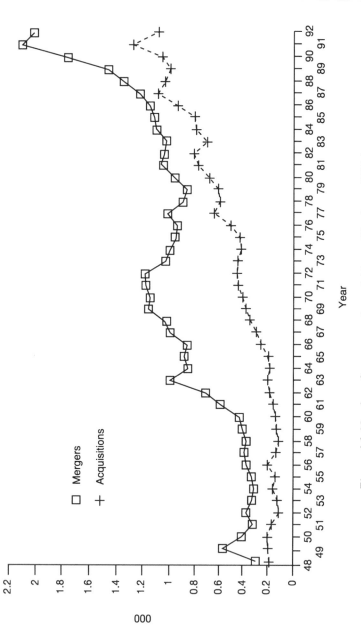

Figure 4.1 Number of mergers and acquisitions of business (000s)
Source: Fair Trade Commission 1993, tables 4.18–9

mergers published by the Fair Trade Commission (abbreviated as FTC in this chapter; not to be confused with the US Federal Trade Commission) is presumed to be comprehensive and reliable. Figure 4.1 gives this number since 1948. The number was more or less stable around the level of 1,000 during the 1960s and 1970s but increased rapidly during the latter half of the 1980s. It reached the peak of 2,091 in 1991 and then slightly decreased to 2,002 in 1992.

The figure also shows the number of 'acquisitions of businesses' which is basically the acquisition of assets and not of equity. As in the case of mergers, companies wishing to make such acquisitions are required to notify the FTC, although whether all of them have been actually following this regulation is less obvious than for mergers and hence the numbers shown may be undervalued. An increasing trend is evident with these acquisitions as well and the number reached the peak of 1,266 in 1991 and then decreased to 1,079 in 1992.

It is noted again that the merger in the FTC statistics is in its strict sense and does not include acquisitions of control of another company through equity acquisitions but without merger (to be simply called acquisitions). Therefore, the total number of mergers and acquisitions must be larger than that indicated in the FTC merger statistics. Also, the latter includes only the mergers among Japanese firms.

In the United States 1,529 mergers were notified to the Department of Justice in 1991 and 1,589 in 1992. The first number is smaller than the number of M&As in 1991 counted by *Mergers and Acquisitions*, which was 2,617. Of these, 1,711 (65 per cent) were of American firms by American firms, 402 (15 per cent) were of foreign firms by American firms, and 504 (19 per cent) were of American firms by foreign firms. They include acquisitions besides mergers and in this regard the coverage is wider than the FTC statistics. However, they do not include those for which the value of acquisition is small and in this regard the coverage is smaller. In conclusion, it is very difficult to compare the number of M&As between Japan and the United States. If we also take into consideration the size difference between the two economies, it becomes even more difficult to argue that M&A activity is less in Japan than in the United States.

MERGERS AND ACQUISITIONS IN JAPAN

Although again there are few comparable data, it seems reasonably accurate to argue that in Japan, first, mergers and acquisitions involving large firms are not many; second, hostile acquisitions are infrequent (though by no means absent); and third, at least among large firms, looser forms of combination are preferred.

Table 4.1 shows that, among the 2,002 mergers in 1992, about half are mergers of firms both of which have total assets of less than a billion yen.[2]

Table 4.1 Number of mergers by total assets of acquiring and acquired firms (billion yen)

Assets of acquiring firm	Assets of acquired firm				
	0–1	*1–10*	*10–100*	*100–*	*Total*
0–1	951 (47.5)	99 (4.9)	8 (0.4)	0	1,058 (52.8)
1–10	447 (22.3)	197 (9.8)	10 (0.5)	0	654 (32.7)
10–100	102 (5.1)	112 (5.6)	28 (1.4)	0	242 (12.1)
100–	6 (0.3)	13 (0.6)	21 (1.0)	8 (0.4)	48 (2.4)
Total	1,506 (75.2)	421 (21.0)	67 (3.3)	8 (0.4)	2,002 (100.0)

Source: Fair Trade Commission (1993), table 4-9.
Note: Figures in parentheses are percentages of the total.

About three-quarters of the mergers are against firms with assets of less than a billion yen and fully 96 per cent are against those with less than ten billion yen. Firms with assets greater than 100 billion yen made forty-eight mergers of which only eight are against firms in the same size class. Of these eight, two are between banks, one is the merger by Japan IBM of its affiliated company, one by the Itochu trading company of its affiliated real estate company, one by a trading company as a rescue operation for another trading company on the brink of bankruptcy, and one by Sumitomo Metal of its affiliated stainless steel maker. The remaining two were associated with more substantial market power issues. The merger between Jujo Paper (506 billion yen in assets) and Sanyo-Kokusaka Pulp (393 billion) was between the third and fifth largest paper manufacturers. Later we will discuss this merger at some length. The merger between Nippon Mining (819 billion) and Kyodo Oil (595 billion) produced the fourth largest oil refiner but the two had been vertically related with Nippon refining and Kyodo marketing the oil products.

The assets of 100 billion yen are very modest in comparison with those of, say, Toyota (6,077 billion), Hitachi (3,907 billion), Nippon Steel (3,431 billion), or even Suzuki (606 billion), the smallest of the eight independent car manufacturers. Clearly, the majority of the mergers are between small or medium-sized firms or those by large firms of smaller firms.

As has been discussed already, the FTC statistics provide the facts on mergers only and not acquisitions of equity. Needless to say, however, acquisitions, at least majority acquisitions, have nearly the same consequence as mergers in that they integrate hitherto separate and independent operations under a single decision-making unit. That is, whether the acquiring firm should place the acquired operation as a division within the company or leave it as a subsidiary is little more than a question of how to create an efficient internal organization and depends on the costs and merits of alternative organizational forms. In fact, several factors, to be discussed below, suggest that acquisitions are usually more advantageous than mergers from these viewpoints.

There are no comprehensive data on mergers and acquisitions combined. Yamaichi Securities counted the M&A cases principally from press reports and found 483 M&As involving Japanese firms in 1992, of which 260 (54 per cent) were by Japanese firms of Japanese firms, 186 (39 per cent) by Japanese firms of foreign firms, and thirty-seven (8 per cent) by foreign firms of Japanese firms. All the M&As involving foreign firms were acquisitions and so were the majority of the acquisitions between Japanese firms.

In view of this weight of acquisitions and in view of the fact that past studies of M&As in Japan concentrated on mergers alone, this author, together with T. Hase, has investigated 243 M&As of Japanese firms by Japanese firms reported in *Nihon Keizai Shimbun* during 1980 to 1987, excluding mergers between subsidiaries and their parent firms.[3] Needless to say, since only major M&As were reported in the press, these are biased towards M&As involving big companies.

We classified them into three categories: mergers (when firms A and B merge into a single company), acquisitions (when A acquires control of B without a merger, usually but not necessarily with majority share ownership), capital participation (when B retains its own control but falls under A's influence, usually with A's minority share ownership). Acquisitions were found to be most popular, with 56 per cent of the cases, followed by capital participation. Mergers accounted for a mere 18 per cent of the cases. Clearly, the majority of firms prefer looser forms of combination. In view of the disadvantages such looser combination is expected to have, such as weaker control and a slower or inaccurate information flow, its advantages in other regards must be large. We will discuss these advantages in the next section.

For 171 of the 243 M&As we could find the reasons for being acquired. Among them 66 per cent raised management difficulty (for instance, due to suboptimal scale, financial difficulty, or simply bad management) as the reason, suggesting that not many Japanese firms are willing to sell themselves unless their survival is threatened. The other 25 per cent raised growth constraint, implying that the acquired firm was doing well but lacked the managerial resources required to expand further, therefore having opted to sell itself. The rest, 9 per cent, were sold owing to the restructuring policy of the former parent firms. None of the reasons suggests that the M&As were made by hostile bidders.

Why is it that few Japanese managers are willing to undertake hostile acquisitions? Yet why are firms under a serious threat of bankruptcy or in need of new resources to attain further growth willing to be acquired? These are the questions vitally related to the essence of the Japanese firm. To investigate this issue, we have to start with a discussion of its human resource management.

THE HUMAN RESOURCE STRUCTURE OF JAPANESE FIRMS AND ITS CONSEQUENCES FOR MERGERS AND ACQUISITIONS[4]

The following are usually believed to be the main features of the Japanese labour system:

1 *Lifetime employment*: the company hires new graduates and retains them until the age of compulsory retirement.
2 *Seniority system*: wages and promotion are determined according to seniority.
3 *Enterprise unionism*: unions are organized on a company basis (as opposed to an occupation basis).

Is there really such a system? Although it is extremely dangerous to give a simple answer, it appears reasonable to say 'yes', with the following reservations. First, not all Japanese workers − in fact, not even a majority of them − are covered by the system. Second, the difference from the American or any other system is not that great. On the one hand, *de facto* lifetime employment and seniority systems do exist in other countries. On the other, even in Japan workers are often made redundant when a company suffers from continuous losses, and wages and ranks vary among the workers of the same seniority. Third, the system started around 1920 in response to the shortage of skilled labour, indicating that it was an outcome of market forces.

These reservations notwithstanding, it is true that the Japanese system is closer to this stereotype than other systems. It is also true that, despite the reality mentioned above, the system is viewed as the norm among Japanese firms. Hence, for instance, while lifetime employment is much less conspicuous among small firms than in large firms, the managers of most small firms try hard to avoid redundancy in times of depression. The result is the prevalence of a long-run company−worker attachment.

Given these practices, M&As are not an attractive strategy for Japanese management. First, corporate growth is sought primarily because of its contribution to utilizing and enriching human resources and in creating promotion opportunities. For instance, firms in stagnating industries desperately seek an opportunity to diversify so as to redeploy surplus workers into new fields. Obviously, only internal growth contributes to this purpose, because an acquisition of a company is also an acquisition of its human resources, thereby hardly creating vacancies in jobs and posts.

Second, workers identify their interests with those of the company, which, as a consequence, is regarded as a sort of community. An acquisition offer may be taken as an intrusion and a hostile takeover attempt is likely to meet furious resistance.

Third, because labour practices are in many ways firm-specific, unifying the practices of two different firms on merger tends to be costly and to create uneasiness and conflicts of interest. Examples relate to the wage system, non-wage fringe benefits, the criteria for promotion and rotation, and even the quality of lunch the company provides. Thus, for instance, the firm created by a merger usually needs to adopt the higher of the wage structures of previously separate companies so as not to disappoint the workers. There are also psychological or sociological costs. In mergers under equal terms, as in the case of Yawata Steel and Fuji Steel merging into Nippon Steel (to be discussed later), great care was taken to prevent an impression that either firm was 'acquired' by the other because, otherwise, the morale of the employees of the supposedly 'acquired' firm will be impaired. Thus it has been said that the choice of the acquiring company in a legal sense (see note 2 above) was made by lottery. Also, for over twenty years since the merger, the presidency has been taken alternately by ex-Fuji officers and ex-Yawata officers. Similarly, great care was taken to equalize the number of ex-Yawata personnel and ex-Fuji personnel at most managerial levels.

Fourth, because the managers of Japanese firms are mostly internally promoted and are less constrained by the stock market evaluation of their company's performance, they are not so worried about short-term results as Anglo-American executives and can stand the initial loss internal growth tends to create during the gestation period.

These factors, together with the presence of stable shareholders, as discussed earlier, explain why M&As are a less attractive means of corporate growth than internal expansion and why hostile M&As are difficult. They also suggest that firms will prefer a loose form of combination to complete integration. By leaving the acquired company under a separate organization the firm can avoid the costs of unifying labour practices, and keep up the morale of the employees, who wish to view their company as an independent organization, however superficial that independence may be. The high percentages of acquisitions and capital participations discussed above clearly support this conjecture.

THE TYPES AND OBJECTIVES OF MERGERS AND ACQUISITIONS

The discussion above does not imply that Japanese firms never use M&As as a strategic means. They use them, but only when internal expansion is expected to be too costly or when the resources of the acquired are expected to complement the internal resources.

In the Odagiri and Hase study the objectives of the acquiring companies were classified into eight categories. Table 4.2 shows the distribution of 243 M&As among these objectives. Among them, categories 1–4 must be self-explanatory. The business community often talks about the need to 'restructure the market' (category 5) when, according to its view, the production capacity of an industry is excessive and the number of producers must be reduced. Naturally, M&As to restructure markets are mostly horizontal and in stagnating or declining industries. A typical example of category 6 takes place when a trucking company in one geographical area acquires a trucking company in another to obtain a licence needed to operate in the latter's area. No. 7 is probably used most often as a strategy for diversification or for acquisition of technology but is listed here as a separate objective. No. 8 indicates that the acquisition was made to save the acquired firm from bankruptcy. Actually the true motivation may have been hidden; for instance, the acquiring firm may have anticipated that it could gain because the acquisition cost was lower than the asset resale price. Or it may have been guaranteed a low-interest loan by the bank(s) with outstanding loans to the failing company.

The table indicates that capacity expansion was raised by acquiring firms in about a quarter of the cases. However, taken together, the following three objectives cover the majority of the cases. These diversifying, marketing-orientated, and technology-orientated objectives are all intended to extend managerial resources into unfamiliar fields. It is therefore suggested that M&As are most often used as a means of diversification. The reason is again

Table 4.2 The objectives of mergers and acquisitions in Japan (per cent)

No.	Objective	Frequency
1	Increasing production capacity	23.0
2	Diversification	19.8
3	Strengthening marketing capacity	18.1
4	Acquisition of technology	14.8
5	Restructuring the market	8.2
6	To deal with regulation	7.0
7	Investment in venture businesses	4.9
8	Rescue	4.1

Source: Odagiri and Hase (1989), table 2.

implied by the earlier discussion. The preference of Japanese firms for internal growth as opposed to external growth, such as M&A, must be particularly strong when the firm intends to grow horizontally, because the required resources, human or informational, are likely to be internally available or can be created without much time or cost. On the contrary, when the firm intends to expand into unfamiliar fields, it lacks the required resources and acquiring them through M&A will complement its internal resources.

The finding suggests that most of the M&As were conglomerate types as opposed to horizontal and vertical ones. Our classification of the 243 M&As into these types in fact indicated that horizontal M&As accounted for 28.8 per cent and vertical ones, 7.0 per cent, while the remaining 64.2 per cent were classified into conglomerate or diversifying type (which was further divided into product extension, market extension, and pure conglomerate categories). The weight of the last type is somewhat larger than that of the 2,002 mergers in 1992 of the FTC statistics in which 33.2 per cent were classified as horizontal, 15.8 per cent as vertical, and 48.4 per cent as conglomerate.[5] One of the reasons for the difference may be that we have classified many of the M&As into the 'product extension' and 'market extension' categories which would have been classified into horizontal or vertical categories by the FTC. In fact, in our study, 37.4 per cent were regarded as 'product extension' types and 16.9 per cent as 'market extension' types, whereas they were, respectively, 8.2 per cent and 11.0 per cent in the FTC statistics. However, the large percentages of these categories seem to accord with the move towards related diversification taken by many Japanese firms as shown in Table 4.2.[6]

Even though the proportion of horizontal mergers was rather small, their impact was large because many of the large-scale mergers were horizontal. In fact 89.5 per cent of the assets acquired through mergers in 1992 were acquired by horizontal mergers and, as shown on p. 72, many of the largest mergers were horizontal. Although this percentage is disproportionately large in comparison with those in previous years (e.g. 56.9 per cent in 1990), the percentage of horizontal mergers in terms of acquired assets has always been larger than that in terms of the number of cases. Therefore, it always made sense to watch mergers carefully from the antitrust viewpoint. To this policy issue we now turn.

THE ANTI-MONOPOLY LAW IN JAPAN: REGULATIONS ON MERGERS AND ACQUISITIONS

The history of anti-monopoly policy in Japan began immediately after the Second World War. The allied occupation army was determined to pursue what it called the economic democratization programme.[7] The major part of this reform consisted of three policies: dissolution of *zaibatsu*, dissolution of firms with excessive market power, and the enactment of the Anti-monopoly Law. Leaving the discussion of the first two to elsewhere (see, for instance, Hadley 1970; Odagiri 1992: chapter 11), we concentrate here on the Anti-monopoly Law (hereafter simply called the law), in particular its provisions on mergers and shareholdings.[8]

Prohibition of particular mergers

Section 15 of the law stipulates that 'no company in Japan shall effect a merger in any one of the following paragraphs: (i) Where the effect of a merger may be substantially to restrain competition in any particular field of trade; (ii) Where unfair trade practices have been employed in the course of the merger.'

To enforce this regulation, the law requires that 'every company in Japan, which is desirous of becoming a party to a merger shall ... file a notification with the Commission' and that 'no company in Japan shall, in the cases coming under the preceding subsection, effect a merger until the expiration of a thirty-day waiting period from the date of the issuance of the receipt of the said report ...'

Clearly, the phrase 'substantially to restrain competition' is ambiguous. In 1980 (revised 1994) the FTC issued a guideline (formally, 'administrative procedure standards') which says that

close examination will be given to any case falling into one of the following categories:

1 The market share of a merging company or the combined market share of the parties concerned in any relevant market where any of the parties to the merger operates; (a) is 25 per cent or more, (b) is ranked first and also 15 per cent or more, or (c) is ranked first and also when the difference between the share of the top-ranked company and that of the second or third largest company is more than a quarter of the market share of the top-ranked company.

2 The market share of a merging company or the combined market share of the merging companies in any relevant market where any of the parties to the merger operates is ranked among the top three and also the aggregate market share of the top three companies is 50 per cent or more.

3 In any relevant market where any of the parties to the merger operates, the number of competitors is seven or less.

4 The total assets of any one of the parties concerned amount to 100 billion yen or more and also those of another amount to 10 billion yen or more.

In the 'close examination', the guideline states, the FTC will consider, in case of horizontal mergers, not only the post-merger market share but also the 'situation regarding competition, etc., in the relevant market where the parties concerned operate', such as 'the number of competitors and their situations, the time-series changes in the market share, the height of entry barriers, the status of imports, and other factors concerning competition in the relevant market', as well as 'the existence or absence of substitute goods', 'the growth potential and other characteristics of the market', and 'the overall business capabilities, etc., of the companies concerned' such as 'the ability to procure raw materials, technical resources, marketing capabilities, and access to credits', and 'their business situation (including their degree of poor business performance)'.

For vertical mergers, the 'extent of foreclosure of the relevant market' and the 'degree of the heightening of entry barriers' will be considered and, for conglomerate mergers, the 'degree of potential competition between the parties to the merger', the 'degree of competitive advantage in the position of the companies following the merger', and the 'degree of heightening of entry barriers' will be considered.

That is, the market share criteria only give the 'standards to select ... mergers for close examination' and by no means imply that every merger that falls into any one of the market share conditions will be forbidden. Nevertheless, the 25 per cent post-merger market share and other conditions have been often taken by the industries as the touchstone on whether the FTC would approve the merger. Examples to be discussed in the next section will illustrate this fact.

Prohibition of particular acquisition of business

This 'acquisition' refers to the acquisition of assets and not of equity as discussed earlier. Section 16 of the law simply states that 'the provisions of the preceding section [prohibition of particular mergers] shall apply *mutatis mutandis* to' such acquisition. Therefore, as in the case of mergers, companies have to notify the FTC in advance of acquisitions.

Prohibition of particular stockholding

Section 10 states that 'no company shall acquire or hold stock of a company or companies in Japan where the effect of such acquisition or holding of stock may be substantially to restrain competition in any particular field of trade, or shall acquire or hold stock of a company or companies in Japan through unfair practices.' The regulation on equity acquisition is thus parallel to that on mergers.

There is a difference, however, in terms of filing requirements:

> every company in Japan whose business is other than financial and whose total assets exceed two billion yen, or every foreign company whose business is other than financial, shall, in cases where it holds stock of another company or companies in Japan, submit ... a report on such stock held in its name or in the name of trustees as of the end of every business year to the commission within three months therefrom.

That is, in contrast to the requirement on prior notification of any merger, a report on stock acquisitions is to be given once a year and after such acquisitions have actually been made. Presumably, this asymmetry came from a belief that dissolving a merger *ex post* is difficult but disposing of the acquired shares *ex post* is not. In view of the common use of acquisitions as the means of business combination, as shown above, it seems to this author more effective to require prior notification of share acquisitions as well, provided the acquisitions are substantial in terms of amount and control and are of a horizontal nature.

The FTC also issued guidelines on stockholding. In addition to the interpretation of 'substantially to restrain competition', which is the same as that on mergers, the guidelines give 'the standards for determining the existence or absence of a joint relationship due to stockholding'. Simply speaking, they say that the FTC holds a joint relationship to exist if the stockholding ratio is 50 per cent or more or the relationship meets the requirement of 'affiliated company' in accounting rules. If the stockholding ratio is between 25 and 50 per cent; or if the ratio is between 10 and 25 per cent and the stockholding company is the largest stockholder; or if the ratio is between 10 and 25 per cent, the stockholding company is among the largest three stockholders, and the companies concerned are competitors with each other, the FTC will examine whether a joint relationship exists. In this examination the FTC will consider not only the stockholding and other financial relationships but also the relationship in markets, personnel, technology, transactions, and others.

Prohibition of holding company

Section 9 stipulates that no holding company 'whose principal business is to control the business activities of a company or companies in Japan by means of holdings of stock' is allowed to be established or to operate.

Restriction on total amount of stockholding by a giant
non-financial company

Section 9-2 (added in the 1977 amendment) stipulates that any large non-financial company 'shall not acquire or hold stock of companies in Japan in excess of its capital or its net assets, whichever is larger.'

Restriction on stockholding rate by a financial company

Section 11 stipulates that 'no company engaged in financial business shall acquire or hold stock of another company in Japan if by doing so it holds in excess of five per cent (ten per cent in the case of an insurance company) of the total outstanding stock'. The effect this regulation has had on the dispersion of stock ownership of Japanese companies has been discussed in Odagiri (1992: chapter 2).

Prohibition of particular interlocking directorates

The regulation is similar to that on stockholding and notification is required within thirty days as from the date of assuming the position.

Prohibition of particular stockholding by a person
other than a company

The regulation is similar to that on stockholding by a company.

THE STEEL AND PAPER MERGER CASES

Nippon Steel

The merger of Yawata Steel and Fuji Steel to form Nippon Steel has been the most important merger case for at least two reasons.

First, Yawata and Fuji were born in 1950 when Japan Iron & Steel, a semi-nationalized company and undisputed market leader before the war, was split under the Law on the Elimination of Excessive Concentrations of Economic Power. In 1964, four years before the Yawata–Fuji merger was proposed, three companies born out of Mitsubishi Heavy Industries under the same law had been allowed to re-merge into Mitsubishi Heavy Industries with only a slight argument from the FTC. Also, three paper companies, Oji, Jujo and Honshu, similarly born out of the prewar Oji, were planning to re-merge around the same time as Yawata and Fuji. The controversy the Yawata–Fuji merger created made the re-merger of the paper companies more difficult (the merger plan was subsequently withdrawn) as well as a few others, most notably Sapporo Beer and Asahi Beer, which were reported to have discussed re-mergers from time to time.

Second, the forthcoming trade and capital liberalization had the Ministry of International Trade and Industries (MITI) worrying about what it regarded as the suboptimal production scales of Japanese firms. The MITI had always regarded the existence of giant foreign firms – US Steel, GM, IBM, and DuPont, to name just a few – as threatening and advocated the pursuit of economies of scale in order to survive the competition against these dominant rivals. Thus when Yawata and Fuji announced the merger plan in April 1968, the MITI immediately announced that it would welcome it. On the other hand, a number of influential economists issued a joint statement opposing the merger. As a result, the FTC's investigation of the case was paid much attention by diverse parties and the decision has been regarded as an important precedent ever since.

The market shares of Yawata before the merger were 22.1 per cent for pig iron and 18.5 per cent for crude steel, and those of Fuji were 22.4 per cent and 16.9 per cent, respectively; the combined shares, therefore, were 44.5 per cent and 35.4 per cent, clearly exceeding the 25 per cent threshold stipulated in the merger guideline which would be set a decade later and even the 30 per cent threshold that the FTC's chairman suggested earlier in the Diet.

The FTC particularly regarded their combined shares in four markets as violating the law: railway rails (100 per cent share by Yawata and Fuji together), tinplate for food cans (61.2 per cent), foundry pig iron (56.3 per cent), and steel piles (98.3 per cent). After thirteen formal hearings, the companies submitted a plan for self-imposed remedies to the FTC, which contained such measures as the transfer of equipment and technological know-how to competitors and the sale of the stocks of subsidiaries. The FTC then issued a consent decision approving the plan as an effective remedial measure. The merger took place in March 1970, creating the present Nippon Steel.

The consent decision does not disclose why the merger, with these remedies, was regarded as not restraining competition except to say, rather generally, that whether market dominance would result depended on a number of economic conditions, such as conditions on the industry in general, the conditions on suppliers and buyers, the presence of imports, the availability of substitute goods, and difficulty of entry. Apparently, MITI's support of the merger must have had an influence, particularly because one of the five FTC commissioners was a MITI ex-official.

More importantly, however, the presence of four major rivals, Nippon Kokan (now NKK), Sumitomo Metal, Kawasaki Steel, and Kobe Steel, and their faster growth than Yawata and Fuji in the preceding two decades seem to have been the critical factor in the FTC's decision. In fact many of the post-war innovations in the industry were started by these rival companies, including the construction of the first large-scale coastal integrated steel mill by Kawasaki, continuous casting by Sumitomo, and the basic oxygen furnace by NKK (see Lynn 1982; Yonekura 1983, 1986; Odagiri and Goto 1996).

By contrast, in the case of the aforementioned merger plan between the three paper manufacturers, the FTC gave a more negative opinion in the informal prior consultation because, although their combined share in paper in general was 32 per cent and about the same as the combined share of Yawata and Fuji in crude steel, no other company had a share of more than 10 per cent, with probably the only comparable competitor, Daishowa Paper, having a 9.5 per cent share.

Whether the merger has produced the intended objectives of cost saving, the elimination of 'unnecessary' parallel investment in facilities, and more efficient R&D activity is difficult to evaluate. According to a simulation study (Yamawaki 1984), the domestic steel price would have been lower and the export price higher during the 1970s were it not for the merger, with only a modest increase in investment. It is difficult to evaluate this effect from the welfare viewpoint.

Another fact is that relative market shares among the big five (Nippon Steel, NKK, Kawasaki Steel, Sumitomo Metal, and Kobe Steel) have been surprisingly stable during the two decades since the merger despite steady erosion of their combined share owing to the growth of non-integrated mills and imports. During the twenty-year period from 1971 to 1991 the combined share of the five firms in crude steel declined from 78.2 per cent to 63.7 per cent and the share of Nippon Steel declined from 34.4 to 26.2. The relative share of Nippon Steel among the five, therefore, declined only slightly, from 44.0 to 41.1, and the relative shares of the other four firms also remained virtually constant. This stability marks a contrast with the preceding twenty-year period, when the combined share of the six firms (with Yawata and Fuji counted as separate) remained rather stable, from 80.8 in 1950 to 78.2 in 1971 but the relative share of Yawata and Fuji combined decreased significantly, from 59.7 to 44.0.[9] Although no evidence has been found of these companies collusively maintaining their relative shares, such stability appears to be too prominent to be dismissed as simply accidental.

Nippon Paper and New Oji Paper

In 1992 Jujo Paper and Sanyo-Kokusaku Pulp announced their intention to merge in April 1993 to become Nippon Paper, which was expected to attain a market share of 17.3 per cent in all paper, exceeding that of the market leader, Oji Paper. Several months later, Oji announced its own plan to merge with Kanzaki Paper in October 1993 to become Shin Oji (New Oji) Paper, with a market share of 19.9 per cent.

Table 4.3 Share of production of paper, 1991 (per cent)

Type of paper	Jujo	Sanyo-Kokusaku	Oji	Kanzaki
All	11.2 (3)	6.1 (5)	16.2 (1)	3.7 *
Newsprint	17.5 (2)	*	28.3 (1)	*
Printing	13.1 (3)	7.5 (5)	13.4 (2)	*
Wrapping	*	*	24.3 (1)	*
Miscellaneous	*	9.9 (1)	5.8 (4)	8.0 (2)

Source: Toyo Keizai Toukei Geppo, December 1992.
Notes: Ranks are in parentheses. * indicates that the rank was sixth or lower.

It is first noted that, as discussed above, Oji, Jujo and Honshu once planned to merge to resurrect the pre-war giant Oji Paper but withdrew the plan when, in their pre-hearing consultation with the FTC, they learned that the FTC would object to the merger. Since then, the merger guideline has been issued which, as discussed earlier, clearly states that the FTC will closely examine any merger that would result in a 25 per cent market share or larger, indicating that its stance against mergers has stiffened since the time of the Yawata–Fuji merger. The post-merger shares of Nippon Paper and New Oji Paper clearly indicate that, in the choice of Sanyo-Kokusaku by Jujo and the choice of Kanzaki by Oji as partners, they were keenly aware of this guideline.

Table 4.3 shows the pre-merger market shares of these companies and their ranking. Although the market share of neither post-merger company would exceed 20 per cent if all kinds of paper are aggregated, in a few more finely defined markets the shares were expected to become substantial; for instance, Kanzaki and Oji together had a share of almost 30 per cent in the market for coated paper and 40 per cent in that for art paper. Given the FTC's concern on these points, Oji sold its production facility for these types of paper to a competitor. In addition, because the FTC was concerned that the combined firm would become a dominant shareholder in both of the two largest paper distribution companies, Oji agreed to sell some of its shares in these companies. Jujo and Sanyo-Kokusaku also agreed to sell some shares in their subsidiaries because the FTC warned that, together with those subsidiaries', their market shares in coated paper, rice paper, and carbon paper were unacceptably large. With these remedial measures the FTC approved both mergers.

CONCLUSION

Has the Japanese anti-monopoly regulation been effective in preventing anti-competitive mergers and acquisitions? The answer appears to be 'yes'. Although formal verdicts in the courts or even formal hearing decisions at the FTC have been rare, this fact alone does not imply that the anti-monopoly regulation has been ineffective. More commonly, the FTC has been preventing undesirable M&As through two means – publication of guidelines and informal consultation. In the paper company mergers, for instance, the guideline influenced the companies' choice of merger partners and, although the FTC did not bring the cases to formal hearings, they were able to persuade the companies to take remedial measures that they regarded as appropriate.

Excessive dependence on guidelines may lead to undesirable consequences, however. Particularly, whereas the market share criteria are basically intended to be 'safe harbours' by the authority, the industry may take it to be 'likely challenge thresholds.' In other words, those mergers that would be approved by the FTC on the basis of conditions other than market shares may never be proposed for fear of the possibility that the combined market share of more than 25 per cent would invite the FTC to challenge the case. The result may be discouragement of procompetitive, efficiency-enhancing mergers. Although no such case has been reported in Japan and the accessibility of the FTC for prior consultation has presumably lessened such a possibility, it would be needed for the authority to convince the industry of its flexibility in applying the guidelines.

The use of informal consultation, counsels, and admonition is common not only in merger cases but also in other anti-monopoly cases. During the 1992 fiscal year the FTC brought one case (not an M&A case) to the courts, issued recommendation decisions in thirty-seven cases, brought no case to a formal hearing, and issued warnings or admonitions to ninety-four cases (FTC 1993). In addition, there must have been numerous cases of consultation that were not reported in the FTC's annual report. On the one hand, such reliance on informal measures and administrative guidance (*gyosei shido*) has the clear merit of minimizing the administrative costs. Legal costs were avoided and the FTC, with about 500 staff, is surprisingly small when compared with the US Federal Trade Commission and the Antitrust Division of the Justice Department.

On the other hand, because the records of these counsels, etc., are not made publicly available, transparency concerning the FTC's evaluations is limited and it is more difficult for outsiders to learn from previous cases. There is clearly a trade-off between these merits and demerits of informal guidance as opposed to legal procedures but the progress of international business activities is making the transparency requirement more and more urgent. The shift towards formal decisions is actually taking place: the number of recommendation and hearing decisions has increased from five in 1988 to ten in 1989, nineteen in 1990, twenty-nine in 1991, and thirty-seven in 1992.

The merger guidelines seem comparable with those in other countries. Clearly, whether the 25 per cent market share makes any economic sense as the threshold level for the restraint of competition (which, as discussed repeatedly, the FTC uses as one of the criteria but by no means the only one) remains a moot question. Mere market share may be a less important factor in the extent of market competition than entry barriers (e.g. is the market sufficiently contestable?) or the mode of rivalrous behaviour (e.g. are the rivals competing *à la* Bertrand or Cournot?). The existence of a powerful foreign rival may function as a threat even if it is not currently operating in the domestic market. Dynamic competition through innovation may be more important than static price competition and, if there are economies of scale or scope in R&D activity, the emergence of firms with high market shares may rather foster dynamic competition. This last argument, however, has been employed too often by businesses, with little convincing evidence.

We have seen in this chapter that a majority of M&As take the form of acquisition rather than merger. Although there have been cases of the FTC challenging acquisitions in the past,[10] far fewer cases have been treated by the FTC by comparison with mergers. Partly this difference reflects the fact that a larger part of acquisitions (and capital participations) have been made for the purpose of diversification, whereas more cases of horizontal combination took the form of mergers (Odagiri and Hase 1989). Another reason may be the lack of any requirement of prior notification of acquisitions. It seems sensible to require prior notification for large-scale acquisitions while reducing the notification requirement for small-scale mergers. Similarly, business alliances without share ownership, for which no notification is currently required, are not easy to detect by the FTC.

Although the majority of such alliances are international and/or diversifying, several horizontal alliances have been also formed, with possible anti-competitive consequences. A typical recent case was the joint venture between Anheuser-Busch and Kirin, the top beer brewers in the United States and Japan respectively, to market Budweiser beer in Japan. Kirin, in particular, is the undisputed market leader, with a 50 per cent share. It was feared that, if Kirin started selling Budweiser together with its own brands, its dominance over rivals would be further enhanced. In consultation with the FTC, the two companies accepted that they should restrict the joint venture to a period of ten years at most after which Kirin would withdraw, Kirin would reduce its share of ownership, they would sell Kirin and Budweiser only in an independent manner, and they would not exchange information on anything unrelated to the joint venture. In view of the possibility that this joint venture would promote the entry of a foreign brewer into the market and, in the long run, would enhance competition, the FTC approved the alliance with these remedial measures.

The consequences for market competition of horizontal alliances, particularly international ones, may depend on a number of factors and are often difficult to assess both theoretically and in actual cases. To maintain a balance between the need for encouraging entrepreneurial activity free from regulation and the need for the government to be informed and prevent any anti-competitive consequence is indispensable, however difficult it actually is.

NOTES

1 The case of hostile share acquisition and greenmailing in 1986 against Fujiya, one of the big five confectionery manufacturers and distributors in Japan, is documented in Kester (1991), chapter 10. Between 1976 and 1987 Kester counted forty-one cases of successful greenmailing. There were also hostile bids by foreign investors, such as those against Minebea and Koito in the late 1980s. However, the transfer of control through hostile bids has been infrequent.

2 Under Japanese commercial code, one of the firms is designated as *kyuushuu kaisha*, namely an acquiring company (or, more literally, absorbing company), while the other firms are designated as *shoumetsu kaisha*, namely an acquired company/ies (or, literally, disappearing company/ies). Although the larger of the merging firms is usually made the acquiring company, it need not be so, and the distinction can be arbitrary.

3 Odagiri and Hase (1989). With slight modification this paper is reprinted as chapter 5 of Odagiri (1992). The results of past merger studies in Japan are also summarized there.

4 See Odagiri (1992), chapters 3 and 5, for the detail of the discussion in this section.

5 These percentages do not add up to 100 because of the presence of sixty-three mergers that were formed to deal with various accounting regulations.

6 See Odagiri (1992), chapter 4, for the characteristics of diversification of Japanese firms.

7 This fact should not be taken as meaning that the pre-war Japanese economy since the Meiji Restoration of 1867 was 'undemocratic', 'controlled', or 'uncompetitive'. In fact, in many industries, rivalrous behaviour and entry activities were surprisingly abundant. See Odagiri and Goto (1996).

8 The English translation of the Anti-monopoly Law (formally, the Act Concerning the Prohibition of Private Monopoly and Maintenance of Fair Trade) is taken from Nakagawa (1984) who was the FTC's director of Administrative Law Judges' Office at the time of writing. The English translation of the FTC's guidelines, as revised in 1995, is taken from the FTC's periodical, *FTC/Japan Views*, No. 19, January 1995.

9 The 1991 and 1971 data were taken from *Toyo Keizai Toukei Geppo*, December 1992 and December 1972. The 1950 data were from Yonekura (1983).

10 The most famous case is the 1957 recommendation decision against Nippon Gakki (now Yamaha), the top piano maker, which acquired 25 per cent of the shares of Kawai Gakki, the second largest piano maker.

REFERENCES

Fair Trade Commission (1993) *Kousei Torihiki Iinkai Heisei 4 Nen-do Nenji Houkoku* [Fair Trade Commission, Annual Report, 1992], Printing Bureau of the Ministry of Finance.

Hadley, Eleanor M. (1970) *Anti-trust in Japan*, Princeton University Press.

Kester, W. Carl (1991) *Japanese Takeovers*, Harvard Business School Press.

Lynn, Leonard H. (1982) *How Japan Innovates*, Boulder: Westview Press.

Nakagawa, Masanao (ed.) (1984) *Antimonopoly Legislation of Japan*, Kousei Torihiki Kyokai.

Odagiri, Hiroyuki (1992) *Growth through Competition, Competition through Growth: Strategic Management and the Economy in Japan*, Oxford University Press.

Odagiri, Hiroyuki and Goto, Akira (1996) *Technology and Industrial Development in Japan: Building Capabilities by Learning, Innovation and Public Policy*, Oxford University Press.

Odagiri, Hiroyuki and Hase, Tatsuo (1989) 'Are Mergers and Acquisitions Going to Be Popular in Japan Too? An Empirical Study', *International Journal of Industrial Organization* 7, 49–72.

Yamawaki, Hideki (1984) 'Market Structure, Capacity Expansion and Pricing: A Model Applied to the Japanese Iron and Steel Industry', *International Journal of Industrial Organization* 2, 29–62.

Yonekura, Seiichiro (1983) 'Sengo Nihon Tekkou-Gyou ni Okeru Kawasaki Seitetsu no Kakushinsei' [The Innovation of Kawasaki Steel in the Post-war Japanese Iron and Steel Industry], *Hitotsubashi Ronso* 90 (3), 387–410.

Yonekura, Seiichiro (1986) 'Tekkou-Gyou ni Okeru Innovation Donyu Process' [The Process of Innovation Adoption in the Iron and Steel Industry], in Kenichi Imai (ed.) *Innovation to Soshiki*, Tokyo: Toyo Keizai.

ACKNOWLEDGEMENTS

The author thanks Neil Campbell and Akira Goto for their comments. The usual disclaimer applies.

5

INTERJURISDICTIONAL CONFLICT IN MERGER REVIEW

A. Neil Campbell and Michael J. Trebilcock

The number of mergers and acquisitions in industrialized countries escalated dramatically over the 1980s, as did the number of foreign acquisitions and mergers of exceptionally large size.[1] Not surprisingly, a concomitant legal trend has emerged over a similar time frame. As recently as 1972 only four countries – Canada, Japan, the United Kingdom and the United States – had enacted merger laws. Since that time, Canada has modernized its merger review regime and numerous jurisdictions including the European Union have introduced merger laws,[2] many of which claim some measure of 'extraterritorial' jurisdiction.[3] The result is that international mergers often engage the attention of antitrust authorities in several countries.[4] This gives rise to transaction costs for merging parties, who are required to meet multiple compliance requirements, introduces the risk of divergent determinations in various jurisdictions, and invites outcomes which are suboptimal from the viewpoint of global economic welfare.[5]

The conjunction of these economic and legal phenomena is an obvious recipe for interjurisdictional conflicts. The potential for conflict is particularly acute in the following scenarios:

1 A multinational enterprise based in country A acquires another multinational enterprise based in country B. Both firms have subsidiaries producing similar lines of products in various domestic markets throughout the world. Here the impact of the merger would presumably have to be assessed market-by-market in the light of alternative sources of domestic or import competition in each market, with the possibility that competition authorities in some jurisdictions would find the merger objectionable while others would not.

2 A foreign firm based in country A acquires a firm based in country B where the relevant products produced by the two firms are traded freely in a regional market (e.g. Canada and the United States or member countries of the European Union). Given that the relevant geographic market for the

product is supranational, domestic antitrust authorities throughout the regional market are each likely to view their jurisdiction as legitimately engaged. The competitive effects should be essentially uniform across a properly defined economic market, but it is possible that the various domestic competition authorities would come to different factual or legal conclusions.

3 A foreign firm in country A acquires a competitor in country B producing a similar product line, but here the geographic market is global rather than national or regional (e.g. the commercial aircraft manufacturing industry). Here, at least in theory, domestic competition authorities in all countries throughout the world where the product is sold may be interested in reviewing the transaction. The probability of divergent decisions obviously increases greatly when a large number of jurisdictions with different laws and enforcement policies have the potential to become involved.

The following section of this chapter provides a brief comparative analysis of the merger regimes in place in the United States, Canada and the European Union in order to identify the extent of commonalities and divergences with respect to regulatory objectives, the scope of merger regulation, substantive issues, and procedural matters. The next section reviews seven models for addressing interjurisdictional conflicts in merger review. The final section contains some concluding observations regarding the institutions that might play a role in harmonization of merger review regimes and, perhaps, competition laws more generally.

COMPARATIVE ANALYSIS OF THREE MERGER REVIEW REGIMES

Merger law in the United States

Regulatory objectives

Control over the exercise of 'market power' is the unifying theme of the 1992 *Horizontal Merger Guidelines*[6] (the '*1992 Guidelines*') issued jointly by the US Department of Justice (DOJ) and the Federal Trade Commission (FTC) (collectively, the 'Agencies').[7] Mergers which create, enhance or facilitate the exercise of market power – whether unilaterally or interdependently – will be opposed.[8] This contrasts dramatically with the populist approach of the US Supreme Court in the 1960s, where even modest trends towards increased industry concentration were viewed with suspicion and arrested in their incipience.[9] Behavioural considerations have also become more prominent, although the *1992 Guidelines* have not entirely abandoned the structural emphasis in the 1960s jurisprudence.

The scope of merger regulation

Section 7 of the Clayton Act applies to acquisitions of shares or assets by any 'person engaged in commerce or in any activity affecting commerce', including corporations, partnerships, other business entities and individual investors.[10] As with US antitrust laws generally, broad extraterritorial jurisdiction is recognized by the US courts.[11]

Although section 7 of the Clayton Act is worded broadly enough to be applicable to horizontal, vertical and conglomerate mergers, the enforcement emphasis is predominantly on horizontal transactions.[12] Mergers in particular industry sectors may be exempted from review if approved by an appropriate regulatory body.[13]

Substantive issues

Defining the relevant market

The US Supreme Court has suggested that product markets should be based on 'the reasonable interchangeability of use or the cross-elasticity of demand between the product itself and substitutes for it'.[14] It has also stated that within a 'broad market' containing reasonably interchangeable products 'well defined sub-markets may exist which, in themselves, constitute product markets for antitrust purposes'.[15] Under the *1992 Guidelines*, a relevant product market is determined in a more technical manner. It includes all products which consumers view as good substitutes for the products of the merging firms at prevailing prices as well as products to which consumers would switch in response to a 'small, but significant, non-transitory' price increase[16] (the 'hypothetical monopolist' approach).[17]

The US Supreme Court has stated that 'the area of effective competition in the known line of commerce must be charted by careful selection of the market area in which the seller operates, and to which the purchaser can practicably turn for supplies'.[18] The geographic market is not necessarily the entire area in which the parties to the merger do business, but where 'within the area of competitive overlap, the effect of the merger on competition will be direct and immediate'.[19] The Agencies employ the hypothetical monopolist paradigm to identify geographic as well as product markets.[20]

Assessment of anti-competitive effects

The threshold   The Clayton Act test – whether the effect of a merger 'may be substantially to lessen competition' – has been interpreted by American courts to mean that a merger between competitors which materially increases a high existing level of concentration is presumptively anti-competitive.[21] The more concentrated the market already is, the more likely it is that even a minor increase in concentration will be presumed to be harmful. Nevertheless, a presumption of illegality may be rebutted by showing that past market share is not a reliable predictor of a firm's future competitive position.

The Clayton Act is regularly applied to mergers which facilitate the exercise of oligopoly as well as monopoly power. The *1992 Guidelines* cite the 'coordinated interaction' of firms as a key method by which the exercise of market power is often facilitated – i.e. 'actions by a group of firms that are profitable for each of them only as a result of the accommodating reactions of the others'.[22]

Market concentration   In the *Brown Shoe* case, the US Supreme Court described market share as 'one of the most important factors to be considered' in predicting a merger's potential anti-competitive effect.[23] A year later it enunciated the rule of presumptive illegality:

> a merger which produces a firm controlling an undue percentage share of the relevant market, and results in a significant increase in the concentration of firms in that market, is so inherently likely to lessen competition substantially that it must be enjoined in the absence of evidence clearly showing that the merger is not likely to have such anti-competitive effects.[24]

While not specifying the minimum threshold that would constitute an 'undue percentage', the court ruled that a bank merger yielding a 30 per cent market share and increasing the two-firm concentration ratio from 44 per cent to 59 per cent was unlawful. Although this presumption of illegality was applied to much lower market shares in subsequent cases,[25] it began to weaken during the 1970s and 1980s, at least in part owing to the increasing influence of the 'Chicago school' of economic analysis. In *General Dynamics*, a merger of two coal producers, the US Supreme Court approved an acquisition after emphasizing the importance of 'other pertinent factors' affecting the nature of the business of the merging parties, such as the dearth of coal reserves possessed by the acquired firm.[26]

Safe harbours and likely-challenge benchmarks   Quantitative benchmarks play a large role in American enforcement policy. The *1992 Guidelines* indicate that the Agencies will not normally challenge a merger where the post-merger Herfindahl–Hirschman Index (HHI) is below 1,000.[27] Conversely, where the HHI exceeds 1,800 and an increase of 100 or more has resulted from the merger, the Agencies will presume that the merger will 'create or enhance market power or facilitate its exercise'.[28] Mergers which fall between the safe harbour and the likely-challenge benchmark will require more detailed analysis of factors such as ease of entry and potential efficiency gains in order to determine whether they are likely to lessen competition substantially.

Other relevant factors   Since *General Dynamics*, merging parties in the United States faced with *prima facie* cases based on concentration data have successfully rebutted the presumption of anti-competitiveness by presenting evidence regarding such factors as ease of entry, efficiencies and changing market conditions.[29] In interpreting market share data, the Agencies will take account of any recent or ongoing changes in market conditions, the financial condition of firms in the market (i.e. the 'failing firm' argument) and special factors affecting the potential competitive significance of foreign firms.[30] With respect to ease of entry, the *1992 Guidelines* establish a three-step methodology [31] to determine whether 'committed entry' would cure the potential anti-competitive effects of concern.[32]

Efficiency gains

American merger policy has historically reflected a strong commitment to consumer rather than total welfare maximization. In *Proctor & Gamble*,[33] the US Supreme Court refused to recognize 'possible economies' as a defence to an otherwise unlawful merger. Although the Agencies do not generally consider efficiencies resulting from scale, scope or other sources of economies as a defence, they will take them into account as one of many factors in determining whether to oppose a merger.[34] However, in one 1984 decision the FTC appeared to treat evidence of 'substantial efficiencies' that would benefit consumers as a valid defence.[35] Some recent lower court decisions have also begun to reflect a similar approach to efficiencies.[36]

Procedural issues

Pre-notification

Section 7A was added to the Clayton Act in 1976 by the Hart–Scott–Rodino Antitrust Improvement Act (the HSR Act) to require that parties to mergers and acquisitions exceeding certain size thresholds make pre-notification filings with the Agencies.[37] A notification must normally be filed if either party is engaged in activity affecting interstate or foreign commerce and the transaction meets the following thresholds:[38]

1 Either the buyer or the acquired enterprise has assets or annual sales exceeding US$100 million and the other party has assets or annual sales of at least US$10 million, and

2 The buyer would end up holding either: 15 per cent or more of the voting securities or assets of the acquired enterprise, or voting securities and assets of the acquired enterprise in excess of US$15 million.

Various transactions which are unlikely to have antitrust implications are exempted from the pre-notification requirements, including purchases of property in the ordinary course of business and investment transactions.[39]

The information required by the initial US notification form is fairly modest. However, if the DOJ or FTC identifies potential competition concerns, an extremely comprehensive 'Second Request' will be issued to obtain all other relevant information from the merging parties.[40] After a notification has been made pursuant to the HSR Act, the proposed transaction may not proceed for thirty days. If a Second Request is issued, the transaction is stayed for a further twenty-day period which does not begin until the parties have fully responded to the request.[41]

Interim injunctions

Preliminary injunctions and hold-separate orders can be obtained by the DOJ and FTC without the need to demonstrate that irreparable harm will result in the absence of an injunction. The DOJ merely has to establish a reasonable probability that it would succeed on the merits, while the FTC must show that, upon consideration of the equities and the Commission's likelihood of success, the granting of a preliminary injunction would be in the public interest.[42]

Time limits

No statute of limitations applies to government challenges of mergers under the Clayton Act. Nor are the US Agencies or courts under any fixed time limits to reach decisions in merger cases.

Remedies

Permanent injunctions and orders for dissolution or divestiture are the primary remedies employed in the United States. The DOJ files enforcement suits in a federal district court, while an administrative complaint by FTC staff leads to adjudicative proceedings before an administrative law judge of the FTC, which is then appealable to the commissioners.[43]

Any person who has suffered injury as a result of a merger which contravenes US antitrust laws may sue for treble damages and/or injunctive relief.[44] State attorneys-general also have standing to bring such actions on behalf of their citizens.[45] Since international transactions are not immune from private and state actions, the US system contains considerable potential to generate interjurisdictional conflict.

Merger law in Canada

Regulatory objectives

Canada regulated anti-competitive mergers using criminal legislation for many years. However, this approach proved ineffective and was abandoned in 1986 in favour of a system of administrative review under the auspices of a newly formed Competition Tribunal.[46]

Competition concerns are paramount in Canadian merger review – there is little or no role for industrial or social policy objectives.[47] Since the release of the Tribunal's first two decisions in contested merger cases[48] in 1992 and the Competition Bureau's issuance of *Merger Enforcement Guidelines*[49] in 1991, it is also clear that:

1 Although structural considerations are not irrelevant, competition is treated primarily as a behavioural process of rivalry between firms which is desirable in order to prevent accumulations of market power that would result in higher prices or reduced choice for consumers.[50]
2 A merger will be found to be anti-competitive if it preserves, enhances or creates market power – i.e. ability of the merged entity to raise prices above competitive levels for an extended period of time.[51]

Transactions which would facilitate the exercise of market power interdependently (i.e. by an oligopoly) as well as unilaterally (i.e. by a dominant firm) are covered.[52]

The scope of merger regulation

The Competition Act applies to any acquisition of control, or even 'significant influence', over a business.[53] It covers purchases of shares or assets, as well as an 'amalgamation' or 'combination' of firms.[54] Although Canada has historically not applied its competition laws extraterritorially, the new merger rules may have some extraterritorial application.[55]

Horizontal, vertical and conglomerate mergers are all potentially within the ambit of the Act, although the Competition Bureau has indicated that vertical and conglomerate mergers will be challenged only in a few discrete circumstances where they would give rise to the exercise of increased market power.[56] Bank, trust and insurance company mergers which have been certified by the Canadian Minister of Finance as being 'in the best interest of the financial system' are exempt from review.[57] Although there is no statutory exemption for acquisitions in other industries that are subject to governmental regulation, case law under the previous merger provisions suggests that such transactions may be immunized by a 'regulated conduct defence'.[58]

Substantive issues

Defining the relevant market

Since the Competition Tribunal has taken the position that 'markets can only meaningfully be defined in a particular context and for a particular purpose',[59] the *Hillsdown* and *Southam* cases presented opportunities for the tribunal to provide guidance on the approach to be used in merger analyses. Unfortunately, the Tribunal in both instances did not adequately address this issue. Analysis of the product market is virtually non-existent in *Southam*, while in *Hillsdown* the Tribunal simply stated that:

> In determining the product dimensions of the market, the first step is to identify the product or products with respect to which, prior to the merger, the two firms were competitors. The second step is to ask whether there are any close substitutes to that product to which consumers could easily switch if prices were raised (an indication of demand elasticity). If two products appear to be close substitutes when both are sold at marginal cost, then the two should be included in the same product market.[60]

The Tribunal chose not to apply the 'hypothetical monopolist' approach contained in the *Canadian Guidelines*,[61] but failed to explain how the open-ended elements of its more qualitative approach (e.g. the term 'close substitutes') should be applied in practice.

With respect to geographic markets, the Tribunal has expressed concern about the use of urban, provincial or regional boundaries as geographic markets purely on the basis of administrative convenience.[62] As with product markets, it has avoided the 'hypothetical monopolist' approach used in the *Canadian Guidelines*.[63] In *Hillsdown*, which involved a merger of meat rendering plants, the Tribunal focused on three key factors in defining the geographic market: distance, borders and consumer preferences with respect to the location of producers.[64] It also accepted that relevant markets may be defined as extending beyond Canada in appropriate cases.[65]

Assessment of anti-competitive effects

The threshold   Under the Competition Act an anti-competitive merger is one which 'is likely to prevent or lessen competition substantially'.[66] In *Hillsdown* the Tribunal indicated that 'a merger will lessen competition if it enhances the ability of the merging parties to exercise "market power".'[67] Determination of whether an exercise of market power (i.e. a lessening of competition) is likely to be 'substantial' requires consideration of market concentration and a number of non-structural factors.[68]

Market concentration The Competition Act explicitly states that a merger may not be found to be anti-competitive 'solely on the basis of evidence of concentration or market share'.[69] This provision was inserted to foreclose importation of the strong structuralist emphasis in American jurisprudence, which was seen as inappropriate, given the much smaller size of the Canadian market place. It does not, however, preclude significant weight being placed on concentration data as long as other factors are also considered.

Safe harbours and likely-challenge benchmarks The Competition Bureau does not formally apply quantitative benchmarks in deciding to challenge a merger. On the other hand, the *Canadian Guidelines* do indicate non-binding safe harbours below which enforcement action is unlikely. In dominant firm situations, a merger which yields a market share below 35 per cent will normally not be challenged. A twofold test is employed for collusion-enhancing transactions: a merger will normally not be challenged if either the post-merger market share of the merged entity is less than 10 per cent or the four-firm concentration ratio is below 65 per cent.[70]

Other relevant factors The Canadian legislation expressly lists seven factors (in addition to concentration data) which are potentially relevant in reviewing mergers: foreign competition, whether a merging party is a failing business, availability of substitutes, entry barriers, effectiveness of remaining competition, removal of a particularly vigorous competitor, and the extent of change and innovation.[71] In addition, 'any other factor that is relevant to competition in a market' may be considered.[72] The Tribunal considered excess capacity to be important in the *Hillsdown* case,[73] and the *Canadian Guidelines* indicate that in collusion-enhancing situations the Bureau will examine market transparency as well as transaction value and frequency under this heading.[74]

Efficiency gains

Canada is unique in having adopted a formal efficiency gains defence in its competition legislation:[75]

1 A transaction is permissible if the efficiency gains are likely to outweigh the anti-competitive effects.
2 The merging parties bear the burden of proving anticipated gains.
3 Only real gains to society are eligible (i.e. redistributive gains accruing to the parties are excluded).
4 Gains which would likely be attained without the merger do not qualify.
5 Gains which cannot be quantified (e.g. many dynamic efficiencies) may still be considered if strong qualitative evidence exists.

To date, neither the Tribunal nor the Bureau has been impressed by the efficiency claims advanced by merging parties.[76]

The *Canadian Guidelines* adopt a total welfare approach: efficiency gains that outweigh a merger's deadweight loss are sufficient to invoke the efficiency defence.[77] However, after concluding in *Hillsdown* that the transaction did not substantially lessen competition, the Tribunal went out of its way to indicate that it had 'difficulty accepting' the Bureau's interpretation of the efficiency defence.[78] It suggested that the efficiency gains may be sufficient only if they outweigh both the deadweight loss arising from an exercise of market power and the expropriation of consumer surplus by producers (i.e. that consumer welfare rather than total welfare is of paramount importance).[79] Citing the *obiter* nature of this decision, the Director of the Bureau has decided to continue with the approach set out in the *Canadian Guidelines*.[80]

Procedural issues

Pre-notification

The Canadian pre-notification requirements do not apply unless two separate size tests are exceeded. A party-size threshold requires that the aggregate Canadian sales or assets of the merging parties and their affiliates exceed C\$400 million.[81] In addition, a transaction-size threshold applies: pre-notification is not required unless the acquired business has Canadian sales or assets of at least C\$35 million.[82] Several exemptions exist for transactions which are unlikely to raise competition concerns (e.g. underwritings, transactions involving affiliates, etc.).[83]

The parties to a merger which is caught by the Canadian pre-notification thresholds can elect to submit either a short-form or a long-form filing.[84] In either case, a description of the proposed transaction and copies of the legal documentation must be supplied, along with basic descriptive and financial material regarding each party.[85] The long-form filing requires substantial additional disclosures, particularly with respect to products and affiliates.

The waiting period during which a transaction cannot be closed depends upon the type of filing which has been made. The minimum statutory waiting periods are seven and twenty-one days for short and long-form pre-notifications, respectively.[86] Time only begins to run once the complete filing is received by the Bureau.

When satisfied that a proposed merger would not be anti-competitive, the Director of the Competition Bureau may issue a formal Advance Ruling Certificate which exempts the parties from the pre-notification obligation and, more important, immunizes the transaction from any future challenge based solely upon the information before the Director.[87]

Interim injunctions

The Canadian Competition Tribunal has broad powers to grant injunctive relief pending the final resolution of any proceedings brought before it.[88] This power has been used to formalize hold-separate arrangements in both contested and consent merger cases.[89] There is also a separate power to make time-limited interim orders, on an *ex parte* basis if necessary, to enjoin actions which would render a proposed merger difficult to reverse ('scrambling of the eggs') or to secure compliance with the pre-notification provisions.[90]

Time limits

The Canadian merger regime does not contain fixed time limits for merger investigations or adjudications. However, there is a three-year limitation period after which proceedings to challenge a completed merger cannot be launched.[91]

Remedies

Only the Director can bring proceedings before the Tribunal. The Tribunal is similar to a regular court, although it has a mixed membership of federal court judges and lay experts.[92] Upon concluding that a merger is anti-competitive, the Tribunal has the authority to issue a prohibition, dissolution or divestiture order (or any other order upon consent) but cannot impose fines or other penalties.[93] While private actions for single damages are available in respect of violations of the criminal provisions of the Act, they are of little relevance in the merger context because no cause of action arises until the Tribunal has made an order regarding a transaction and it has been breached.[94] Provincial government authorities have no standing to challenge mergers, although they do have an automatic right of intervention in any merger proceeding before the Tribunal.[95]

Merger law in the European Union

Regulatory objectives

Although both Articles 85 and 86 of the Treaty of Rome have been held applicable to mergers in limited circumstances,[96] the European Commission began considering a more comprehensive regime for regulating mergers in the early 1970s. The 'Merger Regulation'[97] was finally adopted in 1989 and came into force in September 1990.[98] The Commission has also enacted an 'Implementing Regulation' dealing with the content of pre-notification filings and various procedural matters.[99]

The predominant concern in the European Union has been the need to preserve and develop effective competition in the common market, particularly given the increasing pressures on firms to merge or rationalize in response to the 1992 single market initiative.[100] Whether merger regulation should be based solely on competition grounds or take into account other considerations such as industrial and social policy was the subject of considerable debate within the EU Council. France strongly favoured an industrial policy approach, while Germany and the United Kingdom supported the Commission's view that only competition law criteria should be relevant. The result is a substantive test which focuses on competition, accompanied by a somewhat ambiguous acknowledgement of other considerations in the preamble of the Merger Regulation.[101] During his tenure as Competition Commissioner, Sir Leon Brittan attempted to ensure that the Commission based its decisions only on market power grounds.[102] Although this approach narrowly prevailed in the controversial *De Havilland* decision,[103] industrial policy considerations clearly hover around decision-making by the Commission, which is ultimately a political rather than a judicial or administrative body.[104]

On its face the EU system seems to emphasize behavioural factors, although extensive market share data are also required in the notification process.[105] While the Merger Regulation appears to be focused on mergers which create a dominant position,[106] the Commission has indicated that transactions which facilitate an interdependent exercise of market power by oligopolists will also be a concern.[107]

The scope of merger regulation

A merger ('concentration') is defined as arising where two or more previously independent firms ('undertakings') merge, or one or more persons already controlling at least one undertaking acquire direct or indirect control of the whole or part of another undertaking.[108] 'Control' is further defined as rights, contracts or any other means which confer the possibility of exercising 'decisive influence' on an undertaking.[109] Although the scope of extraterritorial application of EU competition laws has not been articulated as clearly as in the United States, the Merger Regulation on its face would apply to mergers which take place outside the European Union if the parties' sales into the European Union exceed the relevant thresholds.[110]

The notification form developed by the Commission indicates that vertical as well as horizontal mergers will receive close scrutiny, and that conglomerate mergers are also potentially subject to review.[111] An exemption exists for temporary holdings of securities by credit, financial or insurance firms, as well as where securities are acquired in the event of a liquidation, insolvency, or analogous proceedings.[112]

Substantive issues

Defining the relevant market

The European Court of Justice has yet to pronounce on whether market definition under the Merger Regulation should follow the 'reasonable substitutability' approach developed under Article 86.[113] The Commission considers a relevant product market for purposes of merger analysis to comprise all those products which are regarded as interchangeable or substitutable by consumers in light of the products' characteristics, their prices and their intended use. It may in some cases be composed of a number of smaller individual product groups, each of which possesses largely identical physical or technical characteristics and which are fully interchangeable.[114] Market definition analyses tend to focus more on observation and qualitative evidence than on quantitative data.[115]

A relevant geographic market is considered by the Commission to be an area in which conditions of competition are 'sufficiently homogeneous' and which is distinguishable from neighbouring areas having 'appreciably different' conditions. This may be indicated by the nature and characteristics of the products, the existence of entry barriers, consumer preferences and differences in market shares and prices.[116] Relevant geographic markets may be extended beyond EU boundaries if appropriate.[117]

Assessment of anti-competitive effects

The threshold The governing standard under the EU Merger Regulation is whether the merger would 'create or strengthen a dominant position as a result of which effective competition would be significantly impeded'.[118] While Article 86 decisions may be of some assistance in determining what constitutes a dominant position, the reference in the Merger Regulation to competition being impeded appears to impose a less stringent standard than the 'abuse' required under Article 86. Hence a new line of jurisprudence can be expected to develop.[119]

Market concentration The Merger Regulation identifies the 'structure of all the markets concerned' and the 'market position of the undertakings concerned and their economic and financial power' as two among numerous relevant factors in appraising the anti-competitive consequences of a merger.[120] Although there is no indication of the weight to be assigned to market shares, the notification form developed by the Commission places considerable emphasis on such data.[121]

Safe harbours and likely-challenge benchmarks The Merger Regulation contains a general presumption that transactions producing a combined market share of less than 25 per cent are compatible with the common market.[122] Formal likely-challenge thresholds are not employed in the European Union.

Other relevant factors   In appraising a merger's compatibility with the common market, the European Commission is required to take into account, among other things, the market position and economic power of the merging parties, actual or potential competition from undertakings located either within or outside the European Union, alternatives available to suppliers and users, access to supplies and markets, legal and other barriers to entry, supply and demand trends, technical and economic progress,[123] and the interests of intermediate and ultimate consumers.[124]

Efficiency gains

The Merger Regulation instructs the Commission to consider 'the development of technical and economic progress provided that it is to consumers' advantage and does not form an obstacle to competition.'[125] This phrase appears broad enough to include productive and dynamic efficiency gains, provided they are at least partially passed on to consumers. Thus consumer welfare rather than total welfare maximization appears to be the regulatory objective.

Unfortunately, the scope of this provision is not entirely clear. A literal reading suggests that it cannot be invoked when a merger will have anti-competitive effects, even though that is the only occasion where it would logically be relevant.[126] Sir Leon Brittan has stated that the Commission does view efficiencies as a relevant factor in the analysis of a merger although it does not consider them to be a formal defence.[127] On the other hand, some commentators have interpreted early Commission decisions as suggesting that efficiencies may actually count against a merger if they have the potential to reinforce the dominant position of the merged entity.[128]

Procedural issues

Pre-notification

All mergers which have a 'Community dimension' must be pre-notified to the Commission within one week of the conclusion of an agreement, announcement of a public bid or acquisition of a controlling interest, whichever comes first.[129] A concentration has a Community dimension where:

1 The aggregate worldwide sales ('turnover') of all the undertakings is more than ECU 5 billion and

2 The aggregate EU turnover of each of at least two of the undertakings concerned is more than ECU 250 million,

unless each of the undertakings achieves more than two-thirds of its EU turnover within a single member state.[130] Unlike the United States and Canada, the European Union's pre-notification thresholds are jurisdiction-conferring: concentrations which fall below the thresholds are subject to the domestic merger laws of member states rather than review by the Commission.

Notifications to the Commission are made on *Form CO*, which contains extremely detailed information requirements.[131] The automatic waiting ('suspension') period for transactions covered by the Merger Regulation is three weeks after submission of a complete notification, unless the Commission orders an extension or grants a derogation.[132]

Interim injunctions

The Commission may, on its own initiative, extend the suspension period applicable to a transaction or take other interim measures until it renders a final decision.[133]

Time limits

The Commission normally has one month from the date of notification to decide whether or not to initiate formal proceedings.[134] A final decision must be taken within four months after the commencement of such proceedings.[135]

When formal proceedings are initiated, the merging parties are entitled to be informed of the objections to the transaction and to present submissions at a hearing. Before reaching a final decision, the Commission must also consult an Advisory Committee consisting of representatives from the member states.[136]

Remedies

A decision declaring a proposed merger incompatible with the common market is effectively a prohibition order. Where the merger has already been implemented, the Commission may require that the undertakings or assets be separated.[137]

Private parties have no standing to challenge transactions under the Merger Regulation. The Commission may (but is not required to) refer a merger having a Community dimension to the competent authorities of a particular member state upon request where there is an apparent threat to competition in a distinct market within that territory.[138] Mergers which fall

103

below the Community dimension thresholds are intended to be regulated by the domestic competition laws of member states, although provision has been made for the Commission to act in certain circumstances at the request of a member state.[139]

Conclusions

The basic objectives of merger regulation appear to be substantially similar in the United States, Canada and the European Union. All three jurisdictions are primarily concerned with market power being exercised over prices (or other dimensions of competition), and examine behavioural as well as structural factors in making such assessments. The most notable differences are the greater emphasis on structural measures in the United States, and the room for weighing of industrial policy considerations in the European Union.

Notwithstanding the similar objectives, institutional arrangements for merger regulation differ dramatically between the United States, Canada and the European Union. Moreover, mergers are generally regulated using the institutions involved in the administration of other competition laws, which could complicate any attempt to implement merger law harmonization strategies that entail institutional redesign.

With respect to substantive merger provisions, the basic approach in the three jurisdictions is broadly similar. Each begins by ascertaining whether a particular transaction constitutes a merger and then delineating relevant product and geographic markets. Horizontal relationships are of primary concern in assessing anti-competitive effects, although the European Commission also pays relatively close attention to vertical transactions. The primary conceptual difference is the explicit balancing of efficiency gains against non-redistributional anti-competitive effects by the Canadian Competition Bureau (i.e. a total welfare approach), whereas the United States and European Union simply view efficiencies as one among many factors to be considered in the overall analysis (i.e. consumer welfare is the criterion to be maximized).

Notwithstanding the similarities on a conceptual level, the operational differences among substantive provisions are extensive. On the threshold issue of what constitutes a reviewable merger,[140] the standards applicable where less than a controlling interest is acquired vary significantly, there are wide variations in the coverage and structure of statutory exemptions, and each system has a unique approach for dealing with joint ventures. Enforcement agencies in the three jurisdictions appear to accept the possibility of supranational relevant geographic markets, but the European Commission does not employ the highly technical hypothetical monopolist methodology embraced in the United States and Canada. The European Union's anti-competitive threshold is also distinctive: it focuses on market dominance rather than the potentially more lenient substantial lessening of competition approach adopted in the US and Canadian legislation. All three jurisdictions have announced safe harbours based on concentration, yet there are wide variations in both the levels which have been established (e.g. the Canadian thresholds are by far the highest) and the measures of concentration which are employed (e.g. market share versus HHI). The United States places significant weight on structural evidence (and is the only jurisdiction utilizing quantitative likely-challenge benchmarks), whereas Canada and the European Union focus more heavily on behavioural factors in assessing anti-competitive effects. There is also divergence regarding the other relevant analytical factors, their application to particular situations, and the relative priority which should be assigned to each.[141] Finally, in addition to the crucial conceptual difference in the treatment of efficiency gains discussed above, there are important technical variations between the jurisdictions in the analysis of such claims.[142]

The substantive differences are further compounded by variations in terminology and organizing concepts. Moreover, many provisions are broadly framed, leaving considerable discretion for case-by-case decision-making. This results in uncertainty for merging parties and their advisers when attempting to assess the legal position *ex ante* in each jurisdiction which will be affected by a transaction.

With respect to procedural issues, while all three jurisdictions have pre-notification regimes with similar waiting periods, the variations in triggering thresholds and information requirements are substantial. The US system employs very low thresholds and requires a relatively light initial filing. The European Union, in contrast, has very high thresholds but an extremely lengthy filing is required. It would be worth exploring whether the Canadian approach – allowing the merging parties to elect between short-form and long-form filing, subject to the enforcement agency's right to require the long form – could be used to meld into a single system the benefits of a low compliance burden for non-controversial transactions and ability to obtain meaningful information at the outset regarding those which merit close scrutiny.

Timing differences are vitally important, since delay in a single jurisdiction can interfere with the completion of a transaction which has received all other necessary approvals. There is a stark contrast between the tight, fixed time limits governing proceedings in the European Union and the open-ended American process of an HSR Second Request followed by further delay for agency analysis and, if necessary, contested proceedings.[143]

Prohibition, dissolution, divestiture and consent orders are common to all three jurisdictions. Fines do not play a prominent role. However, the possibility of suits by private parties and local governments adds substantial complexity in the United States. This can compensate for lax enforcement by central government agencies, but also increases the uncertainty faced by merging parties and the possibilities of interjurisdictional conflict.

In summary, the procedural differences between the American, Canadian, and European systems are extensive and arise at virtually every stage in the merger review process. Some are administrative practices which would appear to be good candidates for harmonization through negotiations between enforcement authorities. Others are statutory and/or reflect generic competition law procedures. Progress in these areas is likely to be more difficult.

MODELS FOR REDUCING INTERJURISDICTIONAL CONFLICT

The remainder of this chapter outlines three basic approaches for reducing interjurisdictional conflict in international merger reviews: harmonization of domestic laws, use of a 'lead review jurisdiction', and the establishment of a supranational decision-making institution. Each of these approaches contains more and less ambitious variants. While these models may well be instructive with respect to the broader challenges of harmonizing competition laws generally, the discussion which follows is restricted to the merger context.

Harmonization of domestic laws

We use 'harmonization' to mean the development of similar laws in multiple jurisdictions, each of which would retain its own domestic merger review institutions. Harmonization efforts can be directed to procedural harmonization, substantive harmonization, or both. Procedural harmonization is likely to be easier, but leaves many potential benefits unrealized.

Model 1a – procedural harmonization

There are a number of steps which could usefully be considered to reduce the transaction costs incurred by enforcement agencies and private parties during merger reviews, including:

1 Efforts might be made to harmonize pre-merger filing requirements. At present, major discrepancies exist among jurisdictions. Some standardization would seem highly desirable. The ABA *Report* sensibly recommended a light initial filing with the possibility of a subsequent detailed request for information (although much more focused than a typical US HSR Second Request).[144] This has the important consequence of minimizing the compliance burden for the vast majority of mergers which do not pose serious competition concerns. In addition, a question which requires merging parties to disclose all of the competition agencies that have been notified about a transaction would be a simple technique for facilitating greater interagency coordination.[145]

106

2 Differences in the waiting periods before a transaction may be consummated are arbitrary. Eliminating them would reduce logistical complications without undermining the basic function they fulfil.
3 There is much value in the EU approach of specifying fixed time limits within which decisions must be reached. If all major jurisdictions agreed on a common set of time limits, uncertainty for merging parties would be reduced dramatically.
4 Confidentiality rules need to be relaxed in order to permit meaningful exchanges of information between the various agencies reviewing a single transaction.[146]

Harmonized rules in these areas would clearly be a useful advance, and should significantly reduce the transaction costs and uncertainty facing merging parties while increasing the efficiency of agency reviews.[147] Whatever the value of these gains, however, they do not go to the heart of concerns over potential interjurisdictional conflicts in merger review. Specifically, they do little to reduce the likelihood of divergent determinations where mergers engage the jurisdiction of more than one agency. This limitation on the benefits available from procedural harmonization naturally invites an exploration of the potential for substantive harmonization.

Model 1b – substantive harmonization

A preliminary question is whether international mergers possess special characteristics which would warrant different treatment from that given to domestic mergers. The OECD has concluded, correctly in our view, that there is no need for a separate set of substantive standards: the basic economic theory regarding pro-competitive and anti-competitive mergers is equally applicable in both the domestic and international contexts.[148] However, a complicating factor is that the economic theory is unsettled in some important areas (e.g. the significance of market share data versus other factors, what constitutes an entry barrier, etc.).

The substantive differences between merger regimes outlined in this chapter would obviously multiply as further jurisdictions are considered. For example, in the ten OECD jurisdictions it reviewed, the ABA *Report* found that merger law in Canada, Germany and the United States is motivated primarily by competition/efficiency concerns, whereas in other jurisdictions (particularly Ireland, France, Japan,[149] Spain, and the United Kingdom) industrial and public policy play a significant role.[150] It also pointed out that political determinations play an important role in some jurisdictions whereas others rely on judicial or administrative decision-making.[151] Thus it concluded that 'it would be both unrealistic and presumptuous for this Committee to come forward with recommendations for a common substantive approach to international merger control at this time.'[152] In a subsequent chapter reviewing the advantages, disadvantages, and prospects of a World Competition Code, the committee stated that 'perhaps the nations could reach agreement on a code, but it would either be agreement to principles so general that the rules would have no clear meaning, or the agreement would be the result of a process of bargaining in which each representative had to trade away something of value'.[153] This conclusion is a rather gloomy one, in that it leaves the problem of potential interjurisdictional conflict essentially unresolved even if some degree of procedural harmonization is achieved.

Perhaps the conclusion is excessively gloomy. A simple and potentially powerful move in the direction of substantive harmonization would be for merger review agencies (e.g. in all OECD jurisdictions) to commit themselves to promulgating non-binding merger enforcement guidelines (and to make them available in draft form for comment by other agencies).[154] This proposal might be taken a step further by agreeing upon a detailed checklist of issues that each set of guidelines would address.[155] Inducing this degree of articulation and transparency of merger review criteria could well lead to significant convergence over time. An encouraging example is the *Canadian Guidelines*, which borrowed heavily from the US *1984 Guidelines*.

Another strategy worthy of consideration would be to charge an international body of experts (e.g. under the aegis of the OECD Committee on Competition Law and Policy) to formulate a non-binding Model Merger Review Law. Like the Restatements of the American Law Institute, the Uniform Commercial Code and other model laws promulgated by the US Uniform Law Commission, a credible Model Merger Review Law could be expected to have substantial exemplary or exhortatory influence on policy-makers, enforcement authorities, courts and tribunals.

However, as with procedural harmonization, it must be acknowledged that even if major substantive harmonization is achieved, at the end of the day the potential still exists for divergent rulings by national competition authorities on international mergers. No degree of procedural and substantive harmonization can eliminate the qualitative judgements entailed in merger review or the possibility that different agencies will reach different judgements, albeit within similar legal frameworks. Thus one is led to consider models which move beyond purely domestic decision-making.

Designation of a lead review jurisdiction

Employing a 'lead jurisdiction' would allow duplication of effort by enforcement authorities to be minimized. It should also reduce compliance burdens for merging parties. As with harmonization strategies, more and less modest options present themselves within this broad model. All are premised on the assumption that only international mergers which appear to implicate a supranational geographic market would attract this institutional response. Moreover, while bilateral arrangements are possible, geographic markets often do not break down cleanly along bilateral lines. Since a web of parallel agreements presumably would need to be negotiated to circumvent this problem, there is a strong case for multilateral sponsorship.

Model 2a – a coordinating agency

Building on analogies with multi-jurisdictional securities filing regimes that have evolved in Canada and the United States, one could readily contemplate the designation of a lead jurisdiction to play the role of coordinating agency in the case of an international merger that appears to impact on a supranational geographic market. Such an agency would fulfil a centralized information gathering function, solicit comments from those agencies whose markets are potentially affected by a particular transaction, and undertake an initial assessment of the relevant market(s) and the likely competitive effects therein. This assessment would operate merely as a recommendation to national enforcement agencies in the other affected jurisdictions, although presumably some kind of *de facto* presumption operating in favour of the recommendation might exist.

The main difficulty raised by such a model is: how does one go about identifying the lead jurisdiction? As the ABA *Report* pointed out, the 'effects test' of jurisdiction (i.e. the presence of substantial direct and foreseeable effects within a jurisdiction) satisfies the requirements of international law but tends to produce overlaps in jurisdiction.[156] Thus it emphasized the importance of traditional comity factors as a technique for ensuring that the relative interests of each affected jurisdiction are considered.[157] It also suggested that a second question be posed: which agency is best equipped to fashion a remedy if one is required?[158]

As to mechanics, the ABA *Report* recommended that when a merger has been notified to more than one jurisdiction, immediate consultation should take place among the notified agencies. 'A frank discussion of the relative interests involved and the location of assets ought to persuade all but the truly interested jurisdictions to defer.'[159] A three week time was proposed for such consultations. If more than one jurisdiction remains, they should consult throughout their reviews to minimize conflicting or duplicative information requests and use their best efforts to avoid imposing remedies that conflict with the interests of the other jurisdiction(s).

This proposal has some obvious virtues in that it moves beyond existing bilateral and OECD notification obligations[160] to require genuine consultation with a view to narrowing down the number of jurisdictions independently reviewing a merger.[161] However, significant problems remain. First, the legal status of comity in most jurisdictions – including the US – is unclear.[162] In addition, even the comity-type criteria in the *US–EU MOU*[163] are far from self-executing – there is considerable potential for conflict and divergence of opinion. This leaves open the possibility of more than one jurisdiction legitimately remaining involved in reviewing a merger, and thus the possibility at the end of the day of divergent determinations. Moreover, deference by the US federal agencies does not preclude private actions or enforcement initiatives by state attorneys-general.[164] A further barrier to the adoption of a coordinating agency model is confidentiality. While the OECD recommends that communications between enforcement agencies be treated as confidential by the recipients,[165] many domestic confidentiality provisions preclude such communications in the first place. Legislative amendments will be needed to overcome such restrictions.[166]

In summary, a coordinating agency model could reduce transaction costs for the review of international mergers falling into the three scenarios described at the outset of this chapter. However, it would not prevent divergent outcomes. Elimination of conflicting decisions would require a lead jurisdiction with more than coordinating powers.

Model 2b – a lead jurisdiction appointed through consultation

Going beyond the model identified above, one might contemplate multi-lateral agreement on a set of rules which would identify a lead jurisdiction that would be given dispositive power over mergers within its mandate. This would essentially involve converting comity factors which are presently applied on a unilateral basis (if at all) into a jurisdictional balancing test. This would remove the potential for divergent outcomes, but would require that the lead jurisdiction be vested with adequate powers to implement appropriate remedies.

The suggestion in the ABA *Report* that enforcement agencies should consider not only comity factors but also the issue of efficacy of remedy[167] raises a serious dilemma. In some circumstances (e.g. where a local subsidiary exists) it may be possible to use partial divestitures in selected jurisdictions to avoid interjurisdictional conflict.[168] However, the merging parties may be based outside the jurisdiction in which the principal competitive effects of the merger will be felt. As Caves points out, national competition authorities will face considerable political pressure to allow mergers which have minimal effects in their own jurisdiction but enhance the appropriation of rents from foreign consumers (i.e. to take decisions that maximize national income, even at the expense of world income).[169] This is not a tendency to be encouraged by multilateral efforts to harmonize competition laws. Thus, while the decision of the majority of the Federal Trade Commission in the *Institut Mérieux/Connaught BioSciences*[170] case has been widely criticized,[171] if one accepts that the principal anti-competitive effects of that merger were likely to be felt in the US market, it is not clear why a coherent multilateral merger review process would disqualify the United States from effective opposition to the merger. This raises the question of whether comity obligations need to be extended to cover national competition authorities accepting an affirmative obligation to take, or collaborate in implementing, effective remedial action.[172] This far from trivial issue has received less attention than it deserves.

Another problem that has so far received little attention relates to market definition. As has already been emphasized, the lead jurisdiction response is not appropriate unless the relevant market is supranational. However, it is easy to imagine circumstances where various national competition authorities who have been notified or otherwise learn of a merger disagree as to whether a supranational geographic market exists. This suggests that, in addition to formulating some set of multilaterally agreed upon comity rules for identifying a lead jurisdiction and dealing with the question of access to effective remedies, agreement would be needed on a methodology for determining whether the relevant geographic market is supranational or not.[173] In the event of disagreement on this issue, presumably there would not be the necessary consensus to appoint a lead jurisdiction to play the dispositive decision-maker role.

Given the potential for disagreement among national authorities in identifying a single lead jurisdiction – perhaps because of disagreement over the scope of the geographic market, or concerning where the most substantial effects of the merger are likely to be felt, or regarding access to effective remedies – one is then led to consider a further variant of the lead jurisdiction approach.

Model 2c – A lead jurisdiction appointed by an international authority

In cases where it is claimed either by the merging parties or by any of the national enforcement agencies that a supranational geographic market exists, and the consultation process proposed in the ABA *Report* fails to yield a single lead jurisdiction, one might consider giving the merging parties and each national enforcement agency the right to bring the issue before a specialized supranational panel.[174] The panel's function would not be to review the merger on the merits. Rather, assuming some prior agreement on comity rules and methodology for defining geographic markets, the panel would apply these jurisdictional rules to identify the appropriate lead jurisdiction.[175] All signatories to this jurisdictional set of ground rules would agree to accept the panel determinations as binding. A tight time frame would need to be imposed on this adjudication process (e.g. four weeks from the expiry of the consultations) to prevent excessive delay which could undermine potentially beneficial business transactions.

If this approach is to be rendered tractable there would need to be agreement on the principles to be applied in evaluating the relative effects of a merger in different jurisdictions. Essentially what is required is a 'primary effects' doctrine. These principles would need to move beyond the somewhat open-ended comity factors which currently exist. The focus should be on the welfare and efficiency effects of an international merger (e.g. by examining shares of sales by jurisdiction), and not on employment or industrial policy considerations. A total welfare test of the kind adopted in Canadian merger law, while theoretically attractive, raises some problems in this respect. There will be cases where reductions in consumer welfare occur in multiple jurisdictions but the efficiency gains are realized primarily in one.[176] In identifying the jurisdiction most impacted by such a merger, how should these trade-offs be evaluated?

The political difficulties involved in getting countries to cede responsibility for review of mergers to a lead jurisdiction should not be underestimated, particularly where binding determinations are contemplated. It may in fact be more palatable to have the responsibility for substantive decision-making transferred to an international agency than to have the national institutions in another jurisdiction making such decisions.

Decision-making by a supranational institution

The most ambitious approach for eliminating interjurisdictional conflict is to transfer responsibility for substantive decision-making to an international merger review entity. In this area it is convenient to consider the 'strong form' model first, followed by a weaker variant.

Model 3a – supranational investigation and adjudication

This model is exemplified by the European Commission's role under the EU Merger Regulation. Mergers over certain size thresholds are reviewed from the outset by the Commission against the legal norms in the Merger Regulation, with national authorities yielding jurisdiction to the Commission (except for participation on an Advisory Committee), and with the Commission being vested with final dispositive power over all mergers within its mandate.[177] However, as a number of commentators have pointed out,[178] there is room for doubt as to the generalizability of this model to jurisdictions beyond Europe. The European Union is striking in the degree to which member states have been prepared to cede sovereignty to centralized institutions. Moreover, it bears recalling that it took the member states sixteen years to negotiate the EU merger review regime.

The ABA *Report*, after reviewing the prospects for a World Competition Code that might be administered by a supranational authority, such as a specialized branch of the International Court of Justice or the OECD, recommended against the pursuit of such an initiative, at least at the present time.[179] On the other hand, the successful completion of the GATT Uruguay Round and formation of the World Trade Organization indicate that quite substantial economic policy changes can be negotiated among a large number of countries. A group based at the Max Planck Institute has already put forward a draft code which could be grafted on to the GATT/WTO framework, and many others have also suggested that this would be an appropriate forum for the negotiation and implementation of multilateral competition rules.[180] Moreover, it is important to recognize that developing a supranational set of merger rules is a much more modest undertaking than a comprehensive World Competition Code.

Model 3b – supranational dispute resolution

The more modest variant here would involve parallel domestic agency reviews coupled with a supranational appeal or dispute resolution process in the event of divergent determinations. The dispute resolution panels under Chapter 19 of the Canada–United States Free Trade Agreement – which are generally regarded as having worked well[181] – illustrate the potential for this kind of supranational decision-making. However, the mandate of the FTA panels is to review whether domestic trade tribunals have correctly applied domestic law. This would only be a partial solution in the context of international mergers – in the absence of common substantive standards it is entirely possible that divergent outcomes will result when national agencies are correctly applying their own domestic merger control laws.

If countries were to agree to have divergent decisions resolved by a supranational body, it would be essential to develop a process which was responsive to the time sensitivity of merger transactions. In addition, experience with multilateral dispute resolution under the GATT demonstrates both the importance of having well specified governing substantive norms and the ineffectiveness of dispute resolution mechanisms in their absence (e.g. disputes regarding agricultural subsidies).

FUTURE INSTITUTIONAL CHALLENGES

Some progress towards international cooperation and harmonization in merger and other competition law areas could be achieved without creating new institutions. One might contemplate a more ambitious set of bilateral agreements that build upon the state-of-the-art *US–EU MOU*. Treaties could be used to overcome domestic statutory rigidities (e.g. confidentiality restrictions) that memoranda of understanding cannot address.[182] The main drawbacks to these approaches are that they have produced relatively modest gains to date and that, even if more ambitious agreements were to prove feasible, they would run the risk of promoting trade arrangements that were inherently discriminatory and thus inconsistent with the most favoured nation principle that is one of the cornerstones of the multilateral trading system. While it is also possible to envision multilateral memoranda of understanding or treaties that do not require any international institutional infrastructure,[183] most multilateral approaches will entail some institutional support.

One possibility is to graft multilateral merger or other competition rules on to regional trade arrangements, as has been done from the inception of the European Community as a fundamental component of the process of economic integration.[184] More recently, the EFTA nations have accepted EU competition rules as part of the framework for the formation of the European Economic Area.[185] Another logical venue would be the North American Free Trade Agreement, whose three existing signatories have just begun negotiations with Chile regarding its future accession. While NAFTA went beyond the Canada–US FTA by including a chapter on competition, it contains few substantive rules.[186] Instead, a Working Group on Trade and Competition was established with a five-year mandate to report on 'relevant issues concerning the relationship between competition laws and policies and trade in the free trade area'.[187] A task force set up by the American Bar Association Antitrust Law Section has mapped out a comprehensive and visionary agenda for the working group,[188] but how much of it will be realized remains to be seen.

The main difficulty with regional arrangements is that they capture only a portion of the trade of the member countries. As a result, system frictions with external trading partners remain a problem – indeed, they may even increase. This points towards more broadly based multilateral initiatives. Two existing institutions present attractive possibilities for such efforts.

Some commentators favour the OECD Competition Law and Policy Committee as the natural forum, given its substantial history of involvement in the competition law area[189] (perhaps with agreed codes being transferred to the WTO for broader application at a later juncture).[190] While the likelihood of agreement on a common set of competition norms is probably higher in the OECD because of its limited (and primarily industrialized country) membership, significant challenges can still be expected in achieving agreement on many sensitive issues. Even if agreements are reached, they will lack legitimacy with developing countries and countries in transition from command to market economies who are not members of the OECD. Such countries would have little reason to accept any legal norms agreed to or to abide by the determinations of any adjudicative or dispute resolution process set up under the aegis of the OECD.

These limitations could be addressed by reviving the original aspirations of the GATT[191] and including competition rules and dispute resolution processes in the next round of multilateral negotiations.[192] While the added benefits of such broad multilateral coverage would be significant, the difficulties involved in reaching meaningful agreements would also be multiplied. However, the adoption of minimum standards for such trade-related areas as domestic intellectual property regimes (TRIPs) and investment measures (TRIMs) in the recent GATT Uruguay Round Agreement[193] may provide some impetus for this approach.

The *Draft International Antitrust Code* published by a self-appointed International Antitrust Code Working Group (primarily a group of German scholars based at the Max Planck Institute) in July 1993 is an attempt to map out a WTO-based competition law regime.[194] It proposes minimum substantive standards for national antitrust laws that would address horizontal arrangements, vertical restrictions, mergers and abuses of dominant position, as well as the establishment of an independent International Antitrust Authority (IAA) under the auspices of the WTO. The IAA's powers would include: requesting that actions in individual cases be instituted by a national antitrust authority; bringing actions against national authorities which refuse to take appropriate measures against individual restraints of competition; suing private persons or undertakings before national law courts to have restraints of competition enjoined; a right to appeal from decisions of national courts even when it is not a party at trial, but under the same conditions as the parties to the case; and bringing a code signatory before an International Antitrust Panel (IAP) if it appears to have violated the code.[195] The IAP would be a permanent six-member body with a mandate to adjudicate violations alleged by the IAA as well as disputes between signatories regarding violations of the code (provided consultations were tried but failed). If a national judicial decision was found to be inconsistent with the code, the national court or other authority would be required to reconsider the decision to ensure conformity with the findings of the IAP.[196]

The GATT/WTO option has the appeal of being comprehensive in coverage and non-discriminatory in application, but also carries the obvious difficulties of securing agreement among over 100 countries in very different stages of economic development and with very different philosophies regarding the roles of the state and the market in their economies.[197] Opposing risks are thus presented: the norms adopted may be so general, so minimal, or so compromised in order to achieve agreement, that they will mean next to nothing or, worse, will generate additional uncertainty and conflict; or meaningful agreement on a set of operational norms may be achieved at the price of 'freezing' competition law in a complex international treaty that precludes ready adaptability to new industrial organization phenomena or new learning.[198] These risks do not warrant abandoning harmonization initiatives, but they do counsel caution.

However daunting the challenges, until we have achieved a basic reconciliation between international trade and competition policy we will have failed to complete a task that has eluded policy-makers for more than a century – putting in place two economically coherent and consistent framework policies that are major policy determinants of the health of every economy.

NOTES

1 See, for example, A.E. Safarian, 'Trends in the Forms of International Business Organization,' Chapter 3 in the present volume.

2 See generally, Richard P. Whish, *Competition Law* (3d ed.) (London: Butterworth, 1993); J. William Rowley and Donald I. Baker (eds), *International Mergers: The Antitrust Process* (London: Sweet & Maxwell, 1991); American Bar Association Antitrust Section, *Report of the Special Committee on International Antitrust* (June 1991) (the 'ABA *Report*'); Terence Cooke, *International Mergers and Acquisitions* (Oxford: Basil Blackwell, 1988); and OECD, *Merger Policies and Recent Trends in Mergers* (Paris: 1984). The second edition of Rowley and Baker (eds), *International Mergers* (forthcoming, 1995) will contain profiles on the merger control regimes of twenty-nine jurisdictions.

3 See ABA *Report, op. cit.* chapter 7 and appendix III.

4 Nine such high profile cases are reviewed in Richard P. Whish and Diane P. Wood, *Merger Cases in the Real World: A Study of Control Procedures* (Paris: OECD, 1994).

5 For additional discussion of the concept of a 'world welfare standard' see Eleanor M. Fox and Janusz A. Ordover, 'The Harmonization of Competition and Trade Law: The Case for Modest Linkages of Law and the Limits to Parochial State Action', Chapter 16 in the present volume.

6 Department of Justice and Federal Trade Commission, *Horizontal Merger Guidelines*, reprinted in 62 *Antitrust & Trade Reg. Rep.* No. 1559 (April 2, 1992). With few exceptions, the goals and objectives of the *1992 Guidelines* carry forward those established in US Department of Justice, *Merger Guidelines* (1984), reproduced in 4 *Trade Reg. Rep.* (CCH) ¶13,103 (the '*1984 Guidelines*').

7 The decision by the DOJ and the FTC to present a common enforcement policy, together with the recent revision of the National Association of Attorneys General (NAAG), *Horizontal Merger Guidelines*, reprinted in 64 *Antitrust & Trade Reg. Rep.* No. 1608 (March 30, 1993), represents a significant convergence of US merger enforcement policy. For a thorough review of the *1992 Guidelines*, see Paul S. Crampton, 'The DOJ/FTC 1992 Horizontal Merger Guidelines: A Canadian Perspective', 38 *Antitrust Bulletin* 665 (Fall 1993). Unfortunately, early signs indicate that enforcement officials within the DOJ and the FTC are adopting varying interpretations of the *1992 Guidelines*, thereby threatening to undermine the benefits of harmonization (see, e.g., Daniel M. Wall, 'The Guidelines that Almost Weren't,' 6 *Antitrust* 4 (Summer 1992); and William Blumenthal, 'Ambiguity and Discretion in the New Guidelines: Some Implications for Practitioners,' 61 *Antitrust L.J.* 469 (1993) at 483).

8 *1992 Guidelines, op. cit.* §0.1. Market power is essentially equated with supracompetitive pricing, although the possibility of reduced non-price rivalry is also acknowledged.

9 See jurisprudence, discussed below.

10 15 U.S.C. §18.

11 For a brief overview of the US 'effects test' approach to jurisdiction, see A. Neil Campbell and Michael J. Trebilcock, 'International Merger Review: Problems of Multi-jurisdictional Conflict', in E. Kantzenbach, H.E. Scharrer and L. Waverman (eds), *Competition Policy in an Interdependent World Economy* (Baden-Baden: Nomos Verlagsgesellschaft, 1993), at 133–5, and sources cited therein.

12 The *1992 Guidelines, op. cit.* §0, state that they describe '... the present enforcement policy of the Department of Justice and the Federal Trade Commission ... concerning *horizontal* acquisitions and mergers ...' (emphasis added).

13 See Communications Act of 1934, 47 U.S.C. §221(a) (telephone and telegraph – Federal Communications Commission); Interstate Commerce Act, 49 U.S.C. §11341 (transport – Interstate Commerce Commission); and Newspaper Preservation Act of 1970, 15 U.S.C. §1803 (newspapers – Attorney General). While mergers involving banks are not automatically exempted by virtue of regulatory approval, the DOJ has only thirty days to bring an action to block such a transaction: see Bank Merger Act, 12 U.S.C. §1828(c); and Bank Holding Act, 12 U.S.C. §§ 1842–3.

14 *Brown Shoe Co.* v. *United States*, 370 U.S. 294 (1962) at 325.

15 *Ibid.* See also *United States* v. *Aluminum Co. of America (Rome Cable)*, 377 U.S. 271 (1964) at 275–7.

16 Generally, the Agencies consider whether prices in a proposed market could be increased by a 'small but significant and nontransitory' increment (usually, but not necessarily, 5 per cent), for a period lasting into the 'foreseeable future', assuming that the products, as a group, were produced by a single firm ('a hypothetical monopolist'). If such a price increase could not be profitably imposed (because customers would shift to other products), then the proposed product market is expanded and the test is reapplied. This exercise is continued until the smallest group of products that satisfies the test is identified. See *1992 Guidelines, op. cit.* §1.11. The 'foreseeable future' is a period of time that will apparently vary with the industry in question (Paul T. Dennis, 'An Insider's Look at the New Horizontal Merger Guidelines', 6 *Antitrust* 6 (Summer 1992) at 7).

17 For a concise survey of this and other theoretical paradigms, see Paul S. Crampton, *Mergers and the Competition Act* (Toronto: Carswell, 1990), at 266–86.

18 *Tampa Electric Co.* v. *Nashville Coal Co.*, 365 U.S. 320 (1961) at 327. (Although this case involved an exclusive dealing arrangement, the court's comments are often cited in other market definition contexts.)

19 *United States* v. *Philadelphia National Bank*, 374 U.S. 321 (1963) at 357.

20 *1992 Guidelines, op. cit.* §1.21. The market includes all sellers of products among which consumers currently substitute, and each more distant supplier to which consumers would turn in response to a 'small, but significant, nontransitory' increase in price such that the increase would be unprofitable. What constitutes a 'small, but significant and nontransitory' increase in price is determined in the same way as in the product market context.

21 Baker, *op. cit.* at 452.

22 *1992 Guidelines, op. cit.* §2.1. The discussion in the *1992 Guidelines* regarding coordinated interactions of firms has been described as 'pathbreaking' and a 'state-of-the-art treatment of the issue' (Crampton, '1992 Horizontal Merger Guidelines', *op. cit.* at 666 and 688).

23 *Brown Shoe, op. cit.* at 337.

24 *Philadelphia National Bank, op. cit.* at 363.

25 See, for example, *United States* v. *Pabst Brewing Co.*, 384 U.S. 546 (1966); and *United States* v. *Von's Grocery Co.*, 384 U.S. 270 (1966).

26 *United States* v. *General Dynamics Corp.*, 415 U.S. 486 (1974) at 498.

27 *1992 Guidelines, op. cit.* §1.51. The HHI is the sum of the squares of the market shares of each firm in the market. The increase in the HHI resulting

from the merger can be calculated by doubling the product of the market shares of the merging firms.

28 *Ibid.*

29 Baker, *op. cit.* at 455. Ease of entry has played a particularly important role in recent cases where market shares have ranged as high as 76 per cent: see *United States* v. *Waste Management*, 743 F. 2d 976 (2d Cir., 1984); *United States* v. *Syufy Enterprises*, 903 F. 2d 659 (9th Cir., 1990); and *United States* v. *Baker Hughes*, 908 F. 2d 291 (D.C. Cir., 1990).

30 *1992 Guidelines, op. cit.* §§ 1.52 and 5.1. The special factors affecting foreign firms include quotas or other trade restraints that would cause 'actual import sales and shipment data' to overstate the future competitive significance of foreign firms.

31 The three-step methodology is set out in §3 of the *1992 Guidelines*. The first step is to assess whether entry can impact the market significantly within a timely period. The second step requires a consideration of whether entry would be profitable. The third step assesses whether the expected entry would return market prices to pre-merger levels.

32 *Ibid.*, §3.0. 'Committed entry' is defined to mean 'new competition that requires expenditure of significant sunk costs of entry and exit'.

33 *F.T.C.* v. *Proctor & Gamble Co.*, 386 U.S. 580 (1967).

34 Although the treatment of efficiencies under the *1992 Guidelines* has undergone some superficial changes, Crampton has noted that 'it is reasonable to assume that in all other respects the Guidelines were not intended to bring about a change in preexisting policy' ('1992 Horizontal Merger Guidelines', *op. cit.* at 694). Unfortunately, the general approach has never been adequately clarified, particularly in terms of whether the underlying standard is consumer welfare or total welfare.

35 *American Medical International*, 104 F.T.C. 1, 219 (1984).

36 Baker, *op. cit.* at 457. (See, e.g., *United States* v. *Carilion Health Service*, 707 F. Supp. 840, at 849 (W.D. Va., 1989), aff'd. 892 F. 2d 1042 (4th Cir., 1989)).

37 15 U.S.C. §18A.

38 15 U.S.C. §18A(a). There are special tests applicable to US acquisitions by foreign enterprises and purchases of foreign firms by American acquirers: see 16 C.F.R. §§ 802.50 and 802.51; and, for a brief synopsis, Baker, *op. cit.* at 480.

39 15 U.S.C. §18A(c).

40 US Second Requests were described as 'much too onerous' in the ABA *Report, op. cit.* at 175.

41 15 U.S.C. §§ 18A(b) and (e).

42 See Baker, *op. cit.* at 499.

43 See generally Baker, *op. cit.* at 495–502.

44 15 U.S.C. §§ 15 and 26.

45 See 15 U.S.C, §15C; and NAAG, *Horizontal Merger Guidelines, op. cit.*.

46 Comprehensive discussions of Canadian merger law can be found in Crampton, *Mergers, op. cit.*; John F. Clifford, John A. Kazanjian and J. William Rowley, 'Canada', in Rowley and Baker (eds), *op. cit.*; and A. Neil Campbell, 'The Review of Anti-competitive Mergers' (Toronto: University of Toronto doctoral thesis, 1993).

47 *Director of Investigation and Research* v. *Air Canada et al.* (Requests for Leave to Intervene) (1988), 32 Admin. L.R. 157 at 164–5 and 171–2, *per* Strayer J. sitting alone as the Tribunal. See also the purpose clause which prefaces the Competition Act, R.S.C. 1985, c. C-34, as amended, s. 1.1.

48 *Director of Investigation and Research* v. *Hillsdown Holdings (Canada) et al.* (1992), 41 C.P.R. (3d) 289 (*'Hillsdown'*); and *Director of Investigation and Research* v. *Southam et al.* (1992), 43 C.P.R. (3d) 161 (*'Southam'*).

49 Director of Investigation and Research, *Merger Enforcement Guidelines* (Ottawa: Supply and Services Canada, 1991) (the *'Canadian Guidelines'*).

50 See also Competition Act, *op. cit.* s. 92(2), which precludes a transaction being interfered with solely on the basis of concentration data; and Crampton, *Mergers, op. cit.* chapter 3.

51 *Hillsdown, op. cit.* at 314.

52 *Director of Investigation and Research* v. *Imperial Oil et al.* (Reasons and Decision) (CT-89/3, January 26, 1990, not reported), at 36.

53 Competition Act, *op. cit.* s. 91. The *Canadian Guidelines, op. cit.* at 1–2, interpret significant interest very broadly as including any ability to 'materially influence the economic behaviour' of the target firm, which can occur through minority shareholdings or contractual rights.

54 *Ibid.*

55 See Campbell and Trebilcock, 'International Merger Review', *op. cit.* at 133; and Richard F.D. Corley, Geoffrey P. Cornish and Calvin S. Goldman, 'International Mergers and the Canadian Competition Act', [1992] *Fordham Corp. Law Inst.* 217.

56 *Canadian Guidelines, op. cit.* at 41–2.

57 See Competition Act, *op. cit.* s. 94(b).

58 The same interpretation is plausible under the current legislation: Clifford *et al., op. cit.* at 632–3.

59 *Director of Investigation and Research* v. *Chrysler Canada* (Reasons and Order) (1989), 27 C.P.R. (3d) 1, at 10.

60 *Hillsdown, op. cit.* at 299.

61 *Canadian Guidelines, op. cit.* at 7–14.

62 *Imperial Oil, op. cit.* at 21–4.

63 *Canadian Guidelines, op. cit.* at 7–9 and 14–18.

64 *Hillsdown, op. cit.* at 302–10.

65 *Ibid.*, at 311.

66 Competition Act, *op. cit.* s. 92(1).

67 *Hillsdown, op. cit.* at 314.

68 See further discussion below.

69 Competition Act, *op. cit.* s. 92(2).

70 *Canadian Guidelines, op. cit.* at 21.

71 Competition Act, *op. cit.* ss. 93(a)–(g). (The Bureau has elaborated on its interpretation of each factor in *Canadian Guidelines, op. cit.* at 23–40).

72 *Ibid.*, s. 93(h).

73 *Hillsdown, op. cit.* at 318–21.

74 *Canadian Guidelines, op. cit.* at 40–1.

75 Competition Act, *op. cit.* s. 96. The inspiration for this provision can be found in Williamson's 'naive trade-off model': see O.E. Williamson, 'Economies as an Antitrust Defense Revisited: The Welfare Trade-offs', 58 *American Economic Review* 18 (1968).

76 In *Imperial Oil, op. cit.* at 78–81, the Tribunal remarked that the evidence adduced in support of the claimed efficiencies was inadequate. (It ultimately approved a consent order after revisions addressed the merger's potential anti-competitive effects to its satisfaction.) In another case, the Bureau was apparently prepared to approve a merger after an efficiency–welfare trade-off analysis, but circumstances arose which led the Bureau to conclude that the

merger was not likely to substantially lessen competition (see Paul S. Crampton, 'The Efficiency Exception for Mergers: An Assessment of Early Signs from the Competition Tribunal' (1993), 21 *Cdn. Bus. L.J.* 371 at 381). The Bureau has accepted limited efficiency claims in various other cases, but none was sufficiently large to outweigh the anti-competitive effects of the mergers in question: Calvin S. Goldman, *Mergers, Efficiency and the Competition Act* (Ottawa: Industry Canada, October 1988), at 7. See also Don McFetridge, 'The Prospects for the Efficiency Defence' paper presented at the Canadian Bar Association Competition Law Section Symposium on Selected Issues in the Economics of Competition Policy (June 1994).

77 *Canadian Guidelines, op. cit.* at 49. See also Crampton, *Mergers, op. cit.* at 520–9.

78 *Hillsdown, op. cit.* at 337.

79 For discussion of this case and its implications for the efficiency defence, see Crampton, 'Early Signals', *op. cit.*; Larry P. Schwartz, 'The "Price Standard" or the "Efficiency Standard"? Comments on the *Hillsdown* Decision' (1992), 13 *Canadian Competition Policy Record* (no. 3) 42; and John Bodrug and Calvin S. Goldman, 'The *Hillsdown* and *Southam* Decisions: The First Round of Contested Mergers under the *Competition Act*' (1993), 38 *McGill L.J.* 724.

80 H.I. Wetston, *Decisions and Developments: Competition Law and Policy* (Ottawa: Industry Canada, June 1992) at 4–5.

81 Competition Act, *op. cit.* s. 109.

82 *Ibid.*, s. 110. The sole exception is amalgamations, where the transaction size threshold is C\$70 million. An additional voting interest threshold is applicable to share acquisitions: pre-notification is required only when shareholdings in excess of 20 per cent of a public corporation or 35 per cent of a private corporation are acquired (and again when a 50 per cent shareholding is obtained).

83 *Ibid.*, ss. 111–13.

84 *Ibid.*, s. 120. However, the Director of the Competition Bureau may unilaterally require the long form within seven days of receiving a short-form filing.

85 *Ibid.*, ss. 121 and 122.

86 *Ibid.*, s. 123. (An accelerated formula applies to long-form notifications of public takeover bids.)

87 *Ibid.*, ss. 102 and 103.

88 *Ibid.*, s. 104.

89 See *Director of Investigation and Research* v. *Southam et al.* (Reasons for Interim Injunction) (1991), 36 C.P.R. (3d) 22; and *Director of Investigation and Research* v. *Imperial Oil et al.* (Consent Interim Order) (CT-89/3, July 4, 1989, not reported).

90 Competition Act, *op. cit.*, s. 100.

91 *Ibid.*, s. 97.

92 See generally the Competition Tribunal Act, R.S.C. 1985, c. 19 (2nd Supp.).

93 Competition Act, *op. cit.*, ss. 92(1)(e) and (f).

94 *Ibid.*, s. 36.

95 *Ibid.*, s. 101.

96 See *Europemballage Corporation and Continental Can Co.* v. *E.C. Commission* (Case 6/72), [1973] E.C.R. 215 (declaring the applicability of Article 86 to transactions which would enhance an existing dominant position); and *British American Tobacco Co. and R.J. Reynolds Industries* v. *E.C. Commission* (Joined Cases 142 and 156/84), [1987] E.C.R. 4487 (confirming

the potential applicability of Article 85 to acquisitions of a minority shareholding in a competitor).

97 *Council Regulation 4064/89 on the Control of Concentrations between Undertakings*, O.J. L395/1 (1989), corrected version in O.J. L257/13 (1990).

98 Comprehensive commentaries on the Merger Regulation can be found in Whish, *op. cit.*; T. Anthony Downes and Julian Ellison, *The Legal Control of Mergers in the European Communities* (London: Blackstone Press, 1991); Michael Reynolds and Elizabeth Weightman, 'European Economic Community', in Rowley and Baker (eds), *op. cit.*; Christopher Jones, Enrique González-Díaz and Colin Overbury, *The EEC Merger Regulation* (London: Sweet & Maxwell, 1992); and Damien Neven, Robin Nuttall and Paul Seabright, *Merger in Daylight – The Economics and Politics of European Merger Control* (London: Centre for Economic Policy Research, 1993).

99 *Commission Regulation 2367/90 on the Notifications, Time Limits and Hearings Provided for in Council Regulation No. 4064/89 on the Control of Concentrations between Undertakings*, O.J. L219/5 (1990).

100 See Frank L. Fine, 'EC Merger Control in the 1990s: An Overview of the Draft Regulation,' 9 *Nw. J. Int'l Law & Bus.* 513 (1989).

101 See Merger Regulation, *op. cit.* recital 13; and James S. Venit, 'The Evaluation of Concentrations under the Merger Regulation: The Nature of the Beast', 14 *Fordham Int'l L.J.* 412 (1990–1), at 415.

102 Sir Leon Brittan, 'The Law and Policy of Merger Control in the EEC' (1990), 15 *Eur. Law Rev.* 351, at 352–3.

103 See *Re the Concentration between Aerospatiale–Alenia/De Havilland*, [1992] 4 C.M.L.R. M2; and A. Neil Campbell and J. William Rowley, 'The *De Havilland* Case: Implications for International Merger Practice' (1992), 4 *IBTL Newsletter* (no. 1) 10.

104 See, e.g., Christian Marfels, 'The First Two Years of EC Merger Control: Review and Assessment' (1992), 13 *Canadian Competition Policy Record* (no. 4) 45.

105 The notification requirements are reviewed more fully below.

106 See Barry E. Hawk, 'European Economic Community Merger Regulation', 59 *Antitrust L.J.* 457 (1990) at 463.

107 *Re the Concentration between Nestlé and Source Perrier*, [1993] 4 C.M.L.R. M17. See also *Mannesmann/Vallourec/Ilva*, [1994] O.J. L102/15, where the Commission investigated a merger of steel tube manufacturers for potentially creating duopolistic dominance.

108 Merger Regulation, *op. cit.* art. 3(1).

109 *Ibid.*, art. 3(3).

110 See Campbell and Trebilcock, 'International Merger Review,' *op. cit.* at 135–6.

111 *Form CO Relating to the Notification of a Concentration Pursuant to Council Regulation No. 4064/89 (Annex I to the Implementing Regulation, op. cit.)*, ¶ 5. See also Sir Leon Brittan, *Competition Policy and Merger Control in the Single European Market* (Cambridge: Hersch Lauterpacht Memorial Lectures, Grotius Publications, 1991), at 38.

112 Merger Regulation, *op. cit.* art. 3(5).

113 A brief summary of this jurisprudence can be found in Downes, *op. cit.* at 4–5.

114 *Form CO, op. cit.* ¶ 5.

115 Neven *et al.*, *op. cit.* at 90–101. But see Dennis W. Carlton and William D. Bishop, 'Merger Policy and Market Definition under the EC Merger

Regulation', [1993] *Fordham Corp. Law Inst.* 409, at 421–2, who suggest that the Commission is increasingly sensitive to quantitive approaches.

116 *Form CO, op. cit.* ¶ 5.
117 For example, in *De Havilland, op. cit.* at ¶ 20, the Commission found the geographic market for commuter aircraft to be the world except for China and Eastern Europe.
118 Merger Regulation, *op. cit.* art. 2(2) and (3). Unless the area in which anti-competitive effects occur is at least a 'substantial part' of the European Union, the transaction must be declared 'compatible with the common market'. However, small areas have been held to be 'substantial' parts of the common market in Article 86 jurisprudence: Downes, *op. cit.* at 86.
119 Brittan, 'Law and Policy', *op. cit.* at 354.
120 Merger Regulation, *op. cit.* art. 2(1).
121 See *Form CO, op. cit.* particularly ¶¶ 5.3–6 and 5.13.
122 Merger Regulation, *op. cit.* recital 15. Nevertheless, the notification form requires data to be provided for all 'affected markets' which are defined by reference to a 10 per cent market share test: *Form CO, op. cit.* ¶ 5.
123 This factor is discussed in more detail under 'Efficiency gains' below.
124 Merger Regulation, *op. cit.* art. 2(1).
125 Merger Regulation, *op. cit.* art. 2(1)(b).
126 Downes, *op. cit.* at 96.
127 Brittan, 'Law and Policy', *op. cit.* at 353.
128 See Frederic Jenny, 'EEC Merger Control: Economics as an Antitrust Defense or an Antitrust Attack', [1992] *Fordham Corp. Law Inst.* 591; and Neven *et al., op. cit.* at 116–17.
129 Merger Regulation, *op. cit.* art. 4(1).
130 *Ibid.,* art. 1(2). An ECU is approximately equivalent to US$1.25.
131 The ABA *Report, op. cit.* at 174, described *Form CO* as 'much too burdensome'.
132 Merger Regulation, *op. cit.* art. 7(1).
133 *Ibid.,* art. 7(2).
134 *Ibid.,* art. 10(1).
135 *Ibid.,* art. 10(3).
136 *Ibid.,* art. 19.
137 *Ibid.,* art. 8(3) and (4).
138 *Ibid.,* art. 9. This occurs infrequently.
139 *Ibid.,* art. 22(3)–(5). This also occurs infrequently.
140 The ABA *Report, op. cit.* at 225, concluded that a model definition of 'merger' was one of the few promising opportunities for substantive harmonization of merger law. The definition is of special importance because of the complexity and uncertainty which face private parties when an international transaction is subject to merger rules in some jurisdictions but is regulated by other means elsewhere.
141 See, e.g., Paul S. Crampton, 'A Comparative Review of Canada's Merger Enforcement Guidelines', *Int'l Merger Law* (July 1991), at 6–8, who summarizes the factors set out in the Canadian legislation and identifies several areas in which the United States and European Union differ materially.
142 *Ibid.,* at 9–10.
143 Although Canadian practice is closer to that of the United States, the Bureau does attempt to adhere to target completion dates and its requests for additional information are generally less comprehensive than those of American enforcement agencies: see Clifford *et al., op. cit.* at 662 and 665.

144 ABA *Report, op. cit.* at 205–6. While a common notification form was considered to be unrealistic at the time, the ABA *Report* suggested (at 173) that agreement might at least be reached as to the categories or types of information to be provided on an initial notification.

145 This step was recommended by Whish and Wood, *op. cit.* at 107.

146 ABA *Report, op. cit.* at 206. See also OECD Committee on Competition Law and Policy, *Interim Report on Convergence of Competition Policies* (Paris: OECD #C/MIN(94)14, May 1994), at ¶ 52. Unfortunately, the pathbreaking information-sharing legislation enacted recently in the United States explicitly exempts merger filings: see International Antitrust Enforcement Assistance Act of 1994 (S. 2297, H.R. 4781, 103d Cong., 2d Sess.), §5(1).

147 For a more comprehensive discussion of the scope for and mechanics of procedural harmonization, see the appendix to Donald I. Baker, A. Neil Campbell, Michael J. Reynolds and J. William Rowley, 'Harmonization of International Competition Law Enforcement', in Chapter 17 of the present volume.

148 OECD, *International Mergers and Competition Policy* (Paris: 1988), at 14–15.

149 For a concise overview of Japanese merger regulation see Hiroyuki Odagiri, 'Mergers and Acquisitions in Japan and the Anti-monopoly Policy', in Chapter 4 of the present volume.

150 ABA *Report, op. cit.* at 211.

151 *Ibid.*, at 212.

152 *Ibid.*, at 224.

153 *Ibid.*, at 289. (The Task Force of the Antitrust Section of the American Bar Association, *Report on the Competition Dimension of the North American Free Trade Agreement* (1994) (hereafter 'NAFTA Task Force Report'), chapter 7, was only slightly more optimistic about the prospects for harmonization of competition laws within the three NAFTA member countries, suggesting (at 274) that 'any initiative facilitating movement in this direction should be gradual and at first incremental, although there might come a time when an integrated North America needs an integrated competition policy for transactions of a North American dimension'.)

154 The ABA *Report* endorsed this suggestion: see *ibid.*, at 225–6.

155 Suggested issue lists can be found *ibid.*, at 226; and in Baker *et al.*, 'Harmonization of International Competition Law Enforcement', *op. cit.* at p. 492 (n. 193).

156 ABA *Report, op. cit.* at 206.

157 *Ibid.* (The factors in the US Department of Justice, *Antitrust Guidelines for International Operations* (1988), at 32–3 (n. 170), were cited as a useful model. (These factors have been slightly revised and expanded in US Department of Justice, and Federal Trade Commission *Antitrust Enforcement Guidelines for International Operations* (1995), at 20–1.) A bilateral example which employs a very similar approach is *Agreement between the Commission of the European Communities and the Government of the United States of America regarding the Application of their Competition Laws [US–EU MOU]* (1991), reprinted in 15 *World Competition* (no. 1) 155, art. VI:3, which requires that the following factors be considered: the relative significance of conduct in each jurisdiction; any intent to harm customers, suppliers or competitors in the other jurisdiction; the relative significance of each jurisdiction's interests; reasonable expectations that would be furthered or defeated; the degree of conflict with the other jurisdiction's laws or policies; and any effect

on the other jurisdiction's enforcement activities with respect to the same person(s).)

158 *Ibid.*

159 *Ibid.* (There is some uncertainty as to whether competition law enforcement authorities in countries such as Canada have the legal ability to defer without amendment of the legislation which establishes their mandate: see Corley *et al., op. cit.* at 255–6.)

160 For a discussion of the extent and limitations of such obligations, see Edward Glynn, 'International Agreements to Allocate Jurisdiction over Mergers', [1990] *Fordham Corp. Law Inst.* 35, at 39–43.

161 Similar themes also appear in *NAFTA Task Force Report*, chapters 4 and 5.

162 The United States has the best developed comity jurisprudence, but a recent decision of the US Supreme Court casts doubt on whether comity is to be considered by US courts in determining jurisdiction, or is merely a guideline for the executive branch when exercising prosecutorial discretion. See *Hartford Fire Insurance Co.* v. *State of California*, 113 S. Ct. 2891 (1993); and, for a useful commentary, Eleanor M. Fox, 'U.S. Law and Global Competition and Trade – Jurisdiction and Comity,' *Antitrust Report* (October 1993).

163 *Op. cit.*

164 See *California* v. *American Stores Co.*, 110 S. Ct. 1853 (1990), which confirmed that such actions are not barred simply by virtue of the fact that the US federal antitrust authorities have cleared a merger. (The ABA *Report, op. cit.* at 207, proposed that the court hearing a private action should receive input from the executive branch regarding intergovernmental consultations leading to a decision not to initiate enforcement action, but this represents only a partial solution to the problem.)

165 OECD, *Revised Recommendation, op. cit.*, Appendix, ¶ 7.

166 ABA *Report, op. cit.*, at 190–1 and 206. See also Whish and Wood, *op. cit.* at 86–90 and 105–7; and Baker *et al.*, this volume at 455–9 and 470–1.

167 *Ibid.*, at 206.

168 See OECD, *International Mergers, op. cit.* at 37, which reviews several cases where this occurred.

169 Richard Caves, *Multinational Enterprises and Economic Analysis* (Cambridge: Cambridge University Press, 1982) at 129.

170 F.T.C No. 891 0098, 55 *Fed. Reg.* 1614 (January 17, 1990).

171 See, for example, Deborah K. Owen and John J. Parisi: 'International Mergers and Joint Ventures: A Federal Trade Commission Perspective', [1990] *Fordham Corp. Law Inst.* 1; Douglas E. Rosenthal, 'The Potential for Jurisdictional Conflicts in Multistate International Merger Transactions', [1993] *Fordham Corp. Law Inst.* 87; and ABA *Report, op. cit.* at 185–6.

172 This is one possible type of 'positive' (as distinct from traditional) comity. For a general discussion of positive comity see James R. Atwood, 'Positive Comity – is it a Positive Step?' [1992] *Fordham Corp. Law Inst.* 79.

173 For a review of some of the considerations that would need to be addressed see George Hay, John C. Hilke, and Philip B. Nelson, 'Geographic Market Definition in an International Context', [1990] *Fordham Corp. Law Inst.* 51.

174 Sir Leon Brittan has suggested the possibility of an 'arbitration' procedure in the event of jurisdictional disputes, at least in the context of a US–EU bilateral agreement: see Glynn, *op. cit.* at 43–4.

175 In some respects, such a panel would bear analogies to the 'Chapter 19 panels' provided for under the *Canada–US Free Trade Agreement* which rule on anti-

dumping and countervailing duty disputes between the two countries (see further discussion below).

176 An example is the *De Havilland* case, *op. cit.* where the relevant geographic market in which anti-competitive effects would be expected to occur was found to be most of the world, but efficiency gains would be expected to occur primarily at the Canadian manufacturing location being acquired. For a more extensive discussion of these issues see A. Neil Campbell and J. William Rowley, 'Industrial Policy, Efficiencies and the Public Interest – the Prospects for Harmonization of International Merger Rules' (Ottawa: Center for Trade Policy and Law 8th Annual Conference, 1993), at 11–16.

177 See overview presented above.

178 See, e.g., Wernhard Moschel, 'International Restraints of Competition: A Regulatory Outline', 10 *Nw. J. Int'l Law & Bus.*, 76 (1990), at 77; and Karl Meessen, 'Competition of Competition Laws', 10 *Nw. J. Int'l Law & Bus.* 17 (1990), at 20.

179 ABA *Report, op. cit.* chapter 11. See also Whish and Wood, *op. cit.* at 115. (There is already an UNCTAD code dealing with restrictive business practices, but it is non-binding and has had negligible impact: see *Set of Multilaterally Agreed Principles and Rules for the Control of Restrictive Business Practices*, UNCTAD Doc. TD/RBP/Conf. 10/Rev. 1 (December 5, 1980), reprinted in 19 I.L.M. 813; and commentary thereon in ABA *Report, op. cit.* at 281–3.)

180 See further discussion below.

181 See Michael Trebilcock and Thomas Boddez, 'The Case for Liberalizing Trade Remedy Laws', *Minnesota Journal of Global Trade* (forthcoming).

182 For a more detailed analysis see Baker *et al.*, this volume at pp. 448–9

183 An example is the 'International Merger Review System' proposed in Baker *et al., op. cit.*, appendix.

184 A bilateral example is the *Australia–New Zealand Closer Economic Relations Trade Agreement*: see the discussion in Presley Warner, 'The Canada–U.S. Free Trade Agreement: The Case for Replacing Antidumping with Antitrust', 23 *Law & Policy in Int'l Bus.* 791 (1992) at 839–54.

185 See J.H.J Bourgeois, 'Multilateral Competition Rules – Still the Quest for the Holy Grail?' paper presented to the 25th Biennial Conference of the International Bar Association (October 1994), at 7–8.

186 *North American Free Trade Agreement*, reprinted in 36 *Free Trade Law Reports* (1992) (CCH), art. 1502 and 1503, impose some basic disciplines on monopolies and state enterprises.

187 *Ibid.*, art. 1504.

188 See *NAFTA Task Force Report, op. cit.*

189 See, e.g., OECD, *Interim Report on Convergence, op. cit.*

190 See, e.g., Sylvia Ostry, 'Beyond the Border: The New International Policy Arena', in Kantzenbach *et al., op. cit.*

191 The 'Havana Charter' contemplated the creation of an International Trade Organization which would, among other things, administer competition norms, but this concept did not prove politically palatable in the United States and was abandoned. (For a brief summary, see ABA *Report, op. cit.* at 279–81.)

192 See, e.g., Bourgeois, *op. cit.* at 25–6, and sources cited therein.

193 See Michael Trebilcock and Robert Howse, *The Regulation of International Trade* (London: Routledge, 1995), chapters 10 and 11.

194 *Draft International Antitrust Code as a GATT–MTO–Plurilateral Trade Agreement*, reprinted in 65 *Antitrust & Trade Reg. Rep.* S-1 (July 1993).

195 *Ibid.*, art. 19.

196 *Ibid.*, art. 20. This panel process is explicitly acknowledged to have been modelled in part on the *Canada–US FTA* Chapter 19 dispute resolution panels.
197 This difficulty can be partly overcome by allowing GATT/WTO members to opt in (or opt out) of this particular set of obligations, as has been done with many other specific GATT codes. (The *Draft International Antitrust Code, op. cit.* art. 1, contains an accession clause which accommodates this possibility.)
198 See Derek Ireland, *Interactions between Competition and Trade Policies: Challenges and Opportunities* (Ottawa: Industry Canada, Bureau of Competition Policy, Discussion Paper, November 1992), Appendix H.

ACKNOWLEDGEMENTS

This chapter has been adapted and updated from two previous papers which were prepared as part of the Project on Competition Policy in a Global Economy with financial support from Industry Canada (Bureau of Competition Policy). The predecessor papers are 'A Comparative Analysis of Merger Law: Canada, the United States and the European Community' (1992), 15 *World Comp.* (no. 3) 5; and 'International Merger Review: Problems of Multi-jurisdictional Conflict', in E. Kantzenbach, H.E. Scharrer and L. Waverman (eds), *Competition Policy in an Interdependent World Economy* (Baden-Baden: Nomos Verlagsgesellschaft, 1993). The authors gratefully acknowledge the research assistance of Edward Iacobucci. Funding to support the Project on Competition Policy in a Global Economy has been provided by the Japan Foundation, the Center for Global Partnership, Industry Canada (Bureau of Competition Policy), and the Centre for Research in Management, Berkeley.

6

STRATEGIC ALLIANCES

A threat to competition?

Shyam Khemani and Leonard Waverman

INTRODUCTION AND DEFINITION

The term 'strategic alliance' strikes most economists as a marketing tool. All alliances between firms are in a sense strategic, or they would not be undertaken. In addition, interfirm cooperation runs the gamut from a once-for-all spot purchase to complete integration via a merger. What subset of these interfirm agreements is meant by 'strategic' alliances? Moreover, coordination of activities can occur without an alliance – the mutual interaction between oligopolistic competitors who recognize their interdependence through non-collusive but informed price and output setting.

Various definitions of strategic alliances have been suggested. But before these are considered it must be noted that a distinct characteristic of strategic alliances is that they involve two or more *independent* firms. In other forms of interfirm collaborative arrangements such as joint ventures and franchising agreements, this is not the case. For example, joint ventures generally entail setting up a jointly owned and separate entity for a specific project. It involves only a partial and often temporary integration of some of the parent firms' functions which continue to operate, for the most part, as separate units. In contrast, strategic alliances do not require establishing a separate operation. Some forms of strategic alliances may, however, entail acquiring minority share holdings in each other's firm.

Some of the definitions of strategic alliances put forward in the business and economics literature are:

1 'a bilateral or multilateral relationship characterized by the commitment of two or more partner firms to a common goal ...' (Jorde and Teece 1992: 55).
2 A collaborative agreement between two or more companies to 'jointly pursue a common goal' (Hergert and Morris 1988: 15).
3 '... any long-term, explicit agreement amongst two or more firms ... but excluding parent–subsidiary relations' (Mariti and Smiley 1988: 437).
4 '... inter-firm collaboration in product development, manufacture, or marketing that spans national boundaries, is not based on arm's length

market transactions, and includes substantial contributions by partners of capital, technology, or other assets' (Mowery 1988: 2–3).

5 Alliances '… are more than a one-time transfer … they create a continuing dependency' (Contractor and Blake 1988: 3).

We consider that, to be operational, the term *strategic alliances* should be distinguished from spot purchases on one hand and complete integration on the other. Thus the key characteristics of a strategic alliance are as follows:

1 Strategic alliances involve two or more independent firms.
2 The goal is medium- to long-term shared planning of some activity (that is what makes them strategic).
3 They can involve equity swaps or shareholdings but less than what would be considered to be control.

For our purposes, we define a strategic alliance as follows: *Strategic alliances are a form of interfirm agreement or arrangements between independent firms which involves knowledge production or sharing activities aimed at developing products or processes and forms of production. In this regard, the alliance may entail exchange of R&D and/or transfer of various information.*

Strategic alliances are often considered in the literature as a form of joint venture.[1,2] In a joint venture, two independent firms set up a jointly controlled firm (say 50:50 ownership) to accomplish some task. We consider the opposite – that joint ventures are a special case of strategic alliances with a fixed *ex ante* investment and ownership distribution, with a prescribed governance mechanism and decision-making apparatus. A more general strategic alliance has a less defined joint control/decision-making structure.

The literature (see Chapter 3) suggests that strategic alliances are quickly growing both in absolute number and relative to other forms of interfirm coordination such as mergers. Against this backdrop, this chapter examines strategic alliances from three perspectives:

1 Are strategic alliances growing and why?
2 What are the competition concerns of strategic alliances?
3 Can existing competition policies deal with these concerns?

THE GROWTH OF STRATEGIC ALLIANCES?

There is general paucity of data on interfirm collaborative arrangements and of strategic alliances in particular. Most of the information collected is from press reports, the coverage of which tends to be incomplete and varies over time. Two sets of data which unfortunately are not directly comparable are presented in Tables 6.1–2. The first relates to data compiled by the

Table 6.1 Increase in the number of interfirm agreements by form of cooperation (absolute numbers and percentages)

Modes of cooperation	Before 1972	1973–6	1977–80	1981–4	1985–8	Total
Joint ventures and research corporations	83 53.2%	64 41.8%	112 22.6%	254 20.8%	345 17.8%	858 21.6%
Joint R&D	14 9.0%	22 14.4%	65 13.1%	255 20.9%	653 33.7%	1,009 25.5%
Technology exchange arrangements	6 3.8%	4 2.6%	33 6.7%	152 12.4%	165 8.5%	360 9.1%
Direct investment (minority and cross holdings)	27 17.3%	29 19.0%	168 33.9%	170 13.9%	237 12.2%	631 15.9%
Customer–supplier relationship	5 3.2%	19 12.4%	47 9.5%	133 10.9%	265 13.7%	469 11.8%
One directional technology flows	21 13.5%	15 9.8%	71 14.3%	259 21.2%	271 14.0%	637 16.1%
Total	156 100% 3.9%	153 100% 3.9%	496 100% 12.5%	1,223 100% 30.9%	1,936 100% 48.8%	3,964 100% 100%

Source: Hagedoorn (1990), p. 20. About half of these agreements are within Western Europe, the United States and Japan, rather than between these areas. See Hagedoorn and Schakenraad (1989), p. 8. Cited from Safarian (1991).

Table 6.2 Patterns of interfirm agreements: geographical distribution

Geographical areas	High-tech industries		All industries	
	No.	%	No.	%
Intra-area				
US	254	23.9	352	18.7
EEC	150	14.1	282	15.0
Japan	18	1.7	59	3.1
Inter-area				
US–EEC	276	26.0	413	21.9
US–Japan	141	13.3	202	8.6
EEC–Japan	87	8.2	162	10.8
With other areas	135	12.8	413	21.9
Total	1,061	100.0	1,883	100.0

Source: Studies by E. Ricotta and colleagues noted in Chesnais (1988: 68), covering 1,883 agreements set up in 1982–5 between firms in the more industrialized countries. Cited from Safarian (1991).

Maastricht Institute and covers the period from the early 1970s to 1988 and includes information on joint ventures which, as mentioned previously, we consider as being a subset of strategic alliances generally. These data indicate the following: the sheer number of interfirm agreements has increased enormously and shows an accelerating trend (however, this may attest somewhat to the increased popularity of these agreements in the press rather than to an enormous increase in agreements *per se*). It also indicates that joint R&D along with technology arrangements has grown relative to joint ventures and research corporations, minority ownerships and cross-holdings. Customer–supplier relationships and unidirectional technology flows have also increased during the past two decades.

Underlying these trends in Table 6.1 is evidence that these agreements are heavily concentrated in sectors with emphasis on technology transfer and joint research. Forty per cent are in information technology industries, 20 per cent in biotechnology, 10 per cent each in new materials and chemicals and the remaining 20 per cent spread across various manufacturing industries. Production and marketing arrangements are excluded from the database.

The data presented in Table 6.2 cover 1,883 agreements established between firms during the period 1982–5. They indicate that these interfirm agreements are heavily concentrated in or between Japan, the European Union and the United States. US firms are involved in 63.2 per cent of these agreements, 23.9 per cent within the United States, 26 per cent are in US–EEC agreements and 13.3 per cent in US–Japanese agreements. The information underlying these statistics also suggests that the interfirm agreements are primarily in research-intensive industries and between large firms.

A major problem is the lack of a definitive basis on which to judge the significance of strategic alliances and their impact. Three reasons can be given.

First, there are many definitions of strategic alliances: the term is amorphous and, like beauty, may differ across viewers. Many definitions are available and a number were given above.

Second, strategic alliances need not be announced; there is no register of them, nor is notification to antitrust authorities needed in general. This is in contrast with the prenotification procedure required in most countries for mergers of a certain size. The problem is related to the first point above, the lack of a precise, operational definition of a strategic alliance. In Europe, any interfirm agreement (including strategic alliances) which the firms consider as potentially anti-competitive can be registered with the Commission, analysed and, if acceptable, is then granted immunity from antitrust challenge. In the United States research and development joint ventures can also be registered with the FTC; if viewed as pro-competitive, these joint ventures escape treble damages in any private antitrust suit launched.

Strategic alliances are not treated separately under antitrust law and, aside from public announcements, no data series are kept. Thus the data in Tables 6.1–2 reflect the known strategic alliances and, as we have stressed, alliances have come to be good stories in the business press and as a result, the trends may only indicate an increased fascination by the media and not a real growth in strategic alliances themselves.

Third, there are substantial measurement problems in addressing the significance of strategic alliances. If two firms merge, valuation of the asset or market value and other size parameters such as market share or employment of the two separate firms is possible. In many cases, such an assessment of the extent of strategic alliances is not possible. An example indicates why. Take two large firms that announce a strategic alliance in research and development for some product they both produce. What is the measure of the value of interfirm coordination? Consider the Ford–Mazda arrangement. What is the extent of integration? Is it measured by Ford's ownership share, by the value of the assets in the alliance required to produce a car together or by some measure of economic integration or the extent of joint decision-making? These difficulties in measuring the extent of a strategic alliance are reflected in the difficulties of economic analysis.[3]

The work of Coase, Williamson and Teece suggests that the division between the firm, interfirm agreements, and the market is a function of transaction costs, the ability to write *ex ante* contracts for contingencies, the degree of asset specificity and organizational costs.

Strategic alliances especially resemble joint ventures and contracting, as these forms also straddle the border of two or more firms. However, as noted, in joint ventures, cooperation between firms is administered within an organizational hierarchy. It differs from horizontal or vertical integration because the firms involved have ownership claims to the residual value, and control rights over the use of joint assets. Firms presumably choose to share the ownership of these assets because of the diseconomies of acquisition arising from the costs of divesting or managing unrelated activities or the higher costs of internal development. While a corporate governance structure to monitor a joint venture is normally set up, conflict between the parties may erode the value of the project. The venture may generate potential negative externalities through diffusion of proprietary technology, the erosion of reputation and brand labels, disputes over the division of excess profits or adverse competitive effects on common lines of business.

The transactional hazards and negative externalities that may be associated with joint ventures may be resolved by firms through contracting to a third party, or to each other. However, this approach does not preclude the possibility that there may be underinvestment in complementary assets, free-riding on brand labels or technological advantage, or other types of opportunistic behaviour. Generally speaking, contracts cannot envisage all potential contingencies and the enforcement of terms may entail costly litigation.

If the data presented in Tables 6.1–2 are correct, strategic alliances represent a growing share of interfirm agreements. The reasons for this trend are complex.

Strategic alliances tend to represent a more flexible form of interfirm collaboration which overcomes some of the transaction and strategic behaviour hazards. Thus strategic alliances may particularly arise when firms seek to learn and also retain their individual capabilities. Firms may consist of a knowledge base which cannot be easily duplicated because knowledge is organizationally embedded. The transfer of know-how may be severely impaired unless the organization itself is replicated. This may not be possible if such knowledge is a unique firm-specific characteristic which has in part resulted from long experience and historical circumstances.

It is interesting to speculate as to whether the process of globalization has led to strategic alliances becoming an increasing phenomenon. During the past decade a number of distinguishing features have emerged in the patterns of international trade and investment flows reflecting increased global competition. The level and growth of foreign direct investment (FDI) has exceeded merchandise trade. A major component of this FDI is in the form of international mergers and acquisitions and joint ventures. The source and destination of FDI are concentrated among G-7 countries. The trade and investment in 'knowledge intensive' products and services have been most dramatic and again centred amongst the G-7 countries. Against this background, as international competition has intensified, firms have had to become acutely aware of the importance of their relative competitive position for survival – even if they operate solely in domestic markets. Clearly, the large size and risk associated with new investments particularly in pre-competitive R&D, are important explanatory factors. The shift in the distribution of strategic alliances to knowledge production (see Table 6.1) is due to the rise in technology-dependent interfirm arrangements. This signals how the globalization of markets – with its increase in the need for speed to market, speed in reacting to customers and speed of introduction of new technology, new products and new processes – appears to have altered the ways in which firms undertake R&D. This sharing of resources in R&D creates tensions between lower firm costs and greater interfirm interaction. In their book *The Machine that Changed the World* Womack *et al.* (1991) describe the system of production known as lean production. That system is a means of organizing not just the factory floor, but also design, supplies, sales and management:

> Supplier organizations, working to blueprint, had little opportunity or incentive to suggest improvements in the production design ... alternatively suppliers offering standardized designs of their own ... had no practical way of optimizing these parts because they were given practically no information about the rest of the vehicle. The same was true of quality ... finally there was the problem of coordinating the flow of parts on a day-to-day basis. ... the erratic nature of orders from assemblers responding to shifting market demand caused suppliers to build large volumes ...
>
> (p. 59)

> Toyota organized its relationships with suppliers totally differently. Long-term relationships were favoured. Toyota did not wish to vertically integrate its suppliers into a single, large bureaucracy. Indeed, over time, as the system developed, Toyota became less vertically integrated, spinning off its suppliers into quasi-independent first-tier supplier companies in which Toyota retained a fraction of the equity and developed similar relationships with other suppliers ... consequently, the Toyota suppliers were independent companies with completely separate books ... At the same time, these suppliers are intimately involved in Toyota's product development, have interlocking equity with Toyota ...
>
> (pp. 61, 62)

This description of Toyota's lean production system with suppliers describes a set of strategic alliances.

The optimal set of interfirm agreements and the nature of these agreements changes over time reflecting the relative costs and benefits of alternatives. Besides the growth of FDI, other issues are important. A number of books and articles have speculated as to the shortening of the product life cycle. This shortening means that the set-up and exit costs of interfirm agreements become more important. *We hypothesize that strategic alliances are flexible instruments with low set-up and exit costs.* In activities involving allied knowledge production and information-sharing activities, the risk of opportunistic behaviour and appropriation of technology, product design, etc., by one of the member firms cannot be ruled out. Hence strategic alliances may then be subject to high rates of failure, since they are subject to all the problems of recontracting. The failure rates of strategic alliances noted in the literature (see Kogut 1989: 30 per cent of strategic alliances studied failed in three years) are due to the lower sunk costs and hence greater risk of opportunism in strategic alliances than say in joint ventures.

In order to be effective, strategic alliances between firms must be based on mutual trust and compatibility of business objectives; the firms have to co-operate. In order to discourage misbehaviour, the alliance may entail non-control equity investments or share swaps among the firms. This would make the alliance both collaborative and an investment venture. It would serve to forge and align the mutual interests of the firms involved.

For example, in the Ford–Excel and Ford–Mazda strategic alliances, the minority investments have created vested interests, and long-term commitments, and have resulted in critical acceptance of the alliance by internal management, allowing multi-unit coordination, and facilitating the transfer of resources and activities not possible through contracting. The cross-ownership has also created less fear of dominance and ensured the continued independence of the firms from each other. While the percentage of cross-holdings keeps enough public float of the shares, it also serves as a 'hostage' against possible opportunistic behaviour in the interfirm relationship. The sudden liquidation of share holdings by one firm in the alliance could adversely affect the market value of the other firm.

Minority share holdings and exchanges, then, assist in aligning the interests of the parties and are designed to prevent misuse of trust.

Our view of strategic alliances is similar to that of Jorde and Teece (1990). They consider strategic alliances as 'swaps' of know-how where firms have pieces of applicable knowledge and where knowledge is not simply pre-competitive R&D but involves downstream production and marketing know-how and innovation.

MOTIVES AND FORMS OF STRATEGIC ALLIANCES

Various motives have been identified as determining the type of strategic alliances that firms may form. Four general categories can be identified:

Horizontal i.e. the firms involved are engaged in the same type of economic activity in a given market. Especially important would be alliances among actual or potential competitors to engage in pre-competitive R&D or in the commercialization of R&D successes. Among the motives identified for horizontal strategic alliances are:

1 Economies of scale.
2 Lowering and sharing risks.
3 Facilitate transfer of technology.
4 Share information.
5 Surmount barriers to entry and/or reduce entry time.
6 Gain access to markets.
7 Widen product range/lines.
8 Develop product compatibility/standards/improve quality.
9 Adapt and customize products to major client or market needs.
10 Avoid costs of alternative forms of interfirm arrangements such as mergers and joint ventures, including those arising from antitrust actions.

Vertical i.e. the firms involved are engaged in different production–distribution stages of economic activity. These may be driven by such considerations as:

1 Avoid problems of information asymmetry and adverse selection.
2 Respond to government-sponsored industrial policy initiatives.
3 Substitute for vertical integration.
4 Avoid resource dependence.
5 Avoid transaction costs imposed by recurrent negotiations.
6 Avoid problems which limit the use of arm's-length transactions, e.g. difficulties in verifying the assertions of suppliers, uncertainty and irreversible commitments with contracting parties.
7 Hedge against intermediate product price movements in the absence of futures markets.

Complementary i.e. the firms bring complementary assets to bear on a problem.

Market power In addition to the foregoing motives, the strategic alliance may be formed in order to:

1 Foreclose opportunities and inhibit competitors.
2 Create a basis for market power.
3 Facilitate collusion and other anti-competitive practices.
4 Remove the threat of potential competition.
5 Heighten barriers to entry and raise rivals' costs.
6 Engage in a strategy of international pre-emption.

EXISTING ANTITRUST LAW ON STRATEGIC ALLIANCES AND JOINT VENTURES

Strategic alliances as interfirm agreements can be analysed as either akin to mergers or as akin to 'agreements', horizontal or vertical. Thus a broad range of antitrust policy can be brought to bear. Discussions with delegates from various countries to the OECD Committee on Competition Law and Policy suggest that no antitrust authority explicitly singles out strategic alliances as an area of concern.

In the United States joint ventures are interpreted broadly as an interfirm agreement, short of a merger to jointly undertake R&D, manufacturing or marketing (see Areeda, 1986: VII, 348). Thus joint ventures are treated as any agreement in 'restraint of trade' (Sherman Act 1). Under the Sherman Act 1, certain agreements – for example price fixing – are *per se* illegal, thus a joint venture which is a 'sham' and has no plausible efficiencies will be judged *per se* illegal. Other agreements are examined under the rule of reason. A plausible efficiency enhancing joint venture in the United States involves some *risk taking* by the parties who are integrating their activities in some way (see *Arizona* v. *Maricopar County Medical Society* 457 U.S. 332 (1982)).

Jorde and Teece have written extensively on the chilling effects that US antitrust law may have on plausible efficiency enhancing joint ventures. R&D joint ventures are singled out in the United States under the National Cooperative Research Act of 1984–94. R&D (not marketing joint ventures) are tested by a rule-of-reason (not a *per se*) standard and if found not to be anti-competitive (tending to raise prices or lower output) these R&D joint ventures are exempt from treble damages in private antitrust actions. Jorde and Teece as noted argue that R&D and information production are essential components of production and marketing, i.e. the production function is not separable in R&D.

Canada exempts R&D agreements (Section 45(3) (e) of the Competition Act) unless an undue lessening of competition arises (see McFetridge 1992: 29; Wetston 1988). Firms can also cooperate to rationalize production via a specialization agreement. No specialization agreements have been registered to date.

Article 85(1) of the Treaty of Rome explicitly deals with cooperative joint ventures and analyses their potential restriction on competition. However, a strategic alliance that restricts competition can be exempted under Article 85(3) if there is a substantial efficiency gain and effective competition remains in the market. Antitrust analysis examines 'the objective gains of the alliance' (Brittan 1992). While decisions on individual cases are given, block exemptions for R&D (products and processes) and production (unlike in the United States) can be granted if the firms' combined output is less than 20 per cent of the market in the European Union (Regulation No. 418/

85). Joint distribution is not eligible for a block exemption and 'has yet to be the object of an individual decision' (Brittan 1992).

Japan's antitrust law is written in similar language to that of the United States. Agreements are outlawed if a substantial reduction in competition occurs. Exempt are 'cartels that enable small and medium-sized firms to realize economies of scale, rationalization cartels and depression cartels' (McFetridge 1992: 19). While the written law does not exempt strategic alliances and joint ventures, the policy of the Japanese Fair Trade Commission is to consider horizontal R&D, and joint production for commercialization purposes as lawful (Jorde and Teece 1990). There are no reported cases in Japan of joint ventures or R&D strategic alliances being challenged.[4]

COMPETITIVE DYNAMICS OF STRATEGIC ALLIANCES

The analyses conducted in antitrust cases relating to joint ventures are instructional for that pertaining to strategic alliances; most such analyses rest on merger analogues. (See note 1.) The classic case on joint ventures is the Supreme Court decision in *United States* v. *Penn-Olin Chemical Co.*, 378 U.S. 158 (1964). Here two competitors entered into a joint venture in different geographical areas of the United States. The court's decision preventing the joint venture was based on the assumption that each of the two competitors could have entered separately; the court used merger law as its basis of analysis. As the Supreme Court explained in this case:

> The joint venture, like the 'merger' and the 'conglomeration', often creates anti-competitive dangers. It is the chosen competitive instrument of two or more corporations previously acting independently and usually competitively with one another. The result is 'a triumvirate of associated corporations'. If the parent companies are in competition, or might compete absent the joint venture, it may be assumed that neither will compete with the progeny in its line of commerce.

Similar concerns were pertinent to the analyses of the GM–Toyota joint venture undertaken for the government and for Chrysler in its private action against the joint venture (see *FTC decision*, 374, 386 (1984), *Bresnahan and Salop* (1986) and *Reynolds and Snapp* (1986)).

GM–Toyota

The GM–Toyota joint venture (GT) reopened a closed GM plant in Fremont, California, to *jointly* produce an existing Toyota import (the Corolla) and a reskinned Corolla marketed as the GM Nova. The wholesale price of the joint GT car to GM was determined by a basket of other cars, including the Corolla. GM was to learn how to produce small cars and Toyota the means of production in the United States. The antitrust issues were as follows:

1 Did the output of the closed Fremont plant represent output new to the industry (thus raising total market output and lowering price), or would this capacity have been used by someone else?
2 Did the new cooperation between GM and Toyota alter their individual incentives so as to lead to higher prices through: increased information flows; joint sharing of profits of the joint venture, thus an ability to damage the other party, creating new incentives not to compete in existing or new markets; 'enforce better discipline among the other firms in the industry' (Kwoka, 1989: 59)?
3 Did the specifics of the arrangements, principally the wholesale pricing formula, increase incentives to raise price?[5]
4 Did the joint venture inhibit GM's incentive to expand small car output and inhibit Toyota's decision to produce independently in the United States?

The FTC in a split decision provisionally accepted the proposed joint venture but placed finite quantity and time period constraints and also required safeguards against the exchange of competitively sensitive pricing and cost information. In other words the FTC was concerned about 'spillovers' from the joint venture which could give rise to anticompetitive effects. In a Cournot type oligopoly situation, the analyses by Kwoka (1989) suggest that the joint venture may lead to a reduction in output and consequent increase in price. Moreover, there may also be reduced incentives in both price and non-price competition.

R&D joint ventures

Ordover and Willig (1985) examine R&D joint ventures where, besides critical notions of concentration, the speed, timing and extent of R&D are important strategic variables. The authors assume 'that the R&D joint venture does not enable the ventures to coordinate their product market output and pricing decisions' (p. 320). Hence in Ordover and Willig an R&D joint venture is good or bad depending on the outcome of an R&D game taking into account the strategies of non-participants in the R&D joint venture and the state of competition.[6]

There are still important spillovers to the product market, since the time when firms begin to produce affects product market competition. Ordover and Willig examine a merger of the R&D joint venture firms. The merger reduces welfare, since the merged firm can remove one of the products from the market (the R&D joint venture firms do not do so), but if there are high efficiencies in R&D unavailable to the R&D joint venturers then the merger can be socially beneficial.

Can strategic alliances be analysed as mergers?

How can one utilize these analyses to examine the impacts of strategic alliances? We return to the differences between joint ventures and strategic alliances. Alliances take many forms, as mentioned. In a number of these forms it is difficult to utilize the merger analogue analysis of Bresnahan and Salop (1986).[7] For example, the failed alliance between AT&T and Olivetti was designed to 'enrich the organizational capabilities of the partners, such as mastering the convergence between the telecom and computer industries ... AT&T wanted to become after the deregulation an 'informatics company' rather than just a telecom company. Olivetti needed to overcome the narrow boundaries of the European market' (Ciborra 1989: 17). While AT&T and Olivetti overlapped in some product areas, the wide global scope of the alliance (perhaps why it failed) makes market share type analysis difficult. In addition, for many alliances the type of analysis of Ordover and Willig which assumes that spillovers to the product market occur only through new product development is inadequate. Spillovers were key in the GM–Toyota joint venture. The safeguards instituted in the decision, crucial, at least to the FTC, in minimizing anti-competitive spillovers were aimed to reduce cooperative behaviour outside the joint venture. Thus spillovers are a major component of strategic alliances, and one we concentrate on here.

In essence, the analysis of strategic alliances (akin to mergers, joint ventures, R&D joint ventures) requires evaluating the actual and potential effects on competition in the context of present and future markets for existing and/or new products/processes! Assessment of any one of these aspects is undoubtedly complex and appropriately conducted on a case-by-case basis, adopting the rule of reason approach. Particular difficulties are likely to be encountered in assessing any 'potential' anti-competitive versus efficiency effects of strategic alliances. This task is difficult and fraught with controversy in the case of horizontal mergers but is likely to be even more so for amorphous arrangements such as strategic alliances.

We begin by organizing alliances into sets of cases which can be distinguished from each other and we concentrate on spillovers in our analysis of the competition policy issues. The usefulness of procedural safeguards will be discussed.

We assume that the alliance is formed between multiproduct firms where economies of both scope and scale can exist individually and between the venturers. The issue of spillovers (i.e. learning, as in the GM–Toyota joint venture) is then an additional economy of scope.

Figure 6.1 provides a two-by-two tableau with economies of scale denoted on the horizontal axis and economies of scope on the vertical axis. The degrees of scale and scope vary from zero (none) to one (high). Scale and scope refer to activities within each individual firm and between two

139

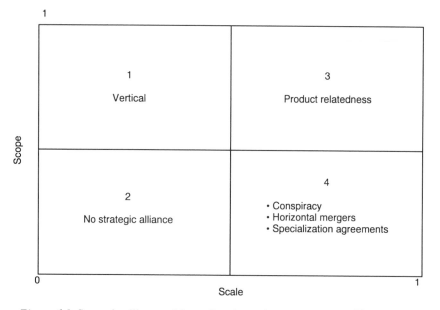

Figure 6.1 Strategic alliance tableau. **Quadrant 1.** C_A $(X_1, X_2; W_1, \Sigma\ W_i)$ and C_B $(X_1, X_3; W_1, \Sigma\ W_i)$; strategic alliance W_1. Possible cases: (1) A produces W_1, input to B. (i) A and B compete in X_1 market. (ii) A and B do not compete in product markets. (2) A and B produce W_1. (i), (ii). (3) W_1 is R&D (Ordover and Willig 1985). (i) Product. (ii) Process. **Quadrant 2.** ● No scale or scope internal to firm or between firms. ● Transaction costs overwhelm the benefits of a strategic alliance. ● 'Sham'. **Quadrant 3.** (i) ● C_A (X_1, X_2); C_B (X_1, X_3): strategic alliance X_1. (ii) ● C_A (X_1, X_2); C_B (X_1, X_3): strategic alliance X_2, X_3. ● Product-relatedness. ● Public-good characteristics, e.g. Ford–Mazda, design trade-off for cheaper entry. Marginal cost of Mazda's design ≈0. ● Spillovers to X_1 market. **Quadrant 4.** ● C_A (X_1, W_1) (no scope economies). ● C_B (X_1, W_1). ● Strategic alliance X_1. ● Substitute for merger-minority cross-holdings. ● 'Hostage' model

multiproduct firms which form a strategic alliance. The tableau is divided into four quadrants.

Where scale and scope are low (quadrant 2), a strategic alliance is not generated – there can be no gains through reduced costs or R&D spillovers and exchanges. In quadrant 2, there is neither scale nor scope internal to each firm nor between the two potential components of the strategic alliance. Thus joining the two firms in a strategic alliance would not generate efficiencies, cost savings or learning.[8] Where economies of scale are high and those of scope low, (quadrant 4), horizontal agreements, conspiracies and mergers are possible. Here, there are potential efficiencies arising from a strategic alliance perhaps in the form of a specialization agreement. Where scope is high but scale low (quadrant 1), vertical or complementary agreements hold. Below we detail the various forms which occur where economies of scope occur between inputs, and impacts on product markets

140

depend on the nature of the economies of scope and scale internal to the firm. Finally, where both scale and scope are high (quadrant 3) alliances for 'product-relatedness' can occur; various impacts on product markets exist.

Below, we expand on the elements of the tableau, indicating the types of spillovers that can occur.

Vertical strategic alliances

We begin at quadrant 1. A number of possibilities exist. Two firms exist, A and B. Firm A produces an input W_i used by firm B and another output, X_1. Firm B uses W_i and other inputs and produces two outputs, X_2 and X_3. Thus the outputs of A and B differ; cost functions are:

$$C_A(X_1, W_1; \Sigma \ W_i)$$
$$C_B(X_2, X_3; \Sigma \ W_i) \tag{1}$$

The outputs of firm A are X_1 and W_1; inputs are $\Sigma \ W_i$. The outputs of firm B are X_2 and X_3; inputs are $\Sigma \ W_i$ and include W_1.

A strategic alliance between A and B is aimed at reducing the cost of W_1; this reduction in cost will increase the output W_1 of firm A and the use of input W_1 by firm B, and thus the outputs X_2 and X_3 produced by firm B with input W_1. An example of this type of strategic alliance is the relationship between Ford and Excel in developing curved windows for automobiles.

> The Ford and Excel alliance facilitates the production of windows compatible with new aerodynamic car designs. Engineers from the two firms work jointly. Excel pays its own costs but, assuming it meets price and quality specifications, it has a long-term contract to supply 70 per cent of Ford's needs. Ford does not have the requisite glass technology, the development of which in-house would be expensive.
>
> (Lewis 1990)

This strategic alliance will be anti-competitive only if the firms have market power in the input or product markets and the strategic alliance reduces the ability of competitors of B to access A's technology or reduces the ability of competitors of A to sell to B. (Neither holds in the Ford–Excel case).

Assume that A is dominant in producing W_1, and B is one of four users of W_1. The strategic alliance between A and B can be examined as a vertical arrangement and the effects of the strategic alliance on competitors to A examined. The spillovers occur when firm A has scope economies in producing its outputs W_1 and X_1. A strategic alliance between firms A and B which lowers the cost of A's producing W_1 benefits firm A in the X_1 market as well. Since firms A and B do not compete in the X_1 market, these spillovers do not cause anti-competitive concerns.

A second example is to complicate the case (1) by having both firms produce output X_1. If the two firms also compete in product X_1, i.e. the cost functions are:

$$C_A(X_1, W_1; \Sigma \; W_j)$$
$$C_B(X_1, X_2; \Sigma \; W_i) \tag{2}$$

firm A has scope economies in producing W_1 and X_1 as outputs, i.e. $C_A(X_1, W_1) \leqslant C_A(X_1) + C_A(W_1)$. Assume that B has scope economies in producing X_1 and X_2. A strategic alliance between A and B in W_1 will then tend to lower costs for both firms: for their common output X_1, and for firm B in the X_2 market (the costs of W_1 fall as before). There is then a clear spillover to the X_1 and X_2 markets. The competition policy issues are in the X_1 market where firms A and B, which have a strategic alliance in W_1, also compete and in the W_1 market, where the spillovers in the X_1 market may affect decisions. Can a strategic alliance between firms A and B in the W_1 market facilitate collusion in the X_1 market? This is the type of analysis undertaken by Kwoka (1989).

Other cases in quadrant 1 are feasible. Suppose both firms produce the input W_1, but produce different products:

$$C_A(X_1; W_1, \Sigma \; W_j)$$
$$C_B(X_2; W_1, \Sigma \; W_i) \tag{3}$$

A strategic alliance in W_1 reduces costs to both firms A and B and expands output in markets X_1 and X_2. Antitrust issues hinge on the market W_1 since whatever new advantages A or B achieve in the X_2 market are due to cost reductions in the W_1 market.

Another variant is where the two firms engage in R&D:

$$C_A(X_1; R_A)$$
$$C_B(X_2; R_B) \tag{4}$$

This is the case analysed by Ordover and Willig. In contrast to the cases analysed above there is no specific input such as W_1 which can be monopolized. Here instead the issue is the appropriate amount of R&D and the speed of innovation. If the strategic alliance results in cooperation such that joint $R_{AB} < R_A + R_B$ economic welfare will be enhanced (through resource savings) if the output of the two firms (X_1, X_2) remains unchanged or increases. If, however, joint R_{AB} results in 'mutual forbearance' such that firm A does not enter into future production of X_2, and similarly firm B does not enter into future production of X_1, then the lessening of potential competition occurs. Various other competitive scenarios can be constructed.

Two subcases are in turn possible – a strategic alliance between A and B for a new product and for a new process. We do not examine these cases.

Horizontal strategic alliances and product-relatedness

We turn to analysing the case where a strategic alliance is formed in product markets; the two multiproduct firms' cost functions are:

$$C_A(X_1, X_2; \Sigma\ W_i)$$
$$C_B(X_1, X_3; \Sigma\ W_i) \quad\quad\quad (5)$$

First we examine a strategic alliance in the X_1 market. Here there are two issues, as in the General Motors–Toyota joint venture – first, how is competition affected in X_1 (e.g. small cars); second, what are the spillovers to the X_2 and X_3 markets? We begin where a strategic alliance is formed and scale exists in X_i. Here scale can involve a specialization agreement so that geographical or product separation occurs. This is a 'traditional' horizontal strategic alliance and would in the X_1 market be analysed by quasi-merger type analysis. However, there can be spillovers to the X_2 and/or X_3 markets. If there are scope economies for firm A (as there are in automobile production, for example) then a strategic alliance in X_1 will affect X_2 output.

When, if ever, are such spillovers anti-competitive? Here we return to the GM–Toyota joint venture. While the authorities and the academics did analyse the X_1 market, the X_2 and X_3 markets were also competitive with each other. Hence the FTC attempted to reduce the flow from cooperation in X_1 to the X_2 and X_3 markets.

A more complicated story is when a strategic alliance is organized in the X_2 and X_3 markets. Assume that there are economies of scope in organizing X_2 and X_3 together. Suppose there is a one-for-one exchange of X_2 for X_3 and this lowers costs. Competition policy officials would not normally investigate a strategic alliance between two firms in two different product market areas. However, it is clear that the X_1 market can be affected if there are economies of scope between X_2 and X_1 and/or X_3 and X_1. If $C_A(X_1, X_2) \leqslant C_A(X_1) + C_A(X_2)$, then an exchange of X_2 for X_3 lowering the costs of X_2 increases A's output of $X_1(X_1{}^A)$. In a Nash–Cournot game this increase in $X_1{}^A$ will *lower* the output of X_1 by B (which has no economies of scope) or by any other competitors of A who do not enjoy a strategic alliance. Therefore, if A alone enjoys economies of scope between X_2 and X_3, a strategic alliance between A and B will act as 'commitment' for firm A – increasing A's profits at the expense of its rivals.

Other possibilities exist in quadrant 3. An example is the Ford–Mazda strategic alliance. Mazda traded off its design abilities against cheaper entry through a strategic alliance with Ford. To Mazda, design was like a public good – the marginal cost of design was close to zero. Ford gained a car of a type it could not build itself. Mazda also substantially lowered its cost of entry into the United States. If the alliance were successful, costs were one-half of the fixed costs of a plant; if the alliance was unsuccessful, Mazda could exit. This suggests modelling the strategic alliance with joint inputs and outputs.

We have here sketched out various ways of examining strategic alliances; the next question is whether existing antitrust law can handle any competition policy concerns which may arise.

IMPLICATIONS FOR COMPETITION POLICY[9]

The information given in Tables 6.1–2 does not provide direct detail on the composition of alliances as between competitors and others. However, the predominance of R&D and 'high-tech' alliances suggests that a large percentage involve direct competitors. Hergert and Morris (1987) examined 839 publicly announced international alliances and determined that 71 per cent were between 'competitors in the same market' (p. 18). However, there is nothing in the paper which details what 'the same market' is. In 1976 Pfeffer and Nowak examined the pattern of domestic joint ventures in the United States and concluded that the majority were horizontal and anticompetitive on the basis of the two-digit SIC industry groupings of the parents. Berg and Friedman (1980) redid the analysis on a three-digit SIC basis and examined the industry groupings of the joint ventures, not exclusively those of the parents. They found the incidence of horizontal joint ventures 'unrelated to parent industry concentration' (p. 154). Mowery (1988) examines a number of US strategic alliances and finds that they are primarily horizontal but not created to avoid antitrust purview of alternatives such as mergers or joint ventures.

The *indefiniteness* of the purpose and time frame of many strategic alliances can be an antitrust concern. As the firms explore areas of mutuality, information-sharing can occur on a broad scale. Lewis (1990) discusses how some alliances allow a great deal of access between firms in R&D, product design, engineering, marketing and even cost and price information. Some of this information-sharing is unintended but results from broad mandates and corporate cultures which allow many points of entry to the firm.[10] However, many other forms of contact or entry already exist between firms – associations, golf tournaments, professional groupings (e.g. civil engineers or membership of the American Economic Association). Thus information flows need not be new or anti-competitive.

Both static and dynamic efficiencies may result from strategic alliances. Since these alliances appear particularly to arise in knowledge-intensive products/industries, they are likely to affect process and product-related technologies. The former can generally be expected to reduce unit production costs while the latter impacts on the introduction of new products and quality improvements. The collaborative arrangements between firms may also result in eliminating socially wasteful duplication of effort and the accompanying misallocation of resources. The interests of competition policy would be served if strategic alliances have these effects.

However, depending on the degree of competition prevailing in the relevant market, strategic alliances may reduce interfirm rivalry, with adverse consequences for the pace of technological change and dynamic efficiency.[11] In particular there is a serious risk that actual or potential competition may be eliminated if the alliance is of a horizontal nature. The alliance may serve as a vehicle to facilitate collusion, entrench the market position of dominant firms and/or be used to engage in various anti-competitive policies. Much depends on the type of alliance, the characteristics of the firms involved and other related factors. As in the case of interfirm arrangements ranging from mergers to conscious parallel firm behaviour, no generalizations regarding strategic alliances can be made. An assessment and balance of the positive and negative aspects of individual alliances is required to draw out the competitive implications. While a particular situation may lead to exercise of market power, there may also be offsetting efficiency gains and other benefits that may flow from the alliance.

INSTRUMENTS OF COMPETITION POLICY

The preceding discussion suggests that, depending on their nature, strategic alliances may have positive or negative effects on market competition. We have stressed that spillovers are important and can involve markets not directly involved, and even markets peripheral to those involved in the strategic alliance. It is the latter types of effect that are of specific concern to competition authorities. In most instances the conventional instruments of competition policy may be sufficient to address these concerns if broadened to include an examination of spillovers (as is done in a number of jurisdictions). For example:

1 The cartel/conspiracy provisions of competition law can be applied if a strategic alliance has been used as a vehicle to fix prices, allocate markets or customers and/or engage in other collusive business practices which significantly reduce competition.

2 The abuse of dominant market position/monopolization provisions can be invoked by competition authorities if a strategic alliance gives rise to dominance and results in price and non-price predation, market foreclosure in the supply and distribution of essential products or inputs, unnecessary restriction of access to vital technology and other business conduct adversely limiting competition.

3 The merger provisions may come into effect if the strategic alliance entails equity purchases or share swaps which may constitute acquiring a 'significant interest' in the operations of the firms involved. In such cases the alliance may create the basis for the exercise of market power and be subject to the normal merger review procedures put into place by competition authorities.

4 The provisions dealing with vertical restraints may be used if the strategic alliance leads to exclusive dealing, geographical market restrictions and resale price maintenance. In a similar vein, provisions dealing with refusal to supply and tied selling may be also applied.

Notwithstanding these types of cases, strategic alliances pose difficulties for the general administration of competition laws. These difficulties stem from the fact that:

1 Many strategic alliances by their very nature tend to be amorphous. As previously indicated, they often entail interfirm cooperation in the form of exchange of information and knowledge sharing relating to production processes, product development and/or distribution arrangements over the medium to long term. They do not necessarily require firms to make specific investments or acquire given assets. The firm or market size dimensions and scope of a strategic alliance may therefore not be easily measurable. Moreover, the alliance may be formed because of unique firm-specific characteristics which may not have alternative commercial value.

2 Compared with more definite forms of interfirm relationships such as mergers and R&D/production joint ventures, present competition laws do not contain specific provisions dealing with strategic alliances. While, in the types of anti-competitive situations mentioned above, the conventional instruments of competition policy could be invoked, there are no formal disclosure, registration or review procedures in place for strategic alliances. No guidelines permitting or proscribing strategic alliances have been formulated outside R&D cooperation (aside from Canada, which has established such guidelines). This increases difficulties in detecting and selecting cases where strategic alliances are likely to give rise to competition concerns.

3 Antitrust law in a number of jurisdictions does explicitly recognize R&D consortia.

4 There is, as yet, insufficient evidence on the size, scope and success of strategic alliances. However, they are difficult to trace and to judge.

It may be recalled that strategic alliances often represent firm responses to changing market conditions. In industries characterized by short product life cycles, increasing costs and risks associated with R&D and the introduction of new products, rapid technological change, intense international competition and problems in accessing and penetrating markets, strategic alliances may essentially be the most flexible and efficient form of interfirm cooperation. From an efficiency viewpoint, more concrete or structured organizational forms between firms may not be feasible or desirable.

Many of these difficulties of information could be surmounted by amending competition laws or by enacting supplementary laws such as the

National Cooperative Research Act 1984–94 in the United States. As in the case of R&D cooperatives, the disclosure and registration of strategic alliances can be encouraged by formulating guidelines and promoting voluntary compliance through such incentives as offering antitrust immunity (or 'safe harbour') for cases which have been officially reviewed and sanctioned. Such measures may also reduce business uncertainty regarding the stance of competition authorities towards strategic alliances. However, before such legislation and policy changes are made, it must be demonstrated that strategic alliances raise significant competition issues. This as yet has not been the case. More definite forms of interfirm cooperation such as R&D and production joint ventures have not resulted in a significant number of antitrust actions. To date, there have also been no specific cases reported where strategic alliances have allegedly led to the substantial lessening of competition. The antitrust treatment of joint ventures has generally been lenient. A parallel treatment of strategic alliances is likely to follow.

In light of these considerations, a case-by-case and a 'rule of reason' approach towards strategic alliances appears to be most appropriate. However, much of the analytical framework used to evaluate strategic alliances is based on criteria designed for merger analysis, or which examine the strategic alliance as an 'agreement'. We suggest that a crucial aspect is spillovers; the analysis of these requires knowledge of the production characteristics internal to the firm.

A question arises as to the degree of permissiveness to be allowed R&D alliances. Jorde and Teece (1990, 1992) argue for a permissive attitude with a safe harbour for R&D and production consortia. Shapiro and Willig (1990) argue that there is no evidence 'to support the view that US antitrust policy stifles innovation by US firms' (p. 124), that the existing rule of reason approach would account for beneficial production joint ventures and therefore that no changes in US antitrust laws are required. However, the 1984 law was changed in 1994 to allow limited joint production.

The distinction between 'R&D' and 'production' is, however, moot, since information is pervasive in the modern corporation and new knowledge is not simply a blueprint for a new product or process but is embodied in the organization of the firm and its day-to-day operations. An unresolved question is whether 'strategic' alliances deserve more lenient anti-trust control than 'non-strategic' interfirm cooperation.

Some thought should be given to the gathering of data on alliances. Perhaps a register of such alliances above some market share (where possible) or absolute size threshold could be considered.[12]

One potential issue is an alliance involving firms operating in different national markets. Little information may be available on such ISAs and the market competition issues may be amenable to international discussion.

CONCLUDING REMARKS

Strategic alliances appear to be a growing phenomenon and occur more often among firms engaged in products/production processes which are knowledge, technology and/or R&D-intensive. In contrast to joint ventures and other types of agreements and interfirm arrangements, these alliances represent a more flexible form of collaboration between firms which overcomes various transaction and strategic behaviour hazards. They generally tend to arise when firms seek to learn and also retain their individual capabilities. In our view, strategic alliances are importantly driven by organizationally embedded firm-specific advantages which cannot be easily replicated without incurring high costs. In effect this gives rise to economies of scope and scale in the generation of knowledge and R&D-intensive products and processes. This makes it feasible for firms to accrue gains in trade from the cooperative exchange of various information, experience and technical know-how. However, there also arise risks of 'spillovers' from such cooperation which can result in anticompetitive effects. While existing instruments of competition policy can, in most situations, be applied to redress these effects, the competitive assessment required is likely to be more complex than is the case, for example, with horizontal mergers and joint ventures. Evaluation of actual and potential competition in present and future markets for existing and new products is likely to be entailed. This is because strategic alliances are generally amorphous in nature, have no defined market share or other size parameter thresholds, and tend to be ongoing relationships between independent firms which span the medium to long term. In light of these aspects of strategic alliances, and the increased importance of the dynamic dimensions of competition, a flexible, case-by-case approach appears to be the most appropriate stance for competition policy to adopt towards strategic alliances.

NOTES

1 The ABA Section of Antitrust Law 'Report of the Special Committee on International Antitrust', October 1991 states, 'For reasons of simplification, we have used merger analysis as a proxy for analysis of mergers and joint ventures' (p. 106, footnote).

2 Strategic alliances are also to be distinguished from industry associations, where member firms also remain independent. Strategic alliances do not involve large numbers of competitors as associations do.

3 See General Motors Corp., 103 F.T.C. 374, 386 (1984).

4 Merger guidelines issued by the Japanese FTC in 1980 suggest that a merger will be examined closely if the three firm concentration rates exceed 50 per cent and one of the merging companies is in the top three, or if either firm in the merger has more than a 25 per cent market share. No mergers have been challenged under these guidelines.

5 'The competitive consequences of such pricing are clear. The transfer pricing formula reduces the fear among the leading small-car companies that others might not follow their price increase. Toyota would know that if it raised the Corolla prices, the price of the joint-venture car must necessarily follow. Ford, Honda, and others would know that if they raised their prices, the joint-venture car would do whatever Toyota did. Effectively, the price of the joint-venture car would no longer be independently set. Rather, it becomes a strict Toyota-price follower, so that GM (or at least that important part of GM's output) is eliminated as a separate player in the oligopoly game. The fact that this has been accomplished without explicit collusion is beside the point. The result is what Toyota's own lawyer conceded to be "lockstep" pricing.' (Kwoka 1989, p. 6.)

6 A R&D joint venture speeds innovation if the primary R&D competition is from firms outside the R&D joint venture. Where primary competition comes from the R&D joint venture participants themselves, the R&D joint venture slows innovation. If no pre-innovation market power exists, the R&D joint venture is 'almost certainly' welfare-improving. If on the other hand, the R&D joint venture participants have market power, pre-innovation, then the R&D joint venture can be welfare-decreasing, depending on the extent of pre-innovation profits.

7 Bresnahan and Salop utilize a modified HHI analysis to analyse how the joint capacity affects concentration.

8 A strategic alliance would then be a 'sham', masquerading for a price-fixing output-restricting agreement.

9 As discussed in the text, the implications of strategic alliances for competition policy have been examined as akin to those that arise from R&D and production joint ventures. A fuller exposition of the relevant issues can be found in OECD (1986), Augustyn (1986), Grossman and Shapiro (1986) and Willig and Shapiro (1990).

10 Lewis notes how Japanese firms tend to limit access in strategic alliances by providing very few people who can be contacted.

11 See Grossman and Shapiro (1986, 1987). In the latter article the authors demonstrate that R&D effort between two firms is greatest when they are about even. If one gains a lead, it has a greater incentive to maintain or increase its R&D effort compared with the second (lagging) firm.

12 This issue was raised by us at the OECD Committee on Competition Law and Policy and was dismissed as unworkable (what is a strategic alliance which is to be notified?) and potentially 'chilling'.

REFERENCES

Areeda, P.E. (1986) *Antitrust Law*, Little Brown, Boston.
Augustyn, F.M. (1986) 'An Antitrust Analysis of Joint Research and Development Agreements in the European Economic Community and the United States', *Georgetown Journal of International and Competition Law* 16, 45–71.
Berg, S. and P. Friedman (1980) 'Causes and Effects of Joint Venture Activity: Knowledge Acquisition vs Parent Horizontality', *Antitrust Bulletin*, spring, 143–68.
Bresnahan, Timothy F. and Steven C. Salop (1986) 'Quantifying the Competitive Effects of Production Joint Ventures' in *International Journal of Industrial Organization* 4, 155–75.
Brittan, Sir Leon (1992) *European Competition Policy, Keeping the Playing-field Level*, Brassey's, United Kingdom.
Buckley, P. and M. Casson (1988) 'A Theory of Cooperation in International

Business', in F. Contractor and P. Lorange (eds) *Cooperative Strategies in International Business.*

Chesnais (1988) 'Technical Cooperation Agreements Between Firms', OECD, *STI Review* 4, 51–120.

Contractor, F.J. and P. Lorange (1988) 'Why Should Firms Cooperate? The Strategy and Economics Basis for Cooperative Ventures', in *Cooperative Strategies in International Business*, Lexington Books, Toronto.

Grossman, G. and C. Shapiro (1986) 'Research Joint Ventures: An Antitrust Analysis', *Journal of Law, Economics, and Organization* 4, 315–37.

Grossman, G. and C. Shapiro (1987) 'Dynamic R&D Competition', *Economic Journal* 97, 372–87.

Gugler, P. (1992) 'Building Transnational Alliances to Create Competitive Advantage', *Long Range Planning* 25, 90–9.

Hagedoorn, J. (1990) 'Organizational Modes of Interfirm Cooperation and Transfer', *Technovation* 10, 17–30.

Hamel, G., Y. Doz and C.K. Prahalad (1989) 'Collaborate With Your Competitors and Win', *Harvard Business Review*, January–February, 133–9.

Harrigan, K. (1988) 'Strategic Alliances and Partner Asymmetries', in F. Contractor and P. Lorange (eds) *Cooperative Strategies in International Business.*

Hergert, M. and D. Morris (1988) 'Trends in International Collaborative Agreements', in F.J. Contractor and P. Lorange (eds) *Cooperative Strategies in International Business.*

Jain, S.C. (1987) 'Perspectives on International Strategic Alliances', *Advances in International Marketing* 2, 103–20.

Jorde, T.M. and D. Teece (1990) 'Innovation and Cooperation: Implications for Competition and Antitrust', *Journal of Economic Perspectives* 4 (3).

Jorde, T.M. and D. Teece, eds (1992) *Antitrust, Innovation and Competitiveness*, Oxford University Press, New York.

Kogut, B. and H. Singh (1988), 'Entering the United States by Joint Venture: Competitive Rivalry and Industry Structure', in F. Contractor and P. Lorange (eds) *Cooperative Strategies in International Business.*

Kogut, B. (1988) 'Joint Ventures: Theoretical and Empirical Perspectives', *Strategic Management Journal* 9, 319–32.

Kogut, B. (1989) 'The Stability of Joint Ventures: Reciprocity and Competitive Rivalry', *Journal of Industrial Economics* 38, 183–98.

Kwoka, J.E. (1989) 'International Joint Venture: General Motors and Toyota', in J.E. Kwoka Jr and L.J. White (eds) *The Antitrust Revolution*, Scott Foresman, Glenview, Ill. pp. 46–79.

Lei, D. and J.W. Slocum (1991) 'Global Strategic Alliances: Pay-offs and Pitfalls', *Organizational Dynamics* 19, 44–62.

Lewis, J. (1990) *Partnerships for Profit: Structuring and Managing Strategic Alliances*, Free Press, New York.

Lorange, P. and J. Roos (1990) 'Why Some Strategic Alliances Succeed and Others Fail', *Journal of Business Strategy*, January–February, 25–30.

McFetridge, D. (1992) 'Globalization and Competition Policy'. Paper prepared for John Deutsch Conference, Queen's University, September 12–19, 1992.

Morris, D. and M. Hergert (1987) 'Trends in International Collaborative Agreements', *Columbia Journal of World Business*, summer, 15–21.

Mowery, D.C. (1988) 'Collaborative Ventures Between U.S. and Foreign Manufacturing Firms: An Overview', in D.C. Mowery (ed.) *International Collaborative Ventures in U.S. Manufacturing*, Ballinger, Cambridge, Mass.

Mytelka, L., ed. (1991) *Strategic Partnerships: States, Firms and International Competition*, Pinter Publishers, London.

OECD (1986) *Competition Policy and Joint Ventures*, OECD, Paris.

Ordover, J. and R. Willig (1985) 'Antitrust for High-technology Industries: Assessing Research Joint Ventures and Mergers', *Journal of Law and Economics*, May, 311–33.

Pfeffer, Jeffrey and Phillip Nowak (1976), 'Joint Ventures and Interorganizational Interdependence', *Administrative Science Quarterly* 21.

Porter, M. (1980) *Competitive Strategy: Techniques for Analyzing Industries and Competitors*, Free Press, New York.

Porter, M. (1985) *Competitive Advantage: Creating and Sustaining Superior Performance*, Free Press, New York.

Porter, M. (1987) 'Changing Patterns of International Competition' in D. Teece (ed.) *The Competitive Challenge*.

Powell, W. (1987) 'Hybrid Organizational Arrangements: New Form or Transitional Development', *California Management Review* 30, 67–87.

Safarian, A.E. (1991) 'Foreign Direct Investment and International Cooperative Agreements: Trends and Issues'. Paper Presented at Canada–Germany Joint Symposium, *Competition Policy in an Interdependent World Economy*, Institut für Wirtschaftsforschung, Hamburg.

Schwartz, W.F. and A. Sheer (1991) 'Antitrust Policy for Research Joint Ventures: In Search of the Optimal Structure of Rivalry in Innovation', Law and Economic Workshop Series, University of Toronto, WSX-4.

Shapiro, C. and R. Willig (1990) 'On the Antitrust Treatment of Production Joint Ventures', *Journal of Economic Perspectives* 4, 113–30.

Teece, D., ed. (1987) *The Competitive Challenge: Strategies for Industrial Innovation and Renewal*, Ballinger, Cambridge, Mass.

Wetston, H.I. (1988) 'The Treatment of Cooperative R&D Activities under the Competition Act', Notes for an Address to the Committee on Science and Technology, Canadian Manufacturers Association, Ottawa.

Williamson, O.E. (1975) *Markets and Hierarchies: Analysis and Antitrust Implications*, Free Press, New York.

Williamson, O.E. (1985) *The Economic Institutions of Capitalism*, Free Press, New York.

Womack, J.P., D.T. Jones and D. Roos (1990) *The Machine that Changed the World*, Maxwell Macmillan International, New York.

ACKNOWLEDGEMENTS

An earlier version of this chapter was prepared for the Competition Law and Policy Committee of the OECD. The authors wish to thank the Canadian Bureau of Competition Policy and the OECD for support. The chapter has benefited from discussion in various forums, notably at the OECD and from project workshops in Paris and Santa Barbara. All errors and views expressed are the authors' alone.

7

CONFIDENTIALITY IN THE ERA OF INCREASED COOPERATION BETWEEN ANTITRUST AUTHORITIES

James F. Rill and Calvin S. Goldman, QC

INTRODUCTION

The thesis is often expressed that cooperation in enforcement between and among antitrust enforcement agencies is good. It is added that cooperation would be materially more effective if enforcement agencies were better able to exchange information. The chief impediment to a better framework for information exchange is the inability of an agency to obtain confidential information from another agency because of statutory or other prohibitions against disclosure of information obtained by an agency in the course of an antitrust investigation.

This chapter will examine the efforts being undertaken by the enforcement agencies in the United States and Canada to improve cooperation through enhanced information-sharing.[1] Both jurisdictions operate under a set of intricate confidentiality safeguards; however, antitrust enforcement authorities in each country have taken a number of steps to facilitate the sharing of confidential information with each other as well as with other nations. The more significant of these initiatives include:

1 The recent enactment in the United States of the *International Antitrust Enforcement Assistance Act* (the 'IAEAA');[2]
2 The signing, on September 23, 1991, of an *Agreement between the United States of America and the Commission of the European Communities Regarding the Application of their Competition Laws*,[3] which was recently ratified by the Council of Ministers of the European Communities;
3 The recent preparation of a draft of a similar agreement between Canada and the European Communities;
4 Efforts by Canadian and US officials to revise the *Memorandum of Understanding between the Government of Canada and the Government of the United States of America as to Notification, Consultation and*

152

Cooperation with Respect to the Application of National Antitrust Laws which was entered into in 1984 (the 'MOU');[4]

5 The signing, on March 18, 1985, of a *Treaty between the Government of the United States of America and the Government of Canada on Mutual Legal Assistance in Criminal Matters*,[5] which came into force on January 14, 1990 (the 'MLAT').

At the threshold, the premise that greater cooperation and increased sharing of sensitive information are desirable should be tested. An affirmative answer might seem self-evident. Serious concerns have been expressed, however, especially by elements of the business community, that the uncontrolled furnishing of information by an enforcement agency to a foreign counterpart can compromise trade secrets and other business sensitive information. Widespread acceptance of this concern could actually cause the agencies to become less effective, through erosion of the confidence of business firms that such information will be protected and a resultant unwillingness to cooperate voluntarily in government investigations. Legal challenges to government information demands can seriously disrupt investigations and, of course, at the very least, cause substantial delay.

Conversely, businesses as well as consumers have an interest in optimally effective antitrust enforcement. Several considerations are relevant. First, businesses as often as not are proponents of governmental antitrust enforcement actions against collusive conduct which raise the prices of goods or services they purchase above competitive levels or against restrictive practices that impede their ability to compete effectively. Second, better coordination at the investigative and decision-making level can substantially reduce the transaction costs inherent in a dual or multiple jurisdiction government investigation, in terms of both out-of-pocket costs and softer costs of divergent enquiries, direction, demands, and timetables. In addition, the focus of an investigation might benefit, and has, from the involvement of an experienced agency in consultation with a less experienced and less predictable agency, thus producing a more rational outcome. Finally, and by no means least important, enhanced cooperation can be the best antidote to what some view as antitrust jingoism – unilateral extraterritorial enforcement – by providing a good foundation for positive comity and resultant mutual confidence in commitment and capacity.

The US and Canadian governments, both of which have statutes providing strong protection of confidential information, are undertaking to balance these conflicting considerations by providing for reciprocal information-sharing, including the sharing of confidential information, in limited circumstances and with strong safeguards protecting against 'downstream' disclosure. The existing MLAT,[6] the revised MOU towards which officials in both countries are now working, and the agreements contemplated by the recently enacted IAEAA are designed to achieve that balance.

Although the focus of this chapter is on the Canada–US context, the issues which arise are generic to the development or expansion of cooperation between antitrust authorities on a bilateral or multilateral basis. The Canada–US relationship, therefore, provides a useful laboratory in which to study these emerging issues for use in future bilateral or multilateral contexts. This is particularly so in the context of the anticipated integration of markets in conjunction with NAFTA.

CONFIDENTIALITY SAFEGUARDS IN CANADA AND THE UNITED STATES THAT LIMIT INTERGOVERNMENTAL INFORMATION EXCHANGES

Canada

Section 29 of the Competition Act (Canada)

In this context, we turn now to the provisions of Canadian law which place restrictions on the ability of the Bureau of Competition Policy (the 'Bureau') to provide confidential information to the US authorities. Such restrictions exist under statute, common law and pursuant to contracts (i.e. undertakings) negotiated with the Bureau. These restrictions will be discussed in turn.

The most important statutory restriction is contained in s. 29(1) of the *Competition Act* (the 'Canadian Act'), which provides:

29(1) No person who performs or has performed duties or functions in the administration or enforcement of this Act shall communicate or allow to be communicated to any other person except to a Canadian law enforcement agency or for the purposes of the administration or enforcement of this Act

(a) the identity of any person from whom information was obtained pursuant to this Act;

(b) any information obtained pursuant to section 11, 15, 16 or 114 [the oral examination, search and seizure and pre-merger notification provisions of the Canadian Act];

(c) whether notice has been given or information supplied in respect of a particular proposed transaction under section 114; or

(d) any information obtained from a person requesting a certificate under section 102 [i.e. Advance Ruling Certificate which confirms that the Director does not have grounds upon which to apply to the Competition Tribunal to challenge a merger].

This statutory protection would not apply to a search and seizure that is carried out by the Bureau pursuant to an MLAT request from the United

States. Such a search and seizure would be done pursuant to the *Mutual Legal Assistance in Criminal Matters Act* ('MLAA')[7] and the provisions of Canada's *Criminal Code*,[8] not ss. 11, 15 or 16 of the Canadian Act.

Violating s. 29 is an indictable offence under the *Criminal Code*.[9] However, the scope of s. 29 is not clear. In particular, it is not clear the extent to which the exception for disclosure to 'a Canadian law enforcement agency or for the purposes of the administration or enforcement of this Act' allows disclosure to foreign authorities. It has been argued that the reference to a *Canadian* law enforcement agency in this phrase implies that s. 29 would not allow disclosure to a US authority of information gathered by compulsory process under the pretext of being 'for the purposes of the administration or enforcement of the Canadian Act'.[10] The Director has publicly stated that he does not share this view. In July 1994, the Director issued a draft Information Bulletin (the 'Draft Bulletin') respecting confidentiality of information under the Canadian Act.[11] The Draft Bulletin contemplates sharing information with foreign antitrust authorities where to do so is necessary to advance a particular investigation.[12]

In response to the Draft Bulletin, the Canadian Bar Association expressed significant concern about both the Director's interpretation of s. 29 and the policy implications of that interpretation, and suggested that amendments to that provision are necessary to give the Director the power he needs to engage in international information-sharing.[13] It may be noted that the Director has recently indicated that he intends to pursue amendments to the Canadian Act in order to clarify his authority to engage in information-sharing with foreign antitrust agencies.

A significant limitation on the protection afforded by s. 29 is that it does not apply to information that is voluntarily supplied to the Bureau, in any context. Thus parties providing information to the Bureau on a voluntary basis – for example, to obtain immunity, request an advisory opinion, support a complaint to the Bureau or oppose a merger – would not have the benefit of s. 29, although the Director has publicly stated that he will treat such information as if s. 29 applied to it.[14] Further, there are other general restrictions on disclosure, which would apply to information gathered by compulsory process as well as to information supplied voluntarily to the Bureau. These restrictions are contained in the Canadian Act, other statutes and the common law. We turn now to these additional restrictions.

Other restrictions

Subsection 10(3) of the Canadian Act provides that enquiries under the Canadian Act must be conducted 'in private'. There appears to be no case law interpreting the phrase 'in private' in the context of the Canadian Act. However, there is reason to believe that the prohibition in s. 10(3) ends when the Director commences an application before the Competition Tribunal or a court proceeding is filed in respect of a criminal matter.[15]

In that context, the words 'in private' probably should not be taken to preclude all disclosure to anyone, since it would dramatically impair the ability of the Director to conduct an inquiry. In the Draft Bulletin and subsequently in the 1995 Statement, the Director stated that the Bureau complies with s. 10(3) by conducting an inquiry in as private a manner as circumstances permit.[16]

In addition to statutory restrictions,[17] there are common law duties of confidentiality to which the Bureau may be subject. For example, the decision of the Federal Court of Appeal in *Crestbrook Forest Industries* v. *The Queen*[18] suggests that the Bureau may not disclose information that is voluntarily supplied to it, including to US antitrust authorities, where to do so would be inconsistent with the purpose for which the information is supplied.

Notwithstanding these apparent common law obligations of the Bureau, parties providing information voluntarily would be well served to clarify the extent to which they expect the information will be kept confidential. In the absence of doing so, the Director may disclose the information where to do so is considered necessary to advance an inquiry or informal investigation. Although he appears to limit the circumstances in which he would do so, the Director has publicly suggested he will provide undertakings to address confidentiality concerns with voluntarily supplied information.[19] Such undertakings, while facilitating the gathering of information by the Director, are not statutorily recognized by the Canadian Act.[20] Given the inability to monitor compliance with such undertakings, parties must rely to a certain extent on the good faith of the staff of the Bureau and its record in maintaining confidentiality.

If an inquiry leads to proceedings before the Competition Tribunal, additional restrictions on disclosure by the Bureau become available. First, confidentiality orders are typically available which prevent the disclosure of information provided by the parties other than for the purposes of the particular proceeding.[21] Further, the Director has in the past been required by the Competition Tribunal, as a condition of receiving information from the other parties to proceedings before it, to sign a confidentiality agreement which precludes the Director from using the information he obtains other than for the purposes of the particular proceeding.[22]

In summary, there are certain statutory prohibitions on disclosure of information in Canada, but the scope of these prohibitions is not clear. Further, the prohibitions do not apply in respect of information that is voluntarily supplied. For that information it is often desirable to ask the Director to agree to maintain the confidentiality of the information.

The United States

An intricate network of statutory provisions safeguards the confidentiality of information obtained by the federal antitrust enforcement agencies in the United States,[23] including the *Hart–Scott–Rodino Act* (the 'HSR Act'),[24] the *Antitrust Civil Process Act*,[25] the *Federal Trade Commission Act* (the 'FTC Act'),[26] the *Trade Secrets Act*[27] and the *Federal Rule of Criminal Procedure* 6(e).[28]

Confidentiality of information obtained pursuant to pre-merger notification under the Hart–Scott–Rodino Act[29]

Section 7A(h) of the *Clayton Act*[30] imposes confidentiality restrictions upon both the Federal Trade Commission (FTC) and the US Department of Justice (DOJ) in connection with information received by those agencies from parties to a merger or acquisition in connection with statutory pre-merger notification requirements.

This provision has generated considerable controversy between the federal enforcement agencies and the attorneys-general of the various states of the United States. In *Mattox* v. *Federal Trade Commission*[31] the Fifth Circuit decided that it was not an abuse of discretion for the FTC to decline to turn over HSR Act documents to the Attorney General of Texas. Later the same year, the US Court of Appeals for the Second Circuit concluded that the above noted statutory provision precludes the antitrust enforcement agencies from making materials available to the state attorneys-general or to any other person or entity except as prescribed by statute.[32] As a result of these decisions, it has been confirmed that the confidentiality of HSR Act materials is protected from disclosure, without the consent of the submitting parties, other than to Congress or committees or subcommittees of Congress. The committees of the US Senate and House of Representatives typically have procedural rules whereby the disclosure of information is governed.[33] As a consequence, the ordinary circumstance is that the committee or subcommittee must vote by a majority to obtain the information; the random request of a maverick member of the Senate or House need not be respected.

The parties submitting pre-merger notification information may waive confidentiality protections such that information may be disclosed on a limited basis. A protocol for the provision of such information pursuant to waiver has been adopted by the DOJ and by the FTC.[34] The rationale for this protocol is that the parties to a merger could be well served by responding to the information request of one rather than several enforcement agencies and permitting the enforcement agencies to coordinate their activity better at less cost to the parties.

Materials obtained through civil investigative demands and other investigatory process

The 'confidentiality-accorded information' obtained by the US Department of Justice in connection with civil antitrust investigations is protected by the *Antitrust Civil Process Act*, in accordance with paragraph 4(c)(3).[35]

There is little authority construing this confidentiality provision. It appears to be co-extensive both in its coverage and in its exceptions with the comparable provisions of the HSR Act. One court has interpreted s. 4(c) as affording adequate protection against disclosure to third parties such that a party issued a civil investigative demand could not avoid compliance on the basis that the documentation it was being forced to produce contained confidential proprietary information.[36]

The general investigatory powers of the FTC are set forth in §6 of the FTC Act.[37] Subsection (f) of that section prohibits disclosure to the 'public' of trade secrets, confidential commercial or financial information, line-of-business data, and subpoenaed documents.[38]

Moreover, s. 14 of the FTC Act, which applies to 'any document or transcript of oral testimony received by the Commission pursuant to the compulsory process in an investigation ... [regarding] any provision of the laws administered by the Commission',[39] affords confidentiality for documents turned over as a result of compulsory process.[40]

Not included within the prohibition against disclosure, however, are requests from Congress and federal and state law enforcement authorities, provided the latter furnish satisfactory assurances of confidentiality.[41]

Section 10 of the FTC Act provides for criminal penalties for disclosure of information by FTC employees when that information is received in connection with an investigation by the FTC and its release has not been authorized by the agency.[42] Since the sanction is applicable only in the absence of agency authorization, it does not provide much protection of confidentiality against agency-directed release, but constitutes merely a safeguard against unauthorized leakage.

Prohibition against disclosure of trade secrets

Section 1905 of Title 18 of the United States Code prohibits and provides criminal penalties for violation of the prohibition against the disclosure of 'trade secrets, processes, operations, style of work, or apparatus or the identity of confidential statistical data, a minor source of income, profits, losses, or expenditures of any person, firm, partnership, corporation, or association ...'.[43] As is the case with §10 of the FTC Act, *supra*, the limitation here is on unauthorized disclosure. This chapter is concerned with the extent to which the antitrust enforcement agencies are themselves permitted to authorize disclosure, not with unauthorized disclosure by their employees.

Federal Rule of Criminal Procedure 6(e)

Rule 6(e)(2) of the *Federal Rule of Criminal Procedure* codifies the common law rule that prohibits disclosure of 'matters occurring before the grand jury', with four specific exceptions, enumerated in Rule 6(e)(3):

(i) when disclosure is to an attorney for the government, and assistants, for use in the performance of such attorney's duty; and

(ii) when directed by a court preliminarily to or in connection with a judicial proceeding;

(iii) when permitted by a court at the request of the defendant, a showing that grounds may exist for a motion to dismiss the indictment because of matters occurring before the grand jury; or

(iv) when the disclosure is made by an attorney for the government to another federal grand jury.[44]

Significantly, Rule 6(e) does not impose any obligation of secrecy on grand jury witnesses.[45] Although the language relating to disclosure in connection with the attorney's official duties is ambiguous regarding foreign governments, the Ninth Circuit has rejected the notion that foreign disclosures could be made by US government attorneys under this exception.[46] Instead, the issue of foreign disclosure falls within 6(e)(3)(C), requiring that a US District Court order disclosure. Such a court-ordered disclosure, however, requires that the parties seeking disclosure satisfy a three-part test:

(i) the material must be sought to avoid possible injustice in another judicial proceeding;

(ii) the need for disclosure must outweigh the need for continued secrecy;

(iii) the disclosure request must be limited to the material necessary to avoid injustice.[47]

The US Supreme Court has indicated, however, that convenience or cost savings alone will not satisfy the test and that the requesting party must first exhaust traditional discovery and investigation techniques.[48]

More recently, however, disclosure of materials produced in response to a grand jury subpoena to foreign enforcement officers has occurred where the materials were in the possession of the US attorney but not yet presented to the grand jury. Courts have allowed such disclosure because the materials were not yet in the possession of the grand jury and, therefore, were not afforded protection from disclosure under Rule 6(e).[49]

With increasing frequency, witnesses called before US federal grand juries for criminal violations are invoking the threat of foreign prosecution as an assertion of their right against compulsory self-incrimination, as established under the Fifth Amendment to the United States Constitution.[50]

Most courts facing such a claim, to date, have rejected it on the basis that Rule 6(e) provides sufficient protection from disclosure of information produced in response to a grand jury subpoena.[51]

Information that presently may be provided to foreign enforcement agencies

Notwithstanding this network of regulatory safeguards of confidentiality, it is beyond dispute that certain information can be shared between US antitrust enforcement agencies and their foreign counterparts. Presently, the three categories of information that can be disclosed to foreign enforcement agencies include: general public information; information obtained in the course of the investigation and not expressly protected under the statutory provisions described above;[52] and information obtained in connection with criminal investigations which may be exchanged under appropriate circumstances with foreign enforcement agencies under mutual legal assistance treaties.

Public information

There is a wealth of public information that may reside in the possession of the US antitrust enforcement agencies that may not be in the possession of or known to the foreign enforcement agency with whom cooperation is under consideration. In this category are government and privately developed but publicly available statistical data, trade association and other business and industrial publications, articles in business and technical and scientific journals, and articles and free-standing trade publications and general news publications. In addition, the US agencies could identify, for their foreign counterparts, experts or other knowledgeable people who could on a voluntary basis provide useful industry information.

Investigatory information not expressly protected by statute

It appears that the US enforcement agencies are of the opinion that they may disclose to their foreign counterparts, in appropriate circumstances, the existence and status of US antitrust investigations. The US–EC Antitrust Cooperation Agreement, for example, calls for notification by a party of the pendency of an investigation that may affect the interests of the other party.[53]

Information provided under the US–Canada MLAT

This topic is discussed in the next section.

INITIATIVES TO FACILITATE CLOSER COOPERATION THROUGH EXTENDED INFORMATION EXCHANGES

The US–Canada MLAT

The MLAT provides for assistance 'in all matters relating to the investigation, prosecution and suppression of offence'.[54] It also provides a non-exhaustive list of the types of assistance that one government can provide to another. The list includes exchanging information and objects, providing documents and records and executing requests for searches and seizures.[55] In short, one government can ask the other to obtain and execute a search warrant and, in the United States, issue a grand jury subpoena, in either case to obtain information located in the other jurisdiction. This is the most common form of assistance under the MLAT. The MLAT also provides, in Article XIII, for the ability of one government (the 'Requesting State') to request the other (the 'Requested State') to provide 'copies of any document, record or information in the possession of a government agency, but not publicly available, to the same extent and under the same conditions as would be available to its own law enforcement and judicial authorities.'[56]

The MLAT requires requests for assistance to be conveyed by the 'Central Authority' of one jurisdiction to the Central Authority of the other. In Canada, the Central Authority is the Minister of Justice or officials designated by him and, in the United States, the Attorney General or officials designated by him. In Canada, as a matter of practice, this means that all requests are routed through the federal Minister of Justice,[57] not directly to or from the Bureau.[58]

The amount of information required to make a request is not subject to a specified limit. For example, the MLAT requires a request for assistance to include 'such information as the Requested State requires to execute the request, including ... a description of the evidence, information or other assistance [and] the purpose for which the evidence, information or other assistance is sought'.[59] It is possible under the MLAT, and indeed may be necessary in some circumstances, for the Requesting State to ask for further information than is initially supplied. In that regard, the courts of the Requesting State are authorized to order 'lawful disclosure' of such information as is necessary to enable the Requested State to execute the request.[60] Ostensibly, the Requested State could acquire all information it considered necessary in order to give it grounds to launch its own investigation under the pretext of asking for more information from the Requesting State for the purposes of carrying out a request.

Both the MLAT and (in Canada) the legislation which implements the MLAT, the *Mutual Legal Assistance in Criminal Matters Act* (referred to above as the 'MLAA'), provide some protection of confidential information, but the protection has significant limitations.[61]

The MLAT does not provide for the right of private parties to be informed that information they provided to the Bureau is being provided to the other country. While this may be understandable when discussing information respecting a criminal offence that was obtained under compulsory process, it is not clear why this protection should not apply in respect of information that is supplied voluntarily to the government of one country. Further, the MLAT is quite clear that it does not grant private parties any right to 'obtain, suppress, or dispute any evidence or impede the execution of a request'.[62]

While it may be expected that the MLAT will be used with increasing frequency in the future, in the four years since it came into force there have been apparently only a few publicly reported requests for assistance going in either direction.[63] There may have been more uses which have not yet been reported.

The US–Canada MOU

The MLAT does not extend to civil matters, but neither is it exhaustive of the extent of cooperation between Canada and the United States.[64] The MOU, mentioned earlier, is a non-binding understanding the purpose of which is 'avoiding or moderating conflicts of interests and policies'.[65] The number of MOU notifications has increased significantly in the last few years. In the Annual Report of the Director for the year ended March 31, 1994, it was disclosed that Canada had received twenty notifications from the United States under the MOU and gave five to the United States. This compares with twenty and eleven, respectively, for the 1993 fiscal year, and with five and eight, respectively, for the 1992 fiscal year.

The principal focus of the Canada–US MOU is dispute avoidance. To this end, the MOU requires the parties to give each other notification in a number of circumstances when an antitrust investigation is in progress that may affect the other jurisdiction. These include:

1 Where an investigation is likely to enquire into activity carried out wholly or in part in the territory of the other party;
2 Where an investigation is likely to enquire into activity carried out wholly or in part outside the territory of the investigating party, and there is reason to believe that the activity is required, encouraged or approved by the other party;
3 Where it is expected that information to be sought is located in the territory of the other party;
4 Where information is to be gathered through the personal visit by enforcement officials to the territory of the other party;

5 Where an investigation, whether or not previously notified, may reasonably be expected to lead to a prosecution or other enforcement action likely to affect a national interest of the other party.[66]

Notably absent from this defensively orientated list are situations where an antitrust enforcement authority becomes aware – for example, through investigation of conduct occurring within its own territory – of anti-competitive effects in the territory of the other party. In addition, despite its focus on dispute avoidance, the MOU does not provide any clear guidance regarding the factors that ought to be considered by the parties in resolving disputes concerning the application of their antitrust laws. In particular, there is no reference to, or elaboration of, comity factors of the kind found in the US–EC cooperation agreement[67] and the 1995 *Antitrust Enforcement Guidelines for International Operations*.

Although paragraphs 1 and 9 of the MOU include references to enforcement cooperation, the achievement of this objective is limited by the absence of specific commitments to provide assistance, the explicit recognition of the constraints imposed by confidentiality laws, and the presence of a vague 'national interest' override.[68] Paragraph 9 of the MOU restricts the exchange of information for enforcement purposes by providing that it 'will be subject to compliance with national laws, considerations of national interest and the establishment of adequate safeguards respecting confidentiality'[69] in relation to intergovernmental communications. Not surprisingly, the confidentiality provisions in the two country's antitrust laws have substantially constrained efforts by enforcement authorities in both jurisdictions to improve cooperation.

Nevertheless, the MOU has provided an important institutional framework for the regular formal bilateral and informal officer-level exchanges between Canadian and US authorities. These contacts have allowed the two countries' antitrust authorities to explore alternative avenues of enforcement cooperation such as the MLAT and, more recently, the Canada–US Extradition Treaty.

Revised US–Canada MOU

On 3 August 1995 Canadian and US antitrust authorities announced the signing of a revised MOU. Formally entitled the *Agreement Between the Government of the United States and the Government of Canada Regarding the Application of their Competition and Deceptive Marketing Practices Laws*, this revised MOU focuses upon:

1 Improving the notification provisions in the MOU, by revising the definition of notifiable circumstances and the provisions regarding the timing of notifications;
2 Amplifying the dispute avoidance provisions, primarily by articulating the comity considerations that ought to guide the exercise of enforcement discretion in matters with cross-border implications;

3 Inserting more specific measures to define the parameters of enforcement cooperation 'within the limits of existing laws'.[70] In this latter regard, it appears that recent experience in enforcement cooperation between the two countries, together with the concept of 'positive comity' developed in the US–EC cooperation agreement, will provide a basis for negotiations.[71]

It appears that a revised MOU, rather than the type of agreement contemplated by the IAEAA, was pursued at this time because of the uncertainty that has been raised regarding the ability of the Director to disclose to foreign enforcement authorities confidential information of the type described in s. 29 of the Canadian Act.

The IAEAA

On November 2, 1994, the *International Antitrust Enforcement Assistance Act* (referred to earlier as the 'IAEAA') was signed into law by President Clinton, with strong bipartisan support from both Houses of Congress, within ten weeks of its introduction. This success was a result of the strong effort of the DOJ under the direction of Assistant Attorney General of Antitrust Anne Bingaman to improve procedural and enforcement convergence with sister competition enforcement agencies in other countries.

The two principal aspects of this legislation are cooperation and information-sharing between the US competition enforcement agencies and their foreign counterparts. Under the IAEAA, cooperation and information-sharing are not mandatory, but instead are conditioned upon the ability of the enforcement officials to enter into bilateral agreements that satisfy the following three criteria:

1 The foreign agency receiving information from the US agencies provides cooperation and information on a reciprocal basis.[72]
2 Before receiving any confidential information from the US enforcement agencies, the foreign agency would provide reasonable assurances of protection 'that is not less than the protection provided under the laws of the U.S. to such antitrust evidence'.[73]
3 The requested cooperation or disclosure by the US enforcement agencies is in the US public interest.[74]

Certain unique aspects of the IAEAA include:

1 Assuming a bilateral agreement that satisfies the above criteria is in place, for the first time confidential information obtained using compulsory process can be shared with enforcement officials of the other country. (Documents or information received under the HSR Act, however, are exempt from disclosure.);
2 Section 3(a) expressly permits the US enforcement agencies to provide confidential information 'without regard to whether the conduct

investigated violates any of the [US] antitrust laws', so long as the assistance is in connection with a foreign investigation or enforcement of competition laws substantially similar to those of the United States. That is, of course, so long as providing the information is consistent with the US public interest. This provision promotes the concept of positive comity because, without raising jurisdictional issues, U.S. officials are able to assist foreign officials in the enforcement of their own competition laws against restrictive practices which may effect market foreclosure;

3 The IAEAA conditions cooperation and information-sharing on reciprocal treatment.[75] If, for example, a foreign country were unwilling to assist US enforcement efforts, US officials would be prohibited from providing those foreign officials with assistance. In effect, this prohibition would constitute at least a temporary *de facto* termination of mutual assistance efforts with that country;

4 Although not subject to US judicial review, the bilateral agreements that the US enforcement officials enter into must provide 'an assurance that the foreign antitrust authority ... will give protection to [the information/ documents, etc.] received ... that is not less than the protection provided under the laws of the United States ... '.[76] Should such protection not be given, agreements can be terminated. The IAEAA, therefore, balances the protection of confidentiality with the need for effective and efficient convergence of antitrust enforcement;

5 Notification to the party providing the information that it is being communicated to a foreign agency is not required or precluded. A US House Of Representatives Judiciary Committee report urges that such notification be given in appropriate cases.[77]

Under the IAEAA, before any information may be shared, a bilateral agreement must be entered into between the United States and the other country. Although there are no final bilateral agreements yet in place, some progress has been made between the United States and Canada and between the United States and the European Union:

1 Discussions with Canadian authorities are ongoing to expand the scope of cooperation to include much of the type of cooperation contemplated by the IAEAA. Under the IAEAA, the confidentiality safeguards are greater than those under the existing MLAT, which governs criminal, including criminal antitrust, law. Accordingly, there remains an issue as to whether the information exchanged in respect of criminal antitrust matters will receive the greater confidentiality protection afforded by the IAEAA, or be subject to the lesser confidentiality standards established by the MLAT.

2 The EC–US bilateral agreement has been restored by vote of the council.

3 The DOJ is now exploring the concept of cooperation agreements contemplated by the IAEAA in several countries.

The IAEAA was created because of inherent difficulties encountered in the United States while attempting to obtain overseas evidence for use in investigations of antitrust violations. The US antitrust agencies in recent years have increased their investigations of violations of US law occurring in the global economic arena. These attempts have often been thwarted by foreign governments unwilling or simply unable to participate in the collection of necessary evidence. The IAEAA was strongly backed by the DOJ and both the current and former Assistant Attorneys General of the Antitrust Division. In testimony before the Subcommittee on Economic and Commercial Law of the House Judiciary Committee, Assistant Attorney General Anne Bingaman conveyed her frustration when confronted by foreign barriers:

> More and more often, the evidence we need is located abroad. Unfortunately, evidence that is located abroad is far too often evidence that is beyond our reach. And when we cannot enforce our antitrust laws against foreign anti-competitive conduct because we cannot get the evidence, it is American consumers and American businesses that bear the cost. Many of [our international] investigations involve straight-out cartel conduct aimed at American businesses and consumers. In several of these investigations, there is a serious possibility we will be unable to get the evidence to prosecute because crucial witnesses or documents are abroad and beyond our reach.[78]

Although the United States has entered into several MLATs and MOUs in recent years, their effectiveness has been hindered by strict confidentiality restrictions placed upon antitrust evidence sharing. US laws such as the *Antitrust Civil Process Act* and the FTC Act, and Rule 6(e) of the *Federal Rules of Criminal Procedure* all impose stringent limitations on information obtained through compulsory process. Further restrictions are dictated by a clause in the HSR Act which enjoins the disclosure of strategic business and market information obtained through the pre-merger notification system. The IAEAA was constructed to circumvent some of these barriers while still taking into account the security of confidential material. By permitting the Attorney General and the FTC to enter into specifically designed mutual assistance agreements, the IAEAA allows for reciprocal information-sharing while also maintaining certain restrictions on the transfer of confidential material.

During congressional hearings on the IAEAA, concerns were raised by American businesses and the House Judiciary Committee as to whether the confidentiality safeguards mandated by the Bill were sufficient protection. One safeguard which was not specifically required by the law is the notification of the party affected by the request for information. Several business groups testified that they believe it is imperative for US agencies to notify companies prior to the disclosure of sensitive information, allowing the affected parties the opportunity to respond to the implications of the exchange. The House Committee concluded that notification of the affected party should be an important consideration; however, it should not be mandated owing to certain situations where criminal investigations are being conducted.

Recent cases

Cooperation between Canada and US antitrust enforcement officials in specific cases is a relatively recent development. However, it has rapidly become a critical element of their respective enforcement policies. The *fax paper* case is an important example, since it was the first joint investigation by the Canadian Bureau and the DOJ. As a result of information which arose in Canada, both the Bureau and the DOJ commenced coordinated investigations that included joint interviews of witnesses and the United States getting document summaries prepared by the Bureau. We are aware of other situations where the two governments have jointly interviewed witnesses in the context of a joint criminal investigation. One of these coordinated investigations culminated on July 12, 1994, when the Bureau announced that a C $950,000 fine had been levied against Kanzaki Specialty Papers ('Kanzaki') for violation of the conspiracy provisions of the Canadian Act.[79] Two days later, the DOJ issued a press release announcing that charges had been laid against Kanzaki, a Japanese officer of a related firm, Mitsubishi Corporation of Tokyo and Mitsubishi International Corporation of New York, and that the defendants had agreed to plead guilty and pay fines of more than US$6 million.[80] On the day the US charges were announced, an unprecedented joint press conference was held in the United States, attended by US Attorney General Janet Reno, US Assistant Attorney General Anne Bingaman and George Addy, Director of Investigation and Research under the Canadian Act.

In another 1994 case, involving manufacturers of plastic dinnerware, US authorities commenced an investigation which included coordinated raids by the Federal Bureau of Investigation in the United States and the Royal Canadian Mounted Police in Canada pursuant to a request by the US under the MLAT. The US investigation led to criminal charges against three plastic manufacturing companies and a number of individuals.[81]

RESTRICTIONS ON DISCLOSURE BY ONE ANTITRUST AUTHORITY OF THE INFORMATION RECEIVED FORM THE OTHER AUTHORITY

On pp. 154–60 we discussed the limitations on the ability of antitrust authorities in each jurisdiction to provide information to the authorities in the other jurisdiction. This section discusses the restrictions on disclosure by the antitrust authorities in one country of information they obtain from the other jurisdiction. This issue has two elements: restrictions on disclosure by the authorities and restrictions that prevent third parties from obtaining access to information from the authorities.

Canada

The MLAT provides that the disclosure or use of information for purposes other than those stated in the request is prohibited without the prior consent of authorities in the disclosing jurisdiction. The Attorney General of the United States (presumably advised by the antitrust authorities) decides whether to permit the use of the information for other purposes. There is no requirement to tell private parties of the request or that the United States has granted its consent.[82] However, it is reasonable to presume that the Bureau would request and consent would be granted only to disclose information to other Canadian law enforcement agencies.[83]

As mentioned earlier, the MOU provides for the assistance between Canada and the US antitrust authorities in the enforcement of their respective antitrust laws through the exchange of information.[84] However, the MOU does not override the confidentiality protections that are part of Canadian law – in fact it allows the United States to request *additional* restrictions on disclosure of information by the Canadian authorities. US persons who wish to control disclosure to the Bureau or the use that the Bureau may make of the information they provide to US authorities should consider seeking the appropriate assurances from the US antitrust authorities when providing information on a voluntary basis.

Section 29 of the Canadian Act has no application to information obtained from US antitrust authorities, whether it was initially provided to the US authorities voluntarily or otherwise. However, s. 10(3) of the Canadian Act and the common law duty of confidentiality described earlier would arguably apply to prohibit disclosure of information obtained from the US antitrust authorities other than for the purposes of the particular investigation. Obviously, those restrictions would not prevent disclosure where the Bureau made disclosure for the purpose of its investigation, for example to a market participant in order to obtain information.

When formal proceedings have been commenced, the Director may invoke a 'public interest privilege' under the *Canada Evidence Act* to resist disclosure requests.[85] In addition, a 'litigation privilege' has been held by the Competition Tribunal to extend to all communications between a complainant and the Director exchanged in preparation of a proceeding before the Competition Tribunal.[86] Finally, Canadian courts have recognized a 'without prejudice' privilege which extends to protect action communications between the Director and a party whose conduct is under investigation from subsequent discovery by third parties.[87] Thus several

168

levels of privilege could apply to requests to obtain information from the Director.

The *Access to Information Act* (referred to earlier as the 'AIA') permits Canadian citizens to obtain access to information under government control. However, the AIA provides two types of exemptions from the general principle of disclosure. First, s. 16 of the AIA provides that the government may refuse to disclose information that contains information obtained by any government institution in the course of lawful investigations pertaining to the enforcement of any law in Canada or information the disclosure of which could reasonably be expected to be injurious to the enforcement of any law of Canada or the conduct of lawful investigation. For this purpose, an 'investigation' includes investigation under the Canadian Act.[88] The Canadian authors understand that the Director traditionally relies on this section when he refuses to disclose information in response to a request under the AIA.

Second, most of the information which is obtained from the United States would likely be exempt from disclosure under s. 20, which protects trade secrets and competitively sensitive information.[89]

It may be noted that the AIA allows for challenges to decisions by the government not to disclose the information. However, it also requires the government to give notice to the party supplying the information in circumstances where the government intends to disclose information.[90]

In summary, there are many protections available in Canada to ensure that third parties cannot get access to information in the possession of the Bureau. Even where disclosure is required, such as in proceedings before the Tribunal, typically protective orders are available. These protections do not prevent the Director or the Bureau from making disclosure, without prior notice to the US firm whose information is being disclosed, where it is considered necessary to advance the Bureau's investigation.

The United States

As previously noted, both the MLAT and the MOU require the information exchanges they facilitate to be made in a manner consistent with the providing country's confidentiality laws. Further, the MLAT, under Article IX, allows the country supplying the information to request additional confidentiality protection for the information it provides. These provisions would appear to provide adequate confidentiality safeguards. To the contrary, however, the existing confidentiality regulatory scheme in the United States is outdated and, in the absence of specifically requested confidentiality agreements, does not prevent the disclosure of confidential information received by US antitrust enforcement officials from their Canadian counterparts.

Each of the confidentiality provisions governing US antitrust enforcement officers, e.g. §18a(h) of the HSR Act, §1313(c) of the *Antitrust Civil Process Act*, §57-b2 of the FTC Act, and *Federal Rule of Criminal Procedure* 6(e) afford confidential treatment to information and documents that private parties are required to produce under each respective statute. In no case does the statutorily imposed confidential treatment extend to information produced voluntarily. Instead, parties that supply information on a voluntary basis typically seek a confidentiality agreement with either the DOJ or the FTC before the information is submitted, to prevent its disclosure. Because information received from Canadian officials is not information that is required to be produced under any of these statutes, there would be no disclosure restriction on the US enforcement official receiving this information from his Canadian counterpart. If Canada, as the 'requested state', has not specifically required that the information it provides the US official be kept confidential, there would be no restriction on the US enforcement official from disclosing the information. For example, if the US enforcement official were to disclose the information it received from Canadian officials to a competitor of a party under investigation in Canada, such a disclosure would not be in violation of Article IX.2 of the MLAT as long as the US official disclosed the information to the competitor in an attempt to gain evidence or use the competitor as a witness for an investigation in the United States. Absent a specific request for confidential treatment by the Canadian authorities, the receiving US official would also be able to disclose the information to other federal and state officials.

With respect to requests under the *Freedom of Information Act* ('FOIA'),[91] by interested third parties, the exemption for not having to comply with a FOIA request also would not be available under the HSR Act or the FTC Act. Although each of these latter Acts exempts, from FOIA disclosure, documents required to be produced under each respective statute, this exemption does not apply to non-required information.[92] *The Antitrust Civil Process Act* does not contain a FOIA exemption. As a result, a FOIA request for documents provided by Canada to either the DOJ or the FTC would be subject only to the general exceptions from disclosures set forth in the FOIA.[93]

ALTERNATIVES TO AGREEMENTS CONTEMPLATED UNDER THE IAEAA

Unilateral action: the US 'effects' test

Historical position

As the US Supreme Court observed in *Hartford Fire Insurance Co.* v. *California*,[94] 'it is well established by now that the *Sherman Act* applies to foreign conduct that was meant to produce and did in fact produce some substantial effect in the United States'.[95] As long ago as the seminal 1945 decision in *United States* v. *Aluminum Co. of America*, it was recognized that conduct engaged in abroad could be found to contravene the *Sherman Act* if it was 'intended to affect imports and did affect them'.[96]

In 1982, the US Congress passed the *Foreign Trade Antitrust Improvements Act of 1982* ('FTAIA'), which provided that the *Sherman Act* applies to conduct which does not involve import commerce but does have a 'direct, substantial and reasonably foreseeable effect' on US commerce, for example on US export trade or export commerce with foreign nations.[97] However, in footnote 159 of the US Department of Justice's 1988 *Antitrust Enforcement Guidelines for International Operations* (the '1988 Guidelines'),[98] it was stated:

> Although the FTAIA extends jurisdiction under the Sherman Act to conduct that has a direct, substantial, and reasonably foreseeable effect on the export trade or export commerce of a person engaged in such commerce in the United States, the Department is concerned only with adverse effects on competition that would harm U.S. consumers by reducing output or raising prices [in the United States].

This provision in the 1988 Guidelines was generally interpreted as indicating that, as a matter of enforcement policy, the DOJ would not pursue matters involving harm to exporters unless there also was direct harm to US consumers.[99]

In 1992, the DOJ effectively repealed the policy reflected in footnote 159 of the 1988 Guidelines. In a statement released on April 3, 1992, the DOJ announced the following position:[100]

> The Department of Justice will, in appropriate cases, take antitrust enforcement action against conduct occurring overseas that restrains United States exports, whether or not there is direct harm to U.S. consumers, where it is clear that:
>
> (i)   the conduct has a direct, substantial, and reasonably foreseeable effect on exports of goods or services from the United States;
>
> (ii) the conduct involves anti-competitive activities which violate the U.S. antitrust laws – in most cases, group boycotts, collusive pricing, and other exclusionary activities; and
>
> (iii) U.S. courts have jurisdiction over foreign persons or corporations engaged in such conduct.

This policy was stated to represent 'a return to the Department's pre-1988 position on such matters'.[101]

US Antitrust Enforcement Guidelines for International Operations

The 1995 Guidelines released jointly by the DOJ and the FTC in April 1995 confirm both the long-standing enforcement policy position with respect to 'inbound' commerce and the 1992 position with respect to 'outbound' commerce. With respect to jurisdiction, the 1995 Guidelines articulate the following general principle:

> Anticompetitive conduct that affects U.S. domestic or foreign commerce may violate the U.S. antitrust laws regardless of where such conduct occurs or the nationality of the parties involved.[102]

The 1995 Guidelines then apply two tests for antitrust subject matter jurisdiction: one for foreign imports, and one for foreign conduct impacting the United States other than through a direct effect on imports. With respect to foreign imports, the 1995 Guidelines state: 'the Sherman Act applies to foreign conduct that was meant to produce and did in fact produce some substantial effect in the United States'.[103] Example A in the 1995 Guidelines, which involves a cartel organized by foreign producers outside the United States having no US production or subsidiaries, illustrates the application of this test. The 1995 Guidelines state that in this example 'subject matter jurisdiction is clear under the general principles of antitrust law expressed most recently in *Hartford Fire*'. They further state: 'Imports into the United States by definition affect the U.S. domestic market directly, and will, therefore, almost invariably satisfy the intent part of the *Hartford Fire* test.'[104]

Example B in the 1995 Guidelines illustrates how the FTAIA's direct, substantial and reasonably foreseeable test applies where the cartel in the previous example does not sell directly into the United States, but instead sells to an intermediary, which is unaware of the cartel, located outside the United States, and which the cartel knows will sell the product into the United States. The 1995 Guidelines provide:

> To the extent that the conduct in foreign countries does not 'involve' import commerce but does have an 'effect' on either import transactions or commerce within the United States, the Agencies apply the 'direct, substantial, and reasonably foreseeable' standard of the FTAIA.[105]

According to the 1995 Guidelines, '[t]he fact that the illegal conduct occurs prior to the import would trigger the application of the FTAIA'.[106]

The 1995 Guidelines also incorporate the jurisdictional tests of the HSR Act and the rules promulgated thereunder, which may apply to acquisitions by foreign firms of assets or subsidiaries outside the United States, but which have substantial sales into the United States.[107] With respect to exports, the 1995 Guidelines apply FTAIA principles to determine whether mergers or acquisitions involving only foreign firms and assets have an effect upon US commerce and are therefore subject to US scrutiny under s. 7 of the *Clayton Act*.[108]

With respect to 'export cases' (i.e. outbound commerce), the 1995 Guidelines confirm the willingness of the DOJ and the FTC to:[109]

> ... take enforcement action against anti-competitive conduct, wherever occurring, that restrains U.S. exports, if (1) the conduct has a direct, substantial, and reasonably foreseeable effect on exports of goods or services from the United States, and (2) the U.S. courts can obtain jurisdiction over persons or corporations engaged in such conduct.

Having said that, the 1995 Guidelines then note that:[110]

> ... if the conduct is unlawful under the importing country's antitrust laws as well, the Agencies are also prepared to work with that country's authorities if they are better situated to remedy the conduct, and if they are prepared to take action that will address the U.S. concerns, pursuant to their antitrust laws.

The simple message here is: 'You take action or we will.'

The 1995 Guidelines have also been amended to make it clear that enforcement action may be taken against *foreign* firms where they engage in conduct which violates US antitrust laws which results in harm to US taxpayers, i.e. where, 'as a result of its payment or financing, the U.S. government bears more than half the cost of the transaction'.[111] The 1988 Guidelines suggested that the DOJ would only consider pursuing such conduct where it was engaged in by 'U.S. firms'.[112] We understand that the change in the wording more accurately reflects long-standing actual enforcement practice.

Another notable addition to the 1995 Guidelines is the statement that 'the mere existence of [blocking statutes which prevent persons from disclosing documents or information for use in US proceedings] does not excuse noncompliance with a request for information from one of the Agencies'.[113] This appears to broaden the approach to personal jurisdiction, relative to the 1988 Guidelines. Unfortunately, the 1995 Guidelines do not distinguish between blocking statutes which are self-executing (i.e. prohibit the sending of certain information outside the jurisdiction), and those which require action by a government authority in the foreign jurisdiction before they become operative. The 1995 Guidelines also do not state what the Agencies' policy is when such action has been taken. We would note that the ABA's comments on the draft Guidelines issued in October 1994 had suggested that the approach to these issues be clarified.[114]

With respect to comity, the approach of the 1995 Guidelines is arguably narrower than in the 1988 Guidelines. For example, the 1988 Guidelines stated that 'the Department considers whether significant interests of any foreign sovereign would be affected *and asserts jurisdiction only when the Department concludes that it would be reasonable to do so'* (emphasis added).[115] The italicized portion of this statement, together with other pro-comity language, has been omitted from the 1995 Guidelines, as has the statement in the 1988 Guidelines that 'the Department may, in extraordinary circumstances, take into account possible effects on the United States' conduct of foreign relations'.[116]

The 1995 Guidelines also added two factors to the list of six factors set forth in the 1988 Guidelines, which are considered in the Agencies' determination of whether to decline to assert jurisdiction on the basis of comity. The original six factors, which are drawn from the decision in *Timberlane Lumber Co.* v. *Bank of America National Trust & Savings Association*,[117] are:

1 The relative significance to the alleged violation of conduct within the United States, as compared to the conduct abroad;
2 The nationality of the persons involved in or affected by the conduct;
3 The presence or absence of a purpose to affect US consumers, markets or exporters;
4 The relative significance and foreseeability of the effects of the conduct on the United States as compared to the effects abroad;
5 The existence of reasonable expectations that would be furthered or defeated by the action;
6 The degree of conflict with foreign law or articulated foreign policies.

The two new factors that have been added in the 1995 Guidelines are:

7 The extent to which the enforcement activities of another country with respect to the same persons, including remedies resulting from those activities, may be affected;
8 The effectiveness of foreign enforcement as compared with US enforcement action.

Assessment factor No. 7 is adopted from the US–EC Antitrust Cooperation Agreement. Footnote 74 of the 1995 Guidelines indicates that assessment factor No. 8 is also derived from that Agreement, although that is not immediately apparent.

The addition of assessment factor No. 8 has given rise to a significant level of concern outside the United States. For example, the UK government stated, in its comments on the draft 1995 Guidelines, that it 'would object to unilateral action based solely on the Agencies' assessment of the adequacy of enforcement in other countries'. It added: 'The apparent absence in a given case of a conflict of enforcement does not on its own justify enforcement activity by the Agencies.'

Although the Canadian government did not file a commentary similar to that filed by the UK government, the Competition Law Section of the

Canadian Bar Association (CBA) submitted a commentary in a letter dated December 23, 1994, to Deputy Assistant Attorney General Diane Wood. In its commentary, the CBA stated that it is concerned about the narrow scope afforded to considerations of international comity in the draft Guidelines. In addition, it raised particular concern about the addition of assessment factor No. 8 to the draft Guidelines. In this regard, it stated: 'In our view, at the very least, this position should be clarified to distinguish between countries such as Canada with well developed antitrust laws in regard to which such judgments by another state would be inappropriate, and those whose antitrust laws are weaker.' The CBA commentary went on to state:

> As a point of general application, however, if comity reflects the 'broad concept of respect among co-equal sovereign nations', then the purported willingness of the U.S. to judge the effectiveness of foreign enforcement appears to be at odds with the principle of comity. Such a judgement would also appear to be at odds with the principle of mutual respect for other national enforcement agencies which underlie the bilateral antitrust cooperation agreements, OECD recommendations and Mutual Legal Assistance Treaties mentioned in Section 2.9, not to mention the implicit recognition of the adequacy of the antitrust laws of Mexico and Canada pursuant to Mexico's obligations under Chapter 15 of the NAFTA to enact legislation in this regard. Indeed, the OECD 'Interim Report on Convergence in Competition Policies' (C/MIN(94) 14, May 18, 1994) recognized that 'comity is an important principle underlying competition policy and its enforcement'.
>
> (p. 7, para. A.2, Annex)

Part of the concern about assessment factor No. 8 has to do with its meaning. It is not clear how the Agencies assess 'the effectiveness of foreign enforcement as compared to U.S. enforcement action'. Does it mean that if a particular country is not as tough as the United States, in terms of imposing jail sentences and heavy fines, it will not be considered to have an effective enforcement policy relative to that of the United States? If this were the case, this factor would almost always mitigate in favour of the United States assuming jurisdiction if the DOJ or FTC believed that it could obtain a significantly more 'effective' remedy.

We would note that this is a concern that was also expressed by the Keidanren (Japanese Federation of Economic Organizations) in its December 21, 1994, letter to Diane Wood in respect of the October 1994 draft of the 1995 Guidelines.

Another notable difference between the 1995 Guidelines and the 1988 Guidelines is that the 1995 Guidelines have qualified assessment factor No. 6, and in doing so may have narrowed its application. The 1988 Guidelines did not elaborate with respect to the approach taken to the six comity assessment factors which it listed. By contrast, the 1995 Guidelines, drawing on the US Supreme Court's 1993 decision in *Hartford Fire Insurance* v. *California*,[118] state:

> With respect to the factor concerning conflict with foreign law, the Supreme Court made it clear in *Hartford Fire* that no conflict exists for the purposes of an international comity analysis in the courts if the person subject to regulation by two states can comply with the laws of both.[119]

To address the misimpression that this statement apparently created in the October 1994 draft, the final Guidelines were revised to include the welcome statement that the 'Agencies also take full account of comity factors beyond whether there is a conflict with foreign law'.[120] Notwithstanding this statement, some, including the Keidanren and the UK government, believe that the *Hartford Fire Insurance* case has given comity considerations a reduced status relative to what they had under earlier decisions such as *Timberlane*.[121]

The above-noted CBA commentary also questioned why, if comity is to be given serious consideration, the draft Guidelines (and now the final Guidelines) required a greater degree of compulsion on the part of foreign governments than is required in respect of actions which are protected by the 'state action' doctrine as applied to US states. The CBA commentary pointed to the fact that the ABA's Antitrust Law Section NAFTA Task Force took the position that there should be a policy of mutual respect regarding government involvement defences by applying such defences in the same manner to actions and policies of governmental authorities in other NAFTA countries as is provided to the actions and policies of that country's own governmental authorities.[122]

The narrowing of the role of comity would be of particular concern to Canada. There is little doubt that if the US government were to adopt a position in the future similar to that taken in respect of the *Institut Mérieux* case discussed below, there would be in all likelihood a very vigorous protest from the Canadian government. Moreover, there would likely be considerable strain to the bridges of cooperation which have developed over the last number of years between Canada and the United States in relation to their operational activities in transborder antitrust investigations.

The various substantive changes from the position articulated in the 1988 Guidelines, as well as the more aggressive overall tone of the 1995 Guidelines, have led a number of commentators to raise a concern that the Guidelines reflect a troublesome extension of the US 'long arm' approach to international antitrust enforcement. The implication for business persons is that anyone involved in (1) global markets, (2) exports to the United States – even if through an intermediary, (3) sales to US agencies or US-funded agencies abroad; or (4) activity which may have an anti-competitive effect on the ability of US firms to penetrate a foreign market, would be well advised to seek the advice of experienced antitrust counsel before pursuing such conduct. This is particularly the case with respect to conduct which may affect US exports, as this result may be quite inadvertent.

Recent cases

United States v. *MCI Corporation and BT Forty-Eight Company*, Civ. No. 94-1317 TFH (D.D.C. 1994) (Settled by Consent Decree With DOJ)

1 Basis for jurisdiction: MCI is a US corporation. BT Forty-Eight Company is a British corporation that transacts business in the United States either directly or through its wholly-owned subsidiaries.
2 Anti-competitive harm alleged: substantial lessening of competition in *foreign* commerce.
   (a) BT will have increased incentive and ability to use its market power in the United Kingdom to discriminate in favour of MCI against other telecommunications providers, lessening competition for US–UK international telecommunications services and seamless global telecommunications services.
   (b) BT will have increased incentive and ability to provide MCI with confidential and competitively sensitive information from MCI's competitors, lessening competition in the United States.
   (c) BT will have increased incentive and ability to favour MCI over its competitors in the allocation of international telecommunications traffic from the United Kingdom, substantially lessening competition in the United States.
3 Outcome: case settled by consent decree, *inter alia*, facilitating access of MCI's competitors to the UK market. Among the provisions was prohibition against MCI providing seamless service through BT unless BT provided comparable access to MCI's competitors. In addition, terms of transactions and linkage between BT and MCI must be made available to DOJ with further disclosure to other carriers seeking to provide international connections through BT.
4 Anne Bingaman indicates substantial discussions were held with UK OFTEL and that the agency was aware of injunctive provisions.

United States v. *S. C. Johnson & Son Inc. and Bayer AG,* CA No. 94-50249 (N.D. Ill 1994) (household insecticides) (Section 1 case)

1 Basis for jurisdiction: S. C. Johnson is a US corporation. Bayer, a German corporation, conducts business through a US subsidiary.
2 Anti-competitive harm alleged: licensing agreements for insecticide ingredient reduced Bayer's incentive to compete with S. C. Johnson in the

manufacture and sale of household insecticides in the United States, and competition generally in that market has been unreasonably restrained.

3 Outcome: case settled by consent decree barring exclusive licensing. S. C. Johnson prohibited from acquiring exclusive licence for insecticide ingredient from licensor anywhere in the world for use in United States without prior approval of DOJ.

United States v. *Pilkington plc and Pilkington Holdings Inc.*, Civ. No. 94-345 TUC (WDB) (D. Ariz. 1994) (glass technology)

1 Basis for jurisdiction: Pilkington Holdings is a wholly-owned American subsidiary of Pilkington plc, both doing business in the United States.

2 Anti-competitive harm alleged: violations of ss. 1 and 2 of the *Sherman Act* by restraining exports of float glass design and construction services by enforcing territorial patent and other intellectual property restraints through licence agreements entered into long ago.

3 Outcome: consent order entered into with DOJ enjoining the Defendants from asserting claims of proprietary technology against US licensees' to prevent their use of float glass technology disclosed or licensed to Pilkington. An exception exists as to trade secrets protected under 'applicable law'.

United States v. *General Motors Corp. and ZF Friedrichshafen AG et al.*, CA No. 93-530 (D. Del. 1993) (heavy automatic transmissions)

1 Basis for jurisdiction: General Motors is a US corporation. ZF is a German corporation that transacts business in the United States through its US directly or indirectly wholly-owned subsidiaries.

2 Anti-competitive harm alleged: elimination of actual and potential competition for the manufacture and sale of automatic transmissions for transit buses in the United States and elimination of worldwide competition in technological innovation in the design, development and production of heavy automatic transmissions. Worldwide research and development market shares measured, *inter alia*, by current worldwide sales.

3 Outcome: transaction abandoned. DOJ indicated that German Cartel Office was conducting a simultaneous investigation of the transaction and that coordination as to process and timing occurred.[123]

United States v. *Microsoft Corp.*, Civ. No. 94-1564 (55) (D.D.C. 1994)

1 Offence alleged: monopolization of worldwide market for PC operating systems through various exclusionary practices.

2 Basis for jurisdiction: Microsoft principal business in the United States.

3 DOJ coordinated with DG IV of European Commission in negotiating settlement. Microsoft facilitated cooperation by waiving confidentiality rights for exchange between enforcement agencies. European Union reportedly entered into undertaking with Microsoft containing provisions comparable to DOJ consent decree.[124]

4 Outcome: settlement, *inter alia*, limits term of exclusive licences and prohibits per processor licence. US District Court disapproved settlement and DOJ appealed. Settlement upheld on appeal. *United States* v. *Microsoft Corp.*, No. 95-5037, 95-5039 (D.C. Cir. June 16, 1995).

Ability to obtain information unilaterally

While the US and Canadian governments have historically had tools for gathering information from another jurisdiction more or less unilaterally, such as international discovery and letters rogatory, these are a poor substitute for the cooperation that is now taking place. Such tools often rely on the willingness of foreign governments to allow such information-gathering to take place.[125] Questions of jurisdiction, comity, the existence of blocking statutes and the delay associated with pursuing letters rogatory mean that cooperative information-sharing results in much more effective antitrust enforcement than one country trying to do it alone.

Effecting service outside the country raises threshold questions of jurisdiction in both the United States and Canada. Further, attempts at international discovery face, in Canada, the possibility of frustration because of the existence of blocking statutes.[126] Blocking statutes are so-called because they can be used to prohibit firms and persons from supplying information to foreign authorities. In Canada, blocking statutes exist at both the federal level, the *Foreign Extraterritorial Measures Act* (the 'Federal Act'), and at the provincial level in both Ontario and Quebec. In the Federal Act, the Attorney General of Canada may make an order precluding production of documents and other acts where a foreign tribunal (which includes a foreign authority which has authority to take or receive information) is exercising or proposing to exercise jurisdiction or powers of a kind that adversely affect or are likely to adversely affect 'significant Canadian interests in relation to international trade or commerce involving a business carried on in whole or in part in Canada' or 'otherwise has infringed or is likely to infringe Canadian sovereignty'.[127]

Letters rogatory ('letters of request') are issued by a court of one country and request a foreign court to invoke its powers in aid of an investigation in the first country. A number of conditions must be satisfied before they are issued and, in the foreign court, before they are enforced through the issuance of compulsory process (such as an order requiring the production of documents). They are comparatively slow, sometimes taking months between the issue of the request and its enforcement in the other jurisdiction.

They are still available to be used, and it appears that the mechanism enforcing letters rogatory has been used in the context of an MLAT request.[128] However, they do not offer the speed or the assurances ensured through obtaining information from a cooperative antitrust agency in the other country.

Trend towards acceptance of the effects test outside the United States

Footnote 51 to the 1995 Guidelines states that 'international recognition of the "effects doctrine" of jurisdiction has become more widespread'. In support of this, the 1995 Guidelines refer to the 'implementation' test that has been adopted by the European Court of Justice, as well as 'the merger laws of the European Union, Canada, Germany, France, Australia, and the Czech and Slovak Republics'.

The American Bar Association's commentary on the October 1994 draft of the 1995 Guidelines takes the position that the 1995 Guidelines overstate the extent to which the effects test has been embraced outside the United States. For example, the ABA commentary notes:

> Although many jurisdictions apply variations of the effects doctrine in cases involving in-bound foreign cartel behaviour, there is no comparable international consensus on the applicability of the effects doctrine to cases involving restrictions on export commerce.

The ABA's commentary further observes:

> [T]he distinction between the 'effects' test and the European Court of Justice's 'implementation' test leads to different results in a narrow, but significant, group of cases. In particular, that group of cases includes those involving ... 'wholly-foreign' conduct that satisfies the jurisdictional test of the FTAIA.[129]

A similar observation was made in the UK government's commentary on the 1995 Guidelines, which further noted:

> It is only under the US interpretation of the 'effects doctrine' that commercial actions that are not implemented within US territory, such as those cited in Examples C and F, are, nevertheless, regarded as falling within US jurisdiction.

The commentary of the Japan Federation of Economic Organizations made essentially the same point in observing that 'it is only the U.S. which extends the "effect doctrine" to a conduct having effect on its export commerce, and no other major countries [have] adopted such an approach'.

In Canada, the trend would appear to be towards embracing the 'effects' test. For example, in its 1979 *amicus curiae* brief in the *Uranium Cartel* litigation,[130] the Canadian government made the following submission:

> The Canadian Government submits that there is no legal basis in international law for the extraterritorial application of United States antitrust laws to the activities of non-United States nationals taken outside the United States in accordance with the laws and policies of other countries. Such action by United States courts would constitute a direct challenge to Canadian sovereignty.

In contrast, thirteen years later in its *amicus curiae* brief in *Hartford Insurance,* the Canadian government asserted:[131]

> Canada's concern does not lie with the tradition in U.S. antitrust enforcement whereby U.S. jurisdiction reaches some persons and conduct that are extraterritorial to the United States. Where Canadian law and policy applied in Canada are compatible with U.S. extraterritorial enforcement, no conflict need arise. Both Canada and the United States are committed to a policy of generally promoting competition and consumer welfare.

Unfortunately, there is no jurisprudence in the competition law area in Canada where the 'effects' test has been addressed. However, the approach that Canadian courts have taken in a number of cases outside the competition law area suggests that they will likely endorse the effects test in the competition law area.[132]

For its part, the Bureau has been quite willing in a number of cases to seriously consider exercising jurisdiction in respect of mergers occurring outside Canada. These include the acquisition of Square D Company by Schneider in May 1991, the proposal by Newell Company to purchase shares of The Stanley Works and the acquisition by Gillette of certain of Wilkinson Sword's worldwide businesses. However, the Bureau has not yet formally pursued a merger or other conduct that has taken place wholly outside Canada.[133]

Disadvantages of unilateral action

The principal drawbacks of the unilateral exercise of jurisdiction by one nation in respect of conduct occurring in another nation are:

1 It has substantial potential for seriously undermining good working relations that may have developed between enforcement agencies in the jurisdictions concerned.
2 It will often be less effective than a more cooperative approach.
3 It may be conducive to converting competition policy into a trade weapon, or to creating the perception that it is being used as a trade weapon.

For example, if US antitrust enforcement agencies actually exercise jurisdiction in an overly aggressive manner not consistent with international comity principles, and without sufficient sensitivity to concerns which may exist as a result of the governmental policies of other jurisdictions, there could be much greater disharmony and much less cooperation in international antitrust enforcement than the 1995 Guidelines appear to contemplate achieving.

In this respect the UK government stated, in its aforementioned comments on the draft 1995 Guidelines:

> the Agencies' approach to comity and personal jurisdiction can be expected to lead to more frequent confrontation with other sovereign states and in appropriate cases to action being taken by states to protect their national interests.

However, in the press release which accompanied the 1995 Guidelines on April 5, 1995, Assistant Attorney General Anne Bingaman stated that: 'the Guidelines also reaffirm our commitment to cooperation with foreign antitrust agencies – cooperation is mutually beneficial to our antitrust goals'. It is hoped that this commitment will lead the DOJ and FTC to resolve extraterritorial issues that arise from time to time on a cooperative, consultative basis, rather than on a litigious basis.

As noted in the ABA's Antitrust Law Section NAFTA Task Force Report, one way of reducing the scope for such tensions is to pursue positive comity.[134] Positive comity is where one country takes enforcement action in its jurisdiction at the request of another country.

Another way of reducing friction is to rely to a greater extent on information-sharing and other forms of cooperation between enforcement agencies. The 1995 Guidelines, like the 1988 Guidelines, suggest that, where effective relief is difficult to obtain, an effort will be made to address the matter by coordinating efforts with foreign authorities. From the perspective of foreign authorities, this is preferable to the situation that occurred in *Institut Mérieux*.[135] In that case, the FTC split 3:2 in favour of imposing an order, albeit ultimately on a consent basis, which governs the terms of a lease of certain facilities wholly located in Canada, as a result of the acquisition of certain assets in Canada. Neither party to the merger maintained relevant production facilities or substantial distribution assets in the United States. In their dissenting opinion two commissioners would have declined to exercise jurisdiction, having regard to principles of comity and the difficulty of obtaining effective relief over assets wholly located in another country. The dissenting opinion also noted that the exercise of jurisdiction was inconsistent with one of the examples (Case 4) referred to in the 1988 Guidelines. The merger had not been challenged by the Bureau, although in the end the Investment Canada agency oversaw the terms upon which the assets in Canada could be disposed.

At the extreme, the unilateral approach to enforcement can result in poisoning the relations between two nations to the point that the target nation begins to perceive that antitrust policy is being converted into a trade weapon. This is a concern that was raised in the comments of both the Japan Federation of Economic Organizations and the UK government on the October 1994 draft of the 1995 Guidelines. Once this perception is raised, it obviously becomes much more difficult to pursue legitimate policy initiatives, let alone work towards developing a cooperative working relationship.

LOOKING FORWARD

Agencies will continue to explore better means of information-sharing

Given the enforcement challenges now facing international antitrust authorities, the US–Canada model of cooperation and information-sharing has not worked badly. There have been both formal and informal examples of cooperation and information-sharing since the MLAT and the MOU came into force and there is substantial latitude for expanding the level of cooperation and information-sharing based on publicly available information. Antitrust authorities in both jurisdictions clearly understand business concerns respecting confidentiality and both enjoy a good record of maintaining information in confidence when asked to do so, in each case consistent with their statutory obligations.

There is a general consensus among antitrust enforcement officials, past and present, that the limits imposed by confidentiality restrictions on cooperation inhibit effective cooperation to a non-trivial extent.[136]

The OECD project

The Competition Law and Policy Committee of the Organization for Economic Cooperation and Development is in the process of examining whether to issue a revised protocol for sharing confidential information among member-state enforcement agencies. Although the OECD has no power to implement any such protocol, of course, its work in the area of antitrust cooperation and convergence has been extensive and well received and it can be anticipated that its recommendations concerning information-sharing will achieve considerable respect.

US marketing of the IAEAA

To date, no agreements authorized by the US IAEAA have been reached. Representatives of the DOJ have been in almost continuous meetings with numerous foreign counterparts to elucidate the characteristics of the legislation and to explain the objectives of the United States in entering into agreements.[137]

As can be seen from the discussion of the IAEAA, the United States is exhibiting increased sensitivity to concerns regarding the confidentiality of shared information. This sensitivity, however, seems limited for now to the possible compromising of confidential information by foreign authorities. Not surprisingly, businesses are also troubled by the security that will be accorded their trade secrets that non-US agencies turn over to the DOJ or FTC. It is certain that, in negotiations with the United States leading up to agreements under the IAEAA, downstream safeguards to be applied by the United States to materials received by DOJ or FTC will be a central topic.

Canadian initiatives

When the Director issued the Draft Bulletin on confidentiality in 1994 a number of commentators, including the CBA, took issue with the Director's stated interpretation of s. 29 of the Canadian Act. In particular, while acknowledging the importance of international cooperation, the CBA expressed the view that the Director was not entitled to provide information to foreign agencies under any circumstances by virtue of s. 29.[138]

The Director subsequently indicated that he would not be finalizing the Draft Bulletin and would instead, in the interests of achieving clarity and certainty in this area, be pursuing statutory amendments to clarify his power to engage in international cooperation and information-sharing. While broad consultations are expected as part of the process of developing amendments, it is to be hoped that such amendments will not only clarify the Director's authority to engage in information-sharing, but also strengthen the confidentiality assurances that are provided to businesses with respect to downstream disclosure of information. The IAEAA is an excellent model and it is to be expected that it will be drawn upon in preparing the Canadian amendments.

Constituent support will/should grow when alternatives are considered

As discussed earlier,[139] a number of business representatives in the United States have expressed serious concern with the manner in which the IAEAA may be implemented. Those concerns have focused predominantly on the downstream confidentiality of sensitive business information, however, they have also included the use of information by foreign authorities for purposes unrelated to legitimate competition purposes and exposure to draconian penalties not contemplated under US law.[140]

Concurrently, foreign business firms have voiced their worries that the IAEAA approach not only threatens the confidentiality of trade secrets but serves as a launching pad for the global expansion of US antitrust.[141] In fact, it is not unlikely that the principal fear of non-US business is of aggressive antitrust enforcement.

However well founded these misgivings, they must be balanced against consideration of what the likely course of enforcement will be in the absence of reciprocal cooperation. When it is realized that not only the US agencies but other nations will use whatever tools are available to enforce their competition laws, the business community may come to the conclusion that cooperation among agencies, including that facilitated by information-sharing, is in their best interests. That was evidently the view of Microsoft in its insistence that the DOJ and DG IV proceed in a coordinated fashion with the monopolization inquiry leading to the recently upheld consent decree.[142]

Essential to the realization of business support, however, are solid assurances of confidentiality, a subject to which we now turn.

Strict assurances of confidentiality are essential

Supplying information to foreign authorities should not be simply a matter of signing a treaty or a memorandum of understanding. Before any country agrees to supply another jurisdiction with confidential information it has obtained from its citizens, voluntarily or otherwise, it has a duty to obtain assurances that the other jurisdiction has rules and measures in place to ensure that the information will remain confidential. This is true whether the information is voluntarily provided or gathered using compulsory process. The rules should be simple and clear – a virtue that, while progress has been made, is still lacking in the US–Canada model. As this chapter has shown, 'knowing the rules' requires considering a number of laws, international agreements and treaties, each of which increases complexity and adds to the difficulty for businesses trying to understand the risk of disclosure, to whom disclosure will be made and in what circumstances. To the extent that businesses think the rules are unclear or create an undesirably high risk of disclosure, the enforcement efforts of agencies will suffer. In particular, the flow of voluntarily supplied information that is grist to the antitrust mill will be slowed and more frequent legal challenges to cooperation will occur. In a world that is becoming more and more competitive, businesses simply have too much to lose if their information is not kept absolutely confidential. Any steps to increasing cooperation have to account for this legitimate concern. This means that, before providing information to a foreign agency, the domestic government must be satisfied that the laws of the foreign country are at least as good as its own at ensuring confidentiality. This carries with it the responsibility to stop the flow of information in appropriate circumstances.

NOTES

1 US Assistant Attorney General Bingaman recently indicated that 'one of my highest priorities is to increase cooperation among antitrust enforcement agencies throughout the world, especially in the collection of information in cases with multi-national implications'. Anne K. Bingaman, *The Role of Antitrust in International Trade*, address before the Japan Society 10 (March 3, 1994) (hereinafter 'Bingaman Japan Society Speech') at 12. A similar comment was recently made by the Director of Investigation and Research under the Competition Act (Canada). See George N. Addy, Remarks to the Canadian Manufacturer's Association, Ottawa, Ontario, March 7, 1995, at 9.

2 Pub. L. No. 103-438, 108 Stat. 4597.

3 Reprinted in 4 Trade Reg. Rep. (CCH) ¶ 13,504 (1991).

4 Reprinted in 4 Trade Reg. Rep. (CCH) ¶ 13,503 (1995).

5 24 I.L.M. 1092.

6 The 1994 Annual Report of the Director states that Canada received two requests for assistance under the MLAT during that fiscal year, while one such request was made to the United States by Canada. In the Director's 1993 Annual Report, it is noted that Canada and the United States engaged in cooperative work under the MLAT in 'three separate inquiries'. The Canadian authors are aware of one case where a grand jury subpoena was requested by US authorities as a result of a request for assistance by Canada under the MLAT. Following the response to the subpoena, the US authorities commenced their own investigation into the activities of the subject companies. The Canadian authors understand that the subpoena made no reference to the fact that the information would be supplied to the Canadian authorities.

7 S.C., chapter C-30 (1985) (Can.) (4th Supp.).

8 R.S.C., chapter C-46 (1985) (as amended).

9 Section 126(1) of the *Criminal Code* provides that everyone who, without lawful excuse, contravenes a federal statute by wilfully doing anything that it forbids is, unless a punishment is expressly provided by law, guilty of an indictable offence and liable to imprisonment for two years.

10 See the commentary of the National Competition Law Section of the Canadian Bar Association on the Director's Draft Information Bulletin respecting confidentiality of information under the Canadian Act, infra, note 13. Further, the reference to 'a Canadian law enforcement agency' implicitly suggests that disclosure to other branches of government in Canada that are not involved in law enforcement is not permitted under s. 29.

11 Director of Investigation and Research, *Confidentiality of Information under the Competition Act*, (Draft Information Bulletin, released July 22, 1994).

12 See, for example, the Draft Bulletin, at 14. The Director did not alter his interpretation of s. 29 in his May 1995 statement (the '1995 Statement') entitled *Confidentiality of Information under the Competition Act*, which was issued in lieu of a finalized Information Bulletin. In the 1995 Statement, the Director states that 'information in the Director's possession may be provided to a foreign law enforcement agency where the Bureau and the foreign agency are working on the same matter and where the Director determines that communication of the information to the foreign agency would assist him in advancing his investigation' (at 3–4). Also see the Director's remarks in Private Rights in the Public Interest under Canada's *Competition Act*: Procedural Guarantees and the Independence of the Director of Investigation and Research, Remarks before the Fordham Corporate Law Institute 12 (October 21–22, 1993).

The Director has commented that disclosure occurs only for the purposes of obtaining information with respect to an investigation on that particular matter, as opposed to generalized 'horse trading' of information on one matter in exchange for information respecting another matter. See the Draft Bulletin, at 14, and the 1995 Statement, at 3. A contrary interpretation would dilute, if not completely eradicate, any benefit from s. 29 at all.

13 Canadian Bar Association, 'Commentary on the Draft Information Bulletin of the Director of Investigation and Research Respecting Confidentiality of Information under the *Competition Act*', December 1994.

14 See the 1995 Statement, cited in note 12, at 2.

15 See, e.g., *Canada (Director of Investigation and Research)* v. *Southam et al.*, 38 C.P.R. 3d 390 (1991) (Competition Tribunal). Also see *Rubin* v. *Clerk of the Privy Council* 2 F.C. 391 (1993), in which the Federal Court Trial Division expressed a similar conclusion with respect to s. 35(1) of the *Access to Information Act* (Canada) (the 'AIA'), which provides that 'every investigation of a complaint under this Act by the Information Commissioner shall be conducted in private'.

16 See the Draft Bulletin at 9 and the 1995 Statement at 1.

17 Additional restrictions may come from the application of the *Canadian Charter of Rights and Freedoms* (the 'Charter'). For example, even though s. 29 permits disclosure of information gathered using a search warrant under the Act where such disclosure is for the purposes of the administration or enforcement of the Act, disclosure of such information to US antitrust authorities may violate the Charter. In addition, it has been argued that the AIA, which grants private citizens the right to obtain information in the possession of the government, implicitly imposes a duty on the government to refrain from disclosing information that is exempt from disclosure. See the commentary of the Canadian Bar Association, cited in note 13, *supra*, on the Draft Bulletin.

18 41 C.P.R. (3d) 34 (1992).

19 In both the Draft Bulletin and the subsequent 1995 Statement, the Director indicated that undertakings might be given in rare circumstances, justified on a case-by-case basis. In the absence of unusual circumstances, the Director has said that he will not provide undertakings. Undertakings are typically provided in a letter to the Bureau confirming an understanding of the commitments the Director is making.

20 Thus the legally binding nature of such obligations is not free from doubt. See P.W. Hogg, *Liability of the Crown* 169–72 (2d ed. 1989).

21 Such orders were obtained, for example, in *Southam*, note 15, *supra* at 390. See *Canada (Director of Investigation and Research)* v. *Hillsdown Holdings (Canada) et al.*, CT-91/1, May 23, 1991.

22 See, e.g., the decisions of the Competition Tribunal in *Hillsdown* and *Southam. Ibid.*

23 This chapter will deal particularly with the federal antitrust enforcement agencies – the Department of Justice Antitrust Division and the Federal Trade Commission. The confidentiality limitations self-imposed by the state antitrust agencies, particularly the offices of the state attorneys-general, are beyond the scope of this chapter; however, the disclosure of information to the state agencies can be somewhat instructive with regard to the disclosure of information by the federal antitrust agencies to their foreign counterparts.

24 15 U.S.C. §18a(h) (1988).

25 15 U.S.C. §1313(c)(3) (1988).

26 15 U.S.C. §57b-2 (1988).

27 18 U.S.C. §1905 (1988).

28 Fed. R. Crim. P. 6(e).

29 15 U.S.C. §18(a) (1988).

30 15 U.S.C. §18 (1988).

31 752 F.2d 116 (5th Cir. 1985).

32 *Lieberman* v. *Federal Trade Commission* 771 F.2d 32 (2nd Cir. 1985).

33 See, e.g., Senate Comm. on Rules and Admin., 102d Cong., 1st Sess., Senate Manual 53 (1992).

34 US Department of Justice, *Justice Department Announces New Procedure to Coordinate Merger Antitrust Investigation with States* (March 6, 1992) (press release); FTC Announcement, 57 Fed. Reg. 21795 (1992).

35 That provision provides: 'Except as otherwise provided in this section, while in the position of the custodian, no documentary material, answers to interrogatories, or transcripts of oral testimony, or copies thereof, so produced shall be available for examination, without the consent of the person who produced such material, answers, or transcripts, and, in the case of any product of discovery produced pursuant to an express demand for such material, of the person for whom the discovery was obtained by any individual other than a duly authorized official, employee, or agent of the Department of Justice. Nothing in this section is intended to prevent disclosure to either body of the Congress or to any authorized committee or subcommittee thereof'

36 *In re Emprise Corporation*, 344 F. Supp. 319 (W.D.N.Y. 1972).

37 15 U.S.C. §46 (1988).

38 Commission regulations undertake to define 'trade secrets and commercial and financial information' to apply to: 'Competitively sensitive information, such as costs or various types of sales statistics and inventories. It includes trade secrets in the nature of formulas, patterns, devices, and processes of manufacture as well as names of customers in which there is a proprietary or highly competitive interest.' 16 C.F.R. §4.10(a)(2).

39 15 U.S.C. §57b−2(b)(1) (1988).

40 That section provides: 'Except as otherwise provided in this section, while in the possession of the custodian, no documentary material, reports or answers to questions, and transcripts of oral testimony shall be available for examination by any individual other than a duly authorized officer or employee of the Commission without the consent of the person who produced the material or transcripts. Nothing in this section is intended to prevent disclosure to either House of the Congress or to any committee or subcommittee of the Congress, except that the Commission immediately shall notify the owner or provider of any such information of a request for information designated as confidential by owner or provider.' 15 U.S.C. §57b−2(b)(3)(C) (1988).

41 15 U.S.C. §57b−2(b)(D)(6) (1988).

42 15 U.S.C. §50 (1988).

43 18 U.S.C. §1905 (1988).

44 Fed. R. Crim. P. 6(e).

45 See Notes of Advisory Committee on Rules, Fed. R. Crim. P. 6(e).

46 *In re Fed Grand Jury Witness (Lemieux)*, 597 F.2d 116, 1168 (9th Cir. 1979).

47 See Note, *Disclosure of Grand Jury Materials to Foreign Authorities under Federal Rule of Criminal Procedure 6(e)*, 70 Va. L. Rev. 1623, 1629 (1979) (citing *Douglas Oil Co.* v. *Petrol Stops Northwest*, 441 U.S. 211 (1979) and *United States* v. *Baggot*, 463 U.S. 476 (1983)).

48 *Smith* v. *United States*, 423 U.S. 1303, 1304–5 (1975), *stay vacated on other grounds*, 423 U.S. 810 (1975); *United States* v. *Sells Engineering*, 463 U.S. 418, 431–5 (1983).

49 See, e.g., *United States* v. *Peters*, 791 F.2d 1270 (7th Cir. 1986), certificate denied, 479 U.S. 847 (1987).

50 See *Disclosure of Grand Jury Materials to Foreign Authorities under Federal Rule of Criminal Procedure 6(e)*, *supra*, note 47, and cases cited therein.

51 *Ibid.*

52 See the statutes cited at p. 159.

53 *Supra*, note 3.

54 'Offence' for Canada means an offence under the federal law of Canada that may be prosecuted upon indictment. *Supra*, note 5, Article I. However, the Canadian Minister of Justice and the Attorney General of the United States may agree, pursuant to Article III(2), to provide assistance in respect of illegal acts that otherwise do not constitute an offence.

55 *Ibid.* Article II.2.

56 Article XIII.2 provides that the Requested State 'may' provide copies of such records and information. There is reason to believe that information is being exchanged on this basis. In a recent interview, Assistant Attorney General Bingaman said: 'We cooperate closely with the Canadian and EC Bureaus of Competition through appropriate exchanges of information. We have a much better agreement in the criminal area with Canada than we do with the EC; we are able to do parallel investigations and obtain confidential documents *while discussing* the matter with the Canadian officials.' Interview with Anne K. Bingaman, Assistant Attorney General, Antitrust Division, Department of Justice (October 1993), reprinted in *Antitrust*, Fall 1993, at 9. Similarly, in Canada, public statements by the Director suggest that the MLAT is being used for more than merely invoking the compulsory procedures in the other jurisdictions. The Director's 1993 Annual Report stated that assistance under the MLAT for the year then ended 'included assisting in the execution of search warrants at the premises in Canada of a firm allegedly party to felony violations of United States antitrust laws; *reviewing and providing documentary and other evidence leading to the initiation of grand jury investigations in the United States*; and, requesting the Antitrust Division to obtain documentary evidence from U.S. corporate offices by compulsory procedures' (emphasis added). The italicized portion of this quotation is at least consistent with providing information that was not obtained using compulsory processes, unlike the first and third examples cited.

57 Department of Justice Canada, *Law Enforcement in the Global Village* 25 (1990) (A Manual for Mutual Legal Assistance in Criminal Matters).

58 At the same time, for practical purposes, it is the Bureau which engages in most front-line investigations and communications.

59 Article VI.3.

60 Article VI.4. As indicated below, this would not override s. 29 of the Canadian Act, which would prohibit the disclosure of information gathered by the Bureau under the compulsory process of the Act's provisions (e.g. under the search powers in the Canadian Act). However, it would not prohibit the voluntary disclosure of information to the Bureau. It is an interesting question whether a court order in Canada would have the affect of overriding any assurances provided by the Bureau with respect to disclosure of information voluntarily supplied to the Bureau. Given Canada's obligations under the MLAT, it is not

clear that the Bureau could resist disclosing information if it would be responsive to a request for additional information from the United States.

61 Article VI.5 of the MLAT requires the Requested State to 'use its best efforts to keep confidential a request and its contents'. However, this obligation does not apply when 'otherwise authorized by the Requesting State'. Further, Article IX.2 provides that the Requesting State shall not 'disclose or use information or evidence furnished for purposes other than those stated in a request'. Once again, this can be overruled if the prior consent of the Requested State is obtained. Finally, Article VII.2 of the MLAT requires that a request 'shall be executed in accordance with the law of the Requested State'. In that regard, s. 3(1) of the MLAA provides that the provisions of any federal statute which prohibits the disclosure of information take precedence over the provisions of the MLAA. As noted earlier, the Director takes the position that the confidentiality provisions of the Canadian Act do not preclude him from providing information to the US agencies where to do so would advance a particular investigation.

62 Article II.4.

63 A former Director indicated in 1992 that Canada's first use of the MLAT was in 1992, when there were two requests. See H.I. Wetston, Developments and Emerging Challenges in Canadian Competition Law, Remarks at the Fordham Law Institute (October 22, 1992) at 22. The 1993 Annual Report of the Director discloses that during the year ended March 31, 1993, there were three outstanding MLAT requests. The Canadian authors believe that this included the two requests referred to by the former Director in 1992.

64 Article III.2 of the MLAT provides that the parties may provide assistance pursuant to other agreements, arrangements or practices. A significant amount of information-sharing can and does go on between antitrust authorities respecting general antitrust theory and disclosure of publicly available information.

65 *Supra*, note 4, at paragraph 1.

66 Paragraph 2(2).

67 *Supra*, note 3.

68 The MOU does not define 'national interests'. It simply notes that 'such interests would normally be reflected in antecedent laws, decisions or statements of policy by the competent authorities' (Article 6.)

69 Such safeguards are a matter of agreement between the parties, not law. In this regard, paragraph 10(1) of the MOU provides that: '(1) The issues of confidentiality that arise in exchanges of information between the Parties are acknowledged to be matters of importance, and each Party will use its best efforts to assure confidentiality to the extent consistent with its national law. The Parties agree that the degree to which either Party discloses information to the other pursuant to this Understanding may be subject to and dependent upon the acceptability of the assurances given by the others with respect to confidentiality and with respect to the purposes for which the information will be used. Each party will oppose, to the extent possible under its laws, any application for disclosure not authorized by the other. In addition, the Parties recognize that there may be limitations imposed by their laws on the disclosure by one party to the other of certain classes of information each possesses.'

70 Letter dated April 26, 1995, to Calvin Goldman from Milos Barutciski, Special Adviser (International Affairs) to the Director of Investigation and Research.

71 *Ibid.*

72 *Supra* note 2, §§ 8(a) and 12(1)(A).

73 *Ibid.* § 12(2)(B).
74 *Ibid.* § 3(a).
75 *Ibid.* §§ 8(a) and 12(1)(A).
76 *Ibid.* § 12(2)(B).
77 H.R. Rep. No. 772, 103rd Cong., 2d Sess., 20 (1994).
78 H.R. 4781, *International Antitrust Enforcement Assistance Act* of 1994; Hearing of the Subcomm. on Economic and Commercial Law, House Comm. on the Judiciary, 103d Cong., 2d Sess., August 8, 1994 'IAEAA Subcomm. Hearings' (Statement of Anne K. Bingaman, at 3–4).
79 See 'Fine Levied under the *Competition Act* in Joint Canada–U.S. Investigation', Bureau of Competition Policy News Release NR-11526/94-15 (July 12, 1994).
80 'Antitrust Division Breaks International Price Fixing Conspiracy in Fax Paper Industry', Department of Justice Press Release (July 14, 1994).
81 'Antitrust Division Breaks Price Fixing Conspiracy in Disposable Plastic Dinnerware Industry', Department of Justice Release (June 9, 1994).
82 MLAT, at Article VI.4.
83 The Director recently indicated that, outside of providing information to law enforcement agencies to assist their investigations, the Bureau does not disclose information to other government departments. In a recent reorganization of the federal government, the Bureau was made a part of what is now called Industry Canada. Remarking on the reorganization, the Director has said the 'reorganization of government departments has not fettered the independence of the [Director]. We do *not* share confidential information with other sectors of the department'. George N. Addy, *Remarks to the Canadian Bar Association National Competition Law Section* (October 1, 1993), at 8 (emphasis in original). The Canadian authors are aware that the Bureau typically provides its views with respect to certain mergers to the branch of Industry Canada that conducts reviews under the *Investment Canada Act* (Canada). However, such communications do not involve providing such government officials with confidential information.
84 MOU, paragraph 9.
85 R.S.C., chapter C-5, §§37–9 (1985). This privilege was recognized in *Canada (Director of Investigation and Research)* v. *Southam et al.*, *supra*, note 15.
86 *Canada (Director of Investigation and Research)* v. *Chrysler*, CT-88-4 Document No. 180, July 5, 1989, at 4.
87 See *Middlekamp* v. *Fraser Valley Real Estate Board*, 96 D.L.R. (4th) 223 (1992) (British Columbia Court of Appeal).
88 Subsection 16(4) of the AIA.
89 With some very limited exceptions, s. 20 requires the government to refuse to disclose information that contains: (a) trade secrets of a third party; (b) financial, commercial, scientific or technical information that is confidential information supplied to a government institution by a third party and is treated consistently in a confidential manner by the third party; (c) information the disclosure of which could reasonably be expected to result in material financial loss or gain to, or could reasonably be expected to prejudice the competitive position of, a third party; or (d) information the disclosure of which could reasonably be expected to interfere with contractual or other negotiations of a third party.
90 Subsection 27(1) of the AIA.
91 15 U.S.C. §552.
92 See the HSR Act, §18a(h); see also the FTC Act, §57-2(f), which provides: '(f) Exemption from Disclosure. Any material which is received by the

Commission in any investigation, a purpose of which is to determine whether any person may have violated any provision of the laws administered by the Commission, and which is provided pursuant to any compulsory process under sections 41 to 46 and 47 to 58 of this title or which is provided voluntarily in place of such compulsory process shall be exempt from disclosure under section 552 of Title 5.'

93 5 U.S.C. §552b(c) (1988).
94 509 U.S. 764 (1993).
95 *Ibid.*
96 148 F. 2d 416 at 444 (2nd Cir. 1945).
97 15 U.S.C. § 6(a) (1988).
98 Reproduced in 4 Trade Reg. Rep. (CCH) ¶ 13, 109 (1988).
99 Department of Justice Policy Regarding Anti-Competitive Conduct that Restricts US Exports, Reprinted in 62 Antitrust & Trade Reg. Rep. 483 (April 9, 1992).
100 *Ibid.*
101 *Ibid.*
102 1995 Guidelines at §3.1.
103 §3.1.
104 §3.11.
105 §3.121.
106 *Ibid.*
107 See, e.g., 16 C.F.R. 801.50–2.
108 §3.14.
109 §3.122.
110 §3.122.
111 §3.13.
112 §4.1.
113 §4.2.
114 American Bar Association (Section of Antitrust Law and Section of International Law and Practice), 'Comments on the Proposed Department of Justice and Federal Trade Commission Enforcement Guidelines for International Operations (1994)' at 36.
115 1988 Guidelines, at §5.
116 *Ibid.* In this regard, the 1988 Guidelines gave as an example the termination, based on foreign policy grounds, of a grand jury investigation into passenger air travel between the United States and the United Kingdom. *Ibid.* at §5, note 171 (citing US Department of Justice Press Release, November 19, 1984).
117 549 F.2d 597 (9th Cir. 1976).
118 *Supra*, note 94.
119 1995 Guidelines at §3.2.
120 *Ibid.*
121 In *Hartford Fire Insurance*, the Court split 5:4 in favour of permitting certain antitrust claims to proceed which were brought by nineteen US states as well as several private plaintiffs under the *Sherman Act* alleging conspiracies among certain London, UK, insurers and reinsurers regarding terms of liability insurance policies made available in the United States. In that case, both the UK government and the Canadian government had filed *amicus curiae* briefs in support of the position of the London insurers. The UK brief argued that the plaintiff's complaint under the *Sherman Act* was completely inconsistent with the requirements of UK law. The majority of the US Supreme Court decided, however, that comity considerations could not be invoked to block the

proceedings because, in its view, the critical question was whether there was a true conflict between US and foreign law; in this respect, there would not be any such conflict if the defendants could have complied with both US law and foreign law simultaneously. In the dissenting opinion, written by Justice Scalia, there was a great deal of direct and specific concern expressed about the majority's narrow application of the comity principles.

122 *Report of the Task Force of the Antitrust Section of the American Bar Association on the Competition Dimension of the North American Free Trade Agreement* (July 20, 1994) at pp. 165–74 and 193.

123 See Address by Deputy Assistant Attorney General Diane P. Wood, *International Enforcement at the Antitrust Division*, before the Greater Cleveland International Lawyers Group, 6 (January 17, 1995).

124 See Address by Assistant Attorney General Anne K. Bingaman, *International Antitrust: A Report from the Department of Justice*, before the Fordham Corporate Law Institute, 11 (October 27, 1994).

125 However, this is not always the case. For example, it may be noted that s. 11(2) of the Canadian Act allows a Canadian court, where a Canadian corporation has a foreign affiliate which has records relevant to an inquiry under the Canadian Act, to order the Canadian corporation to produce the records. This may have the effect of requiring the Canadian corporation to exercise its influence (if any) over the foreign affiliate to supply the sought-after records.

126 See, for example, the comments on blocking statutes of Commissioner Roscoe Starek III in 'What are the limits of Antitrust Cooperation?', Prepared Remarks before the Fourth Annual Symposium on EU Mergers and Joint Ventures: New Commission/New Merger Policy, March 17, 1995, at 7, 8.

127 Orders by the Attorney General can preclude the production before, or disclosure or identification to, or for the purposes of, a foreign tribunal of records that are in the possession or under the control of a Canadian citizen. A 'record' is defined in a very broad manner – basically anything in physical form can be the subject of an order. The Attorney General can also prohibit acts that would result in the production or identification of records to the foreign tribunal or the giving by a person in Canada of information for the purposes of a foreign tribunal in relation to such records. The legislation in Ontario provides that no person shall, under the authority or in compliance with an order of a foreign judicial or administrative authority, send or cause to be sent to a point outside Ontario 'any account, balance sheet, profit and loss statement or inventory or any résumé or digest thereof or any other record, statement, report or any material in any way relating to a business carried on in Ontario' unless certain exceptions apply. Thus no decision of a government official is required before the prohibitions in the statute apply.

128 The Canadian authors are aware of one instance in which the US federal rules of procedure used for responding to letters rogatory were used to authorize a US attorney to gather information from US residents in response to a request from Canada for assistance under the MLAT.

129 Footnote 8 of the ABA's commentary cites as authority for the proposition that the European Court of Justice did not intend to embrace the 'effects' test the following: Joseph P. Griffen, 'EC and US Extra-territoriality: Activism and Cooperation', [1993] *Fordham Corp. L. Inst.* 32, at 68–70 (edited by Barry Hawk, 1994); Sir Leon Brittan, *Competition Policy and Merger Control in the Single European Market* 13 (1991); and Waltern Van Gerven, 'EC Jurisdiction in Antitrust Matters: The Wood Pulp Judgment', [1989] *Fordham Corp. L Inst.*, 451 at 466–7 (edited by Barry Hawk).

130 *In re Uranium Antitrust Litig.*, 480 F. Supp. 1138 (N.D. Ill. 1979).
131 Brief of the Government of Canada as Amicus Curiae in Support of Certain Petitioners, dated November 19, 1992, filed in the Supreme Court of the United States in *Hartford Fire Insurance Co.* v. *California.*
132 C.S. Goldman, G.P. Cornish and R.F.D. Corley, 'International Mergers and the Canadian Competition Act', (July 1993) *International Antitrust Laws* 31.301 at 31.312.
133 The Bureau's willingness to exercise extraterritorial jurisdiction is also reflected in a recent address by George Addy. See *International Coordination of Competition Policies*, HWWA-Institut für Wirtschaftsforschung-Hamburg (Hamburg, October 9–11, 1991). Also see C.S. Goldman, 'Bilateral Aspects of Canadian Competition Policy', 57 *Antitrust L.J.* 401 at 414.
134 *Supra*, note 122, at pp. 230–1.
135 5 Trade Reg. Rep. (CCH) ¶ 22, 779 (August 6, 1990).
136 See, e.g., James F. Rill and Virginia R. Metallo, *The Next Step: Convergence of Procedure and Enforcement*, Address before the Fordham Corporate Law Institute 24 (1992); Bingaman Japan Society Speech, *supra* note 1, at 13. Also see Diane P. Wood, *The Internationalization of Antitrust Law: Options for the Future*, Address before the DePaul Law Review Symposium Cultural Conceptions of Competition: Antitrust in the 1990's, February 3, 1995, at 6 *et seq.*
137 As discussed in the next section, the Director has indicated publicly that he will pursue a statutory amendment to clearly articulate his statutory authority in the area of international enforcement cooperation. Such legislation has not been introduced yet, but the Director has indicated his interest in pursuing amendments in the near future.
138 The CBA's commentary is cited in note 13, *supra*.
139 See pp. 164–7.
140 IAEAA Subcommittee Hearings, *supra*, note 113 (Testimony of R. Blechman).
141 These views have been expressed by representatives of non-US firms at the OECD Competition Law and Policy Committee meeting in November 1994, at the International Chamber of Commerce antitrust meeting in November 1994 and at the International Chamber of Commerce antitrust meeting in May 1995.
142 *United States* v. *Microsoft Corp.*, 1995-1 Trade Cas. (CCH) ¶ 70, 859 (D.D.C. 1995).

ACKNOWLEDGEMENTS

James F. Rill, a partner in the law firm of Collier Shannon Rill & Scott, was the Assistant Attorney General for the Antitrust Division of the Department of Justice from July of 1989 until June of 1992. Mr Rill is grateful to his colleague, Virginia R. Metallo, for her assistance in preparing this chapter. Calvin S. Goldman is a partner in Davies Ward & Beck, Toronto. From May 1986 until October 1989 Mr Goldman was the Director of Investigation and Research, Bureau of Competition Policy, Ottawa. Mr Goldman wishes to acknowledge the valuable assistance of his partners, Joel Kissack and Paul Crampton, in the preparation of this chapter.

Part III

R&D CONSORTIA

8

COLLABORATIVE R&D AND COMPETITION POLICY

Economic analysis in the light of Japanese experience

Kotaro Suzumura and Akira Goto

INTRODUCTION

From the time of Adam Smith to the present, a common belief persists, according to which collusion on prices and quantities among rival firms is detrimental to social welfare in competitive market economies. This being the case, it seems rather peculiar that economists and policy-makers alike are now becoming quite enthusiastic about collaborative R&D through which otherwise competing firms collude on R&D activities and share their costs and benefits. It seems to us that there are at least two reasons behind this recent upsurge of enthusiasm.

First, one of the crucial features of R&D is the rapid diffusion of knowledge once generated, sometimes without compensation, hence the limited appropriability of R&D benefits. Thus collaborative R&D agreements seem to be a natural institutional arrangement which may be effective in coping with the perennial problem of free-riders. Besides, collaborative R&D agreements enable their member firms to avoid wasteful duplication of fixed costs, thus improving the efficiency of resource allocation. From the point of view of the economics of information-sharing and organizational design, therefore, it is quite natural that collaborative R&D has become a focus of serious theoretical research.

Secondly, it is widely thought that the success of Japanese firms in the technology-intensive industries is at least partly due to the widespread collaboration on R&D activities among otherwise competing firms. Various joint R&D projects, the Very Large Scale Integrated Circuit (VLSI) Joint R&D Project being a typical example, are not infrequently cited as the principal vehicle which enabled Japanese computer and semiconductor manufacturers to join the leading players in the world arena. Inspired in part by the Japanese experience, other countries and regions are becoming eager to encourage collaborative R&D among domestic firms. Thus it is of crucial importance to demystify the mechanism of joint R&D projects in Japan and their presumed efficiency.

With this background, the purpose of this chapter is to examine the role and limitations of R&D collaboration in accordance with the following plan. In the next section we examine the theoretical properties of collaborative R&D, capitalizing on some recent literature. The focus of our examination will be twofold. First, we ask whether the existence of R&D spillovers can justify R&D collaboration among oligopolistically competitive firms from the viewpoint of social welfare. Secondly, we ask whether private incentives can sustain R&D collaborations by themselves. In the following section various types of collaborative R&D in Japan are summarized, capitalizing on the 1982 Fair Trade Commission of Japan (JFTC) Survey. In the fourth section we focus on our particular type of collaborative R&D, which is known as the Technological Research Association and construed to be unique to Japan in several important respects. In the fifth section we examine the policy implications of collaborative R&D with special reference to industrial policy and competition policy. The final section concludes this chapter with some observations.

COLLABORATIVE R&D IN THE PRESENCE OF SPILLOVERS

The economics of collaborative R&D is rapidly developing, and the recent upsurge of theoretical research has uncovered several interesting properties.[1] Capitalizing on this theoretical literature, we summarize in what follows several relevant properties of R&D collaborations with special reference to their welfare performance *vis-à-vis* competitive R&D, and their sustainability through private incentives. In so doing, we plan to shed some light on the crucial role of R&D spillovers and information-sharing.

Throughout this section, our analysis is based on a model of oligopoly where firms producing homogeneous products compete in two stages. There are n firms, $2 \leqslant n < +\infty$, where n is fixed throughout this analysis.[2] In the first stage, firms decide on their cost-reducing R&D, either collaboratively or separately. They compete in the second stage in terms of quantities produced.[3] We assume that the cost-reducing benefits of R&D can be diffused to other firms which are not engaging in R&D of their own. In the presence of such R&D spillovers, there are two important questions to ask:

1 Is collaborative R&D always welfare-improving *vis-à-vis* competitive R&D?
2 Is collaborative R&D sustainable through private incentives in the sense that no single firm can secure higher pay-off by unilaterally deviating from R&D collaboration?

These questions are succinctly answered under the two alternative modes of R&D collaborations.

Collaborative R&D without full information-sharing

The first mode of R&D collaboration is pure R&D coordination without actual joint research which generates synergetic effects among member firms. In this extreme polar case, member firms simply coordinate their levels of R&D expenditure so as to maximize joint profits, but they do not share R&D information fully with each other. This institutional mode of collaboration seems to correspond to the model of R&D cooperation formulated by d'Aspremont and Jacquemin (1988).

Let the inverse demand function for the product of this industry be

$$p = f(Q) = a - bQ \qquad (1)$$

where p is the output price, $Q = \sum_{i=1}^{n} q_i$ is the aggregate output, q_i being the output of firm i $(i = 1, 2, ..., n)$, and $a > 0$ and $b > 0$ are constant parameters.[4] Let x_i denote the level of R&D expenditure by firm i and let $c(x_i; x_{-i})$ be the unit cost of production of firm i, where $x_{-i} := (x_1, ..., x_{i-1}, x_{i+1}, ..., x_n)$. The dependence of $c(x_i; x_{-i})$ on x_{-i} is meant to represent the existence of R&D spillovers. We assume that

$$c(x_i; x_{-i}) := c - x_i - \beta \sum_{j \neq i} x_j \qquad (2)$$

where $a > c > 0$, $0 \leqslant \beta \leqslant 1$, and $x_i + \beta \sum_{j \neq i} x_j \leqslant c$. In this formulation, the degree of R&D spillover is measured by the parameter β. Finally, the total cost of undertaking R&D at level x_i is assumed to be

$$\gamma(x_i) := \gamma \frac{x_i^2}{2} \qquad (3)$$

where $\gamma > 0$.

For any R&D profile $x = (x_1, ..., x_i, ..., x_n)$, the profit of firm i in the second stage when an output profile $q = (q_1, ..., q_i, ..., q_n)$ prevails is defined by

$$\pi_i(q; x_i, x_{-i}) := \{f(Q) - c(x_i; x_{-i})\} q_i - \gamma(x_i) \qquad (i = 1, 2, ..., n) \quad (4)$$

which defines a non-cooperative game among n firms, given an R&D profile x, where the pay-off function of firm i is (4) and i's strategic variable is q_i. Let $q^N(x) = (q_1^N(x), ..., q_i^N(x), ..., q_n^N(x))$ be the Cournot–Nash equilibrium of this game. We focus on the symmetrical equilibrium, and assume that $q_i^N(x) = q_j^N(x)$ holds if $x_i = x_j$ does.

199

Turning to the first stage of our game, we define the first stage pay-off function of firm i by

$$\Pi_i(x) := \pi_i(q^N(x); x_i, x_{-i}) \qquad (i = 1, 2, ..., n) \qquad (5)$$

which allows us to define two types of equilibria.

First, if firms choose their R&D levels non-cooperatively, we have a non-cooperative game among n firms where firm i's pay-off function is (5) and i's strategic variable is x_i. The Nash equilibrium of this non-cooperative game is denoted by $x^N = (x_1^N, ..., x_i^N, ..., x_n^N)$. We focus on the symmetrical Nash equilibrium, and assume that $x_i^N = x_j^N (i \neq j; i, j = 1, 2, ..., n)$ holds. The equilibrium pair $\{x^N, q^N(x^N)\}$ is none other than the *subgame perfect equilibrium* of the entire two-stage game.

Secondly, if firms choose their R&D levels cooperatively in full awareness that they compete in the second stage output game, they choose their R&D levels collaboratively so as to maximize $\sum_{j=1}^n \Pi_j(x)$ with respect to x subject to the condition that $x_i = x_j$ $(i \neq j; i, j = 1, 2, ..., n)$. Let x^C be the solution to this constrained maximization problem. Then the pair $\{x^C, q^N(x^C)\}$ is what we should expect to emerge from this institutional mode of R&D collaboration subject to competition in the product market.

It is clear that the welfare performance of this manner of R&D collaboration may be neatly gauged by comparing $\{x^N, q^N(x^N)\}$ with $\{x^C, q^N(x^C)\}$ in terms of some well defined measure of social welfare. To stay within the standard conceptual framework, the welfare measure we invoke is specified by

$$W^S(x) := W(x, q^N(x)) \qquad (6)$$

where

$$W(x, q) := \int_0^Q f(Z) \, dZ - \sum_{j=1}^n \{c(x_j; x_{-j})q_j + \gamma(x_j)\} \qquad (7)$$

which is nothing but the sum of consumer's surplus and producer's surplus.

It turns out that our results on the performance of collaborative R&D *vis-à-vis* competitive R&D from the welfare viewpoint hinge squarely on the extent of R&D spillovers. Note that, because of the existence of R&D spillovers, an increase in cost-reducing R&D by firm i exerts two conflicting effects on the equilibrium output of i's rival firm j $(i \neq j)$. On the one hand, firm i's R&D tends to increase firm j's output by bringing j's unit cost of production down through spillovers of cost-reducing benefits. On the other, firm i's R&D tends to decrease firm j's output by sharpening i's competitive edge against j. Let us say that *the R&D spillovers are sufficiently large if the former effect outweighs the latter* so that $\theta(x) := (\partial/\partial x_i)q_j^N(x) > 0$ $(i \neq j)$ holds. Under the demand and cost specifications (1), (2), (3) and (4), we can easily confirm that $\theta(x) > 0$ holds if and only if $2\beta - 1 > 0$.[5] We may now assert, capitalizing on the work of d'Aspremont and Jacquemin (1988) and Suzumura (1992), that *R&D collaboration along these lines, where firms simply coordinate their R&D levels without full information-sharing, is welfare-improving, viz. $W^S(x^C) > W^S(x^N)$ holds, if R&D spillovers are sufficiently large, but not necessarily so otherwise.*[6]

Let us now turn to our second fundamental question, viz. the question of sustainability of R&D collaboration through private incentives. According to d'Aspremont and Jacquemin (1988: 1135, emphasis added), 'To the extent that profits are higher in the case of cooperative research than in the non-cooperative game, *private incentives, independently of any public policy such as subsidies, can be sufficient to lead to such a cooperation.*' This optimistic assertion notwithstanding, our result on the performance of collaborative R&D in the first mode cannot but be rather pessimistic in this arena.

At the outset, we must introduce several definitions.[7] A *coalition* is any subset T of the set of all firms $N = \{1, ..., i, ..., n\}$. For any R&D profile x, let

$$\Pi_T(x) = \sum_{i \in T} \Pi_i(x) \tag{8}$$

which is nothing but the joint profits of firms in the coalition T when the R&D profile x prevails. A *coalition structure* is any partition of N. Any coalition structure $P = \{T_1, ..., T_k, ..., T_K\}$ naturally induces a K player non-cooperative game with the pay-off function of player k being defined by $\Pi_{T_k}(x)$ ($k = 1, 2, ..., K$). Given a coalition T and an R&D profile x, an R&D profile y is said to be a T *variant* of x if $x_i = y_i$ holds for all $i \in N - T$. We say that an R&D profile x is an *equilibrium relative to the coalition structure P* if, for all $T \in P$, $\Pi_T(x) \geqslant \Pi_T(y)$ holds for any y which is a T variant of x. Thus an equilibrium relative to the coalition structure P is nothing but a Nash equilibrium of the game in which each coalition $T \in P$ acts as a single agent.

We are now ready to clarify what we mean by the sustainability of an R&D collaboration. We say that an R&D collaboration is *sustainable through private incentives* if $\Pi_N(x_{\{N\}}) \geqslant \Pi_{\{i\}}(x_Q)$ holds true for all $i \in N$, where $\Pi_N(x_{\{N\}})$ denotes the profit earned by each firm at the equilibrium relative to the coalition structure $P = \{N\}$, and $\Pi_{\{i\}}(x_Q)$ denotes the profit earned by firm i at the equilibrium relative to the coalition structure $Q = \{\{i\}, N - \{i\}\}$. In that case, no single firm has an incentive to deviate from the R&D collaboration unilaterally, because doing so does not result in a higher profit for the deviant firm.

Despite its rather satisfactory welfare performance *vis-à-vis* competitive R&D, it is unfortunately the case that the R&D collaboration without full information-sharing is likely to be unsustainable through private incentives.

Indeed, Dutta and Suzumura (1993: Proposition 4) have shown that this mode of R&D collaboration is not sustainable for n sufficiently 'large'. Furthermore, for this result to be relevant, it is not necessary that n is unrealistically large. To exemplify this, assume that $a - c = 1$, $b = 2$ and $\gamma = 1$. It can be verified that $\Pi_N(x_{\{N\}})$ and $\Pi_{\{i\}}(x_Q)$ are given by

$$\Pi_N(x_{\{N\}}) = \frac{1}{2[(n+1)^2 - \{1 + \beta(n+1)\}^2]} \tag{9}$$

and

$$\Pi_{\{i\}}(x_Q) = \frac{8(n+1)^2}{D^2} \Delta(n; \beta), \tag{10}$$

where

$$D := 4\{[(n+1)^2 - \{n - \beta(n-1)\}^2][(n+1)^2 - \{2 + \beta(n-3)\}^2]$$
$$- (n-1)(2\beta - 1)^2\{2 + \beta(n-3)\}\{n - \beta(n-1)\}]$$

and

$$\Delta(n; \beta) := [(n+1)^2 - \{n - \beta(n-1)\}^2][(n+1) - (1 - \beta)\{2 + \beta(n-3)\}^2].$$

Table 8.1 summarizes the values of $\Pi_N(x_{\{N\}})$ and $\Pi_{\{i\}}(x_Q)$ for a fixed value of $n = 5$ and for various values of β, where $0.5 < \beta < 1$. It should be clear from this table that $n = 5$ is in fact 'large' enough for all values of β to lead to a welfare improvement through R&D collaboration *vis-à-vis* competitive R&D. We have conducted quite extensive computer simulations to confirm that this is not an accidental result of special parameter combinations, but is indeed a reflection of robust characteristics of the model.

Collaborative R&D with full information-sharing

The second polar mode of R&D collaboration is the establishment of a research association within which not only full R&D coordination but also full information-sharing takes place. As a result, strong synergetic effects among member firms are generated to the extent that the benefits from R&D conducted by any member firm accrue equally and fully to each and every other member. Non-member firms can still enjoy spillover benefits, but the extent thereof is less than that accruing to member firms. This mode of R&D collaboration corresponds to the model of R&D joint venture formulated by Kamien *et al.* (1992).

Because of full information-sharing among member firms, there will now be asymmetrical R&D spillovers among the firms. To capture this important implication of full information-sharing as neatly as possible, let $V(s)$ be the R&D collaboration with full R&D coordination and full

Table 8.1 Instability of R&D collaboration
without information-sharing

β	$\Pi_{\{i\}}(\boldsymbol{x}_Q)$	$\Pi_N(\boldsymbol{x}_{\{N\}})$
0.50	0.0185185	0.0185185
0.52	0.0188699	0.0188582
0.54	0.0192662	0.0192201
0.56	0.0197090	0.0196060
0.58	0.0201998	0.0200179
0.60	0.0207407	0.0204583
0.62	0.0213341	0.0209296
0.64	0.0219824	0.0214349
0.66	0.0226888	0.0219776
0.68	0.0234564	0.0225615
0.70	0.0242889	0.0231911
0.72	0.0251905	0.0238714
0.74	0.0261655	0.0246082
0.76	0.0272189	0.0254085
0.78	0.0283560	0.0262804
0.80	0.0295826	0.0272331
0.82	0.0309051	0.0282779
0.84	0.0323305	0.0294284
0.86	0.0338661	0.0307004
0.88	0.0355203	0.0321138
0.90	0.0373016	0.0336927
0.92	0.0392198	0.0354670
0.94	0.0412849	0.0374745
0.96	0.0435081	0.0397633
0.98	0.0459010	0.0423958
1.00	0.0484765	0.0454544

Source: Dutta and Suzumura (1993).
Note: $\Pi_{\{i\}}(\boldsymbol{x}_Q)$ and $\Pi_N(\boldsymbol{x}_{\{N\}})$ when $n = 5$, $\gamma = a - c = 1$ and $b = 2$.

information-sharing, where s denotes the number of member firms. Then the cost reducing benefits accruing to firm i should now be rewritten as $c(x_i; \boldsymbol{x}_{-i}) := c - \sum_{j=1}^{n} x_j$ if a research association $V(n)$ is formed, $c(x_i; \boldsymbol{x}_{-i}) := c - x_i - \beta \sum_{j \neq i} x_j$ if a research association $V(n-1)$ is formed, to which firm i does not belong, $c(x_i; \boldsymbol{x}_{-i}) := c - \beta x_j - \sum_{h \neq j} x_h$ if a research association $V(n-1)$ is formed, $i \in V(n-1)$ and $\{j\} = N - V(n-1)$, and so forth.

The welfare verdict on this type of R&D collaboration with full R&D coordination and full information-sharing remains essentially the same as before. We may assert that *collaborative R&D along the second mode, where member firms not only coordinate their R&D levels, but also fully* *share information, is welfare-improving, viz. $W^S(x^C) > W^S(x^N)$ holds, if R&D spillovers are sufficiently large, but not necessarily so otherwise.*[8]

It is with respect to the sustainability of R&D collaboration through private incentives that the role of full information-sharing becomes clear. After some seemingly simple yet complicated computations, we may verify that $\Pi_N(x_{\{N\}})$ and $\Pi_{\{i\}}(x_Q)$ can be derived as follows if the condition for solvability $\beta > (n-1)/n$ is satisfied:

$$\Pi_N(x_{\{N\}}) = \frac{1}{b(n+1)^2 - 2n^2} \tag{11}$$

and

$$\Pi_{\{i\}}(x_Q) = \frac{(n+1)^2}{E^2} \Gamma(n; \beta) \tag{12}$$

Table 8.2 Instability of collaborative R&D with information-sharing

β	$\Pi_{\{i\}}(x_Q)$	$\Pi_N(x_{\{N\}})$
Case 1: $b = 2$ and $\beta > 0.97$		
0.98	0.046485	0.045455
0.99	0.047515	0.045455
1.00	0.048476	0.045455
Case 2: $b = 3$ and $\beta > 0.94$		
0.95	0.017497	0.017241
0.96	0.017898	0.017241
0.97	0.018284	0.017241
0.98	0.018656	0.017241
0.99	0.019014	0.017241
1.00	0.019357	0.017241
Case 3: $b = 4$ and $\beta > 0.94$		
0.95	0.010829	0.010638
0.96	0.011022	0.010638
0.97	0.011209	0.010638
0.98	0.011390	0.010638
0.99	0.011566	0.010638
1.00	0.011736	0.010638

Source: Dutta and Suzumura (1993).
Note: $\Pi_{\{i\}}(x_Q)$ and $\Pi_N(x_{\{N\}})$ when $n = 5$ and $\gamma = a - c = 1$

where

$$E := E_1 E_2 - 4(2 - \beta)(2\beta - 1)(n - 1)^2 \{n - \beta(n - 1)\}\{n\beta - (n - 1)\} \quad (13)$$

$$E_1 := b(n + 1)^2 - 2(n - 1)^2(2 - \beta)^2 \quad (14)$$

$$E_2 := b(n + 1)^2 - 2\{n - \beta(n - 1)\}^2 \quad (15)$$

and

$$\Gamma(n; \beta)$$
$$:= [b(n + 1)^2 - 2\{n - \beta(n - 1)\}^2][b(n + 1) - 2(n - 1)^2(2 - \beta)(1 - \beta)]^2 \quad (16)$$

It is clear that the crucial condition $\beta > (n - 1)/n$ is quite stringent, in particular for large n in view of $0 < \beta < 1$ and $\lim_{n \to \infty} (n - 1)/n = 1$. For β close enough to 1 and for small enough n, however, R&D collaboration with full information-sharing may be unsustainable through private incentives. Table 8.2 exemplifies this fact when n is as small as 5. For β realistically small or for n large enough, the condition for solvability is violated, which means that there exists no profitable deviation by a single firm. It is in this sense that R&D collaboration with full information-sharing, besides being clearly welfare-improving *vis-à-vis* competitive R&D, is likely to be a more stable institutional set-up than R&D collaboration without information-sharing.

COLLABORATIVE R&D IN JAPAN: AN OVERVIEW [9]

In 1982 the Fair Trade Commission of Japan conducted an extensive survey of collaborative R&D activity among manufacturing firms, which has provided us with a succinct overview of how Japanese firms collaborate in their pursuit of R&D projects.[10] According to this survey, collaborative R&D can be classified into the following three types:

1 Signing a collaborative research contract with other firms or research institutions, and concomitantly spending R&D funds.
2 Establishing a joint venture with other firms to carry out R&D.
3 Participating in a research association organized under the Law on Technological Research Associations in Mining and Manufacturing Industries.

It should be noted that collaborative R&D activities of firms with their own subsidiaries, which are defined as firms whose parent company owns at least 10 per cent of their total stock, are excluded from the survey. Presumably the reason for this exclusion is that the survey was intended to identify only those collaborative R&D activities which were conducted among independent firms.

The firms surveyed are large and medium-sized ones chosen from four broad categories of industries: (1) electronics and communications, (2) automobiles and auto parts, (3) chemicals, and (4) other materials (which consist of metals and stone, clay and glass). It is clear that the first two industries consist essentially of assemblers of complex final goods using a large number of parts, whereas the remaining two industries consist of manufacturers of intermediate materials using large-scale processing plants.

According to the JFTC survey, collaborative R&D activities of the first type amounted to 94.2 per cent of all collaborative R&D activities as of 1982. Firms which participate in R&D collaboration of this type usually sign a contract which specifies how each firm will share the cost of collaborative R&D, how the R&D fruits are to be divided, and so on. Most R&D collaboration among vertically related firms – for example, collaborative R&D between a ceramics manufacturer and an automobile manufacturer with the purpose of developing a ceramic engine – belonged to this type. The actual R&D activities were carried out at the respective laboratories of participating firms.

Collaborative R&D activities of the second type, where participating firms initiate a joint venture for the purpose of conducting R&D, accounted for only 0.3 per cent of all R&D collaboration as of 1982. They included Sumitomo Ocean Development, established by firms belonging to the Sumitomo group, Mitsubishi Atomic, established by firms belonging to the Mitsubishi group, and Toyota Central Research, established by firms belonging to the Toyota group. In contrast with these projects, which were established by firms belonging to the same corporate group, a joint venture to develop a jet engine was initiated by a collection of firms which were either members of different corporate groups or not associated with any particular group.

Although the share of collaborative R&D belonging to the second type was small at the time of the JFTC survey, it has recently increased and now encompasses new arrangements and features. One notable category of recent R&D joint ventures is that in which collaborative agreements are established by firms and the Key Technology Development Centre. This institution, which is attached to the Ministry of International Trade and Industry (MITI) and the Ministry of Posts and Telecommunications (MPT), invests in high-technology start-up joint ventures, and usually owns between 50 per cent and 70 per cent of the total stock of these newly created joint ventures. The rest of the stock is owned by participating firms.[11] The Optoelectronics Technology Research Corporation is among the joint ventures established under this scheme.

Collaborative R&D activities of the third type, where participating firms form a research association for the purpose of pursuing collaborative R&D, accounted for only 5.5 per cent of all R&D collaborations covered by the 1982 JFTC survey. However, the importance of this type of R&D collaboration should not be underestimated just because of its numerical paucity.[12]

206

On the one hand, whenever the number of firms involved is large, the organizational form of R&D collaboration is usually of this type. On the other, while the first two types of R&D collaboration are quite common, not only in Japan but also in many other countries, the third type of collaboration, which is fairly recent in origin, is quite unique to Japan. The VLSI joint R&D project is presumably the best known example of research associations in Japan. In view of its importance, we will examine this special type of R&D collaboration in more detail below.

According to this survey, half of all responding firms (130 firms out of 237 responding firms) were engaged in some type of collaborative R&D. On average, each firm was conducting 8.7 R&D collaborations, and firms belonging to the materials industries were found to be more active in pursuing collaborative R&D than assembly industries. In most cases (85.8 per cent of collaborative R&D surveyed), the number of partners was just one, so that most R&D collaborations involved only two firms. The majority of R&D collaborations (80.9 per cent of collaborative R&D surveyed) did not involve firms which were competing in the same industry. Indeed, this survey shows that the majority of R&D collaborations occurred among vertically related firms, viz. materials and intermediate goods manufacturers, as well as parts and equipment manufacturers, on the one hand, and users and assembly firms, on the other. Nevertheless, it is still noteworthy that R&D collaboration involving firms in the same broad category of industries was not uncommon.

The kind of research carried out as collaborative R&D projects differed rather sharply from those conducted by the industries in general. According to the JFTC survey, 13.6 per cent of the collaborative R&D expenditures were spent on basic research, 32.1 per cent on applied research, and 54.3 per cent on development research. In contrast, the corresponding figures for the industries in general were 5.5 per cent on basic research, 21.9 per cent on applied research, and 72.6 per cent on development research. It is conspicuous that the percentage of expenditure on development research was much lower, while that on basic research was much higher, in collaborative R&D projects than in independently conducted ones. This seems to be consistent with the often asserted view that R&D collaborations are most suitable for the pre-competitive stage of basic research. Nevertheless, it deserves to be emphasized that the majority of collaborative research expenditures were spent on development research.

COLLABORATIVE R&D IN THE FORM OF RESEARCH ASSOCIATIONS

It was in 1961 that the Law on Technological Research Associations in Mining and Manufacturing was enacted in Japan, which formally introduced a particular type of R&D collaboration formed under the auspices of MITI.

The formal name of this collaborative R&D organization is the Technological Research Association in Mining and Manufacturing, but it is quite commonly called the Research Association. It is useful to understand the background of this formal system of organizing R&D collaboration.[13]

Before the introduction of the law, most collaborative R&D projects were pursued either by signing contracts among participating firms, or by the creation of a loose form of organization within which participating firms shared the costs, activities, and fruits of R&D collaboration. They were established in the automobile parts, camera and chemical industries. In the case of the first two industries, industry associations played a major role in establishing and running their respective research associations. But the last project included not only firms from the chemical industry but also firms from the machinery and steel industries. In a project like this, where the role of the industrial association, if any, is limited because firms from various industries are involved, a new organization that could function as the core of the collaborative research activities was needed. Thus there was growing recognition among firms as well as MITI officials that it would be easier to create an independent entity for the purpose of managing collaborative R&D. After all, it was too costly and cumbersome for member firms to negotiate and manage assets and workers employed for collaborative research, and to administer patent rights generated by it. Accounting and coping with various legal issues concerning collaborative R&D placed a further burden on each firm. It was in response to these needs that the 1961 law was proposed so as to promote collaborative R&D by allowing member firms to create an independent organization to run collaborative R&D, thereby reducing the transaction costs associated with starting and managing such efforts.

The second important event in the background of the 1961 law is the announcement of a major trade liberalization plan in 1960. The plan stated that, by 1963, 80 per cent of imports in terms of the number of tax codes should be automatically approved. As a matter of fact, trade liberalization proceeded more quickly than originally planned, and the automatic approval rate already exceeded 90 per cent of all imports by August 1963. Although imports of manufactured goods had not increased very rapidly, the prospect of competition with foreign firms in the domestic market urged Japanese firms to upgrade their technology as quickly as possible. On its part, the Japanese government was strongly apprehensive that trade liberalization was going to take place while some of the domestic industries were still in the stage of 'infancy'. In this context, the 1961 law can be seen as a policy measure to warn domestic industries and urge them to prepare for trade liberalization.

Although the 1961 law used the existing research association system in the United Kingdom as its prototype, there are two salient and noteworthy differences between the original UK model and the Japanese version.[14] The first difference is that, while the original research associations in the United Kingdom were established on an industry-wide basis mostly in traditional industries, the Japanese research associations were organized to solve certain specific technological problems. Member firms of the Japanese research associations were, especially after the 1970s, mostly large firms trying to enhance their technology base, or to explore the possibility of tackling long-range, risky research subjects.

The second salient feature of the Japanese version of research associations that is distinct from the UK prototype is that the Japanese research associations were designed to be dissolved after the completion of specific research targets. Whether successful or not, these R&D activities usually lasted for several years. This feature of Japanese research associations is important because participants are thereby assured that they need not commit their resources to the project for an indefinite time period. Of 114 research associations established through fiscal 1990, forty-five associations were already dissolved, or in the process of being dissolved.

The actual research at research associations in Japan (JRA hereafter, for brevity) was carried out mainly in two ways. In the first alternative, a JRA established a joint research laboratory of its own, and research was carried out at this laboratory. In the second alternative, the research subject of the collaborative project was divided into several subthemes and these subthemes were assigned to member firms. The member firms carried out their assigned subthemes in their own research laboratories and met occasionally during the course of collaborative R&D to exchange research outcomes.

Not many JRAs had their own joint research laboratories. Indeed, only twelve out of the 114 JRAs established by the end of fiscal 1990 had their own joint research laboratories or some sort of joint research facilities. The case of VLSI Research Association was truly exceptional; the vast majority of JRAs were managed by dividing their research theme into several subthemes and assigning them to member firms. Even in the rare cases where JRAs actually established joint research laboratories, most of the research was allocated to member firms and carried out separately at their respective laboratories.[15] Researchers and research funds were obtained in the following way. As far as researchers were concerned, the situation differed, depending upon whether the JRA in question had its own laboratory or not. When a JRA did not have a laboratory of its own, some of the researchers of member firms were assigned to certain research subjects which coincided with the collaborative research topic. In the case where a JRA had its own laboratory, the staff of the joint laboratory was made up of researchers on loan from member firms; no researchers were hired directly by the JRA. In addition, some researchers joined from national laboratories. In the two well known cases where JRAs had joint laboratories of their own, viz. VLSI RA and Optoelectronics RA, the heads of the joint laboratories were both from national research laboratories.

209

Research funds and the operating costs of JRAs were basically shared by member firms. In some cases they were divided evenly, whereas in other cases they were allocated to member firms in proportion to their sales. The portion of the research which was carried out at each member firm's laboratory was financed independently, except for cases in which equipment was bought on the JRA's account.

Government subsidies were or were not granted, depending on how important the subjects of collaborative research were from the viewpoint of national policy objectives. When government subsidies, contingent loans, and/or national research contracts were nevertheless granted, they proved to be an important source of funds to the JRAs. However, there is no specific government subsidy programme linked with the JRA system. Instead, various existing R&D subsidy programmes were tapped, including the Basic Technologies for Future Industries Programme, the Large Scale Project Programme, and the Programme to Promote Computer and Information Processing. In 1983 forty-four JRAs were active in research, and they spent 64.4 billion yen, which was about 1.5 per cent of total R&D spending in Japan that year. Government subsidies amounted to 32.8 billion yen, or 51 per cent of JRA R&D spending. The subsidies to JRAs accounted for 46.9 per cent of total government R&D subsidies. To apply for these major subsidy programmes, it was often the case that firms had to form a new JRA or join an existing one. If a firm was denied membership in a JRA financed by government subsidies, it meant in effect that the firm would be unable to obtain financial assistance from the government. Special tax breaks, including a scheme of accelerated depreciation, were also provided to JRA member firms and to JRAs themselves.

The number of JRAs established each year, as well as their purpose and background, differed significantly. For instance, twelve JRAs which came into being by 1965 can be classified into the following three groups. JRAs in the first group were established with the focused purpose of developing a standardized testing method for their industry, thereby promoting the improvement of product quality. The second group sought more explicitly to promote manufacturing technologies in industries that were widely recognized to be lagging behind their US and European counterparts. The third group were designed to help small firms in traditional industries, such as textiles, packing materials, casting and lime. This type of JRA was similar to that of the UK prototype model, and was emphasized at the early stage of the development of Japanese research associations.

Only one new JRA was established from 1966 through 1970. Apparently, the experience of JRAs in the early 1960s failed to generate enthusiasm among Japanese firms. During the 1970s, however, the number of newly established JRAs increased. From 1971 to 1980, thirty-four new JRAs were established. One immediate reason for this upsurge is that various government programmes to subsidize and promote R&D had started to use JRAs as the focal organization through which to administer the programme and pool government funds. Several government programmes, including the Large Scale Industrial Technology Research and Development System (started in 1966) and the Subsidy Programme to Promote the Development of Computers (started in 1972) were initiated around 1970 against the backdrop of trade and foreign investment liberalization. Among the thirty-four JRAs established during the seventies, fifteen were linked with these government programmes, while no JRAs were linked with them in the 1960s. Apparently, the government decision to use JRAs as the organization through which to run government subsidized programmes (especially the Large Scale Project System) was one of the major reasons for their proliferation in the 1970s.

Not only did JRAs increase in number, but the size of their budgets also increased during this period. In the 1960s, except for the two very large JRAs, the budgets of JRAs ranged from several million yen to several hundred million yen, with the median being 181 million yen. In the 1970s, however, there were three exceptionally large JRAs, all related to computers, which had budgets of more than 100 billion yen. The rest of the JRA budgets in the 1970s ranged typically from several billion yen to several hundred billion yen. Clearly, the size of JRAs increased saliently in the 1970s even in real terms.

The JRAs in the 1970s included a large number of the computer industry-related ones. There were thirteen computer-related JRAs out of thirty-four established in the 1970s. The four largest JRAs in terms of their budgets in that decade were all related to the computer industry. The reason may be that trade and foreign direct investment liberalization in the computer industry proceeded more slowly than in most other industries. Trade and investment in integrated circuits were liberalized in 1974; mainframe computers in 1975; and information processing in 1976. At this stage, the technology base of Japanese manufacturers was far behind that of their US counterparts, most notably IBM. The government, citing the fact that the R&D expenditure of the six Japanese manufacturers combined was less than one-fifth of that of IBM in 1970, encouraged collaborative research among Japanese computer firms and increased R&D subsidies to them. Although the amount of subsidies was relatively small in comparison with the industry's total R&D expenditure (4.2 per cent in 1972 and 10.3 per cent in 1973), it is worth noting that a significant percentage of the subsidies was granted to the firms through JRAs.[16] The government even created three JRAs in order to consolidate Japanese computer manufacturers into three groups along those lines.

In the 1980s the number of newly established JRAs increased even further, but their essence seems to have changed. The focus of research has gradually shifted to more long-range risky research and research closer to the basic end of the technological spectrum. Some of the long-range futuristic technologies extended across traditional industrial boundaries.

211

The greater number of JRAs in chemicals and non-ferrous metals in the early 1980s reflects changing circumstances. These industries were among the 'structurally depressed' industries that were facing financial problems due to increased energy costs and depressed demand.[17] A significant number of JRAs in the chemical and non-ferrous metal industries were established to find a way to save these afflicted industries. This type of JRA reflects the economic conditions of the early 1980s and the stance of public policy with respect to these conditions. As economic conditions recovered in the late 1980s these JRAs seem to have disappeared. The focus of research at JRAs was gradually moving towards more long range risky research projects which were more akin to basic research.

POLICY IMPLICATIONS OF COLLABORATIVE R&D

The theory of collaborative R&D briefly summarized on pp. 199–205 tells us as follows:

1 Forming an R&D collaboration is welfare-improving *vis-à-vis* competitive R&D irrespective of whether information is fully shared among member firms or not, as long as there exists sufficient spillover of cost-reducing R&D benefits.
2 Collaborative R&D without full information-sharing is vulnerable to the individual motivation to free-ride on other firms, particularly when the number of member firms is large.
3 Collaborative R&D with full information-sharing is more likely to be sustained through private incentives, since there exists no incentive for unilateral deviation as long as *either* the number of member firms is reasonably large *or* the degree of R&D spillover to non-member firms is reasonably low.

In understanding the message of these results, it is crucially important to notice that our theoretical model presupposes that firms are fully aware that they compete in the product market irrespective of whether they cooperate in the R&D stage or not. It is also important that our contrast between collaborative R&D and competitive R&D is focused on *full* cooperation versus *no* cooperation. In other words, the R&D collaboration we have analysed is confined exclusively to collaboration among all firms in the industry.[18]

On the other hand, the following casual observations have been made on the positive role played by R&D collaboration, which seem to underlie the widespread belief in the usefulness of such institutional arrangements for promoting R&D. They are all geared towards a central observation to the effect that R&D collaboration makes it possible to achieve economies of scale in the pursuit of R&D by bringing complementary resources of several firms together, thereby reducing overhead costs and saving time required to complete R&D projects:

1 If firms were to raise funds for R&D individually in imperfect capital markets, it would be necessary for them to reveal at least a portion of information concerning the project, which might negatively affect their incentive to embark on such R&D projects on their own. Collaborative R&D arrangements could overcome this barrier and lead to an increase in aggregate R&D.

2 R&D collaboration may improve R&D efficiency if member firms can bring in expertise from different areas. By combining expertise in complementary areas, a collaborative R&D project may be completed with less time and/or funds.[19]

3 R&D competition encompasses an important feature of rank order competition, since the firm which achieves the R&D goal ahead of its rivals reaps most of the fruits under an effective patent system. Given this feature of R&D competition, many firms may be simultaneously scurrying to accomplish the same R&D objective, resulting in a lower social rate of return on additional private R&D investment. Through R&D collaboration this wasteful duplication of resources may be avoided.[20]

4 Forming an R&D collaboration may provide an efficient mechanism to cope with the appropriability problem, at least partially, thereby increasing aggregate R&D investment. Indeed, by internalizing R&D externalities, the member firms of an R&D collaboration can appropriate the benefits of R&D as a group, although outsiders can still free-ride on R&D spillovers. The diffusion of technological information among member firms can be easier and more assured under R&D collaboration than under a competitive R&D regime.

Against these alleged benefits of collaborative R&D arrangements, some of which were vindicated by our theoretical observations, there seem to be certain drawbacks, which are not properly captured by our theoretical model:

1 R&D collaboration or technology cartels may lead to an excessively high price for technology by reducing competition in the technology market. After all, a technology cartel is a cartel which is anti-competitive in nature.

2 R&D collaboration may lead to dynamic inefficiency by reducing R&D effort collectively. This is a real danger which is exemplified by the case of the American automobile manufacturers' attempt to slow down R&D in pollution control technology.

3 Cooperative behaviour at the R&D level by otherwise competing firms may spill over to the product market. In other words, collusion in the R&D stage may pave the way to collusion in the stage of product market competition.

In the theoretical literature summarized on pp. 199–205 these potentially negative effects of collaborative R&D are not taken into account. Indeed, it is assumed that there is no market for technology, and collaboration in the R&D stage does not exert any long-run negative impact on R&D incentives. It is also assumed that there is no spillover of collusive behaviour from the pre-competitive R&D stage to the stage of product market competition.

It goes without saying that, in order to design a well balanced collaborative R&D policy, it is necessary to pay due attention not only to the positive effects but also to the negative effects.

Using these pros and cons of R&D collaboration as our reference points, let us now evaluate the actual performance of JRAs which we have described in the previous section. Since the formation of JRAs is generally recognized as an integral part of Japanese industrial policy, this exercise may be useful in understanding the role and efficacy of this class of industrial policy.

Recollect that, with rather rare exceptions, JRAs did not have joint R&D facilities. Thus active interaction among researchers from member firms was not as prevalent as it would have been if there had been joint laboratories. Even when joint laboratories were in fact established, the majority of R&D activity took place in each member firm's own laboratory by its own staff, hence the pooling of resources to achieve scale economies in R&D, or to bring together complementary resources, was in fact rarely realized by JRAs. At best, what happened was a limited exchange of information on the research outcomes of each member firm. It is true that member firms could still economize on resources even through this limited exchange of information, as each firm could concentrate on the narrowly circumscribed subthemes and still have privileged access to the research results of the whole team. As in the case of collaborative R&D on computers, however, it often happened that all member firms were manufacturers of the same final product, so that they wanted all the technology required to manufacture the final product. In a case like this, to have access to the technology developed by the other member firms is simply not enough, because it is difficult to codify and transmit all the technological information. It is often necessary that each firm should actually have its own research experience over the entire R&D project if it is to manufacture the final product on the basis of the developed technology. In order to circumvent this problem, member firms must, in addition, pursue research subthemes which are not in fact assigned to them. Thus, R&D collaboration of this type will not actually result in the elimination of effort duplication.

Furthermore, firms purposely tried on occasion to take part in R&D subthemes where they were especially weak, rather than in those where they were strong, so as to gain a free ride on the expertise of other member firms. To the extent that such opportunism prevails, the advantage of organizing R&D collaboration is very limited, and advanced firms have very little, if any, incentive to join.

What about the potentially positive role of R&D collaboration in avoiding duplication due to the so called 'rush to invent'? In the case of JRAs, this argument is not necessarily relevant. Some JRAs were organized with the clear purpose of upgrading the basic technological capabilities of all manufacturers and, as such, have no recognizable relevance to the present question. Other JRAs were geared towards projects whose chances of success were very small but their potential impact quite large, requiring extensive R&D investments and/or long lead times. It is clear that there was hardly anything resembling a 'rush to invent' in those cases. Indeed, most of the projects would not have been started had the government not encouraged the JRAs with funding. Thus, in both cases, the role of JRAs as deterrents to duplicate investment was minimal, if any.

Was the JRA scheme effective in solving the perennial problem of imperfect appropriability? This potentially positive role of R&D collaboration is not very relevant either in the context of JRAs. Those JRAs which tried to raise the general technological level did not create any specific proprietary knowledge. On the other hand, JRAs engaged in projects with a small chance of success, but profound potential impact if successful, may seem to be relevant at first sight. However, most JRAs of this type are partly funded by the government as contract researchers, so that patents thereby generated would be owned by the government. These patents are subsequently licensed to all firms, domestic as well as foreign alike, under the same conditions. Thus, JRA member firms of this type cannot reap any differential benefits from inventions through the patent system. Nevertheless, at least during the joint research process, member firms can obtain valuable skills and know-how that can be retained internally, and possibly provide a head start on production.[21] Thus, although this is not a clear-cut case of the internalization of externalities by a group of firms, firms nevertheless may expect to reap profits through head start production. This may well be one of the major reasons for firms to join this type of JRA.

The second policy context in which JRAs are of relevance is that of technology policy. The JRA scheme is a convenient policy tool through which the government can promote some specific industrial policy goals. An example of such policy objectives is the promotion of the technological capabilities of a domestic industry lagging far behind its American and European counterparts. The JRA scheme was indeed used as a tool to achieve this type of goal by channelling government funds to member firms. Since there was a clear incentive on the part of private firms to upgrade their technological capabilities so as to compete effectively with their foreign rivals, this policy initiative was received positively by private firms. It seems fairly clear to us that the role of JRAs in administering and channelling government funds to industries, where private incentives are largely consistent with policy objectives, may be more important than any other conceivable role.

The third policy context in which JRAs are of relevance is that of competition policy. Since R&D collaboration may generate some negative effects, as identified above, it is clearly important that competition policy be carefully used so that these potentially detrimental effects are effectively kept under control.

In April 1993, the Fair Trade Commission of Japan published the Anti-monopoly Act Guidelines Concerning Joint Research and Development and tried to clarify its general view regarding collaborative R&D arrangements and their implementation. The following salient features of these Guidelines are particularly worth examining:

1 The Guidelines are meant to be universally applicable to all attempts of collaborative R&D to the extent that they may exert an anti-competitive effect in the Japanese market, irrespective of whether the participants are domestic or foreign firms.

2 Collaborative R&D projects that would encounter problems under the Anti-monopoly Act would be those which competing firms collaboratively undertake. There is very little likelihood of non-competing firms undertaking collaborative R&D that would pose problems under the Anti-monopoly Act.

3 In passing judgement as to whether or not competition in the market is substantially restrained by a particular joint R&D project, the number of member firms, and their share of and position in the market, are taken into account. If the combined market share of the participants is no more than 20 per cent, it will usually present no problem under the Anti-monopoly Act. Even when the total share exceeds 20 per cent, however, it does not necessarily pose a problem. Judgement will be made by comprehensively taking matters such as the character of research, the need for collaboration, range of objectives, etc., into consideration.

4 Even where the collaborative R&D presents no problem of its own under the Anti-monopoly Act, arrangements accompanying the actual implementation thereof may affect competition in the product market, thereby creating problems under the Anti-monopoly Act. These problems may occur (a) if an arrangement unjustly restricts the business activities of a participating firm, thereby impeding fair competition, and (b) if competitive business activities relating to the price and quantity of a product are mutually restricted among participating firms. Thus, collaborative R&D presents a problem under the Anti-monopoly Act if there is a spillover of anti-competitive practices from the R&D stage to the stage of product market competition.

5 In principle, under the Anti-monopoly Act, participants of R&D collaboration can be required (a) to disclose information on technologies necessary for the collaborative R&D project, (b) to report on the progress of their share of the research work to other participants, and (c) to keep

secret the information on technologies disclosed to them by other participants in connection with the collaborative R&D.

6 In principle, it does not present problems under the Anti-monopoly Act (a) to restrict, within a reasonable period, the marketing of products utilizing a technology which is a fruit of the collaborative R&D project only to the participants or a designated firm or firms, if deemed necessary to maintain the secrecy of the resulting know-how, (b) to restrict, within a reasonable time, the source or sources of supply of raw materials or parts for products utilizing the technology resulting from the collaborative R&D project only to other participant or to a designated firm or firms to maintain the secrecy of the resulting know-how to ensure the quality of products based on such technology.

7 Other restrictions, even those based on the propriety of one's collaboratively developed technology such as (a) restrictions on production or on the territory where the product may be sold, or (b) restrictions on the production or on the volume of sales of the product, may fall under unfair trade practices.

8 To supplement these Guidelines, a prior consultation system has been established, whereby any uncertainty as to whether a specific collaborative R&D project presents any problems under the Anti-monopoly Act may be resolved. The party eligible to request prior consultation is the firm or the trade association intending to implement the collaborative R&D, irrespective of whether the firm of the trade association is a domestic or a foreign entity.

It is worth while pointing out that the JFTC Guidelines were published for the purpose of facilitating pro-competitive collaborative R&D by making the legal constraints on such collaborations more transparent. Recently, and in a similar spirit, the antitrust laws and the practical implementation of these laws, both in the United States and Europe, have become clearly more lenient towards collaborative R&D associations with the passage of the National Cooperative Research Act in 1984, and the Block Exemption from Article 85 in the European Community for some categories of R&D agreements in 1985. It is against this background that the following observations on the JFTC Guidelines may have some relevance:

1 The first observation is quite a general one which pertains not only to the JFTC Guidelines on collaborative R&D, but also to competition policy in general. It is true that there is a widespread belief in the welfare-improving effects of increased competitiveness. Indeed, as Baumol (1982: 2) has aptly put it, '...the standard analysis...leaves us with the impression that there is a rough continuum, in terms of desirability of industry performance, ranging from unregulated pure monopoly as the pessimal [sic] arrangement to perfect competition as the ideal, with relative efficiency in resource allocation increasing monotonically as the number of firms

expands'. Although some recent studies in theoretical industrial organization have cast serious doubt on the universal validity of this common
belief,[22] the vestige thereof seems to persist in the JFTC Guidelines in that
collaborative R&D is judged to present no problem under the Anti-
monopoly Act only to the extent that it is pro-competitive. It seems to us
that the crucial criterion for approving or not approving any coordinating
device should be whether or not it leads to an improvement in social
welfare, and to be pro-competitive is neither necessary nor sufficient for
this crucial criterion to be satisfied.[23]

2 The second observation pertains to the JFTC Guideline 2. According to
this guideline, horizontal R&D collaboration among competing firms and
vertical R&D collaboration among non-competing firms have strongly
contrasting implications in that the former, but not the latter, has a non-
trivial likelihood of posing problems under the Anti-monopoly Act. It
seems to us, however, that R&D collaboration among vertically related
firms, say a ceramics manufacturer and an automobile manufacturer for
the development of a ceramic engine, if successful, may have a quite
serious impact on competitiveness, both in the ceramics industry and in
the automobile industry. The overly sharp demarcation between horizontal
and vertical R&D collaboration does not seem to be warranted in general.

3 The third observation pertains to the markets whose competitiveness is the
focus of the JFTC Guidelines in judging whether or not R&D collaboration presents problems under the Anti-monopoly Act. We may easily
verify that domestic markets are exclusively focused on in this context,
even though the JFTC Guideline 1 asserts that foreign firms are to be
treated on a par with domestic firms. Thus, the effects of the membership
of foreign firms in Japanese collaborative R&D groupings on the
competitiveness of foreign markets play no role whatsoever in the JFTC
judgement on the pro- or anti-competitiveness of R&D collaborations.
This feature of the JFTC Guidelines may need further examination from
the standpoint of international harmonization of Anti-monopoly Legislation and their implementation.

CONCLUDING REMARKS

The topics we have discussed in this chapter are broad as well as diverse. No
attempt will be made here to summarize the discussion in all respects.
Instead, we conclude by extracting some broad implications of our analysis.

Among various modes of organizing collaborative R&D, the establishment of research associations was unique to Japan, and this mode of
collaborative R&D provides a wealth of policy and theoretical implications.
In particular, those research associations which have joint research
laboratories of their own, where active interactions among researchers from
participating firms with complementary experience and abilities take place,

are capable of generating strong synergetic effects. Thus, this mode of collaborative R&D may be welfare-improving *vis-à-vis* competitive R&D. Besides, it has a high likelihood of being sustainable through private incentives. The VLSI Research Association is a well known example of this type of collaborative R&D in Japan. Although its 'success' should be largely attributed to the rare combination of favourable factors, it is worthwhile to note that the institutional framework of the VLSI Research Association was consistent with what the theory of R&D collaboration most recommends: collaborative R&D in which full information-sharing takes place.

However eye-catching the 'success' of the VLSI Research Association may have been, it should not be construed that it is primarily the organizational mode of research association that makes collaborative R&D welfare-improving and stable. The vast majority of JRAs did not have research laboratories of their own, and, more often than not, failed to generate socially beneficial synergetic effects. One of the major points of this chapter was to demystify this mode of collaborative R&D in factual detail.

From the theoretical point of view, one of the areas where more work is definitely called for is the mechanism through which R&D spillovers are generated. Recall that the theoretical formulation due to d'Aspremont and Jacquemin (1988), Dutta and Suzumura (1993), Kamien *et el.* (1992) and Suzumura (1992) simply start off by assuming some specific form of the spillover functions. In reality, however, the key to the success of R&D collaboration is precisely the successful generation of synergetic effects among member firms which, in turn, create socially useful R&D spillovers. It is clear that the most crucial next step in theoretical research on collaborative R&D is to endogenize the spillover mechanisms.

From the policy-orientated point of view, more work is urgently needed in shedding further light on the channels through which government can assist socially beneficial R&D collaborations. How can government tell socially beneficial R&D collaborations from socially detrimental ones? Supposing that this could be done, should government subsidize socially beneficial collaborative R&D? If the answer to this question is in the affirmative, what should be the policy criterion for the provision of subsidies? Should there be any modification of the Anti-monopoly Act so as to make it more lenient to pro-competitive R&D collaboration?

These are a small sample of the questions which await careful scrutiny. The purpose of this chapter will be served if it succeeds in calling the reader's attention to this selected list of future agenda.

NOTES

1 Recent theoretical works on R&D collaboration include d'Aspremont and Jacquemin (1988), De Bondt *et al.* (1992), Dutta and Suzumura (1993), Geroski (1993), Grossman and Shapiro (1986), Kamien *et al.* (1992), Katz (1986), Katz

and Ordover (1990), Ordover and Willig (1985), Suzumura (1992, 1995: chapter 6), Suzumura and Yanagawa (1993), and Teece (1992). The following observations on the welfare performance of R&D collaborations and the stability thereof capitalize partly on Dutta and Suzumura (1993) and Suzumura (1992, 1995: Chapter 6).

2 A model of oligopolistic competition with R&D commitment where the number of firms is endogenously determined is analysed by Okuno-Fujiwara and Suzumura (1993). See also Suzumura (1995: chapter 7).

3 Those who are interested in knowing how some of the following results would be modified when firms compete in the product market in terms of prices rather than quantities are referred to Suzumura and Yanagawa (1993).

4 There are two interesting directions in which this simple model can be generalized. Firstly, we can generalize the linear demand function (1), which implies that outputs are strategic substitutes, into a non-linear demand function $p = f(Q)$ with $f'(Q) < 0$, thereby allowing for richer analysis on strategic interrelatedness among firms. This direction has already been explored by Suzumura (1992, 1995: chapter 6), who also allows for more general non-linear cost-reduction technology. Secondly, even within the class of linear demand structures, we can introduce a simple form of product differentiation if we replace (1) by (1^*) $p_i = a - b(q_i + \delta \sum_{j \neq i} q_j)$, where p_i is the price of goods produced by firm i and δ, where $0 \leqslant \delta \leqslant 1$, is the substitutability parameter. Products are perfect substitutes when $\delta = 1$, whereas each firm is a monopoly when $\delta = 0$. This possibility has been explored by Kamien et al. (1992), and Dutta and Suzumura (1993).

5 This definition is due originally to d'Aspremont and Jacquemin (1988). See also Suzumura (1992, 1995: chapter 6).

6 This result is due essentially to d'Aspremont and Jacquemin (1988) and Suzumura (1992, 1995: chapter 6). See also Kamien et al. (1992).

7 These concepts are due to Dutta and Suzumura (1993).

8 See Kamien et al. (1992).

9 The following two sections depend heavily on Goto (forthcoming).

10 The findings of this survey are summarized in Rokuhara (1985).

11 Government funds used to create the Japan Technology Development Centre came from the dividends on government-owned stocks of the newly privatized Nippon Telegraph & Telephone (NTT). The idea of promoting R&D-orientated joint venture firms in high technology industries is alleged to have originated with the R&D Limited Partnership System in the United States. There are two similar programmes administered by the Ministry of Agriculture Forestry and Fisheries in the case of biotechnology, and the Ministry of Health and Welfare in the case of pharmaceuticals.

12 Indeed, this type of R&D collaboration is most intriguing as well as theoretically challenging.

13 Concerning the prehistory of research associations, see Kokogyo Gijutsu Kenkyu Kumiai Kondankai (1991).

14 As to the research association system in the United Kingdom, interested readers may consult Johnson (1971/72).

15 For more details see Hayashi et al. (1989).

16 See Wakasugi (1988).

17 Those who are interested in 'structurally depressed' industries are referred to Goto (1988) and Peck et al. (1987).

18 Note, however, that Dutta and Suzumura (1993) have also examined some properties of partial R&D collaborations.

19 For example, a ceramic manufacturer and an automobile manufacturer may develop a ceramic engine more effectively in a collaborative effort than if each of them has to pursue the same R&D project independently.

20 If various approaches are possible to solve the same research subject, and if each firm pursues a separate approach, then competitive R&D may make sense. However, this type of parallel R&D through competition is unlikely to happen. The possibility of duplication is high, because each firm tries to keep its approach secret under the competitive R&D regime. If decision-making is centralized through collaborative R&D, it is possible to diversify the approach deliberately and pursue parallel development strategy intentionally, making the allocation of R&D resources more efficient.

21 As Levin *et al.* (1987) showed, such a head start may be more important than the patent itself as a means to appropriate innovation.

22 See, e.g., Suzumura (1995).

23 Needless to say, this poses many further questions of a serious nature. How should we identify social welfare in the first place? Should we focus exclusively on consumers' welfare, or should we also pay due attention to producers' benefits? If we opt for the latter alternative, what weight should we give to producers' surplus *vis-à-vis* consumers' surplus as an index of consumers' welfare? Although these are formidable questions to tackle even in the single country perspective, the difficulty will multiply if we proceed to discuss the possibility of international harmonization of competition policies.

REFERENCES

Baumol, W.J. (1982) 'Contestable Markets: An Uprising in the Theory of Industry Structure', *American Economic Review* 72, 1–15.

Borda, J. (1990) 'Antitrust Law and Innovation Cooperation', *Journal of Economic Perspectives* 4, 97–112.

d'Aspremont, C. and A. Jacquemin (1988) 'Cooperative and Noncooperative R&D in Duopoly with Spillovers', *American Economic Review* 78, 1133–7.

De Bondt, R., Slaets, P. and B. Cassiman (1992) 'The Degree of Spillovers and the Number of Rivals for Maximum Effective R&D', *International Journal of Industrial Organization* 10, 35–54.

Dutta, B. and K. Suzumura (1993) 'On the Sustainability of Collaborative R&D through Private Incentives', Discussion Paper No. 276, Institute of Economic Research, Hitotsubashi University, Tokyo, Japan.

Geroski, P.A. (1993) 'Anti-trust Policy Towards Cooperative R&D Ventures', *Oxford Review of Economic Policy* 9, 58–71.

Goto, A. (1988) 'Japan: A Sunset Industry', in M.J. Peck (ed.) *The World Aluminum Industry in an Era of Changing Energy Prices*, Baltimore: Johns Hopkins University Press.

Goto, A. (forthcoming) 'Collaborative R&D in Japanese Manufacturing Industries – Innovation in R&D System?' in A. Goto (ed.) *Innovation in Japan: Empirical Studies on the National and Corporate Activities*, Oxford: Oxford University Press.

Grossman, G. and C. Shapiro (1986) 'Research Joint Ventures: An Antitrust Analysis', *Journal of Law, Economics and Organization* 2, 315–37.

Hayashi, I., Hirano, M. and Y. Katayama (1989) 'Collaborative Semiconductor Research in Japan', *Proceedings of the IEEE* 77, 1430–41.

Hirabayashi, H., ed. (1993) *Antimonopoly Act Guidelines Concerning Joint Research and Development*, Tokyo: Shoji-Houmu Kenkyukai. (In Japanese.)

Jacquemin, A. (1988) 'Cooperative Agreements in R&D and European Antitrust Policy', *European Economic Review* 32, 551–60.

Johnson, P. (1971/72) 'The Role of Co-operative Research in British Industry', *Research Policy* 1, 332–50.

Jorde, T. and D. Teece (1990) 'Innovation and Cooperation: Implication for Competition and Antitrust', *Journal of Economic Perspectives* 4, 75–96.

Kamien, M.I., Muller, E. and I. Zang (1992) 'Research Joint Ventures and R&D Cartels', *American Economic Review* 82, 1293–306.

Katz, M. (1986) 'An Analysis of Cooperative Research and Development', *Rand Journal of Economics* 17, 527–43.

Katz, M. and J. Ordover (1990) 'R&D Cooperation and Competition', *Brookings Papers on Economic Activity* 137–203.

Kokogyo Gijutsu Kenkyu Kumiai Kondankai [Forum of Technological Research Association in Mining and Manufacturing] (1991) *Thirty Years' Technological Research Association in Mining and Manufacturing*, Tokyo: Nihon Kogyo Gijutsu Shinko Kyokai. (In Japanese.)

Levin, R.C., Klevorick, A.K., Nelson, R.R. and S.G. Winter (1987) 'Appropriating the Returns from Industrial R&D', *Brookings Papers on Economic Activity*, 783–820.

Levy, J.D. and R.J. Samuels (1991) 'Institutions and Innovation: Research Collaboration as Technology Strategy in Japan', in L.K. Mytelka (ed.) *Strategic Partnerships*, London: Pinter.

Merz, J. (1986) 'The Optoelectronics Joint Research Laboratory – Light Shed on Cooperative Research in Japan', *Science Bulletin* 11, 1–30.

Okuno-Fujiwara, M. and K. Suzumura (1993) 'Symmetric Cournot Oligopoly and Economic Welfare: A Synthesis', *Economic Theory* 3, 43–59.

Ordover, J. and R. Willig (1985) 'Antitrust for High-technology Industries: Assessing Research Joint Ventures and Mergers', *Journal of Law and Economics* 28, 311–33.

Peck, M.J. (1986) 'Joint R&D: The Case of Microelectronics and Computer Technology Cooperation', *Research Policy* 15, 219–31.

Peck, M.J., Levin, R. and A. Goto (1987) 'Picking Losers: Public Policy Towards Declining Industries in Japan', *Journal of Japanese Studies* 13, 79–123.

Rokuhara, A., ed. (1985) *R&D and Anti-monopoly Policy*, Tokyo: Gyosei. In Japanese.

Sigurdson, J. (1986) *Industry and State Partnership in Japan: The Very Large Scale Integrated Circuit (VLSI) Project*, Lund: Research Policy Institute.

Spence, A.M. (1984) 'Cost Reduction, Competition and Industry Performance', *Econometrica* 52, 101–21.

Suzumura, K. (1992) 'Cooperative and Noncooperative R&D in an Oligopoly with Spillovers', *American Economic Review* 82, 1307–20.

Suzumura, K. (1995) *Competition, Commitment, and Welfare*, Oxford: Clarendon Press.

Suzumura, K. and N. Yanagawa (1993) 'Cooperative and Noncooperative R&D in an Oligopoly with Spillovers: Strategic Substitutes Versus Strategic Complements', *Hitotsubashi Journal of Economics* 34, 1–11.

Teece, D. (1986) 'Profiting from Technological Innovation: Implications for Integration, Collaboration, Licensing and Public Policy', *Research Policy* 15, 285–305.

Teece, D. (1992) 'Competition, Cooperation and Innovation', *Journal of Economic Behaviour and Organization* 18, 1–25.

Wakasugi, R. (1988) 'Economic Analysis of Cooperative R&D', *Shinshu Daigaku Keizaigaku Ronshuu*, No. 26, 1–26. (In Japanese.)
Wakasugi, R. and A. Goto (1985) 'Cooperative R&D and Innovation', in Y. Okamoto and T. Wakasugi (eds) *Innovation and Corporate Behaviour*, Tokyo: University of Tokyo Press. (In Japanese.)

ACKNOWLEDGEMENTS

We are grateful to the participants of the project on 'Competition Policy in a Global Economy', especially to Professors Leonard Waverman and William Comanor. Thanks are also due to Professor Bhaskar Dutta, whose joint paper with the first author was instrumental in preparing a part of the section on collaborative R&D in the presence of spillovers. Mr George Samu read the first draft of this chapter carefully and made many valuable suggestions. Needless to say, the usual disclaimer applies.

9

INTERNATIONAL R&D COOPERATIONS

Werner Meißner and Rainer Markl

INTRODUCTION

Economists are used to analysing policies towards R&D in terms of static and dynamic efficiency. On the one hand, it seems reasonable to expect that the supply of goods and services will be improved by the introduction of new processes and products. Whereas, on the other hand, innovations typically give rise to a static efficiency loss due to the additional monopoly power they offer to innovating firms.

R&D cooperations can be considered as a means to damp this fundamental conflict. They promise to promote dynamic efficiency, e.g. by avoiding wasteful duplication of effort, and to reduce the static welfare loss as well. Because of the sharing of R&D results more firms are given access to the newly developed product or technology. And competition will ensure that consumers receive their fair share.

This is what one might call the industrial policy attitude towards R&D cooperations. And – although often expressed only implicitly – it is precisely this view which can be found at the bottom of the recent debate on how R&D cooperations should be treated by antitrust law.[1] If society benefits from more cooperative R&D, one needs to ensure that these arrangements will not be hampered by an antitrust law that is too restrictive. Or, to state the argument in its most aggressive way: the existing antitrust regulations in this field have to be relaxed in order to promote R&D cooperations as the superior way of conducting R&D. Thus, competition law becomes a direct instrument of industrial policy.

However, considering the literature, a few objections arise indicating that the positive picture industrial policy is drawing of R&D cooperations may be too simple. In general there is a tendency to overstate the positive welfare consequences of R&D cooperations.

This is true first of all for the implied gain in dynamic efficiency, which is particularly important when there are technological spillovers between firms. In such situations information from the R&D process of one firm flows over to another firm without any compensation. As recent empirical results show, the involved public-good problem of innovations has probably been overestimated.[2]

The second objection to a more positive welfare view of R&D cooperations follows from theoretical arguments: the gain in dynamic efficiency has to be confronted with the static welfare loss arising from the possible extension of cooperative behaviour to the output market.[3] Compared to a situation without any cooperation at either level – the R&D or the output level – such a scenario may even imply overall welfare losses. Therefore most authors plead for a rule-of-reason treatment. If the industrial policy attitude leads a government to relax competition policy, it may achieve the opposite of the desired result. Instead of a welfare gain, a welfare loss could result as a consequence of increased cooperation.

One may argue, however, that every country should have the right to determine the extent to which it adjusts its competition policy to its industrial policy needs. After all, it is the citizens of the country who have to bear the possibly negative consequences of a misguided government's policy.

Assuming the government acts as a benevolent dictator, there should, thus, be no contradiction between competition policy and industrial policy, since both are bound to achieve a welfare level as high as possible.

As the theory of strategic trade policy demonstrates, this conclusion may, however, not hold in an international context. Strategic trade policy as a variant of international industrial policy is based on the principle that a country's national welfare can be promoted by putting national enterprises in a position which enables them to realize additional profits at the expense of their international competitors. To put it differently, in the field of strategic trade policy governments can no longer be seen as a superposed institution which serves total welfare, but only as a political party which seeks strongly national interests. This implies the possibility that a too permissive competition policy on the international level could be abused to embark on strategic trade policy.

The primary goal of this chapter is to outline the conditions under which R&D cooperations may be used as an instrument of strategic trade policy. Proceeding from there, the second step comprises the issue of how international R&D cooperations should be dealt with in terms of competition policy. Generally there are three suitable options. If one judges the danger of trade policy abuse as being marginal, every country should have the right to decide on its stance towards international R&D cooperations.

In the other case there will be a necessity to counter such an abuse. This requires some form of international competition policy which can either aim to eliminate the existing differences in national antitrust law or, alternatively, can be a policy which relies on binding supranational competition rules allowing transfrontier cooperations to be judged directly.

The chapter is organized as follows. In the next section we refer briefly to the well known case of R&D cooperations which form an obstacle to competition, leading to a welfare loss in terms of forgone consumer rent. From an international point of view R&D cooperations may be interpreted as a new kind of 'beggar-thy-neighbour' policy making the case for harmonization of different national antitrust laws quite convincing.

In the following section we complete the picture by introducing the possibility of rent-shifting which is a common feature of strategic trade policy models. Distinct from what is common in the literature we are therefore focusing on partial, non-industry-wide R&D agreements.[4] Two results stand out. First, when firms have the possibility to exclude rivals from cooperative R&D they will tend to cooperate less than is socially optimal. Secondly, given this pre-emptive motive, national governments have a strong incentive to assure that their national champion is included. However, since this is true of all governments the result is a clear welfare loss. All in all, the antitrust policy implications of this chapter are rather ambiguous.

In the third section global enterprises are included. Their geographical independence poses a new challenge for international antitrust policy. Since it offers countries a chance to attract international cooperations by implementing the most permissive antitrust law it is the efficiency of international direct investments that calls for a quick and strong convergence of different national antitrust policies in this case. Moreover, since R&D cooperations between global firms have the potential to affect markets all over the world, they may be seen as 'natural' candidates for an international antitrust law.

R&D COOPERATIONS AS A NEW FORM OF 'BEGGAR-THY-NEIGHBOUR' POLICY

It is well established that R&D cooperations have the potential to promote the dynamic efficiency of a market system. In particular this can be shown for models where direct R&D competition takes the form of a tournament, i.e. when, roughly speaking, only the winning firm is able to realize a substantial first-mover advantage, with no neighbouring R&D areas for rivals to move to.[5] This, combined with the assumption of technical uncertainty in the R&D process, leads to a situation where more investment in R&D is no longer a guarantee of success. No firm can ever be sure to discover the new product or technology even in the next moment of time. Only the expected time lag before discovery can be reduced – or, which comes to the same thing, the instantaneous probability of discovery at any particular point in time can be increased – by investing more.[6]

However, since each firm considers only its own marginal benefit from investment and does not take into account the reduction it imposes on the expected value of the other firms' investments, such a race results in excessive duplication of effort. The firms collectively forgo intertemporal efficiencies that could be realized by investing at a lower rate over a longer planning horizon.

R&D cooperations are able to correct this market failure. Sharing R&D results internalizes the aforementioned externality imposed on other firms' investments. Joint profits are maximized, R&D efforts are reduced, and discovery takes longer in terms of expected value. 'Overgrazing' is avoided and resources are saved. Thus, joint R&D is typically beneficial in terms of dynamic efficiency.

However, to evaluate the overall welfare consequences of R&D cooperations it is not sufficient to examine just the effect of joint R&D on the level of R&D investments or discovery times. To get a complete picture its implications for the static efficiency of the subsequent output market have to be considered as well. To put the argument in its starkest terms, assume an industry-wide R&D agreement that includes joint exploitation of the newly developed product or process. Clearly, as soon as the innovation is terminated joint production eliminates any rivalry in the product market. Profits rise, whereas consumer rents typically diminish despite the introduction of the new product or process (see Chapter 10 of this volume). Thus, the overall effect in the product market tends to be negative. When output is reduced, the R&D cooperation gives rise to a welfare loss that can be substantial enough to overcompensate for any dynamic efficiency gains.

Thus, society may be better off if R&D had been conducted independently instead. That is the reason why most economists recommend a strict rule-of-reason analysis for R&D cooperations. If the anti-competitive threat cannot be ruled out with certainty – or alternatively if one is not able to define precisely the conditions when the overall welfare effect of joint R&D is undoubtedly positive – rule-of-reason treatment is seen as the sole way to guarantee that only welfare-enhancing R&D cooperations come into existence.

So far, we have examined the welfare effects of R&D cooperations from a purely domestic point of view. Firms were not engaged in international trade, relevant markets were at least geographically well defined, and welfare was simply the sum of consumer and producer rents, generated by economic activities that took place within that strictly confined area. However, as we know from the literature on strategic trade policy, total surplus may become an inappropriate welfare measure when international trade and investment are present. In particular, domestic policy may seek to maximize a welfare function that distinguishes between domestic and foreign consumers or firms, and may seek to raise the home country's welfare at the expense of others.

To present this argument in its starkest terms, assume that a domestic industry consists of a single firm that sells its product only on international markets. Then the country's welfare can be strictly identified with the firm's profit.[7] Given these conditions, privately profitable cooperation between the domestic firm and foreign firms is welfare-improving, irrespective of welfare losses imposed on foreign consumers. Thus, from a purely domestic point of view, it appears justified to treat international R&D cooperations more permissively than national ones. In the extreme, as our example suggests, one might wish to free international R&D cooperations completely from the constraints of antitrust law.

But things are not so straightforward when one considers the possibility that other countries might retaliate by choosing trade policies that have the effect of reducing such one-sided gains from international cooperation.[8] Suppose, for example, that foreign consumers suffer a welfare loss from international cooperation that would have been prohibited if it involved two firms in the same country. In these circumstances, foreign governments may interpret tolerance of cooperation as an aggressive act, to be countered by subsidies (either to investment in R&D or to production) granted to their national firms respectively. Thus, international welfare may be reduced twice. Once by the country that has established an aggressive competition law and a second time by the policy reaction of the foreign governments.

Clearly, in that case the benefits from treating national and international R&D cooperations alike are most obvious. By adopting a more restrictive antitrust law international welfare is improved, exports rise and foreign retaliation is avoided.

On the other hand one has to concede that the conclusions drawn so far depend crucially on one sensible point, namely the assumption of a firm without any connections with national markets. Of course, this assumption will hardly ever be justified by empirical evidence. On the contrary, under reasonable circumstances one may rather expect the opposite case. Normally, the national champions are considered as the type of firms which will most likely be engaged in international cooperations. Hence it seems reasonable to expect that national consumers too will be exposed to the consequences of a cooperation. In that case, direct exemption from antitrust policy would be reasonable only if the rise in profits resulting from participation in the cooperation would outweigh the welfare losses for the national consumers.

Apart from this drastic action there is, however, at least a tendency left to look with a more friendly eye upon an international cooperation than a national one where national consumers alone have to bear the potential static welfare loss from a cooperation which acts exclusively on national markets.

R&D COOPERATIONS: A PRIVATE SUBSTITUTE FOR AND A MEANS OF STRATEGIC TRADE POLICY

Strategic trade policy is based on the idea that government interventions can raise national welfare by shifting oligopoly rents from foreign to domestic firms. As the literature shows, the most direct way to serve this purpose is to grant an export subsidy which establishes a credible pre-commitment in favour of the home firm. However, one can also imagine a more complicated multi-stage process, in which firms themselves attempt to establish commitments to higher output through investment in capital or R&D. In these models, considered in Brander and Spencer (1983), it is the subsidies in investment that play the strategic role. Because they have a deterrent effect on foreign activities, they alter the subsequent game in such a way that domestic firm profits rise by more than the subsidy. Thus national welfare is improved.

In the models of strategic trade policy governments are of crucial importance, because they are doing a 'job' which firms cannot do by themselves. They establish a credible prior commitment to higher output which assigns the leadership role to one particular firm. However, as we know from the industrial organization literature there are other situations where this leadership role may emerge quite naturally. In particular such is the case with entry deterrence models. For example, in the Dixit–Spence model the incumbent firm is allowed to act first, leading to investments in excess capacity to deter or limit entry.[9] Thus, pre-commitments may be seen as a common phenomenon when firms are asymmetrical.

This raises an interesting question with respect to cooperative R&D. Can such an arrangement be considered as an attempt to form a private pre-commitment, provided that the arrangement is partial and not industry-wide? This issue will be addressed in what follows. In order to examine the strategic features of international R&D cooperations properly, a few more assumptions are needed, however.

Firstly, suppose there is an international industry consisting of n identical firms, all located in different countries, whose sole business is to export a homogeneous product to a country '$n + 1$', which is by assumption not able to produce that particular commodity by itself. Again, this is a simplifying assumption that constitutes a scenario where the national welfare of all n countries can be strictly identified with home-firm profits whereas any change in consumer rent is restricted to country $n + 1$. Of course, this simplification is only for analytical purposes. It allows us to concentrate entirely on the profit changes that the cooperation brings with it.

Secondly, let us assume that there exists a certain innovation project, known to all firms, that lowers production costs significantly. There is Cournot competition in the output market. Marginal production costs are constant and the demand curve is linear.[10] All firms have the same interest in realizing the associated profit stream. However, since we intend to model an R&D race, the right to exploit the fruits of successful R&D is strictly confined to the firm that is innovating first.[11] Ex-post licensing is excluded. But firms have the possibility to engage in an ex-ante arrangement that offers all participating firms access to the R&D results, i.e. they can establish an R&D cooperation.[12] Let us assume that m (with $1 \leq m \leq n$) of our n firms have decided to do so, and investigate the consequences of this decision for the other fringe firms who still act independently.[13]

According to the principle of subgame perfectness we will start this examination in the product market. Since this is the final decision, it is influenced by all previous actions: the number of cooperating firms as well as the outcome of the R&D tournament, which is in turn determined by the R&D investments firms have chosen.

Without R&D all firms in the industry were facing the same production costs offering each firm a given profit. Yet, with successful completion of the R&D project, firms' profits differ. Two cases have to be distinguished. The first comes along when one of the non-cooperating fringe firms has succeeded in the R&D race. In this case the innovation is exploited exclusively by that firm. It realizes a winner's profit, exceeding the profit it has earned before. Otherwise there would have been no investment in R&D at all. Apart from the winner all other firms in the industry are losing money. They have to face the same loser's profit, irrespective of whether they are a member of the cooperation or just another fringe firm. Thus, in this case the cooperation size has no effect on the distribution of profits in the output market. The innovator has improved its situation whereas all other firms are worse off.

If, however, the cooperation has won the race, all realized individual profits will depend on m, the number of participating firms. The more firms that join the arrangement the smaller the individual profit of the winning firm and the smaller the profit of a remaining fringe firm will be. Because of the sharing of R&D results, an increase in m implies more firms with superior technology. Assuming a standard Cournot, this leads to an increase in aggregate output that harms both the remaining fringe firms and the cooperation members, which have to face an erosion of their individual competitive advantage. Thus, we can conclude that more cooperation widens the profit gap between winning and losing for outside firms, while it narrows the gap for its members.

Even more important with respect to partial R&D cooperations is, however, that more cooperation also gives rise to a growing difference between the individual winner's profit of a cooperation member and the corresponding profit of a fringe firm. As already mentioned, due to the sharing of R&D results cooperative profits tend to fall with more cooperation, whereas the winner's profits of the fringe firms remain unaltered. Thus, the decision to cooperate is not costless. Cooperation members have to forgo the higher profits from independent R&D. Without that reduction in profit firms would always prefer to establish an R&D cooperation that is industrywide.

On the other hand, there has to be a lower boundary to this profit loss, as well. Otherwise, firms may not cooperate at all. This can most easily be demonstrated by considering an output market with Bertrand competition. If the cooperation members compete on price, the potential profits from innovation are driven down to 0. With no winner's profits left the loss from cooperation will be total, indicating that firms will never cooperate in this case, given the option of staying independent instead.

Another case of unprofitable sharing emerges when the innovation is drastic, i.e. when the cost savings from innovation are substantial enough to offer the innovating firm a monopoly position. A transfer of technology would then only introduce ex-post competition in the product market. The monopolist would lose his privileged position. Because his profits alone exceed any possible duopoly profits a cooperation can earn, a drastic innovation will be shared only when there are additional benefits from cooperative R&D that are substantial enough to overcompensate for the profit loss in the output market.[14]

If, however, firms are engaged in Cournot competition one may conveniently expect that the combined winner's profits of all cooperation members will rise the more firms join in the arrangement. But in fact even this result requires some further assumptions. Generally speaking, the increase in aggregate profit can arise only when the cost reduction from wider dissemination of R&D results offsets the loss in cooperative revenues stemming from more intense competition. Hence this condition will most easily be fulfilled when the demand function is not 'too' concave as in the case of a simple linear demand curve.

To sum up, by assuming a standard Cournot in the output market a situation has been established where more cooperation will cut down the individual winner's profits of the participating firms, but not by so much that it may become unprofitable to cooperate at all.

In the second stage each firm decides how much R&D to do at each instant of time. In common with most other models of an R&D race, we assume that the relationship between the probability of discovery and R&D efforts is time-independent and exponential, leading to constant research intensities.[15]

Moreover, all firms face the same innovation technology z, which is a positive, increasing and convex function of R&D efforts, with $z' \rightarrow +\infty$ when the chosen R&D intensity is very great. Thus there are decreasing returns all round. More intense R&D is more costly, but yields a shorter time to successful innovation.

Thirdly, we are assuming that the individual innovation processes are independent. In particular, we are precluding the public-good case with individual R&D costs that depend on the research efforts of others. Since this assumption guarantees positively sloped R&D reaction functions, it is crucial to our further analysis.

Given these conditions, firms choose R&D intensities to maximize the expected pay-off from innovation. However, the individual pay-offs are not identical for all firms. The exact formulation of the profits and the corresponding R&D reaction functions can be found in appendix 9.1. Here it suffices to note that, according to the decision to establish an m firm cooperation in the first stage, one has to distinguish sharply between the individual pay-off of a cooperation member and that of a fringe firm conducting R&D independently.[16] An independent firm has to compete with other fringe firms on the one hand and cooperation members on the other. Only if none of these competitors has succeeded first is the fringe firm given a chance to win the R&D contest. Thus, the competitive threat a fringe firm faces will be distinct, leading to strong R&D investments in order to forestall the successful completion of the innovation process by its competitors.

Compared with a fringe firm, the cooperation member is in a privileged position. Because of the sharing of R&D results all participating firms are able to realize winner's profits when any of the member firms has succeeded first. Cooperation members compete only with fringe firms. Therefore their competitive threat is reduced significantly. This offers an opportunity for the individual member firm to cut down its R&D investment, which in turn saves R&D costs.

This cost saving is the main attraction of cooperative R&D. It builds up a compensating factor to the individual profit losses in the output market that are associated with that measure. However, owing to the convexity of R&D technology these cost savings will decline the more firms join in. Whereas, in contrast, the combined profit losses all other cooperation members have to suffer when an additional firm is accepted will rise with m.

Hence, depending on the magnitude of either effect, there is a possibility of the cooperation size reaching an upper limit before the cooperation is industry-wide. This is the case of partial R&D cooperations coming into existence when the profit loss caused by more cooperation exceeds the associated benefit from additional R&D cost savings. From then on, it will be unprofitable for the existing cooperation members to admit new firms. The cooperation size will have reached its optimal level.

The necessary condition for the profit maximizing cooperation size is given in appendix 9.1 (eq. 5). Leaving details aside, this condition requires the existence of loser's profits in the output market that come with the Cournot assumption. These profits are part of the total profit losses from more cooperation. And it is precisely owing to them that R&D cost savings may not be sufficient to ensure the profitability of wider cooperation. Two examples, already mentioned, may serve to illustrate this case. When the innovation is drastic, or Bertrand competition is prevalent in the product market, no room is left for loser's profits. Suppose, moreover, that the right to exploit the innovation is restricted to a single firm. Then cooperation profits are given, irrespective of the cooperation size. Thus, compared with the Cournot case, with its increasing aggregate winner's profits, this may seem to be a situation where cooperation is not profitable at all. But the contrary is true. In this case even the slightest cost savings from more cooperation will be sufficient to induce an R&D cooperation that is industry-wide.

To sum up, so far we have derived three equations to determine our three strategy variables: the research efforts of a fringe firm (y), the efforts of a cooperation member (x) and the cooperation size (m). Together they characterize the Nash equilibrium of the game, in which firms (1) choose the appropriate level of R&D cooperation, (2) given that decision, choose research intensities and (3) compete in quantities in the product market.

Unfortunately, this system allows no closed form solution. Thus, in order to characterize the equilibrium, one has to work out the effects that an incremental increase in m will have on the equilibrium values. The cooperation's reduced-form profit function is given by:

$$V(m) = V[x(m), y(m), m]$$

Total differentiation with respect to m yields:

$$\frac{dV(m)}{dm} = \frac{\partial V}{\partial m} + \frac{\partial V}{\partial x}\frac{dx}{dm} + \frac{\partial V}{\partial y}\frac{dy}{dm}$$

From the envelope theorem we know that we can neglect the second derivative. Thus, in order to examine how the optimal V is affected by m, we have to consider two effects: the first is the direct effect indicated by the partial derivative $\partial V/\partial m$ and the second is the indirect – strategic – effect through the change in y. That is:

$$\frac{dV(m)}{dm} = \frac{\partial V}{\partial m} + \frac{\partial V}{\partial y}\frac{dy}{dm}$$

Since $\partial V/\partial y$ is definitely negative, we have to consider two possible equilibria: one where both terms – $\partial V/\partial m$ and dy/dm – are positive and one where they are both negative. This distinction is important, because only the first equilibrium implies a clear-cut profit loss for the fringe firms as a consequence of cooperative R&D. Whereas, if both terms turn out to be negative in equilibrium, fringe firms will possibly benefit from cooperation, because of lower research intensities. Of course, under this condition we can still have a foreclosure equilibrium, provided that the rise in expected profits from more cooperation will be higher for a cooperation member than for a fringe firm. Nevertheless, here in this outline we will concentrate on the more drastic case when $\partial V/\partial m$ and dy/dm are both positive in equilibrium.

A sketch of how to derive the necessary conditions for this result is given in appendix 9.2. Here in the text we will instead turn to discuss the major implications of this case. To begin with: more cooperation leads to higher research intensities – and therefore R&D costs – of those which are excluded. They have to face a profit loss which would become even greater when the cooperation size exceeded its equilibrium value.

This has two important implications. The first is most obvious: no one has an interest in more cooperation. Not the cooperation members, which have chosen m to maximize their expected pay-offs, and not the fringe firms, which would have to suffer an even bigger profit loss from that measure.

The other major implication of this property concerns the membership decision. If fringe firms suffer from more cooperation in equilibrium, one can be certain that up to that point it has always been profitable for them to join in the arrangement. They would never have chosen to stay independent instead. This means that we can exclude the situation where fringe firms have an interest in more cooperation, not because they want to join in but because they can gain from softer R&D competition. Under the condition described above, the decision for a partial R&D cooperation will be consistent with the individual incentives of its potential members.

Considering the results so far, the strategic element of R&D cooperations should be quite obvious. To establish a partial R&D cooperation increases the expected profits of its member firms at the expense of others that are excluded. The deterrent effect comes along with fringe firms' rising R&D intensities. This trend causes a decline in their expected pay-offs. With fixed costs entailed in the research process, rising R&D intensities may even force fringe firms to refrain from any R&D at all.

This scenario requires R&D competition to be tough. Considering the first-order condition for the profit-maximizing choice of m, we know that a partial R&D cooperation will be profitable only when the research intensity of a cooperation member has not yet started to diminish significantly when a new member is adopted. Suppose that markets are not too thin. Then, the cooperation will include only a few members compared with the bulk of fringe firms that are forced to remain outside.

Despite the foreclosure effect, the welfare impact of R&D cooperations will, however, be positive. An R&D cooperation, no matter whether partial or industry-wide, helps to avoid wasteful duplication of R&D effort. It saves the resources of its member firms and reduces R&D costs. Thus, no potential gains of fringe firms from less cooperation could ever be sufficient to outweigh the losses imposed on member firms. R&D cooperations tend to improve the expected pay-offs from innovation, industry-wide.

With respect to welfare, however, even a maximization of industry pay-offs would not be sufficient to achieve the best solution. Given well behaved demand functions in the product market, it is easy to establish that more cooperation improves expected consumer's surplus. Even if joint R&D delays the expected time of innovation, consumers are better off. More cooperation gives more firms access to the new technology. And competition in the product market guarantees that this will result in an increase in aggregate output that consumers can benefit from. Thus, a social planner attempting to maximize the sum of producer and consumer rents would choose a higher level of cooperation than private firms do, when they maximize individual profits. The private incentive to cooperate falls short of society's needs.

Considering the positive welfare effects of partial R&D cooperations, favourable treatment by public policy seems to be justified. If the private incentive to cooperate falls short of the social benefits associated with the measure, the promotion of R&D cooperations seems to be in order.

Moreover – and this is of course of crucial importance when it comes to competition policy – it is even true when production is included. When cooperations are industry-wide one can expect a welfare loss due to monopolization in the product market. With partial R&D cooperations, however, this danger is significantly diminished. Generally, members of a partial cooperation cannot gain from an output reduction. As long as there is still Cournot competition between cooperation members and fringe firms in the product market, cooperating firms would have to face a profit loss if they did not capture the Cournot solution. Thus, if firms have decided to cooperate in both fields, it is most likely that there exist some additional gains associated with that measure. Otherwise there would be no need for joint production. Firms could equally well have chosen to operate as independent Cournot oligopolists instead.

This suggests that the antitrust treatment of R&D cooperations should rely on 'safe harbours' defined in terms of the combined ex-post market shares of the firms involved. Even joint R&D of firms with significant market shares should be permitted only after specific consideration of ex-post market performance.

However, this favourable picture of R&D cooperations may change drastically when firms of different countries are involved. Given that profits directly coincide with national welfare, governments are no longer indifferent as to which firm should be part of the arrangement. When the cooperation is international, governments want their 'national champion' to be included. This raises the question of membership. How do firms decide with whom they want to cooperate and who should belong to the fringe instead?

Perhaps the most direct way to cope with that issue is to relax the assumption that all firms are symmetrical. Suppose, for example, that firms are differently efficient in conducting R&D. Then, given perfect information and differences in R&D technology that are fairly moderate and well distributed, we can expect the partial cooperation to consist of the most efficient firms. Because of lower costs, they spend more on R&D, gain the higher expected pay-offs from innovation and have, consequently, a greater incentive to cooperate.

Having this particular argument in mind, national governments are provided with an opportunity to influence the membership decision in favour of the domestic firm. By subsidizing R&D they can establish a credible pre-commitment for the national firm to become part of the arrangement.[17] As long as their subsidy does not exceed the difference in pay-offs between a cooperation member and a fringe firm, the country is better off.[18]

However, a common feature of strategic trade policy models is that all governments share the same incentive. And if all of them act accordingly, every country will face a welfare loss. This can most easily be seen when the afore-mentioned efficiency differences are weak. In that case every government will pay exactly the profit difference between membership and non-membership. Thus, the basic situation remains unaltered. All countries would be better off, without subsidizing their domestic firm.

This is the traditional story of strategic trade policy. A different interpretation of the model can be given by shifting the focus from the export to the import side. The goal of strategic trade policy will then change from the promotion of exports to the restriction of imports. Owing to their foreclosure effect R&D cooperations have the potential to become a means of defending domestic markets against foreign competitors. Built up by national firms, these arrangements may be seen as a relatively inconspicuous instrument to expand the home country's profits at the expense of others.

And indeed, provided that there are enough domestic firms to form an efficient cooperation, our theoretical considerations can be interpreted as lending support to this argument. However, there is one additional drawback national governments have to have regard to. With domestic markets involved consumers' interests can no longer be neglected. From the perspective of the home country the traditional trade-off between static and dynamic efficiency will be restored. And this implies a change in the domestic attitude towards R&D cooperations. Based on our model with the strict Cournot assumption in the product market, one can expect a stronger incentive to support joint R&D, since domestic consumers will benefit from wider adoption. In that case a purely national cooperation may emerge quite naturally.

However, this is true only of partial cooperations in markets which are not dominated by national suppliers. Otherwise, when there are many domestic firms involved, one has to consider another group that will suffer from a partial cooperation, namely the national firms which are excluded. Thus, even if one is willing to accept that consumers benefit from cooperation, the domestic government will lose interest in who wins the race. Hence in this case one would rather expect the foreign governments to promote a cooperation of their firms in order to open the market, since they are left with the stronger incentive. If, however, the home country's government should adhere to its plans and try to establish an R&D cooperation of all domestic firms even in this case, public policy will definitely be harmful, not only for the foreign firms but also in terms of domestic welfare.

Considering the different welfare effects of national and international R&D cooperations, it may seem justified from an international point of view that competition policy treats international cooperations (including those which serve domestic markets with strong competition from abroad) less permissively than purely domestic arrangements. Not because they raise any specific antitrust concerns, but because of the strategic trade policy element involved. This raises the more fundamental question of whether competition policy should be influenced by non-competition goals. With respect to our problem, the effects of both options are quite obvious: if competition policy gets mixed up, more internationally beneficial cooperation will be hampered, and if it does not, society has to face the welfare losses caused by strategic trade policy. Thus, we are in a situation where one instrument is supposed to serve two goals – a dilemma which cannot be solved without an additional, effective instrument at hand.

On the other side, competition policy is not self-serving. It affects other policy fields. And this makes it necessary to reflect and coordinate its implementation from a broader perspective. Otherwise, society will have to forgo possible welfare gains if competition policy is too tight.

GLOBAL ENTERPRISES: A NEW CHALLENGE

Compared with the difficulties of working out an international standard of competition policy, it is much easier to agree on convergence of different national antitrust policies as a desired goal – in particular, when global enterprises are involved. In the following section we will briefly outline their major impact on international competition policy. Moreover, this allows us to add a few more arguments along less theoretically confined lines.

To this end, we have restricted R&D to the choice of research intensities. Cooperative R&D was defined by the sharing of R&D results. Information was perfect and firms were identical.[19] This helped us to abstract from the particular arrangement firms might have chosen to achieve the common goal. Given these assumptions, organization is irrelevant. No matter whether firms have established an R&D joint venture or a patent pool to share research conducted independently, the research intensities are always the same.

The second major simplification concerns the lack of international linkages. In the model we have considered firms confined to one single activity: the production of a commodity and its export to a distant market. This restriction was due to analytical purposes. Nevertheless, it has to be dropped, in particular, when it comes to international R&D cooperations where global firms are involved.

Introducing international linkages enlarges the scope for domestic firms to act strategically.[20] For example, the sharing of R&D results may substantially strengthen the market position of the domestic firm abroad, leading to profit losses among other foreign firms that are not part of the arrangement. Or, even more directly, the domestic firm may be able to establish an R&D agreement which favours its position onesidedly. This danger is especially severe when foreign firms are competing with each other to enter into strategic alliance with the domestic firm. Thus, the private incentives to establish an international cooperation may well exceed its social benefits.

On the other hand, when it comes to global enterprises, additional positive welfare effects are possible. One argument along these lines would be that such firms make more widespread – international – dissemination of R&D results likely. Another can be related to the fact that such firms typically run several R&D projects simultaneously. Thus, there may be positive spillovers within the firms that are generally much more difficult to evaluate than simple product market profits.

However, these positive effects can easily be outweighed when international competition policy lacks convergence. Global enterprises are geographically independent by definition. This makes them particularly sensitive in deciding where a cooperation should be located. When global firms are involved countries of origin play a minor role. Such firms' international investments are strictly determined by private profitability, which gives them a particularly strong position *vis-à-vis* national antitrust authorities.

Moreover, global firms are able to gain from differences in national antitrust policies. In the extreme, they offer the opportunity to establish an R&D cooperation, irrespective of the antitrust concerns involved. Thus, whereas international welfare suffers, the country with the permissive antitrust law will benefit not only from the higher profits of domestic firms but also from additional direct investment and even from subsequent exports when the R&D arrangement includes production. The locational choice establishes a pre-commitment by itself. When global enterprises are involved, it is the efficiency of international direct investments that requires the convergence of different national antitrust policies in this field. And this goal should be achieved as quickly and completely as possible.

However, global firms are not only geographically independent. The second aspect is that their business activities are not confined to a single area. Such enterprises work on a global scale, selling goods and services all over the world. Hence, if global firms join together and form a cooperative group, one can expect that the welfare effects associated with that measure will spread over markets in many different countries, affecting local consumers and firms as well. Generally, however, the effects will not distribute uniformly. Some countries may benefit whereas others have to suffer a welfare loss. And even with regard to the extent of the effect, one can imagine that some countries will be more affected than others.

Apart from the performance of the global firms involved and their cooperative strategy, the national welfare impact hinges critically on the international competitiveness of the local industries involved. If their performance is low, the country may be confronted with harsh consequences, including the case that the existence of the industries in question may be jeopardized. Moreover, even the potential welfare loss imposed on national consumers tends to rise when domestic firms are less competitive. Since the loss in consumers' rent depends critically on the degree of competition in the post-innovation product market, consumers in other countries with more competitive domestic industries will be better off, in general.

Given this scenario, it becomes clear that the harmonization of competition rules alone may not be sufficient to guarantee an appropriate competition policy on a global scale. As long as countries have a strong incentive to design their competition policy in favour of their own national welfare, there is the danger of diverging assessments building up a potential for international conflict that may even take the form of a trade war.

One possible route of escape from this problem could be the creation of a supranational competition law which makes it possible to judge international cooperations with a significant impact on international trade directly. This is the approach chosen by the European Union. It offers the opportunity to check the overall welfare effect of a cooperation project and to decide on the sole ground of efficiency. It offers no solution to the issue of unevenly distributed welfare effects. However, since they seem to be a problem that cannot, in principle, be tackled with competition policy alone, this argument poses no serious objection. An international antitrust code could at least prevent competition law from becoming a bone of contention that harms both international trade and efficiency.

APPENDIX 9.1

Let Π be the individual profit in the product market without R&D, Π_m^W the winner's profit of a cooperation member with the subscript m indicating that the cooperation has won the race and Π_{n-m}^L the respective loser's profit when the fringe firms have succeeded instead, then the total expected pay-off of a cooperation member will be:

$$V = \frac{\Pi_m^W/r \cdot mx + \Pi_{n-m}^L/r \cdot (n-m)y + \Pi - z(x)}{[mx + (n-m)y + r]} \tag{1}$$

with $r > 0$ as the common interest rate, x denoting the research intensity of a cooperation member and y the R&D effort chosen by a fringe firm.

$\hat{\Pi}_{n-m}^W$ denotes the winner's profit of an independent fringe firm, $\hat{\Pi}_m^L$ its loser's profit when the cooperation has won the race and $\hat{\Pi}_{n-m}^L$ the respective profit when another fringe firm has succeeded first. Hence the expected pay-off of a fringe firm will be:

$$\hat{V} = \frac{\hat{\Pi}_{n-m}^W/r \cdot y + \hat{\Pi}_m^L/r \cdot mx + \hat{\Pi}_{n-m}^L/r(n-m-1)\bar{y} + \Pi - z(y)}{[mx + (n-m-1)\bar{y} + y + r]} \tag{2}$$

with $\bar{y}$ denoting the research effort of another fringe firm.

239

The Nash equilibrium in research intensities is determined by the two reaction functions

$$x \in \arg_x \max V \Rightarrow \Pi_m^W + (\Pi_m^W/r - \Pi_{n-m}^L/r)(n-m)y$$

$$-z'(x)/m[mx + (n-m)y + r] - [\Pi - z(x)] = 0 \quad (3)$$

and

$$y \in \arg_y \max \hat{V} \Rightarrow \hat{\Pi}_{n-m}^W + (\hat{\Pi}_{n-m}^W/r - \hat{\Pi}_m^L/r)mx$$

$$+ (\hat{\Pi}_{n-m}^W/r - \hat{\Pi}_y^L/r)(n-m-1)y - z'(y)[mx + (n-m)y + r] - [\Pi - z(y)] = 0$$

$$(4)$$

showing one firm's profit-maximizing choice to any given research intensity of the other firms.

Yet, to establish the industry equilibrium, the decision to cooperate has to be introduced. Assuming that member firms choose m to maximize their individual profits, their decision is given by

$$m \in \arg_m \max V \Rightarrow [\Pi_m^W/r + (\partial \Pi_m^W/\partial m)/r \cdot m] \cdot x - \Pi_{n-m}^L/r \cdot y - V(x-y) = 0$$

$$(5)$$

APPENDIX 9.2

The basic idea to establish the necessary conditions for $\partial V/\partial m$ and $\mathrm{d}y/\mathrm{d}m$ to be positive in equilibrium runs as follows. Provided that both above-mentioned effects are positive for $m = 1$ (which requires an innovation that offers at least some first-mover advantage without being drastic, initially), one can then examine the function $\mathrm{d}y/\mathrm{d}m$ at $\partial V/\partial m = 0$. This offers a dividing line. If the sign of $\mathrm{d}y/\mathrm{d}m$ should be negative at that particular point, we know from our condition above that $\mathrm{d}V/\mathrm{d}m$ has to be positive:

$$\frac{\mathrm{d}V(m)}{\mathrm{d}m} = \underbrace{\frac{\partial V}{\partial m}}_{=0} + \underbrace{\frac{\partial V}{\partial y}}_{(-)} \cdot \underbrace{\frac{\mathrm{d}y}{\mathrm{d}m}}_{(-)}$$

Thus, in order to establish a maximum, m has to rise further, since that is the only way to drive this condition down to 0. Therefore we can conclude that in equilibrium both effects will turn out to be negative.

If, however, dy/dm should be positive at $\partial V/\partial m = 0$, the expression changes its sign:

$$\frac{dV(m)}{dm} = \underbrace{\frac{\partial V}{\partial m}}_{=0} + \underbrace{\frac{\partial V}{\partial y}}_{(-)} \cdot \underbrace{\frac{dy}{dm}}_{(+)}$$

dV/dm will be negative, indicating that the equilibrium value of m must be lower than that which fulfils the condition $\partial V/\partial m = 0$. But this means on the other hand, since we have established that dy/dm will be positive even for a larger m, we can be sure that it will be positive in equilibrium too.[21]

Thus, provided that dy/dm turns out to be positive at $\partial V/\partial m = 0$, both the direct and the strategic effect of cooperation will be positive in equilibrium and the expected pay-off of a fringe firm will decline.

Yet, in order to derive the sign of dy/dm at $\partial V/\partial m = 0$, we need to examine the equilibrium research intensities more closely. As known already, they are defined by the two reaction functions noted above. In general form these functions can be written as:

$$V_x(x, y, m) = 0$$
$$\hat{V}_y(x, y, m) = 0$$

with the subscript indicating the partial derivative with respect to that variable. Totally differentiating with respect to m yields

$$V_{xx}\frac{dx}{dm} + V_{xy}\frac{dy}{dm} + V_{xm} = 0$$

$$\hat{V}_{yx}\frac{dx}{dm} + \hat{V}_{yy}\frac{dy}{dm} + \hat{V}_{ym} = 0$$

Solving the first of these to obtain dx/dm and substituting into the second establishes that

$$\frac{dy}{dm} = \frac{\hat{V}_{yx}V_{xm}}{A} - \frac{V_{xx}\hat{V}_{ym}}{A}$$

where $A(=V_{xx}\hat{V}_{yy} - V_{xy}\hat{V}_{yx}) > 0$ if the Nash equilibrium in research intensities is to be a stable one.

Thus, dy/dm will only be positive when:

$$\hat{V}_{yx}V_{xm} > \hat{V}_{ym}V_{xx}$$

In the neighbourhood of the respective reaction functions the partial derivatives have the following signs:

$$\underbrace{\hat{V}_{yx}\, V_{xm}}_{(+)} > \underbrace{V_{xx}\, \hat{V}_{ym}}_{(-)\ (+)}$$

Given that the R&D technology is sufficiently convex, this condition will in general be fulfilled even at $\partial V/\partial m = 0$ when V_{xm} turns out to be negative. Thus under these circumstances we can conclude that dy/dm will be positive in equilibrium as well.

NOTES

1 See Jorde and Teece (1990).
2 For a discussion along these lines see Geroski (1993).
3 See d'Aspremont and Jacquemin (1988) for the pioneering model. A more extended version is offered by, for example, Kamien *et al.* (1992).
4 One of the few other models where partial R&D cooperations have been addressed explicitly, though in a different theoretical setting, is due to Motta (1992).
5 See Reinganum (1989) for a deeper discussion of this result. Among the more recent papers relying on R&D races are those which have incorporated the moral hazard problem accruing within R&D cooperations. See in particular Gandal and Scotchmer (1993).
6 For the pioneering models of this type see Loury (1979), Dasgupta and Stiglitz (1980) and Lee and Wilde (1980).
7 Such assumptions are common in models of strategic trade policy. See, for example, Krugman (1989).
8 EC Commission Notice of October 21, 1972, on Imports of Japanese Products may be seen as a proof that this possibility is not too far-fetched. Interestingly, this is a case where the voluntary import restraints on Japanese products form the matter of concern. As the notice indicates these restraints may be seen as infringing European competition law despite the fact that 'the head offices of several or all the participant undertakings are outside the Community'. The Commission sees therefore a strong need to 'propose the appropriate measures of commercial policy with a view to remedying the problems in question'.
9 See Dixit (1979).
10 These assumptions are not crucial to the existence of partial R&D cooperations. However, as our further discussion will show, this standard Cournot setting may serve as an example to demonstrate the properties that are necessary to derive this result.
11 Of course, we could have developed our arguments within a standard model of R&D cooperation as well, where joint R&D results in lower R&D costs, more investment and consequently a greater reduction of production costs potential competitors in the output market will have to face. However, to model the innovative process as a race gives us the additional advantage of being able to incorporate not only technical uncertainty but also R&D competition in the sense that the research undertaken by one firm explicitly depends on the R&D efforts of all others. This has particular importance when it comes to partial R&D cooperations where one would expect the decision to cooperate itself to lead directly to a reaction on the part of those excluded.

242

12 Since firms are completely symmetrical, one can think of an R&D cooperation simply as an arrangement to divide the combined expected pay-offs from innovation, implying that not only R&D costs but also product market profits are shared equally between member firms.

13 Thus, we are restricting the analysis to the highly simplifying case where there is only one R&D cooperation possible. Fringe firms are allowed to react to this measure only in terms of R&D intensities and not by establishing a second cooperation to recoup the profit losses they had to face.

14 The meaning of these examples should not be overstated. As long as the cooperation is free to assign the right to serve the product market to one single firm, the profit loss from sharing can always be avoided. Proceeding further we will therefore have to pick up these cases again.

15 For a more detailed explanation and discussion of the underlying assumptions, see Reinganum (1989).

16 Since we are precluding any additional positive externalities between R&D projects that come along when imitation is very easy, this difference will not be softened.

17 To avoid any direct effects on the subsequent R&D contest, think of the subsidy as a simple lump-sum payment.

18 This contrasts sharply with the negative impact of direct R&D subsidies when all R&D reaction functions are of equal sign. For a discussion of this case, see Beath *et al.* (1989).

19 A recent model based on differences in knowledge is Bhattacharya *et al.* (1992).

20 This line of argument follows Katz and Ordover (1990).

21 Obviously owing to $\partial^2 V/m^2 < 0$, this conclusion will always hold.

REFERENCES

Beath, J., Katsoulacos, Y. and D. Ulph (1989) 'Strategic R&D Policy', *Economic Journal*, 99: 74–83.

Bhattacharya, S., Glazer, J. and D. Sappington (1992) 'Licensing and the Sharing of Knowledge in Research Joint Ventures', *Journal of Economic Theory*, 56: 43–69.

Brander, J. and B. Spencer (1983) 'International R&D Rivalry and Industrial Strategy', *Review of Economic Studies*, 18: 707–22.

Dasgupta, P. and J. Stiglitz (1980) 'Uncertainty, Industrial Structure, and the Speed of R&D', *Bell Journal of Economics*, 11: 1–28.

d'Aspremont, C. and A. Jacquemin (1988) 'Cooperative and Noncooperative R&D in Duopoly with Spillovers', *American Economic Review*, 78: 1133–7.

Dixit, A. (1979) 'A Model of Duopoly Suggesting a Theory of Entry Barriers', *Bell Journal of Economics*, 10: 20–32.

Gandal, N. and S. Scotchmer (1993) 'Coordinating Research Through Research Joint Ventures', *Journal of Public Economics* 51: 173–93.

Geroski, P.A. (1993) 'Antitrust Policy Towards Co-operative R&D Ventures', *Oxford Review of Economic Policy*, 9: 58–71.

Kamien, M.I., Muller, E. and I. Zang (1992) 'Research Joint Ventures and R&D cartels', *American Economic Review*, 82: 1293–306.

Katz, M. and J. Ordover (1990) 'R&D Cooperation and Competition', *Brookings Papers on Economic Activity*, 137–203.

Krugman, P. (1989) 'Industrial Organization and International Trade', in R. Schmalensee and R.D. Willig (eds) *Handbook of Industrial Organization* I, Amsterdam, Elsevier Science Publishers, 1179–223.

Lee, T. and L. Wilde (1980) 'Market Structure and Innovation: A Reformulation', *Quarterly Journal of Economics*, 94: 429–36.

Loury, G. (1979) 'Market Structure and Innovation', *Quarterly Journal of Economics*, 93: 395–410.

Motta, M. (1992) 'Co-operative R&D and Vertical Product Differentiation', *International Journal of Industrial Organization*, 10: 643–62.

Reinganum, Jennifer F. (1989) 'The Timing of Innovation: Research, Development and Diffusion', in R. Schmalensee and R.D. Willig (eds) *Handbook of Industrial Organization* I, Amsterdam, Elsevier Science Publishers.

10

PUBLIC POLICIES TOWARDS COOPERATION IN RESEARCH AND DEVELOPMENT

The European Union, Japan and the United States

Stephen Martin

Just where to draw the line between competition and cooperation among independent firms is a topic of perennial debate in the field of public policy towards private enterprise. US policy-makers have recently shifted that line substantially in the direction of cooperation, largely justifying the move with arguments to the effect that cooperation by rivals in research, development, and production will improve dynamic market performance without adversely affecting static market performance. Comparisons of US policy in this area with those of the European Union and Japan featured prominently in the discussion that led up to this decision.

I wish to suggest, first, that a balanced assessment of the economic analysis of technological progress calls for a more cautious approach to claims that interfirm cooperation in research and development will improve dynamic market performance than has been evident in policy circles; it also suggests that such cooperation is conducive to the exercise of monopoly power in product markets. Second, examination of EU and Japanese treatments of interfirm cooperation suggests that they are structured to maintain effective product market competition, incorporating safeguards that are absent from recently adopted US policy.

JOINT RESEARCH, DEVELOPMENT, AND PRODUCTION IN A MARKET SYSTEM

I begin with a review of what economic models and the economic literature have to say about market structure, cooperation regimes, and dynamic market performance. To foreshadow the main conclusions, formal models suggest that while there are some circumstances in which joint research, development, and production (henceforth, R&D&P) is socially advantageous, it generally involves a trade-off between producer welfare and consumer welfare. Sometimes this trade-off will balance out in favour of consumers; sometimes it will not. Sometimes the net impact on social welfare will exceed that which would be produced by independent R&D and independent production; often it will not. Permitting joint R&D&P ordinarily increases firms' profits, but sacrifices the incentives, recognized since the work of Schumpeter, that product market rivalry provides to invest in innovation.

Innovation race models: simulation results

Innovation involves uncertainty in an inherent way. A decision to invest in the development of a new product or process means committing funds and resources in the short run for a pay-off that will come, if at all, in the long run. Such investments typically take place in a rivalrous 'market for innovation': a firm will understand that if it believes it is profitable to conduct research in a certain area, so will other firms. An R&D project may yield no commercially feasible results; it may be 'beaten to the punch' by a rival project.

Innovation race models describe static and dynamic market performance when firms invest current resources in hopes of being the first to develop, at an uncertain future time, a profitable innovation. The first firm to develop the innovation – the winner of the innovation race – gains an operating advantage over its rivals. That advantage translates into greater profits; exactly how much greater depends on the nature of product market competition, on the extent to which the winner can control use of the innovation (appropriability), and on the extent to which the legal regime permits cooperation, either in R&D or in R&D&P.[1,2]

The models that generate the simulation results reported below have a common structure (described formally in the appendices). Firms have the possibility of competing to discover a cost-saving innovation. Innovation is profitable, in an expected value sense: the first firm to discover the cost-saving innovation is able to produce at lower cost, and is able to license the use of the innovation, for a fee, to its rivals.[3] There are externalities in the production of knowledge: firms benefit from the R&D of other firms, and their own R&D benefits other firms. If a firm undertakes R&D, it does so to maximize its expected present discounted value.

The simulation results describe various aspects of technological performance. Most directly related to technological advance are equilibrium firm R&D levels and the expected time to discovery, which vary depending on the cost of R&D and the extent, if any, to which firms are permitted to cooperate. Results also include expected firm values and a measure of consumer welfare, the expected present discounted value of consumers' surplus.

In a market system, firms will invest in R&D only if doing so increases their value. Thus expected firm values determine whether or not R&D will occur in a market system. Similarly, in a market system, technological progress is valued not for its own sake but rather because it generates products that consumers find more satisfactory or production processes that deliver existing products to consumers at lower prices. Consumers' surplus is an index of the extent to which consumers benefit from technological progress. Cost-saving innovation tends to result in lower prices, leaving consumers better off.

The essential trade-off at the heart of the debate over cooperative research, development, and production is between producer and consumer welfare. If firms are allowed to cooperate in the post-innovation product market, this will increase expected firm profit and firms' incentive to invest in innovation. The resulting cost savings will leave society better off. But product-market cooperation translates into high prices, leaving consumers worse off. The net welfare impact of cooperation in research, development, and production is ambiguous. The alternative simulations discussed below give results for different market structures and cooperation regimes. This permits assessment of the implications of alternative cooperation regimes for static and dynamic market performance.

Costly new product innovation

Table 10.1 reports equilibrium outcomes, under alternative cooperation regimes, for a four-firm race to develop a new product.[4] In relation to the size of the market, the fixed cost of setting up an R&D project is large.

Results are shown for two types of R&D cooperation and two types of product market regimes. An R&D joint venture implies that the four firms divide the cost of a single R&D project; with a patent pool, each firm carries

Table 10.1 Costly new product innovation

R&D	Prod	h	E(disc)	Firm value	Consumers' surplus	Net social welfare
None			Never	0	0	0
Joint	Ind	6.2703	0.1595	−1,707.28	28,158.68	21,329.56
Joint	Joint	6.3606	0.1572	1,144.11	8,519.90	13,096.33
Pool	Ind	2.3816	0.0807	−2,241.32	28,378.60	19,413.33
Pool	Joint	2.3902	0.0806	641.95	8,584.78	11,152.58

Notes: Column 1 indicates the nature of R&D competition, column 2 indicates the nature of product market competition; four firms; R&D cost function $z(h) = 40\ 000 + 10h + 1000h^2$; demand intercept = 100; product differentiation parameter = 0.75; spillover parameter = 0.1; interest rate = 0.1; unit cost after discovery = 25.

out its own R&D project. In either case, all firms have access, upon discovery, to the technology used to produce the new product.

After discovery, each firm produces its own variety of the product. Varieties are close but imperfect substitutes. Price is the post-discovery decision variable.[5] Independent product market behaviour implies that each firm non-cooperatively sets the price that maximizes its own profit, taking the prices of other firms as given. Joint product market behaviour implies that firms set prices to maximize total profit.

The (potential) product is completely new: the first row of Table 10.1 shows values if the market never comes into existence (which explains why net social welfare is zero). Row 2 shows results if firms jointly finance an R&D project, then act independently after discovery. Joint R&D implies that the cost of the R&D project is divided four ways. Independent decision-making in the post-innovation market means firms behave rivalrously, pricing to maximize only their own profit, taking the prices of other firms as given. A consequence is the relatively high levels of consumers' surplus: given that the market comes into existence, consumers are well served by product-market rivalry. Net social welfare is the sum of firms' expected values and expected consumers' surplus. This is positive in row 2, showing that society would be better off if firms' expected losses were covered by a subsidy and the market supplied by independent firms after discovery. There are many practical difficulties associated with such subsidies, however.

But in this example innovation is so costly, relative to the size of the market, that it is not profitable for firms to innovate if they must behave independently after discovery, even though joint R&D means sharing R&D costs: expected firm value in row 2 is negative.

Row 3 of Table 10.1 shows results if firms are permitted to maximize joint profit in the post-innovation market. Such cooperation leaves consumers worse off than they would be under the row 2 regime, but better off than if the product is never developed at all (and under a market system without subsidies, this is the relevant alternative). Observe also that the intensity of the R&D product (h) is greater, and expected time to discovery somewhat smaller, in row 3 than in row 2. Greater expected profit in the post-innovation market is an incentive to increase investment in innovation.

Rows 4 and 5 of Table 10.1 correspond to rows 2 and 3, but assume that firms set up a patent pool, not a joint venture. A patent pool implies that each firm sets up its own R&D project, and all firms have access to the results of the first success. Observe that each firm, in equilibrium, invests less in R&D than with an R&D joint venture – h is substantially smaller in row 4 than in row 2, for example. But because there are four independent projects, expected time to discovery is substantially smaller with a patent pool than with an R&D joint venture. Parallel research projects improve technological performance. Comparing rows 4 and 5, we see once again that product-market cooperation makes it profitable for firms to invest in innovation.

Aside from the fact that expected time to discovery is less under a patent pool than in an R&D joint venture, results for the two cases are qualitatively similar. In what follows, I report results only for R&D joint ventures.

For the case of very costly new-product innovation, consumers are better off with collusive supply of the new product than without the product at all. Allowing static product market cooperation can improve dynamic product market performance, if innovation is costly and provides a new product. It is rare, however, that a product is completely new. Nor is all innovation prohibitively costly, in relation to the benefits it offers. Turn, then, to simulations of the market structure–dynamic performance relationship for cost-saving innovation in the production of existing products.

Monopoly research and development

The market for innovation is plagued with imperfections. A policy of allowing joint production after innovation is a policy of allowing static monopoly power as a remedy for these imperfections. But product market power is not a general cure-all for imperfections in the market for innovation. Even complete monopoly will not ensure some socially desirable innovation; by contrast, oligopolistic rivalry in innovation will sometimes support socially desirable research and development that monopoly will not.

Typical results for cost-saving innovation by a monopolist are shown in Table 10.2. In this example, the innovation leads to a reduction in unit cost from 40 to 25, in a market where a price of 100 would drive the quantity demanded to zero.[6] The table reports results for four cases: no R&D and progressively less costly R&D.

In a market system, a firm will actually undertake an R&D project only if the expected pay-off from doing so exceeds the expected pay-off from using the existing technology and avoiding the cost of running the R&D programme. From row 1 of Table 10.2, if the monopoly supplier of this market does not innovate, its expected value is 9,000. Rows 2 and 3 show results if the fixed cost of R&D is relatively high (20,000 and 10,000, respectively). When the fixed cost of R&D is this high, even complete monopoly power

Table 10.2 Fixed cost and innovation under monopoly

Fixed cost (F_R)	h	$1/h$	Firm value	Consumers' surplus	Net social welfare
No R&D		Never	9,000.00	4,500.00	13,500.00
20,000	4.4294	0.2258	5,193.75	6,975.37	12,169.11
10,000	3.1427	0.3182	7,767.06	6,953.19	14,720.25
5,000	2.2485	0.4447	9,555.59	6,923.47	16,479.05

Notes: $c_1 = 40$; $c_2 = 25$; $z(h) = F_R + 10h + 1000h^2$; interest rate $= 0.1$.

will not make investment in innovation profitable: the monopolist's maximum value with R&D, in rows 2 and 3, is less than its value without R&D. Row 2 shows a case in which the cost of innovation is so high that innovation is socially undesirable as well as privately unprofitable – undesirable, that is, if the goal is to maximize the sum of consumers' plus producer's welfare. If innovation is somewhat less costly, as in row 3, it is socially desirable but privately unprofitable. If innovation is less costly still, as in row 4, it will be privately profitable as well as socially desirable.

In this example, market power is at its maximum: there is one supplier and (by construction) no possibility of entry. But complete monopoly power is not always sufficient to support socially desirable R&D. Reliance on market power to provide incentives to invest in R&D is a second-best solution to imperfections in the market for innovation.

Oligopoly research and development

Table 10.3 shows that rivalry in innovation can sometimes produce results that monopoly market power does not. It extends line 2 of Table 10.2 from monopoly to independent oligopoly innovation. In the market for innovation, each firm sets up its own R&D project, if it is profitable to do so. If a firm sets up an R&D project, it picks the most profitable R&D intensity, taking the R&D intensities of other firms as given.

The first row of Table 10.3 reproduces the corresponding values from line 2 of Table 10.2. The rows that follow show equilibrium values if there are two, three, four, and five firms, respectively, in the market. As one would expect, the greater the number of firms, the lower is expected firm value (with or without innovation) and the greater is expected consumers' surplus.[7]

But expected firm value without innovation falls more rapidly as the number of firms increases than expected firm value with R&D. If an

Table 10.3 Cost-saving innovation under oligopoly

n	h	E(disc)	V_{RD}	V_{ST}	CS_{RD}	CS_{ST}	NSW_{RD}	NSW_{ST}
1	4.4294	0.2258	5,193.75	9,000.00	6,975.37	4,500.00	12,169.11	13,500.00
2	4.2288	0.1075	2,118.60	3,291.43	16,920.02	13,165.71	21,157.22	19,748.57
3	4.2176	0.0659	1,294.62	1,575.00	19,895.13	16,537.50	23,778.98	21,262.50
4	4.2278	0.0455	995.52	915.45	21,293.52	18,308.97	25,275.61	21,970.76
5	4.2416	0.0337	841.96	596.94	22,103.38	19,400.51	26,313.17	22,385.20

Notes: Independent R&D and independent pricing; n is the number of firms; h is equilibrium R&D intensity; subscript RD indicates values if R&D takes place; subscript ST indicates values if R&D does not take place; V = firm value; CS = consumers' surplus; NSW = net social welfare = nV + CS; intercept = 100; $c_1 = 40$; $c_2 = 25$; $z(h) = 20\,000 + 10h + 1000h^2$; product differentiation parameter = 0.75; spillover parameter = 0.1; interest rate = 0.1.

oligopolist sets up an R&D project, it has a chance of gaining a cost advantage that rivals cannot compete away. If there are four or more firms, expected firm value with innovation is greater than expected firm value without innovation. Product-market rivalry can make innovation privately profitable as well as socially desirable.

Increases in the number of firms have other desirable effects on market performance. In Table 10.2, the expected time to discovery falls as the number of rivals increases: the more firms there are in the market, the more independent R&D projects there are, and the more chances, from a social point of view, that some project will succeed. Consumers' surplus and net social welfare rise as the number of rivals increases. These are standard results of oligopoly models: the greater the number of firms, the better is static market performance.

By reducing the initial flow of profits, product market rivalry makes it relatively more attractive for firms to invest in the new technology. This is a very Schumpeterian story: firms invest in innovation to escape product market rivalry, and in doing so leave consumers and society better off, even though a monopolist would not find it profitable to invest in innovation. Comparison of Tables 10.2 and 10.3 confirms that industries where (Villard, 1958: 491)

> 'competitive oligopoly' prevails are likely to progress most rapidly. ...
> The basic point is that progress is likely to be rapid (1) when firms are large enough or few enough to afford and benefit from research and (2) when they are under competitive pressure to innovate-utilize the results of research.

Alternative cooperation regimes

I now compare the implications of alternative product-market cooperation regimes for technological performance. The results reported in Table 10.4 refer to an oligopoly of ten firms, and compare equilibrium outcomes under alternative R&D and product-market cooperation regimes.

Table 10.4 illustrates four cases: no R&D, independent R&D and independent production in the post-innovation market, a complete R&D joint venture (including all firms) with independent production in the post-innovation market, and a complete R&D joint venture with joint profit maximization in the post-innovation market.

The first two lines of Table 10.4 repeat the message of Table 10.3: if there is sufficiently strong product-market rivalry, oligopolists will find even relatively costly innovation to be profitable, in an expected-value sense. Investment in R&D offers each firm a chance at getting a cost advantage over its rivals, an advantage that will allow it to reap greater profits than it can hope for continuing to use the existing technology.

Table 10.4 Innovation under oligopoly, alternative cooperation regimes

R&D	Prod	h	E(disc)	Firm value	Consumers' surplus	Net social welfare
None	Ind		Never	154.65	21,651.65	23,198.19
Ind	Ind	4.2921	0.0123	542.25	23,657.45	29,079.98
Complete JV	Ind	4.3829	0.2281	−635.92	33,559.02	27,199.78
Complete JV	Joint	4.5550	0.2195	902.52	9,342.81	18,368.00

Notes: Column 1 indicates the nature of R&D competition, column 2 indicates the nature of product market competition; ten firms; h is equilibrium R&D intensity; subscript RD indicates values if R&D takes place; subscript ST indicates values if R&D does not take place; V = firm value; CS = consumers' surplus; NSW = net social welfare = $nV + CS$; intercept = 100; $c_1 = 40$; $c_2 = 25$; $z(h) = 20\,000 + 10h + 1000h^2$; product differentiation parameter = 0.75; spillover parameter = 0.1; interest rate = 0.1.

Joint innovation is not profitable, even though it means that the cost of the development project is divided ten ways, if firms make independent decisions in the post-innovation product market. Product market competition among ten firms is relatively severe; consumers benefit greatly from innovation, but firms are left worse off than they would be without innovation.

A complete R&D joint venture with post-innovation joint-profit maximization is the most profitable option in Table 10.4, but also leaves consumers (and society as a whole) worse off. Product-market cooperation allows firms to collude after discovery of the new technique. This benefits firms, but harms consumers.

One of the principal lessons of transaction cost economics for the organization of economic activity is that under conditions of impacted information, economic agents seeking to maximize their own pay-offs should be expected to engage in misrepresentation when it is in their interest to do so. It can be expected, therefore, that firms will make the representation that joint production in the post-innovation market is necessary to make investment in R&D profitable. Institutional arrangements to govern transactions in the public interest should be structured to control for such misrepresentation.

Simulation results: recapitulation

Research and development is a costly and a risky activity. Technological progress is socially desirable if it leaves consumers and producers better off. Cooperation in innovation – R&D joint ventures – spreads the cost of innovation among several firms. This can permit 'big ticket' innovation that would otherwise be beyond the budgets of single firms. Cooperation in innovation, however, sacrifices the stimulus that comes from technological rivalry, the incentive to invest that comes from a hoped-for advantage over rival firms. It also sacrifices the reductions in discovery time that are generated by parallel research paths.

Post-innovation cooperation in production – joint R&D&P – increases the expected profit from innovation. This increases firms' incentive to invest in R&D, but leaves consumers worse off after discovery. Whether joint production in the post-innovation market is socially desirable depends on a trade-off between consumer welfare and producer welfare. For very costly innovations – so costly that the innovation would not otherwise take place – cooperation in production will be socially beneficial. For modest innovations, post-innovation product-market cooperation harms consumers so much that society is worse off, overall, after innovation.

Market structure, cooperation regimes, and market performance

It would be convenient to be able to report that the economic literature on research and development had reached a consensus on the nature of the relationship between market structure and dynamic market performance. The views summarized in Table 10.5, and discussed below, suggest that this is not yet possible.

Spillovers and appropriability

The rationale behind a patent system is that there is a social interest in establishing property rights in new products and processes as a way of creating private incentives to invest in innovation. This does not mean that complete appropriability of the returns from R&D would be desirable, from a social point of view: this might very well lead to an unwelcome degree of product market power.

The relative speed with which information about research plans and developments circulates in the research community (Mansfield 1985; see also Mansfield *et al.* 1981) means that the property rights established by the patent system are inherently limited. But there is also evidence that in some markets product differentiation and first-mover advantages allow innovators to collect economic profits over a very long run (Caves *et al.* 1991). Somewhat more generally (Areeda 1992: 31):

> That an invention can be copied ... does not always mean the imitation will occur quickly, overcome the inventor's head start, or bring about perfectly competitive prices depriving innovators of an adequate return.

Table 10.5 Contrasting views on joint R&D&P

Spillovers and appropriability

Knowledge is transmitted so easily that innovative firms have difficulty appropriating the profits that flow from their investments	It is so costly to transfer information that effective commercialization requires close cooperation between innovators and users

Parallel R&D efforts

Cooperative R&D eliminates shame-fully wasteful duplication	R&D is inherently unpredictable; parallel research efforts increase the probability of successful innovation

User-targeted innovation

Tight vertical links between innovators and users are needed for effective innovation	Empirical evidence suggests that innovative activity in supplying industries is directed toward rapidly growing downstream industries

Joint R&D and static product market performance

Joint R&D has no adverse implications for product market performance	Joint R&D makes it easier for firms to non-cooperatively sustain collusive outcomes, all else equal

Coverage of R&D joint ventures

Unless R&D joint ventures are nearly complete, they may not assure sufficient appropriability	A complete R&D joint venture will restrict investment in innovation below the socially optimal level

Extending joint R&D to joint production

Joint production is often a necessary adjunct if joint research and development is to be profitable	Product market cooperation eliminates competitive pressure to invest in R&D so as not to be left behind by more innovative rivals, and reduces socially desirable parallel research paths

Joint R&D&P and dynamic market performance

Joint R&D&P will increase private investment in innovation	Joint R&D&P will reduce the rivalry that stimulates private investment in innovation

---

There is also a large literature on learning by doing and the transfer of knowledge from one party to another; for example (Jorde and Teece 1992: 51):

> The transfer of technology among the various activities that constitute innovation is not costless. This is especially true if the know-how to be transferred cannot be easily bundled and shipped out in one lot – which is clearly the case when the development activity must proceed

simultaneously and when the knowledge has a high-tacit component. In these cases, the required transfer of technology cannot be separated from the transfer of personnel ...

The presence of such costs makes it more likely, all else equal, that successful innovators will be able to appropriate a substantial portion of the economic profits that flow from their new products and processes.

Parallel research paths

For advocates of joint R&D, parallel research is wasteful duplication (Jorde and Teece 1992: 52):

> Collaborative research also reduces what William Norris, CEO of Control Data Corporation, refers to as 'shameful and needless duplication of effort' ... Independent research activities often proceed down identical or near-identical technological paths. This activity is sometimes wasteful and can be minimized if research plans are coordinated. The danger of horizontal coordination, on the other hand, is that it may reduce diversity.... Unquestionably, a system of innovation that converges on just one view of the technological possibilities is likely to close off productive avenues of inquiry.
>
> However, a private enterprise economy, without horizontal coordination and communication, offers no guarantee that the desired level of diversity is achieved at lowest cost.

The closing point is unconvincing. A private enterprise economy, *with* horizontal coordination and communication, offers no guarantee that the desired level of diversity will be achieved *at all* (Scott 1993: 6):

> much of what might appear to be wasteful duplication may in fact provide the numerous research trials needed to increase the probability of innovation to an appropriate level.... rivalry may increase desirable diversity in R&D effort.

Parallel research paths contribute to dynamic market efficiency, by ensuring that multiple avenues to reach a new product or process are pursued. In addition, if information has a 'high-tacit component' then parallel research efforts are a prerequisite for rivalry in the post-innovation market. Parallel research paths thus contribute to static as well as dynamic market efficiency.

User-targeted innovation

It is sometimes asserted that tight vertical relationships are necessary for successful innovation (Jorde and Teece 1992: 49):[8]

> innovation does not necessarily begin with research; nor is the process serial. But it does require rapid feedback, mid-course corrections to designs, and redesign. ... R&D personnel must be closely connected to the manufacturing and marketing personnel and to external sources of supply of new components and complementary technologies so that supplier, manufacturer, and customer reactions can be fed back into the design process rapidly.

Hypotheses put forward by Jacob Schmookler (1966, 1972) suggest caution about this claim (Scherer 1982: 225):

> Schmookler's main contention ... was that demand played a leading role in determining both the direction and magnitude of inventive activity. His basic underlying premises were two: (1) That the ability to make inventions is widespread, flexible, and responsive to profit-making opportunities; and (2) That the larger an actual or potential market is, the more inventive activity will be directed towards it ...

Scherer's own empirical tests, based on a combination of FTC Line of Business data and a broad sample of patents issued to US industrial corporations, confirm the validity of Schmookler's approach (1982: 236; emphasis added):

> at least for capital goods inventions, the main thrust of [Schmookler's] theory survives. Although weaker than those obtained by Schmookler, the correlations between capital goods patenting and using industry investment are impressive. They persist not only for internal process inventions, but also for capital goods product inventions sold across industry lines. *Markets work, both internally and externally, in transmitting demand-pull stimuli.*

Schmookler's demand-pull hypotheses imply that tight vertical links are not a prerequisite for satisfactory technological progress.

R&D joint ventures and static market performance

Jorde and Teece suggest that cooperation in research and development has no implications, in or of itself, for product market performance:

> market definition should be tailored to the context of innovation...,
> and should focus primarily on the market for know-how; specific

product markets become relevant only when commercialization is included within the scope of the cooperative agreement.

Elsewhere (1989: 22), they dismiss the danger of overt collusion in high-technology industries:

> The difficulty of assembling all the relevant parties to effectuate an international conspiracy is an insurmountable challenge in industries experiencing rapid technological change.

These views miss much of the modern literature on non-cooperative collusion, the essential theme of which is that *without* explicit collusion firms can achieve collusive results if for each firm the expected present discounted value of the profit that would be lost by defecting from a tacitly collusive strategy exceeds the expected present discounted value of the income from tacit collusion. It follows from this that the threat to break up an R&D joint venture can be used to induce firms to independently behave in a way that yields collusive results.

If R&D joint ventures are formed non-cooperatively, then they will occur only where firms expect them to be profitable. But if firms expect participation in an R&D joint venture to be profitable, then the threat to break up an R&D joint venture will help sustain tacit collusion on product markets. One can show formally (Martin 1995) that common ownership of an R&D joint venture makes it more likely, all else equal, that non-cooperative collusion will be an equilibrium strategy.

It is difficult to reconcile the claim that tacit or overt collusion is unlikely in high-technology industries with episodes in which R&D cooperation has served as the vehicle for strategic behaviour. An example from the US automobile industry involved strategic delays in the development of emission control technology.[9]

Coverage of R&D joint ventures

A closely related question involves the appropriate horizontal coverage of R&D joint ventures. It is sometimes asserted that nearly complete coverage is essential for efficiency in innovation (Jorde and Teece 1992: 53):

> A 'research joint venture' may not do enough to overcome appropriability problems, unless many potential competitors are in the joint venture.

Complete R&D joint ventures will generally be less profitable than a system of partial joint ventures (Kamien *et al.* 1993; Martin 1994). They also raise the possibility of dynamic inefficiency (Scott 1989: 111–12, emphasis added):

> the problem that I have illustrated is a general problem that could reasonably be expected to plague many cooperative R&D ventures.

The basic conditions create situations in which society would prefer only one firm or an industry-wide cooperative venture *if only the single decision-making entity would choose socially optimal values for the number of R&D trials and the periodic expenditure for each.* However, the monopolist or industry-wide cooperative venture chooses to underinvest in R&D, and, because of that choice, free-entry non-cooperative rivalry produces an R&D expenditure pattern that results in better R&D performance from society's standpoint.

One would also have to take into account the possibility that complete or near-complete R&D joint ventures could actually be a mechanism for overt collusion; this does not seem an unreasonable interpretation of the patent pool central to *Hartford-Empire Co. et al.* v. *U.S.*[10]

The extension of joint R&D to joint R&D&P

One can find claims that separation of production from joint R&D is a source of inefficiencies (Jorde and Teece 1992: 52):

the imposition of a market interface between 'research' and 'commercialization' activities will most assuredly create a technology transfer challenge, a loss of effectiveness and timeliness, and higher costs.

That Japanese joint R&D does not generally extend to production raises doubts about this position (Scott 1993: 216):

some evidence suggests that Japan's cooperative ventures are more likely than their U.S. counterparts to develop truly generic research results which the individual firms then incorporate in their proprietary products that benefit not only from the cooperative generic research, but also from the purposive diversification of R&D through the *keiretsu* groups. The Japanese firms then compete with one another and with foreign firms in the sale of those products that use the generic knowledge that was developed cooperatively.

At a minimum, balanced views suggest that cooperative R&D&P sets up a trade-off between static and dynamic market performance (Jacquemin 1988: 557):[11]

a regulation of R&D cooperation excluding any cooperation at the level of the final markets could discourage or destabilize many valuable agreements. However, allowing an extension of cooperation from R&D to manufacturing and distribution encourages collusive behavior which impedes competition and ... reduces output.

R&D joint ventures and dynamic market performance

One can find the view that there is no desirable alternative to cooperative research and development (Lee and Lee 1991: 340):

> proponents of [joint R&D] emphasize that in today's world of increased competition from abroad and rapidly changing technologies, cooperation is necessary to remain competitive. They point to the advantages of minimizing the costs of developing new technologies, spreading the risks of research and development, reducing unnecessary duplication of research effort, obtaining immediate access to new technologies, new markets and cheap production sources, and making otherwise formidable projects possible.

The view is also held, however, that it is rivalry, not cooperation, that induces private investment in innovation (Scott 1993: 149):

> Arguably, Schumpeter's vision, though, is that in an evolutionary context competition and monopoly are part of the same process. Greater competition implies a greater incentive to use divergent research strategies to lessen the anticipated erosion of quasi-rents caused by competition among rival innovations in the postinnovation market.

The position that R&D joint ventures will improve dynamic market performance is not supported by early evidence on the actual consequences of the National Cooperative Research Act of 1984 (Scott 1993: 177):

> If the NCRA is to be beneficial, we would expect the act to promote cooperative R&D in those areas where the productivity slump hit hard. To turn around the productivity performance of the economy, the act would stimulate R&D in those industries that were poor performers during the heart of the slump.... the gains expected from the act would be most likely if the act furthered cooperative R&D in the unconcentrated, fragmented industries, in the lower productivity growth industries, and in industries where the salubrious effects of R&D diversification could not work because the R&D activities in those industries had not been combined with the R&D in other industries. In fact, what we find is quite the opposite: NCRA-protected cooperative R&D is largely in those industries which, during the heart of the productivity slump which laid the groundswell for the NCRA, were already concentrated ..., had higher productivity growth, and whose R&D was already purposively combined with the R&D activities of other industries. Further, there appear to be no unusual appropriability problems in the industries where protected cooperative R&D is occurring.

Interfirm cooperation and dynamic market performance: reprise

The most conservative reading that can be given of the economic literature on joint research, development, and production is that there is no compelling reason to think that joint R&D&P will *in general* improve static or dynamic market performance. This is consistent with the simulation results reported above. Joint R&D&P may well be the most effective way, from a social point of view, to obtain very expensive innovations. Unless R&D is extremely costly, however, joint R&D is likely to shut off socially desirable parallel research efforts, reducing the rate of technological progress. It can also facilitate tacit collusion, by providing firms with information about rivals' views of the market and raising the opportunity cost of vigorous product-market rivalry. These effects are more likely if joint activity covers all or almost all firms in the market. Joint R&D thus has the potential to worsen static *and* dynamic market performance. Except for very costly innovation, the same is true of joint R&D&P.

THE RANGE OF RATIONALES OF POLICY TOWARDS JOINT R&D&P

European Union

EU policy towards joint R&D&P

Article 85, paragraph 1, of the Treaty of Rome prohibits interfirm agreements that distort competition in the Common Market.[12] But Article 85, paragraph 3, provides that the European Commission may waive this prohibition for agreements

> which [contribute] to improving the production or distribution of goods or to promoting technical or economic progress, while allowing consumers a fair share of the resulting benefit.

For EU competition policy, 'consumer welfare' means the welfare of consumers, not the welfare of consumers plus the welfare of producers. A prerequisite for action under Article 85(3) is that the restriction of competition be no more severe than necessary to obtain the identified benefit.

The EC Commission's early treatment of cooperative research and development under Article 85(3) was permissive, provided that cooperation did not have the effect of blocking post-innovation rivalry (EC Commission 1972: 46):[13]

> agreements arrived at for the purpose of undertaking joint research do not generally restrict competition on condition that the enterprises are not restricted as far as their own research activities are concerned, and

that the results of the joint research are made available to all participants in proportion to their participation.

This approach is continued in the Commission's 1984 block exemption for R&D cooperation (EC Commission 1985: 38):[14]

> The new regulation leaves intact the 1968 Notice on Cooperation between Enterprises, which states that cooperation agreements relating only to R&D normally do not fall under Article 85(1), but extends the favourable treatment to R&D agreements which also provide for joint exploitation of the results.

Joint research and development is thought to be necessary because of market failures of various kinds (EC Commission 1985: 37–8):

> in many cases the synergy arising out of cooperation is necessary because it enables the partners to share the financial risks involved and in particular to bring together a wider range of intellectual and mental resources and experience, thus promoting the transfer of technology.

Characteristically, the Commission takes a structural approach to ensure that restraints on competition have strictly limited effects (EC Commission 1985: 39):

> (i) where at the time the agreement is entered into, any of the parties are competitors for products which may be improved or replaced by the results of R&D, the exemption applies only if their combined production of such products does not exceed 20% of the market;

> (ii) where no two or more of the parties are competitors at the time the agreement is entered into, the exemption applies irrespective of market shares;

> (iii) after five years of joint exploitation, the exemption continues to apply, whether the parties were initially competitors or not, only if their combined production for the new product does not exceed 20% of the market.

The Commission's 1993 Notice on cooperative joint ventures[15] treats product-market rivalry among independent firms as the normal state of affairs, departures from which are not typically mandated by efficiencies that may flow from R&D cooperation (recital 20):

> The economic pressure towards cooperation at the R&D stage does not normally eliminate the possibility of competition between the participating undertakings at the production and distribution stages. The pooling of the production capacity of several undertakings, when it is economically unavoidable, and thus unobjectionable as regards

competition law, does not necessarily imply that these undertakings should also cooperate in the distribution of the products concerned.

The notice takes a realistic view of the impact of a production joint venture on product market performance (recital 22):

> The restriction of competition ... between parents and joint ventures typically manifests itself in the division of geographical markets, product markets (especially through specialization) or customers. In such cases the participating undertakings reduce their activity to the role of potential competitors. If they remain active competitors, they will usually be tempted to reduce the intensity of competition by coordinating their business policy, especially as to prices and volume of production or sales or by voluntarily restraining their efforts.

The adverse effect of joint R&D&P is explicitly held to exceed that of joint R&D alone (recital 37):

> A research and development joint venture may, in exceptional cases, restrict competition if it excludes individual activity in this area by the parents or if competition by the parents on the market for the resulting products will be restricted. This will normally be the case where the joint venture also assumes the exploitation of the newly developed or improved products or processes.

Once again, the standards outlined by the Commission are structural in nature. If a joint venture's parent firms are very small – aggregate annual turnover less than ECU 200 million and aggregate market shares less than 5 per cent – the joint venture is regarded as having no appreciable effect on competition, and the Article 85(1) prohibition of agreements in restraint of competition does not apply (recital 15). A joint venture that combines research, development, production, and licensing will be exempted under Article 85(3) if its parents' combined market share is less than 20 per cent (recital 48). If the joint venture includes distribution, the standard is more severe: parents' combined market shares must be less than 10 per cent (recital 46).

Joint ventures that do not meet these standards may none the less be exempted, following individual evaluation by the Commission.[16] Once again, the Commission's attitude is more cautious the more closely cooperation approaches the final consumer (recitals 59, 60):

> Pure research and development joint ventures which do not fulfil the conditions for group exemption ... can still in general be viewed positively. This type of cooperation normally offers important economic benefits without adversely affecting competition. ... If the joint venture also takes on the manufacture of the jointly researched and developed product, the assessment for the purpose of exemption

must include the principles which apply to production joint ventures. ... Sales joint ventures belong to the category of classic horizontal cartels. ... The Commission will therefore in principle assess sales joint ventures negatively. The Commission takes a positive view however of those cases where joint distribution of the contract products is part of a global cooperation project which merits favourable treatment pursuant to Article 85(3) and for the success of which it is indispensable ... [including] sales joint ventures set up for the joint exploitation of the results of joint R&D, even at the distribution stage.

Structural standards remain important, even for individual exemptions (recital 64):

To assess whether a full-function joint venture raises problems of compatibility with the competition rules or not, an important point of reference is the aggregate market share limit of 10% contained in the group exemption regulations.

The block exemption for cooperative research and development is entirely consistent with the main line of development of EU competition policy, which is one of qualified reliance on the market as a mechanism for resource allocation. Contracts, combinations and concerted practices that restrain trade may be permitted, under Article 85(3) of the Treaty of Rome, if they promote progressiveness, but only if consumers share in the resulting benefits.

The political economy of EU competition policy

The European Commission certainly highlights the economic benefits that flow from an active competition policy (EC Commission 1972: 11; see also 1985: 15):

Competition is the best stimulant of economic activity since it guarantees the widest possible freedom of action to all. An active competition policy ... makes it easier for the supply and demand structures continually to adjust to technological development. ... Through the interplay of decentralized decision-making machinery, competition enables enterprises continuously to improve their efficiency ... competition policy is an essential means for satisfying ... the individual and collective needs of our society.

Despite economists' advocacy of competition because of its perceived affirmative effects on market performance, however, there is little doubt that EU political support for an active competition policy stems from the perception that, without such a policy, European integration would ultimately fail (Spaak Report, 1956, p. 53):

> Le marché commun ne conduirait pas par lui-même à la répartition la plus rationnelle des activités si les fournisseurs gardaient la possibilité d'approvisionner les utilisateurs à des conditions différentes, en particulier suivant leur nationalité ou le pays de leur résidence. C'est dans ces termes que se pose le problème de la discrimination.

In point of fact, EU competition policy permits various restrictions of competition that are forbidden under US antitrust law. The general conditions required are that the restriction on competition be (at least in principle) temporary, that it be no more severe than necessary to accomplish some approved-of goal, and that consumers eventually benefit.

EU competition policy permits independent firms to agree to specialize in the production of certain lines of products – that is, to agree not to compete in certain lines (EC Commission 1973: 19):[17]

> specialization agreements generally contribute to improving the production process ... they are particularly suited to strengthening the competitive position of small- and medium-sized firms. The favourable economic effects of specialization lie in the achievement of economies of scale or ... in rationalization measures which enable the firms to cut costs by concentrating operations; it can be expected that these measures will lead, in conditions of effective competition, to lower prices and will thus benefit the user.

For similar reasons, and under similar conditions, exclusive purchasing agreements can be permitted (EC Commission 1978: 23–4):

> exclusive purchasing agreements can contribute to improving the production and distribution of goods, because they make it possible for the parties to the agreement to plan their production and sales more precisely and over a longer period, to limit the risk of market fluctuation and to lower the cost of production, storage and marketing. And in many cases agreements of this kind give small and medium-sized firms their only opportunity of entering the market and thus increasing competition. However, exemption can only be given where the firms involved do not retain the whole of the benefit. Consumers must be allowed their fair share as well. ... These tests are not satisfied if the exclusive arrangements make it more difficult for other firms to sell on the market, and especially if they raise barriers to market entry.

Firms may restrict competition to coordinate the reduction of excess capacity (EC Commission 1983: 43–4):

> Structural overcapacity exists where over a prolonged period all the undertakings concerned have been experiencing a significant reduction

in their rates of capacity utilization, a drop in output accompanied by substantial operating losses and where the information available does not indicate that any lasting improvement can be expected in this situation in the medium term.

... the Commission may be able to condone agreements in restraint of competition which relate to a sector as a whole, provided they are aimed solely at achieving a coordinated reduction of overcapacity and do not otherwise restrict free decision-making by the firms involved.

... production can be considered to be improved if the reductions in capacity are likely in the long run to increase profitability and restore competitiveness, and if the coordination of closures helps to mitigate, spread and stagger their impact on employment. ...

... consumers can be considered to enjoy a fair share of the benefits resulting from the agreement if, at the end of the agreement, they can rely on a competitive and economically healthy structure of supply in the Union, without having been deprived during its operation, despite the effects of the capacity cutbacks, of their freedom of choice or the benefit of continued competition between the participating firms ...

And, of course, there is affirmative regional and sectoral aid, by the member states and by the Union's structural funds, that aims to spread the social costs of the working of the market system (EC Commission 1972: 17):[18]

Even though the operation of market forces is an irreplaceable factor for progress and the most appropriate means of ensuring the best possible distribution of production factors, situations can nevertheless arise when this in itself is not enough to obtain the required results without too much delay and intolerable social tension. When the decisions of the enterprises themselves do not make it possible for the necessary changes to be made at an acceptable cost in social terms, then recourse to relatively short-term and limited intervention is necessary in order to direct such decisions towards an optimal economic and social result. The purpose of such aids must be to re-integrate the sectors and regions benefiting from them within a practicable and efficient system of competition while reducing the social cost of change ...

As its acceptance of these limited and controlled restrictions of competition shows, the European Union's competition policy neither seeks nor relies upon the untrammelled workings of the market system. It begins from the premise that it is in the nature of a market system to adjust slowly to long-run equilibrium, and that the adjustment often generates social costs that can be ameliorated by accepting short-term restrictions on competition.

Restrictions on competition are accepted where they have the effect of maintaining support for the ongoing process of economic integration. Research and development joint ventures, permitted where market structure suggests continued effective competition, fit naturally into this system.

Japan

Encouragement of research and development has been a persistent feature of Japanese industrial policy. As is well known, it is industrial policy that has shaped the characteristically Japanese version of competition policy (Okimoto 1989: 14):

> The Japanese government has found ways of reconciling industrial policy with antitrust enforcement. The [J]FTC and MITI have been able to work out differences through negotiations. In Japan's latecomer system, the commitment to principles of antitrust has not been allowed to shape the content of industrial policy. There are not very many examples that can be cited in which the [J]FTC has ordered MITI to make major changes in industrial policy in order to conform to antitrust statutes. MITI officials try to take antitrust factors into account in formulating industrial policy.

In the early post-war period, controls on foreign exchange were used to channel imports of state-of-the-art equipment towards industries and firms thought to have the greatest prospects for growth. Tax incentives have also been used to induce firms to invest in R&D. Active industrial policy has been used to ensure that cooperative behaviour contributed to public as well as private goals. Joint research associations have been formed with the encouragement and often the funding of the Japanese government. They are not, in general, frameworks within which firms undertake research and development on a cooperative basis (Odagiri 1986: 407):

> Most well-known among the research associations is that on very-large-scale integrated circuits (VLSI), which was composed of five computer producers and active from 1976 to 1979. This association, having yielded numerous patents, is said to have established a foundation for the following Japanese success in the semiconductor industry. This well-publicized 'success', however, is not typical of research associations. In fact, most of the associations did not have any joint research associations (which the VLSI had), each member firm receiving its share of research funds (partly financed by the government) and carrying out research in its own research institution. Thus they often worked as no more than a channel through which the funds were delivered from the government to the member firms.

The effect of the research association is to ensure rapid dissemination of the results of research and development, ensuring competition in the post-innovation market (Audretsch 1989: 107):

> Research undertaken under the auspices of a Japanese research association frequently is not carried out in a joint laboratory where the members engage in cooperative research. Rather, the R&D is usually carried out in each member's own research laboratory. The resulting information and scientific knowledge is subsequently exchanged in a coordinated manner directed by the research association. This effectively speeds up the process of the diffusion of technological change. Upon completion of the project, the research association is usually dissolved.

The typical form of industrial organization in Japan accentuates this tendency to ensure rivalry in the use of new technologies (Komiya 1993: 52):[19]

> The industrial organization in [Japan's mass-production machinery industries] is characterized by a relatively large weight of 'loose' vertical integration long-term, continuous and cooperative relationship between parent makers and manufacturers of parts and equipment, and by low weights of both 'tight' vertical integration and 'arm's-length' transactions, concerning the production, processing, designing and R&D of parts and manufacturing equipment. These characteristics make possible the long-term, continuous and close cooperation among companies that could not develop through 'arm's-length' transactions, while creating competition through multilateral transactions that could not exist in the 'tight' vertical integration.
>
> Under such industrial organization, a new technology or a new product developed by one firm tends to spread to other firms in the industry rapidly through the network of 'loose' vertical integration. Thus the structure of Japan's mass-production type machinery industry is more conducive to the diffusion of new technologies among firms, and therefore to the overall technological process of the industry, than that of its counterparts in other industrialized countries ...

Thus cooperative R&D in Japanese industry promotes spillovers, with consequent positive effects on competitiveness.

United States: a policy pendulum

According to the 1980 Antitrust Guide Concerning Research Joint Ventures, R&D joint ventures are to be encouraged if they promote research and development that would not otherwise have taken place (USDJ 1980: 8–9):

> If the cost and risk of the research in relation to its potential rewards are such that the participants could not or would not have undertaken the project individually, then the venture will have the effect of increasing rather than decreasing innovation. This may happen, for example, if individual firms lack the resources to finance independent research projects on a reasonably efficient scale or the risks involved in that research are so high that the effort must be shared to make a research project practicable. It may also occur in industries in which the firms are small in size and there is a history of little or no investment in research, so that only joint effort between several firms (or even an industry-wide project) can be expected to produce innovation. If, on the other hand, the joint research replaces existing individual research by the participants or causes those firms to forego research which, in the absence of the joint project, they would have performed individually, the formation of a joint project might well slow the rate of technological progress in the industry, unless the project involves substantial efficiencies.

The 1980 Joint Venture Guidelines embody a cautious approach to restrictions on competition that are ancillary to the functioning of the R&D joint venture (USDJ 1980: 16–17):

> collateral restraints on competition that are clearly closely related to achievement of the venture's essential purposes are ... likely to be legal, while those that are more remotely related to the purposes of the venture are generally of less certain legality, and those whose relationship to the venture's purposes is tenuous or nonexistent and which are significantly anticompetitive are almost certain to be unlawful.
>
> Examples of closely related collateral restraints include: the obligation to exchange any results from research undertaken previously in the field of the joint research, the duty not to disclose results of the joint research to outside parties until patents are obtained, and the division of particular aspects of the research between the venturers.
>
> ...
>
> Restraints more remotely related to the legitimate purposes of the joint venture include restrictions on individual development, production and marketing of the inventions resulting from the research. These restrictions imply collaboration extending beyond mere research efforts, resulting in projects which closely approximate joint manufacturing ventures or even mergers. While in some instances these more remote restraints may be reasonably necessary to the success of the joint research, joint research normally does not necessitate joint

development or manufacture. If such extensive collaboration is necessary ... , it should be limited to the results of the joint research and should not encompass other competing products or services marketed by the cooperating firms ...

The National Cooperative Research Act of 1984 was designed to improve productivity by encouraging joint R&D (Scott 1988: 181):

The framers and supporters of the law hoped ... that the promotion of cooperation would increase [the] net social benefit of R&D investment by improving appropriability, lowering costs, lowering risks, decreasing wasteful overbidding (in the sense of too many trials), and reducing actual duplication ...

The NCRA mandates the use of the rule of reason in antitrust cases involving research joint ventures (Scott 1989: 65):

It provided, inter alia, that the behavior of a research consortium, if challenged under the U.S. antitrust laws, would be judged under a rule of reason asking whether the alleged restraints of trade were ancillary to the pursuit of efficiency. For those research ventures notifying the government of their participants and purposes, any subsequent antitrust violation would be assessed single, not treble, damages.

The National Cooperative Production Amendments of 1993 extends rule of reason treatment to production joint ventures. Provided that production facilities are located within the United States,[20] antitrust action against a production joint venture that has been notified to enforcement agencies would involve the possibility of single, rather than treble, damages.

Significantly, the legislation made no provision for a structurally defined 'safe harbour', despite the fact that such a provision had appeared in many preliminary proposals.[21] The legislation also declined to assign an exemption power to government agencies (Committee on the Judiciary 1993: 725):

One bill has proposed giving the Federal antitrust agencies the power to exempt joint ventures from all penalties and liabilities under the antitrust laws. ...

The principal difficulty with this proposal lay in its elimination of any threat of private enforcement to ensure that market power is not unreasonably exercised against domestic producers.

The logic of relying on private antitrust enforcement while raising the costs of carrying out a private antitrust action (by mandating the use of the rule of reason) and reducing the possible benefits of a private antitrust action (single rather than treble damages) is not immediately obvious.

CONCLUSION

The economic analysis of technological structure–performance relationships suggests that it is a combination of rivalry and cooperation that delivers the best dynamic market performance. Cooperation in innovation allows firms to spread the cost and risk of investing in uncertain R&D projects. Independent product market behaviour ensures that consumers eventually benefit from successful innovation.

The European Union tolerates strictly limited cooperation among independent firms. Before such cooperation is permitted, it is required that the market structure should support effective product market competition and that consumers will eventually benefit in some demonstrable way.

Japan implements an active industrial policy that aims to promote research and development. By subsidy and tax incentives, government encourages firms to invest in innovation. As a *quid pro quo* the government establishes institutional frameworks that have the effect of disseminating R&D output and ensuring that there is rivalry in the exploitation of the results of R&D projects.

Both approaches are consistent with what economics has to say about the determinants of dynamic market performance.

The United States has adopted a permissive attitude towards cooperation in research, development, and production, even by large firms and even where market structure gives no assurance of the maintenance of effective competition. In adopting this policy, US policy-makers have ignored substantial evidence that product-market power is not a desirable, or even an effective, tool to promote innovation. It is safe to predict that this policy will increase private profits. It is much less clear that it will improve market performance or benefit consumers.

In the context of US antitrust, which lacks the natural brake on anticompetitive agreements that the drive to integration provides in the European Union, toleration of product-market cooperation will undermine the reliance on rivalry as a resource allocation mechanism that has characterized US policy for a century and which (paradoxically) is in large measure responsible for the Japanese success that motivates suggestions for change. If it is rivalry that promotes desirable market performance, as most industrial economists continue to believe, such toleration will worsen US economic performance.

APPENDIX 10.1 RACING MODELS OF INNOVATION

Monopoly research and development

Consider a situation in which a monopolist uses a technology with constant marginal and average cost c_1. The monopolist has the option of setting up an

R&D project to develop a new technology that allows production at unit cost $c_2 < c_1$.

Let the random variable τ denote the uncertain time of discovery, and suppose that the relationship between research effort h and the probability of success is exponential,[22]

$$F(t) = \Pr(\tau \leqslant t) = 1 - e^{-ht} \tag{1}$$

with corresponding density function

$$f(t) = F'(t) = he^{-ht} \tag{2}$$

The probability that discovery has not occurred at time t is

$$\Pr(\tau \geqslant t) = 1 - F(t) = e^{-ht} \tag{3}$$

The probability of discovery in a short interval of time dt, given that discovery has not occurred at the start of the interval, is then constant,

$$\frac{F'(t)\,dt}{1 - F(t)} = h\,dt \tag{4}$$

Integrating by parts, the expected time of completion of a project run at intensity h is

$$E(\tau) = \int_0^\infty \tau h e^{-h\tau}\,d\tau = \frac{1}{h} \tag{5}$$

Let $z(h)$ denote the cost of an R&D project run at intensity h, with $z'(h) > 0$, $z''(h) > 0$. Greater research intensity is therefore more costly but yields a shorter expected time to successful innovation.

If the monopolist undertakes an R&D project, it will select research intensity h to maximize the present discounted value of its expected income stream:

$$V_{RD} = \int_{t=0}^\infty e^{-(r+h)t}\left[\pi_m(c_1) - z(h) + h\,\frac{\pi_m(c_2)}{r}\right]dt$$

$$= \frac{\pi_m(c_1) - z(h) + h\,\dfrac{\pi_m(c_2)}{r}}{r+h} \tag{6}$$

The first two terms in the numerator on the right are the monopolist's flow of income while it is using the original technology and operating an R&D project. The third term is the expected present discounted value of monopoly profit using the new technology, from the moment of discovery, weighted by h. The interest rate r is used to discount future income.

The first-order condition for maximization of equation (6) is

$$V_{RD} = \frac{\pi_m(c_1) - z(h) + \dfrac{h\pi_m(c_2)}{r}}{r + h} = \frac{\pi_m(c_2)}{r} - z'(h) \qquad (7)$$

Let h_m denote the solution to (7). For the quadratic cost function $z(h) = F_R + uh + vh^2$, which is used for the simulations reported in the text, h_m is the (positive) solution to the quadratic equation

$$vh^2 + 2rvh - [\pi_m(c_2) - \pi_m(c_1) - ru + F_R] = 0 \qquad (8)$$

A profit-maximizing monopolist will undertake R&D only if its present discounted value with an R&D project, (6), evaluated for the solution to (7), exceeds its value if it does not undertake R&D,

$$V_{ST} = \int_{t=0}^{\infty} e^{-rt}\pi_m(c_1)\,\mathrm{d}t = \frac{\pi_m(c_1)}{r} \qquad (9)$$

The expected present discounted value of consumers' surplus if there is R&D is

$$\int_{t=0}^{\infty} e^{-(r+h_m)t}\left[CS_m(c_1) + \frac{h_m CS_m(c_2)}{r}\right]\mathrm{d}t = \frac{CS_m(c_1) + h_m \dfrac{CS_m(c_2)}{r}}{r + h_m} \qquad (10)$$

where $CS_m(c_1)$ is instantaneous consumers' surplus under monopoly when the old technology is in use and $CS_m(c_2)$ is instantaneous consumers' surplus after discovery of the new technology. If there is no R&D, the expected value of consumers' surplus is

$$\frac{CS_m(c_1)}{r} \qquad (11)$$

It follows that the change in expected consumer welfare due to research and development under monopoly is

$$\frac{h_m}{r + h_m}\frac{CS_m(c_2) - CS_m(c_1)}{r} > 0 \qquad (12)$$

A profit-maximizing monopolist will set a lower price when marginal cost is lower; this benefits consumers. If R&D is privately profitable for a monopolist, it raises social welfare.

Oligopoly R&D

Independent R&D with spillovers, independent post-innovation production

Suppose each firm in an n-firm oligopoly carries out a single R&D project.[23] Let τ_i be the random discovery time of firm i, which operates an R&D project of intensity h_i at cost $z(h_i)$, $i = 1, 2, ..., n$. To allow for possibility of spillovers in R&D activity, let the distribution function of τ_i be

$$\Pr(\tau_i \leq t) = 1 - \exp(-g_i t) \tag{13}$$

where

$$g_i = h_i + \sigma \sum_{j \neq i} h_j \tag{14}$$

The parameter σ lies between zero and one and indicates the degree of spillovers in R&D. $\sigma = 0$ implies that a firm benefits only from its own R&D efforts. For $\sigma = 1$, spillovers are complete; a firm benefits as much from other firms' R&D efforts as from its own.

The probability that no firm has discovered at time t is

$$\prod_1^n \Pr(\tau_i > t) = \exp\left(-\sum_1^n g_i t\right) \tag{15}$$

If no firm has discovered at time t, firm i's instantaneous pay-off is

$$\pi_N(c_1) - z(h_i) \tag{16}$$

where $\pi_N(c_1)$ is the non-cooperative oligopoly pay-off when only the first technology is known.

The probability density that firm i discovers first in the time interval dt is the product of the probability that it discovers for the first time during the interval and the probability that no other firm has discovered at the start of the interval,

$$g_i \exp(-g_i t)\, \mathrm{d}t \times \exp\left(-\sum_{j \neq i}^n g_j t\right) = g_i \exp\left(-\sum_{j=1}^n g_j t\right) \mathrm{d}t \tag{17}$$

In this case, firm i's value, from the moment of discovery, is

$$\frac{\pi_W}{r} \tag{18}$$

where π_W is the instantaneous profit of the firm that wins the exclusive right to control the use of the new technology. π_W depends on the nature of product-market competition and on the appropriability regime, and will be discussed below.

The probability density that some other firm discovers first during the time interval dt is

$$\left(\sum_{j \neq i} g_j\right) \exp\left(-\sum_{k=1}^{n} g_k t\right) dt \tag{19}$$

In this case, firm i's value, from the moment of discovery, is

$$\frac{\pi_L}{r} \tag{20}$$

If firm i undertakes an R&D project, its expected present-discounted value is

$$V_{RD}^i = \frac{\pi_N(c_1) - z(h_i) + \dfrac{g_i \pi_W + \displaystyle\sum_{j \neq i} g_j \pi_L}{r}}{r + \displaystyle\sum_{1}^{n} g_j} \tag{21}$$

Using

$$\sum_{j \neq i} g_j = (n-1)\sigma h_i + [1 + (n-2)\sigma] \sum_{j \neq i} h_j \tag{22}$$

and

$$\sum_{j=1}^{n} g_j = [1 + (n-1)\sigma] \sum_{j=1}^{n} h_j \tag{23}$$

the first-order condition to maximize (21) is

$$V_{RD}^i = \frac{\pi_N(c_1) - z(h_i) + \dfrac{\pi_W + (n-1)\sigma \pi_L}{r} h_i + \dfrac{\sigma \pi_W + [1 + (n-2)\sigma]\pi_L}{r} \displaystyle\sum_{j \neq i} h_j}{r + [1 + (n-1)\sigma] \displaystyle\sum_{j=1}^{n} h_j}$$

$$= \frac{1}{1 + (n-1)\sigma}\left[\frac{\pi_W + (n-1)\sigma \pi_L}{r} - z'(h_i)\right] \tag{24}$$

The second equality implicitly defines firm i's R&D intensity reaction function.

Partially condense (24) by setting $h_j = h_{-1}$ for all $j \neq 1$, to obtain an expression for the first-order condition that defines firm 1's profit-maximizing R&D level as a function of the equal R&D levels of all other firms:[24]

$$0 = \frac{\pi_W - \pi_N(c_1) - (n-1)\sigma[\pi_N(c_1) - \pi_L]}{1 + (n-1)\sigma} + z(h_1) - h_1 z'(h_1)$$

$$- \frac{rz'(h_1)}{1 + (n-1)\sigma} + (n-1)h_{-1}\left[(1-\sigma)\frac{\pi_W - \pi_L}{r} - z'(h_1)\right] \quad (25)$$

In like manner, obtain an expression for the condensed R&D reaction function of all other firms,

$$0 = \frac{\pi_W - \pi_N(c_1) - (n-1)\sigma[\pi_N(c_1) - \pi_L]}{1 + (n-1)\sigma} + z(h_{-1}) - h_{-1}z'(h_{-1})$$

$$- \frac{rz'(h_{-1})}{1 + (n-1)\sigma} + [h_1 + (n-2)h_{-1}]\left[(1-\sigma)\frac{\pi_W - \pi_L}{r} - z'(h_1)\right] \quad (26)$$

In equilibrium (setting $h_1 = h_{-1} = h$), the slope of firm 1's R&D reaction function is

$$\left.\frac{\partial h_1}{\partial h_{-1}}\right|_{eq} = \frac{(n-1)h}{\left[nh + \dfrac{r}{1+(n-1)\sigma}\right]z''(h)}\left[(1-\sigma)\frac{\pi_W - \pi_L}{r} - z'(h)\right] \quad (27)$$

This is positive for σ near zero, and negative for σ near one. The slope of the condensed reaction function of all other firms is

$$\left.\frac{\partial h_{-1}}{\partial h_1}\right|_{eq} = \frac{(1-\sigma)\dfrac{\pi_W - \pi_L}{r} - z'(h_1)}{\left[nh + \dfrac{r}{1+(n-1)\sigma}\right]z''(h) - (n-2)\left[(1-\sigma)\dfrac{\pi_W - \pi_L}{r} - z'(h)\right]}$$

$$(28)$$

Stability requires that the slopes of the resulting functions be less than one in absolute value at equilibrium; see Henriques (1990) and Suzumura (1992). These conditions are met for the simulation results reported in the text.

Given the symmetry that characterizes the model, all firms will choose the same R&D level in equilibrium.[25] Letting $h_i = h$ for all i, (24) becomes

$$V_{RD}^i = \frac{\pi_N(c_1) - z(h) + [1 + (n-1)\sigma]\dfrac{\pi_W + (n-1)\pi_L}{r}h}{r + [1 + (n-1)\sigma]nh}$$

$$= \frac{1}{1 + (n-1)\sigma}\left[\frac{\pi_W + (n-1)\sigma\pi_L}{r} - z'(h)\right] \tag{29}$$

Let h_N denote the solution to (29). For a quadratic R&D cost function, h_N is the solution to the quadratic equation

$$(2n-1)vh^2 + \left[\frac{2rv}{1 + (n-1)\sigma} - (n-1)(1-\sigma)\frac{\pi_W - \pi_L}{r} + (n-1)u\right]h$$

$$- \left[\frac{\pi_W + (n-1)\sigma\pi_L - ru}{1 + (n-1)\sigma} - \pi_N(c_1) + F_R\right] = 0 \tag{30}$$

Under oligopoly with independent R&D and independent post-innovation production, expected consumers' surplus is

$$\frac{CS_N(c_1) + [1 + (n-1)\sigma]nh_N\dfrac{CS_N[(n-1)c_1, c_2]}{r}}{r + [1 + (n-1)\sigma]nh_N} \tag{31}$$

Here $CS_N(c_1)$ is instantaneous consumers' surplus in non-cooperative equilibrium if all firms produce with unit cost c_1; $CS_N[(n-1)c_1, c_2]$ is instantaneous consumers' surplus if $n-1$ firms produce with unit cost c_1 and one firm produces with unit cost c_2.[26]

Instantaneous consumers' surplus without R&D is

$$\frac{CS_N(c_1)}{r} \tag{32}$$

The change in expected consumers' surplus with independent R&D and independent production in oligopoly is

$$\frac{1 + (n-1)\sigma}{r + [1 + (n-1)\sigma]nh_N}nh_N\frac{CS_N[(n-1)c_1, c_2] - CS_N(c_1)}{r} \tag{33}$$

Product-market rivalry normally implies that in non-cooperative equilibrium instantaneous consumers' surplus will rise after innovation;[27] we expect (33) to be positive.

276

Complete R&D joint venture, post-innovation rivalry

If there is a complete R&D joint venture, firms together finance a single R&D project.[28] After innovation, all firms have access to the new technology. Research intensity h is chosen to maximize expected present-discounted firm value,

$$V_{RD}^{Ji} = \frac{\pi_N(c_1) - \dfrac{z(h)}{n} + h\,\dfrac{\pi_N(c_2)}{r}}{r + h} = \frac{\pi_N(c_2)}{r} - \frac{z'(h)}{n} \tag{34}$$

The first expression is the definition of firm value; the second equality is the first-order condition that defines the privately optimal R&D level. Let h_N^J denote this value; for a quadratic R&D cost function, h_N^J is the solution to

$$vh^2 + 2rvh - \{n[\pi_N(c_2) - \pi_N(c_1)] - ru + F_R\} = 0 \tag{35}$$

With a complete R&D joint venture and independent post-innovation decision-making, expected consumers' surplus is

$$\frac{CS_N(c_1) + h_N^J\,\dfrac{CS_N(c_2)}{r}}{r + h_N^J} \tag{36}$$

Expected consumers' surplus without R&D is given by (32). The change in expected consumers' surplus due to R&D is

$$\frac{h_N^J}{r + h_N^J}\,\frac{CS_N(c_2) - CS_N(c_1)}{r} \geq 0 \tag{37}$$

Complete R&D joint venture, post-innovation joint production

If firms are able to set up a production joint venture after development of the new technology, then a single firm's post-innovation pay-off is its proportional share of monopoly profit, $\pi_m(c_2)/n$, rather than the non-cooperative equilibrium profit $\pi_N(c_2)$. The relevant expressions follow by making the appropriate substitutions in the previous section. Let $h_{j\pi m}^J$ denote the equilibrium R&D intensity. Expected consumers' surplus with R&D is

$$\frac{CS_N(c_1) + h_{j\pi m}^J\,\dfrac{CS_{j\pi m}(c_2)}{r}}{r + h_{j\pi m}^J} \tag{38}$$

Once again, expected consumers' surplus without R&D is given by (32). The change in expected consumers' surplus due to R&D is

$$\frac{h^J_{j\pi m}}{r + h^J_{j\pi m}} \frac{CS_{j\pi m}(c_2) - CS_N(c_1)}{r} \tag{39}$$

which is of ambiguous sign. For very great cost savings, consumers can be better off with joint profit maximization in the post-innovation market than with non-cooperative decision-making in the pre-innovation market. But if the cost saving is modest, consumers will be worse off after innovation. The net welfare effect of innovation will then depend on a trade-off between increased economic profit and reduced consumers' surplus.

Complete R&D patent pool, post-innovation rivalry

Each firm carries out its own R&D project; if any firm develops the new technology, all firms have access to its use. R&D intensity h_i is chosen to maximize

$$V^i_{PP} = \frac{\pi_N(c_1) - z(h_i) + [1 + (n-1)\sigma]\left(\sum_{j=1}^{n} h_j\right) \dfrac{\pi_N(c_2)}{r}}{r + [1 + (n-1)\sigma]\sum_{j=1}^{n} h_j}$$

$$= \frac{\pi_N(c_2)}{r} - \frac{z'(h_i)}{1 + (n-1)\sigma} \tag{40}$$

In equilibrium, all firms will choose the same research intensity; (40) becomes

$$\frac{\pi_N(c_1) - z(h) + [1 + (n-1)\sigma]nh \dfrac{\pi_N(c_2)}{r}}{r + [1 + (n-1)\sigma]nh} = \frac{\pi_N(c_2)}{r} - \frac{z'(h)}{1 + (n-1)\sigma} \tag{41}$$

Let h^{PP}_N denote the solution to (41). Evaluated for a quadratic R&D cost function, (41) h^{PP}_N is the solution to the quadratic equation

$$(2n-1)vh^2 + \left[\frac{2rv}{1 + (n-1)\sigma} + (n-1)u\right]h$$

$$- \left[\pi_N(c_2) - \pi_N(c_1) - \frac{ru}{1 + (n-1)\sigma} + F_R\right] = 0 \tag{42}$$

Expected consumers' surplus with R&D is

$$\frac{CS_N(c_1) + [1 + (n-1)\sigma]nh_N^{PP} \dfrac{CS_N(c_2)}{r}}{r + [1 + (n-1)\sigma]nh_N^{PP}} \qquad (43)$$

The change in consumers' surplus due to research and development is

$$\frac{1 + (n-1)\sigma}{r + [1 + (n-1)\sigma]nh_N^{PP}}\ nh_N^{PP}\ \frac{CS_N(c_2) - CS_N(c_1)}{r} \geq 0 \qquad (44)$$

One may take the view that σ is a parameter that describes the flow of information in the research community, and that its magnitude will not be affected by the formation of a patent pool.[29] Alternatively (Kamien *et al.* 1992; Choi, 1993) one may argue that the cooperation implied by a patent pool translates into a greater value of σ (perhaps even to 1). The relevant expressions are obtained by altering the value of σ in the preceding expressions.

Complete R&D patent pool, joint production

The expression that determines equilibrium R&D intensity $h_{j\pi m}^{PP}$ follows from those of the previous section, substituting $\pi_m(c_2)/n$ for $\pi_N(c_1)$. Expected consumers' surplus with R&D is

$$\frac{CS_N(c_1) + [1 + (n-1)\sigma]nh_{j\pi m}^{PP} \dfrac{CS_{j\pi m}(c_2)}{r}}{r + [1 + (n-1)\sigma]nh_{j\pi m}^{PP}} \qquad (45)$$

The change in consumers' surplus due to R&D is

$$\frac{1 + (n-1)\sigma}{r + [1 + (n-1)\sigma]nh_{j\pi m}^{PP}}\ nh_{j\pi m}^{PP}\ \frac{CS_{j\pi m}(c_2) - CS_N(c_1)}{r} \qquad (46)$$

which is of ambiguous sign and can lead to the same trade-off identified for the case of an R&D joint venture with post-innovation joint production.

APPENDIX 10.2 INSTANTANEOUS PAY-OFFS

The general expressions given above can be applied to any model of product market behaviour. In this chapter I have chosen to simulate results assuming that firms set price and produce substitute varieties of a differentiated product. Friedman (1982: 505) regards this case as being of greatest interest. Results are robust to alternative specifications of the nature of product market competition.

Demand and consumers' surplus

Let the inverse demand curve for variety 1 be

$$p_1 = a - [q_1 + \theta(q_2 + \cdots + q_n)] \tag{47}$$

with corresponding expressions for other varieties. This is a standard model of demand for differentiated products, due among others to Spence (1976). The parameter θ, assumed to lie between zero and one, measures the degree of product differentiation. $\theta = 1$ implies products are perfect substitutes; if $\theta = 0$, demand for one product is completely independent of the outputs of other products.

The inverse demand curves (47) are consistent with the representative consumer utility function

$$U = m + a \sum_{i=1}^{n} q_i - \frac{1}{2} \left\{ \sum_{i=1}^{n} \left[q_i^2 + \theta \sum_{j \neq i} q_i q_j \right] \right\} \tag{48}$$

where m is a numeraire good and the budget constraint is

$$Y = m + \sum_{1}^{n} p_i q_i \tag{49}$$

Evaluated at the appropriate equilibrium values, this yields an expression for instantaneous utility:

$$U = Y + \sum_{i=1}^{n} (a - p_i) q_i - \frac{1}{2} \left\{ \sum_{i=1}^{n} \left[q_i^2 + \theta \sum_{j \neq i} q_i q_j \right] \right\} \tag{50}$$

The last two terms on the right measure consumers' surplus from consumption of the differentiated product group.[30]

Equilibrium prices

In the pre-innovation market, all firms produce with constant cost c_1 per unit. If there is a complete R&D joint venture or a complete patent pool, then in the post-innovation market, all firms produce with cost c_2 per unit. To deal with these cases of identical unit costs, consider the more general case, in which unit costs can differ, since this occurs under some cooperation regimes after innovation. Write c^i for the marginal cost of firm i and rewrite the demand curves in terms of deviations from unit cost as

$$p_i - c^i = a - c^i - \left(q_i + \theta \sum_{j \neq i} q_j \right) \tag{51}$$

Inverting the system of equations of which (51) is a part yields demand curves of the form[31]

$$(1 - \theta)[1 + (n - 1)\theta]q_1 =$$

$$[1 + (n - 2)\theta]a^1 - \theta \sum_{j=2}^{n} a^j - [1 + (n - 2)\theta](p_1 - c^1) + \theta \sum_{j=2}^{n} (p_j - a^j)$$

$$(52)$$

writing $a^j = a - c^j$ for notational compactness.

From (48) we obtain an expression for firm 1's instantaneous profit,

$$(1 - \theta)[1 + (n - 1)\theta]\pi_1$$

$$= (p_1 - c^1)\left\{[1 + (n - 2)\theta]a^1 - \theta \sum_{j=2}^{n} a^j\right.$$

$$\left. - [1 + (n - 2)\theta](p_1 - c^1) + \theta \sum_{j=2}^{n} (p_j - a^j)\right\} \quad (53)$$

The first-order condition for maximization of (53) gives the equation of firm 1's price reaction function,

$$2[1 + (n - 2)\theta](p_1 - c^1) - \theta \sum_{j=2}^{n} (p_j - c^j) = [1 + (n - 2)\theta]a^1 - \theta \sum_{j=2}^{n} a^j \quad (54)$$

Note that (54) implies that anywhere along firm 1's price reaction function, and in particular in equilibrium,

$$q_1 = \frac{1 + (n - 2)\theta}{(1 - \theta)[1 + (n - 1)\theta]} (p_1 - c^1) \quad (55)$$

so that firm 1's pay-off satisfies

$$\pi_1 = \frac{1 + (n - 2)\theta}{(1 - \theta)[1 + (n - 1)\theta]} (p_1 - c^1)^2 \quad (56)$$

The system of equations of price reaction functions can be written in matrix form as

$$\{[2 + (2n - 3\theta)]I_n - \theta J_n J_n'\}(P - C) = \{[1 + (n - 1)\theta]I_n - \theta J_n J_n'\}(aI_n - C) \quad (57)$$

where I_n is the identity matrix, J_n a column vector of ones, P a column vector of prices, C a column vector of unit costs, and subscripts indicate dimension. Inverting the coefficient matrix on the left in (57), equilibrium prices have the form

$$p_1 - c^1 = \frac{[2 + 3(n-2)\theta + (n^2 - 5n + 5)\theta^2]a^1 - \theta[1 + (n-2)\theta] \sum_{j=2}^{n} a^j}{[2 + (n-3)\theta][2 + (2n-3)\theta]} \quad (58)$$

In the pre-innovation market, $c^i = c_1 \ \forall \ i$; (58) reduces to

$$p - c_1 = \frac{1-\theta}{2 + (n-3)\theta} (a - c_1) \quad (59)$$

The non-cooperative equilibrium pay-off in the pre-innovation market is obtained from (56). There is a similar expression for equilibrium price if all firms have the right to use the new technology in the post-innovation market.

Post-innovation, independent production

In the post-innovation market, the winner of the patent race has an exclusive right to control the use of the new technology. Assume that the winner is able to license use of the new technology to losers, who pay a royalty fee $c_1 - c_2$ per unit of output.[32] The winner's and losers' pay-offs are

$$\pi_W = (p_W - c_2)q_W + (n-1)(c_1 - c_2)q_L \quad (60)$$

and

$$\pi_L = (p_L - c_1)q_L \quad (61)$$

respectively. p_W and p_L are found by evaluating (58) for the appropriate values of unit cost; equilibrium outputs follow from (55).

Post-innovation, joint profit maximization

If there is a complete R&D joint venture or a complete patent pool and firms are able to coordinate decisions after the new technology is discovered, they will set joint-profit maximizing prices in the post-innovation market,

$$p_{j\pi m} = c_2 + \tfrac{1}{2}(a - c_2) \quad (62)$$

Output per variety is

$$q_{j\pi m} = \frac{1 + (n-2)\theta}{(1-\theta)[1 + (n-1)\theta]} \frac{a - c_2}{2} \quad (63)$$

NOTES

1 Innovation race models are one of the two leading ways of modelling innovation that appear in the literature; see Loury (1979), Lee and Wilde (1980), Reinganum (1983, 1989) and Martin (1993a, 1994, 1996). The leading alternative model, due to d'Aspremont and Jacquemin (1988, 1990), assumes a deterministic relationship between R&D inputs and R&D output; see also Henriques (1990), Katz and Ordover (1990), Kamien et al. (1992, 1993), and Suzumura (1992). An advantage of the patent race model is that it permits analysis of the impact of market structure and appropriability regimes on the expected time to discovery.

2 Jorde and Teece (1989: note 11) assert that innovation race models apply only if patents ensure appropriability of the profit that flows from successful innovation. This is simply incorrect. There are mechanisms other than the patent system that allow firms to appropriate some of the returns from successful innovation; businessmen are aware of these mechanisms (Levin et al. 1988). In some cases, they can protect economic profits long after patent protection evaporates (Caves et al. 1991). From a strictly modelling point of view, one can allow for imperfect appropriability in specifying the pay-offs to successful innovation; see appendix 10.2.

3 There are substantial transaction costs associated with the negotiation of such licensing agreements; see Levin et al. (1988: 794), Kay (1992). A specification that allows for partial licensing is indicated in appendix 10.2; see also Simpson and Vonortas (1994).

4 The simulation results reported here are generated by a set of BASIC programmes that are available on request from the author.

5 Neither the assumption that varieties are differentiated nor the assumption that firms set price is essential to the results that follow. Results for Bertrand competition and Cournot (quantity-setting) competition with homogeneous products, which are qualitatively similar to those reported here, are available on request from the author.

6 The inverse demand curve is linear ($p = 100 - Q$). Monopoly profit is 900 per time period with unit cost 40, 1,406.25 per time period with unit cost 25.

7 Note that if there are two firms in the market, instead of one, the innovation is socially desirable. With oligopolistic rivalry, the cost-saving innovation is used to produce a greater output, generating larger welfare gains than under monopoly.

8 See also Jorde and Teece (1992: 57)

> the NCRA is not sufficiently permissive. The NCRA unwisely precludes joint manufacturing and production of innovative products and processes, which are often necessary to provide the cooperating ventures with significant feedback information to aid in further innovation and product development, and to make the joint activity profitable.

9 *United States* v. *Automobile Manufacturers Association* 1969 Trade Cases (CCH) Para 72,907 (C.D. Cal. 1969)(consent decree), modified 1982–3 Trade Cases (CCH) Para 65,088 (C.D.Cal. 1982). I am indebted to William L. Baldwin and John T. Scott for this reference. For those unfamiliar with the fine points of US legal procedures, a consent decree implies that the parties alleged to have violated the law decline to admit that they did so and promise never to do so again.

10 323 U.S. 386 (1945).

11 See also Stockdale (1992: 283):

> The [production joint venture] also increases the likelihood of either tacit or explicit collusion among the participants in other downstream product markets and in upstream research markets.

12 For a summary of EC competition policy provisions as of the end of 1989, see EC Commission (1990); more recently Commission Notice regarding restrictions ancillary to concentrations *OJ* No. C 203/5, 14 August 1990, and Commission Notice concerning the assessment of cooperative joint ventures pursuant to Article 85 of the EEC Treaty *OJ* No. C 43/2, 16 February 1993. See also Comanor *et al.* (1990), Goyder (1992), and Geroski (1993).

13 See EC Commission, Notice concerning agreements, decisions and concerted practices in the field of cooperation between enterprises, *OJ* No. C75, 29 July 1968, corrected by *OJ* No. C84, 28 August 1968, p. 14, and reprinted in EC Commission (1990).

14 Regulation (EEC) No. 418/85 of 19 December 1984 on the application of Article 85(3) of the Treaty to categories of research and development agreements, *OJ* No. L 53, 22 February 1985, reprinted in EC Commission (1990).

15 Commission Notice concerning the assessment of cooperative joint ventures pursuant to Article 85 of the EEC Treaty, *OJ* No. C 43/2, 16 February 1993; see also Commission Regulation (EEC) No. 151/93 of 23 December 1992 amending Regulations (EEC) No. 417/85, (EEC) No. 418/85, (EEC) No. 2349/84 and (EEC) No. 556/89 on the application of Article 85(3) of the Treaty to certain categories of specialization agreements, research and development agreements, patent licensing agreements and know-how licensing agreements, *OJ* No. L 21/8, 29 January 1993.

16 One example is a Commission decision of 23 December 1992 (*OJ* No. L 20/14 28 January 1993) treating a joint venture between Ford and Volkswagen to produce a multipurpose vehicle in Portugal, with each parent to distribute its own versions of the vehicle. The decision recognized that the exchange of information among the two parents could affect their behaviour in related markets (recital 21), but saw countervailing benefits in the effective entry of two firms into the market (recital 24), installation of state-of-the-art production capacity in the Community (recital 25), and product improvement (recital 26).

17 See Regulation No. 2779/72/EEC 21 December 1972, *OJ* No. L 292, 29 December 1972. For applications, see EC Commission (1973: 55; 1976: 45).

18 See Evans and Martin (1991, 1994). These aspects of EC policy are reinforced by the commitment to social and economic cohesion added to the EEC Treaty by the Single European Act.

19 See also Jorde and Teece (1989: 27): 'Once the technology is mastered, Japanese firms will then often invest in it with the object of becoming the world cost leader. At this stage, strong competition will emerge to complement earlier cooperation' and (1989: 30): 'It is important to note that the Japanese have rejected the model of national champions, and seem to promote cooperation among firms that are rivals. The level of cooperation fades, but does not necessarily disappear, as new products approach the point of sale.'

20 And provided also that parties to the production joint venture are US firms or from countries that accord corresponding treatment to US firms that are parties to overseas joint ventures.

21 See, for example, Jorde and Teece (1992: 75–7).

22 This is the distribution function when the time to discovery is a Poisson process; see Freeman (1963).

23 This assumption is made for simplicity; the results are qualitatively similar if a firm carries out multiple research projects.

24 This is without loss of generality, since all firms set the same R&D level in equilibrium.

25 One can investigate non-symmetrical equilibria, in which a single firm would undertake an R&D programme if and only if its expected value with an R&D programme exceeded its expected value if it did not undertake an R&D programme but all other firms did. This leads to a model in which, in equilibrium, some firms undertake R&D, some do not, and a firm's expected value falls if it changes its R&D decision. The appropriate stability conditions are analogous to those of d'Aspremont et al. (1983).

26 This includes the particular cases in which the winning firm licenses the use of the new technology to losing firms and in which the cost advantage of the new technology is so great that losing firms shut down in the post-innovation market.

27 This is the case, for example, with Cournot competition or Bertrand competition.

28 Once again, this assumption can be relaxed without fundamentally altering the nature of the results.

29 This view is supported by evidence that parties to research joint ventures are often reluctant to share strategic information; see Stockdale (1992: 288–9).

30 Additional simplifications are possible. Substituting in (50) from the expression for the inverse demand curves to eliminate $a - p_i$ yields

$$U = Y + \frac{1}{2} \left\{ \sum_{i=1}^{n} \left[q_i^2 + \theta \sum_{j \neq i} q_i q_j \right] \right\}$$

(which is valid when evaluated for optimal quantities). Substituting from the expressions for the demand curves (52) then yields the indirect utility function.

31 I limit discussion here to the case in which equilibrium demand for all varieties is positive. The necessary adjustments in the contrary case are straightforward.

32 A specification that encompasses the one used here is

$$\pi_W(\alpha) = [p_W(\alpha) - c_2] q_W(\alpha) + \alpha(n-1)(c_1 - c_2) q_L(\alpha)$$

where α, lying between zero and one, measures the degree of appropriability.

REFERENCES

Areeda, Phillip (1992) 'Antitrust law as industrial policy: should judges and juries make it?' in Thomas M. Jorde and David J. Teece (eds) Antitrust, Innovation, and Competitiveness. New York: Oxford University Press.

Audretsch, David B. (1989) 'Joint R&D and industrial policy in Japan', in Albert N. Link and Gregory Tassey (eds) Cooperative Research and Development: The Industry–University–Government Relationship. Dordrecht: Kluwer Academic Publishers.

Brodley, Joseph F. (1990) 'Antitrust law and innovation cooperation', Journal of Economic Perspectives 4, 3, 97–112.

Caves, Richard E., Whinston, Michael D., and Hurwitz, Mark A. (1991) 'Patent expiration, entry, and competition in the U.S. pharmaceutical industry', Brookings Papers on Economic Activity Microeconomics, pp. 1–48.

Choi, Jay Pil (1993) 'Cooperative R&D with product market competition', International Journal of Industrial Organization 11, 4, 553–71.

Comanor, William S., George, K., Jacquemin, A., Jenny, F., Kantzenbach, E.,

Ordover, J.A., and Waverman, L. (1990) *Competition Policy in Europe and North America: Economic Issues and Institutions.* Chur: Harwood Academic Publishers.

Committee on the Judiciary, U.S. Senate (1993) The National Cooperative Production Amendments Act of 1993, Report, Antitrust and Trade Regulation Report, 10 June, pp. 725–732.

d'Aspremont, Claude and Jacquemin, Alexis (1988) 'Cooperative and noncooperative R&D in duopoly with spillovers', *American Economic Review* 78, 5, 1133–7.

d'Aspremont, Claude and Jacquemin, Alexis (1990) 'Cooperative and noncooperative R&D in duopoly with spillovers: erratum', *American Economic Review* 80, 3, 641–2.

d'Aspremont, Claude, Jacquemin, Alexis, Gabszewicz, Jean Jaskold, and Weymark, John A. (1983) 'On the Stability of Collusive Price Leadership', *Canadian Journal of Economics* 16, 1, 17–25.

EC Commission (1972) *First Report on Competition Policy.* Brussels and Luxembourg, April.

EC Commission (1973) *Second Report on Competition Policy.* Brussels and Luxembourg, April.

EC Commission (1976) *Fifth Report on Competition Policy.* Brussels and Luxembourg, April.

EC Commission (1978) *Seventh Report on Competition Policy.* Brussels and Luxembourg, April.

EC Commission (1983) *Twelfth Report on Competition Policy.* Brussels and Luxembourg.

EC Commission (1985) *Fourteenth Report on Competition Policy.* Brussels and Luxembourg.

EC Commission (1990) *Competition Law in the European Communities, I, Rules Applicable to Undertakings.* Brussels and Luxembourg.

Evans, Andrew and Martin, Stephen (1991) 'Socially Acceptable Distortion of Competition: EC Policy on State Aid', *European Law Review* 16, 2, 79–111.

Evans, Andrew and Martin, Stephen (1994) 'Reform of the Structural Funds', in Stephen Martin (ed.) *The Construction of Europe.* Dordrecht: Kluwer Academic Publishers, 41–70.

Freeman, Harold (1963) *Introduction to Statistical Inference.* Reading, Mass. Addison-Wesley.

Friedman, James W. (1982) 'Oligopoly Theory', in Kenneth J. Arrow and Michael D. Intriligator (eds) *Handbook of Mathematical Economics* II. Amsterdam: North-Holland.

Geroski, Paul A. (1993) 'Antitrust policy towards co-operative R&D ventures', *Oxford Review of Economic Policy* 9, 2, 58–71.

Goyder, D.G. (1992) *EEC Competition Law.* Second edition, Oxford: Clarendon Press.

Henriques, Irene (1990) 'Cooperative and noncooperative R&D in duopoly with spillovers: comment', *American Economic Review* 80, 3, 638–40.

Jacquemin, Alexis (1988) 'Cooperative agreements in R&D and European antitrust policy', *European Economic Review* 32, 2/3, 551–60.

Jorde, Thomas M. and Teece, David J. (1989) 'Innovation, cooperation and antitrust', *High Technology Law Journal* 4, 1, 1–112.

Jorde, Thomas M. and Teece, David J. (1992) 'Innovation, cooperation, and antitrust', in Thomas M. Jorde and David J. Teece (eds) *Antitrust, Innovation, and Competitiveness.* Oxford: Oxford University Press.

Kamien, Morton I., Muller, Eitan and Zang, Israel (1992) 'Cooperative joint ventures and R&D cartels', *American Economic Review* 82, 5, 1293–1306.

Kamien, Morton I. and Zang, Israel (1993) 'Competing research joint ventures', *Journal of Economics and Management Strategy* 2, 1, 23–40.

Katz, Michael L. and Ordover, Janusz A. (1990) 'R&D cooperation and competition', *Brookings Papers on Economic Activity* Microeconomics, 137–203.

Kay, Neil (1992) 'Collaborative strategies of firms: theory and evidence', in Alfred Del Monte (ed.) *Recent Developments in the Theory of Industrial Organization.* Ann Arbor: University of Michigan Press.

Komiya, Ryutaro (1993) 'Japan's comparative advantage in the machinery industry: industrial organization and technological progress', Jean Monnet Chair Lecture, European University Institute, Florence, Italy, March.

Lee, Michelle K. and Lee, Mavis K. (1991) 'High technology consortia: a panacea for America's technological competitiveness problems?' *High Technology Law Journal* 6, 2, 335–62.

Lee, Tom and Wilde, Louis L. (1980) 'Market structure and innovation: a reformulation', *Quarterly Journal of Economics* 94, 2, 429–36.

Levin, R.C., Klevorick, A.K., Nelson, R.R., and Winter, Sidney G. (1988) 'Appropriating the returns from industrial R&D', *Brookings Papers on Economic Activity*, pp. 783–820.

Loury, Glenn C. (1979) 'Market structure and innovation', *Quarterly Journal of Economics* 93, 3, No. 372, 395–410.

Mansfield, Edwin (1985) 'How rapidly does new industrial technology leak out?' *Journal of Industrial Economics* 34, 2, 217–23.

Mansfield, Edwin, Schwartz, Mark and Wagner, Samuel (1981) 'Imitation costs and patents: an empirical study', *Economic Journal* 91, 364, 907–18.

Martin, Stephen (1993a) *Advanced Industrial Economics.* Oxford: Basil Blackwell.

Martin, Stephen (1993b) *Industrial Economics*, Second edition, New York: Macmillan.

Martin, Stephen (1994) 'Private and social incentives to form R&D joint ventures', *Review of Industrial Organization* 9, 2, 157–71.

Martin, Stephen (1995) 'R&D joint ventures and tacit product market collusion', *European Journal of Political Economy* 11, 733–41.

Odagiri, Hiroyuki (1986) 'Industrial policy in theory and reality', in H.W. de Jong and W.G. Shepherd (eds) *Mainstreams in Industrial Organization* II. Dordrecht: Kluwer Academic Publishers.

Okimoto, Daniel I. (1989) *Between MITI and the Market Japanese Industrial Policy for High Technology Industries.* Stanford: Stanford University Press.

Reinganum, Jennifer F. (1983) 'Uncertain innovation and the persistence of monopoly', *American Economic Review* 73, 4, 741–8.

Reinganum, Jennifer F. (1989) 'The timing of innovation: research, development, and diffusion', in Richard Schmalensee and Robert D. Willig (eds), *Handbook of Industrial Organization* 1. Amsterdam: North-Holland.

Scherer, F.M. (1982) 'Demand-pull and technological invention: Schmookler revisited', *Journal of Industrial Economics* 30, 3, 225–37.

Schmookler, Jacob (1966) *Invention and Economic Growth.* Cambridge, Mass.: Harvard University Press.

Schmookler, Jacob (1972) *Patents, Invention, and Economic Change: Data and Selected Essays.* (Zvi Griliches and Leonid Hurwicz, editors). Cambridge, Mass.: Harvard University Press.

Scott, John T. (1988) 'Diversification versus cooperation in R&D investment', *Managerial and Decision Economics* 9, 3, 173–86.

Scott, John T. (1989) 'Historical and economic perspectives of the National Cooperative Research Act', in Albert N. Link and Gregory Tassey (eds) *Cooperative Research and Development: The Industry–University–Government Relationship*. Dordrecht: Kluwer Academic Publishers.

Scott, John T. (1993) *Purposive Diversification and Economic Performance*. Cambridge: Cambridge University Press.

Shapiro, Carl and Willig, Robert D. (1990) 'On the antitrust treatment of production joint ventures', *Journal of Economic Perspectives* 4, 3, 113–30.

Simpson, R. David and Vonortas, Nicolas S. (1994) 'Cournot equilibrium with imperfectly appropriable R&D', *Journal of Industrial Economics* 42, 1, 79–92.

Spaak Report (1956) *Rapport des chefs de délégation aux Ministères des affaires étrangères*, Comité intergouvernemental créé par la Conférence de Messine, Brussels, 21 April.

Spence, A. Michael (1976) 'Product differentiation and welfare', *American Economic Review* 66, 2, 407–14.

Stockdale, Donald K. (1992) 'Antitrust and international competitiveness: is encouraging production joint ventures worth the cost?' *High Technology Law Journal* 7, 2, 269–314.

Suzumura, Kotaro (1992) 'Cooperative and noncooperative R&D in an oligopoly with spillovers', *American Economic Review* 82, 5, 1307–20.

US Department of Justice, Antitrust Division (1980) *Antitrust Guide Concerning Research Joint Ventures*. November.

Villard, Henry H. (1958) 'Competition, oligopoly, and research', *Journal of Political Economy* 66, 6, 483–97.

Williamson, Oliver E. (1968) 'Economies as an antitrust defense: the welfare tradeoffs', *American Economic Review* 58, 1, 18–36.

ACKNOWLEDGEMENTS

I am grateful for comments received at the Competition Policy in a Global Economy workshop, at the International Institute of Management, Berlin, the University of Sienna, the September 1993 meetings of the European Association for Research in Industrial Economics, the University of Berne, and INSEAD. Responsibility for errors is my own.

11

INNOVATION, MARKET STRUCTURE AND ANTITRUST

Harmonizing competition policy in regimes of rapid technological change

Thomas M. Jorde and David J. Teece

The harmonization of competition policy is a laudable goal, but one which is still quite remote. In this chapter we argue that the full convergence or harmonization of competition policy on a global basis must await the adoption of a common intellectual framework, common political and social goals, and perhaps common legal and administrative structures. This is clearly an unlikely outcome, possibly even an undesirable one. However, the global economy can benefit if competition policy everywhere adheres to at least a few superordinate goals and some common themes. In this chapter we suggest that economic welfare ought to be adopted as the principal goal of antitrust, requiring that economic analysis inform competition policy. We furthermore suggest that commanding insights into the nature of competition can be derived by recognizing the importance of technological innovation to competition. Indeed, we suggest that if competition policy develops and adopts a pro-innovation framework, it will assist economic development and competition more assuredly than policies which are blind to the centrality of innovation to competition. No country has yet fully recognized in its policies the importance of innovation to competition, and competition to innovation. We suggest ways in which competition policy can assist innovation. Our framework is generally applicable to all developed countries interested in economic growth and prosperity.

THE GOALS OF COMPETITION (ANTITRUST) POLICY

Almost two decades ago Robert Bork (1978: 7) wrote that

> the overriding need of antitrust today is a general theory of its possibilities and limitations as a tool of national social policy. Yet there exists a surprising lack of agreement concerning the most basic

questions. The disagreement, though variously phrased, is finally about two issues: (1) the goals or values the law may legitimately and profitably implement; and (2) the validity of the law's vision of economic reality.

While much has been accomplished on both counts over the last twenty years, there is still considerable dissonance with respect to both issues.

However, there is an emerging consensus globally that economic welfare ought to be the goal of antitrust policy. Nevertheless, when the economic welfare goal is accepted, it is sometimes not correctly implemented. One reason is that so much of the economic theory that is used to help guide courts, tribunals, agencies, and policy-makers is extraordinarily static – that is, it tends to look at the impact on consumer welfare today, and not in the future. This thinking is because much of the apparatus of applied microeconomics that underpins contemporary antitrust economics is single period in its focus. The focus on static analysis may also be the result of greater data and measurement difficulties associated with long-run analysis. Unfortunately – and importantly – in static analysis there is almost no reference to innovation and its importance to competition and to economic welfare.[1]

It is widely recognized in scholarly works that innovation and its rapid and profitable commercialization are the key factors driving productivity improvement and economic welfare. Consumer welfare is enhanced through the generation and application of new technology and new organizational forms. Efforts to link competition policy with consumer welfare may fall wide of the mark whenever the focus is on present consumer welfare, which is the common focus of microeconomic theory. Accordingly, if consumer welfare is to be the goal of competition policy, it needs to be couched in a forward-looking context. Otherwise, competition policy may have the perverse effect of hindering technological progress and the creation of national wealth. At minimum, when the promotion of static consumer welfare and innovation are in conflict, the courts should favour future impact. This may well make analysis less tractable, but at least it will be focusing on the correct issues.

THE NATURE AND IMPORTANCE OF COMPETITION

Americans and most Europeans have a long-standing and well-founded belief in competition. This tradition is rooted in part on political beliefs. Competitive systems that are open to newcomers provide important checks and balances on monopoly power; monopoly power is often seen as being correlated with political influence. Open and competitive systems are commonly seen as a corollary of democracy.

The economics profession, particularly in the post-war period, has spilled a great deal of economic content into the development and enforcement of competition laws in many countries. However, the dominant image of competition that is embedded in mainstream thinking is often that of perfect competition. In textbook descriptions of competition, firms compete on price,[2] and typically employ identical technologies. The profit motive ensures marginal revenue equal to marginal cost at all times, and perfect competition ensures zero profits, and prices equal to marginal cost. In this world, monopolists create unfortunate welfare losses by restricting output and charging prices above competitive levels. The textbook model of perfect competition supposedly provides useful insights into how the world ought to look, at least with respect to prices and output.

Although this highly stylized view of economic reality can sometimes be helpful, we are concerned that it overlooks important aspects of the competitive process and distorts others. Indeed, as Schumpeter (1942) suggested half a century ago, the kind of competition embedded in standard microeconomic analysis may not be the kind of competition that really matters if enhancing economic welfare is the goal. Rather, it is dynamic competition propelled by the introduction of new products and new processes that really counts. If competition policy and antitrust laws were more concerned with promoting dynamic rather than static competition, the law would look somewhat different from what we see today.

There are at least two types of innovative regimes that require analysis. Incremental innovation occurs when new products are introduced in rapid succession, each one such an improvement on the prior product that the new drives out the old. In regimes characterized by incremental innovation, the population of firms in an industry is likely to be relatively stable. However, established firms will fall into relative decline if they do not keep up with changing technology. Good contemporary examples of industrial regimes characterized by incremental innovation are the aircraft, chemical, and VCR industries.

The other regime is one where radical innovation is predominant. Few industries are characterized by this form for long periods of time. However, when the transistor arrived, it clearly did more to invigorate competition and provide economic benefits than did any level of rivalrous behaviour among the manufacturers of vacuum tubes (valves). Likewise, the invention of the compact disc engendered competition in the recording business of a kind that firms competing with vinyl records could not supply. And the arrival of the steamship sharpened competition in ocean freight in ways that intense competition among sailing ships could never have done.

Conceding the importance of dynamic competition flowing from both of these regimes of innovation would not give rise to any tension with existing competition law if the world of perfect competition envisaged in the textbook was the ideal structure for supporting innovation, be it incremental

291

or radical. However, there is no evidence that the world of perfect competition to which antitrust doctrine frequently aspires is in fact ideal for promoting innovation. Nor is there evidence that the world of monopoly is ideal.

In fact the weight of the evidence would appear to suggest that the structure of markets – whether competitive or monopolized – has little impact on innovation (Cohen and Levin 1989). The evidence does suggest that monopoly is rarely a barrier; most truly radical innovations emerge outside an established industry, and access to the infrastructure provided by incumbent firms is rarely important for ultimate success. Incremental innovation is not much affected by market structure either.

What, then, does innovation require? The evidence is sketchy. However, we can identify several classes of factors that are important: the availability of a labour force with the requisite training and technical skills; decentralized economic structures that recognize private property and permit considerable autonomy, entrepreneurship, and wealth creation; economic systems that permit and encourage a variety of approaches to technological and market opportunities; access to 'venture' capital, either from a firm's existing cash flow or from an external venture capital community; good relations between the scientific community, especially the universities,[3] and the technological community, and between users and developers of technology; protection of intellectual property, and the availability of contractual arrangements to enable innovating firms to capture a return from their investment (unless social returns are equal to the private returns, firms will underinvest in the development of new technology); in fragmented industries, the ability to build quickly or contractually access cospecialized assets inside or outside the industry.[4]

Few of these relate to competition (antitrust) policy. But while competition policy may not be central to the innovation process, it would be wrong to assume that it is unimportant. The ability of innovating firms to cooperate by striking necessary vertical and horizontal agreements, or entering into alliances, often raises issues in antitrust, as do other elements of business strategy. For instance, if innovating firms engage in exclusionary behaviour to exclude 'me too'-type imitators, they can sometimes entangle themselves in a web of costly litigation.

In short, (1) dynamic, not static, competition is what competition laws in advanced nations should promote to advance the goal of enhancing economic welfare, and (2) the implicit adoption of frameworks derived from the model of perfect competition – which is inherently short-run – can lead to significant policy errors. Yet perfect competition as the ideal still holds considerable sway and influence over antitrust economics and legal scholarship, particularly in the United States.

COMPETITION THROUGH INNOVATION:
IMPLICATIONS FOR MARKET DEFINITION AND
FOR COOPERATION

Market definition

There is no area where competition policy so clearly displays its focus on static competition as in its treatment of market definition.[5] In many countries, market definition is a key pillar in the design of competition policy and its enforcement. In the United States, for instance, in the absence of market power, practically every form of business behaviour, other than price fixing, market divisions, or customer allocation, is legal. Once market power is proven, business practices will be closely scrutinized to determine whether they are reasonable. In standard treatments, market power itself may be proved by evidence of a firm's ability to restrict output or exclude competition, by prices above costs, or profits above 'competitive levels'.

Standard approaches to competition can assign market power incorrectly to an innovating firm. Even though the market power associated with innovation is often quite transitory, entry barrier analysis – with its one-to-two-year fuse for entry[6] – will often not undo a finding of market dominance and associated market power for an innovator. Accordingly, innovators may sometimes need to constrain severely their business conduct in order to avoid violating competition laws.

With a Schumpeterian concept of competition in mind, one finds the methodology for defining product markets used in the United States rather troublesome. Clearly, market power can be ephemeral in industries – like computers, biotechnology, telecommunications equipment – characterized by rapid technological change. Such considerations are not readily incorporated into the standard analytical frameworks used to define relevant antitrust markets.

For example, consider how the US Department of Justice (DOJ) approaches market definition.[7] As explained in the *U.S. Department of Justice Merger Guidelines* (1984), the DOJ will include in the product market a group of products such that 'a hypothetical firm that was the only present and future seller of these products ("monopolist") could profitably impose a small but significant and nontransitory increase in price – generally five per cent lasting one year'. The focus here is not so much on the 5 per cent threshold – which has in any event been subsequently abandoned – as on the fact that the implicit assumption embedded in this framework is that products in a market are homogeneous and that competitors compete on price. This is often not so. As a result, application of the 5 per cent test in an industry where competition is Schumpeterian rather than neoclassical is likely to create a downward bias in the definition of the size of the relevant product market, and a corresponding upward bias in the assessment of market power.

Consider the minicomputer industry as it existed in the 1970s in the United States. A variety of systems competed on price and performance while exhibiting price differences of several hundred per cent.[8] Too literal an application of the DOJ's test would suggest that each manufacturer is in a different market; otherwise product substitution would occur that would stimulate pressures for price equalization.

Such an interpretation, however, would have ignored the realities of competition in the computer industry. A variety of systems with quite different price–performance attributes successfully occupied the same market at a given point in time. As new systems were introduced and the prices of existing systems changed, it took some time for resulting price–performance implications to be digested and understood by the market in the early days of the industry. One reason is simply that it takes time for users to experience and test the products. Moreover, to the extent that a product is durable and a replacement for existing equipment, purchase decisions may be complicated by the need to retire existing equipment. In addition, new computer systems sometimes required new support systems, including applications software, so that even computer systems that are consensually superior on price and performance dimensions may take time to diffuse and be adapted. In such situations 5 per cent or even 25 per cent price increases may be met with no substitution until the performance of the products can be assessed and existing equipment can be economically replaced. Even a 25 per cent price increase may seem insignificant if accompanied by a performance enhancement. In such circumstances, where competition is performance-based, the DOJ's one-year/5 per cent rule is not likely to identify markets that are in any way meaningful.[9] We outline a brief version of our approach to this problem, which is more fully developed in Hartman *et al.* (1993).

When competition proceeds primarily on the basis of features and performance, the pertinent question to ask is whether a change in the performance attributes of one commodity would induce substitution to or from another. If the answer is affirmative, then the differentiated products, even if based on alternative technologies, should be included in the relevant product market. Furthermore, when assessing such performance-induced substitutability, a one-year or two-year period is simply too short because enhancement of performance attributes involves a longer time to accomplish than price changes. While it is difficult to state precisely (and generally) what the length of time should be, it is clear that the time frame should be determined by technological concerns. As a result, it may be necessary to apply different time frames to different products and technologies.

When assessing performance-based competition among existing producers, the product changes to be included as a metric should involve the re-engineering of existing products using technologies known to existing competitors. Product changes, which depend on anticipated technologies that are not currently commercial, should be excluded. Thus if firm A, by modifying its product X using its existing proprietary product and process technology and public knowledge, could draw sales away from product Y of firm B, such that B would need to improve its products to avoid losing market share to A, then X and Y are in the same relevant market. If such changes are likely to occur, yet would take longer than one year, the one-year rule should be modified.

When assessing potential competition and entry barriers, the two-year/5 per cent rule must also be modified to include variations in the performance attributes of existing and potentially new technologies. In high-technology innovative industries it is this potential competition that is often most threatening, also the most important from a welfare standpoint,[10] takes the longest time to play out, and is the most difficult to fully anticipate. A more realistic time frame must be determined over which the new products and technologies may be allowed to enter. The precise length of time allowed for the entry of potential competitors must also reflect technological realities. Hence it too may vary by product and technology.

The need to assess performance competition argues for the use of 'hedonic methods'. A growing body of hedonic literature has addressed the importance of product attributes in economic behaviour. This literature has been both theoretical and empirical and has focused on product demand and production cost (hence supply). The demand literature has addressed the importance of product attributes in determining prices[11] and market share.[12] The cost literature demonstrates and measures the impact of product attributes on production costs.[13]

Thus assume that several firms offer various products with different attributes. Assume that one product improves the performance of a certain attribute, holding price and other attributes constant. If a decrease in the demand for a similar product results, there exists a performance cross-elasticity between the two products. If this cross-elasticity is high enough, the products are in the same market. However, if the producer were to improve the performance of a certain attribute, while simultaneously raising the product's price such that no substitution occurred, it would not necessarily mean that the products were in different markets.

This framework allows one to analyse and quantify both price and performance (attribute) competition. Using it, one can retain the 5 per cent price rule while extending the DOJ approach to incorporate performance competition. For example, analogous to the 5 per cent price rule, one could assess the effects of percentage changes in performance. However, such an extension is far from straightforward. One needs to specify rules of thumb carefully regarding the threshold size of performance competition and the time period over which such competition is allowed to unfold.

In general, performance changes are more difficult to quantify than price changes because performance is multidimensional. As a result, quantification requires measuring both the change in an individual attribute and the relative importance of that attribute. Unlike price changes, which involve altering the value of a common base unit (dollars), performance changes often involve changing the units by which performance is measured. None the less, rough quantification is possible, based on the pooled judgements of competent observers, particularly product users.

In terms of threshold effects, we suggest introducing a 25 per cent rule for a change in any key performance attribute. This threshold implies the following. Assume that an existing manufacturer lowers the quality of a key performance attribute of an existing product up to 25 per cent, *ceteris paribus*. If no substitution of other products occurs, the original product constitutes a distinct antitrust market. If substitution of other products does occur, those other products share the market with the original product. Conversely, assume that a new product is introduced that is identical to an existing product in all ways except that it offers up to a 25 per cent improvement in a key performance attribute. If there is no substitution of the new product, the products represent distinct markets. If there is substitution from the existing product to the new product, the two products share the same antitrust market.

The criterion of 25 per cent performance improvement for a single key performance attribute is conservative. Not only is a 25 per cent improvement small compared with those that commonly occur in industries experiencing rapid technological change, but a 25 per cent improvement in a single attribute is likely to imply an overall performance improvement of considerably less than 25 per cent. This performance threshold must furthermore be judged in terms of feasibility. While it is always feasible to raise prices, it is not always feasible to increase performance. This problem is most severe in the case of quantum changes, such as the introduction of a specific application for a device. Following introduction, however, most product changes take place along a relatively continuous trajectory of technological movement. Many product users are familiar with the key development programmes of their suppliers and are able to assess the likelihood that a particular product change will emerge in the near future.

An effective measurement procedure, therefore, could be to rely on the informed judgement of users of exiting products. This procedure would involve identifying market experts, asking them to list key performance attributes, and then asking them to assess the substitutive effects of changes in the attributes. The sample of product users could be supplemented by a corresponding sample of commercial participants, although care would be required to avoid introducing competitive bias into the judgements.[14] A sample of such participants could be asked whether a 25 per cent change in the performance of any one attribute would lead to product substitution.

In addition to threshold rules regarding performance changes, market definition requires the identification of a time frame for the competitive product changes – that is, a definition of the 'near future'. We argued above that the DOJ one-year and two-year rules are too short for almost any case of serious technical advance. Indeed, because there is significant variation among products, no single number will be appropriate for all cases. None the less, we suggest that a four-year period be established as a default time frame, with the option of adjusting the period if strong evidence suggests that it would be appropriate in an individual case. Like the DOJ's one-year rule or the patent law's seventeen-year grant, a fixed four-year rule will not be optimal in all cases. It could provide too broad a market definition in some cases and too narrow a definition for others.

Finally, one needs to address the question of the appropriate Herfindahl–Hirschmann Index thresholds for determining market power, or for assessing merger risk. In the United States, the *Merger Guidelines* selects critical HHIs at 1,000 and 1,800. It is difficult to hypothesize and propose alternative HHIs for mergers in technologically dynamic markets. However, the inclusion of performance competition and the extension of the time frame of competitive response may mean that it is not necessary to change the threshold HHIs. Furthermore, we believe that, with technologically dynamic markets, the dynamics of market structure in the past should provide some guidance to assessing market definition and predicting likely changes in market concentration. Key factors are the change in concentration and the trend in the number of competitors. Nevertheless, a dominant market position maintained over a long period of time may still be quite fragile in a market characterized by rapid innovation.

Failure to recognize that competition is often on the basis of performance attributes and not price will lead courts, tribunals, and the antitrust enforcement agencies to underestimate the breadth of product markets in industries characterized by rapid technological change. This process, in turn, may lead courts and agencies to exaggerate antitrust dangers in some cases and to underestimate it in others. As a consequence, technological development and economic welfare may be retarded.[15]

Cooperation

There appears to be little room in accepted antitrust creed for cooperation if it involves 'competitors', despite the obvious importance of cooperation to economic activity and to the innovation process in particular. The primary reason why economists are sceptical of the benefits of interfirm cooperation is that the coordination function which an economy requires is almost uniformly perceived to be executed with present and forward dispatch by the price mechanism. Indeed, the 'Chicago years' have probably strengthened antitrust hostility towards horizontal cooperation, at least in the United States.

However, the price mechanism does not achieve coordination well when no market exists for the inputs needed, or if the markets are 'small numbers' markets. By small numbers markets we are referring to circumstances where trading is relatively infrequent because user demands are specialized. Such circumstances are ubiquitous, particularly where innovation is involved. Thus the developer of a new instant camera may discover that it requires a new type of instant film. The number of potential developers of the instant film may be quite small ex-ante, and even if large ex-ante may be small ex-post because of what Oliver Williamson (1985) has referred to as the 'fundamental transformation'. In such circumstances the ability of a camera developer to contract with a film developer in an arm's-length, open market is likely to be quite restricted.

If one recognizes the need for cooperation to spur and commercialize innovation, even among firms that may be competitors, then one is likely to be sceptical, as we are, of the antitrust hostility towards horizontal cooperation. If one is prepared to abandon this hostility, there are at least three ways to go. (1) The more radical approach is to abandon large pieces of antitrust law altogether.[16] We do not favour this at all. Indeed, an economically sound antitrust policy can facilitate the privatization and deregulation of industries – like telecommunications and electricity – where historical concern about the potential for monopoly power has led to regulation or possibly even governmental control. (2) An alternative approach, and one advanced by Richard Schmalensee (1992), would be to abandon the *per se* illegality of price fixing and market allocation and adopt a rule-of-reason approach instead. We support such an approach, although it is not our preferred alternative for advancing innovation. (3) A third approach, and the one we favour as an interim solution, would be to permit a 'safe harbour' for cooperative agreements among competitors innovating and commercializing innovation, if their combined market share is less than 25 per cent of the relevant market (Jorde and Teece 1992: chapter 3). We would favour rule-of-reason analysis for shares greater than 25 per cent. Our rule-of-reason analysis would pay close attention to the requirements of the innovation process, and the intellectual property protection available to innovators if the cooperative activity is designed to help facilitate the development or the commercialization of new technology.

ANTITRUST AS INDUSTRIAL POLICY

We define a nation's industrial policy as the aggregate of policies that directly and indirectly affect industrial performance through its impact on microeconomic variables. Key elements of industrial policy include adjustment assistance, certain aspects of tax policy, government procurement policy, regulation, science and technology policy, and competition (antitrust) policy.[17] Antitrust policy, it seems to us, ought to be assessed not just on a stand-alone basis, but also on how it integrates with other aspects of industrial policy. For the United States, antitrust laws are a more central aspect of industrial policy than in Europe or Japan. Without judging whether antitrust or other components of industrial policy are at fault, it seems appropriate to flag certain areas of tension, if not conflict.

Antitrust and trade policy are often at odds, particularly in the United States. The semiconductor trade agreement between the United States and Japan – which required Japanese firms to collude in reducing exports to the United States – was in conflict with antitrust policy, as were the orderly marketing agreements for steel and automobiles negotiated during the 1970s.

Antitrust law and patent law, while they both purport to have enhancing economic welfare as their goal, sometimes conflict, although they need not. Market power obtained from a patent is not illegal. Nevertheless, a not uncommon response to a patent suit is an antitrust counter-claim from the infringer.

US telecommunications regulation, up to the divestiture, required AT&T to provide universal service and to engage in cross-subsidization. But when AT&T moved to cripple new entrants, whose actions systematically served to undo the structure of cross-subsidies regulators had imposed, AT&T had sufficient antitrust exposure to cause it to enter a settlement agreement with the government. Telecommunications policy and antitrust policy have thus been at odds with each other. But antitrust policy prevailed.

These conflicts suggest that, at least in the United States, antitrust policy is frequently in conflict with other aspects of industrial policy. Where it exists, this tension needs to be recognized, and addressed and resolved where possible. Furthermore, as markets become increasingly global, antitrust policy needs to become global in scope as the reach of policies and governance systems must match the domain of the activity in question. But US antitrust policy can only impact foreign business behaviour through its impact on US commerce, and then only if the behaviour in question is not sanctioned by foreign government(s). Thus the most egregious anticompetitive structure of the post-war period – the Organization of Petroleum Exporting Countries (OPEC) cartel – has not been touched by US antitrust law, despite the fact that it has tremendous impact on US consumer welfare. Indeed, by preventing countervailing cooperative strategies by US oil companies, US antitrust has strengthened, not weakened, OPEC's power. Retaliatory cooperative acts by US oil companies that could have served to destroy the cartel are decidedly illegal. Ironically, the most far-reaching exercise of market power in the US marketplace has been completely untouched by US antitrust laws, while these same laws have prevented efforts to exercise countervailing market power by US petroleum companies.

Our point is simply that as foreign commerce continues to become increasingly important, competition policy often looks antiquated as the guardian of economic welfare.[18] There is no administrative apparatus in place in the United States to enable antitrust policy to be integrated with trade policy or science and technology policy.[19]

CONCLUSION

The integration of competition policy with other aspects of industrial policy is obviously a worthwhile goal. Once it has been accomplished, policy-makers can usefully turn to harmonization. Perhaps, when they do so, intellectual frameworks will have evolved to the point where the importance of innovation to competition will have been globally recognized. If this happy state transpires, the harmonization of competition policy will be facilitated, and economic welfare will advance. Absent the development of such frameworks, harmonization is premature and likely to retard rather than advance economic welfare.

NOTES

1 For an excellent exposition of static microeconomics as applied top antitrust analysis, see Posner (1976).
2 This follows in part from the homogeneous goods assumption that underlies perfect competition.
3 This ensures access to technological opportunities due to discoveries in basic science.
4 For a good survey of some of the relevant literature, see Dosi (1988).
5 This section is based on Jorde and Teece (1988) and on Hartman *et al.* (1993). Our treatment here is preliminary.
6 See *U.S. Department of Justice Merger Guidelines*, June 14, 1984.
7 While frequently criticized, this approach is widely accepted by scholars and the courts. For a critique, see Harris and Jorde (1983).
8 See Hartman and Teece (1990).
9 In Section 3.411, the *U.S. Department of Justice Merger Guidelines* state that with heterogeneous products 'the problems facing a cartel become more complex. Instead of a single price, it may be necessary to establish and enforce a complex schedule of prices corresponding to gradations in actual or perceived quality attributes among competing products ... Product variation is arguably relevant in all cases, but *practical considerations dictate a more limited use of the factor.*' As a rule of thumb, if the product is completely homogeneous (very heterogeneous), 'the Department of Justice is more (less) likely to challenge the merger.'
10 As noted earlier, Schumpeter (1942) stressed that potential competition from new products and processes is the most powerful form of competition, stating: 'in capitalist reality, as distinguished from its textbook picture, it is not that kind [price] of competition that counts but the competition that comes from the new commodity, the new technology, the new source of supply. ... This kind of competition is as much more effective than the other as bombardment is in comparison with forcing a door, and so much more important that it becomes a matter of comparative indifference whether competition in the ordinary sense functions more or less promptly.'
11 See Brown and Mendelsohn (1984); Brown and Rosen (1982); Epple (1987); Hartman (1987); Hartman and Doane (1987); Hartman and Teece (1990); Ohta and Griliches (1976); Rosen (1974).

300

12 See Atkinson and Halvorsen (1984); Hartman (1982); Hausman (1979); Mannering and Winston (1984).

13 See Epple (1987); Friedlaender *et al.* (1983); Fuss (1984); Fuss and Waverman (1981); Spady and Friedlaender (1978).

14 For instance, if an employee of a competitor firm for which the market power was being determined was included in the sample, that person would have an incentive to overestimate the difficulty of performance improvement. In the United States the need to inform these economic decisions with technological reality would argue for a closer working relationship between the Antitrust Division of the Justice Department and the National Science Foundation or the Office of Technology Assessment.

15 One example was the Justice Department's challenge to the sale of EMI Inc's US operations to General Electric.

16 George Stigler (1985: 8) has noted that 'if a nation wished to foster competition, it would be at least a tenable position that the common law doctrine of non-enforceability of restrictive agreements was sufficient legal action'.

17 We realize that for a brief period in US history – in the late 1970s and early 1980s – industrial policy became an ideologically loaded phrase describing quasi-national planning activities such as 'picking the winners' and 'weeding out the losers'. Few people ever took the notion of heavy-handed interventionist planning apparatus seriously, and the debate died a natural death. We trust we will not be misinterpreted here in our use of the term 'industrial policy'.

18 Witness the AT&T divestiture. The severing of the vertical supply links between Western Electric – the equipment arm of the Bell system – and the Bell operating companies created tremendous opportunities for foreign telecommunications equipment suppliers. US interests would undoubtedly have benefited if the divestiture could have been used to leverage concessions from trading partners.

19 Phillip Areeda in chapter 2 of Jorde and Teece (1992) explicitly explores the links between antitrust policy and industrial policy in the US context.

REFERENCES

Armentano, Dominick T. (1986) *Antitrust Policy: The Case for Repeal*. Washington, D.C.: Cato Institute.

Atkinson, Scott E. and Roger Halvorsen (1984) 'A New Hedonic Technique for Estimating Attribute Demand: An Application to the Demand for Automobile Fuel Efficiency', *Review of Economics and Statistics* 66: 417–26.

Baxter, William F. (1985) 'Antitrust Law and Technological Innovation', *Issues in Science and Technology* (Winter): 80–91.

Bork, Robert (1978) *The Antitrust Paradox: A Policy at War with Itself*. New York: Basic Books.

Bowman, Ward D. (1973) *Patent and Antitrust Law*. Chicago: University of Chicago Press.

Brown, Garoner, Jr and Robert Mendelsohn (1984) 'The Hedonic Travel Cost Method', *Review of Economics and Statistics* 66: 427–33.

Brown, James N. and Harvey S. Rosen (1982) 'On the Estimation of Structural Hedonic Price Models', *Econometrica* 50: 765–8.

Cohen, Stephen, David J. Teece, Laura Tyson and John Zysman (1985) 'Competitiveness', *Global Competition: The New Reality* 3. Washington, D.C.: President's Commission on Industrial Competitiveness.

Cohen, Wes M. and Richard C. Levin (1989) 'Empirical Studies of Innovation and

Market Structure', in Richard Schmalensee and Robert Willig (eds) *Handbook of Industrial Organization* 2. Amsterdam: North Holland.

Dosi, Giovanni (1988) 'Sources, Procedures and Microeconomic Effects of Innovation', *Journal of Economic Literature* 26 (September): 1120–71.

Epple, Dennis (1987) 'Hedonic Prices and Implicit Markets: Estimating Demand and Supply Functions for Differentiated Products', *Journal of Political Economy* 95: 59–80.

Friedlaender, Ann F., Clifford Winston and Kung Wang (1983) 'Costs, Technology and Productivity on the U.S. Automobile Industry', *Bell Journal of Economics* 14: 1–20.

Fuss, Melvyn A. (1984) 'Cost Allocation: How Can the Costs of Postal Services Be Determined?', in Roger Sherman (ed.) *Perspectives on Postal Service Issues.* Washington, D.C.: American Enterprises Institute, pp. 30–52.

Fuss, Melvyn A. and Lawrence Waverman (1981) 'Regulation and the Multiproduct Firm: The Case of Telecommunications in Canada', in G. Fromme (ed.) *Studies in Public Utility Regulation.* Cambridge: MIT Press.

Harris, Robert G. and Thomas J. Jorde (1983) 'Market Definition in the Merger Guidelines: Implications for Antitrust Enforcement', *California Law Review* 71: 464–96.

Hartman, Raymond S. (1982) 'A Note on the Use of Aggregate Data in Individual Choice Models: Discrete Consumer Choice Among Alternative Fuels for Residential Appliances', *Journal of Econometrics* 18: 313–36.

Hartman, Raymond S. (1987) 'Product Quality and Market Efficiency: The Effect of Product Recalls on Resale Prices and Firm Valuation', *Review of Economics and Statistics* 39: 367–72.

Hartman, Raymond S. and Michael J. Doane (1987) 'The Use of Hedonic Analysis for Certification and Damage Calculations in Class Action Complaints', *Journal of Law, Economics and Organization* 32: 351–72.

Hartman, Raymond S. and David J. Teece (1990) 'Product Emulation Strategies in the Presence of Reputation Effects and Network Externalities: Some Evidence from the Minicomputer Industry', *Economics of Innovation and New Technology* 1: 157–82.

Hartman, Raymond S., David J. Teece, Will Mitchell and Thomas M. Jorde (1993) 'Assessing Market Power in Regimes of Rapid Technological Change', *Industrial and Corporate Change* 2: 317–50.

Hausman, Jerry A. (1979) 'Individual Discount Rates and the Purchase and Utilization of Energy-using Durables', *Bell Journal of Economics* 10: 33–54.

Jorde, Thomas M. and David, J. Teece (1988) 'Product Market Definition in the Context of Innovation', University of California, Berkeley: Working Paper No. BPP-29, Center for Research in Management (February).

Jorde, Thomas M. and David J. Teece (1992) *Antitrust, Innovation, and Competitiveness.* New York: Oxford University Press.

Mannering, Frederick and Clifford Winston. (1984) 'Consumer Demand for Automobile Safety', *American Economic Review* 74: 316–18.

Ohta, Makoto and Zvi Griliches (1976) 'Automobile Prices Revisited: Extensions of the Hedonic Hypothesis', in Nester E. Terleckyj (ed.) *Household Production and Consumption.* Washington, D.C.: National Bureau of Economic Research Conference on Research in Income and Wealth, Studies in Income and Wealth, pp. 325–90.

Posner, Richard (1976) *Antitrust Law: An Economic Perspective.* Chicago: University of Chicago Press.

President's Commission on Industrial Competitiveness (1985) *Global Competition: The New Reality* 1. Washington, D.C.: Superintendent of Documents.

Rosen, Sherwin (1974) 'Hedonic Prices and Implicit Markets: Product Differentiation in Pure Competition', *Journal of Political Economy* 82: 34–55.

Schmalensee, Richard (1992) 'Agreements between Competitors', in Thomas M. Jorde and David J. Teece (eds) *Antitrust, Innovation and Competitiveness*. New York: Oxford University Press.

Schumpeter, Joseph A. (1942) *Capitalism, Socialism and Democracy*. New York: Harper Brothers.

Spady, Richard H. and Ann F. Friedlaender (1978) 'Hedonic Cost Functions for the Regulated Trucking Industry', *Bell Journal of Economics* 9: 159–79.

Stigler, George (1985) 'The Origins of the Sherman Act', *Journal of Legal Studies* 14: 1–11.

US Department of Justice, Antitrust Division (1984) *U.S. Department of Justice Merger Guidelines*, June 14, Washington, D.C.: GPO.

Williamson, Oliver E. (1985) *The Economic Institution of Capitalism: Firms, Markets, Relational Contracting*. New York: Free Press.

303

Part IV

VERTICAL ARRANGEMENTS

12

VERTICAL INTERFIRM RELATIONS

A competition policy issue?[*]

Annette Bongardt

VERTICAL INTERFIRM RELATIONS AND GLOBALIZATION

In post-war economic history three phases with changing trade patterns may be distinguished in geoeconomic terms, i.e. exports, internationalization and globalization. The first comprises exports by firms from their national market base and extends to the emergence of newly industrialized countries as export powers. The subsequent period is characterized by the internationalization of production by multinational firms (MNEs). These MNEs established themselves as local players with direct distribution of their goods in relevant markets but shifted production activities abroad to exploit factor price differentials. The present era of globalization implies that firms need to plan their insertion in clusters of firms without frontiers in the medium to long run (compare OECD 1992b). Globalization thereby denotes growing synergies of national economies by means of a certain degree of functional integration of activities that may be dispersed at world scale.

It should be noted that the substitution of the concept of internationalization for globalization goes hand in hand with a different understanding of the organization of firms, often referred to as clusters or networks. The importance of network organization for firm competitiveness and for the competitiveness of a given region or country is by now widely recognized (e.g. see Porter 1990). While the impact of vertical firm relations and globalization on trade and foreign direct investment patterns has received more attention, its ramifications for the underlying nature of competition and for competition policy have as yet been less discussed.

[*] I thank Len Waverman, Bill Comanor and participants in the project's Seminar at the University of California, Santa Barbara, and workshop in Paris for helpful comments. Part of this paper was written while the author was at the Rotterdam School of Management, Department of Strategic Management and Business Environment, and at the International Centre for Economic Research (ICER), Turin.

According to the OECD, the relation between firm strategy encompassing cluster organization and globalization can be sketched out as follows:

1 *Increasing weight of intermediate goods and services.* In the 1980s the increasing weight of procurement of intermediate goods and services in world markets as compared to domestic markets has emerged as a clear trend in the principal industrialized countries. This opens up a window of opportunity for the export of intermediate products from third countries, especially since some of today's products are of a multinational nature.

2 *Foreign direct investment as the most dynamic factor.* At the same time, foreign direct investment rather than exports was the driving force of globalization throughout the last decade. Its growth rate (28.9 per cent) outperformed the growth of world GDP (7.8 per cent) and global exports (9.4 per cent) by four and three times, respectively, between 1983 and 1989.

3 *Cluster organization as a key in a firm's globalization strategy.* Foreign direct investment or the shift of production facilities abroad to exploit factor price differentials or to overcome market barriers nevertheless represents only the very first step in a firm's globalization process. Rather, in a world of global competition these short-term measures have to be embedded in a medium-to-long-term global network strategy in which the firm positions itself within a cluster of firms as a global exporter of goods and services from a foreign platform.

4 *Regional insider strategy in the Triad.* In geoeconomic terms, a firm should aim at a strategic position as a regional insider within the Triad's trading blocs or of emerging markets.

Interfirm vertical relations thereby emerge as a centerpiece for firm competitiveness on a global scale. This change of industrial organization towards networks of firms is a reflection of the ongoing shift of production philosophy from the former mass ('Fordist') production system to the lean ('Toyotist') production system. Spearheaded by the automobile industry, Western firms are emulating Japanese best practice. One of the most important features of lean production lies in the separation and delegation of tasks between firms in the supply chain and a more cooperative, as opposed to adversarial, attitude within the network structure.

In a world of globalizing competition, it is self-evident that a more efficient organization of the supply chain that leads to cost and performance advantages (and which originated in one particular country) should be felt by many firms across the world and stir up calls for protection from national industries. At present firms operate in an environment which requires that they master increasingly complex goods that are subject to an often high pace of technological change. Under these conditions the tightly coordinated Japanese industrial groups practising lean production could in the past make inroads into the EU and the US markets, for instance in the car, electronics and semiconductor industries. The automotive industry, presented hereafter as an illustration, is by no means an isolated phenomenon, in that the EU Commission and the US government rushed to offer it protection from 'unfair' competition by restricting imports.

Although this shift of production philosophy to practices invented by Japanese firms in the 1950s and 1960s is recognized as a global phenomenon (OECD 1992a), the different vertical relations between Japanese as compared with Western firms have given rise to recurrent trade friction between the European Union and the United States on the one hand and Japan on the other over recent years. The US structural impediments initiative and the latest US–Japan dispute over trade in cars and car parts aimed at opening up the Japanese market provide a good example of the fact that this trade friction is often rooted in competition policy divergences, that is, policies that are domestic by nature. Japanese-type networks of firms (the so-called *keiretsus*) were singled out as foreclosing market access to Western firms. The US argument was that these organizations might be illegal under US antitrust law, that Japanese antitrust law was similar to that in the US and was not being applied.

System friction related to vertical firm relations might have its roots in diverging competition policies rather than in the trade arena *per se*, in that a laxer national competition policy or laxer enforcement might give domestic industry a competitive advantage over its foreign competitors or might indeed be used as a strategic trade instrument. This chapter sets out to shed light on the issues associated with networks of vertically related firms. As outlined above, these issues are on the one hand a country's openness to trade (exports and imports of intermediate goods) and to FDI and, on the other, a country's attitude and the facility of building up a cluster organization and the related issue of whether a foreign firm can become a regional insider or whether there are barriers to entry due to the need to enter two production stages simultaneously. Although the latter issues are clearly the domain of competition policy, they have an obvious effect on trade and FDI patterns.

The focus of this chapter is first on how the nature of competition changed with lean production, globalization and vertical interfirm relations (clusters) and secondly on competition policy. Despite their real-world importance in terms of firm competitiveness and trade (friction), the roots of success of interfirm vertical arrangements, their workings and impact on the changing nature of competition are still somewhat sketchy in many respects. It is, however, important to establish how the nature of competition changed with lean production before turning to competition policy and to whether the philosophy behind these policies proves still adequate in the light of the new realities. Hence this chapter compares in some detail customer–supplier relations in the automotive industry, an industry that assumed a leading role in terms of industrial organization right from the beginning, and considers likely developments in terms of competitive behaviour and variables in the Triad, in the first place in the European Union and in Japan. The goal is firstly to increase our understanding of vertical relations between firms and the time factor (i.e. cycle times) as the new drivers of competition. Second, it is aimed at identifying the differences that are likely to last in the vertical organization of firms. On that basis we shall then examine whether friction as to vertical restraints ultimately originates in different competition policies.

THE NATURE OF VERTICAL FIRM RELATIONS: THE CASE OF THE AUTO INDUSTRY

This chapter draws on the automotive industry to compare the structures, workings and innovation performance of Japanese and EU industrial groupings (cf. Bongardt 1993, 1995). It investigates the different coordination modes between industrial customers and suppliers and ramifications for competitiveness. The industry lends itself particularly well to the analysis of supply chain coordination in the Triad. The car industry has led other industries in the reorganization of the production process, thus initiating shifts from craftsmanship to mass production (or 'Fordism') to the present new production philosophy invented and perfected by Toyota ('Toyotism') in the 1950s and 1960s. This new production regime, widely applied in Japan since the 1970s, centres around tight coordination of industrial customers and suppliers. In the 1980s the different Japanese organization of the value chain changed the rules of the competitive game in the global automotive industry. The car producers had little choice but to face up to competition that presupposed better coordination within a streamlined supply chain and a faster and more continuous innovation pace.

In the ensuing part the focus is on the coordination of the supplier interface in the EU automotive industry and its implications for EU competitiveness *vis-à-vis* the Japanese motor industry. Car producers and parts and component suppliers coordinate their activities in supplier systems. In the past, the predominant production philosophy and the structure and cohesion of automotive supplier systems differed markedly between the European Union and the United States on the one hand and Japan on the other hand. The performance implications have been well known since the 1990 study of the global automotive industry by Womack *et al.* that showed that Japanese producers outperformed Western mass producers because of their superior internal and external organization. Whereas Japanese supplier systems are organized along so-called 'lean production' principles, Western supplier systems used to organize manufacturing and supply according to mass production principles. The classic US model of mass production has been associated with short-term, adversarial relations with suppliers or vertical integration. Car producers selected suppliers by competitive tender on the basis of blueprints of components developed in-house. In contrast, while EU supply relations have been adversarial, they have been relatively long-standing and characterized by significant involvement of suppliers in component development. For historical reasons the supplier interface in the EU automotive industry has displayed elements of both mass production and lean supply systems.[1]

The challenge for the Western motor industry to emulate Japanese-type lean production practices in order to improve performance and increase efficiency was formidable. In 1986, Adams reported a total Japanese production cost advantage for a typical subcompact car produced in Japan of US$2,201 (or US$1,718 net, excluding shipping costs). The European motor industry reacted to the challenge ten years later than its American competitors when Japanese car makers shifted their attention from the American to the European market. It should therefore not come as a surprise that, as recently as 1992, Mercedes-Benz estimated that the Japanese car makers had a production cost advantage over their German competitors amounting to 35 per cent (*Financial Times* survey, 25 June 1992: iv). This production cost advantage was not the result of single improvements but the sum of multiple improvements throughout the production and sourcing process. Of this differential about 10 per cent is attributable to relatively low capital costs and the longer working hours in Japan, advantages that are hence subject to 'natural' erosion with the ongoing globalization of capital markets and social evolution. The need for increased efficiency is highlighted by the estimate that only a 15 per cent production cost differential is sustainable (F. Piëch, head of the VW group). Before restructuring in the EU motor industry took place, Japanese producers only required about half of the man hours per standard car. They had reduced defects per car to less than half of the European figure. The Japanese firms achieved a larger variety of models with a lower average life span and smaller production runs than EU producers. They boasted seventy-two models against forty-nine in Europe, with a life span of 2.1 as compared with 3.9 years, while their average production series was less than a third of European producers' (Jones and Womack 1988). Perhaps the most noteworthy achievements were the reductions of cycle times as compared with the best Western producers, evidenced by marketing, orders and distribution within six to eight days versus sixteen to twenty-six days, car production within two to four days against fourteen to thirty days and new product development and market introduction within two and a half to three years against four to six years, respectively (Stalk and Hout 1990: 29).

With vertical relations and timing as key competitive variables, restructuring was a must for survival and restored competitiveness for the EU motor industry in the recent recession. With vertical interfirm relations being crucial for the superior performance of Japanese lean producers *vis-à-vis* Western producers in terms of cost, performance and cycle times, the EU automotive industry addressed its two major weaknesses, both of which were related to coordination of the supplier interface. Firstly, since competition shifts from interfirm competition to competition between networks, changes in the relationship between car producers and suppliers became crucial. The second key competitive variable – intricately related to the first – consisted in the significantly lagging speed of new product development and market introduction of new models. The European motor industry responded to this challenge by remodelling vertical relations. Supplier systems were rationalized with a view to pyramidal structures, characterized by the separation and delegation of responsibilities to suppliers and single sourcing of parts and components systems from direct suppliers.

In the ensuing sections we shall examine the nature and performance features of vertical relations in the European Union and in Japan as well as possible limits on the emulation of Japanese patterns in the European Union. The aim is to establish the efficiency properties and possible anti-competitive behaviour associated with vertical structures as a basis for the concluding section on competition policy (enforcement) as a source of friction in the Triad.

COMPARATIVE SOURCING IN THE EUROPEAN UNION AND JAPAN

This section compares the coordination of the supplier interface in the European Union and in Japan in order to assess the strengths and weaknesses of the EU supplier systems. Given that the Japanese car networks set the performance standards for the EU automotive industry, their supply structure and car producer–component supplier relationships will be discussed first.

Organization of the supply chain in Japan

In the Japanese car market, eleven domestic car producers, five of which qualify as major car makers (Toyota, Nissan, Honda, Mitsubishi and Mazda), compete fiercely. They are usually classified as volume producers, although all have entered the specialist segment by building up their own luxury marques.[2]

The Japanese supplier systems are characterized by tight group cohesion and little overlap between them. Japanese car producers are associated with industrial groupings of suppliers that are largely dedicated to a specific car maker. The supply structure resembles a pyramid composed of strictly hierarchical tiers. First-tier suppliers are affiliated with one or sometimes several car producers by means of minority equity stakes. Group cohesion is reinforced by interlocking cross-shareholdings and industry practices like joint directorships or full exchange of cost information (i.e. value analysis

312

and value engineering of parts and components). Second- and third-tier subcontractors are more independent in terms of ownership structure and form a common supplier base. The first-tier suppliers have the capacity to subassemble and supply entire component systems. Responsibility for total quality, just-in-time delivery and relations with lower-tier suppliers rests with them. Of the 40,000 firms in the auto sector, 320 are direct, first-tier suppliers. Each of these major suppliers in turn relies on a group of around twenty to sixty second-tier suppliers. The third tier of suppliers, more than 10,000, takes advantage of the wage differential between large and small firms and performs simple, more labour-intensive tasks. The Japanese supplier firms have tight organizational and financial links with auto makers. The majority of them belong to groups that centre around a major car maker. For instance, Nippondenso, the largest Japanese producer of car parts and components, is affiliated with Toyota by means of equity links. Numerous Japanese suppliers possess equity links with several car makers. This system has created a supply industry that is more specialized and more concentrated than the European supply sector (Commission of the European Communities 1994: 11/22).

These Japanese vertical arrangements achieve operational coordination and structural control over the supply base which is usually associated with vertical integration. Vertical integration figures for Japan that reflect ownership boundaries, usually put at around 20 per cent of total component requirements, therefore understate the tightness of coordination of the supplier interface by Japanese car producers. Coordination of the supply chain in Japan has been rationalized by means of a tier system and the sourcing of entire component systems. Moreover, Japanese car producers have limited the number of direct suppliers to a few first-tier suppliers. Contrary to widely held belief, single-sourcing is by part number only. Suppliers per part average 2.2. One of these suppliers is typically affiliated with the car producer (Boston Consulting Group 1990: 168, 170). Affiliated first-tier suppliers do the thrust of business with their parent car company, but are encouraged to compete for business beyond. In contrast to sourcing, there is no direct competition between suppliers in component development. Component development and technology transfer are delegated to only one, affiliated first-tier supplier. Leading-edge technology development and supply are always kept within the industrial group.

Japanese car producers attach more importance to long-term supplier performance than Western car makers have traditionally done. Affiliation of first-tier suppliers and tight network cohesion mean that the benefits from coordination accrue to the network under car assembler control. The distribution of benefits is less subject to a conflict of interest between customers and suppliers and can be more 'cooperative'. Supply relations with first-tier suppliers are long-term, based on multi-year contracts. In contrast to unilateral price determination by the customer or price fixing on the basis of supplier quotations, as was common practice in the West, prices are usually determined bilaterally (Nishigushi 1989: 200). A supply quota and a target price are agreed on for a given component, with planned cost-cutting in line with anticipated savings due to learning economies in the course of component supply. Improvements beyond that enhance supplier profits so that suppliers have an incentive to further cost-reducing efforts. The price is fixed on the basis of exchange of supplier cost information and car producer cost calculations for the market price of the vehicle. The supply quota is awarded on the basis of past supplier records. Competition between typically dual suppliers is instilled by adjusting their quota and thus profits according to regular detailed performance evaluations with respect to multiple criteria like quality, design, delivery and price.

To summarize, the strength of the Japanese network structure is that it facilitates supply relations that combine the coordination benefits usually associated with vertical integration with built-in efficiency checks concerning multiple performance criteria. Tight vertical coordination – often backed up by equity links – overcomes hold-up problems otherwise associated with a bilateral bargaining situation and a supplier first-mover advantage from product development and hence facilitates the realization of both the cost and timing advantages (notably just-in-time delivery, simultaneous product development) outlined above.

Organization of the supply chain in the European Union

The European Union is the world's largest market for passenger cars (before the US and Japan) and maintained that position throughout 1992–4, despite the deep dip in production and sales due to the severe recession in 1993. The EU automotive industry has in the past been fragmented along national borders, with the result that smaller national car producers were unable to realize economies of scale and vertically integrate into component manufacture to the same extent as the large US producers. On average, and including affiliated component divisions, they sourced out between 60 per cent and 70 per cent of total component requirements in 1994, as compared with 40–50 per cent in the United States and around 80 per cent in Japan (Commission of the European Communities 1994: 11/25). There are, however, very large variations between the car makers.

There are seven major domestic producers – Volkswagen group (VW, Audi, Seat, Skoda), Fiat group (Autobianchi, Alfa Romeo, Lancia), PSA group (Peugeot, Citroën, Talbot), Renault, Mercedes-Benz, Rover (taken over by BMW in 1994) and BMW – that compete in the European market. Of these, five have market shares between 10 per cent and 12 per cent; only Volkswagen group possesses a 17.5 per cent market share. The six largest producers (without Rover) accounted for 75 per cent of the EU market in

1994, whereas Japanese producers increased their market share from 10.9 per cent in 1989 to 12 per cent in 1993.

Competition in the EU market is heating up, owing to two major developments. First, with the ever more integrated internal EU market mobility barriers between member countries are coming down, eroding the hitherto strong domestic bases of European car makers. On the other hand, voluntary export restraints limit Japanese imports only until 1999 and are scheduled to gradually increase until then, while the newly competitive US car makers and South Korean auto producers in particular could increase their exports to Europe significantly. Several Japanese car makers have set up production plants in the European Union, predominantly in Britain, thereby circumventing trade barriers. New plants in Eastern Europe contribute to overcapacity in the sector. In the resulting fight for market share, and with most European car makers still highly dependent on the EU market (globalization moves are inadequate and a relatively recent phenomenon), their efficiency and performance in global terms are crucial to survival. Over the last couple of years, lean production techniques have led to more outsourcing and substantial changes in the relationship between car makers and their suppliers, the coordination of product development and production, production and logistics, and the responsibility, flexibility and qualification levels of the workforce. Although their best plants already match world standards with the significant changes made in response to the competitiveness of Japanese rivals, most European car makers still face the challenge of bringing their old plant and all their activities up to the new standards (Commission of the European Communities 1994: 11/15–16). In particular, they still have to match the best US plants, whose adaptations were fuelled by next-door Japanese transplants and joint ventures with Japanese producers.

Internal efficiency apart, the management of external relationships assumes particular importance for the competitiveness of EU car producers. The unit cost performance of manufacturing is highly dependent on the effectiveness of procuring parts and assemblies, and suppliers are ever more crucial to ensuring quality and quick delivery. The European component supply sector in turn, relatively protected in the past, is facing up to competition not only at a national and European, but at a global level. The creation of the European single market requires suppliers to effect cross-penetration of national markets, whereas the internationalization moves of European car makers implies geographically enlarged sourcing bases and intensifies competition. On the other hand, the Japanese production establishments in Europe draw the attention of Japanese components suppliers to the European market.

The Japanese components sector still enjoys several serious competitive advantages compared with the European supply sector. In Europe a million persons are employed by first-tier, direct automotive component suppliers, compared with 280,000 in Japan. The European components sector is much more small-scale and fragmented and is still building up the pyramidal structure that is well established in Japan. The majority of EU component suppliers are small or medium-sized, more than 64 per cent of suppliers employing fewer than 100 persons. In Europe 3,200 companies qualify as first-tier suppliers, compared with only 320 in Japan. Their average size is 270 employees, compared with the 900 of an average Japanese first-tier supplier. Including lower-tier suppliers, the European average is merely 5.5 employees. Whereas 45 per cent of Japanese firms employ more than 500 persons, in Europe the proportion is only 10 per cent (Commission of the European Communities 1994: 11–23). The role of large suppliers in the European Union is, however, crucial, not only in terms of EU employment, but also for the technological competitiveness of EU car networks (see pp. 318–22). While it is only the top 4 per cent of EU automotive suppliers that have more than 1,000 employees, they account for 50 per cent of total employment in the sector.

The EU supply structure that has emerged to date is characterized by large, diversified suppliers such as Bosch and Siemens, large specialized automobile suppliers such as Valeo and Magneti Marelli and hundreds of SMEs with smaller-scale production. The number of independent suppliers has fallen by up to 50 per cent (although estimates vary) with increased rationalization of supply networks in terms of outsourcing and systems sourcing. Suppliers that could not qualify as first-tier suppliers became second or third-tier suppliers. Moreover, over the last five years mergers, acquisitions and consolidation of former rivals and firms with synergies set the pace in the motor industry. With the exception of Italy and to some extent France, EU component suppliers tend to be independent of car producers. Only two suppliers in France and Italy out of the top twenty European suppliers are closely associated with major car producers. There has nevertheless been significant coordination within EU supplier systems, owing to their national character, essentially nationally focused sourcing habits and legal requirements relating to vehicle testing and compulsory maintenance. Despite the emergence of large international firms, the sector remains rather fragmented. EU car makers' sourcing habits have largely remained nationally focused: for instance, Mercedes-Benz sources 90 per cent nationally, Renault 70 per cent and Fiat 85 per cent.

Supply structures in the EU car industry used to resemble overlapping and unstructured pyramids. This situation has been changing rapidly, although the restructuring process is not complete. The competitive pressures in terms of cost, price, quality and delivery cycles have prompted a restructuring process similar to the one in the assembler firms. The parts and components suppliers compete on the basis of quality, fast delivery and price. Substantial productivity gains have been made by the implementation of JIT, total quality, CAD/CAM, electronic data exchange, etc., and supplier flexibility and quality assurance have been improved. However, this process, which presupposes very large investments and qualified labour, is far from complete, in particular in the small and medium-sized firms. As a result, the Japanese network structures have created an industry that as yet is more specialized and more concentrated than the European auto sector. While the European sector remains competitive *vis-à-vis* its Japanese counterparts in terms of technology, its weakness is rooted significantly in the fact that the first-tier segment is less competitive in terms of labour productivity, product quality, logistics and delivery cycles and product design and development cycles (Commission of the European Communities 1994: 11/21–3).

Conversely, EU groupings resemble Japanese car networks in terms of long-standing relations and supplier involvement in product development. The relations between independent EU parts and components suppliers and car producers are, however, more adversarial. Unlike in Japan, the often long-standing supplier relations in the past were not matched by long-term contracts; short-term contracts were awarded by competitive tender on the basis of price that consequently blocked any full exchange of cost information.[3] After hesitating initially, EU producers have embarked on long-term contracts with single suppliers in return for increased supplier responsibility for component development, more efficient delivery and quality/warranty. Although EU car producers, like the Japanese to date, used to prefer multiple direct suppliers that competed with each other (see Womack *et al.* 1990: 157), the European motor industry found that the need for a more cooperative stance in vertical interfirm relations to realize Japanese-type performance features was compatible only with long-term supply contracts and a single supplier status for its large, independent suppliers.

As in Japan, increased dependence of car makers on outsourcing implies fundamental changes in the structure of the supply sector, notably owing to the increase in outsourcing of high value-added components, the rapid growth of R&D expenses and the need for the organizations to adapt to new standards of quality, fast delivery, price and, not least, flexibility. In addition, suppliers have to share continuously productivity gains with car assemblers and undertake production investments (tools and specific equipment) for manufacturing specific products. In exchange, car assemblers cooperate more tightly with their suppliers and with a long-term horizon which increases the stability of their mutual relations.

What are the strengths and weaknesses of EU supplier systems as compared with Japanese networks? In the European Union car producers tend to share independent first-tier suppliers in new product development and sourcing. In contrast, Japanese first-tier suppliers are affiliated to car producers. As a result of the different supply structures, benefit-sharing in Japanese car networks is 'cooperative', while attitudes have been more adversarial in the EU. The restructuring of the EU supply base towards a pyramidal structure and overlapping supplier systems and the clear-cut division of labour within given supplier systems (i.e. first-tier suppliers with a global presence, proprietary technology and economies of scale that design and supply component systems and subcontracting to second and third-tier suppliers) increases supplier bargaining power and hence mutual dependence between the parties in the vertical chain. Vertical interfirm coordination by means of long-term contracts and a single sourcing status for developing suppliers indicate that the European motor industry found a market solution to coordinating an otherwise adversarial interface and decreasing the scope for bilateral haggling by means of a more equitable sharing of value added in the network in the longer run.

As to the performance of this coordination mechanism, Japanese car makers that set up production plants in Europe report better performance than in their Japanese plants, likewise using independent European component suppliers and single sourcing. They have generally built up more constructive partnerships than their European counterparts, thereby helping their European suppliers to live up to Japanese performance standards while being as tough on price as their European rivals. In the long run, the arrival of Japanese transplants in Europe is expected to accelerate the restructuring of the components sector, raise its competitiveness and ultimately the competitiveness of European car assemblers (European Commission 1994: 11/23).

COMPONENT DEVELOPMENT: INNOVATIVENESS AND R&D EFFICIENCY

This section focuses on the technological performance of EU supplier systems in the context of their structure and supply relations. Two complementary factors determine competitiveness in technological terms, namely the innovativeness and managerial efficiency of the R&D process. They are subsequently discussed.

EU technological standing

As indicated above, independent EU automotive suppliers have performed well in terms of innovativeness. The large number of EU licences to Japanese suppliers bears witness to this fact. In addition, the EU components sector displays no technological gaps. Japanese suppliers that entered the European market did so via joint ventures with indigenous suppliers (Ruigrok *et al.* 1991: 171–3). In certain fields, the EU parts and components sector is thought to have a technological lead *vis-à-vis* its Japanese competitors. This technological advantage pertains in particular to anti-lock brakes, electronic fuel injection and automotive electronics, constantly variable transmissions, constant velocity joints and water-based paints. Japan's technological strengths, on the other hand, lie in ceramics, four-wheel steering, memory seats, multi-valve engines and turbochargers (Boston Consulting Group 1990: 331).

The technological prowess of the EU components industry is related to a number of underlying factors. Notably, on the demand side, the presence of car producers in the up-market segment for which technology has been a key competitive variable has spurred innovation. On the supply side, the existence of a strong EU engineering industry, particularly in Germany, and large and independent component suppliers with R&D capability has been an asset. EU automotive suppliers spend 3–6 per cent of sales (weighted average of component groups) on R&D. German suppliers spend most, namely 6.6 per cent. Independent EU suppliers apply their know-how to component development with several car producers. Thereby they accumulate know-how with respect to development and manufacturing that in turn increases the technological level of components. It is noteworthy that the large, independent EU suppliers are largely responsible for the EU technological lead *vis-à-vis* Japan. The activities of the top twenty EU suppliers mirror the European technological advantage in automotive electronics, brakes, fuel systems and transmissions. Six of them specialize in one product category and are world leaders in their field. Eight of the top twenty have dedicated activities in the strategically important electrics/electronics sector (Boston Consulting Group 1990: 331, 339, 151).

The technological strengths of the EU components industry and its capacity to sustain a high pace of innovation were decisive for car producers' competitiveness in the past and will be even more so in the future. Rapid technical change in the automotive industry has prompted a shift to increased supplier responsibility for component development. First, product life cycles are shortening while R&D outlays are rising. Second, new technologies need to be incorporated into the vehicles, such as electronics and new materials. Electronics is commanding an ever-growing share of the value-added of vehicles. Electronics know-how lies beyond the traditional expertise of car producers that pertains to mechanics. Electronics suppliers with systems integration know-how are increasingly critical for the performance of mechanical parts and the entire vehicle.

EU car producers responded to the need to delegate costly component development to large specialist suppliers that have the required know-how and the critical mass to sustain high R&D investments and can reap economies of specialization in the course of shorter product life cycles. The reliance of car producers on suppliers with problem-solution capability and strong development capacities grows, in particular in automotive electronics. Car producers have adopted essentially three strategies in order to cope with the resulting hold-up problem. First, in the area of strategically important automotive electronics, EU car producers have aimed to reduce their reliance on suppliers. They have pursued tapered integration by acquiring suppliers to enhance in-house expertise on component design and pricing and have encouraged new entry by large suppliers like Siemens into the industry to decrease reliance on a few key suppliers, such as Bosch. Second, car producers have formed joint ventures for in-house component development of mechanical parts deemed critical, e.g. axles and motors. Third, the direct suppliers of particular components or subsystems are granted long-term contracts and single-supplier status in exchange for their increased responsibilities, in particular higher R&D outlays, and for accepting car producer interference in their management and production operations to ensure supplier performance, timely delivery and quality.

To summarize, European networks are characterized by single supply and the development of a certain component (system) by large, independent suppliers, whereas there is competition in product supply but not as regards development in Japanese networks. Next we shall see that the reason for the difference in network organization lies in ownership structures in Japan that curb possible opportunistic behaviour owing to a supplier first mover advantage that stems from product development.

Management of the R&D interface

Whereas in technological proficiency the EU components sector compares favourably with its Japanese competitors, the industry proved uncompetitive in terms of timing, i.e. longer new model cycles and higher R&D costs. It is, however, cycle times that with lean production have become the new and critical competitive variable in the motor industry and beyond. The remainder of this section focuses on the second determinant of EU technological competitiveness, i.e. the extent to which the efficiency of component development is conditioned by vertical structures. The management of the development process between car producers and component suppliers influences development speed and cost.

EU car producers have traditionally pursued a superior technological performance strategy coupled with product distinctiveness and model variety that somewhat insulated them from cost pressures. This strategy has been reflected by the primacy given to the R&D department over the other functions in order to ensure a product design focus on technological refinement. Japanese producers on the other hand have tended to compromise product design features in the process of consensus-seeking with other departments (Nonaka 1992). The European car makers' strategy of focusing on technological performance at the expense of cost and charging high prices has become less sustainable, because the Japanese lean production system has spurred pressures for efficient management of R&D in terms of speed and cost across market segments. Japanese car networks display high technological performance and at the same time have achieved shorter component development and new model cycles and a higher variety of components and models, compared with their European counterparts.

Component standardization and less design novelty across models did not explain faster development and more variety, with Japanese new car models containing more unique parts and fewer carryover and common parts than European models.

Already in 1987 Clark *et al.* showed that faster product development cycles were at the root of faster new model cycles in Japanese supply systems and that Japanese car networks achieved superior product development performance without spending more on R&D than EU supplier systems (Clark *et al.* 1987). It emerged that on average Japanese networks spent less on R&D in proportion to sales than their European counterparts (car makers and suppliers), while development productivity (engineering hours per new model) was higher in Japan. The explanation for the gap in development productivity could be attributed not to greater delegation of design responsibility by Japanese car producers to suppliers, but to the differential involvement of Japanese and EU car producers in component development and the efficiency of the organization of the R&D process in the supply chain. Table 12.1 gives a more detailed break-down of the relative contributions of car producers and suppliers to component development in the past. Figures for US volume producers are included for reference. The table mirrors the fact that European car producers had a major role in component development, whereas European suppliers contributed proprietary parts to an extent comparable with Japanese suppliers. It illustrates that EU and Japanese automotive supplier systems used to differ significantly regarding the responsibility that component suppliers or car producers assumed in the component development process and that Western car makers were especially reluctant to delegate black-box development to suppliers. As indicated above, lacking capacity of the EU components industry to develop components or entire systems cannot have been the reason for the lower black-box development ratio.

Let us now turn to the link between European car producers' reluctance to undertake black-box development and the R&D productivity gap. Comparing the management of the component development process, the typical patterns differ markedly between the European Union and Japan. In Japan,

Table 12.1 Component development between car producers and suppliers prior to the adoption of lean production in the Western motor industry (%)

Component development pattern	Japanese	American	European
Engineering carried out by suppliers[*]	51	14	35
Supplier proprietary parts	8	3	7
Black box parts	62	16	39
Assembler-designed parts	30	81	54

[*] In per cent of total hours
Source: Womack *et al.* (1990: 157).

only one affiliated supplier conducts the entire component development process. This black-box supplier is selected already at the component concept stages. Upon selection, the supplier is assured of supplying the component in question over the car model life cycle. The price is established late and adjusted throughout the model cycle on the basis of full provision of cost information. Simultaneous actions in terms of investments in R&D and equipment are possible from the outset. In Europe, suppliers were often involved in component development as a condition of bidding for the supply contract. Multiple suppliers and/or the assembler conducted component development. It was the sequential nature of component development and supplier selection that slowed down component development and new model cycles, while the duplication of R&D efforts raised total development costs. The price for the component used to be established in a competitive tender for one- to two-year supply contracts. Price rises were associated with design changes or controllable cost increases (Boston Consulting Group 1990: 351).

Ultimately, therefore it was the nature of the coordination of EU vertical interfirm relations that accounted for its competitive disadvantages. The EU component sector has been competitive on a technological level. While its technological strengths are due to its large, independent suppliers that conduct component development with several car producers (in overlapping supply networks), the sequential management of the R&D process within the supply chains proved uncompetitive in terms of speed and total development costs. EU supplier systems coordinated the supplier interface by large car producer involvement in component development and/or R&D competition between suppliers and direct competition between suppliers for supply contracts. In contrast, it is the very structure of Japanese car networks that has facilitated coordination of the interface at lower cost and with timing advantages, since an affiliated supplier conducts component R&D and technology transfer. Supplier interaction with a long-term time horizon furthermore promotes organizational and technological learning within the supplier system. No competition in component development is required to achieve dual or multiple sourcing.

We shall next address the reason why European networks used to be so reluctant to delegate R&D to suppliers and whether European car networks can emulate Japanese patterns and efficiency properties associated with lean production despite different interfirm relations and network structures.

AN ILLUSTRATION: THE CASE OF MERCEDES-BENZ

Having compared the different component development and sourcing patterns in EU and Japanese supplier systems, this section looks in more depth at the respective roles of car producers and suppliers in component development and at the relationship between component development and sourcing patterns, presenting concrete cases on component development and supply drawn from Mercedes-Benz AG of Germany (cf. Bongardt 1990).

The choice of Mercedes-Benz

To illustrate the rationale of the previous EU model of vertical interfirm relations and to sketch out the strengths and weaknesses of the new model that aims to emulate the Japanese pattern in the European setting, the Mercedes-Benz case is particularly interesting with respect to the firm's network structure, supply relations and performance for four reasons:

First, Mercedes-Benz is a leading EU car producer. It operates globally from the open and competitive German market and, together with Volkswagen group and BMW, in the recent past contributed to the German car industry's positive car trade balance in value terms with Japan.

Second, Mercedes-Benz represents a European version of a vertical learning network (Ruigrok *et al.* 1991). Its supplier base, in line with the typical EU setting, is independent. It boasts an outstanding innovation record. Important areas of EU technological strength have resulted from the development of components with its suppliers, notably with Bosch in automotive electronics (anti-lock braking systems and electronic fuel injection systems).

Third, like other EU car makers, Mercedes-Benz had to close the productivity gap with respect to Japanese producers while keeping up superior technological performance. To do so it found that it had to devise a new manufacturing strategy modelled on Japanese-style lean production, logistics and manpower management, but adapted to the German setting. Its recent greenfield production facility at Rastatt was set up as a proving site. Mercedes-Benz's difficulties in switching to lean production practices have been comparable to those of other EU car makers as far as the nature of EU supplier systems is concerned.

Finally, Mercedes-Benz is part of an industrial group, Daimler-Benz AG. With its portfolio of traditional and high-technology sectors and its link with the Deutsche Bank, the group structure is reminiscent of a medium-sized Japanese industrial group; as a rule, suppliers are not part of the group, with the exception of some areas that are considered strategic (e.g. electronics). Its diversification in the middle to late 1980s was explicitly aimed at creating synergies between group members. In 1990 the Daimler-Benz group and the Mitsubishi group of Japan announced a strategic alliance in various fields that was confirmed again in 1994. In regard to their respective car divisions, it includes agreements on mutual dual sourcing of components and strengthened involvement of Daimler-Benz in Mitsubishi's subcontractors (Ruigrok *et al.* 1991: 95). However, up to the present these agreements seem not really to have been put into practice.

323

With the advent of lean production practices that lowered entry barriers into the luxury market segment (via the resulting simultaneous reduction of costs, high quality and shorter innovation cycles) Mercedes-Benz's strategy of charging high prices in the luxury car segments via product differentiation on quality, safety and technological leadership became more vulnerable to both cost and performance pressures applied by Japanese rival products that moved up-market. Formerly, Mercedes-Benz's reputed superior quality and technology used to be key in a traditionally price-inelastic upmarket segment and its investment in R&D accordingly was higher than the German industry average. BMW, equally pursuing a technological leadership strategy, used to be its main competitor. Upon the up-market move of Japanese car producers, Mercedes-Benz and BMW lost market share to the lower-priced Japanese luxury brands, especially in the US market. Mercedes-Benz compared unfavourably with its Japanese rivals in terms of productivity and cost competitiveness. Its superior quality but low productivity plant in Sindelfingen was found to require four times the man hours per vehicle of Japanese plants, owing to the fact that quality control proceeded in a mass-production framework with craft-like practices at the end of the assembly process (Womack *et al.* 1990: 89). Its model cycles were eight years. At a time of recession and environmental concern, Mercedes-Benz's long product cycles proved a major disadvantage for its necessary refocus of its product strategy towards smaller, less luxurious cars.

It is hence obvious that Mercedes-Benz was under profound pressure to improve its performance by adopting lean production practices, notably by delegating responsibility to suppliers for quality and development activities, and to overhaul its model policy. Its recent model and price policies and the production of the so-called Swatchmobile, to be assembled in France as of 1996, bear witness to its resolution to do so.

Component sourcing with adversarial vertical relations

The cases presented here concern sourcing relations and development patterns associated with six automotive component innovations, i.e. anti-lock braking system (hereafter ABS), electronic fuel injection (hereafter EFI), air bags, electronic front-window wipers, flywheels (clutch) and spark plugs. They concern the first half of the 1980s. At that time Mercedes-Benz produced 48 per cent of value added in-house and procured the remaining component requirements from independent suppliers. This latter ratio has been gradually increasing.

Supply structure and relations in the case studies reflect patterns typical of EU supplier systems: nationally focused sourcing, independent suppliers and short-term contracts. Mercedes-Benz still sources 90 per cent of its component requirements locally (Commission of the European Communities 1994: 11/26). All suppliers, without exception, were independent of

Mercedes-Benz. The studied supply relations were long-standing, but based on short-term contracts. The bilateral relation with Bosch, the supplier of ABS and EFI, dated back more than 100 years. In the other cases relations ranged from a minimum of five years (air bags) to more than fifty years. The specific component sourcing relations had lasted from five to twelve years. The minimum of five years before taking up a new component sourcing relationship corresponds to normal procedure with Mercedes-Benz to ensure supplier reliability, quality and performance standards.

The cases reflect the importance of large, independent suppliers for component development in the European Union. The suppliers that Mercedes-Benz chose for component development and as main suppliers were all large (more than 1,000 employees), with the exception of the medium-sized air bag suppliers (500–1,000 employees). The air bag is a case apart, since suppliers with the required pyrotechnical know-how had to be found beyond the automotive industry. Supply contracts consisted of long-term framework contracts and one-year supply contracts. They were equal across components, corresponding to the standardized contracts used in the German automotive industry. Supply contracts were not differentiated according to, for instance, supplier investment in component development or the strategic importance of components.[4]

Component development: the hold-up problem

This section addresses the question of whether and why component development might have differed across components. It analyses cases of component development in the Mercedes-Benz supplier system with reference to Japanese-style learning networks. In Japanese automotive supplier systems one affiliated supplier is entrusted with component development and technology transfer. This black-box development means that car producers define product specifications, while the supplier is responsible for the entire component development process. Affiliated suppliers do not transfer know-how that involves strategic components to another supplier(s). EU car producers used to retain a higher share of development activities in-house and delegate less black-box development to suppliers than the Japanese car makers.[5]

The Mercedes-Benz learning network operates in the German automotive context, that is, supplier systems are overlapping in that major suppliers generally work with several car producers in component development and sourcing. Independent component suppliers have been a prime source of innovation in the German automotive industry. By cooperating with car makers in component development, suppliers pool industry know-how. They create know-how by technological cooperation with car producers and in turn diffuse it to other car makers by applying it to specific technological problem solutions. Thereby German components suppliers have fulfilled a beneficial function of know-how exchange between car producers and have promoted a high industry technological standard.

In the cases studied, Mercedes-Benz selected the suppliers involved in component development from a limited number of large, independent suppliers with adequate development capability. In line with Japanese practices, the car producer defined product functional and technological specifications for components. Only for ABS, a leading-edge innovation, were specifications developed jointly with the supplier, Bosch. Bosch is the largest auto component supplier in the world, with a leading position in automotive electronics.

In contrast with the Japanese component development pattern, the car producer's and the supplier's roles in the component development process are less clear-cut in the cases studied. The Mercedes-Benz component development pattern constitutes a half-way house between European component development with several suppliers and the Japanese pattern with one supplier conducting black-box development. There was no case of supplier black-box development of a significant component innovation. Instead, component development was done by one independent supplier in three cases, i.e. the leading-edge automotive electronics (ABS and EFI) and the flywheel, but in all cases in cooperation with Mercedes-Benz. The other two components with a major degree of novelty, the air bag and the electronic window wiper, were essentially assembler-designed. The only entirely supplier-designed component was a minor innovation, the spark plug. Accordingly, there was no supplier patent on proprietary innovation know-how. Patents were joint patents or car producer patents according to the parties' contributions to component development. Mercedes-Benz thus maintained a major role in the design and development process of all significant component innovations.

The case studies illustrate that the observed development patterns had a strategic dimension from the point of view of the car assembler for the coordination of the supplier interface. They highlight the sequential nature of component development and supplier selection. The developing supplier(s) invest in component development before having concluded a supply contract regarding supply quota, price, etc., with Mercedes-Benz. The R&D investment was thus the precondition for a supply contract. The developing supplier was subsequently granted a supply contract with a higher price over a one-year period than other suppliers. Although the supplier could acquire a learning advantage vis-à-vis other suppliers in the course of component development that translates into an ability to offer better price and quality, this learning advantage from single component development did, however, lead to single-sourcing only in the EFI case. In all other cases the number of actual component suppliers increased to at least two. It appears that Mercedes-Benz achieved dual or multiple sourcing by the joint patent and the shared learning that enabled the car producer to

Table 12.2 Case evidence on component development and supply from Mercedes-Benz

| Components | Novelty | Component development | | | No. of component suppliers | (Contractual) arrangements beside supply contract |
		Developers	Classification	Owner of proprietary know-how/patent		
Anti-lock braking system	Leading edge technology	Car producer +one supplier	Joint development	Joint	2	Sharing of development costs and informal one-year exclusive supply
Electronic fuel injection system	Leading edge technology	Car producer +one supplier	Joint development	Joint	1	Development contract; formalized one-year exclusive supply
Air bag	Major innovation	Car producer	Assembler-designed	Car producer	3	None
Electronic window wiper	Major innovation	Car producer	Assembler-designed (two suppliers only at prototyping/testing stage)	Car producer	2	None
Flywheel (clutch)	Major innovation	Car producer +one supplier	Joint development	Joint	3	None
Spark plug	Minor innovation	One supplier	Supplier-designed	No patent	2	None

transfer the know-how to another supplier(s) not selected for their problem-solving capabilities.

In Mercedes-Benz's learning network know-how was diffused, in line with the European pattern, between suppliers and between networks. The R&D cooperation of the car maker with one supplier seems, however, less wasteful than multiple suppliers in component development and, judging by an impressive innovation record, appears to have promoted innovativeness. Mercedes-Benz confirms our above observations that it is the sequential coordination of adversarial development and supply relations aimed at ensuring competitive component supply that has contributed to longer model cycles. The next section illustrates that the reason why R&D coordination that seems costlier and slower than Japanese interaction patterns has been preferred in the Mercedes-Benz supplier system lies in the hold-up problem. That is, in such a bilateral bargaining situation the car maker would have to share the rents in a more equitable way with its powerful supplier.[6]

Coordination of the supplier interface in the absence of equity links

Car makers' reluctance to delegate black-box development and single-source a (strategic) component was related to bargaining problems between two major parties. The cases of automotive electronics, ABS and EFI, which concern a small numbers situation in component development and sourcing, illustrate this. ABS and EFI both constituted leading-edge developments in which the car assembler had a very strategic interest but little in-house expertise. The large and independent supplier, Bosch, was in a strong bargaining position. Only in the cases of ABS and EFI could a supplier translate a development advantage into single-supply of the innovative component. However, extra provisions were made regarding both component development and supply. ABS involves complementary braking and electronics technologies. Mercedes-Benz and the developing supplier, Bosch, contributed complementary know-how and each paid half of the total development costs of DM10 million. For EFI, the locus of expertise lies predominantly with the supplier. Mercedes-Benz and Bosch concluded a development contract for the development of the EFI system. In both cases, the parties agreed on one-year exclusive supply of the innovative component to the car producer. In the ABS case, the one-year exclusive supply agreement was informal, in the EFI case it was formalized.

Note that the ABS development preceded the development of EFI. Both components were initially single-sourced from the developing supplier. Bosch, however, interpreted the informal exclusive supply agreement for ABS differently and supplied the system to BMW, Mercedes-Benz's main competitor, before the end of the agreed one-year period. Mercedes-Benz then transferred the know-how to Teves, part of ITT of the United States. Teves at that time had lost out to the newest technological developments, but possessed the required know-how, testing equipment and financial resources for component supply. Conversely, Bosch remained the single supplier of the EFI system. It is conceivable that the move from informal agreements at both development and sourcing levels to formalized contractual agreements implies a learning effect on the part of the car producer.

With the need for lean production practices, the playing off of suppliers against each other has become inefficient as a vertical coordination mechanism. Rapid technical change, cost considerations and increasingly large, independent suppliers which are specialists in their field have meant a shift towards more black-box development, sourcing of entire component systems and single-sourcing to cut costs and improve performance. This confers more bargaining power on suppliers and erodes the basis of the mechanisms used or potentially usable to achieve dual sourcing, i.e. forced licences or assembler property rights. A development contract which confers a property right on the innovative know-how can be an alternative to achieve dual or multiple sourcing. The findings suggest that coordination of independent, adversarial parties requires explicit contractual arrangements at both development and sourcing stages if multiple sourcing is to be achieved. Trust, even when based on a long history of interaction, was not sufficient.

The action taken by Mercedes-Benz with respect to coordinating the supplier interface already illustrated that coordination would then be achieved in the market by mechanisms like explicit contractual agreements and/or the threat of loss of business to other potential suppliers. First, development contracts were designed in conjunction with longer-term supply contracts. Moreover, single sourcing with long-term supply contracts has become the rule. Second, the Daimler-Benz group has diversified into those sectors with the largest potential for conflict, i.e. electronics and new materials. This in-house expertise facilitates bargaining with suppliers, since tapered integration gives access to know-how concerning product design and pricing and provides a fall-back production capacity. Third, the alliance with Mitsubishi includes common sourcing of components and establishes Mercedes-Benz's involvement in Mitsubishi's supplier base. This increases demand power by enlarging the pool of possible suppliers across component groups and notably in the field of electronics.

To conclude, both the Japanese and the European car networks face the challenge of overcoming the hold-up problem created by specific investments. Japanese network structures can rely on their interlocking equity links,[7] whereas European networks (without unified goals and often still with adversarial attitudes) had to find a market solution. This market solution implies bilateral dependence between the car maker and first-tier suppliers and a solution of the bilateral bargaining problem by way of a more equitable sharing of rents, that is, value added in the supply chain and a long-term time horizon. European car makers were reluctant to contemplate this course while their home market was less competitive, but have now generally embarked on long-term contracts and single sourcing from major suppliers.[8] Japanese car networks operating in Europe likewise resorted to single-sourcing from European, independent suppliers. Their performance and the performance of the best European car makers seem to suggest that the looser character of European car networks is not an impediment to realizing Japanese-type performance, but that the independence of large suppliers and their cooperation with various car networks may create rather effective learning networks and thus contribute to generally high technological standards. After all, Japanese car makers in Japan seem to be moving in the same direction.

VERTICAL FIRM RELATIONS AS A COMPETITION POLICY ISSUE

The nature of competition under lean production

On the basis of a detailed analysis of the structure and workings of the Japanese supplier systems and their EU counterparts, this chapter has shown that the Japanese car networks realized important efficiency gains by tight coordination of their supply chains in conjunction with a clear-cut separation of tasks between vertically related firms. Competition under the so-called lean production paradigm became driven by their superior coordination of their value chains and their use of time as a competitive variable, not least by means of faster and more continual innovations. Thus the highly competitive Japanese automotive groupings were able to change the tune of competition in the automotive industry on a global scale. Compared with the binary industrial organization alternatives – vertical integration or adversarial, rather short-term orientated customer–supplier relations (the make or buy decision) – previously practised in the West, Japanese-type, more cooperative and longer-term customer–supplier relations afford ampler information flows and greater flexibility in reacting to market changes. Shorter innovation and product life cycles increased their competitive advantage. The above analysis of the EU automobile industry and of Mercedes-Benz's past sourcing patterns underscored that performance improvements associated with lean production are intricately linked with coordination across firm boundaries, i.e. vertical interfirm relations.

More efficient internal production and work organization in assembler plants apart, it was long-term relations with a few, selected suppliers of components and component systems and clear-cut separation and delegation of tasks within rationalized supply networks that facilitated the superior performance and efficiency of Japanese car networks in terms of cost, quality and cycle times. In the past Western industry used to be particularly outclassed by the fact that tightly coordinated Japanese car networks could thereby reduce cycle times (JIT production and short assembly throughput times, but in particular new product development and model cycles) dramatically and turn model cycles into a new and critical competitive variable; again, the tight vertical coordination and delegation of black-box R&D to a reduced number of suppliers has been a precondition for like performance. In the meantime, the Western automobile industry adapted Japanese-type practices and organizational structures to its particular settings (with the notable exception of interlocking cross-shareholdings between firms in vertical networks). As a result, the best Western auto firms or plants now match or even exceed Japanese performance standards. The resulting mixture of cooperation in the vertical chain (and occasionally with some rivals) went hand in hand with intensified competition in the European Union and in world markets (Nagel and Eger 1992).

In the light of the superior performance features of network configurations, it is not surprising that the OECD found that network forms of industrial organization have been proliferating in the West and that they have become a centrepiece of firms' globalization strategies. The Western automobile industry merely spearheaded the switch to lean production methods that can be observed as well in other sectors that benefit from the integration of procurement and the production/assembly of inputs (railway equipment, electrical engineering and electronics, computers, biotechnology, to name but a few). Lean production and interfirm relations tend to have a twofold impact on the nature of competition in those industries:

1 The nature of competition, with lean production and network organiz-ation, is now characterized by a mixture of cooperation within the vertical chain (intra-brand coordination) on the one hand and concurrent fierce competition between car assemblers (final producers) in product markets (inter-brand competition) on the other.
2 This vertical network organization facilitates important timing advantages and the time factor, i.e. cycle times, has thus emerged as the key competitive variable, in the form of JIT delivery and assembly and, in particular, innovation cycles (new model and model development cycles).

Yet, the fact that Western industry is recognizing on a large scale the efficiency properties of Japanese structures, and is adapting its own structures and practices accordingly, has not prevented system friction within the Triad that points to these practices. Given that the tightly integrated supply networks manage to realize the efficiency properties of vertically integrated structures by introducing various efficiency checks both of an administrative nature and competition to avoid the inefficiencies usually associated with vertical integration, the crucial question is whether these Japanese vertical relations would be qualified as anti-competitive in the West despite their efficiency properties. What are the remaining differences that could give rise to friction in the motor industry?

Although we have seen that the differences between car network organization and practices in Europe and in Japan under the lean production paradigm are getting ever smaller, two differences seem to be of a rather persistent nature:

1 While Western vertical interfirm relations have become more cooperative and long-term in nature, in Europe suppliers tend to be independent of car assemblers, in contrast to the straight ties, often associated with interlocking equity cross-shareholdings, in Japanese car networks and other cohesion-enhancing mechanisms.[9]

2 Single sourcing and product development by a sole supplier in European car networks contrasts with product development (typically by one, affiliated supplier) and dual sourcing with performance-dependent supply quotas in Japan.

With economics furnishing the theoretical groundwork for competition policy, several authors in this volume address vertical firm relations and innovation with a view to their competition policy implications. In Chapter 13 Comanor and Rey look at the efficiency properties of vertical restraints (vertical mergers and vertical ties) and competition, that is, the effect that vertical intra- and interfirm relations can have on market conditions at both stages of production. While vertical restraints facilitate intra-brand coordination, their ultimate impact on competition depends on the degree of inter-brand competition and market power in the final market. Of the three effects of vertical restraints – higher intra-brand coordination (as a response to miscoordination and externalities), reduced interbrand competition and higher entry barriers – the welfare effect of the first two critically depends on the degree of final product market competition, whereas the latter effect assumes more immediate relevance for international trade and investment. It is then up to policy-makers to weigh the positive and negative effects and to model competition policy in line with their evaluation, as vertical restraints can promote efficiency by doing away with double marginalization and free-riding, but at the same time may reduce interbrand competition and render market access more difficult for foreign producers. Thereby, it is the resulting firmness or laxity of a nation's competition policy stance that not only allows more or less vertical restraints but leads as well to higher or lower entry barriers for foreign firms at one production stage. Comanor and Rey point out that there is competition policy divergence in the Triad, as both US and Japanese competition policy towards vertical restraints happens to be lax in practice though not in letter, in contrast to EU competition policy towards vertical restraints, which is firmly enforced.

In Chapter 10 Martin expands on R&D cooperation motivated by the well-known market failures revolving around the production of information. While cooperative R&D can facilitate non-cooperative collusion, the welfare effects of cooperative R&D depend on the rivalry in product markets. With respect to the firmness or laxity of a country's competition policy stance, Martin finds that policy stances in terms of the permissiveness of R&D cooperation differ in the Triad. Both the European Union and Japan authorize joint R&D and research associations, while ensuring effective competition in product markets and the use of research results. Conversely, the US stance was characterized by the greatest permissiveness regarding joint production. In Chapter 9 Meißner and Markl elaborate on the effect of R&D associations from the viewpoint of strategic trade policy and globalization. They put forward the argument that weak national competition policy standards on international R&D cooperations (R&D joint ventures or patent pools) can be used as a strategic trade instrument that affords national firms a competitive advantage in product markets over their foreign competitors, hence transferring rents from foreign countries to augment national welfare.

Despite convergence on the need for competition in product markets, the chapters suggest that different domestic competition policy stances regarding vertical restraints and cooperative R&D may have resulted in a non-level playing field in the Triad. With the general adoption of lean production practices that presuppose a kind of network organization the question is whether this system friction is to persist or will be of a temporary nature in the light of the now globally applied new production and supply practices. A recent study commissioned by the European Commission's competition directorate argues that the European automobile industry does in fact experience competitive disadvantages *vis-à-vis* its Japanese rivals that stem from EU competition policy and that EU competition policy requires amendment to recreate a level playing field with international competitors (Nagel and Eger 1992).

The EU competition policy stance on vertical firm relations

EU competition policy was not prepared for the shift to vertical interfirm relations based on single sourcing upon the adoption of lean production practices. What is at stake here is a certain competition policy model. The nature of competition under lean production in the motor industry has come to be characterized by a mixture of cooperation (in particular in the vertical chain) and concomitant fierce competition between car networks. The emerging concept of competition hence responds less to Adam Smith's concept of atomistic competition (who however focused rather on horizontal cooperation) than to Porter's notion that companies can create a competitive advantage by optimizing horizontal and especially vertical cooperation, and thus increase their performance in terms of logistics, order processing, R&D, after-sales service, etc. (Porter 1990). Rather than being a trade-off as under mass-production principles, the adoption of lean production practices made possible the simultaneous achievement of cost reduction and performance improvements (quality, innovation cycles, etc.). In addition, timing or cycle times emerged as a new and critical competitive variable. In the motor industry vertical cooperation appears not to have prejudiced competition (and consumer welfare) but rather to have been associated with a hotting up of rivalry between car networks. Consumers benefit in terms not only of lower prices, but also of increased performance and more choice.

EU competition policy does not yet embody this lean production notion of competition despite the fact that in the European Union there exists a tendency in classical competition policy to view cooperation more favourably and overcome the entrenched distrust of cooperation.[10] The underlying competition policy concept, for the practical purposes of EU competition policy, may be summarized as making sure that the markets are kept open or are opened up in order to keep up competition between actual or potential competitors; protection thereby extends not only to rivals, but also to the vertical chain and supply and sales (Nagel and Eger, expertise for EU Commission, 1992: 100).

The lean production notion – in its European form – has, however, not yet been implemented in the European competition policy stance. Nagel and Eger argue that the European motor industry was put at a disadvantage *vis-à-vis* its Japanese rivals and that a level playing field with Japanese networks could be created only by amending legislation and facilitating single sourcing in Europe. The motor industry evidence clearly supports these affirmations and shows the root of the EU industry's competitive disadvantage. The above analysis of the EU motor industry and of case studies of Mercedes-Benz illustrate that the emulation of lean production practices in the European setting implies product development by a single supplier and single sourcing. Recall that R&D coordination in the motor industry takes the form of strict separation and delegation of design and product development tasks in the vertical chain (the suppliers undertake product innovation of components and component systems according to the specifications of the car assembler) rather than of cooperation in the product development process of the same product. The case studies of Mercedes-Benz in particular show that independent components suppliers will only take over such responsibilities – i.e. in product innovation – provided that they are granted single-supplier status and their proprietary know-how is thus protected from being leaked out to a rival supplier. Put differently, the exclusive purchasing agreements that have by now become a characteristic feature of the European motor industry compared with dual sourcing in Japan are motivated by possible market failure (intellectual property right protection in the vertical chain).

However, there is a gap in EU competition legislation concerning single-sourcing arrangements.[11] In principle, single sourcing falls under the prohibition of Article 85/1 of the Rome Treaty, although the European Commission is entitled to permit it under certain circumstances and provided that consumers get their fair share and that barriers to market entry are not raised for other firms that sell on the market (1978: 23–4).[12] However, while Article 85(3) of the EU Treaty allows block exemptions for joint R&D and under some circumstances joint production if market structure safeguards efficient competition, the same does not hold true of single sourcing as a response to market failure related to R&D. That is, owing to the problems outlined above – intellectual property in the case of black-box product development and transaction-specific investment – European car networks face a hold-up problem that does not exist in Japanese car networks owing to equity links and institutional arrangements. European car networks aim to solve this problem by means of long-term contracts with single suppliers, i.e. a bilateral relationship with reciprocal dependences. Nagel and Eger advocate that single sourcing be given a block exemption on the basis of Article 85(3) of the EU Treaty. Although single-sourcing agreements would usually benefit from exemptions under Article 85(1), they reckon that this procedure is more lengthy, uncertain and costly, thus imposing a competitive disadvantage on the European motor industry.

More specifically, Japanese equity-based vertical cooperation is forbidden in the European setting, as vertical bilateral coordination between a single supplier and the car assembler is subject to the cartel prohibition of Article 85(1) of the Rome treaty if it prejudices competition.[13] This is in contrast to the laxer Japanese policy stance under which vertical networks cum equity links are permitted in Japan.[14] Japanese-type interlocking shareholdings between firms in a network are qualified as anti-competitive in the European Union despite the fact that evidence from the European (and indeed global) motor industry suggests that (in contrast to much of the economic literature that tends to highlight the anti-competitive effects on product markets of vertical arrangements and R&D cooperation rather than economic efficiency gains) the emergence of Japanese tightly coordinated car networks has, if anything, increased competition in the automobile market in Europe (Nagel and Eger 1992). Given the negative opinion of the European Commission in the light of market foreclosure and unequal access, Japanese car assemblers investing in the European Union accordingly have refrained from building up their equity-based networks in the European Union and have resorted to single sourcing instead. Japanese car assemblers in the European Union have built up their pyramidal network structures with predominantly European and independent suppliers (often with better performance results than in Japan), whereas a laxer US competition policy stance allowed the replication of Japanese networks with their affiliated suppliers in the United States. In both cases the networks are, however, more open to longer-run competition by third suppliers and have not been challenged on competition grounds in the European Union or in the United States.

The fact that under EU competition law bilateral relationships fall under Article 85(1) does not preclude the application of Article 85(3) that, adopting a wider view of the rationalization advantages and increased competition between car assemblers overall, could justify an exemption, given that with strong competition in the car sector competition is unlikely to be reduced. However, the tedious, lengthy and uncertain procedure for applying for exemption from the EU Commission for each case of vertical, bilateral cooperation clearly puts EU firms at a disadvantage in a global lean production system. Block exemptions for typified contracts under Article 85(3) are as yet limited to joint R&D (regulation 418/85) that may extend to production if competition is not impaired. As indicated by our case study above, car assemblers adopt Japanese-type sourcing practices, adapted to the European setting of typically independent suppliers, that necessarily make use of single sourcing (and not dual sourcing) in an effort to constrain opportunistic behaviour in supply and product development and enhance efficiency. Our findings hence underscore that it is this gap in EU competition legislation granting block exemptions for typified single-sourcing agreements in the vertical chain that implies that European networks are prejudiced in terms of transaction costs and time compared with networks based beyond the EU that benefit from laxer legislation. The typical contractual configuration of vertical cooperations could then be subject to a block exemption of single-sourcing relationships. That is, if the typified preconditions apply, single sourcing should be exempted from the cartel prohibition of Article 85(1); Article 86 should still check abuse of a dominant position. Although the EU Commission is empowered by the Council to such a directive on group exemptions (regulation no. 19/65), up to the present it has seen no need for such action.[15]

While the Japanese and US competition policy stances are laxer towards Japanese vertical networks cum equity links, the stricter competition policy stance towards vertical restraints in the European Union (regarded as an essential precondition for the undistorted functioning of the internal market) plus the competition policy gap regarding single sourcing put European industry in the European Union market at a competitive disadvantage for comparative efficiency and strategic trade reasons. It is well known that the laxer Japanese competition policy towards vertical restraints plus heavy regulation (affiliations between customers and suppliers, exclusive dealerships and repair facilities) and domestic sourcing habits rendered market access in Japan difficult for Western auto firms, thus impairing Japan's openness to trade in cars and in auto parts. Interlocking cross-shareholdings in the Japanese car industry raise barriers to entry not only for foreign suppliers (although Japanese structures seem to be slowly opening up, owing to efficiency reasons) but, with suppliers and distributors centring around large car assemblers (by equity and other cohesion-enhancing ties), as well for foreign car assemblers that find it more troublesome to set up local distribution operations. Exclusive dealerships are common practice in

Japan as, to date, in the European Union,[16] contrasting with multiple dealerships in the United States.

Therefore, the conflict between Europe and Japan revolving around the motor industry that apparently takes place in the trade arena can be traced back to divergences in competition policy law and enforcement, that is, a different evaluation by domestic policy-makers of the trade-offs in terms of positive and negative effects of coordination and/or of the use of vertical restraints as a strategic trade instrument that gave national (Japanese) industry a head start over foreign competitors in the past and extracted rents from third countries. The analysis of the motor industry supports the view of Nagel and Eger that there is a gap in EU competition legislation that should be closed as soon as possible to curb one source of system friction in the global motor industry. It is up to the European Union to recreate a level playing field within the EU market by closing the competition policy gap on single sourcing. On the other hand, system friction caused by market foreclosure in Japan by affiliations between auto makers and their suppliers is subject to Japanese, domestic competition policy. Vertical restraints based on interlocking cross-shareholdings gave Japanese firms a competitive advantage in the past by protecting the domestic market from foreign competition and granted Japanese firms an advantage over foreign competitors abroad. However, even if competition policy (stance) differences concerning network structures remained in the Triad, the global spread of lean production practices combined with macroeconomic factors should be and is pushing towards *de facto* harmonization of practices and the erosion of the perceived unfair practices.

A NEED FOR HARMONIZATION OF COMPETITION POLICIES IN THE TRIAD?

The latest US–Japanese trade dispute again centred around the motor industry, namely vehicles and car parts, and the large bilateral US trade deficit with Japan in this domain. The United States threatened unilateral sanctions if Japan failed to comply with its various market-opening demands. The dispute was settled just before the deadline of June 28, 1995, set by the United States for trade sanctions to come into force under s. 301 of US trade law. The European Union, while largely in agreement with the United States on the issue of claimed anti-competitive practices, accused the United States of undermining the newly created multilateral forum, the World Trade Organization (WTO), by resorting to unilateral means.

This trade row once more can be traced back to divergent competition policies. In principle, the WTO that came into being only in January 1995 after the completion of the Uruguay round in 1994 has been equipped with a reinforced mechanism for settling trade disputes. However, considering the global shift to network structures that span countries and trading blocks and different competition policies and their enforcement on network structures, two main problems remain:

1 A gap in trade rules. Barriers to foreign investment, given changed trade patterns, often act as barriers to imports. Just consider that roughly one-third of all trade consists of intra-firm transactions and that the best way for firms to enter a foreign market is often to set up shop locally; in many service industries it is almost impossible to sell otherwise. Trade-related investment measures (TRIMs) agreed under the Uruguay round offer only a patchy coverage (for instance, it obliges WTO members to scrap rules on local content, but leaves other practices untouched such as establishing no right to national treatment for foreign firms) that in any event is limited to trade in goods.[17]

2 Competition policy is beyond WTO rulings. The key issues in the US–Japanese trade dispute over the motor industry were firstly the deregulation of Japan's replacement auto parts market (the aftermarket), secondly the expansion of dealerships selling US cars and thirdly an increase in purchases of US car parts by Japanese auto manufacturers. The United States reportedly chose the two-track approach of filing a case with the WTO plus the bilateral move of threatening sanctions under its trade laws because of the gaps in the WTO's competence. As yet, the WTO does not encompass every practice through which governments or industries can protect their home markets. The United States took to the WTO a case against the standards and technical barriers erected by the Japanese government towards replacement auto parts. It argued that this is covered by the WTO and works to deny US companies benefits agreed under the Uruguay round. Conversely, the United States held that affiliations between car makers and their suppliers (and dealerships) are not covered by the WTO. The bilateral challenge of practices deemed anti-competitive such as the *keiretsu* relationships in Japanese auto networks aims to force open the Japanese market by challenging practices that make import penetration difficult.

The bilateral settlement of the trade dispute reflects these differences, as Japan agreed to deregulate the aftermarket for replacement parts, whereas Japanese car makers made voluntary pledges to increase the share of US auto parts (instead of fixing a quota, as the United States had insisted). The United States was almost sure to lose the WTO ruling in the latter case, given that, competition policy being beyond its competence, vertical networks with affiliations are not covered with respect to their impact on trade. As concerns the former, the United States disregarded the procedures of the WTO.[18] To that extent the US approach set a dangerous precedent and might have toyed with the credibility of the multilateral forum.

Nevertheless, the dispute and its solution did have the merit of highlighting the issue of competition policy as a cause of trade disputes and the limits of the WTO's powers. The United States' basic complaint that the Japanese economy is still geared towards exporting and lacks the fair access for imports that a leading industrial nation should provide can hence only partially be solved under the umbrella of the WTO as it stands. Therefore, should competition policies in the Triad be harmonized to solve system friction or can a case be made for the coexistence of the different models? Economics provides no clear-cut guidelines as to the desirability of vertical networks – the chief issue in the motor industry – and unsurprisingly policy-makers' evaluations and competition policy stances differ in the Triad. However, the above analysis of the motor industry has indicated that although there are different vertical network configurations in the Triad, practices are getting more similar with the general adoption of lean production practices. These changing practices necessarily imply more long-term customer–supplier relations (with or without equity links) on a global scale, i.e. more long-term competition, hence entry/import penetration by third parties (domestic or foreign) becomes longer-term as well. With global competition on the basis of the same production philosophy, is there still a need to harmonize competition policies? As far as the European Union is concerned, amending its competition policy and granting block exemptions for single sourcing could recreate a level playing field in the Union. Recent developments in Japan indicate a loosening of Japanese networks in terms of equity links and sourcing habits that is due to efficiency reasons. Macroeconomic developments, notably the strength of the yen (i.e. against the US dollar), have made imported car parts and cars radically cheaper (up to 40 per cent) and have been pushing towards the relocation abroad of Japanese auto and auto parts production and the increased use of imported auto parts in Japan. The strong yen seems to be more effective in breaking up inefficient structures, changing local sourcing habits and prompting deregulation in Japan than other (trade) mechanisms. Imported vehicles are gaining market shares in Japan, albeit from a rather small base. Foreign car part makers have been experiencing a steady upward trend in their sales to Japanese car assemblers. With the potential for conflict in the motor industry getting smaller due to market forces, there seems no urgent need for the harmonization of competition policies as far as this particular industry is concerned.

NOTES

1 Lean production, in contrast to mass production, is a relatively novel concept. Developed and perfected by Toyota, it is widely applied not only in the Japanese car industry, but across industrial sectors in Japan. Lean production is driven by two complementary factors pertaining to manufacturing and supplier relations (Jones and Womack 1988). On the manufacturing side, the lean factory concept denotes the use of teams of multi-skilled workers with problem-solving skills at all organizational levels and the deployment of highly flexible, increasingly automated equipment to produce lower volumes of products in great variety. The

reorganization of the supply chain is a prerequisite for rendering effective organizational innovations like just-in-time delivery or total quality control. Lean supply requires cooperative, long-term supply relations in conjunction with the early involvement of the supplier in component development. Japanese customer–supplier relations have resulted in learning networks that facilitate an ongoing stream of product, process and organizational innovations on the part of both car producers and suppliers.

2 Note that lean production has rendered the scale-based distinction between volume and specialist producers obsolete in practice. For instance, the European specialist car maker Mercedes-Benz has significantly higher production runs per model than Japanese 'volume' producers. The performance pressures due to lean production therefore now apply across market segments. As a consequence, the price to technological performance ratio is an important variable not only for EU volume producers but increasingly for EU specialist producers as well.

3 As would be predicted, profitability differences between car producers and first-tier suppliers in Japan were minimal, whereas car producers had consistently higher profitability than the component sector in 1984–8 (de Banville and Chanaron 1985: 16–19, and Boston Consulting Group 1990: 281, respectively).

4 The cases involve components that mirror to a different extent EU technological advantage and the extent to which the locus of technological expertise is with suppliers. The ABS and EFI innovations constitute leading-edge technology, in which the EU has maintained a technological lead up to the present. Air bags, electronic front-window wipers and flywheels represent innovations with a major element of novelty. The spark plug is a standard item with only minor functional or technological modifications. In the cases of ABS and EFI, the locus of technological expertise (automotive electronics) is beyond the car maker's traditional field of mechanics expertise. The same applies to a lesser extent to the pyrotechnical know-how for the air bag. The difference lies in the differential capacity of the car producer to act as systems integrator for (sub)systems. Electronics know-how is critical for systems integration not only of component subsystems but increasingly for vehicles. For Mercedes-Benz's technological leadership strategy, the strategic importance of the component innovations corresponds to the degree of novelty inherent in components and their share of value-added in the vehicle. These are precisely the components in which it possesses the least in-house expertise. The question therefore arises whether and why development patterns differ according to component strategic importance and whether (contractual or other) arrangements are made in addition to standard supply contracts.

5 The distinction between black-box development and assembler-designed parts put forward by Womack et al. (1990: 157) is based on the Japanese model. It fails to take into account cooperation patterns in component development observed in the German automotive industry where a less clear-cut separation of tasks existed.

6 This is in line with Helper's (1992) findings on the US motor industry, which suggest that cooperation in vertical networks increases with the intensity of competition in the final market.

7 Recall that cross-shareholding of minority equity positions in supplier firms is a frequent feature of Japanese firms that manufacture complex goods such as cars. Taken by themselves, these participations are quite small, but adding up the intricate web of cross-shareholdings between the upstream customer and its suppliers results in a significant degree of control. Japanese car networks achieve the coordination benefits associated with vertically integrated firms, but avoid

their costs by inducing competition by administrative mechanisms. Input prices are not subject to a Western-style bidding process. The car maker sets a target price for the vehicle in the envisaged final market segment and works its way backward to components prices. The final input price is agreed between the parties on the basis of a far-reaching exchange of supplier cost data and includes planned cost-cutting. Japanese car *keiretsus* practise preferential trading with group suppliers.

8 Our analysis has shown that vertical interfirm relations in the European and Japanese motor industries go hand in hand with intense competition. In Japan, eleven car networks compete fiercely. With the Japanese firms entering the European market, European auto makers have likewise had to increase vertical cooperation. On the basis of observations of the US motor industry, Helper (1992) suggests that the level of rent in the car market is inversely related to cooperation in the vertical chain in the United States, in that US car makers have shifted to vertical cooperation only with lower rents in the car market. Vertical interfirm relations in the motor industry have not limited competition in the final product market.

9 Realized efficiency properties require long-term, stable customer–supplier relations, notably with respect to the cost-reducing delegation of tasks and to innovation. Input pricing in Japanese vertical networks resembles transfer pricing more than Western-style bidding and competition is long-term.

10 This is well illustrated by the fact that block exemptions granted under Article 85(3) are not confined to vertical cooperations, but even extend to horizontal cooperations.

11 The question then is whether competition policy in the European Union allows these vertical links or their European version to the extent Japan does or whether there is a potential for friction. Articles 85 and 86 of the Treaty of Rome provide the legal basis for EU competition policy towards vertical firm relations. Under both articles firms in the vertical chain and horizontal rivals are free to cooperate, unless cooperation causes anti-competitive effects and abuses that may affect trade between EU member states and that are substantial. More specifically, Article 85 of the Treaty of Rome covers concerted actions with anti-competitive effects. In addition, Article 86 covers unilateral acts to the extent that they are abuses of a dominant position within the single market or in a substantial part of it. Anti-competitive actions can be exempted from the prohibition of Article 85(1) under the individual or block exemptions of Article 85(3). This does not rule out the application of Article 86. Article 85(1) does not prohibit concerted actions in terms of interfirm cooperation irrespective of firm size, unless they restrict the scope of action of the participating firms and these firms coordinate their conduct (Commission notice on concerted practices between enterprises of 29 July 1968).

12 Quoted in Chapter 10 of this volume, p. 255.

13 In terms of the motor industry, Article 85 of the European Union's Rome Treaty chiefly covers anti-competitive effects that consist in the restriction of a supplier's freedom of action *vis-à-vis* third persons and vice versa. Conversely, Article 86 covers only dominant manufacturers that abuse their position with respect to suppliers by means of exploitation, discrimination, binding arrangements, unfair obstruction, etc. A car assembler commands a dominant position if the supplier is more interested in the contract and hence has higher exit costs. Moreover, a manufacturer's dominance must have an impact on a substantial part of the European single market; however, given the Europe-wide sourcing and long-term contracting by car assemblers this will usually be the case.

341

14 European Commission notice of 21 October 1972, quoted in Meißner and Markl in Chapter 9 of this volume, p. 227. Recall as well that EU competition law claims extraterritoriality.

15 In its most recent regulation proposal concerning the motor industry single sourcing agreements are not included. See regulation proposal by the European Commission, no. C 387/16-33, December 1994.

16 The new block exemption, coming into force on 1 October 1995 for seven years, is to curb car assemblers' hold over distributors. Among other things it will give dealers the right to establish multiple dealerships and to buy spare parts from independent suppliers as opposed to original equipment.

17 Negotiations on trade in service industries, handled by the General Agreement on Trade in Services (GATS), are still under way, and so far obligations only concern the services specified in WTO commitments.

18 The first step in any action under WTO rules is consultation over the issue, followed by ten days of reply for the defendant and a twenty-day period for bilateral consultations; should consultations fail, a dispute panel set up under the WTO rule is empowered to impose sanctions in the event of non-compliance with the rule (unlike GATT).

REFERENCES

Adams, W. (1986) *The Structure of American Industry*, seventh edition, New York: MacMillan.

Banville, E. de and J.J. Chanaron (1985) *Le système automobile français: de la sous-traitance au partenariat? Eléments d'une problématique*, Paris (Centre de Prospectives et d'Evaluation), 56.

Bongardt, A. (1990) 'Coordination between customers and suppliers in intermediate goods markets and associated patterns of R&D collaboration: Market power and efficiency', Ph.D. dissertation, Florence (European University Institute).

Bongardt, A. (1993) 'The automotive industry: supply relations in context', in H.W. de Jong (ed.) *The Structure of European Industry*, third edition, Boston and Dordrecht: Kluwer Academic Publishers.

Bongardt, A. (1995) 'L'industria dell'auto nella penisola di Setúbal (Portogallo)', in Torino Incontra, *Le Regioni Europee dell'Auto*, Milan: Franco Angeli.

Boston Consulting Group (1990) *The EC automotive components sector in the context of the single market*, 1 and 2, Commission of the European Communities.

Clark, K.B., T. Fujimoto and W.B. Chew (1987) 'Product development in the world motor industry', *Brookings Papers on Economic Activity* 3, 729–71.

Commission of the European Communities (1978) *Seventh Report on Competition Policy*, Brussels: EC.

Commission des Communautés Européennes (1994) Véhicules automobiles/ Equipement, accessoires et pièces détachées pour automobiles, *Panorama de l'Industrie Communautaire 1994*, Luxembourg: Office des Publications Officielles des Communautés Européennes, 11/9-27.

Commission of the European Communities (1994) Regulation proposal by the Commission concerning the application of article 85/3 of the EC Treaty on certain categories of distribution and sales and after-sales service agreements of automobile vehicles, *Official Journal of the European Communities*, C 378/16-33.

Financial Times (1992) 'Mercedes-Benz: new car plant will be test-bed for "lean production"', *Financial Times survey*, Executive cars, 25 June: iv.

Helper, S. (1992) 'Long-term relations and product-market structure', *Journal of Law, Economics and Organization* 8, 3, 561–81.

Jones, D.T and J. Womack (1988) 'The real challenge facing the European motor industry', *Financial Times*, 28 October.

Nagel, B. and T. Eger (1992) *EG-Wettbewerbsrecht und Zulieferbeziehungen der Automobilindustrie*, Gutachten im Auftrag der EG-Kommission, Generaldirektion Wettbewerb (IV), Luxemburg (Amt für amtliche Veröffentlichungen der Europäischen Gemeinschaften).

Nishigushi, T. (1989) 'Strategic dualism: An alternative in industrial societies', Ph.D. dissertation, Oxford (Nuffield College).

Nonaka, I. (1992) Nissan Motor Co., Ltd. Development of Primera, Nomura School of Advanced Management (Tokyo).

OECD (1992a) *La mondialisation industrielle – Quatre études de cas*, Paris (OECD).

OECD (1992b) *Science, Technology and Industry Review*, special issue on globalization, no. 13, Paris (OECD), December.

OECD (1993) *Echanges intra-entreprises*, série Problèmes de politique commerciale, Paris (OECD), October.

Porter, M. (1990) *Competitive Advantage of Nations*, London and Basingstoke: Macmillan.

Ruigrok, W., R. van Tulder and G. Baven (1991) *Cars and Complexes: Globalization versus Global Localisation Strategies in the World Car Industry*, MONITOR–FAST Programme, Prospective Dossier no. 2: vol. 13, Commission of the European Communities.

Smith, A. (1776) *An Inquiry into the Nature and Causes of the Wealth of Nations*, I–III, London. (Reprinted Baltimore 1974.)

Stalk, G. and T.M. Hout (1990) *Competing against Time*, New York: Free Press.

United Nations Centre on Transnational Corporations (1991) *World investment report – the Triad in foreign direct investment*, New York: United Nations.

Womack, J.P., D.T. Jones and D. Roos (1990) *The machine that changed the world*, New York: Rawson Associates.

13

COMPETITION POLICY TOWARDS VERTICAL FORECLOSURE IN A GLOBAL ECONOMY

William S. Comanor and Patrick Rey

The foreclosure of firms from upstream suppliers or downstream distributors is a long-standing problem for competition policy. At times, it has been strongly condemned,[1] but in other periods it has been considered as primarily efficiency-enhancing and not challenged at all.[2] This vacillating approach towards the problem of vertical foreclosure reflected its uncertain treatment in the economic literature. As this treatment has varied, so have policy standards.

The prospect of vertical foreclosure arises most commonly from the complete integration of a firm at succeeding stages of production. In that situation, either suppliers or distributors who had previously dealt with its separate divisions can now be foreclosed from those sales or purchases. So long as an integrated firm deals only with itself, single-stage rivals are excluded from some degree of market access.

Foreclosure can also arise through contractual relations among independent firms. When buyers and sellers agree to deal only with each other, or impose costs from dealing with others, their single-stage rivals are again excluded from suppliers or distributors with whom they might deal.

When it is relatively easy for single-stage firms to obtain needed supplies or gain effective distribution of their products, then vertical integration or exclusive dealing arrangements can have little market impact. Only where supplies or distribution outlets are limited, for one reason or another, can exclusion occur. In effect, the problem of foreclosure is the problem of market access because these vertical arrangements may prevent single-stage firms from producing or distributing their products.

An important setting where this problem can arise is in foreign trade. Where either contractual or ownership integration is achieved and foreclosure results, a foreign manufacturer may be unable to distribute his product effectively, so his alternatives become either to leave the market or to construct his own outlets. In either case, costs can increase and exporters

344

may be placed at a substantial disadvantage. On the other hand, where established distribution facilities are open to all producers, there are greater prospects for international trade. How these arrangements are evaluated, therefore, is an important matter for foreign economic policy.

In this chapter, we review the treatment of vertical foreclosure under current economic doctrine. We also recount the history of vertical arrangements in the US automobile industry and draw conclusions from this experience for international competition. Finally, we consider appropriate competition policy standards towards practices leading to vertical foreclosure.

THE RECENT LITERATURE ON VERTICAL FORECLOSURE

Most of the literature on market foreclosure has considered the effects of full integration. These studies typically examine the conduct of a vertically integrated firm that competes with non-integrated rivals at both stages of production. In principle, the same effects could result from contractual arrangements, which can be called integration by contract. While the agreement must benefit both parties, that condition applies as well to vertical integration achieved through merger. In either case, there must be a net gain to both parties.

In this discussion, we first survey the literature on market foreclosure achieved by integrated firms. And then we examine recent work that deals with the foreclosure effects of vertical restraints.

Vertical integration and market foreclosure

The extent to which vertical integration leads a firm to foreclose rivals at one or another stage of production has been the subject of much controversy. The original argument was that foreclosure followed directly from differences in the market shares of a newly integrated firm at the two stages of production. If the firm's parts dealt only with each other, as was assumed, then the division with the smaller share would expand at the expense of its single-stage rivals, and concentration levels at that stage would increase. It was this increase in concentration at one stage of production, and the corresponding demise of single-stage rivals, that was considered the primary vice of such arrangements.

To be sure, this position attracted considerable criticism. Some writers argued that vertical integration by itself could not increase the profitability of the combined firm as compared with what it would earn as separate units, so the quantity produced could not be further limited and the price could not be raised.[3] Even with market power, they contended, a vertical stream of production gives rise to a certain maximum amount of profits, that depends on demand conditions for the final product and costs at all constituent stages. These profits can be earned by a monopolist at any single stage of production, and cannot be increased even if monopoly positions are extended from one stage to another. Therefore, foreclosure cannot lead to an increase in market power and can have no additional anti-competitive effects.

An early response by one of the authors of this chapter was to avoid the concept of foreclosure entirely and to emphasize instead the possible effects on entry conditions. Since single-stage firms can now be at a disadvantage relative to their multi-stage rivals, effective entry can require operations at both stages of production. And where multi-stage entry is more costly or difficult than entry at either stage separately, the height of entry barriers can increase as a direct result of vertical integration.[4]

More recently, however, several studies have sought to rehabilitate the concept of foreclosure, which specifically concerns the effect of vertical integration on non-integrated rivals. In one such article, and in direct opposition to the Bork–Posner position, Salinger (1988), argues that a vertical merger 'eliminates an independent supplier of the intermediate good and, as a result, can cause the intermediate good price to increase. If it does, the remaining unintegrated producers become less competitive, which, other things equal, causes the price of the final good to increase' (p. 350). Since there are fewer firms in the market for the intermediate product after the merger, there will be higher prices for the intermediate good, which in turn leads to higher prices for the final products sold by single-stage producers.

Salinger concludes that vertical integration can lead to higher prices and greater profits so long as there is imperfect competition at both stages of production. If foreclosure leads to fewer suppliers of the intermediate product, its price can rise; then if the market price for the final product is set by the single-stage producers, which means only that they are the marginal producers, vertical integration can well have anti-competitive effects. An essential condition is that full monopoly returns are not gained at either stage, so there is still the possibility of increased profits.

This analysis is extended by Ordover *et al.* (1990). These authors acknowledge the long-standing charges against the theory of foreclosure and seek to answer them. One issue is that, even after vertical integration, the upstream part of an integrated firm may still find it profitable to supply downstream rivals. The mere fact of integration does not always mean that downstream firms are foreclosed from their supplies. A second issue is whether intermediate good prices necessarily rise when rivals integrate, and whether higher downstream prices always follow from higher upstream prices. And finally there is the question of whether non-integrated rivals may respond by vertically integrating themselves.

While the authors acknowledge that vertical integration does not always lead to foreclosure, they suggest conditions which make foreclosure particularly likely.[5] One is that the integrated firm's profits must increase with the price set in the non-integrated upstream market, at least to a point. But this condition is not very limiting, for it holds whenever sellers of differentiated products raise their prices in response to higher rival prices. However, without this condition, foreclosure is not a profitable strategy.

Another condition is that, for small increases in the price of the intermediate products, the gain to single-stage upstream firms must exceed the loss to downstream firms so that competing integration is not a feasible strategy. The effects of market foreclosure cannot then be evaded.

Foreclosure by contract

The analysis of foreclosure by contract is not so different from that achieved through the exchange of ownership rights. When integration is accomplished through contractual agreements, both parties must be rewarded, as in the case with merger agreements. To achieve foreclosure following a merger, the upstream division of an integrated firm does not supply the rivals of its downstream division. For independent firms to achieve this result, they must agree on an exclusive dealing arrangement through which distributors refrain from buying and reselling the rivals' products. In either case, these actions can be used to raise rivals' costs and restrict them from the producer's markets.[6]

In an important paper on this topic, Aghion and Bolton (1987) demonstrate that established buyers and sellers can use contractual provisions between themselves to retard the entry of a more efficient seller. By including a provision for liquidated damages in which the buyer must pay the original seller a certain amount if he purchases from a rival, new entrants can be foreclosed from the market, or at least limited to buyers who have not made these contractual arrangements.

In their model, there are gains from excluding the new seller, which are then divided between the two incumbents. To be sure, as Aghion and Bolton point out, if the new seller has sufficiently low costs, it is preferable to permit his entry but to allocate a share of the resulting profits to the original seller. In effect, the new seller compensates the distributor for his required payment of liquidated damages. The analysis demonstrates that a more efficient supplier can be foreclosed from a specific distributor if the latter has already agreed to sell only the original supplier's products or pay a specific penalty. New suppliers are then excluded from the segment of the market occupied by the distributor.

A related paper by Rasmusen et al. (1991) considers the prospect that an incumbent supplier can take advantage of the lack of coordination among his buyers to reach exclusionary contracts with some of them. The authors demonstrate that there is an equilibrium outcome in which the supplier can pay a minority block of buyers to sign these contracts by using the rents extracted from the rest of them. This strategy requires that potential rivals face a minimum efficient scale of entry and that this minority block is sufficient to deny entrants the required scale of output. Under these circumstances, established suppliers can use exclusionary contracts to exclude potential rivals.

However, the conclusions reached in both these studies were disputed by Innes and Sexton (1994). They consider market settings 'where buyers have free reign [sic] to form coalitions among themselves and to contract with either the incumbent or an entrant' (p. 566). Note that this setting stands in sharp contrast to the one employed in the Aghion–Bolton model, which specifically does not permit renegotiation of the original contract between buyer and seller. For this reason, the buyer and the new entrant must take the original contractual provisions into account in any dealings between them. These authors write that 'a central purpose of [their]... analysis is to consider whether this important result is robust to a generalized contracting environment wherein buyers can behave strategically and elicit entry in response to potential monopoly or seller cartel behavior' (p. 567). In effect, they find that it is not.[7]

The essential reason for the conflicting results is the extent of contracting permitted. If all buyers and sellers, whether actual or potential, can connect at any time, then it is more difficult to deter low-cost entrants. On the other hand, when a model incorporates practical limitations on contracting, such as these between existing and potential firms, then very different results are obtained. The exclusionary effects of vertical foreclosure appear to depend on factors such as inherent differences between existing and potential firms that inevitably affect their prospects for contracting.[8]

Consider another situation where an incumbent producer has a monopoly position and sells his product through a group of distributors in a certain area, and assume that it is prohibitively costly to establish a new distribution network. In that setting, an exclusive arrangement with these distributors effectively deters the entry of a new manufacturer who seeks to sell in the area. If the probability of entry is not too high and/or the potential entrant does not have much lower costs, distributors may accept a moderately lower wholesale price to commit themselves not to deal with an alternative supplier. And since the exclusive arrangement deters the entry of a potential competitor, it increases his expected profits, part of which are then allocated to the distributors.

An essential condition for this to be a feasible strategy is that the established producer must have some (possibly limited) market power. That is, the upstream market must not be so competitive that there are no rents to be protected from potential competitors. In that case, he will generally enjoy some bargaining power in his relationships with his distributors. In addition, a similar strategy can be used by dominant distributors to impede the entry of more efficient rivals.[9]

Other types of restraints can also be used to foreclose markets. For example, by assigning exclusive territories, firms can deter entry by committing themselves to a more aggressive reaction if entry does occur. New firms typically do not enter an entire market at once but rather do so originally through particular market segments or in limited geographical areas. An incumbent producer can then assign specific areas to distributors, which encourages a strong price response to new entrants. In the absence of territorial assignments, he would be more reluctant to contest entry in this manner, since he would then have to reduce prices for all buyers. With specific territories, entry into the geographical area or market segment is more difficult and so is entry into the broader market.[10]

Although the effects of foreclosure are typically considered in the context of buyer–seller (or vertical) relations, they are also present in other circumstances. For example, Whinston (1990) describes circumstances where firms tie the purchase of one product to another and thereby foreclose sales by rival sellers of the tied product. He presents various models in which a tying strategy is profitable 'precisely because of this exclusionary effect on market structure' (p. 855). What his study indicates is that the effects of foreclosure can arise in horizontal as well as vertical situations.[11]

AN HISTORICAL EXAMPLE

In this section, we describe a particular historical example where the vigorous enforcement of competition policy towards vertical restraints not only promoted competition but also stimulated the flow of international trade. Indeed, in this example, international factors were largely responsible for the expanded competition that occurred.

The example concerns the US automobile industry in the years immediately following the Second World War. In that era, the industry was a tight oligopoly that displayed the classic symptoms and problems of such structures.[12] It earned very high returns and largely avoided price competition.[13] The industry was dominated by its two largest firms: General Motors and Ford, who together accounted for 72 per cent of unit retail sales in 1967. The third largest seller was Chrysler, which added another 16 per cent. In the same year, all imports together accounted for about 10 per cent of total sales, with Volkswagen representing 5 per cent.[14]

An important feature of the industry in that era was the widespread policy of exclusive dealing. With few exceptions, automobile dealers sold only the products of a single manufacturer. Between 1950 and 1955, for example, the number of General Motors dealerships dualled with another brand of automobiles was only between 6 per cent and 8 per cent of the total number.[15] And most Ford dealerships were equally exclusive.[16]

The competitive impact of that exclusive distribution system is explored by Pashigian (1961). His conclusions follow from the presence of significant

349

scale economies at both the manufacturing and the distribution stages of production. At the manufacturing stage, most economies were exhausted at approximately 600,000 units per year.[17] If a producer could not sell that quantity, his unit costs were higher than those of larger firms. This requirement was particularly burdensome for domestic entrants into the industry; foreign producers who sold their output at home as well as in the United States were not affected as much.

In addition to scale economies at the manufacturing level, Pashigian found distribution economies that persisted to about the same level of output.[18] These economies arose because car buyers respond to selling efforts and also as to the availability of repair services and replacement parts, and these activities can be supported only by dealers who sell a substantial number of cars per year. Smaller dealers were not able to provide these services or, if they did, would need to add a higher distribution margin on to the price of the automobiles sold to cover their costs.

In major metropolitan areas, and other large markets, Pashigian reported that this requirement was not too burdensome because demand was sufficient to support at least one large dealership. In small cities and rural areas, on the other hand, that was not the case. In those markets, it was more difficult for single-brand dealers to achieve full distribution economies. Only those who sold the products of manufacturers with large market shares could do so, which essentially meant only those selling General Motors and Ford automobiles. Smaller manufacturers and new entrants were at a substantial disadvantage, since prospective buyers were forced to travel longer distances to find a full service dealer.

The final element of Pashigian's argument turned on the distribution of sales between large and small markets, which corresponded to the distribution of sales where smaller manufacturers and new entrants were or were not at a disadvantage in terms of distribution costs. Where a manufacturer could primarily sell to large market areas and still achieve the requisite volume needed to achieve full production economies, then any disadvantage in distributing his product in small market areas could be overcome. On the other hand, where sales in small market areas comprised a substantial share of demand, a small firm or new entrant could not achieve full economies of scale in production by selling only in large markets but needed to sell in small markets as well; but in those markets he faced higher distribution costs.

As compared with a manufacturer selling the number of automobiles required to achieve full production economies, Pashigian estimated increased distribution costs of about 10 per cent per unit for a manufacturer selling 120,000 cars per year and about 7 per cent per unit for one selling 300,000 cars.[19] He concluded that the volume of output required for production economies

> cannot be easily obtained because of the difficulty in securing representation in small markets.... Entry will not be successful because the combined sales of dealers located in relatively large markets are not sufficient to exhaust the production economies, and additional dealers cannot be placed in relatively small markets to obtain additional sales.[20]

To be sure, this disadvantage would not exist if dealers could sell more than a single brand of automobiles. In that case, retailers located in small markets could achieve full distribution economies by selling the products of various manufacturers. Small producers and new entrants would then not incur higher distribution costs. The culprit, following the Pashigian analysis, was a system that limited dealers to a single brand of automobiles.

While this distribution system persisted into the 1960s, it incurred various attacks before it was finally dissolved. As early as 1941, the Federal Trade Commission ordered General Motors to refrain from cancelling any dealer 'for purchasing or dealing in accessories or supplies not obtained from [them]'.[21] This early skirmish was followed in 1949 by the *Standard Stations* case where exclusive contracts by sellers with large market shares were deemed to violate the antitrust laws. The case dealt with the major suppliers of petroleum products who had prevented their distributors from selling a rival's products. The court decided:

> it would not be far fetched to infer that their effect has been to enable the established suppliers individually to maintain their own standing and at the same time collectively, even though not collusively, to prevent a late arrival from wresting away more than an insignificant portion of the market.[22]

This decision called directly into question the legality of the exclusive dealing arrangements employed in the automobile industry.

In the succeeding decades, the explicit requirement of exclusive dealing was omitted from dealer franchise agreements, although the practice remained. As recently as 1968, an official of the National Automobile Dealers Association testified as follows:

> *Senator Monroney.* You are not allowed, are you, as a franchised dealer of X cars to handle a competitive car in the same price category?
> *Mr. Slack* (Vice-president, National Automobile Dealers Association). Well, the answer to that is that we are allowed to, so far as our sales contract is concerned. There is no prohibition. However, it is pretty well understood when the dealer signs the selling agreement ... it will be an exclusive representation.[23]

Even though the leading manufacturers preferred exclusive dealing, they abandoned the requirement if not the practice under the pressure of competition policy. As White observed in 1971, 'the major effect of exclusive dealing preferences is probably to limit the retailing opportunities open to foreign manufacturers'.[24]

What actually occurred generally confirmed this analysis. The removal of the exclusive dealing requirement from automobile dealership agreements facilitated the eventual entry of new manufacturers, although the process did not occur until the 1970s – some twenty years after the court decision. Various foreign manufacturers entered the US market through distributors, many of whom also sold American cars as well as other foreign makes. In the process, the exclusive dealing of automobiles ended in fact as well as by contractual provision. Although it took many years, the policy actions had a substantial impact on the market.

By the 1990s, the US market had become much more competitive. The aggregate market share occupied by General Motors and Ford had declined to 56 per cent by 1992. Together with Chrysler, the Big Three accounted for only 65 per cent of unit retail sales as compared with 88 per cent twenty-five years earlier. And imports had expanded to fully 35 per cent of the total number of cars sold.[25] Under the pressure of new entry, American manufacturers set lower prices and improved the quality of their products. There is little doubt but that competition in the industry today is far more vigorous than it was thirty or thirty-five years ago.

A relevant question is whether the widespread entry of foreign manufacturers would have occurred at all, or as rapidly, if exclusive dealing requirements had continued to limit the distribution system available to them. It may be that foreign manufacturers would have entered by constructing new dealerships, as Volkswagen did during the late 1950s. Still, the elimination of exclusive dealing facilitated the entry of new producers, particularly by promoting distribution to small market areas.[26] Through this process, competition was fostered, and also there was a substantial expansion of international trade in automobiles. By all accounts, the active enforcement of competition policy towards vertical restraints was an important factor in achieving these results.[27]

IMPLICATIONS FOR COMPETITION POLICY

Both the economic literature and the case study presented above suggest that competition policy towards vertical restraints affects international as well as domestic competition. Because exclusive distribution can retard the entry of foreign manufacturers, these restraints can limit a nation's openness to foreign trade. For that reason, the relaxed policies of recent years towards these restraints in both the United States and Japan may have artificially raised entry barriers between the two countries.

In both nations, there have been few recent government actions against vertical restraints. Since the revolutionary change in US antitrust policy that followed Ronald Reagan's inauguration as president in 1981, and through the end of 1992, neither federal enforcement agency brought a single action against vertical price or non-price restraints. However, the policy climate towards these restraints changed with the new administration that took office in January 1993, and we have just begun to see cases brought against them.

The ruling Supreme Court decision in this area is that which decided the *Sharp Electronic* case of 1988.[28] In that action, a divided court determined that a manufacturer's actions to terminate a price-cutting distributor did not limit competition, 'because of the usual presence of interbrand competition and other dealers' at the retail level (p. 727 n.). Indeed, the court suggested that contractual arrangements between manufacturers and dealers are typically 'beneficial to consumers' (p. 731).

Although there is no recent decision specifically on the effects of foreclosure, it is unlikely that the *Brown Shoe*[29] decision of 1962 would withstand re-evaluation. In fact the lack of recent cases on these issues may be one reason why it has not been directly overruled. Despite the renewed economic literature on the prospective anti-competitive effects of foreclosure, the case law in the United States remains stuck on earlier concepts.

In Japan, however, there is a sharp contrast between the form and substance of policy measures towards vertical restraints. Under the general anti-monopoly laws,[30] most practices are adjudicated under the rule of reason, and vertical restraints constitute unfair business practices if they have a 'tendency to impede fair competition'.[31] Indeed, the Japan Fair Trade Commission promulgated guidelines in 1991 which include the following provisions:

> In cases where a restriction of handling competing products is imposed by an influential manufacturer in a market, and if the restriction may result in making it difficult for new entrants or competitors to easily find alternative distribution channels, such restriction is illegal.[32]

Yet, according to a review of Japanese practices written prior to these guidelines, 'the sanctions are so weak that the law is widely flouted'.[33] And another commentator observed more recently:

> the unusual number of such [vertical] restraints employed in many markets and their widespread use across markets has contributed to making the Japanese distribution system much more tightly controlled by manufacturers than is the case in Western industrialized nations.[34]

The contrast between policy standards and actual practice is striking. As described by an official of the Economic Planning Agency in Tokyo, relations between manufacturers and distributors are governed not by legal requirements but rather by longstanding personal relationships which provide suppliers with substantial control over their distributors. This system of vertical control is known as *keiretsuka* in the Japanese distribution system.[35]

A possible interpretation of this system of distribution is that there are significant transaction costs associated with gaining traditional distribution outlets for foreign manufacturers, where there are no personal relationships. Another interpretation is simply that small distribution outlets do not maximize profits alone but rather include stable business dealings in their objective function. In either case, these practices can effectively foreclose foreign manufacturers from Japanese consumer markets unless non-traditional distribution facilities are created. An alternative is to enforce more vigorously the Japanese anti-monopoly laws against business practices that lead directly to the exclusion of foreign entrants.

The weak policy standards in both the United States and Japan can be contrasted with the policy of the European Commission. The Treaty of Rome prohibits

> as incompatible with the common market; all agreements ... which may affect trade between Member States and which have as their object or effect the prevention, restriction or distortion of competition within the common market.[36]

However, such agreements may specifically be exempted from this provision if they improve production or distribution efficiency and provide consumers with a share of the resulting gains.[37] The European Commission thus has broad powers to fashion an effective competition policy.

From the beginning, the Commission recognized the negative impact that vertical restraints can have on international trade. With its focus on promoting European integration, it sought to prevent these restraints from impeding trade between European countries. At the same time, the Commission has been less attentive to the effects of vertical restraints on trade between the European Community and other countries.

To further these purposes, the European Commission has ruled that specific limitations placed on the number of dealers are restrictions of competition and exemptions are permitted only in 'exceptional circumstances'.[38] Producers are thereby prevented from restricting the number of distributors who serve their products. In addition, distribution agreements are not acceptable if qualified dealers are excluded specifically to maintain prices.[39] Producers must set objective criteria for their dealers and only terminate dealers when the criteria are breached. In this manner, the

Commission has sought to prevent selective distribution networks that could be used to restrain intra-Community trade.

The first policy action in this area led to the Grundig-Consten decision of 1966.[40] Consten was the exclusive distributor of various Grundig consumer electronics products in France and had agreed not to permit its products to reach the French market through indirect routes. Nevertheless, other distributors were in fact importing Grundig's products into France and selling them in competition with Consten. When Grundig moved against the parallel importers, the European Commission acted and the European Court of Justice agreed that vertical restraints could not be used to stop such imports. Their purpose was to prevent these restraints from limiting trade among European countries.

These principles are now embodied in various regulations. The Commission has issued 'block exemptions' for both exclusive distribution and exclusive purchasing arrangements,[41] which specifically permit exclusive territories and also the requirement that dealers purchase exclusively from particular suppliers. 'Such agreements are acceptable, however, only if they do not prevent parallel imports.'[42] In effect, vertical restraints are permitted in Europe so long as they do not limit intra-Community trade.

Particularly in Europe, policy-makers have recognized that vertical restraints can have major implications for international trade and competition. This result follows because potential entrants into many markets are often foreign producers. Where imports are concerned, a foreign manufacturer is a non-integrated supplier who seeks to use the distribution system of the host country. When he is impeded from doing so, and when this result occurs because of vertical restraints or the actions of vertically integrated firms, then the failure of competition policy authorities to move against these restraints can have protectionist effects.

In effect, a relaxed competition policy can be used for protectionist purposes. To be sure, this result is not limited to upstream manufacturers. In some situations, a downstream firm can be a foreign contractor or large distributor who requires local suppliers but is impeded from getting them. Where these difficulties follow from vertical restraints or from the actions of vertically integrated firms, the same problems exist. A tolerant attitude towards these restraints can therefore discriminate against foreign producers and in favour of domestic ones. On the other hand, a vigorous policy against these restraints can promote international trade.

As exemplified by exclusive dealing in the US automobile industry, these restraints are particularly relevant to international trade precisely because foreign manufacturers are often not able to create their own distribution facilities. While it may be feasible for individual firms or industries to establish their own distribution network when they deal with one product or a small number of products, it can be impossible to do so when economies of scope are substantial so that it is more efficient for a distributor to sell hundreds or even thousands of products. In that situation, it may not be economically possible to find new distribution facilities even if that were required for the entry of a low-cost manufacturer.

Marvel has argued that exclusive dealing arrangements between manufacturers and distributors can contribute to economic efficiency by protecting the 'property right to the customers which its advertising or design investments [have] generated'.[43] Otherwise, distributors will switch customers to less advertised and imitation products that sell for less even while distribution margins are higher. Only through exclusive distribution is the switching of customers prevented and the rewards maintained from investing in this form of intangible capital.

However, before permitting his argument to determine policy conclusions, there are two issues to consider. The first concerns the extent to which the incentives for these types of outlays require exclusive dealing and how much spending on advertising and product design would remain without these arrangements. Merely suggesting that rewards are increased through exclusive dealing is not a sufficient answer.

And, second, there is the important distinction between public and private gains from these outlays. Even if the marginal returns from the outlays warrant the expenditures to the firms involved, that fact by itself does not determine their social benefits, which instead turn on their average returns.[44] And where marginal returns exceed average returns from any given set of expenditures, private firms can spend more on these activities than is socially optimal.

For these reasons, it is not so evident that exclusive dealing arrangements promote economic efficiency, although there can be circumstances where it does so. However, even then, these restraints can limit international trade flows and the entry of foreign manufacturers. There is no necessary conflict between the two effects; both can exist at the same time. In that case, policymakers would need to compare the efficiency gains from exclusive dealing with those from greater competition and expanded foreign trade. While making the comparison is difficult, the mere finding of private advantages to manufacturers from exclusive vertical arrangements is not sufficient to justify their presence.

From this discussion, we conclude that the enforcement of competition policy towards vertical restraints can have serious implications for the flow of international trade. These restraints can pose an important barrier towards such trade. In this realm, as in many others, competition policy cannot entirely be separated and distinguished from trade policy.

NOTES

1 In the United States, see the Supreme Court decision in *Brown Shoe Co.* v *U.S.*, 370 U.S. 323 (1962).

2 In 1985 the US Department of Justice published its 'Vertical Restraints Guidelines' which dealt explicitly with exclusive dealing arrangements. Shortly thereafter, one commentator wrote that these guidelines 'would if adopted by the courts, virtually terminate all litigation involving non-price restraints' (Hay 1987: 116–17).

3 Bork (1954) and Posner (1976).

4 Comanor (1967).

5 In response to a later comment, the authors write that: 'the notion that vertically integrated firms behave differently from unintegrated ones in supplying inputs to downstream rivals would strike a businessperson, if not an economist, as common sense. We show that there is theoretical merit to that commonsense view' (Ordover *et al.* 1992: 698.)

6 Comanor and Frech (1985) provide an analysis of the foreclosure effects of exclusive dealing arrangements.

7 The Innes and Sexton analysis can be viewed as a direct application of the Coase theorem, which finds that unrestricted contracting always achieves maximum efficiency. See Coase (1960). The issue then is whether unrestricted contracting is a valid way to represent all vertical economic relationships.

8 See Hart and Tirole (1990) for an elaborate model that allows for multi-party contracting arrangements and still finds anti-competitive foreclosure under certain conditions.

9 These circumstances are explored in Bayet and Rosenwald (1992) and also in our companion paper: Comanor and Rey (1995).

10 See Rey and Stiglitz (1986).

11 While this discussion deals with the foreclosure effects of vertical restraints, the latter can have other anti-competitive effects. In particular, they can be used to reduce interbrand as well as intra-brand competition. See Rey and Stiglitz (1988, 1995) for a discussion of these effects.

12 White (1971) p. 1.

13 *Ibid.*, pp. 248–75.

14 *Ibid.*, pp. 6–7.

15 Pashigian (1961), p. 122 n.

16 *Ibid.*, p. 122.

17 *Ibid.*, p. 239.

18 *Ibid.*

19 *Ibid.*, p. 236.

20 *Ibid.*, p. 219.

21 *General Motors Corporation*, 34 FTC 58 (1942), as quoted in Hewitt (1956), p. 104.

22 *Standard Oil* v. *United States*, 337 U.S. 293 (1949).

23 U.S. Senate, Hearings, p. 11.

24 White (1971), p. 152.

25 *Automotive News*, May 26, 1993, p. 19.

26 To be sure, the relative importance of small market areas declined over time, so the effect described by Pashigian declined as well. However, that fact does not diminish the foreclosure effects that occurred in earlier years.

27 After completing this section, we encountered Scherer's discussion of this example, where he reaches a similar conclusion. He writes: 'With the law hovering above their heads, the principal U.S. automobile manufacturers refrained from making exclusivity a formal condition of their dealer franchises. This greatly facilitated the entry of Japanese autos into the U.S. market, which in

turn had profound international trade and competitive implications' (Scherer, 1994, pp. 75–6).

28 *Business Electronics Corporation* v. *Sharp Electronic Corporation*, 485 U.S. 717 (1988).

29 See note 1 above.

30 The Act Concerning Prohibition of Private Monopoly and Maintenance of Fair Trade, Law No. 54 of 14 April 1947, as amended.

31 The degrees of impediment identified are 'without good reason', 'unduly', and 'unduly in the light of normal business practices'.

32 Japan Fair Trade Commission (1991), p. 8.

33 Flath (1989), p. 187.

34 Marvel (1993), p. 154.

35 Kuribayashi (1991), p. 55.

36 Article 85(1).

37 Article 85(3).

38 European Commission, *Fifth Report on Competition Policy*, paragraph 13, 1976.

39 European Commission, *Thirteenth Report on Competition Policy*, paragraph 34, 1984.

40 Nos. 56/84 and 58/84, ECR 299 (1966).

41 Regulation Nos. 1983/83 and 1984/83 respectively.

42 OECD (1994), p. 86

43 Marvel (1982), p. 8.

44 See Spence (1975) for the path-breaking analysis of this distinction. See also Scherer (1983), Comanor (1985), and Cailland and Rey (1987).

REFERENCES

Aghion, Philippe and Patrick Bolton (1987) 'Contracts as Barriers to Entry', *American Economic Review* 77, 388–401.

Automotive News, May 26, 1993.

Bayet, Alain and Fabienne Rosenwald (1992) 'Vertical Restraints and Entry Barriers', INSEE discussion paper.

Bork, Robert H. (1954) 'Vertical Integration and the Sherman Act: The Legal History of an Economic Misconception', *University of Chicago Law Review* 22, 196.

Cailland, Bernard and Patrick Rey (1987) 'A Note on Vertical Restraints with Provision of Distribution Services', INSEE discussion paper.

Coase, Ronald (1960) The Problem of Social Cost', *Journal of Law and Economics* 3, 1–44.

Comanor, William S. (1967) 'Vertical Mergers, Market Power, and the Antitrust Laws', *American Economic Review* 57, 254–65.

Comanor, William S. (1985) 'Vertical Price Fixing, Vertical Market Restrictions, and the New Antitrust Policy', *Harvard Law Review* 98, 983–1002.

Comanor, William S. and H.E. Frech (1985) 'The Competitive Effects of Vertical Agreements', *American Economic Review* 75, 539–46.

Comanor, William S. and Patrick Rey (1995) 'Vertical Restraints and the Market Power of Large Distributors', unpublished manuscript.

European Commission (1976) *Fifth Report on Competition Policy*.

European Commission (1984) *Thirteenth Report on Competition Policy*.

Flath, David (1989) 'Vertical Restraints in Japan', *Japan and the World Economy* 1, 187–203.

Hart, Oliver and Jean Tirole (1990), 'Vertical Integration and Market Foreclosure', *Brookings Papers on Economic Activity, Microeconomics*, pp. 205–86.

Hay, George A. (1987), 'The Interaction of Market Structure and Conduct', in Donald Hay and John Vickers (eds) *The Economics of Market Dominance*, Oxford: Basil Blackwell.

Hewitt, Charles Mason (1956) *Automobile Franchise Agreements*, Homewood, Ill.: Irwin.

Innes, Robert and Richard J. Sexton (1994) 'Strategic Buyers and Exclusionary Contracts', *American Economic Review* 84, 566–84.

Japan Fair Trade Commission (1991) 'Outline of the Anti-monopoly Act Guidelines Concerning Distribution Systems and Business Practices', July 11. Tokyo.

Kuribayashi, Sei (1991) 'Present Situation and Future Prospect of Japan's Distribution System', *Japan and the World Economy* 3, 39–60.

Marvel, Howard P. (1982) 'Exclusive Dealing', *Journal of Law and Economics* XXV, 1–25.

Marvel, Howard P. (1993) 'Contracts and Control in Japanese Distribution', *Managerial and Decision Economics* 14, 151–62.

Mathewson, G. Frank and Ralph A. Winter (1984) 'An Economic Theory of Vertical Restraints', *Rand Journal of Economics* 15, 27–38.

Ordover, Janusz A., Garth Saloner and Steven C. Salop (1990) 'Equilibrium Vertical Foreclosure', *American Economic Review* 80, 127–42.

Ordover, Janusz A., Garth Saloner and Steven C. Salop (1992) 'Equilibrium Vertical Foreclosure: Reply', *American Economic Review* 82, 698–703.

Organization for Economic Cooperation and Development (1994) *Competition Policy and Vertical Restraints Franchising Agreements*, Paris: OECD.

Pashigian, B. Peter (1961) *The Distribution of Automobiles, An Economic Analysis of the Franchise System*, Englewood Cliffs, N.J.: Prentice-Hall.

Posner, Richard A. (1976) *Antitrust Law: An Economic Perspective*, Chicago: University of Chicago Press.

Rasmusen, Eric B., J. Mark Ramseyer and John S. Wiley, Jr (1991) 'Naked Exclusion', *American Economic Review* 81, 1137–45.

Rey, Patrick and Joseph E. Stiglitz (1986) 'The Role of Exclusive Territories in Producers' Competition', INSEE discussion paper.

Rey, Patrick and Joseph E. Stiglitz (1988) 'Vertical Restraints and Producers' Competition', *European Economic Review* 32, 561–8.

Rey, Patrick and Joseph E. Stiglitz (1995) 'The Role of Exclusive Territories in Producers' Competition', *Rand Journal of Economics* 26, 3, 431–51.

Salinger, Michael (1988), 'Vertical Mergers and Market Foreclosure', *Quarterly Journal of Economics* 103, 345–56.

Scherer, F.M. (1983) 'The Economics of Vertical Restraints', *Antitrust Law Journal* 52, 687–707.

Scherer, F.M. (1994), *Competition Policies for an Integrated World Economy*, Washington, D.C.: Brookings Institution.

Spence, A. Michael (1975) 'Monopoly, Quality and Regulation', *Bell Journal of Economics* 6, 417–29.

US Senate, Committee on Commerce (1968) Special Subcommittee on Automobile Marketing Practices, Hearings: *Unfair Competition and Discriminatory Automobile Marketing Practices*, 90th Congress, 2nd session, July 25.

Whinston, Michael D. (1990) 'Tying, Foreclosure, and Exclusion', *American Economic Review* 80, 4, 837–59.

White, Lawrence J. (1971) *The Automobile Industry since 1945*, Cambridge, Mass.: Harvard University Press.

ACKNOWLEDGEMENTS

This chapter is part of a larger project on 'Competition Policy in a Global Economy' that is supported by the Japan Foundation, Center for Global Partnership.

14

KEIRETSU

Interfirm relations in Japan

Akiro Goto and Kotaro Suzumura

Like other business practices in Japan, *keiretsu*, or business groupings, are attracting vigorous attention from various angles. During the trade talks between the United States and the Japanese government, US trade representatives claimed that the presence of *keiretsu* was impeding foreign imports and investment, because the firms in *keiretsu* tended to trade with each other and held each other's stocks, excluding outsiders.[1] Japanese officials claim that close, long-lasting business relationships are an integral part of the Japanese industrial system and one of the important factors of its efficiency.

These policy disputes aside, the problem of interfirm relations is attracting widespread interest among economists, management scientists, and corporate managers. Recent developments in applied microeconomics, including transaction cost economics and the economics of contracts are focusing on the various forms of transactions under imperfect information. They seem to suggest that long-term transaction relationships among specific parties based on trust, or, to use Hirschman's terminology, the voice relationship, can be an effective mode of transaction under certain circumstances. The user–supplier relationship is investigated in the light of these new developments, and some managers in the United States are reorganizing their relations with suppliers along similar lines.[2]

Unfortunately, the term *keiretsu* is more journalistic than academic and not well defined. This seems to be the cause of unnecessary confusion. In this chapter we try to identify two types of so-called *keiretsu*, and discuss their nature and background. The organization of the chapter is as follows. The next section explains two types of *keiretsu*, horizontal and vertical. It then explains how firms in each type of *keiretsu* are related to other firms of the same *keiretsu*. The following section enquires how these interfirm relationships evolved historically in Japan. The economic implications of *keiretsu* are discussed in the last section.

INTERFIRM RELATIONS IN *KEIRETSU*

As mentioned, *keiretsu* is not a well defined term. It is used in different ways by different people. However, it usually refers to the loose alliance of firms linked through various ties such as long-standing business transactions, stockholding, and interlocking directorates. It is also customary to identify *keiretsu* as being one of two types.[3] The first type, which is often called horizontal *keiretsu*, is the alliance of large firms belonging to different industries. The major horizontal *keiretsu* has its origin in pre-World War II *zaibatsu*, although the structures of *keiretsu* and *zaibatsu* are quite different. The second type of *keiretsu* is made up of a large manufacturing firm such as Toyota or Matsushita and its suppliers. Large manufacturing firms procure a large portion of their parts and semi-finished materials from suppliers with whom they have long-lasting transaction relationships. The relationship among firms in these two types of *keiretsu* can be summarized as follows.

Horizontal *keiretsu*

Usually, six large horizontal *keiretsu* are identified, namely, Mitsubishi, Mitsui, Sumitomo, Fuyo, Daiichi-kangin, and Sanwa. Among them, the first three are referred to as former *zaibatsu* groups, owing to their historical origin.[4] As is discussed below, *zaibatsu* were large conglomerate-type organizations that played a major role in the Japanese economy before World War II. They were broken up by the occupation forces after the war as a part of the 'Economic Democratization Policy'. Even though their organizational structure markedly differs from that of pre-war *zaibatsu*, most of the member firms of these three groups have their origins in the *zaibatsu*.

The second three groups among horizontal *keiretsu* are formed around large banks, namely Fuji Bank, Daiichi-Kangin Bank, and Sanwa Bank, with firms borrowing from these banks. Essentially, the second three groups were formed by banks which tried to emulate the model of former *zaibatsu* groups. The links between firms in this type of group are weak, and the significance of the groups is very limited. Therefore we will concentrate mainly on former *zaibatsu* groups when we discuss horizontal *keiretsu*.

Usually the presidents of the major firms in horizontal groups meet once a month, and the firms whose presidents attend are identified as group member firms. According to this criterion, Mitsui group has twenty-four member firms, Mitsubishi twenty-nine, and Sumitomo twenty. Firms in a group belong to various industries, but all groups include commercial, or 'City' banks, insurance companies, and trading companies. Other member firms belong to various manufacturing industries such as chemicals, steel, and electric appliances. In this sense, it might be appropriate to refer to these groups as 'conglomerate groups' rather than 'horizontal groups', because the term 'horizontal' usually pertains to the relationship of firms within the same industry.

Mitsui group has twenty firms excluding financial institutions, and its total assets, if such total matters at all, amount to 24,280 billion yen, or 2.29 per cent of the total assets of all Japanese firms taken together, excluding financial institutions, in 1989. Mitsubishi group's twenty-five non-financial firms combined had assets of 25,163 billion yen (2.37 per cent), and Sumitomo group's sixteen firms had 14,083 billion yen (1.33 per cent) worth of assets in the same year. Needless to say, these figures which show the share of a group or groups with respect to the overall Japanese economy make sense only when groups are judged as realistic entities having strong ties and a form of coordination mechanism between member firms. These conditions are not readily observed, however.

Firms in a horizontal *keiretsu* are linked in several ways. (As explained above, the scope of our discussion is limited to three former *zaibatsu* groups, namely Mitsui, Mitsubishi, and Sumitomo, unless mentioned otherwise.)

Each firm owns the outstanding stocks of other firms in the same group. Although the percentage of the stocks owned by each other member firm in the same group is small (averaging around 1 per cent for firms of these three groups), a total of 27.46 per cent of outstanding stocks of member firms is owned by the same group's firms.[5] However, the implication of this figure should be evaluated in the context of general patterns of stock ownership in Japan. In 1988, 46.6 per cent of the stocks of listed Japanese companies were owned by financial institutions, and 24.9 per cent were owned by non-financial corporations. The percentage owned by individuals and others was only 22.4 per cent. Stockholding by firms itself is very common in Japan, and a large proportion thereof is held by firms (including banks and insurance companies) that have longstanding business relationships with the firm in question.[6] It is a widespread practice among Japanese firms to ask trading partners to own their stocks and become 'friendly stockholders', or 'stable stockholders'.

It might be possible to characterize these stockholdings as hostages to prevent opportunistic behaviour by trading partners. However, as this practice is based only on a tacit mutual understanding between both parties, it is not uncommon that supposedly 'friendly and stable' stockholders sell their stocks, especially when they do not have other means to raise cash quickly, as is happening more often in the recession of the early 1990s. In the case of horizontal *keiretsu* firms, the member firms own other member firms' stock and act as each other's 'friendly and stable stockholders'. Their stock ownership pattern is often described by an input/output matrix-like table.

A second link between firms in groups is interlocking directorates. Among seventy-three firms belonging to the three groups, forty-four firms had directors from firms in the same group in 1989.[7] The number of directors from other groups is small, averaging 1.8 directors per firm. It should be noted that the number of directors is much larger in Japanese firms than in US firms. For instance, in 1981 the number of directors at GM was twenty-five while that of Toyota was thirty-nine, and that of GE was twenty, IBM twenty-one, US Steel sixteen, while that of NEC was twenty-nine, Fujitsu thirty, and Nippon Steel fifty-two. (See Kagono *et al.* 1983.)

The third link consists of loans from banks and other financial institutions in the same group. The ratio of loans to firms in a group from financial institutions in the same group to the total amount of loans of these firms was 21.61 per cent on average among three former *zaibatsu* groups in 1989. Again, the above figure should be evaluated in the context of the relationship between banks and borrowing firms in Japan in general. The ratio of loans to 1,581 firms listed on the Tokyo Stock Exchange from the largest lending bank (which is often called the main bank) to the total amount of loans of these firms was 27.89 per cent in the same year. Another interesting fact is that among firms in these three groups, the main banks of 36.15 per cent of the firms were not the banks in the same group. Thus the relationship between firms and banks in the same group should be evaluated in the light of the vast demand for bank loans firms need to finance their active expansion, and the highly intense competition among banks to lend to these largest and least risky firms in Japan.

The fourth link between firms in a horizontal *keiretsu* is intra-group sales and purchases, a practice which is often the focus of trade talks. It is claimed that these *keiretsu* firms prefer to buy from firms in the same group, making it difficult for newcomers, who are often foreign firms, to penetrate the Japanese market. According to a JFTC survey (Fair Trade Commission 1992), the ratio of sales of member firms of a group to other member firms of the same group (excluding financial institutions) to the total sales of firms in the group averaged 11.11 per cent for three former *zaibatsu* groups in 1989. On the purchase side, the ratio of purchases from member firms of the same group to the total was 8.1 per cent. As there are no appropriate benchmarks, it is difficult to determine whether these figures are high or low, but it can be said safely that the majority of business transactions by member firms are with outside, non-member firms.

However, these figures may not be an accurate measure of the degree of trading within groups. There are goods and services whose seller or buyer does not exist within the same group. In these cases, member firms have no choice but to trade with outside firms. On the other hand, there may be goods and services whose major buyer and supplier happen to belong to the same group. Thus an accurate measure should include only such goods and services as can be sold or bought by both member firms and outside firms. In other words, what is needed is the information on whether member firms prefer to deal with other group members when outside alternatives exist.

Unfortunately, no such figure is available. However, the results of a JFTC survey (Fair Trade Commission 1992) are of interest concerning this point. The survey pertained to the use of mainframe computers among group member firms. The Mitsubishi group and Sumitomo group have mainframe computer manufacturers as member firms (Mitsubishi Electric and NEC, respectively), while Mitsui group does not. According to the report, among all mainframe computers owned by firms in the Mitsubishi group combined, 7.45 per cent were made by Mitsubishi Electric, 31.06 per cent by other domestic firms, and 61.49 per cent by foreign manufacturers in 1989. The corresponding figures for Sumitomo firms were, 45.57 per cent by NEC, 1.27 per cent by other domestic firms, and 53.16 per cent by foreign manufacturers. As for Mitsui, 41.34 per cent were domestic and 58.66 per cent were made by foreign manufacturers. Thus the share of foreign firms is reasonably high. Sumitomo firms, with a major computer firm (NEC) as a member, tend to buy from within, especially when they buy domestic products, despite the fact that there are other equally major firms such as Fujitsu outside the group.

On the other hand, even though Mitsubishi Electric manufactures mainframe computers, their product is not considered to be very competitive. In this case, Mitsubishi firms tend to buy from foreign firms and domestic firms outside their group such as NEC or Fujitsu, rather than from Mitsubishi Electric. This indicates the plain fact that while group firms may prefer to deal with each other, in actuality they buy from outside firms when they are not satisfied with the group firm's product. This is especially true when the product in question is an essential input whose quality affects the efficiency and the competitive position of the buying firm in their own intensively competitive product market. However, at the margin, group affiliation seems to have a significant impact on the purchasing decisions of group firms. When the prices and/or products of sellers in the same industry differ only marginally because of, for instance, regulation, this effect may be substantial.

Vertical *keiretsu*

Another type of *keiretsu*, which is often called vertical *keiretsu*, consists of large manufacturing firms and their suppliers. Parent companies own stocks, nominate directors, and provide financial assistance to some of their suppliers, but these types of relationship are limited. The major tie is, needless to say, long-lasting transactions in parts and materials. Another JFTC survey (Fair Trade Commission 1991) on user–supplier relationships reveals interesting aspects of these relations in four industries; electric appliances, shipbuilding, synthetic fibres, and gas fittings. Taking the case of colour TV manufacturing as an example, let us briefly outline the user–supplier relationship in the Japanese manufacturing industries.

JFTC investigated six colour TV manufacturers and their suppliers in 1990–1. A manufacturer buys parts from 271.3 suppliers on the average, and with five manufacturers where data were available, 10.2 out of this 271.3 suppliers were foreign or foreign-owned companies. The manufacturers had maintained relationships of more than five years with 232.2 of them. However, within the last ten years, they had started to buy from forty-eight new suppliers. On the other hand, they had stopped buying from nine existing suppliers within the last three years. Thus, though a long-lasting relationship is very common, there exists entry and exit, especially when a manufacturer plans to introduce new models, and the relationship is not very inflexible. According to this JFTC survey of user–supplier relations, some of the larger suppliers sell their products to almost all of the TV manufacturers, and therefore, do not value a long-lasting relationship with a specific manufacturer particularly highly.

As to this non-exclusivity of user–supplier relations, an independent study by Shioji (1987) of Toyota's relations with its suppliers shows that

Table 14.1 Major suppliers to the Toyota Group

Supplier	% sales to Toyota Group[a]	Other buyers[b]
Nihon Denso	59.5	Mitsubishi, Mazda, Isuzu, Fuji (Subaru), Honda
Toyota Gosei	54.0	Mitsubishi, Mazda, Isuzu, Honda
Aisin Seiki	82.8	Mitsubishi, Isuzu, Honda
Aisan Kogyo	81.5	Mitsubishi, Mazda, Isuzu
Koito Seisakusho	52.2	Nissan, Mitsubishi, Mazda, Isuzu, Fuji (Subaru), Honda
Jeko	51.8	Mitsubishi, Mazda, Isuzu, Fuji (Subaru), Honda
Tokai Rika Denki	59.7	Mitsubishi, Mazda, Isuzu, Fuji (Subaru), Honda
Takaoka Kogyo	81.3	
Taiho Kogyo	69.3	Mitsubishi, Fuji (Subaru), Honda
Chuo Hatsujo	48.1	Nissan, Mitsubishi, Mazda, Honda
Tsuda Kogyo	88.0	

Notes: (a) Ratio of sales to Toyota Group firms to total sales to each firm (1979–85 average). (b) Other automobile manufacturers who also purchase from each firm (1985). Thus for instance, Nihon Denso sold 59.5 per cent of its products to Toyota Group firms, but it also sold to Mitsubishi, Mazda, Isuzu, Fuji (Subaru), and Honda.
Sources: This table is derived from table 2-5 (p. 61) and table 2-6 (p. 64) in Shioji (1987). As to the original source of the figures, see Shioji (1987) and the articles cited there.

same pattern exists in the automobile industry. Toyota's suppliers sell their products to various manufacturers. Table 14.1 lists Toyota's major suppliers. Even though they depend heavily on Toyota as an outlet for their products, they also sell to other automobile manufacturers. Smaller suppliers' dependence on the largest buyer may or may not be greater.

Holding of suppliers' stocks by their buyer-manufacturer is limited. According to the JFTC survey of user–supplier relations mentioned above, among 271.3 suppliers per manufacturer of colour TV, only 14.8 suppliers' stocks were owned by their user-manufacturer, and where a stockholding relationship did exist, the percentage of stocks owned by their manufacturer was less than 1 per cent.

Sending directors to suppliers by their buyer-manufacturer was even rarer. Of six manufacturers, only three sent directors to their suppliers. Further, these three manufacturers sent directors to only one to four suppliers. Manufacturers often try to avoid becoming involved with specific suppliers by sending directors and owning stocks because that reduces their flexibility.

The characteristics of user–supplier relationships in other industries reported in the JFTC survey are more or less the same. There exist widespread long-lasting user–supplier relationships. Nevertheless, entry and exit from these relationships is not uncommon, and the relationships are not exclusive. Suppliers often deal with more than one manufacturer. Other ties between user and supplier are not very strong.

EVOLUTION OF THE *KEIRETSU* RELATIONSHIP—THE HISTORICAL AND INSTITUTIONAL BACKGROUND

This section investigates how these two types of *keiretsu* relationships evolved. It is shown that these relationships are the product of the responses of Japanese firms that tried to defend themselves from the threat of takeovers and to promote production efficiency, given Japan's historical events and the legal and institutional framework. However, it should be noted here that business groupings or long-lasting interfirm relationships exist in almost any market economy. Industrial groups in continental Europe are a well known example.[8] So are Choebols in Korea. Leff (1978) provides an interesting account of business groups in the developing countries. Chandler (1982) states that multi-unit, multi-functional, multi-industrial firms in the United States serve as industrial groups even though each unit of them is legally not an independent firm but rather a division for tax and legal reasons.

Long-lasting user–supplier relationships are also not uncommon. The classic study by Macaulay (1963) reports many such user–supplier relationships through his field study in Wisconsin. There are quite a few studies that refer to 'quasi-vertical integration' in the United States and

United Kingdom, including those by Crandall (1968), Monteverde and Teece (1982a,b), Levy (1985), MacDonald (1985), and Caves and Bradburd (1988), among others.

Therefore, firms in real world market economies are not isolated islands but are often connected through bridges of long-lasting transactions, stockholding and other ties. In some countries, firms are more closely connected with each other than in other countries. By what means the firms are connected, how closely the firms are connected, and what are the relative sizes of the resultant groups are questions that depend on the historical, legal and institutional background of each economy.

Horizontal *keiretsu*

As can be seen from the discussion in the previous section, the unique feature of horizontal *keiretsu* is cross-stockholding among member firms. Thus, by focusing on the evolution of cross-stockholding, we can approach the fundamental feature of horizontal *keiretsu*.

It is shown by Miyajima (1992) that cross-stockholding already existed among *zaibatsu* firms before World War II. *Zaibatsu* were essentially controlled and owned by a holding company and its founding family. However, during the rapid expansion of heavy industries in the 1920s and 1930s, *zaibatsu* started to sell stocks of their member firms in the stock market, partly because they needed large amounts of capital to finance the rapid expansion of the firms in the heavy industries, and partly because they felt the need to 'modernize' in order to appease the growing hostility of the public towards them. However, being wary of interference by outsiders, financial institutions and other firms of the same *zaibatsu* bought a certain percentage of stocks. By the end of World War II in 1945, 12–17 per cent of the stocks of major firms of three *zaibatsu* groups, Mitsui, Mitsubishi and Sumitomo, were owned by other firms of the same *zaibatsu*, a majority being owned by each holding company.

With the end of World War II, *zaibatsu* were dissolved as part of the 'Economic Democratization Policy' implemented by the occupation forces. All the stocks of *zaibatsu* owned by the holding companies, the members of the founding families, and the firms within the same *zaibatsu*, were consolidated and then sold to the public on the stock market, beginning in 1947. According to Miyajima (1992), the amount of stocks that went through this process was about 45–70 per cent of those of the firms that belonged to the four largest *zaibatsu* groups, Mitsui, Mitsubishi, Sumitomo, and Yasuda. This means that for those firms, 45–70 per cent of stocks that used to be in friendly hands, or owned by stable stockholders, disappeared and largely went to individual stockholders all at once.

The consequences of these events were predictable. Quite a few of the firms became the target of takeovers and greenmail. According to Miyajima

(1992) and Kikkawa (1992), firms that used to be members of now dissolved *zaibatsu*, such as Fuji Electric, Sumitomo Electric, NEC, Taisho Marine & Fire, Yowa Real Estate, Kanto Real Estate, and Mitsui Real Estate were involved in takeover battles and greenmail. In addition, Yafeh (1994) shows in his original study that the firms that went through the process described above showed poorer performance in terms of price–cost margin than non-reformed firms because of the monitoring problem by dispersed stockholders.

The response of the firms to the threat of takeovers and greenmail was cross-stockholding. From 1951 to 1952 the cross-stockholding ratio (the ratio of stocks of former *zaibatsu* firms owned by the firms that belonged to the same *zaibatsu* to the total outstanding stocks of these firms) increased sharply; for Mitsui firms, it increased from 1.9 per cent to 4.0 per cent, for Mitsubishi firms, 2.7 per cent to 8.6 per cent, and for Sumitomo firms, from 0.3 per cent to 9.5 per cent. The cross-stockholding ratio increased gradually afterwards, as the firms asked friendly stockholders, firms in the same group, including banks and insurance companies, to own a part of the newly issued stocks which were needed to finance their rapid expansion in the 1960s. It rose sharply again around 1965. The Japanese economy experienced a recession in 1965. Its growth rate fell to 6.4 per cent from a double-digit growth rate trend. Stock prices fell sharply, and one of the major securities firms was on the verge of bankruptcy. In order to avoid a collapse of the financial system, the Bank of Japan provided emergency loans to this firm, and two organizations were established to purchase stocks on the market in order to stop further decline of stock prices. The amount of stocks bought and frozen was 5.1 per cent of the entire stock of all listed companies.

As the economy and consequently stock prices recovered in 1966, these buy-up institutions started to sell the stocks they had purchased. The timing of the sales happened to coincide with the liberalization of foreign direct investment into Japan, which started in 1967. The Japanese firms were concerned that these stocks would be bought by large foreign firms, which could be the first step towards takeover. Thus they asked friendly stockholders and firms with long-standing relationships to purchase such stocks and increase their holdings. According to Kobayashi (1980), from 1965 to 1973, when the fifth round of direct investment liberalization took place, the cross-stockholding ratio of Mitsui group firms rose from 10.04 per cent to 17.25 per cent, that of Mitsubishi group firms from 17.20 per cent to 26.04 per cent, and that of Sumitomo group firms from 18.79 per cent to 24.39 per cent.

In any country, the incumbent management, and often employees, try to defend themselves from takeovers by various measures. Such resistance may be stronger in Japan because of labour practices that emphasize job security and corporate identity. As we have explained above, Japanese firms responded to the threat of takeovers and greenmail with efforts to increase the share of stocks in the hands of friendly or stable stockholders. In the case of former *zaibatsu* firms, they acted as friendly, stable stockholders to each other. Cross-stockholding among *keiretsu* firms should be viewed in the general context of this 'friendly and stable stockholding' practice among Japanese firms.

As mentioned above, cross-stockholding existed between *zaibatsu* firms to a certain extent to supplement stable stockholding by holding companies and *zaibatsu* families. This being the case, it is natural for those firms to rely on cross-stockholding as a means to protect them from potential threats. But it also reflects the legal and institutional framework that shapes the market for corporate control (or lack of it) in Japan.

Under the Japanese system, firms have few options to counter takeover threats and greenmail other than to increase 'stable' stockholding. In the United States, the Securities Exchange Act mandates the disclosure of the identity of purchasers when more than 5 per cent of stock in a firm changes hands. The Japanese Securities Exchange Act did not have such a provision until 1989. Thus managements were unable to detect takeover attempts during the early stages and take appropriate measures to counter them.

The Japanese Companies Act prohibits companies from repurchasing their own stocks.[9] As Bagwell and Shoven (1989) document, stock repurchase is widely used in the United States with the purpose of deterring takeovers. Bagwell (1991) shows that stock repurchase raises the cost of takeover when the valuations of investors are diverse. Cross-stockholding can be seen as an incomplete substitute for stock repurchase.

It should be noted also that the Japanese Companies Act contains no provisions similar to those of the Company Act at the state level in the United States, which provides various measures to protect the incumbent management.

Furthermore, Japan's banking system is different from that in Germany, where a 'universal' bank plays a significant role in protecting firms from takeovers. Japan's Security Exchange Act has provisions similar to those of the Glass–Steagal Act, under which 'City banks' are not allowed to engage in investment banking.

Even though banks are allowed to own stocks, Japan's Anti-monopoly Law sets limits to stockholding of other corporations by financial and non-financial corporations. It also prohibits the establishment of 'pure' holding companies, whose main line of business is to control other firms through stockholding.

Thus, Japanese managements possess few of the measures to counter takeovers and greenmail[10] which are available in other countries. It was under these legal and institutional constraints that Japanese management developed the practice of 'stockholder stabilization'. In the case of former *zaibatsu* groups, it took the form of cross-stockholding with the firms with historical ties.

Vertical *keiretsu*

The development of user–supplier relationships in Japan can be examined by taking the automobile industry as an example, because it is one of the industries having a very extensive user–supplier network and is studied by scholars most. According to Smitka (1991), Japanese auto manufacturers made their parts and components in-house to the same extent as their counterparts in the United States before World War II. It was during the 1950s and 1960s that the user–supplier relationships which exist today started to develop. The background of this development was as follows.

Before World War II, the main buyers of Japan's automobiles were the military and taxi companies. The private passenger car market first started to develop in the late 1950s and the 1960s, and grew very rapidly. Constrained by capital and managerial resources, automobile firms concentrated their operations on manufacturing essential components such as engines and on assembling. They relied on outside suppliers for other parts and components. At that time there were a large number of small machinery firms eager to become suppliers to the rapidly expanding automobile firms. As a consequence of the continuing economic development which started before the turn of the century, and owing to the intensified militarization of the economy, the number of plants in the machinery industry increased very rapidly during the 1930s and 1940s. According to Miyazaki and Itoh (1989), it increased from 10,250 in 1935 to 24,910 in 1942. It decreased to some extent immediately following the war, but there were still 20,961 machinery shops remaining in 1950, even though Japan's military industry had completely disappeared. This large reservoir of small machine shops were natural candidates to become parts suppliers to automobile manufacturers, who were experiencing extremely rapid growth but were still severely constrained by the limited availability of funds and managerial resources.

In addition, there was, and still is, a large difference in the wages paid by large firms and small firms. According to Ono (1983), the wages paid by firms with ten to nineteen employees were about half of those paid by firms with 1,000 or more employees in 1978. In the United States and Europe, wages in smaller firms are also lower, but the difference is much less.

Thus, under these circumstances, Japanese automobile manufacturers bought parts and components rather than making them in-house. However, as claimed by Williamson (1975), Klein *et al.* (1978), and others, the market mechanism may not be an efficient mode of transaction for customized or semi-customized products such as auto parts and equipment. Transaction costs would be high and hold-up problems may render market transactions difficult. Vertical *keiretsu* are, at least partially, an institutional arrangement to cope with this problem. In vertical *keiretsu* a long-lasting relationship and repeated transactions between user and supplier based on trust and a continuous flow of information are usual. Opportunistic behaviour is unlikely and unprofitable in such a situation. Continuous cost reduction and quality improvement were made possible by cooperation between suppliers and users through transaction-specific investments on both sides.

As is evident from the above, the user–supplier relationship in Japan is the product of the behaviour of firms under the specific economic and institutional conditions of post-war Japan, just as the changing user–supplier relationship in the United States reflects the basic conditions and environment of US industry in each era.[11]

Rapid progress of globalization in recent years may change the user–supplier relationship in Japan in a profound way. The Japanese transplants in the United States and Europe started business with local suppliers. The sharp appreciation of the yen is forcing Japanese parts suppliers into offshore production. These new trends will change the user–supplier relationship in Japan as well as in other countries.

DISCUSSION: ECONOMIC IMPLICATIONS

Corporate governance and *keiretsu*

The major issue of horizontal *keiretsu* from the standpoint of economic welfare and public policy lies in cross-stockholding. As mentioned above, it developed as a response of management to the threat of takeovers by domestic as well as foreign firms. Under the Japanese legal and legislative framework, few measures were available to management other than increasing the proportion of stocks in the hands of 'stable and friendly' stockholders. Cross-stockholding is the specific form of this practice used by *keiretsu* firms that have historical ties with each other. Thus most of the following discussion on the implication of cross-stockholding can be applied to the 'stable and friendly stockholding' practice in general.

It may be possible to argue that the managements of *keiretsu* firms were insulated from takeover threats by cross-stockholding and could pursue 'long-term goals', investing heavily in plant and equipment, R&D, and human capital. This, in turn, was said to have served as the source of the competitiveness of Japanese firms. However, this popular argument needs further investigation.

It is not easy to determine whether Japanese management actually had a longer-term perspective in comparison with its US and European counterparts, to whom takeovers are more familiar. Nor is it clear whether takeover activity leads to reduced levels of long-term investment. Hall, in her empirical study (1987), reports no negative relationship between takeover and R&D spending in the case of US manufacturing firms. Even if we accept this popular view of long-termism in Japan, the underlying reason may be the lower cost of capital in Japan, which seems to be the case, at least until the end of the 1980s.[12]

There are several possible economic disadvantages of cross-stockholding. The first pertains to the corporate governance of Japanese companies. There is no guarantee that the management of the *keiretsu* firms will pursue long-term goals in enhancing the efficiency of their firm as they are freed from stock market discipline. It is also possible that the incumbent management of *keiretsu* firms will collusively turn a blind eye to each other's discretionary behaviour. They may invest in high-profile, prestigious projects without giving serious consideration to their feasibility and profitability. They may retain too many employees or simply seek extravagant perks.

However, in the case of Japan, these problems may have been mitigated by other mechanisms, which tended to discipline the management to a certain extent. Intense competition at the product market level forced firms to use their resources efficiently. Their 'main banks', which possess detailed information and the resources and ability to analyse it, monitor the activity of the firms and force them, if necessary, to use their resources efficiently. It should be noted that the fact that the majority of the stocks of Japanese firms are owned by firms and not by individuals means stock ownership is more concentrated and concentrated in the hands of firms which have more detailed information and the ability to analyse it than individuals.[13] Thus, according to Jenkinson and Mayer (1992), it may be possible to claim that the Japanese governance structure deters takeovers and 'obviates the need for them'.

The second possible cost of cross-stockholding to the economy is that it makes the entry and restructuring of firms through takeovers difficult. Naturally this is the other side of the coin of cross-stockholding, which was originally intended to discourage hostile takeovers. Mason's study (1992) of foreign direct investment in Japan provides a detailed account of the difficulty foreign firms face when they try to enter the Japanese market. After official barriers were largely removed in the late 1960s and 1970s, he contends, private business practices such as cross-stockholding became the major obstacle for foreign firms. This argument can be applied also to takeover attempts by domestic firms. Mergers of firms across *keiretsu* boundaries are extremely rare.[14]

Long-lasting transactions

As was discussed in the previous section, the vertical *keiretsu* is essentially the user–supplier relationship as widely seen in Japanese manufacturing industries. It had developed against the historical and institutional background of the Japanese economy. From a theoretical point of view, it can be thought of as a mechanism to reduce transaction costs and increase efficiency through long-lasting, repeated transactions. However, the following caveats are in order.

First, the much praised efficiency of the Japanese user–supplier system is essentially due to the production efficiency of users and suppliers. It is rather easy to see that a cooperative solution is better for the two parties involved than a non-cooperative solution. However, efficiency with regard to the economy as a whole, including consumers, is still not very clear. Conventional wisdom suggests that if the final market is competitive, efficiency gains in the production sector will be passed on to the consumer. However, further investigation is needed. First, it is conceivable that if one firm organizes its suppliers into its *keiretsu*, the best response of other firms is to also form their own *keiretsu*. The price of the final product may be higher under this type of equilibrium situation.[15] It is necessary to evaluate the level of welfare of the whole economy under this type of arrangement.

Second, as we have described above, the user–supplier relationship as it exists in Japan is not actually as rigid as is usually thought. Still, in so far as long-lasting relationships are the key, a certain degree of foreclosure is inevitable. There seem also to be cases where horizontal *keiretsu* firms prefer to trade with each other, especially when the price and/or quality of the product offered on the market does not differ substantially. There have been several attempts to determine whether these *keiretsu* relationships are detrimental to imports.[16] The results of these studies are mixed. It should be noted that even though there exists foreclosure due to long-term relationships, it is still possible for newcomers to start business with *keiretsu* firms, and competition between *keiretsu* firms and outside firms always exists, as the Fair Trade Commission study illustrates. In this sense, the harm to competition is limited and it should be compared with the benefits from the long-term relationship.

Third, even though long-standing, continuous transactions between users and suppliers may facilitate the smooth flow of large amounts of information, the process is nevertheless not costless. For instance, Japanese companies spend 5 trillion yen on expense accounts. It takes a lot of money and possibly a lot of time to maintain this process.

The above discussion suggests that what is casually called the *keiretsu* problem involves diverse issues such as the corporate governance structure and the organizational arrangements of the production system. These are highly important and interesting problems into which economists have started to enquire with new theoretical tools and understanding. It is not constructive to frame the attempt to analyse these problems with such a vague term as *keiretsu*. Instead, we should examine the alternative structure of corporate governance and the alternative structure of production systems, and their advantages and disadvantages. Corporate governance and the structure of the production system are the most fundamental basis of the market economy. If we agree to maintain the diversity of the various types of market economies, they should be allowed to be diverse too. It is necessary to find a way to maintain this diversity and, at the same time, to guarantee the compatibility of the diverse market economies.

NOTES

1 Lawrence (1991) examined the effect of *keiretsu* relationships on Japanese imports using simple regression analysis and concluded that it reduced the level of Japanese imports.
2 See 'Learning from Japan', *Business Week*, January 27, 1992.
3 The so-called distribution *keiretsu* can be counted as the third type of *keiretsu*. It refers to the relationship between manufacturers and other wholesalers and retailers connected through various vertical restrictions. The reason we did not include this type of *keiretsu* is that, in addition to space limitations, it involves rather different issues and backgrounds that demand different treatment.
4 Fuyo group, also known as Fuji group after the name of its leading bank, Fuji Bank, is also related to the pre-war Yasuda *zaibatsu*. However, the Yasuda *zaibatsu* was not only small but also concentrated mostly in banking and financing, and had few activities in manufacturing. Thus the post-war Fuyo group is regarded as a bank-related group rather than an ex-*zaibatsu* group.
5 See Fair Trade Commission (1992). All data on horizontal *keiretsu* are taken from this report unless otherwise stated.
6 According to Odagiri (1992), the percentage of stocks owned by households is also low, around 20 per cent, in the United Kingdom, Germany, France and Italy, while in the United States and Canada it is a little less than 70 per cent. As Odagiri (1992) suggests, the international differences in this figure reflect various institutional differences such as the treatment of retirement allowances and pension funds.
7 The member firms, or the firms of a group, are defined as the firms attending the group's presidents' meetings.
8 With regard to French industrial groups, see Levy-Leboyer (1980) and Encaonua and Jacquemin (1982). See also Scherer (1990), chapter 3.
9 The process to amend this provision of the Companies Act is in progress at the time of writing. After the amendment, stock repurchase will be allowed under limited circumstances.
10 'Lock-up', which means to issue new stock and ask friendly stockholders to own it, is another possible measure to counter takeovers. It was used once recently, but generally is rarely used.
11 Helper (1990) provides an excellent account of the changing user–supplier relationship in the US automobile industry from the viewpoint of the changing environment surrounding it. One interesting point made by Helper (1991) is that the type of user–supplier relationship is related to the degree of competition in the final product market. She asserts that, as the rent in the final market was large (at least until the Japanese automobile manufacturers increased their share), the Big Three not only did not feel the need to maintain close relationships with suppliers, but in fact avoided them. If they were to establish close relationships with suppliers, they might have had to share the rent in the lucrative car market. Using this line of argument, close user–supplier relationships in Japan can be explained by the fact that there were eleven passenger car

manufacturers competing intensely in a market much smaller than that of the United States.

12 As to the comparison of the cost of capital between Japan and the United States see McCauley and Zimmer (1989).

13 Prowse (1992) shows that corporate ownership is more concentrated in Japan than in the United States, and that the degree of concentration does not differ between *keiretsu* firms and non-*keiretsu* firms.

14 It is very rare, but not impossible. For instance, a shipping firm of the Mitsui group merged with a shipping firm of the Sumitomo group.

15 Bonanno and Vickers (1988) investigate this problem in a manufacturer–retailer context.

16 As to a survey of the literature, see Lawrence (1993) and Saxonhouse (1993).

REFERENCES

Bagwell, L.S. (1991) 'Share Repurchase and Takeover Deterrence', *Rand Journal of Economics* 22, 72–88.

Bagwell, L.S. and Shoven, J.B. (1989) 'Cash Distribution to Shareholders', *Journal of Economic Perspectives* 3, 129–40.

Blois, K.J. (1972) 'Vertical Quasi-integration', *Journal of Industrial Economics* 20, 253–72.

Bonanno, G. and Vickers, J. (1988) 'Vertical Separation', *Journal of Industrial Economics* 36, 257–65.

Caves, R.E. and Bradburd, R.M. (1988) 'The Empirical Determinants of Vertical Integration', *Journal of Economic Behavior and Organization* 9, 265–79.

Chandler, A.D. (1982) 'The M-form Industrial Groups, American Style', *European Economic Review* 19, 3–23.

Crandall, R. (1968) 'Vertical Integration and the Market for Repair Parts in the United States Automobile Industry', *Journal of Industrial Economics* 16, 212–34.

Cusumano, M.A. and Takeishi, A. (1991) 'Supplier Relations and Management: A Survey of Japanese, Japanese-transplant, and U.S. Auto Plants', Center for International Studies, MIT.

Encaonua, D. and Jacquemin, A. (1982) 'Organizational Efficiency and Monopoly Power: The Case of French Industrial Groups', *European Economic Review* 19, 25–51.

Fair Trade Commission (1991) *Survey on the Current Status of Inter-firm Transaction*, Tokyo (in Japanese).

Fair Trade Commission (1992) *On the Current Status of Business Groups* (in Japanese).

Goto, A. (1982) 'Business Groups in a Market Economy', *European Economic Review* 19, 53–70.

Hall, B.H. (1987) 'The Effect of Take-over Activity on Corporate Research and Development', NBER Working Paper No. 2191.

Helper, S. (1990) 'Comparative Supplier Relations in the U.S. and Japanese Auto Industries: An Exit/Voice Approach', *Business and Economic History*, Second Series, 19, 153–62.

Helper, S. (1991) 'How much has really changed between U.S. Auto Makers and their Suppliers?' *Sloan Management Review* 32, 15–28.

Helper, S. and Levine, D.I. (1991) 'Long-term Supplier Relations and Product Market Structure: An Exit–Voice Approach', Center for Research in Management, University of California at Berkeley.

Hirshman, A.O. (1970) *Exit, Voice and Loyalty*, Cambridge, Mass.: Harvard University Press.

Jenkinson, T. and Mayer, C. (1992) 'The Assessment: Corporate Governance and Corporate Control', *Oxford Review of Economic Policy* 8, 1–10.

Kagono, T., Nonaka, I., Sakakibara, K., and Okumura, A. (1983) *Comparison of the Management in the U.S. and Japan*, Tokyo: Nihon Keizai Shinbunsha (in Japanese).

Kikkawa, T. (1992) 'Formation of Post-war Type Business Groups', in J. Hashimoto and H. Takeda (eds) *Development of Japanese Economy and Business Groups*, Tokyo: Tokyo University Press (in Japanese).

Klein, B., Crawford, R.G. and Alchian, A.A. (1978) 'Vertical Integration, Appropriable Rents, and Competitive Contracting Process', *Journal of Law and Economics* 21, 297–326.

Kobayashi, T. (1990) 'Fundamental Value of Shares', in K. Nishimura and Y. Miwa, (eds) *Share Price and Land Price in Japan*, Tokyo: Tokyo University Press (in Japanese).

Kobayashi, Y. (1980) *Analysis of Business Groups*, Hokkaido University Press (in Japanese).

Lawrence, R.Z. (1991) 'Efficient or Exclusionist? The Import Behavior of Japanese Corporate Groups', *Brookings Papers on Economic Activity*, pp. 311–41.

Lawrence, R. Z. (1993) 'Japan's Different Trade Regime: An Analysis with Particular Reference to *keiretsu*', *Journal of Economic Perspectives* 7, 3–19.

Leff, N.H. (1978) 'Industrial Organization and Entrepreneurship in the Developing Countries: The Economic Groups', *Economic Development and Cultural Change* 26, 661–75.

Leff, N.H. (1979) 'Monopoly Capitalism and Public Policy in Developing Countries', *Kyklos* 32, 718–38.

Levy, D.T. (1985) 'The Transaction Cost Approach to Vertical Integration: An Empirical Examination', *Review of Economics and Statistics* 67, 438–45.

Levy-Leboyer, M. (1980) 'The Large Corporation in Modern France', in A.D. Chandler and H. Daems (eds) *Managerial Hierarchies*, Cambridge, Mass.: Harvard University Press.

Macaulay, S. (1963) 'Non-contractual Relations in Business: A Preliminary Study', *American Sociological Review* 28, 55–67.

MacDonald, J.M. (1985) 'Market Exchange or Vertical Integration: An Empirical Analysis', *Review of Economics and Statistics* 67, 327–31.

Mason, M. (1992) *American Multinationals and Japan*, Cambridge, Mass.: Harvard University Press.

Mathewson, G.F. and Winter, R.A. (1984) 'An Economic Theory of Vertical Restraints', *Rand Journal of Economics* 15, 27–38.

McCauley, R.N. and Zimmer, S.A. (1989) 'Explaining International Differences in the Cost of Capital', *Federal Reserve Bank of New York Quarterly Review* Summer, 7–28.

Miyajima, H. (1992) 'Dissolution of Zaibatsu', in J. Hashimoto and H. Takeda (eds) *Development of Japanese Economy and Business Groups*, Tokyo: Tokyo University Press (in Japanese).

Miyazaki, M. and Itoh, O. (1989) 'Industry and Firm During and After the War' in T. Nakamura (ed.) *Japanese Economic History* 7, Tokyo: Iwanami (in Japanese).

Monteverde, K. and Teece, D.J. (1982a) 'Supplier Switching Costs and Vertical Integration in the Automobile Industry', *Bell Journal of Economics* 13, 206–13.

Monteverde, K. and Teece, D.J. (1982b) 'Appropriable Rents and Quasi Vertical Integration', *Journal of Law and Economics* 15, 321–8.

Odagiri, H. (1992) *Growth Through Competition, Competition Through Growth*, Oxford: Clarendon Press.

Ono, A. (1983) *Labor Economics*, Tokyo: Toyo Keizai (in Japanese).

Prowse, S.D. (1992) 'The Structure of Corporate Ownership in Japan', *Journal of Finance* 67, 1121–40.

Saxonhouse, G.R. (1993) 'What Does Japanese Trade Structure Tell Us About Japanese Trade Policy?', *Journal of Economic Perspectives* 7, 21–43.

Scherer, F.M. (1990) *Industrial Market Structure and Economic Performance*, Third edition, Boston, Mass.: Houghton Mifflin.

Shioji, H. (1987) 'Production and Capital Linkages of Keiretsu Parts Manufacturers: Case of Toyota' in K. Sakamoto and M. Simotani (eds) *Business Groups in Contemporary Japan*, Tokyo: Toyo Keizai (in Japanese).

Smitka, M.J. (1991) *Competitive Ties: Subcontracting in the Japanese Automotive Industry*, New York: Columbia University Press.

Tucker, I.B. and Wilder, R.P. (1977) 'Trends in Vertical Integration in the U.S. Manufacturing Sector', *Journal of Industrial Economics* 16, 81–94.

Ueda, K. (1989) 'On the Level of Stock Prices in Japan', *Nihon Keizai Kenkyu* 18, 4–15

Williamson, O.E. (1975) *Markets and Hierarchies: Analysis and Antitrust Implications*, New York: Free Press.

Williamson, O.E. (1979) 'Transaction-cost Economics: the Governance of Contractual Relations', *Journal of Law and Economics* 22, 233–61.

Yafeh, Y. (1994) 'Corporate Ownership, Profitability and Bank–Firm Ties: Evidence from the American Occupation Reforms in Japan', mimeo.

Part V

COOPERATION, HARMONIZATION, CONVERGENCE?

15

TRADE LIBERALIZATION AND THE COORDINATION OF COMPETITION POLICY

Damien Neven and Paul Seabright

INTRODUCTION

The conclusion of the Uruguay Round of negotiations under the General Agreement on Tariffs and Trade (GATT) has led among other things to a sense that competition policy is coming to occupy an important place on the international agenda. This is partly because of the avowed desire of the GATT participants to replace trade policy instruments (whose use had been defended as necessary for policing competition but whose practice has often been avowedly protectionist) by a more objective and less discriminatory set of policy instruments for ensuring fair competition between firms in the international market place. It is partly because of a belief, not always explicitly articulated, that if the Uruguay Round achieves its purpose of increasing the proportion of the world's output of goods and services traded across international frontiers, the opportunities for and temptations to anti-competitive behaviour by various parties will likewise increase. Increased trade may, it is feared, lead to increased anti-competitive behaviour. And finally, the growing importance of competition policy as an international issue is motivated by a sense that, regardless of whether competition policy interventions become more or less important over time, an increasing proportion of those that are undertaken will raise international issues with which the present set of national institutions with overlapping jurisdictions are increasingly ill equipped to cope.

The purpose of this chapter is to investigate the second and third of these claims. Is it indeed reasonable to fear that increased trade will lead to increased anti-competitive behaviour? And are present institutions increasingly ill equipped to police international competition?

Strikingly incompatible answers to the first question have been advanced in policy discussions in recent years. In the economic reforms undertaken by the formerly planned economies of Central and Eastern Europe, a liberal trade regime has in many cases been implemented with the specific aim of exposing domestic firms to more competitive discipline than it is realistic to expect from rivalry between domestic firms. According to this view, a liberal trade regime and national competition policy are to some degree substitutes for one another. However, the opposite view – namely that liberalized trade and national competition policy are complements rather than substitutes – has been advanced with equal conviction in both academic and political discussion of trade reform with the European Union (see Smith and Venables, 1988; Emerson *et al.*, 1988). According to the latter view, the removal of trade barriers merely encourages firms to erect new barriers to competition to replace the old ones; consequently increased vigilance by the competition authorities becomes appropriate once a systematic programme of multilateral trade reform such as the single European market is put in place. For example, the process of integration which had been taking place in Europe since the mid-1980s was a major driving force behind the institution of a European merger control procedure, as explicitly stated in the Council regulation of 1989 which created it.

We analyse the question whether trade liberalization and national competition policies are substitutes or complements in a variety of models of imperfect competition in the next section. Our analysis supports the presumption that trade liberalization enhances domestic competition so that trade policy and domestic competition policies affecting barriers to entry tend to be substitutes for one another. Turning in the following section to the abuse of dominant position, collusion and mergers – the more familiar preoccupations of competition authorities – we identify some circumstances where increased vigilance at the national level is indeed warranted when trade is liberalized. Predation may sometimes become more frequent under these conditions. We find also that whether the scope for collusion is enhanced when trade barriers are removed depends on the magnitude of the trade liberalization and the type of factors giving rise to trade. We find no presumption, however, that the liberalization of trade in goods enhances the incentive to undertake uncompetitive mergers across jurisdictions. This suggests that increased vigilance towards international mergers should be appropriately associated with the liberalization of capital flows rather than the liberalization of trade. Indeed, easier capital flows may lead to a surge in mergers that were previously constrained.

Overall, our analysis suggests that unalloyed confidence that trade liberalization will address the problems of uncompetitive market structure in Eastern Europe would be inappropriate. Nevertheless, it supports the general presumption that trade and domestic competition policies are substitutes, albeit imperfect ones.

In light of these results, the second part of the chapter discusses the appropriate institutional framework for organizing international cooperation in competition policy. In the context of the Uruguay Round, there has been much discussion of the proposal that competition policy should be handled within the GATT; Sir Leon Brittan has been a strong advocate of this view. According to Hoekman and Mavroidis (1994a), the current provisions of the GATT treaties, if forcefully implemented, could go a long way towards the objective of coordinating competition policies across countries. However, it is less clear that the intergovernmental structure of GATT is the adequate institutional form to deal with competition policy. Given the importance of discretion in the implementation of competition policy, alternative institutional forms like a central institution with some executive power (as in the case of the European Commission) or an international agreement which allocates jurisdictions (as in the case of the European Economic Area [EEA] agreement) may be more appropriate. This issue is taken up in the fourth section.

TRADE AND DOMESTIC COMPETITION POLICY

In this section, we examine how the removal of trade barriers affects competition in domestic markets. We use a variety of models of competition and review the main findings that emerge from these models. First we consider the effect of trade liberalization on competition in the domestic market, in general using static models. We address the issue of whether the need for a structural domestic competition policy is reduced when trade is liberalized. We then consider the incentive to undertake predation, collusion and mergers.

Trade and structural competition policy

The extent to which a liberal trade policy can act as a structural competition policy has often been addressed in the context of static oligopoly models (see, for instance, Hazledine 1992 for a recent survey). This approach evaluates the effect of a tariff reduction on domestic prices as an indicator of the extent to which trade policy is a substitute for a structural domestic competition policy.

Some early contributions consider perfect competition abroad and evaluate the effect of tariff cuts on different market structures at home. In this context, models that assume a domestic cartel, limit pricing and perfectly elastic foreign supply typically predict that a change in tariff will be fully reflected in domestic prices (e.g. Stykolt and Eastman 1960). As the elasticity of foreign supply is reduced (see, e.g., Ross 1988) domestic prices will fall by less than the tariff cut. The same happens when the domestic structure is assumed to be more competitive. These results support the basic intuition that trade and domestic competition are indeed substitutes and that trade policy is most effective when it matters most (i.e. when the domestic market is collusive).

There are at least two shortcomings of this approach. First, the extent to which domestic firms can collude is presumably affected by the trade regime, so that collusion should be partly endogenized. This is most naturally considered in the context of repeated games (see below). Second, the assumption that foreign firms are non-strategic, if convenient, is not entirely satisfactory. Accordingly, we now examine how the basic presumption that trade and structural domestic competition policies are substitutes when foreign firms are strategic.

Let us consider a given product market in two countries, one domestic and one foreign. Domestic and foreign firms operate in their respective countries but also undertake some export so that there is some bilateral trade. We consider quotas and increased (marginal) costs of exports as alternative forms of trade barriers.

Assume that a tariff in the domestic economy is reduced or that trade costs fall. This has the effect of increasing the foreign firm's marginal revenue in the domestic market or of reducing its marginal cost. The optimal reaction of the foreign firm is to become more aggressive, i.e. to increase output or reduce price. In turn, the reaction of domestic firms will depend whether products are strategic substitutes or strategic complements (see Bulow *et al.* 1985): if the products are strategic substitutes, an aggressive move by the foreign firms reduces the marginal profit of domestic firms which is associated with an aggressive response, so that it triggers a soft response. The domestic firm will thus reduce output but aggregate sales still increase. When products are strategic complements, the reverse happens: domestic firms become more aggressive. Of course, aggregate output increases and domestic prices fall as both firms increase sales.

To the extent that firms face scale economies, competition in the foreign market is also affected by the removal of the tariff/quota in the domestic economy. With scale economies, the aggressive move by the foreign firm in the domestic economy will be accompanied by an aggressive move in its own market. This, in turn, will trigger a reduction (soft response) or an increase (aggressive response) in exports by the domestic firms, depending on whether the products are strategic substitutes or complements.

Overall, the extent to which competition is enhanced will therefore depend on whether products are strategic substitutes or complements but competition (as measured by the overall level of prices, and aggregate margins) will not be reduced.[1] Static models therefore confirm the widely held presumption that trade liberalization has pro-competitive effects.

How large is the effect of trade liberalization on domestic prices? To set a benchmark, consider the standard case of strategic substitution, where firms sell a homogenous product, produce under linear costs, face a linear demand and compete *à la* Cournot. In that case, the elasticity of the domestic price with respect to the level of cost faced by a foreign firm is given by the product of the market share of imports and the cost/price ratio of the foreign firms.[2] For the sake of illustration, if we consider a cost/price margin of 0.8 and import penetration of 20 per cent, one obtains an elasticity of 0.16. This number can be seen as a lower bound but still suggests that the substitution between trade and domestic competition policy should not be exaggerated.

The main thrust of the analysis presented so far, which considers a reduction in tariffs or trade costs, applies to the case of a quota, to the extent that the marginal revenue of foreign firms is increased when the quota is reduced. The discrete nature of the quota may, however, induce a discrete change in the strategies used by domestic firms and, by contrast with the case of a tariff, the removal of the quota may actually decrease imports. To illustrate, consider an extreme case where there are two markets, one domestic and one foreign firm and a quota in the domestic economy. Assume that C_2 is the marginal cost of export for the foreign firm. (C_1, the marginal cost of the domestic firm is set to zero, without loss of generality.) Demand in the domestic market is given by $P = 1 - Q$, where Q denotes total sales. The domestic firm can either fight the foreign firm, by competing à la Bertrand, or accommodate the foreign competition, in which case it allows the foreign firm to fulfil the quota and sets a monopoly price facing the corresponding residual demand (the market demand shifted by the quota). The accommodation strategy will lead to an equilibrium price:

$$p' = \tfrac{1}{2}(1 - q^*) \tag{1}$$

It will be a mutual best reply if

$$q^* < \tfrac{1}{3}(1 - 2C_2) \tag{2}$$

(i.e. fulfilling the quota is the best reply for the foreign firm). The fighting strategy yields an equilibrium price $p'' = C_2$. Since at this equilibrium the quota is non-binding, this is also the price which obtains after the quota has been removed. The accommodation strategy will be more profitable than price competition if

$$C_2(1 - C_2) < \tfrac{1}{4}(1 - q^*) \tag{3}$$

It is easy to check that there is a range of parameters where conditions (2) and (3) are fulfilled at the same time. Accordingly, in the presence of a quota, an equilibrium obtains when domestic firms accommodate the foreign competition. When the quota is removed, the domestic firm prices the foreign firm out of the market. Accordingly exports to the domestic market fall to zero.

This simple example illustrates that a quota can act as a commitment to a limited fight, at least in the context of a model of Bertrand competition where alternative commitment mechanisms are lacking. The cost of not fighting the foreign firm is limited by the quantitative restriction.

The models presented so far support the presumption that trade and domestic structural policies tend to be (somewhat imperfect) substitutes. Structural policies are, however, not the central preoccupation of competition authorities. Their concern tends to focus on the abuse of a dominant position, co-ordinated behaviour and anti-competitive mergers. We now turn to these issues.

Predation, mergers and collusion

Abuse of a dominant position can take various forms, including the refusal to supply, the limitation of production or the imposition of contracts which harm competitors. Article 86 of the Treaty of Rome provides a list of such practices, which has subsequently been enlarged by a substantial case law. Most of the practices have in common aggressive behaviour towards other firms which goes beyond normal business practices and whose purpose is to weaken their ability to compete effectively in the future. Predation, understood as the attempt to induce the exit of a competitor, is merely the strongest form of such behaviour. In what follows, we focus on exit inducement mechanisms and analyse whether the removal of trade barriers enhances the probability that these practices will be used. The basic intuition that we try to scrutinize here is the idea that because of the more competitive environment brought about by trade liberalization, a dominant firm may undertake more predation towards smaller rivals.

The literature on predation in industrial organization has emphasized the parallel between predation and entry deterrence (see, for instance, Tirole 1988: chapters 8 and 9). In both cases, a dominant firm attempts to modify the conditions of competition or the belief of competitors to such an extent that it will decide to give up (either leave the market or abandon entry plans). This is modelled in a two-stage game where initially the dominant firm bears a cost in order to modify either the conditions of competition at a later stage or the beliefs of other firms regarding that competition.

In what follows we focus on a simple analysis where the dominant firm invests in some strategic variable that will make it aggressive in later competition and accordingly induce exit. We will thus not consider predation through limit pricing where, in the presence of asymmetrical information on cost, the dominant firm induces competitors to believe that later competition will be tough. The reason for neglecting this formulation is that trade liberalization does not clearly change the information structure regarding costs among domestic firms.[3]

Let us consider a domestic industry where there is a dominant firm and a fringe (which could be either a single firm or a collection of them). We do not specify the underlying reason why one firm is dominant. This asymmetry in market shares could be due to a number of different reasons. For instance, in a Cournot model, differences in marginal cost will typically generate such asymmetries. The dominant firm contemplates using mechanisms to induce exit, and we analyse whether its incentive is enhanced by the removal of trade barriers.

Let $\pi(d, d)$ denote the profit of the dominant firm if exit does not occur; $\pi(f, d)$ is the profit of a fringe firm if it stays in the market; $\pi(d, m)$ is the profit of the dominant firm if exit of the fringe firm occurs. All pay-offs are a function of the trade barriers (say T) in place, which can take the form of a quota or a non-tariff barrier. The static competition models reviewed in the previous section suggest that, in general, the removal of trade barriers enhances competition and accordingly we assume that

$$\frac{\partial \pi(d,d)}{\partial T} > 0; \qquad \frac{\partial \pi(f,d)}{\partial T} > 0; \qquad \frac{\partial \pi(d,m)}{\partial T} > 0$$

Let I represent the investment in a strategic variable undertaken by the dominant firm, which affects the outcome of competition with fringe firms. For instance, I can represent an investment in excess capacity, advertising or product proliferation. $C(I)$ is the total cost associated with the investment I. The pay-off of the dominant firm in the case of exit is then given by $\pi(d, m) - C(I^*)$, where I^* is such that

$$\pi(f, d) = 0$$

where

$$\frac{\partial \pi(f,d)}{\partial I} < 0$$

Predation will then occur as long as $\pi(d, d) < \pi(d, m) - C(I^*)$.

Consider how the removal of trade barriers will affect the incentive to undertake predation against domestic firms: as barriers are removed, the pay-off of the dominant firm falls whether or not exit of the fringe takes place. However, the profit of a fringe firm if it stays in also falls. Accordingly I^* falls, which enhances the probability that predation will take place. Overall, the incentive to undertake predation will be enhanced when the following condition is met:

$$\frac{\partial \pi(d,d)}{\partial T} < \frac{\partial \pi(d,m)}{\partial T} - \frac{\partial C}{\partial I}\frac{\partial I^*}{\partial T} \qquad (4)$$

where

$$\frac{\partial I^*}{\partial T} = -\frac{\partial \pi(f,d)}{\partial T} \bigg/ \frac{\partial \pi(f,d)}{\partial I}$$

using the implicit function theorem. The incentive to undertake predation will thus be determined by the sensitivity of profits to the removal of the barriers and by the marginal productivity of the exit inducement mechanism used by the dominant firm.

To fix ideas, assume that the extent to which profits fall as barriers are removed is proportional to output (this assumption will be discussed later). Accordingly, we can write

$$\frac{\partial \pi(d,d)}{\partial T} = kq(d,d); \qquad \frac{\partial \pi(d,m)}{\partial T} = kq(d,m); \qquad \frac{\partial \pi(f,d)}{\partial T} = kq(f,d)$$

Condition (4) can then be rewritten as:

$$k[q(d,m) - q(d,d)] > -kq(f,d)\,\frac{\partial C/\partial I}{\partial \pi(f,d)/\partial I} \qquad (5)$$

As a benchmark consider the least effective exit inducement mechanism, where the dominant firm can do no better than bribe the fringe for staying out: in this case, we can write

$$\frac{\partial C/\partial I}{\partial \pi(f,d)/\partial I} = -1$$

and (5) can be rewritten as:

$$[q(d,m) - q(d,d) - q(f,d)] > 0 \qquad (6)$$

Under normal conditions, the overall level of output if exit has taken place will be lower than the level of output if the fringe firm stays in the market, so that this condition will not be met. Under these standard conditions, the dominant firm has less incentive to induce exit after trade has been liberalized because the increased effectiveness of this exit inducement mechanism is overcompensated for by the dilution of the benefits that accrue to him from inducing exit.

In general, though, this analysis helps to indicate a number of circumstances where trade liberalization is likely to enhance the incentive to undertake predation: high marginal productivity of the exit inducement mechanism, and a distribution of the costs associated with trade liberalization which is less than proportional with output will both tend to have this effect.

In Appendix 15.1 we show that our assumption that when trade barriers are removed profits fall proportionately to output is not entirely *ad hoc*, but is a property that holds in a model with Cournot behaviour and linear costs. This is true whether the trade barrier takes the form of a tariff or a quota. If the dominant firm is a Stackelberg leader, it is hurt more than proportionately by the trade reform.

The incentive to merge when trade policy is liberalized has been analysed by Ross (1988). He shows that lower tariffs will in general lessen the incentive to merge among domestic firms; the main reason is that a smaller proportion of the benefits associated with reduced competition can be internalized by merging parties when trade is liberalized.

The model presented above can also be used to shed some light on the incentive to merge: indeed, bribing a fringe firm to stay out is akin to a takeover of the smaller rival by a dominant firm. Condition (6) therefore implies that output-enhancing mergers are more likely to be encouraged by trade liberalization than are output-decreasing mergers.

Regarding the scope for collusion among domestic firms, there is a similar presumption that imports will destabilize incumbent cartels. This is analysed by Feinberg (1989), who suggests that a surge of imports following the tariff reduction will make cheating harder to detect for incumbent firms and accordingly increase the frequency of price wars (in the spirit of Green and Porter 1984). According to this author, trade liberalization was indeed the key factor beyond the breakdown of cartel behaviour in the US bulk aspirin industry.

Overall, increased emphasis on structural policies or increased vigilance towards domestic cartels and mergers do not seem warranted when trade is liberalized. Some concern may still arise with respect to predation but on the whole the analysis presented here supports the general presumption that trade and domestic competition policies are substitutes.

TRADE LIBERALIZATION AND SUPRANATIONAL COMPETITION POLICY

The claim that trade liberalization and market integration enhance the need for a supranational competition policy relies on two arguments: first, that the number and importance of cases involving firms and non-competitive practices across jurisdictions will increase and, second, that a supranational authority will perform better than decentralized decisions by national jurisdictions. In this section, we tackle the former issue, leaving the latter for the next section. Accordingly, we first analyse whether trade liberalization and market integration will enhance the incentive to undertake predation, the scope for collusion and the incentive to undertake uncompetitive mergers across jurisdictions.

Predation among international firms

As trade is liberalized, it is commonly feared that foreign firms, enjoying improved competitive conditions, may undertake more predation towards small domestic rivals, or that domestic firms may react to deteriorating domestic conditions by undertaking more predation towards foreign firms. We address these issues in the context of two alternative models which emphasize respectively the profit reallocation effect and the market enlargement effect of trade liberalization.

The model of predation used above can be readily adapted to study the profit reallocation effect. This model suggests that the incentive to undertake predation depends on the marginal effectiveness of the exit inducement mechanism and the relative sensitivity of profits among firms to the removal of barriers. We observed that, when domestic profits fall in proportion to output, additional predation is unlikely. If, rather than a domestic firm, we consider a foreign competitor, additional predation is, other things equal, more likely; indeed, the profit of a foreign firm is likely to be much less affected by trade liberalization than that of a domestic firm. There are now two countervailing tendencies: profits of the foreign firm will increase as its costs in the domestic market are reduced. They will also fall as before, because competition in the domestic market is enhanced. For a large class of competitive models (for instance, with Cournot and linear costs) the latter effect will exceed the former, so that profits of the foreign firms will still fall but by much less than that of a domestic competitor. Accordingly, additional predation, or hostile takeovers of small rivals by foreign competitors may become more likely as trade is liberalized simply because profits are reallocated in favour of them. By the same token, predation by a domestic firm against a foreign rival becomes less likely.

Besides the reallocation of profits, trade liberalization has the effect of enlarging the pool of potential competitors for domestic firms. This may in turn affect the incentive to undertake predation by the domestic firm. On the one hand, one may argue that the domestic firm will have an incentive to fight early to keep off additional prospective entrants. One may also argue that it may prefer to give up altogether. The issue can be modelled as follows.

Consider a domestic monopolist who produces a homogeneous good at a marginal cost c, with zero fixed cost. There are n foreign firms capable of producing the same good, but they have variable (and uncertain) costs. The unit cost to firm i of selling on the domestic market is given by $c_i + t + \Theta_i$, where t is a tariff and $\Theta_i \in [\Theta^L, \Theta^H]$ is a random variable which is observed by the entrant only after it has entered and committed itself to a certain level of production capacity. The distribution of Θ_i is assumed to be the same for all firms, taking the value Θ^L with probability s and Θ^H with probability $(1 - s)$. Demand conditions are characterized by the inverse demand function $p(q)$. All firms are risk-neutral.

We can without loss of generality rank firms in ascending order of c_i, and we can then assume (with some loss of generality, but not unreasonably) that these firms decide sequentially whether or not to enter the domestic market, with firm 1 deciding first, then firm 2 and so on. So the game proceeds as follows: each period has two subperiods, labelled a and b. Firms choose capacity commitments at the beginning of period a and are committed to them for both subperiods, but they have the option of exiting the market costlessly at the end of any subperiod. In period 1 firm 1 decides whether to enter and commits itself to a production capacity q_1; the incumbent decides on its own capacity Y_1; the cost variable Θ_i is realized (and observed by both parties), and production takes place. At the end of sub-period a the two players simultaneously decide whether to stay in the market or to quit. If one firm exits the other has a period free of challenge until period 2. Then in period 2 firm 2 decides whether or not to enter, and the game goes on. It is assumed (rather restrictively) that firms that stay in the market expect to face no new entry or exit play Cournot for ever. There is a discount rate Γ per subperiod.

We can solve the entry decision for any firm i on the assumption that, when it enters, there is at most one firm already in the market. In addition, the marginal entrant will balance the discounted future profits to be gained if its costs turn out to be low against the one-period losses it will sustain if its costs are high; since it is the marginal entrant it is also the last entrant, and can therefore assume that future output will be determined by Cournot behaviour. Then we can denote by $Y_H(c_i + t)$ the lowest value of the incumbent's capacity Y_i such that an entrant with costs $[c_i + t + \Theta^H]$ facing that capacity will decide to exit at the end of the subperiod. We can likewise denote by $Y^L(c_i + t)$ the lowest value of the incumbent's capacity Y_i such that an entrant with costs $[c_i + t + \Theta^L]$ facing that capacity will decide to exit at the end of the subperiod. $Y^*(c_i + t)$ is the capacity chosen by an incumbent playing Cournot against an entrant with costs $(c_i + t)$. It follows immediately that $Y^L(c_i + t) > Y^H(c_i + t)$; and both exceed $Y^*(c_i + t)$ for any firm for whom entry is expected to be profitable. Both $Y^L(c_i + t)$ and $Y^H(c_i + t)$ represent in these circumstances predatory actions by the incumbent; that is, both represent capacity choices that are only profit-maximizing if they induce exit by the entrant, and the former is the more extreme form of predation since it is designed to induce exit by both low- and high-cost firms. We can then explore the effect of changes in the tariff t on the relative profitability of these various capacity choices by the incumbent.

Imagine that initially t is at a level at which the expected profitability to the incumbent of setting $Y^L(c_1 + t)$ exceeds that of setting $Y^H(c_1 + t)$. Then there will be no entry, since that would immediately be met by predation that would force out both high- and low-cost entrants. Predation will not, however, be observed, and the incumbent will remain a monopolist. As t is reduced it will reach a point t_1 at which the incumbent will (just) decide it is not profitable to seek to induce exit by the low-cost entrant, and so will set $Y^H(c_1 + t)$ in the event of entry in period 1. This will ensure positive profits for the low-cost entrant, and for a sufficiently low discount rate will make entry an attractive option for firm i even before it discovers its cost level. At this point, entry is met by predation that is effective against high-cost firms. However, as t falls further it will reach a point t_2 at which the profitability to the incumbent of setting $Y^L(c_2 + t)$ falls below that of setting $Y^H(c_2 + t)$. In other words, even if it succeeded in inducing exit by firm 1 it would still face a challenge from firm 2, whereas accommodating the entry of firm 1 diminishes the likelihood of a challenge from firm 2. This reduces the profitability of engaging in predation against firm 1.

Figure 15.1 illustrates this. The further t falls, the larger the number of firms for which the profitability to the incumbent of setting $Y^L(c_i + t)$ falls below that of setting $Y^H(c_i + t)$, and for which therefore entry will be profitable if costs turn out to be low. To put it another way, the further t falls, the longer the queue of potential challengers faced by the incumbent,[4] and the less incentive the incumbent has to resist the first entrant. The role of competition policy, therefore, which is (*inter alia*) to diminish the incentives to predatory action by incumbent firms, may be most important when trade liberalization results in a relatively short queue of potential entrants to the domestic market, but relatively unimportant when the queue of entrants is sufficiently long to provide the appropriate incentives by itself.

If this simplified account bears any resemblance to reality, it may provide some clues as to why competition policy has a different urgency in the context of a regional liberalization such as that of the European Union's single market, compared with the liberalization relative to the rest of the world implicit in the policies recommended for Eastern Europe. Simply put, regional liberalization opens up domestic markets to a relatively short queue of potential entrants, and consequently requires strong backing from competition policy. If true, this is another disadvantage of regional liberalization as compared with global liberalization, to add to the catalogue of such disadvantages already familiar from the theory of customs unions.

The argument also suggests, of course, that technological factors (and specifically the dispersion of cost levels across potential foreign entrants compared with the magnitude of the cost reduction implicit in the trade

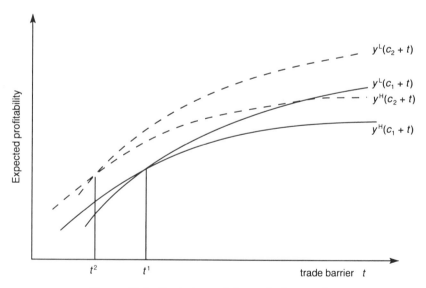

Figure 15.1 Predation and the pool of competitors

392

liberalization) will help in identifying those sectors in which trade liberalization is most in need of supplementing by competition policy.

On the whole, we find that both domestic and foreign firms may have additional incentives to undertake predation against their (respective) foreign competitors as trade is liberalized. Predation by foreign (domestic) firms is more likely when trade is fully (partially) liberalized.

Multi-market competition and the prospects for collusion

In this section we examine how the removal of trade barriers will affect firms' ability to collude. Let us consider a repeated game where firms compete in price. In this context, firms will refrain from deviating by the (credible) threat that Bertrand price competition would take place for ever afterwards (see Abreu *et al.* 1986).

The effect of a reduction in trade barriers in this context may actually depend on the extent of bilateral trade. The scope for collusion will in general be lower when trade arises from comparative advantage, relative to what happens when trade arises from scale economies and product differentiation and occurs within industries.

Let us first consider that trade is associated with comparative advantage (with less than complete specialization). Assume that two firms compete in the domestic market and that the foreign has a higher level of marginal cost (cf) than the domestic firm (cd), despite the comparative advantage of foreign production. (The cost advantage of foreign production is more than compensated for by transport costs and trade barriers.) In this context, collusion can be sustained as long as the foreign firm is allowed a sufficient market share (see Bernheim and Whinston 1990). Indeed, as the market share of the foreign firm decreases, its incentive to undercut the domestic firms is enhanced and the cost of reverting to Bertrand competition is reduced (it does not have much to lose). In turn, the lower the cost difference between domestic and foreign firms, the more attractive is collusion to the domestic firm: when cost differences are high, Bertrand competition may turn out to be more attractive to the domestic firm than accommodating the foreign firm to sustain collusion; accordingly, one would expect in this case that a reduction in trade barriers will actually enhance the probability of collusion and implicit market sharing arrangements. In that case, competition policy in the domestic market is a clear complement to the liberalization of trade policy.

Let us now consider intra-industry trade such that foreign and domestic firms compete on both the domestic and the foreign market. A basic insight into this matter can be gained from the analysis of Bernheim and Whinston (1990). They investigate the possibility that multiple market contacts may help firms to sustain tacit collusion and suggest that multi-market competition effectively pools the incentive constraints of the various markets involved; firms will realize that a deviation will trigger retaliation in all markets where competition take place. The incentive to deviate is therefore lessened. The immediate benefit from deviation will, however, increase with the size of the overall market. However, when the former effect outweighs the latter, multi-market competition allows a wider set of collusive outcomes.

When competition takes place between identical firms in identical markets, both the incentive to deviate and the punishment change proportionately so that firms' ability to collude is unaffected. However, when costs differ across firms, the scope for collusion may be enhanced and will lead to the creation of spheres of influence. Indeed, a strategy whereby firms retreat to their own market becomes sustainable; retreating to the domestic market will enhance the profits from not deviating (as firms concentrate on the market where they are efficient) and reduce the incentive to deviate (as a larger share of the profits from deviating would come from the market where firms have the higher level of costs).

As trade barriers are reduced, cost differences across firms will be reduced and the additional scope for collusion allowed by multi-market contact will vanish, which suggests that in this case trade liberalization is a substitute for competition policy.

Mergers

There is an obvious way in which merger activity may be enhanced by trade liberalization if it is meant to include factor movement; merger activity may be initially constrained by restrictions on capital movements and the lifting of those may give rise to additional mergers. The focus on this section is, however, more on the (rather less straightforward) link between the incentive to undertake potentially uncompetitive mergers and the removal of barriers to the movement of goods.

Let us first consider a simple model of mergers where a merger of two firms is akin to the reduction of the number of firms by one unit (in the spirit of Salant *et al.* 1983). This is an extreme description of mergers which focuses exclusively on the competitive effect (so that a merger is effectively a lock-up). In this context, mergers between symmetrical firms are rather unlikely because merging firms bear the whole cost of closure (the profit of one firm in an n firm oligopoly) whereas all firms get an equal share of the benefit (an increase of profit from an n firm to an $n - 1$ firm oligopoly). Is it that in such a context mergers of asymmetrical firms (one low-cost domestic firm merging with a high-cost foreign counterpart) are more likely? Anderson and Neven (1994) show that when the asymmetry between foreign and domestic firms is very large (so that foreign firms sell little in the domestic market) some mergers between them may indeed be profitable. The reason is simply that for a given reduction in output, and hence for a given marginal benefit, forgone profits from the locked-up operation are very small when foreign firms have very high costs. However, the incentive to merge quickly disappears in this model as cost differences are reduced.

Typically mergers do, however, involve the takeover of assets or production capacity so that mergers cannot be adequately described as lock-ups. Following the formulation of Perry and Porter (1985), we now consider that there is an initial capital endowment in the industry equal to one unit. Let s_i denote the share of this capital available to firm i. Its marginal cost function is then given by $MC_i = c_i + (1/s_i)q_i$. This formulation reflects the idea that a larger capital base will endow the firm with a lower marginal cost function (which rotates around the intercept on the vertical axis as the capital base expands). In this context, a merger is represented by the addition of two capital stocks of the parties involved. Such operations have a clear efficiency benefit to the extent that they reduce the marginal cost of the merging parties; there is a rationalization motive behind mergers in addition to the lock-up motive.

In the absence of asymmetry across firms in the intercept of the marginal cost curve, Perry and Porter (1985) show that firms will often have an incentive to merge (by contrast with their incentive to undertake a lock-up). In what follows, we extend their model by allowing for a different marginal cost curve across firms: we assume that domestic firms have a lower intercept of the marginal cost curve than foreign competitors; the difference is meant to represent trade costs. As before, we wonder whether trade liberalization, modelled as a reduction in trade cost, will enhance the incentive to undertake a merger. In other words, does the rationalization motive for mergers increase when trade costs are reduced?

To illustrate, consider two domestic firms operating with one-third of the capital base each and two foreign firms each endowed with one-sixth of the capital. Assume that firms compete à la Cournot. A merger between a domestic and a foreign firm not only leads to a higher capital base and hence rotates the marginal cost, but it also shifts the intercept to an intermediate value between the domestic and foreign levels. In Appendix 15.2 we derive the incentive to undertake a merger between a domestic and a foreign firm as a function of the intercept of the marginal cost of the foreign firms.

First, we find that indeed there are some incentives to undertake mergers in this model, in particular when trade costs are high and when the marginal cost of the merging entity is close to that of a domestic firm. Second, the merger outcome becomes less profitable as trade costs are reduced. This reflects the fact that, as the market is becoming more competitive, output reduction becomes relatively more costly and that the rationalization effect becomes less important as the equilibrium becomes more symmetrical. Third, the combined profit of the independent entities, which initially falls as trade costs decrease from their maximum value (compatible with positive output), increases for intermediate values of the trade costs. The reason is that the profits from foreign firms increase at a faster pace than that at which profits of the domestic firm fall. That is also to say that, for those intermediate values, the incentive to undertake mergers is reduced as trade costs fall.

Hence it seems that, for intermediate values of trade costs, mergers become less attractive, both because output restrictions become more costly when the market is becoming more competitive and because the rationalization effect becomes less important. It also seems that such intermediate values of the trade costs for which the incentive to undertake mergers may actually fall are empirically reasonable. Indeed, according to Smith and Venables (1988), the allocation of output and market shares across EU markets is consistent with a tariff equivalent of the order of 30 per cent (on average across a sample of industries). For such a value of the trade cost, our model actually predicts that the incentive to undertake mergers falls as trade is further liberalized.

Overall this analysis suggests that the liberalization of trade in goods may not increase merger activity. It is only when integration includes the liberalization of factor movements that a surge in mergers may be expected.

THE SCOPE FOR INTERNATIONAL COMPETITION POLICY

Our arguments so far have suggested that, although there is considerable force in the claim that internationalization of trade and capital movements may substitute to some extent for intervention by competition authorities, it cannot do so completely, and there are even some circumstances in which more vigorous action by these authorities may be required after liberalization than before. We must now consider the fact that the competition authorities, when they do act, will as a consequence of this same internationalization be taking decisions whose consequences extend across national boundaries to a greater extent than before.

Competition authorities are creatures of the nation state. They are not neutral technocratic organizations whose policies and goals can be straightforwardly adjusted to reflect internationalist considerations. They are answerable (sometimes in subtle and indirect ways) to the political authorities of the countries in which they are established, and their priorities reflect those of these authorities as well. When refereeing competition between firms of different nationalities, and evaluating the harm to consumers in a variety of countries, it is unrealistic to expect national competition authorities to be entirely objective and impartial. And, to the extent that they are not, the fact that their decisions extend across national boundaries will create spillovers that distort competition policy from the point of view of the world as a whole. Anti-dumping policy, for example, is likely to lead to a more stringent response to alleged predation than would otherwise be desirable, discouraging firms from competing keenly and protecting the inefficient domestic firms at the expense of efficient foreign ones and of consumers. Merger policy, on the other hand, may in many circumstances be laxer than is desirable, since the customers of the merging firms may well be located in several different countries, and the authorities of a single nation may well treat too lightly the costs to consumers of market power.

What is the appropriate institutional response to problems of this kind? One of the results of the completion of the Uruguay Round of the GATT negotiations was increasing emphasis on competition policy in the agenda of the new World Trade Organization (WTO). However, the actions of the WTO are constrained by the scope of international agreements, and the GATT treaty in its present form covers only part of the range of competition policy matters that are likely to arise. Hoekman and Mavroidis (1994a) have reviewed the details of GATT provisions and examined the extent to which they overlap with the concern of competition authorities. They conclude that entry barriers associated with discrimination between domestic and foreign firms can be adequately tackled within the GATT framework. They conjecture that failure to enforce domestic competition policy in a way that favours domestic firms could be seen as a discrimination falling under GATT provisions.

There are two reasons for thinking that this is not on its own an adequate response to the kinds of difficulty we have anticipated. The first is that it is likely to be very hard to demonstrate in any given case that competition policy has been applied in a discriminatory fashion, because policy necessarily involves a degree of discretion in its implementation. The standards of proof required to overturn national decisions will necessarily be stringent, otherwise the appeal procedure would be a source of great instability – but evidence of discrimination that meets such standards may be impossible to obtain. The second is that discrimination between domestic and foreign firms is only one of the sources of bias we have identified. Treating the interests of domestic firms as more important than those of foreign consumers is another, and one which the GATT provisions are inherently unsuited to tackling. Indeed, any mechanism which relies on redress against the decisions of national authorities (rather than a ceding of those decisions to international authorities) will find this issue virtually impossible to deal with, since giving inadequate weight to consumer interests is an endemic failing of competition authorities everywhere, and it is hard to imagine how one could demonstrate that the failing resulted in a particular case from discrimination on grounds of nationality.

It seems clear, therefore, that international mergers, international cartels (besides exports and import cartels) and at least some forms of abuse of a dominant position (for instance, in the field of intellectual property) do not fall under existing GATT provisions. As we have already discussed, such practices can nevertheless be encouraged by trade liberalization. Indeed, many international conflicts have already arisen in the field of international mergers and cartels (Hawk 1992; Campbell and Trebilcock 1992). This suggests that the GATT framework is even now inadequate; and, more important, its inadequacy may increase over time to the extent that the removal of trade impediments induces firms to engage in non-competitive behaviour of the kind that the GATT does not cover.

Current arrangements for the resolution of conflicts between the United States and the European Community rest on bilateral negotiations between the countries involved and the custom that national courts will take into account the interests of foreigners. The United States has signed a bilateral agreement with the EU regarding the principles that should be followed in deciding to exercise jurisdiction. But the implementation of these principles is capable of giving rise to much debate (Campbell and Trebilcock 1992). The agreement contains provisions regarding notification of pending actions and a commitment to take into account the views of the other party before proceeding. Overall, however, current arrangements between the United States, Japan and Europe are widely perceived to be inadequate (see American Bar Association 1991; Hawk 1992; OECD 1988).

Within the European Union potential conflicts are managed more explicitly. With respect to restrictive practices that fall under Articles 85 and 86 (collusion and the abuse of a dominant position), Union rulings take precedence over domestic decisions. Regarding mergers, the Regulation of December 1989 clearly establishes that the Union has jurisdiction over mergers, provided that the overall turnover of the companies involved exceeds ECU5 billion and that the Union-wide turnover of at least two parties exceeds ECU250 million. There are also a number of specific exceptions to these principles (as discussed in Neven et al. 1993).

There is also a formal agreement between the European Union and European Foreign Trade Agreement (EFTA) countries, as part of the EEA Agreement, though this is evidently much diminished in practical significance now that most of these countries have joined the European Union. The agreement stipulates that jurisdictional control is exercised by two separate entities, namely the Commission and the EFTA Surveillance Authority. The agreement provides objective criteria for the allocation of jurisdiction in cases of overlap. When a merger or a restrictive practice affects trade only within EFTA, the Surveillance Authority will be deemed competent; conversely the Commission will exercise its prerogative if trade is affected in the common market. In cases of overlap, the agreement stipulates that the Commission should be responsible, except when 33 per cent or more of the undertakings' activities occur in EFTA, in which case the Surveillance Authority would be responsible. This clause was introduced to avoid parallel proceedings and the risk of diverging decisions. The agreement also provides for the regular exchange of information, co-operation and consultation between the two authorities.

Finally, for a number of years the OECD has been active in encouraging member countries to meet and discuss competition policy concerns with a view to alleviating sources of friction. Though the OECD is only a meeting forum and has no formal power there is evidence that competition authorities take its activities and its views seriously and that these views have been influential in determining the form of competition policy in those countries establishing it for the first time.

What lessons can be learned from these various arrangements for dealing with potential international conflicts over competition policy? Can we say anything about the relative merits of centralized discretionary power (the EU); rules for the allocation of jurisdiction (EU–EFTA); agreements to cooperate (EU–US); and information-sharing and coordination (OECD)?

Discussions of the appropriate institutional mechanisms for dealing with conflicts of interest in economic policy usually turn on an enumeration of the costs and benefits of centralizing power (see Begg *et al.* 1993 for a discussion of the subsidiarity issue in the European Union). The benefits of centralization usually consist primarily in the internalization of economic spillovers across national boundaries, thus ensuring that all the effects of a particular policy decision are taken into account and are not given differential consideration according to the country on whose citizens they happen to fall. There may also be benefits from scale economies in the development of certain specialized technical policies, though the evidence suggests that these scale economies can be adequately achieved at the regional level and are not significantly greater for the world as a whole: expertise is not that scarce! However, as we have already indicated, the extent of external effects between countries and regions can only increase as world trade expands, and the case for centralizing competition policy will continue to strengthen in consequence.

However, centralization also has costs, notably the risk of making regulatory policy-makers more remote from the economies whose firms and consumers they influence by their actions. Such remoteness may result simply in lack of awareness of local conditions: policies designed in Washington D.C. may overlook the particularity of conditions in Vladivostock or Tokyo. More important, remoteness can result in a lack of accountability: regulators who are unaccountable do not necessarily pursue policies of Olympian detachment, but may simply use their discretion to favour whichever parties they happen to like (for reasons that may be innocent or sinister). This lack of accountability may in turn be due to one or more of several factors. First, citizens and voters may have less information about the operation of centralized institutions than about those of their own country or region, so there may be less political pressure to ensure that these institutions function well, except on the part of those firms directly affected by them, whose conception of 'good functioning' may be very much directed to their own particular interests. Secondly, even with adequate information, citizens and voters may have difficulty holding such institutions to account because this relies on concerted action among all those affected, which is much harder to achieve at a centralized level than for local or regional groups. Thirdly, holding centralized institutions to account is often difficult because it is hard to see how alternative policies would function; one of the advantages of decentralization is that 'competition among regulators' helps to reveal by comparison the strengths and shortcomings of any particular system or set of policies.

Overall, then, centralization is most appropriate when externalities across countries are large relative to the risks of 'capture' of centralized institutions. Short of full centralization, alternative cooperative arrangements can also be considered. For example, coordination of decision-making across countries can attempt to correct for international spillovers either by making side payments (usually disguised as political concessions in other fields of negotiation) or by countries taking it in turn to act, on the understanding that each will take the spillovers into account in its deliberations. Recently, Kowalczyk and Sjöström (1992) have derived the side payments that would be necessary to implement a Pareto-efficient trade equilibrium, and their analysis may be extendable to the present context. The recent EEA agreement, on the other hand, provides a useful model of the second approach.

Common sense suggests that, in areas of policy where implementation involves an unavoidable element of discretion, cooperative mechanisms for internalizing international spillovers will tend to work adequately when not too many parties are involved. The larger the number of interested parties the harder it will be to preserve trust between them and to monitor departures from the collectively agreed procedure. This may be one reason why the European Union has felt the need to centralize its merger control procedures, while the European Union and EFTA are happy with a cooperative but non-centralized mechanism. Cooperation between twelve parties is harder to monitor than cooperation between two.

Pure information-sharing, by contrast (on the OECD model) is useful primarily for achieving economies of scale in expertise rather than for overcoming genuine conflicts of interest between members, since information-sharing by itself provides no incentives stronger than good manners for countries to stick to a collectively preferable but individually constraining policy.

The conclusion must be that cooperative rather than centralized mechanisms for resolving international competition policy issues are likely to work only if there is reasonable homogeneity of interests between the members of a few international groups (represented perhaps by the European Union, the United States and Japan). If conflicts of interest within these regions make it difficult for their respective authorities to speak on behalf of all the important interest groups in the world economy, then cooperation may fail and the alternatives will be global centralization or decentralized muddling-through.

Our arguments in this chapter have suggested that, although there will be circumstances under which trade liberalization may actually increase the incentives for firms to engage in anti-competitive behaviour, on balance it is likely that liberalization will substitute for positive action on the authorities' part. Nevertheless, increased world trade means that a growing proportion of the gains and losses from anti-competitive behaviour will tend to spill across national borders, and to this extent cooperative action to police competition is likely to become an increasing necessity in the future. Is cooperation without centralization the right way to manage this problem, or should the world's nations be seeking to cede more power to the new World Trade Organization (or to some other)?

It is still too early to say with confidence how the WTO is going to function, though the lengthy international wrangles over the appointment of its director suggest that many important issues of accountability as well as organizational effectiveness still need to be resolved. We have argued that international spillovers in competition policy implementation can only increase in coming years, and that the existing powers of the WTO can deal adequately with only some of the sources of these spillovers. What is less clear is whether international cooperation between the main affected parties can cope adequately with the remainder. Will the European Union, the United States and Japan prove able to represent coherently and effectively the interests of other countries in their respective regions, and to build up trust in each other's willingness to abide by cooperative agreements? If so, strengthening the powers of the WTO may prove to be unnecessary, a conclusion that would reduce the need to face some hard questions about the accountability of the WTO and its vulnerability to capture by special interests.

APPENDIX 15.1: THE IMPACT OF TRADE LIBERALIZATION ON DOMESTIC PROFITS IN OLIGOPOLY

The purpose of this appendix is to analyse the change in firms' profits that takes place when trade is liberalized. We first consider a Cournot oligopoly with linear costs and demand, where different firm sizes are obtained from differences in costs. We show that, in this context, profits fall in proportion with output, as trade is liberalized either through a reduction in a quota or through a reduction in trade costs. We also consider a Stackelberg model and show that the dominant firm would be hurt more than proportionately by trade liberalization.

Consider an aggregate (inverse) demand in the domestic market of the form $P = 1 - Q$. Firms sell homogeneous products and compete in quantities. There are three firms: one low-cost domestic firm operating with a constant marginal cost c_1 (set to zero without loss of generality), a high-cost domestic competitor operating with a marginal cost c_2 and a foreign competitor with cost c_3. Equilibrium output levels in this game are given by:

$$q_1 = \tfrac{1}{4}(1 + c_3 + c_2)$$
$$q_2 = \tfrac{1}{4}(1 + c_3 - 3c_2)$$
$$q_3 = \tfrac{1}{4}(1 + c_2 - 3c_3)$$

And the equilibrium price is given by: $P = \tfrac{1}{4}(1 + c_3 + c_2)$.

As before, trade liberalization is first modelled as a reduction in c_3. Accordingly, in order to evaluate the effect of trade liberalization on domestic firms we take the derivatives of equilibrium profits for each domestic firm with respect to c_3. We obtain:

$$\frac{\partial \pi_1}{\partial c_3} = \frac{1}{8}(1 + c_3 + c_2)$$

$$\frac{\partial \pi_2}{\partial c_3} = \frac{1}{8}(1 + c_3 - 3c_2)$$

So that changes in profits following trade liberalization are proportional to output.

Next, we model trade liberalization as a change in the quota q^* imposed on the foreign firms. Equilibrium outputs are now given by:

$$q_1 = \tfrac{1}{3}(1 - q^* + c_2)$$
$$q_2 = \tfrac{1}{2}(1 - q^* - 2c_2)$$

The derivatives of equilibrium profits with respect to the quotas are given by:

$$\frac{\partial \pi_1}{\partial q^*} = -\frac{2}{9}(q_1) \quad \text{and} \quad \frac{\partial \pi_2}{\partial q^*} = -\frac{2}{9}(q_2)$$

Finally, we consider a Stackelberg game and a quota (the case of a change in trade costs can be dealt with along similar lines as above and gives similar results to that of a quota). We obtain the following equilibrium output:

$$q_L = \tfrac{1}{2}(1 - q^* + c_2)$$
$$q_F = \tfrac{1}{4}(1 - q^* - 3c_2)$$

where q_L is the output of the leader and q_F that of the follower. It is then easy to compute that:

$$\frac{\partial \pi_L}{\partial q^*} = -\frac{1}{4}(q_L) \quad \text{and} \quad \frac{\partial \pi_F}{\partial q^*} = -\frac{1}{8}(q_F)$$

So that the leader is more affected by trade liberalization than the follower.

APPENDIX 15.2: TRADE LIBERALIZATION AND THE INCENTIVE TO MERGE

We consider two large domestic firms with one-third of the capital base each, and two foreign firms endowed with one-sixth each. The aggregate (inverse) demand is given by $P = 1 - Q$. The marginal cost of domestic firms is given by $MC_i = c_L + (1/s_i)q_i$ and that of a foreign firm is given by $MCi = c_H + (1/s_i)q_i$.

We first compute the profits of independent entities. Routine calculations yield the following equilibrium output for a domestic and a foreign firm:

$$q_d = (\tfrac{9}{50})(1 - c_L - (1 - c_H)\tfrac{2}{9})$$
$$q_f = (\tfrac{6}{50})(1 - c_H - (1 - c_L)\tfrac{2}{6})$$

The combined profit of independent entities (one domestic/one foreign) is then given by:

$$\Pi_I = \frac{(14 + 7c_L + 4c_H)}{25} \frac{(11 - 7c_L - 4c_H)}{50} - c_L \frac{(7 - 9c_L + 2c_H)}{50}$$

$$\Pi_I = \frac{(14 + 7c_L + 4c_H)}{25} \frac{(11 - 7c_L - 4c_H)}{50} - c_L \frac{(7 - 9c_L + 2c_H)}{50}$$

$$\Pi_I = \frac{(14 + 7c_L + 4c_H)}{25} \frac{(11 - 7c_L - 4c_H)}{50} - c_L \frac{(7 - 9c_L + 2c_H)}{50}$$

$$-\frac{3}{2}\left(\frac{7 - 9c_L + 2c_H}{50}\right)^2 - c_H \frac{(4 - 6c_H + 2c_L)}{50} - \frac{6}{2}\left(\frac{4 - 6c_H + 2c_L}{50}\right)^2$$

Assuming that after the merger the new entity would enjoy a marginal cost intercept equal to kc_L, one can easily derive the equilibrium output in the configuration where firm 1 is the merger between a domestic firm and a foreign firm, and firms 2 and 3 are respectively the domestic and foreign independent entities;

$$q_1 = \frac{4}{21} + c_L \frac{1}{21} - c_L k \frac{17}{63} + c_H \frac{2}{63}$$

$$q_2 = \frac{3}{21} + c_L \frac{9}{42} - c_L k \frac{1}{21} + c_H \frac{1}{42}$$

$$q_3 = \frac{2}{21} + c_L \frac{1}{42} + c_L k \frac{2}{63} + c_H \frac{19}{126}$$

The profit of the merged entity can then be derived as:

$$\Pi_M = \left(\frac{12}{21} + c_L \frac{3}{21} + c_L k \frac{4}{21} + c_H \frac{2}{21} \right) \left(\frac{4}{21} + c_L \frac{1}{21} - c_L k \frac{17}{63} + c_H \frac{2}{63} \right)$$

$$- c_L k \left(\frac{4}{21} + c_L \frac{1}{21} - c_L k \frac{17}{63} + c_H \frac{2}{63} \right)$$

$$- \left(\frac{4}{21} + c_L \frac{1}{21} - c_L k \frac{17}{63} + c_H \frac{2}{63} \right)^2$$

Taking the derivative of the combined profits of independent entities and that of the merger with respect to c_H, one obtains:

$$\frac{\partial \Pi_M}{\partial c_H} = \frac{2}{63} \left(\frac{16}{21} + c_L \frac{4}{21} - c_L k \frac{68}{63} + c_H \frac{8}{63} \right)$$

$$\frac{\partial \Pi_I}{\partial c_H} = \frac{1}{50} \left(-\frac{3}{25} - c_L 2 + c_H 6 - \frac{1}{50} (98 - c_L 26 - c_L 72) \right)$$

It is easy to check that (as c_L, $c_H < 1$ and $c_L < c_H$)

$$\frac{\partial \Pi_M}{\partial c_H} > 0$$

Using the non-negativity constraint on output, one can check that for the largest admissible value of c_H

$$\frac{\partial \Pi_I}{\partial c_H} > 0$$

and that

$$\frac{\partial^2 \Pi_I}{\partial c_H^2} > 0$$

404

and that

$$\frac{\partial \Pi_I}{\partial c_H} = 0$$

for some value $c_H > c_L$.

NOTES

1 In the case of trade costs, welfare might still fall (because increased resources are spent on bilateral trade – see Krugman 1983).
2 For a proof of this result, see Dornbusch (1987), who considers the effect of a permanent change in exchange rates (which is formally analogous to a change in tariff).
3 This is not to deny that equilibria in asymmetrical information models may be responsive to changes in trade parameters, but space forbids their consideration here.
4 We leave aside the question of how many successful entrants the market as a whole can support.

REFERENCES

Abreu, D., D. Pearce and E. Stacchetti (1986) 'Optimal cartel equilibria with imperfect monitoring', *Journal of Economic Theory*, 39 (1), 251–69.
American Bar Association (1991) Report of the Special Committee on International Antitrust, ABA Report.
Anderson, S. and D. Neven (1994) 'Merger waves', mimeo, University of Lausanne.
Begg, D., J. Cremer, J.-P. Danthine, J. Edwards, V. Grilli, D. Neven, P. Seabright, H. W. Sinn, A. Venables and C. Wyplosz (1993) *Making Sense of Subsidiarity*, CEPR, London.
Bernheim, D. and M. Whinston (1990) 'Multimarket contact and collusive behavior', *Rand Journal of Economics* 21 (1), 1–26.
Brander, J.A. and P. Krugman (1983) 'A reciprocal dumping model of international trade', *Journal of International Economics* 11, 1–14.
Bulow, J., J. Geanakoplos and P. Klemperer (1985) 'Multimarket oligopoly: strategic substitutes and complements', *Journal of Political Economy* 93 (31), 488–511.
Campbell, N. and M. Trebilcock (1992) 'International Merger Review: Problems of multi-jurisdictional conflict', mimeo.
Dornbusch, R. (1987) 'Exchange rates and prices', *American Economic Review* 77, 93–106.
Emerson, M. *et al.* (1988) *The Economics of 1992*, Oxford: Oxford University Press.
Feinberg, R. (1989) 'Imports as a threat to cartel stability', *International Journal of Industrial Organization* 7, 281–8.
Green, E. and R. Porter (1984) 'Noncooperative collusion under imperfect price information', *Econometrica* 52, 87–100.
Hawk, B. (1990) 'European Economic Community merger regulation', *Antitrust Law Journal* 457.

Hawk, B. (1992) 'Antitrust in a global environment: conflicts and resolutions; introductory remarks', *Antitrust Law Journal* 60, 525–30.

Hazledine, T. (1992) 'Trade policy as competition policy', in S. Khemani and W. Stanburgh (eds) *Competition Law and Policy at the Centenary*, Institute for Research on Public Policy, Halifax, N.S.

Hoekman, B. and P. Mavroidis (1994a) 'Antitrust based remedies and dumping in international trade', CEPR Discussion Paper No. 1010, August.

Hoekman, B. and P. Mavroidis (1994b) 'Competition, competition policy and the GATT', CEPR Discussion Paper No. 876, January.

Kowalczyk, C. and Sjöström, T. (1992) 'Bringing GATT into the core', mimeo.

Neven, D., R. Nuttal and P. Seabright (1994) *Merger in Daylight: The economics and politics of merger control in the EC*, CEPR, London.

OECD (1988) *International Mergers and Competition Policy*, OECD, Paris.

Perry, M. and R. Porter (1985) 'Oligopoly and the incentive for horizontal merger', *American Economic Review* 75 (1), 219–27.

Ross, T. (1988) 'On the price effect of mergers with freer trade', *International Journal of Industrial Organisation* 6, 233–46.

Salant, S., S. Switzer and R. Reynolds (1983) 'Losses from horizontal merger: the effects of an exogenous change in industry structure on Cournot–Nash equilibrium', *Quarterly Journal of Economics* 98 (2), 185–213.

Smith, A. and T. Venables (1988) 'Completing the internal market in the European Community: Some industry simulations', *European Economic Review* 32 (7), 1501–26.

Stykolt, S. and H. Eastman (1960) 'A model for the study of protected oligopolies', *Economic Journal* 70, 336–47.

Tirole, J. (1988) *The Theory of Industrial Organization*, Cambridge, Mass.: MIT Press.

16

THE HARMONIZATION OF COMPETITION AND TRADE LAW

The case for modest linkages of law and the limits to parochial state action

Eleanor M. Fox and Janusz A. Ordover

INTRODUCTION

Trade law concerns nations' restraints of trade. Competition law, or antitrust, concerns private restraints of trade. With the successful completion of the Uruguay Round and the increasing internationalization of markets, attention has been turned to the international dimension of antitrust and the fit of competition policy with the world trading system. Proposals have been made for an international antitrust system, for harmonizing the antitrust laws of trading nations, and for harmonizing antitrust and trade law in general or at key intersections such as market access. This chapter first examines the motivations for harmonization and world policy. It then methodically examines whether there is a case to be made for convergence in each key substantive area of antitrust law, including each point of intersection of trade and competition. Using a vision of community, the chapter concludes that certain modest linkages should be forged at world level; that national law is not sufficient to the task; and that particular attention should be devoted to eliminating parochial restraints of nations that impose anti-competitive costs on neighbours and, as a consequence, on the world trading system and on the citizen/consumers of the world.

The inspiration for harmonization and convergence

First we examine the factors that have inspired initiatives to harmonize the antitrust laws of nations and to link antitrust and trade law. We seek to identify those points at which harmonization and coordination are important to the world competition/trading system, and we make a proposal for the use of competition policy to achieve the benefits of free trade and competition in a global economy.[1]

There are three major reasons why there has been growing interest in the problems of harmonizing competition policies among market economies, in bringing emerging market economies into the 'antitrust family', and in converging antitrust and trade law principles. The most obvious reason lies in the growing international linkage of market economies. These linkages take many forms, from international trade to direct investment to complex transnational joint ventures and mergers. There are clear virtues in assessing transnational business conduct, wherever it takes place, by the same or compatible criteria. Common modes of assessment would simplify business planning, and if the modes conduced to efficiency, they would direct business activity to its most efficient location.

Second, a wise common policy on the rules of competition could counter the centrifugal force that generates pressures by businesses on governments to obtain special treatment – pressures that increase as jurisdictions compete for foreign direct investment.[2] After seven rounds of the General Agreement on Tariffs and Trade (GATT), tariffs have become on average only a minor impediment to international trade in manufactured products. As indicated in Figure 16.1, the average tariff on manufactured products has fallen from 40 per cent in the late 1940s to approximately 5 per cent by the 1990s. This remarkable decline has not signalled an end to trade distortions. Non-tariff barriers have emerged to take up the slack, often if not usually in response to business pressures. (See Figure 16.2.) Voluntary export restraints, anti-dumping actions, countervailing duty measures, retaliatory trade 'sanctions' against real and imaginary 'unfair' traders, and private restraints often facilitated by government are adversely affecting international trade and investment, often in ways less transparent and more costly, and therefore more invidious, to home consumers than were the old-fashioned tariffs.[3]

Third, with the tariff walls down, 'system friction' stemming from different market models used by different nations has revealed itself more distinctly.[4] A source of this friction is the asserted prerogative of the sovereign (or a group of sovereigns, such as the European Union) to deploy or countenance macroeconomic and microeconomic policies that negatively affect its international trading partners. The ongoing system friction between the United States and Japan centres on Japan's $60 billion trade surplus with the United States, which some attribute in part to structural conditions and practices in Japan, governmentally and culturally or historically nurtured, which operate as impediments to trade.[5] (See Table 16.1.)

It is in this politically charged context that the matter of harmonization of competition systems and trade and antitrust law arises.

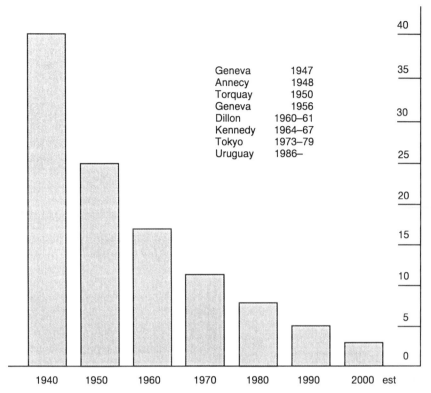

Geneva	1947
Annecy	1948
Torquay	1950
Geneva	1956
Dillon	1960–61
Kennedy	1964–67
Tokyo	1973–79
Uruguay	1986–

Figure 16.1 GATT rounds and the industrial countries (average tariffs, %)
Source: Centre for International Economics, GATT

Definition and model

We use the word 'harmonization' generically to signify a process or phenomenon that relieves tensions between and among the laws and policies of different nations in a liberal world competition/trading system by bringing those laws and policies into a state of greater compatibility. Harmonization can be achieved in many ways. Adoption of common law and policy – a single law interpreted and applied by the same institutions – is the ultimate harmonization. Alternatively, nations may adopt and implement common goals. The legal implementing rules may be differently phrased, but none the less their evenhanded enforcement, i.e. enforcement even when non-nationals are victims, can yield harmony and synergy as opposed to tensions and costs. More passively, law tends to drift into harmony through cross-fertilization.[6]

National enforcers' and courts' exercise of discretion not to enforce national law whenever the wrongdoers are non-nationals (e.g. offshore

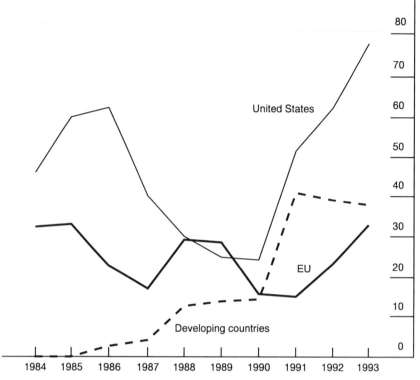

Figure 16.2 Anti-dumping cases (years ending June)
Source: GATT

Table 16.1 Potential increase in US sales to Japan if barriers lifted ($ million)

Sector	Potential sales
Food	101
Steel	138
Paper	6,671
Textiles	132
Aerospace	2,190
Automobiles	20,520
Equipment/tools	3,939
Computing/software	18,979
Electronics	10,702
Telecommunications	514
Chemicals	9,820

Source: Economic Strategy Institute, courtesy
Financial Times, February 14, 1994, p. 4, col.5

cartelists) could also modulate some tensions and could thereby produce a kind of harmony, but, to the extent that such non-enforcement undermines the world competition/trading system by closing the eyes to international restraints, this kind of national restraint does not produce positive, linked harmony.

Moreover, even similarly formulated law may not mean harmonious law. Exemptions from antitrust, though commonly recognized by nations, can produce the greatest perturbations to the world system. State action exemptions (e.g. the 'right' of a state to order export cartels) may create tensions and disharmony even if all nations have exactly the same law which, although prohibiting domestic and inbound cartels, sanctions export cartels.[7]

A model. The European Union, for its internal market, has the most developed law and policy in the world on the harmonization of laws in pursuit of free competition/free trade. Although, to be sure, the starting point for the European Union is a common market without frontiers and the degree of market integration contemplated is more complete than that envisioned for the world, the economic framework of 'undistorted competition' in the European common market offers an important model. Rules of the model include no government barriers to trade – tariff or non-tariff – and rules of non-discrimination, national treatment, and acceptance of regulatory standards imposed in the member state where the goods were first put on the market ('mutual recognition'). Within this model, Europe has proceeded to harmonize regulatory laws, principally to remove distortions of competition. At the one extreme, on matters of great importance such as competition law, the European Union has a common policy with common institutions for enforcement and adjudication. For other matters, mechanisms are put into place to bring national laws closer together. For example, EU legislation sets minimum standards on product safety with rights of states to adopt higher standards, as long as the higher standards are publicized and transparent. Moreover, the European Union has adopted enhanced free trade agreements with the nations of EFTA (the European Free Trade Association), and the EFTA countries have eliminated anti-dumping measures in the free trade area and have undertaken to adopt both the primary and the secondary law of the European Union for conduct affecting trade with the European Union. Meanwhile the Visigrad countries (Hungary, Poland, the Czech Republic and the Slovak Republic), in 'Europe Agreements' with the European Union, have undertaken to 'approximate' their major bodies of economic law, including competition law, to the law of the European Union.[8]

Informed by the EU model, which shifts trade law for the internal market into law against public or private distortions of competition, we use the word 'harmonization' in the context of our primary concern: law, its enforcement or non-enforcement, as a barrier, obstruction or deterrent to a liberal world competition/trading system.

Obstacles and opportunities

Harmonization of the competition laws of nations faces serious obstacles. First, even at the level of pure theory of antitrust law and economics, there is substantial disagreement as to the proper scope and analytical methods that should be deployed in assessing the conduct of firms and the extent to which analytical methods may be deployed in assessing conduct by state-owned business and even by government itself. In this respect, antitrust policy rests on much less secure and transparent economic foundations than does the traditional theory of international trade that has informed trade liberalization during the last four decades. This phenomenon is unavoidable. Competition policy must deal with market structures that deviate substantially from the 'perfectly' competitive benchmark. In real market settings, the assessment of short-term and long-term welfare consequences of firms' conduct generally does not lead to unambiguous answers; the enquiry is intensely fact-specific.[9] These ambiguities are complicated further by the fact that nations differ with respect to the goals of antitrust. Most particularly, they differ on whether their law should protect opportunities for small and middle-sized business; the extent to which the law should control 'abusive' pricing and other conduct that may be thought exclusionary, coercive or otherwise unfair, and the extent to which industrial policy may be a limit on antitrust.

To avoid the pitfall of these 'details', one could resort to very broad principles around which substantive harmonization could be accomplished. For example, policy-makers in advanced market economies could all agree that cartel behaviour – at home and abroad – is welfare-reducing and undesirable. It is debatable, however, whether much would be accomplished from the standpoint of international trade and investment policy by harmonization only on a cartel principle without removing tensions at other notable points; for example, market access problems and anti-competitive government action.

Second, the benefits of convergence of the antitrust laws of nations would have to flow from common interpretation of broad principles, and the implementation of them.[10] Yet we observe that nations differently define and apply even the word 'anti-competitive' and the concept 'market definition'; and we anticipate that these differences would be magnified if interpretation and enforcement of an international rule were to devolve to national competition authorities.[11]

This tendency could suggest that, if meaningful common principles of law are desired, a supranational competition authority could be useful. Such an authority could have competence to take up antitrust matters that meet certain threshold criteria of size and international dimension. It could act as would the US Supreme Court, resolving matters of legal interpretation.

Yet such a suggestion would face the opposition of many nations, which often assert their right to decide the fate of their own economy and the 'right to do it their way', and who may not trust an international body of experts to act non-politically and to 'get it right', much less to protect their national interests.

Finally, while some considerations support self-conscious efforts to advance harmonization of the antitrust laws of nations, other considerations point in the other direction. Diversity, flexibility, and ground-up evolution may be preferred for their own sake, and for the benefits of competition among systems, to enforced uniformity. While some differences in nations' law are arbitrary (e.g. the length of the pre-merger waiting period), others are rooted in culture, context, and a nation's choice of political economy (e.g. a focus on allocatively efficient outcomes versus a concern for opportunity for small business or a focus on the competition process).[12]

Recognizing the value of diversity and of ground-up evolution of law, we might approach harmonization with a finer sculpting knife and ask what is to be gained from harmonizing antitrust rules as applied to specific types of transactions and conduct. We might further ask, what are the specific tensions in our world competition/trading system that can be alleviated by other forms of convergence (e.g. linkages between antitrust and trade law). By asking these questions, we focus on specific problems and we offer a programme for convergence where, we believe, convergence will make a difference.

Before we proceed with this agenda, we comment on modes and methodologies of convergence, the principal models of substantive antitrust law (which will surely be guideposts for convergence), and the plan of the chapter.

Modes and methodologies

Convergence and perhaps some common policy could take a number of forms. Forms that have been considered include a World Code, with detailed rules of competition law, enforced largely in national courts but with substantial duties for an international antitrust authority.[13] In accordance with a different vision, to which we return, contracting nations could state a few strong shared principles of competition law at the interface of trade law, to be adopted into national law, with a role, albeit minimal, for dispute resolution in the event of global impacts and conflicts.[14] Under either concept, nations might agree to extend the scope of their antitrust law to proscribe anti-competitive conduct in their territory that would inflict anti-competitive harm elsewhere in the community of contracting nations; they might eliminate the right of nations to take beggar-thy-neighbour government action; nations might open their courts to harmed nations in the contracting community; and, to the extent that appeal to an impartial body would be necessary, a dispute resolution system could be available.

413

The principal models of substantive law

We express antitrust principles and the potential for harmonization principally in terms of the law of the United States and the law of the European Union. This is because US and EU law and their comparison provide a good sample case of harmonies and disharmonies in substantive law and legal systems and thus a good microcosm of possibilities of convergence. The United States and the European Union have the two most developed bodies of antitrust law in the world, save for Germany, which was one of the models for EU law. EU law has been accepted by the EFTA countries for transactions in the European free trade area, and most of the Eastern European countries have agreed to approximate their competition laws to those of the European Union.

Japanese antitrust law, while less fully judicially developed than US law, is close in language and concept to the two principal models (although Japanese vertical restraint law may be more constricting, at least on its face). However, Japanese antitrust law is not as well rooted in its culture as US and EU law are rooted in their cultures. Industrial policy rather than competition policy has shaped the Japanese economy. Interpretations of the Japanese antitrust law are often opaque and not predictable, and enforcement has been selective and not systematic.

Canadian law closely resembles US law in many respects. It does, however, provide an efficiencies defence for mergers, a defence that has not been officially recognized in the United States or the European Union. Like EU law, it has explicit concern for opportunities for small and middle-sized business and for the impact of abusive practices on excluded competitors.

We believe that most of the problems and possibilities of harmonization are captured by the US–EU example, while recognizing special problems of convergence with regard to systems shaped largely by government and business cooperation.[15]

With the growing scope for EU law, it may well be standard-setting. In fact, it is likely that within the next decade virtually all of Europe will have adopted EU substantive antitrust standards. Thus, if there is a perceived need for one rule worldwide, the pressures for harmonization towards an EU standard are likely to be strong.

To the extent that US and EU law diverge, however, it is unlikely either that the United States will accept EU standards or that the EU will accept US standards. Consequently, for the foreseeable future and to the extent of such divergence, two distinct focal points of substantive harmonization will coexist: one around the EU standard, the other around the US standard, even while the two systems continue their process of cross-fertilization. The interfocal 'battle' between these two standards will reflect the system tension between the Anglo-Saxon conception of advanced market capitalism and the

EU conception of a social market economy. How this contest will ultimately resolve itself will not depend on which standard proves 'better', for there is no applicable metric, and optimality may be a function of culture and traditions. The resolution or directions of the cross-fertilization may be influenced by the overall balance of economic and political forces between the United States (and the NAFTA signatories) on one hand and the enlarged European Union on the other.[16]

Plan of the chapter

Competition increasingly expands markets but tensions remain because of some bad fits of law and because law has evolved nationally with a view towards enhancing the interests of nations against nations even while transactions and businesses supervene nations.

If we need or desire convergence of some sort, we must ask: convergence towards what? The answer need not be, and presumptively should not be: towards US antitrust law because (some Americans might say) it is right, or towards EU law because (some might say) it is becoming the model for most of the world. The answer must be found in looking past nationalism towards globalism, for national solutions may be cut from too narrow a cloth.

We start here with a view of the appropriate guiding light. We then turn to particular areas of antitrust law and ask: is harmonization important, and what are the problems associated with this area of the law that reveal themselves as obstructions in the world trading system? Finally, we offer a proposal.

THE ASPIRATION AND GUIDING LIGHT – WORLD WELFARE, APPROPRIATE SOVEREIGNTY AND NATIONAL AUTONOMY

If nations act in their own individual interests, viewed from an inward-looking, nationalistic standpoint, they may regard their economic task as maximizing net national welfare.

Net national welfare is the economic concept that represents the total 'real' income of a nation's population. It is not an accounting measure of a nation's output deflated by a price index, although it is related to that concept. Rather, it is the total willingness of the population to pay for the goods and services it consumes, less the willingness-to-pay for the labour, capital, natural resources, and other productive factors it supplies. Under this measure, sales at supracompetitive prices that extract surplus from foreign consumers and transfer it into the profits of home firms are seen as a positive contribution rather than as a subtraction.[17]

The net national welfare standard, seen short-term, would welcome private export-cartel conduct, government action to facilitate export cartels, and mergers to monopoly or tight (non-competitive) oligopoly where most of the buyer population is abroad; hence beggar-thy-neighbour conduct.[18] It may welcome subsidies and other state aid where the value of the gain from 'saving' jobs and empowering workers to spend more money exceeds the investment.[19] If vision is especially myopic, the nation may welcome tariffs and anti-dumping duties when low-priced imports threaten domestic jobs and businesses, or even when they do not.

Past the very short run, retaliatory measures and counter-measures taken to offset the first nation's distortion of trade and competition tend to degenerate into a downward spiral of increasing impediments to trade. The prospect and reality of the downward spiral have been the impetus to agreements among nations on world trade[20] – particularly in the context of the GATT (succeeded by the World Trade Organization). The message that such nationalistic games are harmful was first brought home to nations with regard to government-imposed quotas, tariffs, Voluntary Export Restraints (VERs), and similar impediments. It has only recently been brought home with respect to government-imposed non-tariff barriers, including foreign investment limitations, unreasonably exclusionary standards (e.g. in telecommunications) and discriminatory procurement policies.

The lesson has not yet been brought home, however, with respect to private restraints, or (perhaps peculiarly, because it *is* government action) facilitation by governments of restraints by firms within their territory. Yet governments quite perceptibly and pervasively facilitate private restraints, and the costs to the world possibly amount to billions of dollars a year in lost income.[21] Governments may act in numerous anti-competitive ways. National legislatures may limit the coverage of antitrust laws so as not to reach beggar-thy-neighbour restraints. Executive or administrative decisions may be taken not to enforce antitrust law where the gain from harm to foreigners is judged greater than the loss to the nation's own constituency.

An alternative to the national welfare standard is a world welfare standard. By world welfare we mean the aggregate level of consumer benefits and profits realized by consumers and firms in all pertinent countries. The case for a world welfare standard to guide the two residual areas identified above – private restraints of international dimension, and government facilitation of them – seems rather compelling but is not uncomplicated. The complication is twofold. First, most purely private action is not anti-competitive and not harmful to world welfare; careful fact-specific analysis must underlie any conclusion that it should be condemned. Few private restraints are like government restraints in terms of their predictable distorting effect on competition and trade. Second, nations must be accorded a rather broad range of discretion to act in (their conception of) the public interest of their citizens. Every nation pursues all sorts of industrial policies, and ruling out this prerogative would undermine the function of government.

The challenge is to formulate a consensus definition of impermissible industrial policies, and to devise sufficient incentives for nations to honour their agreement to refrain from impermissible actions. One approach would specify that government action is impermissible where the harm it causes to world welfare perceptibly outweighs the benefit to the nation's citizens in correcting a market imperfection or otherwise protecting a national interest.[22] National industrial policy with a perceptibly negative external effect could be subject to a reporting and justification requirement. Justification would involve not only identification of the interest as a proper (not parochial) one, but also, as in the European Union for its internal market, it would involve showing that national measures that perceptibly impact trade or competition among nations are tailored to and proportionate to a proper national interest.[23]

A second approach for assessing the permissibility of state action would involve specifying a hierarchy of social policy goals served by various industrial policies. For example, at one end of the hierarchy, policies designed to cure a cognizable market failure within the state (such as pollution or inadequacy of private R&D due to a substantial deviation of social returns from private rates of return on R&D) could be accepted as permissible, irrespective of their external effects on the trading partners. At the other end of the hierarchy, policies that have as their main objective the shifting of profits from foreign firms to home firms could be categorized as impermissible, irrespective of the impact on aggregate welfare.[24]

Some difficulties inhere in both approaches. Under the first, it might be difficult to obtain and assess the necessary information and to devise an acceptable plan for choosing the decision-makers and assuring that they are free from political influence. Regarding the second, placement in the hierarchy will depend upon a nation's stated reasons, and the true reasons for any particular policy can be camouflaged because any type of industrial intervention can be consistent with more than one objective. For example, supporting nuclear electric power could arguably be justified by the high pollution cost of coal-fired generators (i.e. correcting an externality) or by the desire to subsidize indirectly energy-intensive industries that compete in export or import markets. Also, it is not clear that the countries could ever reach agreement on a hierarchy of remediable market failures and permissible industrial policies.[25]

Despite the difficulties, we believe that both approaches or variations on them are potentially workable and should be considered. Both offer the same guiding light: a world-welfare model subject to proper scope for national and local autonomy.

With that, we turn to substantive law to enquire what if any action is called for at this stage to put us firmly on a course towards the one-world-with-appropriate-autonomy vision. We review substantive law with a view to identifying problems that relate to trade.

HARMONIZATION

Substantive law

Cartel law

Cartel law is the law against agreements among competitors solely to eliminate their competition against one another. Cartel agreements may fix prices, allocate quotas or divide customers or territories in order to control the market.

Almost all nations have a law against private cartel agreements. Some allow justifications, such as for crisis or depression cartels. Almost all nations either have export exemptions from their cartel laws, or their law expressly does not reach outbound trade. The law of almost all nations prohibits import cartels, including competitor agreements to boycott foreign imports, but some nations are lax in enforcing their law against such cartels, presumably on a theory of national advantage.

Almost all nations respect (as lawful) government action ordering or allowing, and supervising, cartel activity, whether that action is taken by a domestic government (federal or state) or by a foreign government.

Cartels lead the list of private restraints that may harm world competition. Despite rather strong national law, however, transnational cartels continue to exist.[26] Often they are facilitated by government restraints, including tariffs and VERs, as in steel and aluminium, or are actually carried out by governments, as in oil (OPEC), so that there may be no private illegal action at all.

We take, first, the case in which private cartel action probably exists and harms competition in more than one nation. In this case, enforcement at national level by one or more nations is normally sufficient to deal with the matter. The problem is not insufficiency of the substantive law. There are, however, three concerns. First, it is sometimes difficult to obtain jurisdiction over foreign actors. This problem has been alleviated by long arm statutes (for personal jurisdiction), and by consensus on the effects doctrine (for subject matter jurisdiction). Second, the cartel may be suspected, not documented, and information may be difficult to obtain. Foreign antitrust enforcers may be a fruitful source of information, but information may be confidential and not subject to being shared. This problem is addressed in part by mutual cooperation agreements among governments. It is further addressed by the enactment of the International Antitrust Enforcement Assistance Act of 1994,[27] which authorizes the United States to enter into mutual assistance agreements and to share certain confidential information in connection with mutual assistance. Third, the cartel may be shielded by state action; and while forward-looking policy may impose limits on excessively anti-competitive and cost-shifting state action, national law seldom does so now.

Second is the case of the export cartel, which is normally not covered by national law. The reasons ordinarily given by a nation in support of this exclusion are: (1) harm abroad is not its business, and (2) export collaboration enhances the nation's exports and is therefore good for the nation. The first justification would disappear if nations agreed that they are all better off if they mutually prohibit export cartels. Though often ardently stated, the second reason seems to be a make-weight if the proponent means that efficient and pro-competitive export collaborations would be caught by a rule against export cartels. In the domestic context we distinguish every day between collaborations that result in better, more efficient delivery and those that are simply designed to override the market (i.e. cartels). There is no reason why the same distinguishing tests cannot also be applied to exports.

Third is the case of selective non-enforcement against cartels that boycott foreign imports. Here the problem is government inaction that itself restrains trade and competition. The problem can be addressed by nations' agreement to enforce their own laws, and the provision of a right of action, with meaningful discovery and remedies, by harmed nations if the nation defaults in enforcing its law. Anticipating the possibility that all of the foregoing means of recourse may be inadequate, nations might agree to accept the jurisdictional legitimacy of antitrust action in the harmed nation's courts. To defuse a defendant's claim of unfairness (i.e. 'I did not know and could not know that I would be subject to your law'), the enforcing court could be required to apply the law of the nation on whose soil the conduct and principal effects occurred,[28] or alternatively to accord the defendant the right to defend on grounds that, under the law of the defendant's country, even if the conduct and all of its harms occurred within that country, the conduct would be lawful.

Now that we have assessed the national cartel laws and their limits, we are ready to ask whether, in the cartel area, more should be done in the spirit of world welfare. In view of the effects doctrine (and thus the ability to catch beggar-thy-neighbour export cartels and possibly, though less clearly, import cartels), and given initiatives for information-sharing and other enforcement agency cooperation, are all cartel problems sufficiently soluble on a national level?

The answer to us is no, even though national initiatives can carry us far in the right direction. World competitors must play by international rules of the game, in competition no less than trade law. Certain basic international rules must be visible, some assurance of their enforcement must exist, and some limits must be placed on nationalistic strategies to harm other nations.[29] Nations must begin to understand the benefits to their citizens of a world welfare model (subject to the subsidiarity principle developed below), and must understand the community interest in preventing private conduct and controlling government action that causes antitrust harm anywhere in a transnational market. It should no longer be acceptable to disclaim antitrust injury[30] on the grounds that the harm is 'extraterritorial'.

Accordingly, we might begin to formulate a world competition policy model with four simple cartel-related rules, offered for agreement by all nations that choose to join the compact (e.g. offered to all members of the GATT/WTO) with respect to cartel conduct of a transnational dimension:

1 All nations should maintain and enforce a rule of law prohibiting cartels.
2 The prohibition should include conduct that causes antitrust harm anywhere in the community of contracting nations.
3 No nation or its subdivisions should order cartels or exempt cartels that significantly harm transnational competition, except that these rules should not prohibit them from taking action they deem necessary to address internal market problems as long as the action is no broader than proportional to the problem, and even then only upon notification of the terms and scope of the government action and justification therefor.[31]
4 All nations should provide and assure meaningful access to enforcement of the law against cartel conduct that harms non-nationals.[32]

Market access law

Equally important on the substantive antitrust international agenda is market access law – law that prohibits private anti-competitive restraints that block access to markets. This item surfaces on the international agenda because it is so visible, being so distinctly felt, from the trade point of view; and because antitrust as well as trade law has a set of rules to deal with market access.

Governments are accustomed to negotiating with governments to open their markets, i.e. to remove government barriers to access. As government trade barriers have become lower, existing non-tariff barriers and private barriers have become more visible. Moreover, as domestic firms are exposed more frontally to foreign competition, private firms may have the incentive to erect or reinforce their own restraints to keep the foreign competition at bay.

Artificial private barriers can be erected in three ways. First, competitors that cartelize may employ mechanisms to keep foreign competitors out, thus protecting their supra-competitive profits. For example, in a market where it is difficult to set up a distribution system, cartelizing competitors may agree with one another to bind their distributors not to carry the goods of a competitor (e.g. a foreigner) who is not a member of the cartel.[33] The same can be accomplished by producers of inputs who may, to protect their cartel, bind their customers (e.g. car makers who need windshield glass) not to buy from foreign suppliers. These are examples of cartels with boycotts. They are illegal virtually everywhere. They are included by necessary implication in the cartel discussion in point 1 above, and thus are included by implication in the minimal agreement suggested with respect to cartels.

Second, artificial barriers can be erected by a monopolist[34] in much the same way – tying up non-duplicable distribution systems or requiring financially linked beholden buyers to refuse to deal with foreign sources of supply. Single-firm conduct is more ambiguous than cartel conduct, however. While there is no *bona fide* reason for competitors to agree with one another that each will require its distributor not to deal with its competitors, there may be efficiency reasons for a firm acting unilaterally to choose an exclusive distribution system or an assured outlet (which terms have the effect of requiring the distributor not to deal with the competitors of the firm imposing the restraint). Under US law, which probably is the most permissive monopolization law in the world today, such 'vertical' conduct may be accepted as valid if justified by an efficiency reason that could not be satisfied in an obviously less exclusionary way.[35] Thus, if a vertical restraint violates the US monopolization law, the same restraint probably violates the monopolization or abuse-of-dominance law of all the trading partners of the United States and can be classified as a consensus prohibition.

Accordingly, one might wish to include, on a short list of commonly understood offences, certain narrowly delineated practices by monopoly firms designed only to keep competitors out, likely to exclude or retard even efficient competitors, and not justified by good business reasons. Such a principle would apply with particular strength to network industries, such as telecommunications, pipelines, and electricity, in which access to the network is essential for competitive success.

Third, artificial barriers can be erected by vertical restraints imposed by firms that are neither cartelists nor monopolists. This is a more hazardous area for a short international list, however, for firms without monopoly power that impose vertical restraints unilaterally are likely to be acting from efficiency impulses rather than from anti-competitive impulses. Indeed, if they have no market power, efficiency and responsiveness to buyers is presumptively the explanation for their conduct. There is none the less a class of cases in an imperfectly competitive market wherein there is no monopolist but a few firms have market power (oligopoly power); they use vertical restraints – e.g. they impose exclusive purchasing arrangements – in a market which, at the level of the tied-in purchaser, is hard to enter, and the restraints elevate entry barriers and lessen both domestic and international competition.[36] US antitrust law would examine the market to see whether, despite this foreclosure effect, the competitive pressures within the market are sufficiently strong to keep price near cost; if so, the case would probably be dismissed. Even if the market is not so competitive, US law would examine the pervasiveness of the restraints; if few firms used them, the exclusionary impact might be minimal and if so the case would probably be dismissed. Even if all firms used the restraint and the market was not fully competitive, US law would entertain the claim that the restraint was efficiency-justified and if so would examine whether the cost savings or technology-improving aspects outweighed the loss from the forgone additional market pressure.

Vertical restraints can result from express contracts or implied contracts, from coercion by the more powerful firm in the supplier–buyer pair or from mutual desire, and may be one-way restraints or may entail reciprocal dealing. They can effect partial or complete market foreclosures. In all cases the US analysis is guided by the same principles, but facts differ, and therefore the effect on competition and the antitrust treatment may differ. Major variables include the tightness or looseness of the restraint (i.e. the freedom of the 'promisor' firm to go outside of the supplier–buyer channels), the relationship of the market segment foreclosed to the whole market, and the height of barriers.

Under US law, in most circuits, the enquiry is focused on market power and the law is indifferent to the claim that the vertical restraint excludes small and middle-sized business from opportunities to serve a market.[37] In other nations, such an effect is more central to analysis. Some nations treat access to markets as more or less an antitrust *right*, rather than as a possible by-product of a consumer-centred analysis that looks first and foremost at whether incumbents face sufficient incentives to serve consumers.

Because of the difficulties of establishing the existence of welfare-reducing, foreclosing, private restraints imposed other than by cartelization or dominant firm conduct, one might be reluctant to include the matter on a world agenda. On the other hand, when one views foreclosing restraints from the perspective of international trade, one sees them as impediments and sometimes unreasonable impediments to trade, and will understand their place in a world trading system whose members have agreed, more or less, to keep their markets open to one another.

Trade law focuses on rights of access and equates blockage from market entry by government action with harm to the world trading system.[38] The trade paradigm calls for the justification of government restraints when they tend to prevent goods and services from moving freely across borders. Only in recent years, when governments have been called to account more fully for the non-tariff restraints they impose, has it become apparent that restraints that impede market access may remain even after governments appear to have fulfilled their trade obligations. There is suspicion that the residual restraints may be private, not public, and the nation on whose territory they occur is simply condoning them when they hurt foreigners; or that these residual restraints may be hybrid government and private action that has slipped through the net of GATT obligations.

Eastman Kodak evoked these factors in a petition filed in May 1995 pursuant to s. 301 of the US Trade Act of 1974. It alleges that the Japanese government, when faced with the lowering of trade barriers on consumer photographic film and paper, and thus with the reality of diminished government-sponsored protection, initiated a programme of 'liberalization counter-measures' which constituted delegating the protectionist function to private industry (largely Fuji), thus 'privatizing protection'. Fuji denies all material facts that underlie the charge, and alleges that Kodak anti-competitively represses Fuji's competition in the US market. The trade and competition issues are intricately intertwined, as are the Japanese anti-monopoly law issues with the US antitrust law issues.

These are the principal reasons why competition law is expected to be on the next agenda of the GATT/WTO; and they explain why it would be unwise to shrug off the issue of vertical restraints and single-firm restraints on the grounds that they are normally pro-competitive and therefore not a subject for concern.[39]

To the extent that antitrust law or concepts are relevant, the trade/competition problem has not been lack of antitrust law that bears on market access. Instead, the problems have been lack of clarity regarding what the existing law demands, lack of enforcement of existing law, as in the persistent problem of alleged *keiretsu*-related restraints in Japan, and a possible gap in coverage regarding hybrid public/private restraints.

Accordingly we would add to the short list of principles for international antitrust:

All nations should maintain and enforce a rule of law prohibiting enterprises with significant market power, including government enterprises, from engaging in exclusionary practices that foreclose market access, when such conduct harms consumers and the competitive process. Each nation's rule of law should be transparent.

Points 2 and 4 under 'Cartel law', above, would apply.

Government entities may sometimes need more flexibility in order to fulfil their duty to act in the public interest, and therefore for government entities a clause should parallel the EU exception: 'except as necessary to fulfil their public duties'.[40]

The above provision designedly does not state how a nation should formulate its law. It would leave intact each nation's formulation and interpretation. Some nations' law will continue to be more 'pro-access' than others. As discussed below, the law to be applied is the law of the nation wherein the foreclosing restraint operates, so that firms are not held accountable for violating foreign law whose application may be unexpected and unforeseeable and the contours of which may not be fully understood.

Vertical restraints other than foreclosing restraints

Most vertical restraints are restraints in the course of distribution and directly concern intra-brand competition. They may limit the autonomy of the dealer, sometimes in order to produce efficiencies in distribution. Vertical restraints may at times be price-raising; or they may be neutral or pro-competitive.

Differences among nations exist in the law on vertical distribution restraints. EU law prohibits tight territorial restraints at member state lines, without regard to the intensity of interbrand competition. Thus a producer may not absolutely confine its distributor to a member nation.[41] This prohibition is based on the European Union's important goal of market integration and on the significance attached to the principle of free movement. In contrast, US law liberally allows restraints in the course of distribution other than resale price maintenance agreements, as long as they do not preserve or increase market power at the level of interbrand competition.

US analysis is based in large part on acceptance of the position that single-firm vertical behaviour is normally pro-consumer. It recognizes that there may be a free-rider problem (corner-cutting distributors may free-ride on the investment of service-providing distributors), and it preserves producers' freedom to impose restraints that protect the service-provider's investment. EU case law attaches much less importance to the free-rider problem than does US case law.[42]

Moreover, the EU procedure of block exemptions,[43] to which the United States has no counterpart, steers European transactions into a common mould, constraining their form. Thus a procedural as well as substantive gap is perceptible.

Vertical restraints other than foreclosing ones have little impact on international trade and competition. If the use of resale price maintenance or vertical divisions of customers or territories should raise the price of one brand, sellers of competing products in international trade have all the more opportunity and incentive to sell into that territory and satisfy the deprived consumers. If the vertical restraint law of one nation or region favours autonomy on the part of dealers or preserves the flow of parallel imports of the same brand (as does the European Union for market integration purposes) and if this law handicaps producers by ruling out the most efficient distribution strategies, again opportunities for foreign sellers could be increased, or at least they would remain neutral to the extent that foreign sellers would be bound by the same restrictive law as domestic sellers when they established their distribution systems in the regulating nation.

The very fact of different legal regimes governing vertical distribution restraints can be costly to producers, who must design their distribution to conform with the rules of each country in which they do business. The prospect of cost savings and a free flow of trade across borders could put pressure on less efficient national systems to converge their laws and procedures regarding distribution restraints. This is especially likely to happen in North America, where the three NAFTA countries' laws and procedures are quite similar and the prospect of a free flow of goods in a North America without frontiers is almost tangible. But it is unlikely that the distribution restraint law of the United States and the European Union will converge much more than it already has, in view of the quite different procedures and some different goals.

We see little reason to raise non-foreclosure vertical restraint law to an international dimension.

Monopolization and abuse of a dominant position

Virtually all nations have a law against monopolization and abuse of a dominant position. Some nations, especially recently decommunized nations, have a law authorizing break-ups with particular but not exclusive regard to state enterprises. All have laws regulating anti-competitive conduct on the part of monopoly or dominant firms.

Nations have differing tilts to their laws against monopolization or the abuse of a dominant position. The US law is relatively permissive towards the unilateral behaviour of firms even with substantial market power, on the theory that society is better off if firms are allowed to compete vigorously, even if the conduct disadvantages competitors and increases a firm's dominance.[44] EU law finds dominance to exist at much lower levels than US law finds monopoly power, and EU law imposes a variety of constraints on the dominant firm. These include a constraint against excessive pricing, a duty to continue dealing with existing customers, and sometimes a duty to deal with new customers. The EU law also prohibits dominant firms' exclusive contracts where they shelter too much market share or significantly increase market share. Even while US antitrust jurisprudence endorses allocative efficiency as the guide to antitrust law and discounts concern about fairness and about opportunity for small competitors, EU law self-consciously incorporates values of fairness, opportunity and legitimacy; it pays special regard to the viability of small and middle-sized businesses, and it rejects the notion that a gain to smaller competitors must be a loss to consumers.

Monopolization and abuse of dominance have not been such high-profile offences in world competition that international law seems needed. To be sure, dominant firms can sometimes block market access. This issue is treated separately herein in point 2, above, and can be treated separately for the international agenda.

It is theoretically possible for a monopoly firm in one nation to be also a monopolist in world markets and thus have the power to exploit consumers worldwide. If, however, there are no government-imposed barriers, and no anti-competitive conduct (which national law can catch), we think the right 'remedy' is the US remedy: let others enter the market and challenge the monopolist. High price tends to invite entry and to inspire challenges that correct the defect.

In sum, dominant firms' foreclosing conduct should be dealt with on the world agenda under the rubric of market access. Exploitative pricing and suboptimal performance should not be raised to an international level, although any artificial barriers that facilitate the exploitation and that otherwise blunt competitive pressures should be removed.

Mergers

Virtually all nations' laws prohibit anti-competitive mergers, although some countries allow a competition agency to consider the industrial policy advantages of the merger or (more commonly) allow a Minister to override the competition agency's negative decision on industrial policy grounds.

The most common industrial policy reasons offered in justification of anti-competitive mergers are jobs and national champions. It is not usual, however, for a merger both to increase market power and to save jobs that the market would eliminate; therefore, it cannot be expected that industrial policy would counsel approval of an anti-competitive merger because of jobs. (Preserving redundant jobs is an inefficiency and a cost and could therefore dissipate market power.) On the other hand, the creation of a national champion by a market-power-increasing merger implies a scenario for exploitation in the world (unless the nation itself is a market and the nation is willing to let its citizens be exploited in order to achieve advantages that make the firm merely a robust player in the world market place – in which case the rest of the world has no standing to complain).

Merger analysis is similar all over the world, but analytical frameworks, methodologies and emphases differ. For example, analysis in the European Union is looser, less technically economic, and more likely to be politically influenced than analysis in the United States.

While in rhetoric EU merger law seems much more sympathetic to the plight of foreclosed competitors than does US merger law, the European Union is essentially indulgent to merging firms. The Commission almost never prohibits a merger. The one outright prohibition[45] caused enormous political turmoil in the name of industrial policy and may have triggered increased conservatism by the EU Commission.[46] Also, the European standard of prohibition does not clearly cover mergers that increase oligopoly as opposed to monopoly power, but future interpretations may close this gap. Japan, like the European Union, seldom prohibits a merger.

Neither the United States nor the European Union has an explicit efficiencies defence or set-off that could sanction mergers which enhance market power,[47] as Canada does,[48] although in both jurisdictions efficiencies may be relevant in analysing competitive effects. Jurisprudence regarding efficiencies is still developing.

Even the first step in merger analysis – market definition – is differently approached in different nations. Moreover, 'anti-competitive' means different things to the enforcers and courts in the different jurisdictions. Thus even a similarly worded law against anti-competitive mergers may not constitute a harmonized law.

Merger law presents itself as a candidate for international scrutiny for two reasons, one relating to the effects on competition and one relating to procedure and jurisdiction.

Mergers may have price-raising and foreclosing effects in areas beyond the nations in which the merging parties are located.[49] It may be contended that we need international concepts to keep the anti-competitive effects of mergers from radiating throughout the world.[50]

For price-raising problems, one might say, as we did regarding monopolies, that if there are no government barriers, entry opportunities normally constitute a sufficient safeguard. There is, however, an important difference between merger law and monopoly law. The monopolist presumably achieved its place on the map by being the most efficient competitor, and we may not wish to interfere with incentives to be the best. In mergers to monopoly or to tight oligopoly, however, the merging firms are 'buying' market power, and an injunction may stop them from doing so without interfering with organic efficiencies. For these reasons, one may be less reluctant to interfere with mergers.

On the other hand, the decision to allow or disallow a merger affects the structure of a nation's economy. This observation plays into the sovereignty claim of nations that the structure of their economy is a matter for them alone to choose. An inclination to defer to sovereignty interests may make one reluctant to interfere with the 'industrial policy' decisions of nations. More in keeping with the thesis of this chapter, however, nations' claim as of right to pursue industrial policy may suggest the need for international dialogue with a view to drawing the line between appropriate national autonomy and inappropriate spillovers.

The second set of issues is procedural and jurisdictional. Notification of the same merger may be required by a dozen jurisdictions. Each jurisdiction has its own filing and notification requirements. Each may require a different waiting period. The merger notification and information process alone may cost many hundreds of thousands of dollars for a single transaction, and manifold duplicated time and energy in dealing with the various nations' antitrust enforcers. Moreover, after the filing and information period, many authorities may sue at once, sometimes seeking different relief.[51]

The second set of issues is more easily addressed than the first. Indeed, much thought has been given to the matter, and initiatives to alleviate some of the problems are under way. Recommendations have been made, which we support, that nations' enforcement authorities should try to agree to a single notification form and a single waiting period, or they should accept as first notification that which was filed first. To the extent that parties waive confidentiality, a central filing system can be established, and the central office may be obliged to provide the documents to the competition agencies of all contracting nations that assert an interest in the transaction. Also, to the extent that the parties waive confidentiality, the interested agencies can share their analyses with one another, identify common problems, and, if they wish, adopt a common approach to common problems.[52] Where appropriate, enforcement authorities can develop a protocol specifying a framework for determining which agency proceeds first and which takes the lead in a given case of overlapping interests.[53]

Is the foregoing coordination enough to solve the world welfare problems of international mergers? We think not, because of the problems of externalities and industrial policy overrides. Our solution, however, is modest and accords with our proposal for an overarching principle. Nations should agree to the following:

1 Nations should maintain and enforce a law against anti-competitive mergers.
2 Anti-competitive harm anywhere in the community of contracting nations should be treated as seriously as harm within the regulating nation's borders.
3 If a nation designates a process for the authorization of certain anti-competitive mergers under specified circumstances, such process and the decision-making thereunder should be transparent, the criteria necessary for a grant of approval should be clear, anti-competitive harm to nationals should not be treated more seriously than harm to non-nationals, and gains from anti-competitive harm to non-nationals should not be permitted to weigh in the balance in favour of approval of the merger.
4 Nations' enforcement authorities should adopt a common form of pre-merger notification and a common waiting period, and should provide, and make available at the merger parties' option, a central filing system for mergers with an international dimension.

Joint ventures and alliances would be accorded the same treatment.

Certain collaborations and behaviour that are essentially pro-competitive, efficient and progressive for the world

We have thus far analysed proscriptive law where there may be a need for world coordination. There is also a category of cases in which the collaboration or behaviour of firms is so likely to enhance world welfare that the danger is not that it will escape proscription by individual nations but that it will be enjoined by one judge or one agency and its benefits will be lost for all. If the costs and benefits fall predominantly in one nation, there could be little cause for concern, for that nation should have the incentive to do what is appropriate. But if the benefits are widely dispersed, or the nation's incentives are skewed (e.g. by lobbying), there may be a need for freedom-preserving international rules.

Transactions, conduct and behaviour that may fall into this category are:

1 Research and development joint ventures.
2 Certain alliances, especially involving high technology.
3 Sustainable cross-border low pricing (which may risk being condemned as unfair or predatory).

A related situation is the problem of excessive antitrust intervention by one nation where the enforcement or relief spills over and undermines competition, efficiency or technological progress in the community of nations. An example is the proposed relief of the European Community against IBM Europe in the 1980s requiring IBM to disclose planned interface changes in its computer system to customers and competitors so that the competitors would be at the starting line with IBM in supplying compatible peripheral equipment. The EC Competition Directorate believed that the relief would enhance competition and not undermine inventiveness. IBM and the US Department of Justice believed that the relief would undermine incentives to invent and would harm technological progress.[54]

The proposition that certain proscriptions and injunctions have a tendency to harm world welfare and should be examined under and possibly pre-empted by higher law is, as a practical and political matter, difficult to maintain at this early stage of world antitrust coordination. At a later point in time an optimal system may involve a world institution for economic law, entrusting one body with the obligation of examining such transactions 'from the top' and make appropriate dispositions in view of world welfare. At this stage, however, a realistic solution would be the following. *Nations should agree to consider pro-competitive, efficiency and technological benefits of challenged transactions or conduct and of proposed relief against such transactions or conduct everywhere in the community of contracting nations, and to take these effects into account to the same extent that they would if such effects fell within their own territory.* The principle according injured nations a meaningful right of action in the regulating nation's courts would help to keep regulating nations true to their agreement.

This solution preserves nations' right to formulate their own law. For example, efficiency benefits abroad of a competition-reducing merger would count for no less (or more) than efficiency benefits at home.

Controlling anti-competitive government action

We have already glimpsed the problem that government action can be far more anti-competitive and far more obstructive of world competition than private restraints; yet, with respect to antitrust restraints, government action is largely accepted as a trump, in the name of sovereignty.

It is time to recognize the overuse and misuse of the word 'sovereignty', particularly in the arena of world competition. Sovereignty is good, indeed vital, in its place, but nationalistic agendas can undermine the common economic good and nations can agree to pursue the common good without suffering an 'infringement of sovereignty'. We specify some areas in which anti-competitive government action might be contained.

Cartels – government involvement

Government action to cure internal market failures may be warranted, but at some point the negative spillover effect is significant and may be adjudged excessive. Nations should be accountable for imposing costs on others. We stated a principle to govern this problem above.[55] The principle applies to invocation of the defences of act of state and foreign sovereign compulsion[56] – defences frequently invoked in cartel cases.

Subsidies and state regulation

The Treaty of Rome requires member states to notify to the European Commission all state aids, including subsidies, which the states must then justify or eliminate. The law has worked reasonably well, though far from perfectly, tending to give governments the strength to resist private-interest lobbying.[57]

The EU model is a useful one. Sunlight may be a step towards a later, more ambitious programme of justification or elimination. For an agenda, we propose: *nations and their state subdivisions agree to catalogue all state aid that impacts international competition and to provide annual reports disclosing such state aid and explaining the justification therefor.*

Countervailing duty law is made necessary or appropriate only because of state aid. As state aid diminishes, so, too, will the need to countervail it.

Anti-dumping law

In most nations anti-dumping law is easily triggered to keep out low-priced imports that materially injure a domestic industry. In contrast, antitrust law on price predation is designedly permissive, condemning only sales below a level of cost by a firm with market power that can rationally expect to destroy its competitors, raise prices, and keep prices high for a sufficiently long period of time to recoup its investment in predation through monopoly or tighter oligopoly. The antitrust law is designedly permissive in order to encourage low pricing, even low pricing that harms competitors, because low pricing is competition itself. The EU law on price predation is not so demanding – the Commission need not prove the probability of recoupment – but otherwise EU law, too, favours competitive low pricing.

430

Thus, the antitrust laws and the anti-dumping laws conflict. The anti-dumping laws, liberally invoked, harm consumers, intermediate buyers that must compete in world markets, and world welfare.

The area is fraught with political pressures. There is much literature studying the tensions and proposing solutions. In view of the political pressures, we make only a modest, preliminary proposal for the agenda. *Nations should agree to consider the tension between their anti-dumping laws and world welfare, and to modify their antidumping laws to bring them more closely into line with their antitrust price-predation laws.*

Other government action

We mentioned above anti-competitive action by government as a market player, and suggested that such government entities should normally be subject to the same rules as other commercial entities, with a gateway, as in the European Union, for carrying out public duties. We mentioned also that government sometimes enacts unduly anti-competitive legislation. Anti-dumping legislation is one example.

We might do well to be guided by the EU internal market principle prohibiting legislation that discriminates against foreign goods or services unless tightly justified by specified standards. This may be an idea before its time for an international action list. For now, the matter might be left to national autonomy with a plea for conscience and perhaps publicity for legislation affecting international trade that ostensibly falls short of cosmopolitan standards. Examples of such shortfall are the US Exxon *Florio* law,[58] the US joint production venture law,[59] and buy-national and national content laws. Thus we propose: *nations should publish an annual report compiling all federal and state laws that impact on international trade and that ostensibly discriminate against foreign goods and services, stating the justification for the discrimination.*

CONCLUSION

Global competition is driving businesses and trading nations closer to one world. Legal institutions are already in place in the area of trade laws, with the mission, however difficult, of moving the world towards world welfare. In the area of anti-competitive private action and anti-competitive government restraints beyond GATT treatment, however, the law has lagged.

Efforts are proceeding to work from 'the bottom up'. Enforcement cooperation among government agencies has reached a new level. Moreover, certain procedural harmonization, such as the harmonization of merger notification forms, is a subject of conversation. These bottom-up and horizontal initiatives are praiseworthy and important steps, but they do not take the place of a vision from the top guided by a world welfare principle subject to appropriate national autonomy.

A world competition system does not require a compendium of world rules of antitrust law. Nor does it require investigation into the minute differences between the antitrust laws of nations or a determination to harmonize the laws or converge them towards any existing model. Rather, it requires a guiding standard (world welfare), and an understanding of how transactions and action, government and private, may impact world trade and competition in world-welfare-reducing ways. It then requires procedures for steering the world towards its goals, which we suggest should be largely self-executing at national level.

Disputes among nations will predictably arise. The design of an acceptable system for dispute resolution is imperative.

We have presented the pieces of the system under the appropriate headings above. We combine them here.

1 All nations should maintain and enforce a rule of law prohibiting cartels, prohibiting firms with significant market power, including government enterprises, from anti-competitive foreclosure of market access, and prohibiting anti-competitive mergers. Any derogations should be clear and narrowly tailored. The rules of law should be transparent.

2 The prohibitions should include conduct that causes antitrust harm anywhere in the community of contracting nations. Harm in the contracting community but outside of the regulating nation's borders should be treated as seriously as harm within the regulating nation's borders.

3 Nations should agree to consider the pro-competitive, efficiency and technological benefits of challenged transactions and conduct everywhere in the community of contracting nations, and should take these effects into account to the same extent that they would if such effects fell in their own territory. Similarly they should consider and take into account spillover harm to competition, efficiency and technological progress that may result from relief ordered in antitrust proceedings.

4 No nation or its subdivisions should order or exempt cartels that significantly harm transnational competition; except that nations may take necessary action to address internal market problems if the action is no broader than proportional to the problem, and even then only upon notification of the terms and scope of the government action and justification therefor.

5 Any process for authorization of anti-competitive mergers should be transparent, the criteria necessary for a grant of approval should be clear, a merger should not be approved if anti-competitive harm to non-nationals exceeds any harm to nationals, and national gains from anti-competitive harm to non-nationals should not weigh in the balance in favour of approval of the merger.

6 All nations should provide and assure to other nations meaningful access to their enforcement system so as to allow other nations to challenge prohibited anti-competitive conduct that harms non-nationals.

7 Nations' enforcement authorities should adopt a common form of pre-merger notification and a common waiting period, and should provide a central filing system for mergers with an international dimension.

8 Nations should agree to consider the tension between their anti-dumping laws and world welfare, and to modify their anti-dumping laws to bring them more closely into line with their antitrust price-predation laws.

9 Each nation should publish an annual report disclosing and compiling all national and state government aid and all laws that discriminate against foreign goods and services, stating the justification.

Through world welfare standards, with sunlight and appropriate national autonomy, the trading nations of the world may begin to meet the promise of convergence.

NOTES

1 This chapter focuses on convergence of substantive law, with occasional reference to procedural convergence. For procedural harmonization in the merger process, see Chapter 17 of this volume. For coordination among national and regional antitrust agencies, see Chapter 7.

2 This process is taking place in Eastern Europe, where foreign firms demand and obtain favourable trade, tax and conduct treatment from local governments.

3 See, e.g. J.A. Ordover and L. Goldberg, *Obstacles to Trade and Competition: A Report to the Secretariat*, Organization for Economic Cooperation and Development ('OECD') (1993), for a summary of the empirical research on the costs of voluntary export restraints.

4 The concept of 'system friction' was introduced by Sylvia Ostry. See S. Ostry, 'Exploring the Policy Options for the 1990's' in OECD Forum for the Future, *Support Policies for Strategic Industries: Systemic Risks and Emerging Issues* (1991).

5 See, e.g. the debate between R. Lawrence and G. Saxonhouse on whether Japan imports 'too little'. R. Lawrence, 'Japan's Different Trade Regime: an Analysis with Particular Reference to *Keiretsu*', 7 *J. Econ. Perspectives* No. 3 (1993), 3–20, and G. Saxonhouse, 'What does Japanese Trade Structure Tell Us About Japanese Trade Policy?' *ibid.*, 21–44. Trade frictions exist also between the United States and the European Union. Although agriculture could be said to head the list, it plainly does not fit any of the now standard models of international high-technology competition. Trade frictions exist, for example, in the aircraft industry. There the bone of contention has been the decision by certain EU countries to subsidize the joint development of the Airbus, which is in competition with US aircraft manufacturers. The effect of these subsidies has been to harm the economic interests of the United States and, potentially, to benefit the economic interests of the EU member countries. The EU member countries have responded to the US complaints regarding these subsidies by noting that the US aircraft industry has long been a beneficiary of indirect subsidies from the US Defense Department, which, in turn, enabled the US

defence industry firms to dominate the civilian aircraft industry. See Laura D'Andrea Tyson, *Who is bashing whom? Trade Conflict in High-technology Industries*, chapter 5 (1992), for a somewhat one-sided review of the debate.

6 See David Leebron, 'An Analysis of Harmonization Claims: Lying Down With Procrustes', in J. Bhagwati and R. Hudec (eds), *Fair Trade and Harmonization: Prerequisites for Free Trade*, in publication (1996), for an analysis of claims that law should be harmonized; Eleanor Fox, 'Competition Law and the Agenda for the WTO: Forging the Links of Competition and Trade', 4 *Pac. Rim Law & Policy J.* 1 (1995).

7 See *The Report of the ABA Antitrust Section Task Force on the Competition Dimension of the North American Free Trade Agreement* (1994), chapters 3 and 4; *The Report of the ABA Antitrust Section Special Committee on International Antitrust* (1991), chapter 3.

8 See Joel Trachtman, 'International Regulatory Competition, Externalization, and Jurisdiction', 34 *Harv. Int'l L. J.* 47 (1993); Joel Trachtman, 'L'Etat, c'est nous: Sovereignty, Economic Integration and Subsidiarity', 33 *Harv. Int'l L. J.* 459 (1992); 'Vision of Europe: Lessons for the World' (introduction to symposium issue), 18 *Fordham Int'l L. J.* 379 (1994); Eleanor Fox, *The Developing Antitrust Law of the Visigrad Countries – Central Europe Moves into Step with the European Union*, Antitrust Report (Matthew Bender, October 1995); George Bermann, Roger Goebel, William Davey & Eleanor Fox, *Cases and Materials on European Community Law* (1993) (Supp. 1995).

9 When imperfect competition is injected into standard models of international trade, some of the sharpness of the welfare results regarding the benefits of free trade is lost. See P. Krugman, 'Is Free Trade Passé?', 1 *J. Econ. Perspectives* No. 2, 131–44 (1987).

10 International application of broad principles may generate dispute resolution problems. The GATT dispute resolution mechanism caused such problems as its broad principles were applied to more and more cases of growing complexity. See 'GATT: The Eleventh Hour', *The Economist*, December 4, 1993.

11 Even among the twelve federal US circuits, there is disagreement on matters of interpretation, such as the legal standard for price predation and whether there is an offence of monopoly leveraging, and how to apply the rule of reason in a vertical non-price restraint. For example, there is disagreement whether pricing above average variable cost or even above average total cost can ever be a violation. Compare *Barry Wright Corp.* v. *ITT Grinnell Corp.*, 724 F. 2d 227 (1st Cir. 1983), with *McGahee* v. *Northern Propane Gas Co.*, 858 F. 2d 1487 (11th Cir. 1988).

12 See generally David Leebron, note 6 supra. The literature on environmental law raises similar problems. See Benedict Kingsbury, 'The Tuna–Dolphin Controversy: The World Trade Organization, and the Liberal Project to Reconceptualize International Law', 5 *Yearbook of International Environmental Law* (in publication).

13 See Draft International Antitrust Code as a GATT–MTO–Plurilateral Trade Agreement ('Munich Code'), 64 *BNA Antitrust & Trade Reg. Rep.* August 19, 1993 (Special Supp., No. 1628).

14 E. Fox, Handler Lecture, 'Antitrust, Trade and the 21st Century – Rounding the Circle', 48 *Record of the Association of the Bar of the City of New York* 589 (1993). See also Introduction to Munich Code, *supra*, at S-7 to S-9.

15 We have considered whether it is necessary or important to deal separately with the antitrust laws of less developed countries and newly industrializing or newly reindustrializing economies. We decided that it is not, because, to the extent that

such nations' antitrust laws are different from US antitrust, the substantive differences are largely along lines of protecting small and middle-sized business, providing them with opportunity, or protecting them against abuses by powerful firms. This tilt goes in the direction of (though sometimes further than) EU law and the concept can normally be captured by differences between US and EU law.

The antitrust law of the recently decommunized nations also has a mission to open markets at vertical stages of competition, in order to allow market forces to determine the efficient degree of vertical integration. Such nations may face a complicated calculus in balancing the need to provide incentives to invest in creating markets where none existed for forty to ninety years and the virtues of freer access to markets. Experts continue to debate whether various state monopolies should be broken up (and their markets open to competition) prior to privatization, or thereafter. See, e.g. P. Joskow and R. Schmalensee, 'Competition Policy in Russia during and after Privatization', *Brookings Papers on Economic Activity (Microeconomics)*, 301–74 (1994). Thus, different conditions may lead to differences in law. Also, the circumstance of enormous monopolies created by state command has led to a mandate for demonopolization which is not paralleled in nations whose economies have grown by free enterprise.

LDC and NIC competition policy is often most divergent from US and EU law not on the substantive content of the law but with respect to exceptions and derogations from it, e.g. allowing state-facilitated cartels. This state action/industrial policy problem must be considered separately, for if antitrust policy is overwhelmed by government restraints in areas of international trade and foreign competition, harmonization of antitrust rules would have little meaning.

16 This conclusion is especially apt when it comes to assessing the direction of Japanese competition policy. There we may expect to see increasing adoption of portions of US and EU competition policy, along with enforcement that lags behind good intentions. Absorption of US and EU principles is likely to reflect continuing pressures on Japan to open up its markets and thus to stimulate 'fair' competition in the allegedly protected sectors of the economy and to reduce collusive practices, such as 'dango', which could not work if foreign suppliers were not blocked from competition with the members of the informal cartels.

17 For further explanation of this welfare measure, see J. A. Ordover, 'Transnational Antitrust and Economics', in B. Hawk (ed.), 1984 *Fordham Corp. L. Inst.*, especially at 237–41 (1985).

18 See E. Helpman and P. Krugman, *Trade Policy and Market Structure* (1989), chapter 5.

19 If a subsidy calculated to carry the beneficiary over 'rough times' is withdrawn gradually but according to a tight schedule and it is expected that the firms' future revenues will be sufficient to pay back the subsidy, the subsidy may be appropriate. This could be the case if the firms' exit would have adverse external consequences which the firms disregard in making their exit decisions.

20 The downward spiral, however, is not the only reason to embrace a one-world view. Even without the downward spiral problem, there are gains to be made in trade and competition from removing rather than devising market impediments. Although aggregate figures on the costs of various impediments to international competition are difficult to obtain and evaluate, some insights can be obtained from considering the potential gains from trade liberalization. Thus, a recent study by the GATT secretariat predicts an annual potential gain in world income from the Uruguay Round in excess of $500 billion by the year 2005. See

'Sutherland warns of US "mortal blow"', *Financial Times*, November 11, 1994, p. 5. According to the study, the European Union would gain $163.5 billion from the ratification of the agreement reflecting the results of the round, while the gains to the United States would be in the order of $120 billion. A similar study by Schott and Buurman estimates that the tariff cuts would increase US economic output by $65 billion a year by 2004. See J. Schott and J. Buurman, *The Uruguay Round: an Assessment* (1994).

21 See J.A. Ordover and L. Goldberg, *supra* note 3, for some summary statistics on the economic costs of quotas and voluntary export restraints.

22 The European Union follows such a standard in principle, with the 'world welfare' standard narrowed to the welfare of the EU. In approving or disallowing state aid, the European Commission must assess the consequences of such aid to intra-community trade and competition. When state aid significantly distorts intra-community trade, it threatens the overriding objectives of the European Union, as stated in the Treaty of Rome. The treaty and implementing legislation set forth demanding standards for justification.

23 The standard could be informed by the EU law on the four freedoms and on the member states' obligation to facilitate the achievement of a common market. See *Procureur du Roi* v. *Dassonville*, Case 8/74, [1974] ECR 837. *Dassonville* has recently been weakened by *Keck and Mithouard*, Cases C-267 and 268/91, [1993] ECR (November 24, 1993), and its progeny.

24 For a fuller discussion of this proposal based on a hierarchy of industrial policies, see J.A. Ordover, 'Conflicts of Jurisdiction: Antitrust and Industrial Policy', 50 *Law & Contemporary Problems* 165–79 (1988).

25 If nations cannot agree on the hierarchy, they may, for the same reasons, be unwilling to subscribe to the 'world welfare' principle.

26 Recently, the United States and Canada jointly prosecuted, and obtained plea agreements, regarding an alleged thermal facsimile paper cartel in North America. See *United States* v. *Kanzaki Specialty Papers*, D. Mass. (July 14, 1994). Newspaper accounts report apparent price-raising activity in aluminium, partially facilitated by involvement of governments. See 'Foiled Competition: Don't Call It a Cartel, But World Aluminum Has Forged a New Order', *Wall St. J.*, June 9, 1994, p. 1.

27 Pub. L. No. 103-438, 108 Stat. 4597 (1994), amending 15 U.S.C. §§1311 *et seq.*

28 Switzerland has incorporated such a principal into its positive law. Private International Law of Switzerland, Art. 137(1).

29 Indeed, new cartel issues that are distinctly international are on the horizon. The UNCTAD secretariat has been working on the design of a global system of tradable permits for CO_2 emissions in order to reduce net CO_2 emissions in the world and thereby protect the climate. Nations would receive initial allotments of permits, which, thereafter, could be bought and sold. Anti-competitive strategies could distort the system and undermine its environmental benefits. For example, sets of oligopolists in industrialized nations could buy up permits, warehouse them, and raise the price of permits, which less developed countries need in greater quantities than developed countries. They could thereby raise the costs of their rivals in targeted markets. Or LDCs, which might be favoured with more permits than they initially need for their (usually) state-owned businesses, might in concert lease the rights at monopoly prices to their rivals in industrialized countries. Cartel questions, jurisdictional and choice-of-law questions, and government action questions all combine. Problems of monopolization and abuse of dominance are also implicated.

30 Antitrust injury is injury that flows from the anti-competitive aspect of a transaction or conduct. It is to be contrasted with injury from competition itself.

31 For justification, the restraints authorized must be designed to address a cognizable internal market problem and must be narrowly tailored to address that problem.

32 We use the term 'non-national' to mean any person or firm not located in the regulating nation.

33 See U.S. Government's Antitrust Enforcement Guidelines for International Operations, §3.131, Illustrative Example C (April 1995), printed at 4 *CCH Trade Reg. Rep.* ¶ 13,107.

34 See *Aspen Skiing Co.* v. *Aspen Highlands Skiing Corp.*, 472 U.S. 585 (1985); *United States* v. *American Telephone & Telegraph Co.*, 524 F. Supp. 1336, 1348–57, 1370–2 (D.D.C. 1981). Other nations and the European Union, under their abuse-of-dominance law, give greater weight to the exclusionary effect on small and middle-sized firms. See E. Fox, 'Monopolization and Dominance in the United States and the European Community – Efficiency, Opportunity, and Fairness', 61 *Notre Dame L. Rev.* 501 (1986).

35 Cf. *SCFC ILC* v. *Visa USA* 36 F. 3d 958 (10th Cir. 1994), cert. denied, ●●● U.S. ●●● (June 19, 1995). See also *Eastman Kodak Co.* v. *Image Technical Services*, 112 S. Ct. 2072 (1992).

36 US firms have made such claims regarding the Japanese automobile and glass markets.

37 See *U.S. Healthcare* v. *Healthsource*, 986 F. 2d 589 (1st Cir. 1993); *Valley Liquors* v. *Renfield Importers* 822 F. 2d 656 (7th Cir. 1987). But cf. *United States* v. *Pilkington plc*, 59 Fed. Reg. 30604 (June 14, 1994) (Proposed Final Judgement and Competitive Impact Statement).

38 See Andreas F. Lowenfeld, *Public Controls on International Trade* §2 and generally (2d ed. 1983).

39 It may be that most anti-competitive vertical restraints are, at core, horizontal restraints. It is therefore important that efficiency justifications for true vertical restraints be fully aired.

40 See, for application of the EU standard, *Gemeente Almelo & Ors* v. *Energieibedriif IJsselmij* (Case C-3939/92) (not yet reported), judgement delivered 27 April 1994 (ECJ), decision summarized at 4 *Comm. Mkt. Law Rep.* (CCH) ¶ 97,409.

41 *Consten* and *Grundig* v. *Commission*, [1966] ECR 299.

42 For EU case law, see, e.g. *Scholler Lebensmittel GmbH & Co.* [1993] 2 CEC 2,101 and *Langnese-Iglo* [1993] 2 CEC 2,123.

43 Agreements that distort competition must be notified to the EU commission, and they are subject to exemption or disapproval. 'Block exemptions' exist for some of the most common forms of transactions, such as exclusive dealing. The regulations enacting the block exemptions list clauses that are permitted and clauses that are prohibited. If an agreement contains only permissible clauses, it falls within the block exemption and the enterprise need not undertake the cumbersome and uncertain individual notification procedure.

44 But compare *United States* v. *Microsoft Corp.*, D.D.C. 1994 (consent decree), *CCH Trade Reg. Rep.* ¶ 50,764.

45 *Aerospatiale-Alenia/de Havilland*, O.J. L 334/42 (Commission Decision 1991).

46 See, e.g. *Mannesmann Vallourec/Ilva*, O.J. L 102/15 (Commission Decision 1994).

47 The US agencies, however, explicitly take efficiencies into account in deciding whether to sue. See 1992 *U.S. Agency Merger Guidelines* at point 4. See B. Fox and E. Fox, 2 *Corporate Acquisitions & Mergers* §8.02 [2][j] (revised 1995).

48 Canadian Competition Act §96 (1985).

49 For harm in the nations in which the merging parties are located, national law should be adequate.

50 The US agencies may assert jurisdiction in cases of mergers of two foreign firms with no assets or subsidiaries in the United States. See International Guidelines, *supra* note 33, Example H, and *Matter of Institut Mérieux S.A.*, 1990 FTC Lexis 291 (consent order August 6, 1990). This outreach, however, may create international tensions. See Y. Ohara, 'The New U.S. Policy on the Extraterritorial Application of Antitrust Laws, and Japan's Response', 17 *World Competition* 49 (1994).

51 See *Merger Cases in the Real World: a Study of Merger Control Procedures* (1994), known as the Whish/Wood Report. For proposals regarding convergence of merger process, see chapter 17 of this volume.

52 Perhaps ironically, the US statute recently passed to facilitate information exchanges (see note 27 *supra*) excludes pre-merger notification filing from the qualified waiver of confidentiality.

53 See the protocol developed by the ABA Antitrust Section NAFTA Task Force. NAFTA Task Force Report, *supra* note 7, chapter 4.

54 See E. Fox, 'Monopolization and Dominance', *supra* note 34, 61 *Notre Dame L. Rev.* at 1,011.

55 See p. 420.

56 Foreign sovereign compulsion is largely an equity doctrine devised lest innocent persons or firms get caught in the middle of conflicting state commands. The foreign sovereign compulsion defence would currently be available if, for example, nation A ordered its firms that wished to export widgets to join an export cartel for widgets. If, under the agreement suggested herein, nation A should agree not to order export cartels, its order would be unlawful and should give the exporter no protection. In any event, the foreign sovereign compulsion defence should at least be limited as follows. No one shall have the advantage of a foreign sovereign compulsion defence unless the compulsion is disclosed to the importing nation's antitrust authorities before the 'compelled' action is commenced. Even then, if the importer into the regulating nation receives supracompetitive profits by reason of its anti-competitive action, it may fairly be required to disgorge the extra profits.

57 While US law does not prohibit state subsidies as such, the Supreme Court has recognized their parochial nature and their interference with trade and competition on the merits, and it has recently stricken, under the Commerce Clause, a state plan to subsidize state milk farmers linked with a non-discriminatory milk tax. *West Lynn Creamery* v. *Healy*, 129 L. Ed. 2d 157 (1994).

58 Defense Production Act of 1950 as amended, §721, 50 U.S.C. §§2,062 *et seq.*

59 National Cooperative Research and Production Act of 1993, §7, 15 U.S.C. §§4,301–5.

ACKNOWLEDGEMENTS

Eleanor M. Fox is Walter Derenberg Professor of Trade Regulation at New York University School of Law. Janusz A. Ordover is Professor of Economics at New York University. The authors thank William Comanor and Leonard Waverman for their helpful comments.

17

THE HARMONIZATION OF INTERNATIONAL COMPETITION LAW ENFORCEMENT

Donald I. Baker, A. Neil Campbell,
Michael J. Reynolds and J. William Rowley

INTRODUCTION

This chapter explores how competition law agencies can make enforcement activities more effective and efficient when two or more countries are involved. Some benefits may be available through greater cooperation within the framework of existing legal rules and institutions, while others will depend upon the development of common standards. The term 'harmonization' is used here to refer to both cooperation and convergence.

Reasons for pursuing harmonization

Two driving forces have put harmonization on the policy agenda. The first is the globalization of economic activity over the past quarter of a century. This has expanded trade and investment flows, increased competitive interactions which cut across individual national economies, and generated an explosion of international mergers, joint ventures and strategic alliances.[1] The second is the enactment or expansion of competition laws, including merger pre-notification requirements, by many nations, and the extraterritorial application of such laws.[2] Both these developments have contributed to uncertainty, complex legal disputes, political conflicts and multiplying costs.

The three main rationales for harmonization are enhanced global economic efficiency, reduced 'system friction',[3] and decreased transaction costs.[4] As the OECD has observed, 'trade liberalisation and globalisation change the basic features of competition in ways that increase the potential benefits to be derived from greater competition policy convergence and greater international cooperation'.[5] However, harmonization also has costs associated with it, while diversity respects cultural differences, preserves sovereignty and allows experimentation.[6] Thus, although quantification is difficult, the up-front costs of any harmonization initiative should be viewed as an investment which needs to be justified by the global benefits (net of costs) expected to be generated.

Harmonization of enforcement activities and procedures (as distinct from substantive laws) seeks primarily to reduce public and private transaction costs. However, as the OECD has recognized, this also 'appears to hold considerable potential' for 'reducing friction' and for promoting the objective of global allocative efficiency which is at the heart of both competition and trade policy.[7] In other words, effective international enforcement is important for the same reason as effective domestic enforcement: halting and deterring economic welfare losses (e.g. the discovery and prosecution of an international cartel).

Progress on process matters may also smooth the path of substantive harmonization. While enforcement harmonization need not precede substantive harmonization, this chapter is based on the assumption that material differences in substantive competition laws will remain for the foreseeable future, whether because of differing policy goals, legal traditions or inertia. It has also been assumed that the basic institutional design of domestic competition law agencies will continue largely unchanged, with the result that the division of responsibility for investigation, prosecution and adjudication activities will vary considerably between jurisdictions.[8] The purpose of the chapter is to explore what progress might be made in the context of existing substantive laws and institutions,[9] without denigrating more ambitious efforts to develop a world antitrust code and/or international antitrust agencies.

Ex-ante and ex-post investigations

Opportunities for public and private transaction cost savings depend heavily upon the nature of the investigation and the incentives of the parties involved. Mergers and other forward-looking transactions are typically time-sensitive. If a transaction is subject to ex-ante review in a number of jurisdictions, the parties will typically prefer the various reviews to run on a parallel and expeditious time track.[10] A coordinated approach may also be beneficial for the enforcement agencies (e.g. by facilitating information gathering and a faster, more refined analysis of relevant markets, the transaction's competitive effects and any remedial measures which may be required). Enforcement agencies may have less to gain from pursuing simultaneous investigations of past conduct unless cross-border evidence-gathering is necessary.[11] The targets of an investigation will also often have less enthusiasm for parallel investigations and prompt decisions by all enforcement agencies in these situations.

As a practical matter, mergers seem to be the area where governments, businesses and antitrust enforcement agencies are all likely to obtain significant benefits from harmonization initiatives. Thus, while the possibilities of increased enforcement cooperation in all areas of competition law are worth exploring, appendix 17.1 attempts to apply the general principles discussed below to the design of harmonized procedures for reviewing international mergers.

FUNDAMENTAL PRINCIPLES

Six fundamental principles would provide a foundation for progress towards enforcement harmonization. Since none of them seems radical, they should form a workable point of departure for concrete bilateral and/or multilateral discussions.

National treatment

National treatment is a cornerstone of most international trade agreements.[12] The OECD has identified it as a basic principle in the competition as well as the trade policy context.[13] Not surprisingly, such a non-discrimination provision was also included in the *Draft International Antitrust Code* published in 1993 by a group based at the Max Planck Institute.[14] The most obvious application of a national treatment principle in the competition policy context is to tear down blatantly discriminatory substantive provisions such as export cartel exemptions.[15] At the same time, there is simply no good reason to countenance procedural rules or enforcement practices which discriminate against foreign firms or activities.[16]

National treatment is a 'one-way' non-discrimination principle. It precludes foreign entities being treated less favourably than domestic ones, but not the reverse. For example, imposing more rigorous pre-notification obligations on mergers which involve a foreign rather than a domestic acquirer would be inconsistent with the principle of national treatment. On the other hand, a law which treats foreign firms more leniently (as occurs under certain aspects of the US pre-merger notification rules[17]) is generally unobjectionable – such an approach will tend to lower system friction risks and compliance burdens.

A broader 'two-way' non-discrimination principle would be neither necessary nor desirable. Domestic firms might like, but normally do not have any real need of, protection against discrimination (relative to foreign entities) by their own governments and enforcement agencies. The main effect of a rigid two-way discrimination rule would be that countries which otherwise might voluntarily elect to reduce legal risks or burdens for foreign entities would be discouraged from doing so.

Extraterritoriality tempered by comity

While extraterritorial application of competition laws is often criticized (particularly outside of the United States), Fox and Ordover point out that 'if each nation draws into its shell, transnational restraints will go unremedied'.[18] Thus, absent a seamless international antitrust code, global allocative efficiency is better served by overlapping jurisdiction (e.g. based on an 'effects test') than by gaps in jurisdiction which would allow anti-competitive conduct to fall between the cracks of domestic competition law regimes.[19] Extraterritoriality becomes even more desirable if its major disadvantages – the potential for inefficiency and system friction – are effectively moderated by comity, which the OECD has described as 'an important principle underlying competition policy and its enforcement'.[20]

'Traditional comity' (sometimes referred to as 'negative comity', although no pejorative connotation is implied[21]) is essentially a doctrine of politeness and good manners between nations. It deals with the host of factors that one sovereign ought to consider in deciding whether or not to pursue a case involving firms or conduct in another jurisdiction. Traditional comity may enter into competition law decision-making in two places:

1 *The enforcement stage.* An enforcement agency in one country may decide that, instead of pursuing a case, it will defer to the interests and efforts of an agency in another country. For example, the groundbreaking '*US–EU MOU*' sets out a non-exhaustive list of six relevant factors which will be considered 'in seeking an appropriate accommodation of the competing interests'.[22] Unilaterally, the US Department of Justice ('DOJ') applies a similar set of eight comity factors in deciding whether to prosecute cases where 'significant interests of any foreign sovereign would be affected'.[23]

2 *The adjudication stage.* If an enforcement agency acts, with or without consultation with its foreign counterparts, it still may face a motion that the case should be dismissed.[24] Whether and when a court in the United States (the jurisdiction with the most extensive comity jurisprudence) will exercise its discretion to dismiss proceedings brought by the DOJ or FTC on the basis of comity considerations remains somewhat uncertain.[25] The role of comity in actions initiated by private or state plaintiffs is also unclear, and could well differ in light of their lack of responsibility for the conduct of foreign relations.[26]

The US Supreme Court's closely divided 5:4 decision in *Hartford Insurance* confirmed the broad jurisdiction of US antitrust laws while paying scant attention to comity on the ground that there was no express conflict between the US and foreign laws in question.[27] As a result, the status of the comity doctrine in the United States is 'in a state of uncertainty'.[28] If comity is to temper the conflicts resulting from broad extraterritorial jurisdiction meaningfully and consistently, neither *ad hoc* decision-making by prosecutors and courts, nor a Memorandum of Understanding ('MOU') between enforcement agencies will be sufficient. A treaty which specifies the rules under which one nation's courts or enforcement agencies would defer to another's on the basis of comity is needed. Were such an exercise to be undertaken, the US *International Enforcement Guidelines*, the *Timberlane* decision and the *US–EU MOU* provide useful models upon which to build.[29]

Repeal of blocking statutes

Motivated in large part by perceived over-aggressiveness in the enforcement of US antitrust laws, many nations have enacted 'blocking statutes'.[30] Such legislation typically seeks to:

1 Ensure that local authorities are notified by private parties when another jurisdiction is attempting to take extraterritorial action.
2 Prevent the transmission of documents and other potential evidence to foreign enforcement agencies or private plaintiffs (on pain of a fine or perhaps even imprisonment).
3 Preclude local courts from assisting foreign enforcement agencies or private plaintiffs to gather evidence through discovery or other means.
4 Deny recognition and enforcement of foreign damage awards (or at least the portion exceeding single damages) in local courts;
5 Provide a right of action under which local parties can attempt to 'claw back' all or part of damage awards which have already been paid.

As befits the political nature of sovereignty disputes, the activation of such blocking devices is commonly left to the discretion of the executive branch of government on a case-by-case basis.[31]

Blocking statutes are plainly incompatible with the objectives of enforcement harmonization. They tend to escalate rather than reduce system friction. More important, they throw up roadblocks to effective enforcement action against anti-competitive activity which has an international dimension, with the result that global allocative efficiency can be undermined. Successful enforcement harmonization would entail replacing sovereignty-orientated blocking statutes with strengthened comity commitments and closer collaboration on information gathering and exchanges.[32] This can be expected to be politically difficult,[33] but one hopes that countries will ultimately recognize their long-run interests are best served by reciprocal commitments not to impede legitimate and effective enforcement of competition laws.[34]

Positive comity

'Positive comity' differs from traditional comity in that the focus is on affirmative acts of assistance rather than on minimizing the negative effects of conflicts through restraint and deference.[35] It is not a buffer against conflict resulting from extraterritoriality; it provides a framework for cooperative initiatives. Application of this concept to the field of competition law is one of the key innovations in the *US–EU MOU*:

> If a Party believes that anticompetitive activities carried out on the territory of the other Party are adversely affecting its important interests, the first Party may notify the other Party and may request that the other Party's competition authorities initiate appropriate enforcement activities ....[36]

Positive comity should assist countries to prosecute conduct which both have an interest in but only one has the enforcement tools to reach effectively. Under the *US–EU MOU*, however, the notified agency is only obligated to consider the request for assistance and retains complete discretion as to whether to initiate or expand enforcement activities.[37] Stronger positive comity obligations could overcome this uncertainty, but might also result in scarce enforcement resources being diverted from other domestic priorities. This could be politically difficult to implement in many jurisdictions even though, looked at over the long term, there should be net benefits to all jurisdictions from reciprocal commitments which ensure effective cross-border enforcement of competition laws.

Transparency

Transparency of laws and law enforcement reduces uncertainty for private parties, fosters consistency in case-by-case decision-making, encourages public confidence in the law enforcement process and promotes learning. These benefits are particularly relevant in the international context because foreign laws and practices are more likely than domestic ones to be poorly understood and treated with suspicion. The OECD has accepted that transparency is a basic principle in both the competition and the trade policy contexts.[38]

As markets become more integrated, the actions of one competition law agency are increasingly likely to have an impact on business enterprises located in other countries. This being so, it becomes important for enforcement agencies in each nation to make information about their policies and specific decisions accessible not only to their foreign counterparts but to business enterprises and advisers in such countries.

Transparency obviously has costs associated with it, and ought therefore to be optimized rather than maximized. Unfortunately, officials in government departments or administrative agencies who are faced with many of the direct costs have little incentive to consider the significant public benefits associated with transparency. Indeed, there will often be a personal incentive to avoid transparency in order to minimize the risk of embarrassment or criticism which results when decision-making is open to close public scrutiny. As a result, it may be necessary to specify minimum standards of transparency in domestic legislation and/or international agreements.

General guidance about enforcement policies and practices can be provided through a number of vehicles, including:

1 *Annual reports.* The European Commission produces annual reports on competition policy whose comprehensiveness and analytical commentary are worthy of emulation.

2 *Speeches.* The speeches of agency officials can provide a valuable mechanism for informing the interested public of leading-edge develop-ments and policy changes, especially if the written text is subsequently made available (as is often done by competition law enforcement officials in countries such as Canada and the United States).

3 *Guidelines.* Agencies in several countries have published detailed guidelines with respect to particular competition law matters. To date most have focused on mergers, and the ABA's *International Antitrust Report* rightly encouraged the expansion of this practice.[39] The publication of enforcement guidelines could usefully be extended to many other areas where uncertainty exists, including procedural as well as substantive matters. For example, a sensible recommendation of the OECD's *Merger Convergence Project* is that each country draw up guidelines outlining the practical operation of its confidentiality laws and their application in cross-border situations.[40] Guidance on other international issues (e.g. extraterritorial jurisdiction), as has been provided by the US enforcement agencies,[41] is also extremely useful.

4 *Repository.* A central repository of competition legislation and related regulations, policies, enforcement guidelines and the like would be invaluable.[42] This depends on having a suitable international institution to take on the administrative responsibilities. Two existing institutions which might fulfil this function in the competition law context are the OECD's Committee on Competition Law and Policy and the Antitrust and Trade Committee of the International Bar Association.[43]

5 *'Country reports'.* An external device with great potential for promoting transparency is the preparation of periodic reports on individual countries' practices by an institution with appropriate expertise and impartiality. This currently occurs with respect to trade policy matters under the GATT. It has also been used by the OECD in areas such as capital movements.[44]

While general disclosure about policies and practices is invaluable, the application of laws and/or enforcement guidelines to individual cases cannot fully be appreciated without case-specific disclosures. Here too, many vehicles are available including:

1 *Adjudicative decisions.* In most competition law systems ample information becomes publicly available when a case proceeds through adjudication. A written decision will typically summarize issues, key facts, major arguments, legal interpretations and the reasons for the decision, all of which may be further supplemented by an extensive public record of the proceedings.

2 *Announcement of enforcement actions.* Disclosure about significant competition law enforcement or non-enforcement decisions in most jurisdictions is spotty. Simple techniques such as press releases could be utilized much more frequently and the depth of information disclosed could be improved.

3 *Administrative guidance.* In some countries it is possible for private parties to obtain oral and/or written advice from enforcement officials regarding the legality of proposed conduct.[45] Although such mechanisms are useful even if the advice is not made available to the public, much more could be done to disseminate the gist of important policy determinations while preserving the anonymity of the parties involved.[46]

4 *Case settlements.* The consent decree formalities in the US *Tunney Act* are a good illustration of how transparency can be achieved when enforcement agencies enter into settlements with private parties.[47] Most jurisdictions currently disclose much less information about the nature and reasons for acceptance of settlements.

For investigations which involve more than one country, it generally would be beneficial for enforcement agencies, private parties and the public in each jurisdiction to be aware of significant steps taken elsewhere. One way to promote this objective would be for enforcement agencies to agree to notify each other when an investigation is commenced, formal adjudicative or injunctive proceedings are launched, or a file is closed.[48] Greater use of press releases or similar announcements regarding both enforcement and non-enforcement decisions[49] would further contribute to transparency in cases with an international dimension, especially if made available in translated form in the various countries affected.

Situational opting in (or opting out)

It is difficult to predict precisely when specific enforcement harmonization steps will yield sizeable benefits. Even though there is a strong general trend towards globalization, the benefits from cooperation and convergence will depend on marketplace factors specific to each individual transaction or investigation. For example, a merger involving direct competitors in a truly global market usually will be well suited to interagency collaboration because similar issues will need to be addressed in each jurisdiction. On the other hand, the benefits from a harmonized approach to merger review will be much more modest where few jurisdictions are affected, the relevant geographic markets are clearly local rather than supra-national,[50] market structure and competitive conditions differ greatly, and competition concerns arising in any country would most naturally be remedied by divestiture of one of the merging parties' local subsidiaries.[51]

For these reasons harmonization initiatives should seek to provide enforcement agencies and private parties with the flexibility to capture the benefits which they perceive to be available. For example, enforcement agencies could agree to follow an international merger review protocol for transactions which merging parties so elect (e.g. because of potential time or cost savings).[52] Similarly, it is easier to envision acceptance of permissive rules for exchanging confidential information between enforcement agencies than mandatory obligations.[53]

While it is convenient to think in terms of an 'opt-in' concept, in some areas the more sensible alternative may be to establish a generally applicable scheme from which individual enforcement agencies or private parties can opt out, either in specified circumstances or at their absolute discretion. The default arrangement which is chosen may or may not be significant, depending upon the cost, timing, symbolic and other incentive implications facing the decision-maker. In general, an opt-out approach is appropriate where the objective is to soften a mandatory rule by building in a 'safety valve', whereas an opt-in approach works well when good incentives for participation are available.[54]

The *US–EU MOU* contemplates coordination of enforcement activities where the agencies in each jurisdiction 'agree that it is in their mutual interest'.[55] The factors to be considered in reaching such decisions are noteworthy: making more efficient use of enforcement resources, relative abilities to obtain information relevant to the investigation, attainment of enforcement objectives and the possibility of reducing costs incurred by persons under investigation.[56] Absent confidentiality constraints,[57] this type of general framework would appear to be promising, but it remains to be seen whether the incentives to agency participation will be sufficient to ensure that the potential benefits are captured.[58]

BILATERAL COOPERATION AND CONVERGENCE

Finding common ground for harmonization will be simplest on a bilateral basis. Greater cooperation and convergence should also be possible because interagency trust and monitoring are easier to achieve and maintain when only two parties are involved.[59] However, a patchwork of differing bilateral arrangements would introduce complexities and anomalies, would be cumbersome when dealing with conduct which extends beyond a particular bilateral pairing, and would fail to capture the full potential benefits of widespread multilateral harmonization. Ideally, bilateral progress in the short term will blaze the trail for more broadly based harmonization over time.

There are three main techniques for bilateral cooperation amongst competition law authorities: informal contacts, memoranda of understanding and treaties.

Informal bilateral contacts

The simplest approach, yet one whose importance should not be underestimated, is regular informal bilateral contact. Such contact already occurs often and more could be done without resort to legislative or regulatory enactments. The benefits are likely to be maximized if contacts occur at the level of line officials in addition to the higher echelons. Analytical methods and emerging issues are among the areas where collaboration may be especially fruitful. Case-specific contacts would also be invaluable, although at present they are inhibited by confidentiality rules.[60]

Memoranda of understanding

Memoranda of understanding can be negotiated and implemented more readily than formal treaties.[61] These 'executive agreements' may just memorialize existing working relationships, or they may effect real change in the nature and extent of agency interactions and internal activities. An MOU enables the enforcement agencies in two countries to monitor each other from a close vantage point and act accordingly (albeit unilaterally). In this sense it provides something of an accountability system.

To the extent that harmonization entails an expansion of cooperation among enforcement agencies, MOUs can achieve significant results.[62] Of course, where harmonization is constrained by existing statutory rules (e.g. legislated confidentiality provisions, which are common in many countries) an MOU will not be sufficient.[63] Similarly, the rights and interests of parties independent of a federal government (including those of state governments and private plaintiffs, which are so important in the United States[64]) often cannot be bound except by a formal treaty.

Bilateral treaties

Generic mutual legal assistance treaties ('MLATs') typically do not apply to the realm of competition law. (The notable exception is the *Canada–US MLAT*,[65] which has recently been invoked effectively by the Canadian and US enforcement agencies.[66]) Nor have customized competition law treaties yet been used to combat the limitations of MOUs. The key advantage of these treaty mechanisms (perhaps supported by implementing legislation[67]) is the potential to overcome limitations imposed by domestic statutory rules. This opens up many additional information gathering and exchange possibilities.[68]

An MLAT normally entitles signatories to request various types of assistance from each other, including the use of formal investigative powers. MLATs are potentially powerful tools, but they have traditionally been restricted to criminal matters.[69] To the extent that competition law in many jurisdictions is non-criminal, an MLAT will not be helpful. This restriction may even have the perverse effect of deterring the enforcement agency in the requesting jurisdiction from switching to a civil investigation when that is the better and fairer course of action.

A bilateral competition law treaty offers two main advantages over an MLAT. It could readily be designed to cover civil as well as criminal aspects of competition law. It could include those areas of competition law where the signatories have similar policy orientations and exclude others where they do not (e.g. the European Union's state aid provisions have no parallel in many other nations' competition laws). In addition, procedural arrangements could be tailored to the needs of competition law enforcement rather than being constrained by rules which have been created for more general use. Although bilateral competition law treaties have not yet been developed, these advantages make them an attractive mechanism for improving international competition law enforcement in the future.

MULTINATIONAL COOPERATION AND CONVERGENCE

The advantages and disadvantages of a multilateral approach are largely the converse of those of proceeding bilaterally.[70] Greater jurisdictional coverage will increase the potential magnitude of benefits available from harmonization. However, the likelihood of a clear and far-reaching agreement will tend to decrease as more jurisdictions become involved, and there may be a serious 'lowest common denominator' effect.

There are several possible approaches for pursuing multilateral cooperation and convergence at the enforcement level. This chapter considers three existing institutions which could play a significant role, and also examines the possibility of a multilateral competition law treaty which would be implemented by signatory nations without any new institutional infrastructure.

GATT and the World Trade Organization

There have been many suggestions that competition policy (or at least trade-related aspects of it) is a prime subject for the new World Trade Organization.[71] A group at the Max Planck Institute has gone so far as drafting a detailed proposal setting out how this might work.[72] The broad membership of the GATT/WTO makes this concept appealing because international competition concerns can arise wherever international trade flows exist.[73] Building upon the GATT/WTO is also likely to be easier and more credible than establishing a customized institutional framework for international competition law enforcement from scratch.

Making progress would be challenging because of the great diversity between countries which must be addressed and the political complexities of negotiations involving many participants. Nevertheless, the successful completion of the GATT Uruguay Round illustrates that these kinds of challenges can be overcome.

GATT procedures and culture might also require adaptation to meet the needs of competition regulation. Government-to-government dealings are the focus in GATT, whereas competition law is primarily concerned with states policing private conduct and litigation between private parties. There is also a risk that trade policy concepts and approaches would overwhelm and dilute competition policy in such a venue (e.g. anti-dumping regimes might continue to be supported notwithstanding their anti-competitive character).

In any event, it seems unlikely that the GATT/WTO would become a forum of competition law harmonization at the enforcement level unless or until a substantive 'world competition code' is put in place. Assuming for present purposes that this is not imminent (an assumption which is reinforced by the cool reception the *Draft International Antitrust Code* has received), this chapter focuses on other institutions and mechanisms which appear to offer better prospects for short-term progress on enforcement harmonization.

The Organisation for Economic Cooperation and Development

The OECD's Committee on Competition Law and Policy ('CCLP') provides a regular forum for discussions between enforcement agencies and fosters the development of professional relationships among senior officials. The CCLP has compiled annual reports and other useful surveys on various aspects of competition laws in OECD countries.[74] It is also examining possibilities for convergence of substantive competition laws and, in conjunction with the OECD's Trade Committee, the interface between competition and trade policies and the prospects for integrating competition rules into a multilateral framework.[75]

The OECD's limited membership is both a blessing and a constraint. The development of a consensus on any issue is likely to be easier among two dozen (mostly industrialized) countries than among a much larger and more diverse group as would be involved through the GATT. On the other hand, to the extent that economic activity straddles OECD member and non-member countries, some of the potential benefits from harmonization may be left on the table by proceeding through the OECD.

The OECD's *Recommendation Concerning Restrictive Business Practices*[76] can be thought of as the multinational equivalent of bilateral MOU's. It is the enforcement analogy to a non-binding model competition law, and as such provides a benchmark for unilateral or bilateral convergence. However, the OECD's pronouncement has now been eclipsed by the more sophisticated *US–EU MOU*. Thus it would be worth while for the CCLP to revisit this area with a view to incorporating features of the US–EU model as well as breaking new ground in some of the challenging areas outlined below.

The International Bar Association

Bar associations in many countries serve a valuable function in monitoring the activities of competition law enforcement agencies and providing input regarding matters of policy and practice. The comparable international institution is the Antitrust and Trade Committee of the International Bar Association ('ATC').[77]

Historically, the ATC has tended to focus on seminars and studies dealing with mergers and other competition matters. More recently it has also begun to explore formal liaison with major competition law agencies and the preparation of annual country reports. With a membership of 1,500 practising lawyers and corporate counsel, drawn from virtually every country with competition laws, the ATC is well positioned to take on a more prominent role as a proponent for, monitor of and adviser regarding enforcement harmonization initiatives.

A multilateral enforcement treaty

A multilateral treaty focusing on enforcement would not need to await the development of a substantive world competition code, nor would an international institution be required for implementation. As already noted, the primary significance of the treaty approach is that statutory barriers to enforcement harmonization can be tackled.[78]

How to get from here to there presents a challenge. An initial arrangement amongst a small group of countries would be the easiest way to start. This could facilitate increasing harmonization over time by either providing a model for others to follow and/or by including an accession clause allowing new members to join once certain minimum entrance qualifications are met.

Various multilateral groupings might be good candidates for the development of such a treaty. The US–EU–Japan 'triad' or the 'G-7 nations' are attractive possibilities because they account for a large portion of global economic activity. Regional trading blocs are also promising alternatives because they have shared interests in the effective functioning of their markets for goods and services. The European Union is obviously most advanced in this respect, but does not provide a readily generalizable model because the level of economic and political integration is unusually high (i.e. approaching a federation in many ways). NAFTA, on the other hand, creates a loosely integrated free trade area in which Canada, the United States and Mexico have announced an intention to 'cooperate on issues of competition law enforcement policy, including mutual legal assistance, notification, consultation and exchange of information' and to establish a working group to explore the relationship between competition and trade policies.[79] Existing Canada–US bilateral arrangements[80] provide a foundation which could be built upon in the course of this process.

INFORMATION GATHERING

Information gathering is a critical facet of almost every competition law investigation. Thus the public and private transaction cost savings from improving this process are potentially substantial. The key question is how coordinated approaches can be used to make the information gathering process more effective and efficient for enforcement agencies and/or less burdensome for private parties.[81]

Formal investigative powers

Most enforcement agencies gather information through both voluntary cooperation of private parties and the use of statutory investigative powers. Harmonizing these formal powers would not be easy because they are shaped by each country's culture, traditions and legal system.[82] However, the transaction cost savings in the area of information gathering have little to do with the specific formalities which a particular agency must follow. The main opportunities for gains come from coordination of information requests and from agencies assisting each other to gather relevant information, irrespective of how they go about doing so. Initiatives on either of these fronts would also require that the protection of legal privileges be given careful consideration.

Coordinated requests for information

A requirement that agencies coordinate information requests on all international investigations obviously would be too rigid. However, enforcement agencies should have this option available for cases where cost savings or other benefits seem attainable. There will certainly be situations where agencies in multiple countries would benefit by jointly considering (even in quick, informal telephone exchanges) what information is likely to be relevant, as well as in knowing that each is asking for the same information (or at least complementary information in the same form based on different geographical markets).[83] Equally, there are bound to be some advantages to recipients in responding to coordinated requests, especially if common definitions and search limitations (e.g. time periods for which documents must be produced) are used.[84]

Three basic levels of collaboration could be considered. The most extensive would be a single request for information designed jointly by multiple agencies (perhaps under the leadership of a 'lead jurisdiction') and issued to the relevant parties in each country. This would be most appropriate where the subject matter is not country-specific (e.g. product market definition[85]). Alternatively, individual agencies could issue separate information requests which are tailored to each country on the basis of general collaboration as to issues to be covered, terminology, time periods, and perhaps standard questions. An even less integrated approach which nevertheless may be useful in some situations is for an agency to seek input from other agencies on a request for information which it is preparing unilaterally.

There do not appear to be major legal barriers to enforcement agencies coordinating requests for documents or other information requests. It should be possible without violating existing confidentiality laws in most cases, so long as the information request does not recite facts received in confidence.[86] Whether coordinated requests for information will actually come into common use depends on whether enforcement agencies perceive the cost savings and/or increased effectiveness of such collaboration to be worth the effort. In many cases the benefits may not be substantial, and separate investigations will be appropriate.[87]

If coordinated information requests are issued, it becomes necessary to consider how modifications and limitations should be handled. Ideally, a private party which obtains a limitation on a request from one enforcement agency (e.g. on the scope of a question or the time period to be covered in a response) would like the limitation to apply to all agencies' requests. It would therefore be desirable for the cooperating agencies to agree that one will act as a 'lead jurisdiction' with responsibility for negotiating such matters.[88] Time and resource savings should result for both the enforcement agencies and private parties.

Obtaining assistance from other agencies

Seeking the assistance of a foreign enforcement agency is the key ingredient of positive comity. The positive comity principle embodied in the *US–EU MOU* is purely voluntary.[89] Moreover, it is only contemplated that the assisting agency will use formal investigative powers upon the suspicion that its laws may have been violated in connection with conduct which is subject to its jurisdiction.[90] As long as the matter has a potential competitive effect in the jurisdictions of both the requesting agency and the assisting agency, the latter should be able to use its powers to assist the former. However, the European Commission would not be expected to aid the US DOJ or FTC in gathering evidence related to a purely US antitrust violation, or vice versa.

A more expansive approach has been employed in the securities law area. Under several recent MOUs, the US Securities and Exchange Commission ('SEC') can be deputized at the request of a foreign securities authority for the purpose of taking testimony and gathering evidence on behalf of that authority.[91] This can be done even if the incident being investigated does not involve a violation of US law. The SEC essentially has been granted the legal authority to do in civil matters what an MLAT would allow in the criminal area. As has been noted, this kind of cooperation is now also occurring with respect to criminal competition law matters under the *Canada–US MLAT*.[92]

There are clearly times when one enforcement agency would like to obtain the assistance of another in developing its own case. To make this work, existing statutory rules would have to be changed in two main ways:

1 The assisting agency would need to be authorized to use its investigative powers at the request of the foreign agency even where no violation of domestic competition laws is suspected.
2 Confidentiality rules would need to be relaxed to permit transmission of the evidence obtained to the requesting agency.[93]

Legislation enacted recently by the US Congress provides a model for implementing this approach in the competition law context. The *International Antitrust Enforcement Assistance Act of 1994*[94] ('*IAEAA*') is enabling legislation which allows the DOJ and FTC to enter into reciprocal Antitrust Mutual Assistance Agreements ('AMAAs') with competition law enforcement agencies in other jurisdictions, subject to certain confidentiality and other safeguards.[95] This two-tiered approach is attractive because customized agreements developed with various jurisdictions do not require individual approvals from the US Congress provided they comply with the minimum statutory standards.

The assistance which the DOJ and FTC are empowered (but not required) to provide to their foreign counterparts is to invoke their general powers in order to 'conduct investigations to obtain antitrust evidence relating to a possible violation of the foreign antitrust laws ... without regard to whether the conduct investigated violates any of the Federal antitrust laws'.[96] The US Attorney General may also apply to a Federal District Court for orders compelling testimony or documents to be provided in furtherance of an investigation by a foreign agency.[97] This is potentially very substantial assistance indeed.

Legal privileges

Several legal privileges may come into play in connection with a competition law investigation. Depending on the jurisdiction, these include privileges associated with obtaining legal advice, legal work product, contemplated litigation, self-incrimination, and perhaps business secrecy.[98] It is difficult to envision convergence on a common set of rules, since privileges are not specific to competition law – they have developed as part of the general legal system of each jurisdiction.[99] Fortunately, a single standard is not necessary to allow harmonized information gathering to go forward.

Reducing legal privileges which currently exist under domestic laws is not likely to be politically acceptable in most countries. Basic considerations of fairness would suggest the following:

1 *Information gathering.* In the jurisdiction where information is being gathered by an enforcement agency, whatever privileges exist in the domestic law should be available even if the investigation is being made at the request of a foreign agency.

2 *Transmission of non-privileged information.* If information which is not privileged in one jurisdiction is transmitted to an enforcement agency in another jurisdiction, private parties should be able to invoke whatever privileges may exist in the recipient jurisdiction.[100]

3 *Transmission of privileged information.* Information which is privileged in the transmitting jurisdiction should not be shareable with foreign agencies without the consent of the holder of the privilege.

EXCHANGES OF INFORMATION

Once agencies have gathered information, to what extent can they exchange or discuss it? Currently, there are few constraints if information comes from the public domain. Much information gathered in an investigation will be subject to confidentiality restrictions, however, with the result that opportunities for case-specific collaboration are seriously impaired.

Three basic approaches are available: limited or no exchanges of confidential information (essentially the *status quo*); allowing agencies the option of exchanging information when they so choose; or requiring an agency in possession of relevant information to make it available to other interested agencies, either automatically or upon request. The latter approach carries a risk of excessive, unnecessary and even counterproductive exchanges, while the former inhibits harmonization. The opting-in approach is clearly preferable.[101] Once the possibility of exchanges of confidential information is introduced, 'downstream' confidentiality protections and third party access must also be addressed.

Transmission of confidential information

Most countries provide protection for information given to competition law agencies under compulsion, and perhaps voluntarily as well.[102] The main reasons they do so are to protect commercially sensitive information, shield targets against harmful rumours at the investigational stage and encourage cooperation with investigations (including voluntary information disclosures) by both informants and targets. Since confidentiality rules are frequently legislated, the ability of enforcement agencies to cooperate with respect to what they receive is currently much more limited than with respect to what they request. For example, in the *US–EU MOU*, lofty-sounding promises under the heading 'Exchange of Information' are qualified by a reference to all existing domestic laws remaining unchanged as well as by the statement that 'neither Party is required to provide information ... [if it] ... (a) is prohibited by the law of the Party possessing the information, or (b) would be incompatible with [its] important interests ....'[103]

The OECD's CCLP has concluded that:

While recognizing the need to protect commercially sensitive information, effective enforcement of competition laws in a global economy would be facilitated if appropriate mechanisms existed for the sharing of confidential information among competition law enforcement officials. *Such mechanisms already exist in other policy fields, including taxation, money laundering and securities regulation.*[104]

Similarly, the ABA's *International Antitrust Report* recommended that concrete action be taken to break down the impediments to information exchange:

The sharing of information among enforcement agencies helps to ensure expedition and coordination in multilateral investigations. We applaud the information exchanges that currently take place between agencies, and initiatives to expand such exchanges. However, they are at present restricted to non-confidential information. This greatly limits the potential utility of these exchanges, since much of the truly pertinent information will have been received in confidence from the parties themselves or third parties.

We therefore propose that national confidentiality laws be amended to allow agencies to disclose facts submitted to them in confidence to another agency for the purpose of consultation and subsequent review.[105]

However, this recommendation was conditional upon the establishment of solid downstream protection against leaks or retransmission of information received by an agency.[106]

The logic of the ABA recommendation is compelling. The essential concept is a 'closed loop' which facilitates interagency cooperation without unfairly prejudicing the position of private parties to whom information belongs. Whether such an approach would be acceptable politically in a large number of jurisdictions is open to question.[107] However, the rapid passage of such enabling legislation in the United States[108] – and its reciprocal structure – provide a model which may generate momentum in other jurisdictions.

The *IAEAA* allows (but never requires) the US DOJ and FTC to provide to a foreign enforcement agency (which has entered into an AMAA) antitrust evidence in the possession of the US agencies that may assist in the enforcement of the foreign competition law.[109] While this provision is extremely broad, certain additional thresholds apply with respect to grand jury evidence, and merger pre-notification filings under the *Hart–Scott–Rodino Act* are completely exempt from disclosure.[110] Before any information is transmitted, the US agency must also make an affirmative 'determination' that the exchange is 'consistent with the public interest of the United States'.[111] This provision is one of the wild cards which will determine how successful the AMAA concept proves to be in practice; if the discretion is exercised too conservatively, foreign agencies may conclude that they are not much further ahead.

Downstream confidentiality protections

As has been noted, the ABA's *International Antitrust Report* directly linked interagency exchanges of confidential information to appropriate protection for such information once it is in the hands of the recipient agency:

> We recognize that governments and affected parties will be legitimately concerned about the submission of sensitive information to foreign government agencies: we therefore also propose that amending legislation be passed, where necessary, to ensure that the staff members of an agency to which such information has been disclosed are bound, on pain of criminal sanction, not to disclose that information to any other person.[112]

The *US–EU MOU* contains a simple provision which addresses downstream confidentiality:

> Each Party agrees to maintain, *to the fullest extent possible*, the confidentiality of any information provided to it in confidence by the other Party under this Agreement and to oppose, *to the fullest extent possible*, any application for disclosure of such information by a third party that is not authorized by the Party that supplied the information.[113]

This type of best efforts approach may be adequate in the context of an MOU which does not override existing statutory confidentiality rules.[114] However, it lacks the sanctions and full bullet-proofing against third party penetration necessary to create a closed loop which is sufficiently secure to justify the relaxation of domestic confidentiality restrictions.[115]

It is debatable whether sanctions need to be personal (as opposed to institutional) and criminal. The compatibility of personal criminal sanctions with legal traditions (not to mention constitutional constraints) and cultural factors in various jurisdictions is also open to question. However, the basic principle is sound: there must be sufficiently clear and strong incentives to discourage deliberate or careless leakages of information. Otherwise, countries are unlikely to be willing to enter into a regime which involves information exchanges, nor will private parties be inclined to disclose information to domestic agencies voluntarily in situations where there is a potential international dimension.

The public interest in effective competition law enforcement requires one obvious exception to the closed loop concept. Recipient agencies need to be able to use the confidential information they receive in any formal proceedings which result from an investigation, even if such proceedings are public.[116]

The negotiation of downstream confidentiality protection along these lines should not be overly problematic. Reciprocity and a basic level of trust are the building blocks. There are undoubtedly many nations which have a high degree of familiarity with, and confidence in the integrity of, each other's competition law enforcement agencies. Reciprocity in this context need not imply identical sanctions so long as each jurisdiction perceives the sanctions adopted elsewhere to be adequate deterrents to breaches of confidentiality.

The *IAEAA* addresses downstream confidentiality by placing the DOJ and FTC under a strict obligation not to disclose any information received from a foreign agency under an AMAA.[117] The sole exception is an accommodation to fairness: the defendant in a proceeding brought by the DOJ or FTC is entitled to whatever access (e.g. discovery rights) would otherwise be available under US law. Whether this chink in the armour will be viewed by foreign agencies as a concern remains to be seen.

The question of what constitutes 'confidential information' does not have to be a stumbling block. While one could contemplate a grandiose multilateral agreement regarding the types of information that would qualify as confidential, a much simpler approach is available. A workable default rule would be that any information exchanged between agencies must be treated as confidential by the recipient agency, unless:

1 The transmitting agency expressly indicates that the information is not confidential under its domestic law (e.g. because it is already public[118]).
2 A waiver of confidentiality is received from the party which provided the information.[119]

That said, it would be useful to attempt to develop criteria for individual jurisdictions to take into account in determining the types of information which will be accorded confidential status.[120]

Preventing third party access

Prevention of voluntary or accidental disclosure by recipient agencies is not sufficient to ensure the integrity of a closed loop. It is also essential to foreclose the possibility that third parties could use requests under freedom of information legislation and/or discovery processes in private litigation[121] – in either the transmitting or the recipient jurisdiction – to gain access to otherwise confidential information.[122]

It is currently possible that transmission of non-public information by an enforcement agency to its foreign counterparts could constitute a waiver of confidentiality. If so, other parties – particularly private parties or state attorneys-general in the United States – inevitably will seek to obtain confidential information that has been shared with a foreign agency.[123] Absent clear legislative protection, this scenario (or even uncertainty as to the possibility of it occurring) would seriously undermine the incentives to voluntary cooperation – both between enforcement agencies and to private parties considering whether to respond to requests for information.

There is a straightforward solution to this issue. Any treaty or legislation used to relax confidentiality rules should contain an affirmative provision that interagency transmissions of information do not destroy the confidential status of the material being exchanged, and do not make it subject to disclosure through freedom of information requests or discovery in private actions. This will ensure a truly closed loop which cannot be prised open by third parties in either the transmitting or the receiving jurisdiction.

The downstream confidentiality provision in the *IAEAA* forecloses third parties using US access to information legislation[124] to obtain material received by the DOJ or FTC from a foreign agency pursuant to an AMAA.[125] Moreover, the discovery of information in the hands of the US agencies is available only to defendants in proceedings the federal agencies have initiated.[126] However, it remains to be seen whether the creative US antitrust bar will be able to indirectly erode what appears to be an almost completely closed loop system.[127]

INTERAGENCY COMMUNICATIONS

There are many opportunities for productive interagency consultation beyond information gathering and exchange. They include notification of action taken or proposed; collaboration in areas of mutual interest; and formal consultations to avoid or resolve conflicts related to such matters as evidence gathering and appropriate remedies.

Notification

Notification is a central feature of the OECD's *Recommendation Concerning Restrictive Business Practices* as well as of most bilateral MOUs. The role of notification obligations is to guarantee a bare minimum level of awareness about the activities of other agencies, some of which may merit more extensive consultation. The OECD's *Recommendation* currently indicates that notifications should be made when the 'important interests' of another country are affected.[128] In practice this provision has not always operated as well as might be expected, which led the *Merger Convergence Project* to suggest that notification requirements should be clarified and expanded.[129] The ABA's *NAFTA Report* also emphasized the importance of notifications – including, to the extent possible, for private and state actions as well as proceedings initiated by federal agencies.[130]

Collaboration

Collaboration can be as simple as case officers informally discussing an issue of mutual interest such as market definition. At the other end of the spectrum is comprehensive coordination of an investigation[131] or even joint settlement negotiations with multinational corporations.[132] Individual circumstances will determine whether, when and what kind of discussions would be useful. This is an area where enforcement agencies should have the option – but not any obligation – to communicate as they see fit, subject to the confidentiality principles discussed above (i.e. officials should have unencumbered ability to discuss confidential information, but there must be a secure closed loop beyond which such information will not be retransmitted).[133]

The OECD's *Merger Convergence Project* discovered through interviews that there is little interagency contact at the case officer level,[134] and there is no reason to believe that the usual experience in non-merger cases is any more favourable.[135] At a minimum, it was suggested that 'it should be as easy as possible to discover who the relevant official to contact would be'.[136] However, it would have been useful to go further and explore how bureaucratic impediments and historical inertia might be replaced by an environment which actively encourages direct contacts among line officials.

Formal consultations

The appropriate rule for formal consultations has both opt-in and mandatory components. Since the primary objective is to address conflicts or divergent interests, it is sensible to allow consultations to be requested by any agency at any time while requiring that any such request be responded to promptly and in good faith. The ABA's *NAFTA Report* contains the useful suggestion that, when a notification is made, the agencies involved should consult with respect to choosing between deference to the jurisdiction most affected, coordinated investigations with a 'lead jurisdiction', and multiple investigations with no lead jurisdiction.[137]

The OECD's *Recommendation Concerning Restrictive Business Practices* requires that a request for consultations be given 'full and sympathetic consideration'.[138] Bilateral MOUs typically also provide a formal framework for consultations. Crisp timing norms for starting and ending such consultation processes would be useful – subject, of course, to the agencies involved agreeing upon different timing if they so desire. Even more valuable would be an agreed list of the criteria which would be taken into account, perhaps along the lines of the traditional and positive comity factors in the *US–EU MOU*.[139]

CONCLUDING OBSERVATIONS

The principal reasons for pursuing harmonization of competition law enforcement are to promote efficiency (i.e. transaction cost reductions for both agencies and private parties), to reduce system friction, and to enhance global economic welfare by ensuring effective detection, prosecution and deterrence of anti-competitive conduct having an international dimension. Regular close contact between enforcement agencies may also create a climate in which substantive harmonization is more readily attainable.

The fundamental principles which provide a basis for enforcement harmonization are neither complex nor controversial. National treatment simply requires that jurisdictions which are purporting to work cooperatively should not discriminate against each other – hardly an unreasonable expectation. A broad extraterritorial reach for domestic laws is better than leaving international anti-competitive conduct unregulated. Greater attention to traditional comity principles is preferable to the use of blocking statutes for resolving conflicts arising from the resulting overlaps in jurisdiction. Once positive as well as traditional comity considerations achieve recognition as appropriate balancing principles, the focus of debate can shift to the specific comity factors to be included in MOUs and/or treaties. Transparency – both at the level of policy and in case-by-case decision-making – is critical if enforcement agencies and private parties are to realize the potential benefits of harmonization. Finally, initiatives which rely to the maximum extent possible on voluntary opting in (or opting out) by enforcement agencies and private parties will allow cooperation and convergence to flourish where real gains appear to be attainable, without the counter-productive rigidity of mandatory rules.

Bilateral MOUs between enforcement agencies are the cornerstone of current international cooperation efforts. Formal treaties (or statutory amendments) should also be considered to overcome confidentiality and other legislative barriers to harmonization. In the long run, a broad-based multilateral approach would be better suited to the borderless nature of economic activity than a patchwork quilt of differing bilateral arrangements, but bilateral initiatives may be an important stepping stone.

Appendix 17.1 attempts to apply the foregoing principles and concepts to the area of merger review, which is a top candidate for initial harmonization efforts. It demonstrates that much could be accomplished through a multilateral treaty without the need for any additional institutional framework. The key features of such an 'International Merger Review System' include:

1 Simple rules for identifying transactions which would be subject to the system, supplemented by appropriate opt-in opportunities for merging parties and enforcement agencies.
2 Two-stage pre-notification with a relatively light initial filing.
3 Tight but attainable common time limits at each stage of the review process.
4 Clear rules permitting the sharing of confidential information between, but not beyond, the enforcement agencies reviewing a transaction.
5 Regular interagency communication.
6 A fairly high degree of transparency with respect to both general approaches (e.g. through enforcement guidelines) and case-specific decisions (e.g. through press releases).
7 Ideally, the availability of time-limited 'clearance' and/or 'authorization' mechanisms in each jurisdiction, at least for international merger transactions.[140]

APPENDIX 17.1
AN INTERNATIONAL MERGER REVIEW SYSTEM

Both the ABA's Special Committee on International Antitrust and the OECD's Committee on Competition Law and Policy have identified merger review procedures as a promising area for harmonization efforts.[141] It is the possibility of significant private, as well as public, transaction cost savings (including benefits related to reductions of delay and uncertainty) which makes this area attractive as an initial focus. Applying the principles in the main chapter, this appendix outlines concrete proposals which could form a basis for going forward.

Proposed approach

Some of the steps set out below could be implemented administratively, while others would involve legislative changes. There are political difficulties inherent in opening up legislative provisions to amendment in the US, the EU and probably most other jurisdictions. While these complications cannot be neglected, neither should they be allowed to deter the development of worthwhile harmonization proposals. One way to enhance the prospects of success is to work towards a treaty which leaves existing domestic merger review regimes untouched but commits the signatory jurisdictions to accept an 'overlay' of standardized timing rules, filing forms, information-sharing protocols and other procedures for transactions having a clear international dimension. This concept will be referred to as an International Merger Review System ('IMRS').[142]

The components

The remainder of this appendix describes the twelve core components of an IMRS which would not entail any separate institutional structure.

Pre-filing consultations with merging parties

In some jurisdictions there is a well established practice of enforcement officials being accessible for consultation with merging parties before any formal filing is made or an investigation is under way. This may relate to narrowing the scope of filing requirements and/or preliminary discussions of substantive or even remedial issues. For example, the Canadian Competition Bureau strongly encourages such consultations as a mechanism to facilitate timely, effective and compliance-orientated merger regulation. The availability of extensive pre-notification guidance is also one of the key reasons why the relatively young EU merger control system has worked well. It would be counter-productive if an IMRS undermined the provision of such guidance.

Merging parties will be loathe to seek pre-merger guidance from domestic agencies if faced with uncertainty as to whether sensitive information will be passed to authorities in other jurisdictions. It would therefore be important for an IMRS to include two clear rules along the following lines:

1 Confidential guidance received (or even the fact that guidance was sought) from an agency in an IMRS jurisdiction will not be disclosed to other IMRS jurisdictions unless or until the transaction becomes reviewable under the IMRS.[143]
2 Once a transaction does become subject to IMRS review, information received from and/or advice given to the merging parties by a domestic agency may (not must) be exchanged with other IMRS agencies reviewing the same transaction,[144] but only in accordance with the general 'closed system' confidentiality rules which would be an integral feature of any workable IMRS.[145]

Pre-notifiable transactions

Unlike many jurisdictions, the EU's pre-notification thresholds are jurisdiction-conferring.[146] While it would be a misnomer to use the term 'jurisdiction' with respect to an IMRS, some straightforward method is necessary to determine the transactions which would be subject to the IMRS rather than individual country regimes.

Most existing pre-notification regimes employ party and/or transaction size thresholds based on revenue ('turnover') and/or assets. The same approach could be used to design a 'universal' pre-notification threshold which would identify large transactions that also involve a sufficiently international dimension. The European Union's three-part threshold test[147] is probably the best available model if this approach were to be pursued, since it addresses degree of international activity as well as size.

However, a much simpler solution commends itself. Since the primary rationale for an IMRS process is to save public and private transaction costs which result when mergers are reviewed in multiple jurisdictions, the IMRS should be triggered automatically whenever a transaction is pre-notified under the domestic regimes of two or more IMRS signatories.

Non-pre-notifiable mergers are subject to substantive review in most jurisdictions. Thus merging parties may face multiple merger reviews even if their transaction is pre-notifiable in one or no country. In these situations, it would be desirable for merging parties to have the right to opt in to the IMRS if they desire the timing, certainty or other benefits which are available.[148]

A further useful possibility would be to allow any enforcement agency to 'bump' a merger under domestic review into the IMRS system.[149] This approach is not likely to be employed frequently, but might be attractive in cases where an agency desires international gathering of evidence or consultations about remedies. It is hard to see any serious down side to having such an option available.

Once a transaction becomes subject to the IMRS (either by being pre-notifiable in two separate jurisdictions or through merging parties or an enforcement agency opting in), all signatory jurisdictions in which the merging parties (or legal affiliates) have assets or sales should be entitled to prompt notification of the transaction. Such a rule is necessary to guard against fragmentation; without it, some IMRS signatories with jurisdiction over the merger might not be aware of and participate in the coordinated review process. It would also discourage opportunistic behaviour by merging parties (e.g. seeking the benefit of IMRS review in some jurisdictions where it appears tactically beneficial, but not in others).

Disclosure of domestic notifications

The OECD's *Merger Convergence Project* recommended that individual enforcement agencies 'agree to require parties to inform them of which other agencies have already received formal notification of a transaction', and that merging parties be under a continuing obligation to disclose promptly any future notifications to other agencies.[150] This salutary proposal would be useful in an IMRS because any transaction which had been pre-notified in at least two participating jurisdictions would immediately become apparent. In addition, the interested IMRS member jurisdictions would be alerted to any non-IMRS jurisdictions which would be reviewing a particular transaction. The cost of compliance for merging parties should be minimal, since the fact and date of local notifications are readily available information.

One stage or two stage pre-notification?

The US pre-notification rules reflect a 'law enforcement' approach to mergers. The merging parties file a very short form and, unless the reviewing agency perceives competition concerns, the transaction goes forward. However, if the agency does identify competition issues, then a detailed, almost adversarial, 'second request' for information is issued. By contrast, an 'approval' system, such as exists in the European Union, tends to work with a much larger initial filing but less disruptive follow-up requests. In Canada there are both a short form and a long form; the initial choice rests with the merging parties, but the Director of the Competition Bureau may require the filing of a long form at any time before the expiry of the seven-day 'waiting period' applicable to a short form filing.[151]

The ABA's *International Antitrust Report* expressed a preference for two stage pre-notification systems over unitary ones because the compliance burden involved in providing extensive information can be limited to the minority of transactions which raise genuine competition issues.[152] This reasoning is especially persuasive in an IMRS context, where merging parties would be providing relevant information regarding each jurisdiction in which they have assets or sales.

The objective of an enforcement agency in the first stage is simply to determine whether a detailed investigation is warranted. Some transactions may be 'no brainers' (e.g. most conglomerate and – in many jurisdictions – vertical mergers). Others may require a preliminary assessment or 'quick look' at such issues as possible relevant markets and concentration levels before an enforcement agency reaches a sufficient level of comfort to conclude its investigation. Canada's short form/long form approach offers a nicely balanced incentive structure which could be adapted to deal efficiently with these possibilities in the first stage of an IMRS:

1 The 'Short Form' would cover only the bare minimum information that enforcement agencies would need to know about the parties and the transaction in order to be satisfied that it did not raise competition issues.

2 The 'Long Form' would still be a relatively modest filing but would include enough additional information about the product and geographical scope of the merging parties' operations, estimated market demand, competitors and other basic matters to allow an enforcement agency to decide whether or not a detailed investigation and supplementary information request would be warranted.

3 The merging parties would initially have the option of submitting a Short Form or a Long Form filing.

4 If a Short Form filing was made, the recipient enforcement agencies would each have a brief time period in which to require a Long Form (with the effect that the waiting period for the first stage would not start to run until after filing of the complete Long Form) or to move directly to a second stage information request.[153]

At the second stage, an enforcement agency's objective is to gather enough information to decide whether or not to challenge a proposed transaction. Accordingly, fairly extensive supplementary information requests might be anticipated. However, one would hope that US-style second requests, which 'have a potential to be much too onerous',[154] would be avoided through various steps discussed below.[155]

Time limits

Every jurisdiction with pre-notification rules has its own timetables for responses and decision-making, many of which are legislatively prescribed. The OECD's *Merger Convergence Project* observed that 'both the length of the different review processes, and the fact that some do not have a fixed end point, creates costs and uncertainty for companies and complicates the task of interagency cooperation'.[156] A common timetable would greatly facilitate the review of international mergers, even where somewhat different information is sought by each jurisdiction. It would also reduce the risk that 'the remedy ordered by an authority that finished earlier would prejudice the options available to one that needed more time'.[157] Thus efforts to harmonize the time periods for making decisions are a priority activity.[158]

The design of appropriate time limits is obviously closely linked with the type of pre-notification system which is adopted. For the two stage approach suggested above, the following timing would seem feasible:[159]

1 *Stage One with Short Form filing.* Each enforcement agency reviewing a

transaction would have two weeks from receipt of a complete filing to review its contents, consult other agencies if desired, and decide to: (1) request a Long Form; (2) move immediately to a Stage Two Supplementary Request; or (3) close its investigation.[160]

2 *Stage One with Long Form filing.* Each enforcement agency reviewing a transaction would have one month from receipt of a complete filing to review its contents, consult other agencies if desired, and decide to: (1) make a Stage Two Supplementary Request; or (2) close its investigation.[161]

3 *Stage Two.* Each enforcement agency making a Supplementary Request would have one month from receipt of the completed response to: (1) commence formal proceedings; or (2) close the investigation.[162] Agencies should probably also have the flexibility to extend this waiting period unilaterally (e.g. by a further two or three weeks, one-time only) in complex cases.

Placing enforcement agencies under time limits which are too short and inflexible can be counter-productive.[163] The time frames listed above are merely suggestions. They are intended to be tight yet workable; if enforcement agencies have a systematically different view this should emerge in any negotiations to establish an IMRS.

Regardless of the specific time limits adopted, cases may arise (hopefully infrequently) where one or more agencies would prefer more time before having to make a formal decision carrying significant resource implications for both the agency and the merging parties (e.g. requiring a Long Form filing, issuing a Supplementary Request, or commencing formal proceedings). The current US and EU time limits have a rigidity which may motivate enforcement agencies to err on the side of caution – with the unfortunate result that additional public and private transaction costs are incurred. In an IMRS, it would be preferable to allow merging parties the flexibility to consent to extensions of any of the time limits. The merging parties and their advisers could then decide whether they preferred to permit slippage from the standard timetable or force a decision within the time limit at the risk of it being unfavourable.

An ambitious system would also place time limits on the duration of formal proceedings. This would be a radical step in some jurisdictions, particularly where merger challenges are adjudicated in the ordinary courts.[164] However, the benefits of guaranteed expedition coupled with reduced timing uncertainty are highly desirable,[165] and the European Union has demonstrated that such an approach can work. The European Union's four month time frame for formal contested proceedings[166] would seem to be a reasonable target for an IMRS as well.[167]

Stage One: filing requirements

The ABA's *International Antitrust Report* observed that '[national] agencies do in fact require different information; they are examining different markets'.[168] It went on to conclude that 'one could imagine, however, having a single form type, only parts of which need be completed for each different authority' and that it 'should be possible to achieve some sort of agreement on the classes of information to be provided, and more particularly, as to the level of detail'.[169] This is one of the most promising areas for reducing transaction costs. It should also facilitate interagency consultations and more expeditious decision-making.

The kinds of information which would be sought in an IMRS initial pre-notification can be grouped into three categories:

1 *Common information.* The Short Form and the Long Form in an IMRS will undoubtedly cover some matters which are of interest to all enforcement agencies reviewing a transaction.[170] Examples include a description of the parties and relevant legal affiliates, the nature and objectives of the transaction, and the proposed closing date. Each enforcement agency should obviously receive such material.

2 *Parallel information.* Some types of information will be relevant to merger analysis in virtually any jurisdiction, but the data will vary by country. Examples include the parties' product lines and sales in particular geographical areas, the identity of major competitors in each jurisdiction, and 'market' size, share or other statistics. For such situations, country-specific annexes which follow a single format and use standardized terminology would be the logical approach.[171] (When it appears that the relevant geographic market may be transnational, the agencies involved could exchange the information collected in parallel so that all would have a common set of aggregate data.[172])

3 *Unique information.* As long as differences in substantive merger laws persist in various jurisdictions, there will be types of information which are highly relevant under one statutory regime but have little significance in other jurisdictions. For example, the European Union requires certain information to assess whether joint ventures are 'concentrative' (and hence reviewable under its *Merger Regulation*) or 'cooperative' (and hence governed by Article 85 of the Treaty of Rome).[173] Such material could be accommodated in additional country-specific annexes which are designed and administered solely by a particular jurisdiction.[174]

Ideally, the unique information category would be small relative to the common and parallel information requirements which each IMRS signatory would agree to accept in place of its usual domestic pre-notification disclosures.[175]

It is beyond the scope of this chapter to map out the specifics of a standard IMRS Short Form or Long Form. In designing such forms there would undoubtedly be worthy elements to draw upon from many domestic pre-notification regimes. Based on the current Canadian, EU and US systems, the following general approach might be reasonable:

1 *Short Form.* The standard Short Form should be at least as streamlined as the current Canadian short form requirements or an initial *Hart–Scott–Rodino Act*[176] filing in the United States.

2 *Long Form.* The standard Long Form should be slightly broader, and more focused on competition issues, than the current Canadian long form requirements (which place heavy emphasis on affiliated legal entities), but noticeably less detailed than the European Union's Form CO.

Negotiating waivers or derogations from the standard Short Form or Long Form could be cumbersome and time-consuming when multiple enforcement agencies are involved. Nevertheless, there is no reason to foreclose this possibility. Accordingly, the IMRS system should include a commitment on the part of each enforcement agency to participate in pre-filing discussions with merging parties and/or other enforcement agencies with respect to reducing the scope of a filing. However, the consent of all enforcement agencies reviewing a particular transaction should be required for any waiver or derogation of the common information requirements.[177]

Stage two: supplementary requests for information

The starting point of an effective Stage Two procedure would be to develop a standardized Supplementary Request form.[178] All IMRS enforcement agencies would agree to work from this standard model in designing supplementary information requests in specific cases. Each enforcement agency in the IMRS should also be required to make good faith efforts to omit non-critical items from the standard Supplementary Request and only add customized questions which relate to issues of real importance. In addition, it would be useful to have a short window period during which the enforcement agencies involved in a particular case would be available for negotiations with merging parties to narrow the scope of proposed Supplementary Requests.

Assuming Short Form and Long Form filing requirements along the lines outlined above,[179] it would be logical for the standard Supplementary Request to be roughly as extensive as the European Union's Form CO, subject to additions or deletions in various areas to achieve more universal relevance. In any event, it should be considerably less extensive than second requests which are often issued under the US *Hart–Scott–Rodino Act.*

Information sharing and confidentiality

To maximize the potential for cooperation and coordination, the enforcement agencies reviewing a transaction would need to be able to exchange and discuss freely the information which each has gathered.[180] This could include information received in country-specific annexes to a pre-notification filing, a Supplementary Request or other communications with the merging parties or their advisers. It could also include information obtained by an agency from such sources as competitors, customers, suppliers and other government departments.

In light of the commercial sensitivity of much of the information in merger reviews, it is unlikely that anything short of the 'closed loop concept' discussed above[181] would be acceptable to governments and business enterprises contemplating the creation of an IMRS. The remainder of this section outlines how the closed loop concept might be operationalized in the context of an IMRS.

To begin with, each jurisdiction would need to enact an exemption authorizing its enforcement agency to transmit otherwise confidential information to other enforcement agencies involved in an IMRS review of a particular transaction.[182] Each jurisdiction would also have to impose an obligation on its enforcement agency(ies) and officials[183] to keep strictly confidential all non-public information received from other IMRS enforcement agencies.[184] In addition, third parties in both the transmitting and the receiving jurisdictions must be precluded from using freedom of information requests, discovery procedures or the like to access the information exchanged between enforcement agencies. The result would be a set of reciprocal exemptions and protections allowing information to be transmitted and discussed within the IMRS while maintaining a completely closed system.

The issue of downstream dissemination of information once it has been received by an enforcement agency is of fundamental importance. Broader information sharing is unlikely to be politically acceptable without a system which is perceived as a truly closed loop, and merging parties may become loathe to seek pre-notification guidance or provide information voluntarily if uncertain as to the integrity of the system.

There is currently a perceived problem with the institutional exchange of information which is built into the EU merger control regime, under which the competition authorities in member states receive documents from and are consulted by the European Commission at a number of stages during the review process. There has been concern that, if leaks are going to occur, it will be not at the level of the Commission but when files are transmitted to the member states. Once a file is passed to the competition authority of a member state, it is difficult to control where that information may end up – it could, for example, be passed to another branch of government where its confidentiality will not be so carefully respected. A rule prohibiting confidential IMRS information from one agency being transmitted by a second agency to local government agencies (including the provinces or states within a federal system) would therefore be appropriate. The practical effect of this rule in the EU context would be that the Commission would exchange confidential information with the enforcement agencies only of member states which were independent signatories of the IMRS.[185]

Interagency communications

The OECD's *Merger Convergence Project* found a surprising lack of consistency in the use of formal notifications pursuant to the OECD *Recommendation Concerning Restrictive Business Practices*, as well as very limited direct contact at the case officer level in the nine international mergers selected as case studies.[186] An IMRS would by its very nature tend to encourage more interagency contact. Most of these communications should be left to the voluntary initiative of the agencies and officials reviewing a transaction.[187] The symbolic value of including an IMRS provision which encourages interagency consultations, including direct contacts between case officers, should also be considered.[188]

Nevertheless, there are a few critical points in an IMRS review where awareness of steps being taken by the various jurisdictions would need to be ensured through notifications and/or formal consultations (see Table 17.1)[189].

Enforcement guidelines

Domestic merger enforcement guidelines already exist in both the United States and Canada (and, indeed, contain notable similarities, including the use of a complex 'hypothetical monopolist' approach to market definition).[190] To date the European Union has avoided the publication of general guidelines, although the Commission has issued two 'notices' regarding specific technical issues which arise under the *Merger Regulation.*[191]

As has been discussed, enforcement guidelines are one of the important ways of achieving a level of transparency which would facilitate interagency cooperation, reduce uncertainty for private parties and potentially promote convergence towards economically enlightened, administratively feasible competition laws and practices.[192] It would therefore be appropriate for an IMRS to encourage, or perhaps even require as a condition of participation, that member enforcement agencies issue guidelines describing their approach to key facets of merger review.[193]

An agency's enforcement practices and/or its interpretation of domestic law may change over time. Where embellishments of or departures from

Table 17.1 Minimum formal interagency communications in an IMRS

Event	Communication
A jurisdiction which plans to require a Long Form filing should be obliged to notify the other reviewing agencies in advance because of the impact on timing of the review process	Notification
Within a short preliminary review period,[a] enforcement agencies should hold consultations to determine which have significant, moderate or no interest in further examining a transaction. In the context of the IMRS pre-notification regime proposed above, it would be sensible to require agencies to be prepared to consult by way of conference call one week prior to the expiry of the Stage One waiting period	Formal consultations (mandatory)
An agency which intends to issue a Supplementary Request should be obliged to consult other reviewing agencies one week before doing so in order to identify possible opportunities for collaboration. It should also be required to formally notify the other agencies when the Supplementary Request is issued and make copies available	Formal consultations (mandatory) Notification
An agency should have the right to request consultations regarding assistance in gathering evidence, information-sharing, substantive issues, possible remedies for addressing competition concerns or other matters at any time, and the other IMRS agencies should have a duty to participate promptly in such consultations	Formal consultations (upon request)
When one agency decides to go forward with formal contested or consent proceedings, it should be required to notify and provide copies of relevant documentation to other reviewing agencies	Notification
Whenever an agency closes its investigation of an IMRS transaction, it should be required to notify the other reviewing agencies promptly	Notification

Note:

[a] ABA Special Committee, *International Antitrust Report*, pp. 189–90, suggested that this should occur within a time period of three weeks.

published merger guidelines occur, there should be an obligation to notify other IMRS member agencies of the changes.[194]

Announcement of filings and decisions

An IMRS, like the current European Union system, would be designed to handle a relatively modest volume of sizeable transactions which would have a material impact in two or more countries. Transparency is fostered in the European Union by the requirements that a brief public announcement be made when a pre-notification filing is submitted and that the European Commission publish its final decision.[195] The initial announcement alerts interested parties who may wish to make submissions regarding the transaction, while the published decision contributes to agency accountability by making the interested public aware of the action taken and the underlying reasons.

A similar level of case-specific disclosure would be worthwhile in any IMRS system. The merging parties should be required to issue an initial press release identifying all jurisdictions which will be reviewing the transaction (and this announcement should be made available in each jurisdiction in the relevant official language(s)). Every enforcement agency undertaking a review should then be responsible for issuing a prompt announcement when it has either commenced formal adjudicative proceedings or closed its investigation.

Clearances and authorizations

Various jurisdictions offer the possibility of situation-specific 'exemptions', 'clearances', 'notifications', 'authorizations' and the like for mergers or other proposed activities. The general concept is that private parties make fair advance disclosure of their plans to the relevant agency in exchange for some reduction in their potential competition law exposure. Two such devices for immunizing mergers from future attack are of particular interest for present purposes: the 'Advance Ruling Certificates' ('ARCs') available under the Canadian *Competition Act* and merger 'authorizations' pursuant to the *Trade Practices Act* in Australia.[196]

ARCs may be issued at the discretion of the Director of the Competition Bureau. Once issued, an ARC precludes the Director (who is the only person in Canada with the standing to attack a merger – private actions are not available) from challenging a transaction 'solely on the basis of information that is the same or substantially the same' as that considered in issuing the ARC.[197] An ARC also exempts the merging parties from the pre-notification rules.[198] In practice ARCs are sought when one or more of the merging parties desires a high degree of certainty. They can usually be obtained fairly expeditiously (although the Director is under no fixed time limit) and tend to be used for relatively 'straightforward' situations because the Director has been reluctant to bind his discretion to challenge transactions if competition concerns subsequently emerge.[199]

The ARC mechanism is unique to Canada. It offers real benefits to merging parties in some cases, contains an appropriate incentive to full and fair disclosure by applicants,[200] and appears to be viewed by the Competition Bureau as a positive element of the merger review process rather than a burden. The certainty offered by this type of clearance procedure could be especially valuable in complex international transactions. It would be desirable for all jurisdictions participating in an IMRS to have a clearance mechanism available (at least for transactions being reviewed under the IMRS, even if not for domestic ones). The Canadian system appears to provide a good model, although the addition of reasonable time limits for agency responses to such requests and greater transparency would be useful improvements.[201]

The Australian authorization mechanism also insulates proposed mergers from future challenge, yet it differs greatly from Canadian-style ARCs in both purpose and operation. Authorizations are for 'hard' cases, not easy ones, and are most commonly sought when efficiency gains or other public interest considerations are put forward as justification for an otherwise potentially anti-competitive merger. The process is initiated by the merging parties, involves a formal proceeding before the Trade Practices Commission in which enforcement officials and interested third parties may participate, and is subject to crisp timing rules (but surprisingly broad rights of appeal).[202]

Under a world competition code, one could envision multi-jurisdictional authorization proceedings being available to merging parties which seek certainty that their transaction will not be challenged in any jurisdiction which is a signatory to the code. The availability of parallel authorization processes in individual jurisdictions would be a less ambitious but none the less powerful step towards harmonization. Merging parties might decide to pursue an authorization in all jurisdictions, or might focus on those where uncertainty is especially high while ignoring others where the risk of a challenge is perceived to be low.

Two of the co-authors of this chapter have argued previously that authorizations can be used as a 'second-best' solution if countries are unwilling to harmonize the substantive test for evaluation of mergers to a pure competition law standard.[203] Any jurisdiction wishing to retain an efficiency defence, industrial policy criteria or broad public interest considerations in its merger law would agree that such claims be asserted by merging parties through a time-limited and transparent proceeding (before a domestic adjudicative body) in which third parties would also have fair participation opportunities. However, authorization proceedings need not be limited to dealing with such defences. The parties to an international merger might well decide that uncertainty arising from other substantive or technical issues (e.g. market definition, entry barrier levels, etc.) is worth removing.

Of particular interest is the role which authorizations could play in reducing the complications and uncertainties resulting from the possibility of private and/or state actions in jurisdictions such as the United States. An IMRS could require all participating jurisdictions to make available to merging parties the option of initiating an authorization proceeding which, if successful, would preclude future challenges by private or state plaintiffs as well as the federal enforcement agency.[204] Such a process would obviously have to afford notice, standing, and other appropriate procedural safeguards to potentially interested states and private parties. The incentive for them to participate is that, once the merging parties had commenced an authorization proceeding, it would become the only forum for opposing the transaction.

Summary of IMRS proposals

The IMRS contemplated in this chapter would be structured as a multilateral treaty amongst jurisdictions with well developed domestic merger control systems. New institutions would not need to be established. It would have twelve core components:

1 *Pre-filing consultations with merging parties.* IMRS jurisdictions should be encouraged to make officials available where merging parties request consultation regarding jurisdictional, substantive, remedial, timing or other procedural issues. Information received or advice given may (not must) be disclosed to the enforcement agencies in other IMRS jurisdictions, but only after an IMRS review of the transaction has commenced.

2 *Pre-notifiable transactions.* Mergers should be subject to review under the IMRS rather than domestic review procedures (although each jurisdiction would continue to employ its own substantive laws) in the following situations:

   (a) *Mandatory.* Any transaction which is subject to pre-notification in two or more IMRS jurisdictions.

   (b) *Opt-in by merging parties.* Any transaction subject to substantive review in two or more IMRS jurisdictions which the merging parties voluntarily choose to have reviewed under the IMRS rather than under a multiplicity of country-specific procedural regimes.

   (c) *Opt-in by an enforcement agency.* Any transaction with international aspects which an enforcement agency elects to 'bump' from domestic review into the IMRS process.

   Once a transaction becomes subject to IMRS review, all signatory jurisdictions in which the merging parties (or their legal affiliates) have assets or sales should be entitled to prompt notification of the transaction.

3 *Disclosure of domestic notifications.* Each IMRS jurisdiction should include in its standard domestic pre-notification regime a requirement that merging parties list all foreign agencies to which the transaction has previously been notified and to promptly disclose any future notifications.

4 *Two stage pre-notification.* The IMRS pre-notification process should consist of two stages:

    (a) *Stage One.* The purpose of the first stage would be to use quick examinations to weed out transactions which clearly do not require extensive review. Merging parties should have the option of submitting a very brief Short Form or a somewhat longer, but still modest, Long Form filing. During the mandatory waiting period for a Short Form filing, any enforcement agency could request a Long Form filing instead.

    (b) *Stage Two.* The purpose of the second stage would be to allow an enforcement agency to conduct a detailed investigation in order to determine whether to challenge or seek restructuring of the transaction. The primary basis of information gathering should be a largely standardized Supplementary Request form.

5 *Time limits.* To reduce uncertainty and promote expedition, there should be tight but attainable fixed time limits (during which the transaction could be not closed) at each of the major stages of the IMRS process. The following time limits would seem to be realistic:

    (a) *Stage One with Short Form.* Two weeks from the submission of a complete filing.

    (b) *Stage One with Long Form.* One month from the submission of a complete filing.

    (c) *Stage Two.* One month (with an agency option to extend by a further two or three weeks in complex cases) from receipt of a complete response to a Supplementary Request.

    (d) *Contested proceedings.* Four months from initiation of the formal proceeding by the enforcement agency.[205]

    (e) *Consent proceedings.* Two months from the commencement of the proceeding.[206]

All time limits should be extendable indefinitely with the consent of the merging parties.

6 *Filing requirements (Stage One).* The standard Short Form and Long Form should be divided into:

    (a) *Common information requirements.* A single response would be submitted to all reviewing agencies.

    (b) *Parallel information requirements.* Each reviewing agency would receive a separate but similarly-structured annex containing data or responses relevant to that jurisdiction.

    (c) *Unique information requirements.* Each jurisdiction would have the option of designing customized annexes for obtaining information relevant only to its particular domestic merger control law.

Enforcement agencies should be prepared to participate in discussions with merging parties to reduce the scope of a filing, but common information requirements should be waivable only with the consent of all the reviewing agencies.

7 *Supplementary Requests for Information (Stage Two)*. IMRS agencies should agree to work from a comprehensive, standardized Supplementary Request questionnaire, should delete non-critical items and minimize customized additions whenever possible, and should be prepared to participate in discussions with merging parties to narrow the scope of such requests.

8 *Information sharing and confidentiality*. Each IMRS jurisdiction would need to amend its existing confidentiality rules in three respects:

(a) *Transmission of information*. Each agency should have the unrestricted ability (but not any obligation) to disclose confidential information to other IMRS agencies reviewing a transaction.

(b) *'Downstream' confidentiality protection*. Each agency should be required to keep strictly confidential all non-public information received in confidence from another IMRS agency. Retransmitting the information to other government agencies, or to state enforcement agencies, would be prohibited.[207]

(c) *Third party access*. Third parties should be precluded by law from using freedom of information requests, discovery procedures or other means to access non-public information which has been transmitted by, or received by, an agency reviewing a transaction under the IMRS.

9 *Interagency communications*. IMRS agencies involved in reviewing a particular transaction should interact according to the following framework:

(a) *Notifications*. The following events merit a formal notification:
   (i) An agency requests a Long Form filing after receipt of a Short Form filing.
   (ii) An agency issues a Supplementary Request.
   (iii) An agency commences a formal contested or consent proceeding.
   (iv) An agency closes its investigation.

(b) *Informal discussions*. Agencies should be encouraged, but not required, to communicate regularly with each other during the course of an IMRS review (especially at the case officer level).

(c) *Formal consultations*. Agencies should be required to participate in consultations at the following times during an IMRS review:
   (i) One week prior to the expiry of the Stage One waiting period, with a view to identifying agencies having moderate or no interest in a Stage Two review.
   (ii) One week prior to issuing a Supplementary Request, with a view to identifying opportunities for collaboration and efficient information gathering.

477

    (iii) At any other time at the request of any reviewing agency, with respect to information sharing, substantive issues or possible remedies for addressing competition concerns.

10 *Enforcement guidelines*. To promote transparency (and possible future convergence of merger laws), each IMRS agency should publish (and periodically update) enforcement guidelines which address six key substantive issues,[208] any unique features of their domestic laws and significant process matters.

11 *Announcement of filings and decisions*. The merging parties should be required at the commencement of an IMRS review to publicly announce the proposed transaction in each reviewing jurisdiction in order to allow interested third parties to have timely input. Every enforcement agency which reviews the transaction should then be responsible for publicly announcing when it has either closed the investigation or commenced formal proceedings.

12 *Clearances and authorizations*. IMRS jurisdictions should be strongly encouraged to make available to merging parties either or both of the following options for reducing uncertainty as to whether a transaction will be subject to a possible future challenge:

  (a) *Clearances*. Modelled along the lines of the Canadian Advance Ruling Certificate system, a clearance would involve the enforcement agency binding itself not to challenge a transaction on the basis of information provided by the merging parties and perhaps other sources. It would provide an expeditious method for approving mergers which do not appear to raise serious competition concerns.

  (b) *Authorizations*. Modelled upon the Australian authorization system, this mechanism could be initiated by merging parties in situations where potential competition concerns are apparent but they seek an early and definitive ruling that the transaction will not be blocked. In exchange for going through a time-limited, predominantly public hearing process with broad standing rights for interested third parties, success on an application would insulate a transaction from any future challenge by either federal or state enforcement agencies in the relevant jurisdiction and would extinguish any private rights of action which would otherwise exist.

NOTES

1 See, for example, Chapter 3 of the present volume, by A.E. Safarian.
2 The literature on the extraterritorial application of antitrust laws is voluminous. For a brief summary, see A.N. Campbell and M.J. Trebilcock, 'International Merger Review: Problems of Multi-Jurisdictional Conflict', in E. Kantzenbach, H.-E. Scharrer and L. Waverman (eds) *Competition Policy in an Interdependent World Economy* (Baden-Baden, Germany: Nomos Verlagsgesellschaft, 1993), pp. 133–6, and sources cited therein.

3 The term 'system friction' was coined by Ostry to describe the impact of differing domestic policies on trade and investment flows and the linkages between countries in an increasingly global economy: see S. Ostry, 'Beyond the Border: The New International Policy Arena', in Kantzenbach *et al.*, *Interdependent World Economy, supra*, note 2.

4 Campbell and Trebilcock, 'International Merger Review', *supra*, note 2, p. 129.

5 Organisation for Economic Cooperation and Development, *Joint Report on Trade and Competition Policies by the Committee on Competition Law and Policy and the Trade Committee* (Paris: May 17, 1994, #C/MIN (94) 7), p. 2, ¶ 2.

6 E.M. Fox, 'Harmonization of Law and Procedures in a Globalized World: Why, What and How' (1991), 60 *Antitrust Law Journal* 593, pp. 596–7. The concept of subsidiarity which has attained great momentum in the European Union illustrates the strong political appeal of diversity and respect for sovereignty. For a more extensive discussion of how appropriate sovereignty interests can be reconciled with a 'world welfare' standard for competition laws, see E.M. Fox and J.A. Ordover, in Chapter 16 of the present volume.

7 Organisation for Economic Cooperation and Development, *Joint Report on Trade and Competition Policies, supra*, note 5, p. 6, ¶ 23.

8 In the merger area, for example, the United States essentially employs a 'law enforcement' approach: a merger can be blocked only after an adversarial evidentiary hearing before a federal District Court judge. The process in the European Union is more of an 'administrative approval' approach. Canada is somewhat in the middle, with the Competition Bureau having a very central role and proceedings before the quasi-judicial Competition Tribunal – whether on a contested or on a consent basis – being a rarity.

9 Since harmonized approaches to enforcement will have to retain sufficient flexibility to accommodate broad substantive and institutional differences, providing enforcement agencies and private parties with opportunities to voluntarily 'opt in' (or 'opt out') is likely to be more acceptable, and more efficiency-enhancing, than mandatory approaches in many areas: see pp. 446–7.

10 R.P. Whish and D.P. Wood, *OECD Merger Process Convergence Project – Final Report* (Paris: OECD, 1993), p. 80, ¶ IV.A.1.ii, observed that 'it is of course possible that the parties in a hostile case or in a questionable case would like to drag matters out as long as possible, but we do not count the temptation to abuse process as a legitimate concern'.

11 A sequential approach may be attractive in saving resources, especially if the agencies are able to share the fruits of investigation and are not constrained by domestic statutory limitation periods.

12 See, for example, *General Agreement on Tariffs and Trade*, art. III; *Treaty of Rome*, various provisions; *Canada–United States Free Trade Agreement*, ch. 5; and *North American Free Trade Agreement*, art. 301 and 1202 and various other specific provisions.

13 See OECD, *Joint Report on Trade and Competition Policies, supra*, note 5, p. 6, ¶ 23; and Organisation for Economic Cooperation and Development, *Interim Report on Convergence of Competition Policies by the Committee on Competition Law and Policy* (Paris: May 18, 1994, #C/MIN(94) 14), p. 4, ¶ 8, and p. 7, Annex ¶ A.2.

14 International Antitrust Code Working Group, *Draft International Antitrust Code as a GATT–MTO–Plurilateral Trade Agreement* (Munich: Max Planck

Institute, 1993), art. 2:2(b). (The minority which did not support development of a detailed code nevertheless endorsed national treatment as one of fifteen 'minimum principles': *ibid.*, ¶ VIII.4.)

15 To the extent that changes in domestic laws are required, a formal treaty rather than a memorandum of understanding between domestic antitrust agencies would be necessary to fully implement the principle of national treatment: see *infra*, pp. 448–9.

16 For examples of how a national treatment principle could be applied to competition law enforcement in the *North American Free Trade Agreement* ('NAFTA') area, see American Bar Association Antitrust Section Task Force, *Report on the Competition Dimension of the North American Free Trade Agreement* (Chicago: 1994), pp. 175–7 and 193 (Recommendation IV.F). (One of the authors of this chapter, Donald Baker, was a member of the Task Force.)

17 See 16 C.F.R. §§802.50–52 (1994); and summary in United States Department of Justice and Federal Trade Commission, *Antitrust Enforcement Guidelines for International Operations* (Washington: April 1995), pp. 31–2.

18 E.M. Fox and J.A. Ordover, 'Antitrust – Harmonization, Accommodation and Coordination of Law', paper presented at the Tokyo meeting of the Project on Competition Policy in a Global Economy (April 1994), p. 22.

19 This approach has been endorsed by ABA Task Force, *NAFTA Report, supra*, note 16, pp. 159–64 and 191 (Recommendation IV.C); and American Bar Association Section of Antitrust Law, *Report of the Special Committee on International Antitrust* (Chicago: 1991), p. 164 (Recommendation VII.I). (One of the authors, William Rowley, was a member of the Special Committee.)

20 OECD, *Interim Report on Convergence, supra*, note 13, p. 7, Annex ¶ A.2.

21 See, for example, J.R. Atwood, 'Positive Comity – Is It a Positive Step?', (1992) *Fordham Corporate Law Institute* 79, p. 81.

22 *Agreement Between the Commission of the European Communities and the Government of the United States of America Regarding the Application of their Competition Laws* (1991), reprinted in 15 *World Competition* (no. 1) 155, art. VI:3. (This agreement has been ruled invalid by the European Court of Justice (see *infra*, note 61), but is likely to be re-approved by the EU Council and this chapter proceeds on that assumption.)

23 See US DOJ and FTC, *International Enforcement Guidelines, supra*, note 17, pp. 20–1. (See also the predecessor guidelines, which adopted a similar approach: United States Department of Justice, *Antitrust Enforcement Guidelines for International Operations* (Washington: 1988), pp. 32–3, n. 170.)

24 *Timberlane Lumber Co.* v. *Bank of America N.T. & S.A.*, 749 F. 2d 597 (9th Cir. 1976) is the leading case which spells out the factors to be considered by a US court.

25 The US DOJ maintains that comity analysis is solely within the purview of the executive branch. Hence a prosecutorial decision to proceed with a case after a comity analysis should not be second-guessed by the courts: see US DOJ and FTC, *International Enforcement Guidelines, supra*, note 17, pp. 21–2. This approach was followed by the court in *United States* v. *Baker Hughes*, 731 F. Supp. 3 (D.D.C.), *aff'd* 908 F. 2d 981 (D.C. Cir. 1990). (But see ABA Special Committee, *Report on International Antitrust, supra*, note 19, p. 164 (Recommendation VII.III); ABA Task Force, *NAFTA Report, supra*, note 16, pp. 173 and 191–3 (Recommendations IV.D and E); and Canadian Bar Association Competition Law Section, *Commentary on the Competition*

Dimension of the North American Free Trade Agreement (March 1995), p. 23; all of which concluded that courts should have an obligation to apply comity principles.)

26 See, for example, *Laker Airways* v. *Sabena Belgian World Airlines*, 731 F. 2d 909 (D.C. Cir. 1984), pp. 950 and 952, where the court concluded there was no legal requirement under US or international law to decline jurisdiction on the basis of comity considerations.

27 *Hartford Fire Insurance* v. *California*, 113 S. Ct. 2891 (1993), *per* Souter J. on behalf of a 5:4 majority.

28 ABA Task Force, *NAFTA Report*, *supra*, note 16, p. 166. See also E.M. Fox, 'U.S. Law and Global Competition and Trade – Jurisdiction and Comity', *Antitrust Report* (October 1993), pp. 3–7, who notes that the majority decision explicitly left open the possibility that comity could apply in other cases, and who argues that Scalia J.'s strong dissent might emerge 'as a guide to the future'.

29 ABA Special Committee, *International Antitrust Report*, *supra*, note 19, p. 164 (Recommendation VII.II), endorsed the six comity factors in the *1988 International Enforcement Guidelines* (*supra*, note 23) as a desirable approach.

30 See, for example, the UK *Protection of Trading Interests Act, 1980*; and the Canadian *Foreign Extraterritorial Measures Act*, R.S.C. 1985, c. F-29. Such legislation has been the subject of numerous commentaries including A.V. Lowe, 'Blocking Extraterritorial Jurisdiction: The British *Protection of Trading Interests Act, 1980*' (1981), 75 *American Journal of International Law* 257; W.C. Graham, 'The *Foreign Extraterritorial Measures Act*' (1985), 11 *Canadian Business Law Journal* 410; and, more generally, P.C.F. Pettit and C.J.D. Styles, 'The International Response to the Extraterritorial Application of the United States Antitrust Laws' (1982), 37 *Business Lawyer* 697.

31 For example, under the UK's *Protection of Trading Interests Act* and Canada's *Foreign Extraterritorial Measures Act* (see *supra*, note 30), an order must be issued by the Secretary of State or the Attorney General (with the concurrence of the Minister of External Affairs), respectively, before the various blocking devices become applicable to a specific assertion of extraterritoriality.

32 Blocking statutes might be retained for application against jurisdictions which have not entered into satisfactory bilateral or multilateral enforcement harmonization arrangements, and perhaps also in strictly limited 'safeguard' situation where a country is not complying with the letter or spirit of its commitments under such arrangements. However, the norm should be collaboration, not blocking.

33 If complete elimination of blocking statutes cannot be obtained in the present political climate, it would at minimum be useful to seek agreement that all automatic blocking rules will be replaced with regimes that require an affirmative decision to block and that specify the criteria which can legitimately be considered in the exercise of such discretion.

34 A promising example of this kind of change in focus is the enabling legislation recently passed by the US Congress to facilitate information-sharing and enforcement assistance: see *infra*, note 94, and following text.

35 See Atwood, 'Positive Comity', *supra*, note 21, pp. 83–5.

36 *US–EU MOU*, *supra*, note 22, art V:2.

37 *Ibid.*, art. V:3 and 4. (The notifying agency also retains complete discretion with respect to its enforcement activities, including any extraterritorial application of competition laws which would be otherwise available.)

38 See OECD, *Joint Report on Trade and Competition Policies, supra*, note 5, p. 6, ¶ 23; and OECD, *Interim Report on Convergence, supra*, note 13, p. 4, ¶ 8, and pp. 7 and 15, Annex ¶¶ A.2, F.39 and F.41.

39 ABA Special Committee, *International Antitrust Report, supra*, note 19, pp. 225–6 (Recommendation III.II).

40 Whish and Wood, *Merger Process Convergence Project, supra*, note 10, pp. 85–6, ¶ IV.C.3. For a more detailed discussion of confidentiality issues, see *infra*, pp. 455–9.

41 See US DOJ and FTC, *International Enforcement Guidelines, supra*, note 17.

42 The *Draft International Antitrust Code, supra*, note 14, art. 2:1(b), contains the attractive proposal that each country 'inform the International Antitrust Authority of its existing law at the date of accession and of any changes in its laws and regulations relevant to this Agreement and in the administration of such laws and regulations'.

43 Both are discussed *infra*, p. 450.

44 See A.E. Safarian, in 'Policy Harmonization and International Mergers, Joint Ventures and Strategic Alliances' (1994) mimeo, p. 9.

45 Examples are the Canadian Competition Bureau's Program of Advisory Opinions and the US DOJ's Business Review Letter mechanism.

46 For example, the Canadian Competition Bureau publishes useful summaries of advisory opinions in the misleading advertising area on a no-names basis: see the *Misleading Advertising Bulletin* (Ottawa: Industry Canada, quarterly).

47 See the *Antitrust Procedures and Penalties Act*, 15 U.S.C. §§16(b)–(h); and commentary in D.I. Baker and W.T. Miller, 'United States', in J.W. Rowley and D.I. Baker (eds) *International Mergers – The Antitrust Process* (London: Sweet & Maxwell, 1991; 2nd ed. 1995), pp. 1671–8.

48 Obligations of this sort already exist in some MOUs between enforcement agencies and in the OECD's recommended protocol for cooperation regarding restrictive business practices (which is discussed *infra*, note 76, and related text). However, the OECD guidelines are not consistently followed, owing, at least in part, to the fact that 'different countries interpret its scope in different ways': see Whish and Wood, *Merger Process Convergence Project, supra*, note 10, p. 83, ¶ IV.C.1.

49 Public announcements of decisions not to launch formal merger proceedings are regularly made by the European Commission. The Canadian Competition Bureau has also done this from time to time, although generally only in high profile cases.

50 For a general discussion of the link between harmonization approaches and the scope of relevant geographical markets, see Chapter 5 of the present volume, pp. 89–90 and 106–15.

51 Even in these circumstances, however, there may be benefits from inter-agency consultation with respect to general issues such as product market definition and entry barriers. A coordinated and streamlined review process might also be of value.

52 This concept is somewhat analogous to the interface between US federal and state enforcement agencies with respect to merger reviews under the *National Association of Attorneys General Voluntary Premerger Disclosure Compact*; the *Protocol for Coordination in Merger Investigations Between the Antitrust Division and State Attorneys General*; and the FTC's *Program for Federal–State Cooperation in Merger Enforcement*. (This type of opt-in option is included in the International Merger Review System outlined in appendix 17.1.)

53 See further discussion *infra*, pp. 455–9.
54 One would ideally want incentive structures which lead the decision-maker to consider global costs and benefits. Realistically, there will almost always be costs and/or benefits which are externalities to the decision-maker, but incremental improvements over the *status quo* may still be very valuable.
55 *US–EU MOU*, *supra*, note 22, art. IV:2.
56 *Ibid.*
57 See *infra*, note 107, and, more generally, pp. 455–9.
58 For concrete illustrations of how incentive arrangements can be designed, see the International Merger Review System outlined in appendix 17.1.
59 We are indebted to Professors Damien Neven and Paul Seabright for this point.
60 This issue is addressed infra, pp. 455–9.
61 However, they may pose constitutional issues in certain jurisdictions. For example, the *US–EU MOU* (see *supra*, note 22) was ruled invalid by the European Court of Justice on the basis that the European Commission lacked the authority to enter into such an agreement: see *Application for a Declaration that the Agreement Between the Commission of the European Communities and the Government of the United States of America Regarding the Application of their Competition Laws, which was Signed into Force on 23 September, 1991, is Void*, E.C.J. No. C-327/91 (August 9, 1994). (See also A.J. Riley, 'Nailing the Jellyfish: The Legality of the EC/US Government Competition Agreement', [1992] 3 E.C.L.R. 101.)
62 The United States is the leading participant in MOUs, having developed such arrangements with Germany, Australia, Canada, and the European Union. The *US–EU MOU*, *supra*, note 22, is currently state of the art. The US DOJ is understood to be seeking out additional MOUs which may incorporate new features.
63 A variation which may overcome these limitations is for multiple jurisdictions to unilaterally enact enabling legislation which gives their enforcement agencies the ability to develop agreements with each other will operate under a flexible statutory framework. An example is the new US information sharing and enforcement assistance legislation which is discussed in detail *infra*, note 94, and following text.
64 Many US state enforcement agencies actively enforce federal as well as local antitrust laws. They do not necessarily defer to the federal agencies, even in the international arena. (See, for example, *Hartford Insurance* v. *California*, *supra*, note 27, a case initiated against numerous foreign reinsurers as well as domestic defendants by nineteen state attorneys-general.) Private antitrust remedies – encouraged by mandatory trebling of damages and fee shifting for successful plaintiffs – are also a central part of the US antitrust enforcement scheme, and 'private attorneys-general' do not defer to the federal agencies at all. (See, for example, *International Association of Machinists & Aerospace Workers* v. *Organization of Petroleum Exporting Countries*, 477 F. Supp 553 (C.D.C.L. 1979), *aff'd* 649 F. 2d 1354 (9th Cir. 1981), certiorari denied 454 U.S. 1163 (1982) (private suit against OPEC members for conspiring to raise prices).)
65 *Treaty Between the Government of Canada and the Government of the United States of America on Mutual Legal Assistance in Criminal Matters* (March 18, 1985), 24 I.L.M. 1092 (entered into force January 24, 1990).
66 Coordinated investigations have led to the prosecution of cross-border price-fixing activity in the plastic dinnerware and thermal fax paper industries: see 'Plastic Dinnerware Price Fixing Probe Nets Indictment, Guilty Plea Agreements', 66 A.T.R.R. 662 (1994); and 'U.S. and Canadian Prosecutors Attack Cartel Behaviour by Fax Paper Distributors', 67 A.T.R.R. 108 (1994).

67 In some countries (e.g. the United States) a ratified treaty has the force of law. In many others (e.g. Canada), implementing legislation is required.
68 See further discussion *infra*, pp. 452–9.
69 Some MLATs (although not the Canada–US one) contain 'dual criminality' provisions that require that a violation for which assistance is requested be criminal in both countries. Thus an agency investigating a violation which is criminal in its own jurisdiction may be out of luck if the conduct is not criminal in the assisting jurisdiction.
70 See *supra*, pp. 447–8.
71 See, for example, J.M.J. Bourgeois, 'Multilateral Competition Rules – Still the Quest for the Holy Grail?', paper presented to the Twenty-fifth Biennial Conference of the International Bar Association (October 1994), pp. 25–6, and sources cited therein.
72 See *Draft International Antitrust Code*, *supra*, note 14.
73 UNCTAD also has an extremely broad membership base. This chapter focuses on the GATT/WTO because of the momentum and credibility resulting from the successful completion of the Uruguay Round, and because the non-binding *Set of Mutually Agreed Principles and Rules for the Control of Restrictive Business Practices*, UNCTAD Doc. TD/RBP/Conf. 10/Rev. 1 (December 5, 1980), has not proven to have much of an impact.
74 See, for example, *Competition Policy in OECD Countries 1990–91* (Paris: December 1993); *Competition Policy and Intellectual Property Rights* (Paris: June 1989); and *International Mergers and Competition Policy* (Paris: December 1988).
75 See OECD, *Interim Report on Convergence*, *supra*, note 13; and OECD, *Joint Report on Trade and Competition Policies*, *supra*, note 5.
76 Organization for Economic Cooperation and Development, *Revised Recommendation of the Council Concerning Cooperation Between Member Countries on Restrictive Business Practices Affecting International Trade* (Paris: 1986) [C(86)44(Final)].
77 Three of the authors of this chapter have been actively involved in the ATC: Michael Reynolds and William Rowley are past chairmen, and Donald Baker is a past secretary.
78 See *supra*, note 67 and related text, pp. 448–9.
79 *North American Free Trade Agreement*, art. 1501:2 and 1504.
80 See *Canada–US MLAT*, *supra*, note 65; and *Memorandum of Understanding Between the Government of Canada and the United States of America as to Notification, Consultation and Cooperation With Respect to the Application of National Antitrust Laws* (March 9, 1994), 21 I.L.M. 275.
81 These issues, and the related subject of information sharing between enforcement agencies (which is discussed in the following section – see *infra*, pp. 455–9), are timely because increasing its effectiveness in international enforcement has become a top priority for the US DOJ: see, for example, A.K. Bingaman, 'Change and Continuity in Antitrust Enforcement', [1993] *Fordham Corporate Law Institute* 1, pp. 2–4.
82 For example, civil investigative demands ('CIDs') and grand juries are available in the United States, while the Director of the Canadian Competition Bureau can obtain search warrants and orders for the production of documents or compelling responses to written interrogatories. The basic functions are similar, but implementation differs in many respects.
83 The attractiveness of joint information requests is likely to increase if agencies can expect to share the fruits of their common efforts. The issue of exchanging

information is explored *infra*, pp. 455–9; for present purposes, the assumption is that collaboration occurs only with respect to the design of the information request.

84 Such a process would reduce the ability of recipients to give different answers on the basis that agencies were asking somewhat different questions, but this tactical point is entitled to no weight.

85 There will, of course, be differences in the way that individual agencies approach economic concepts such as market definition, but a fairly high degree of overlap should exist on the core types of information to be analysed.

86 The Canadian Competition Bureau is believed to take a conservative view on this issue, and other agencies may well also follow a cautious approach. It would therefore be useful for any competition law treaty and/or implementing legislation in individual jurisdictions to clarify that appropriate flexibility is available.

87 Ideally, enforcement agencies would also consider any private transaction cost savings in deciding whether to proceed by way of a joint request for information. To the extent that they fail to do so, there will be a suboptimal amount of collaboration.

88 Absent such an agreement, there would be little reason to expect the remaining agencies to view a compromise agreed to by one agency as dispositive, although it might have persuasive value.

89 See discussion *supra*, note 37 and related text.

90 *US–EU MOU*, *supra*, note 22, art. V.

91 The enabling legislation is the *Securities Exchange Act of 1934*, 15 U.S.C. §78u(a)(2).

92 See discussion *supra*, notes 66 and 67, and related text; and also Chapter 7 of the present volume, pp. 161–2.

93 See further discussion *infra*, pp. 455–9.

94 *International Antitrust Enforcement Assistance Act of 1994*, S. 2297, and H.R. 4781 (103rd Cong., 2nd Sess.) (1994). For a more detailed commentary, see A.N. Campbell and J.W. Rowley, 'The U.S. *International Antitrust Enforcement Assistance Act of 1994*' (November 1994) (copy available from authors).

95 The information exchange and confidentiality provisions are discussed *infra*, notes 109, 117 and 125, and related text. Making reciprocal assistance available to the US agencies and providing at least as much protection for confidential information as exists in the United States are among the eligibility criteria for an AMAA: see *IAEAA*, *supra*, note 94, §12(2).

96 *IAEAA*, *supra*, note 94, §§3(b) and (c).

97 *Ibid.*, §4.

98 Privileges normally provide protection against documents or other evidence being used in formal proceedings and may also be invocable as a shield against the information-gathering powers of enforcement authorities.

99 An example is lawyer–client advice: communications from in-house as well as external counsel are privileged in the United States, whereas the European Union only protects communications with external counsel.

100 Whether a privilege can or should be shareable amongst separate legal entities within a single economic enterprise is an issue which is beyond the scope of this chapter.

101 For a general discussion of the opting-in principle, see *supra*, pp. 446–7.

102 For a detailed survey of the Canadian and US regimes, see Chapter 7.

103 See *US–EU MOU*, *supra*, note 22, art. VIII:1 and also art. III and IX.

104 OECD, *Interim Report on Convergence, supra*, note 13, p. 17, Annex ¶ F.52 (emphasis added).

105 ABA Special Committee, *International Antitrust Report, supra*, note 19, p. 190.

106 See further quotation reproduced *infra*, p. 457.

107 Although private parties could benefit indirectly from information exchanges to the extent that enforcement agencies become more deferential to each other once uncertainty as to information possessed and likely enforcement intentions is reduced, they can be expected to prefer that there be no scope for interagency exchange of their confidential information without consent. Weighing against this is the public interest in more effective and efficient competition law enforcement against anti-competitive conduct which cuts across borders.

108 There has been historical reluctance in the United States for the federal agencies to disclose information to their state counterparts, which makes the decision to allow international disclosure all the more remarkable. There is a similar historical tension in the relationship between the European Commission and member state competition authorities.

109 *IAEAA, supra*, note 94, §2.

110 *Ibid*, §5,

111 *Ibid*, §8(a).

112 ABA Special Committee, *International Antitrust Report, supra*, note 19, pp. 190–1.

113 *US–EU MOU, supra* note 22, art. VIII:2 (emphasis added).

114 See *supra*, note 103, and related text.

115 As to the status of information exchanged under the current *Canada–US MLAT*, see Chapter 7 *supra*, pp. 161–2.

116 This a common exception to domestic confidentiality protections: see, for example, the Canadian *Competition Act*, R.S.C. 1985, c. C-34, s. 29(1). Transparency at the adjudicative stage will tend to facilitate accountability and public confidence in decision-making. However, the court or tribunal will typically also have some discretion to issue appropriate protective orders.

117 *IAEAA, supra*, note 94, §8(b).

118 See for example, *Competition Act, supra*, note 116, s. 29(2).

119 The agency transmitting the information should not have the ability to waive confidentiality because that would create uncertainty and potential unfairness for private parties.

120 A procedural step which could be of value in this area would be to put private parties under the onus of identifying and providing brief rationales for the information which they view as confidential. An example of this approach can be found in the European Union's merger pre-notification system. *Form CO*, ¶ E requires that: 'If you believe that your interests would be harmed if any of the information you are asked to supply were to be published or otherwise divulged to other parties, submit this information separately with each page clearly marked "Business Secrets." You should also give reasons why the information should not be divulged or published.'

121 The main concern with respect to discovery in litigation between private parties is not that the agency will be forced to divulge information (although third party discovery is available in some countries), but that one party will seek to discover 'all documents given to agency X' in relation to an investigation covering issues similar to those raised in the private action. Thus in the United States, and perhaps various other jurisdictions, a legislative amendment would likely be needed to preclude discovery requests based on information gathered and exchanged by agencies conducting an international investigation.

122 For a thorough discussion of these possibilities under the current Canadian and US systems, see *supra*, Chapter 7, particularly pp. 168–70. See also Director of Investigation and Research, *Draft Information Bulletin – Confidentiality of Information under the Competition Act* (July 22, 1994), pp. 21–5.

123 *Ibid.*

124 *Freedom of Information Act*, 5 U.S.C. §552.

125 See commentary in United States House of Representatives Committee on the Judiciary, *Report on the International Antitrust Enforcement Assistance Act of 1994*, 67 A.T.R.R. 448 (1994), p. 454.

126 See *supra*, p. 458.

127 See, for example, the discussion *supra*, note 121.

128 OECD, *Recommendation Concerning Cooperation on Restrictive Business Practices*, *supra*, note 76, art. I:1(a). This is defined to include information gathering in the foreign territory, investigation of a practice carried out at least in part in the foreign territory, and taking enforcement action in respect of a previously notified matter: *ibid.*, appendix, ¶ 2.

129 Whish and Wood, *Merger Process Convergence Project*, *supra*, note 10, pp. 82–3, ¶ IV.C.1. (This proposal is as relevant to non-merger situations as it is to merger investigations.)

130 ABA Task Force, *NAFTA Report*, *supra*, note 16, pp. 150–5 and 189–90 (Recommendation IV.A).

131 See the Canada–US cartel investigations cited *supra*, note 66, in which, among other things, agency officials conducted joint witness interviews and depositions and coordinated their use of formal investigative powers: see G.N. Addy, *Luncheon Address to the Canadian Bar Association Competition Law Section* (Hull: Bureau of Competition Policy, September 30, 1994), p. 6.

132 A rare example is Microsoft's recent simultaneous agreements with the US DOJ and the European Commission to revise various contractual practices that had been under investigation in both jurisdictions: see 'Microsoft Settles Accusations of Monopolistic Selling Practices', 67 A.T.R.R. 106 (1994).

133 See additional discussion *supra*, pp. 455–9.

134 Whish and Wood, *Merger Process Convergence Project*, *supra*, note 10, p. 83, ¶ IV.C.1. Interagency communications tended to be limited to formal 'horizontal' contacts between the international units of the agencies involved.

135 For the exceptions that prove the rule, see *supra*, notes 66 (coordinated investigations under the *Canada–US MLAT*) and 132 (the *Microsoft* settlement).

136 Whish and Wood, *Merger Process Convergence Project*, *supra*, note 10, p. 83, ¶ IV.C.1.

137 ABA Task Force, *NAFTA Report*, *supra*, note 16, pp. 155–6 and 190 (Recommendation IV.B). In the United States there may also be a need for coordination among the two federal agencies and/or state authorities as to which is going to take responsibility for a particular merger or other civil investigation. Only in the criminal area does one agency, the DOJ, have exclusive responsibility.

138 OECD, *Recommendation Concerning Cooperation on Restrictive Business Practices*, *supra*, note 76, art. I:3(b).

139 *US–EU MOU*, *supra*, note 22, particularly art. VI.

140 The authorization mechanism is especially appealing because it can be used to reduce the uncertainty related to private and state actions in jurisdictions such as the US.

141 See ABA Special Committee, *International Antitrust Report*, *supra*, note 19; and Whish and Wood, *Merger Process Convergence Project*, *supra*, note 10.

142 This approach is quite different from the *Draft International Antitrust Code, supra,* note 14, which envisions both minimum common substantive merger rules and new institutions, namely an International Antitrust Authority with enforcement responsibilities and dispute resolution by International Antitrust Panels. An IMRS treaty might well begin as a bilateral or trilateral arrangement amongst jurisdictions which already have well developed MOU relationships (e.g. the United States, the European Union, Canada). A fairly open accession provision (e.g. containing only a few minimum criteria with respect to matters such as confidentiality protection) would facilitate expansion of the system over time to cover a large number of jurisdictions. The participating jurisdictions would ideally include both the European Union and individual European Union member states which have merger control laws. This would ensure that international mergers with a European component would be included regardless of whether they were ultimately found to exceed or fall below the thresholds in *Council Regulation 4064/89 on the Control of Concentrations Between Undertakings,* O.J. 1990, L 257/14, art. 1:2.

143 This rule should apply even if the subject matter of the guidance is advice as to whether the transaction would be subject to review under the domestic regime or the IMRS.

144 The more restrictive alternative of making all guidance prior to notification non-sharable amongst IMRS agencies would be attractive to merging parties, but inconsistent with the objective of facilitating timely and effective agency collaboration.

145 A closed system which should provide adequate confidentiality assurances to private parties is outlined *infra,* pp. 470–1.

146 The European Commission has no jurisdiction to deal with a transaction if the total worldwide turnover of the parties is less than ECU 5 billion, the total EU turnover of the parties is less than ECU 250 million or each of the parties achieves more than two-thirds of its EU turnover within a single member state: see *Merger Regulation, supra,* note 142, art. 1:2. (There is a narrow exception which allows an individual member state to request the Commission to intervene with respect to a merger affecting its territory: see art. 22:3-5.)

147 See *ibid.*

148 The only minimum qualification which would seem to be appropriate is that the merger be potentially subject to substantive review in at least two IMRS jurisdictions.

149 *Ibid.* There should also be a cut-off date (e.g. two weeks after an agency receives formal notification of the merger) to ensure that such elections are made before separate domestic reviews become too far advanced.

150 Whish and Wood, *Merger Process Convergence Project, supra,* note 10, p. 82, ¶ IV.C.1.

151 More comprehensive descriptions of these three systems can be found in ¶ 5 of the following chapters in Rowley and Baker, *International Mergers, supra,* note 47: chapter 8 (EU – by M.J. Reynolds and E. Weightman), chapter 29 (USA – by D.I. Baker and W.T. Miller) and chapter 5 (Canada – by J.F. Clifford, J.A. Kazanjian and J.W. Rowley). See also ABA Special Committee, *International Antitrust Report, supra,* note 19, pp. 209–10 and appendix II: and A.N. Campbell and M.J. Trebilcock, 'A Comparative Analysis of Merger Law: Canada, the United States and the European Community' (1992), 15 *World Competition* (no. 3) 5, pp. 21–5, ¶ IV.A.

152 ABA Special Committee, *International Antitrust Report, supra,* note 19, pp. 173 and 205 (Recommendation VII.I.B). The European Union's *Form CO* was

described as 'much too burdensome': *ibid.*, p. 174. While the European Commission has defended the comprehensiveness of *Form CO* on the basis that derogations can be negotiated with Merger Task Force officials prior to filing, simultaneous negotiation of derogations with multiple jurisdictions in an IMRS would be unwieldy.

153 The Canadian experience indicates that professional advisers quickly develop the ability to counsel merging parties on whether a transaction is sufficiently clear-cut to take advantage of the short form option or whether prudence would suggest a long form filing at the outset. An average of about eighty-five filings per year are made (see data in A.N. Campbell, 'The Review of Anti-competitive Mergers' (University of Toronto doctoral thesis, 1993), p. 214), most of which use the short form approach. According to an official in the Mergers Branch, the number of situations in which the Director bumped the parties from a short form to a long form filing was negligible.

154 ABA Special Committee, *International Antitrust Report*, *supra*, note 19, p. 175.

155 See *infra*, p. 469.

156 Whish and Wood, *Merger Process Convergence Project*, *supra*, note 10, p. 74, ¶ III.B.2.

157 *Ibid.*, p. 90, ¶ IV.C.7. A further benefit is that it would become 'more difficult for parties to try to play one agency off against another, by strategically seeking approval in one place and then attempting to use that approval to their advantage in another': *ibid.*, p. 89, ¶ IV.C.7.

158 *Ibid.*, p. 89, ¶ IV.C.7.

159 All of these time limits would have to be applied on a filing-by-filing basis in individual jurisdictions. Merging parties could obtain common waiting period expiry dates by aligning the date of filing in each jurisdiction.

160 The model here is the Canadian short form waiting period of seven days, but an extra week seems appropriate in order to allow for interagency consultations. To make this time limit viable in the United States, the interagency clearance process between the DOJ and FTC would have to be further expedited. This should not be an insurmountable obstacle, since IMRS cases would likely represent only a small fraction of mergers reviewed by these agencies. (The clearance process deadline for pre-notification mergers was recently reduced from twenty days to ten days: see US Department of Justice, *Press Release – Department of Justice, FTC Streamline Jurisdication Procedures* (Washington: December 2, 1993).)

161 A one-month waiting period would appear to be reasonable in light of the Canadian twenty-one-day long form waiting period, the US thirty-day initial waiting period (during which the US DOJ and FTC interagency clearance procedure is completed), and the one-month limitation period for commencing formal proceedings in the European Union (during which the extensive information required on *Form CO* is evaluated).

162 The model here is the US statutory second request waiting period of twenty days, with additional time allowed to facilitate interagency consultations.

163 We are indebted to George Addy for highlighting this point.

164 There may be constitutional constraints on limiting the autonomy of courts in some jurisdictions, and in others highly judicialized procedures may be incompatible with speedy decision-making. Thus it might be necessary to allow for the possibility of a recommended 'target' time frame which IMRS signatories would simply be required to use best efforts to meet.

165 Whish and Wood, *Merger Process Convergence Project*, *supra*, note 10, p. 82, ¶ IV.B.3, reported that 'vague deadlines are the worst enemy of transnational mergers and acquisitions, according to the parties involved in our nine cases'.

166 In recognition of their lesser complexity and to provide an incentive for both merging parties and enforcement agencies to negotiate resolutions which avoid litigation, consent order proceedings should be subject to a significantly shorter time limit – perhaps two months, which is the notice and comment period in the United States under the *Tunney Act*, 15 U.S.C. §16(b)–(h).

167 *Merger Regulation*, *supra*, note 142, art. 10:3. In an IMRS there would need to be time for interagency consultations (see further discussion *infra*, p. 471), but this would be no more onerous than the existing EU requirement that the Commission liaise with member state competition authorities and that draft decisions be submitted to an advisory committee consisting of representatives from all the member states before being adopted (art. 19).

168 ABA Special Committee, *International Antitrust Report*, *supra*, note 19, p. 173.

169 *Ibid.*

170 See Whish and Wood, *Merger Process Convergence Project*, *supra*, note 10, p. 87, ¶ IV.C.6.

171 This approach has been endorsed by the ABA Special Committee, *International Antitrust Report*, *supra*, note 19, pp. 173 and 205 (Recommendation VII.I.A).

172 See further discussion of information sharing and confidentiality issues *infra*, pp. 470–1.

173 See *Form CO*, ¶¶ 2.1 and 7.2; and the guidelines from the Commission on this subject which are cited *infra*, note 191.

174 Whish and Wood, *Merger Process Convergence Project*, *supra*, note 10, pp. 87–8, ¶ IV.C.6, endorse the concept of country-specific annexes, but suggest that the timing rules should be left to the individual jurisdictions. We believe that it is neither necessary nor desirable to invite departures from a common timetable.

175 There is a modest parallel here with 'blue sky' securities regulation in the United States: each state tends to have its own forms for securities and broker–dealer registration filings, but each will generally accept a so-called 'uniform' form in lieu of its own.

176 15 U.S.C. §18a.

177 With respect to parallel or unique information, there would be no objection to derogations from a country-specific annex being made unilaterally by the relevant enforcement agency.

178 Given variations in the substantive merger laws in different jurisdictions, there would undoubtedly be the need for some country-specific components. However, attempts should be made to keep these to a minimum by ensuring that similar types of information are not requested in different ways.

179 See *supra*, pp. 468–9.

180 It would be going too far to make interagency disclosure mandatory – an opt-in approach whereby the agencies involved in a case have the flexibility to determine how much (if any) information may usefully be exchanged is more appropriate: see *supra*, note 101, and related text.

181 M.J. Trebilcozk and T.M. Boddez, 'The Case for Liberalizing North American Trade Remedy Laws' (1995), 4 *Minnesota Journal of Global Trade* 1.

182 Although the United States has passed enabling legislation allowing the DOJ and FTC to enter into Antitrust Mutual Assistance Agreements which would come very close to a pure closed loop system, merger pre-notification filings have been explicitly excluded: see *IAEAA, supra*, note 94, §5(1).

183 For practical purposes it would also be helpful for each enforcement agency to be able to share received information with any external experts or advisers retained to assist with the review of a transaction. This possibility could be accommodated with safeguards such as requiring that the identity of any external experts or advisers be notified to the agency which originally provided the confidential information, having such experts or advisers execute a standard form of confidentiality undertaking (which would preclude use of the information for other purposes and provide for its return or destruction) and making them subject to whatever types of sanctions are applied to agency officials. The sanctions for breach of confidentiality by a recipient agency should also be applicable to leakages arising from its use of experts or advisers, which will provide the agency with an incentive to closely supervise their activities.

184 The only exception is that a recipient agency be entitled to use such information in any formal merger proceedings it initiates. The IMRS might also usefully include a protective order regime to address confidentiality of exchanged information which is entered as evidence in formal proceedings.

185 It is recognized that this would require an amendment to the *Merger Regulation, supra*, note 142 (as would many other features of an IMRS). However, this protocol would only supplant the standard EU consultation regime in the small number of transactions which would be subject to IMRS review.

186 See Whish and Wood, *Merger Process Convergence Project, supra*, note 10, pp. 82–3, ¶ IV.C.1.

187 *Ibid.*, p. 8, ¶ I.D.i.b, reported that agency officials do not necessarily want to be bombarded with copious files of documents from other jurisdictions when they are working on a merger within tight regulatory time limits. They would prefer to receive more focused information.

188 While nothing should preclude in-person meetings, phone and fax communication would presumably be the norm for both speed and cost reasons. Moreover, it would generally be desirable for contacts to be at the case officer level in the first instance, with more senior officials becoming involved on an as-needed basis.

189 For a general discussion of the importance of making certain notifications and consultations mandatory, see *supra*, pp. 460–1.

190 See US Department of Justice and Federal Trade Commission, *Horizontal Merger Guidelines* (1992); and Director of Investigation and Research, *Merger Enforcement Guidelines* (1991).

191 See *Commission Notice Regarding its Interpretation of Concentrative and Cooperative Situations under Council Regulation No. 4064/89 on the Control of Concentrations Between Undertakings*, O.J. 1990, C 203/10; and *Commission Notice Regarding its Interpretation of Restrictions Directly Related and Necessary to the Implementation of Concentrations*, O.J. 1990, C 203/5.

192 See the general discussion of transparency *supra*, pp. 444–6. As to the possibility that promulgation of merger guidelines might induce gradual convergence on substantive issues, see ABA Special Committee, *International Antitrust Report, supra*, note 19, pp. 225–6 (Recommendation III.II); and chapter 5 *supra*, p. 108.

193 Expanding slightly on the ABA's approach (see ABA Special Committee, *International Antitrust Report, supra*, note 19, pp. 225–6 (Recommendations III.II.C and D)), it would seem desirable for each nation's guidelines to address the following topics: (1) the definition of a 'merger'; (2) applicability of the law to oligopoly concerns (i.e. 'collusion-enhancing' mergers) and to vertical and conglomerate mergers and joint ventures; (3) market definition, including the treatment of supranational economic markets; (4) the anti-competitive threshold, including any public interest elements; (5) the factors considered in assessing anti-competitive effects, with special attention to how entry barriers and foreign competition are approached; (6) the availability of failing firm, efficiency or other defences/justifications for anti-competitive mergers; (7) any other unique and important features of the domestic law; and (8) significant process matters.

194 For example, see the obligation to inform in the *Draft International Antitrust Code* which is reproduced *supra*, note 42.

195 *Merger Regulation, supra*, note 142, art. 20.

196 See *Competition Act, supra*, note 116, ss. 102 and 103; and *Trade Practices Act 1974* (Cth), as amended, ss. 88–90; respectively. For a comparative analysis of these two approaches, see A.N. Campbell and J.W. Rowley, 'Commonality and Divergence in Canadian and Australian Competition Law', [1992] *Fordham Corporate Law Institute* 261, pp. 287–9.

197 *Competition Act, supra*, note 116, s. 103.

198 *Ibid.*, s. 113(b).

199 See discussion in J. Barker (then Acting Deputy Director of the Canadian Competition Bureau's Merger Branch), 'The Merger Review Process Under the Competition Act' (Vancouver: Canadian Bar Association Competition Law Conference, 1993), pp. 6–8.

200 See *supra*, note 197, and related text.

201 The notion of an enforcement official giving legally binding approval to proposed transactions may run counter to legal traditions and/or political realities in some jurisdictions. An IMRS should encourage the adoption of clearance mechanisms, but making this a condition of participation would be going too far.

202 See generally R. Miller, 'Australia', in Rowley and Baker, *International Mergers, supra*, note 47, pp. 34–5, 44, 51–4 and 64–5.

203 See A.N. Campbell and J.W. Rowley, 'Industrial Policy, Efficiencies and the Public Interest – The Prospects for Harmonization of International Merger Rules' (Ottawa: Center for Trade Policy and Law Eighth Annual Conference, 1993), particularly pp. 20–2.

204 Merging parties might well decide to forgo such a proceeding and live with the uncertainty of future challenges, but it would be useful to give them the option of investing in the reduction of uncertainty if they so desire.

205 This time limit might have to be structured as a best-efforts target rather than a mandatory limit in certain jurisdictions where constitutional constraints or legal/cultural traditions make it infeasible to place formal timing limitations on the relevant domestic adjudicative body.

206 *Ibid.*

207 In the European Union the effect of this rule would be to prevent the European Commission from retransmitting IMRS confidential information to the competition authorities of a member state unless the country were also an IMRS signatory.

208 The specific issues are listed *supra*, note 193.

ACKNOWLEDGEMENTS

This is a revised version of a paper originally prepared for the meeting of the Global Forum on Competition and Trade Policy ('Global Forum') in Tokyo in April 1994. We are grateful to George Addy, Cornelis Canenbley, Eleanor Fox, Damien Neven, Paul Seabright, Paul Victor, Leonard Waverman and other participants at the Tokyo meeting for helpful comments. Funding to support the Global Forum has been provided by the Japan Foundation, the Center for Global Partnership, Industry Canada (Bureau of Competition Policy), and the Center for Research in Management, Berkeley. Ongoing funding is now provided by the International Bar Association, the World Bank and Industry Canada (Bureau of Competition Policy).

INDEX

foreign enforcement agency 453–4
Foreign Extraterritorial Measures Act
see Federal Act
foreign ownership, desirability 60
Foreign Trade Antitrust Improvements
Act (1982) (FTAIA) 171–3, 180
Freedom of Information Act (FOIA) 170
Fuji 423
Fuyo 362, 375

G–7 countries 132
GATT *see* General Agreement on
Tariffs and Trade
General Agreement on Tariffs and Trade
(GATT) 113, 114, 381, 383, 397;
harmonization 408, 416, 431, 434;
WTO agreement 3, 113, 115, 449–50
General Motors 178, 349–52
Germany: antitrust laws 414; automotive
industry 323, 325–6
Glass–Steagal Act 370
globalization 1, 30–2, 307
GM-Toyota, joint venture 137–8, 143
governments: anti-competitive action
429–31; procurement policy 298
Grundig-Consten decision 355

harmonization: competition policy
289–303; merger law 106–8; *see also*
competition harmonization
Hart-Scott-Rodino (HSR) Act 157, 170,
172
Hartford Fire 170, 176, 181
Herfindahl–Hirschmann Index (HHI)
297
horizontal alliances 86–7
horizontal collusion 12, 35
horizontal cooperation, USA 297–8
horizontal *keiretsu* 362–5, 368–71
horizontal strategic alliances 134–5,
143–4
human resource structure, Japan 74–5

IAEAA *see* International Antitrust
Enforcement Assistance Act
IBM 211, 429
IMRS *see* International Merger Review
System
independent R&D 273–9
industrial policy: antitrust 298–300;
competition law 224
information exchanges, law enforcement

455–9
information gathering, law enforcement
452–5
information seeking, IMRS 468
information sharing: antitrust authorities
183–4; confidentiality 470–1; R&D
199–205, 212
innovation: antitrust 289–303;
competition policy 293–8; component
development 318–22; cost-saving
247–9; joint 252–3; race models
246–9, 270–2; *see also* post
innovation
instantaneous payoffs 279–82
Institut Mérieux 182
interagency communications 459–61;
IMRS 471, 472, 477
interfirm agreements 53, 54, 56; *see also*
international corporate alliances; joint
ventures
interfirm relations, *keiretsu* 362–7
International Antitrust Enforcement
Assistance Act (IAEAA) 418;
alternatives 170–83; antitrust 152,
153; Canada 184; constituent support
184–5; USA 164–7, 183–5
International Bar Association 451
international competition policy
389–93, 396–401
international corporate alliances (ICAs)
40–1, 51–9, 60–1; biotechnology 52,
55; desirability 60; growth 57;
semiconductors 52, 55
international corporate organization 7–8
International Merger Review System
(IMRS) 462–78; proposal summary
475–8
international mergers and acquisitions
(IMAs) 46–51; barriers 59;
desirability 60
international R&D cooperations 224–44
international strategic alliances (ISAs)
12–13
internationalization 307
investigative powers, law 452, 455
investment policy 37; *see also* foreign
direct investment

Japan: acquisitions 71–2, 73–4, 76, 86;
anti-monopoly policy 77–81, 84–5;
antitrust laws 137, 266, 414;
automobile industry 310–18, 329–36,

497